Global Perspectives for Conservation and Management of Open-Air Rock Art Sites

Global Perspectives for the Conservation and Management of Open-Air Rock Art Sites responds to the growth in known rock art sites across the globe and addresses the need to investigate natural and human-originated threats to them as well as propose solutions to mitigate resulting deterioration.

Bringing together perspectives of international research teams from across five continents, the chapters in this book are divided into four discrete parts that best reflect the worldwide scenarios where conservation and management of open-air rock art sites unfolds: (1) ethics, community and collaborative approaches; (2) methodological tools to support assessment and monitoring; (3) scientific examination and interventions; and (4) global community and collaborative case studies innovating methodologies for on-going monitoring and management. The diverse origin of contributions results in a holistic and interdisciplinary approach that conciliates perceived intervention necessity, community and stakeholders' interests, and rigorous scientific analysis regarding open-air rock art conservation and management. The book unites the voices of the global community in tackling a significant challenge: to ensure a better future for open-air rock art.

Moving conservation and management of open-air rock art sites in from the periphery of conservation science, this volume is an indispensable guide for archaeologists, conservators and heritage professionals involved in rock art and its preservation.

António Batarda Fernandes is an archaeologist currently heading the Division for Inventory, Study, and Safeguard of Archaeological Heritage of the Directorate-General for Cultural Heritage, an institution under the Ministry of Culture of the Portuguese Government.

Melissa Marshall is an archaeologist, GIS technician and Early Career Research Fellow based at the Nulungu Research Institute, the University of Notre Dame, Australia.

Inés Domingo is an ICREA Research Professor at the University of Barcelona and Vice-president of the World Archaeological Congress.

Global Perspectives for the Conservation and Management of Open-Air Rock Art Sites

Edited by
António Batarda Fernandes,
Melissa Marshall and Inés Domingo

Routledge
Taylor & Francis Group

LONDON AND NEW YORK

First published 2023
by Routledge
4 Park Square, Milton Park, Abingdon, Oxon OX14 4RN

and by Routledge
605 Third Avenue, New York, NY 10158

Routledge is an imprint of the Taylor & Francis Group, an informa business

© 2023 selection and editorial matter, António Batarda Fernandes, Melissa Marshall, and Inés Domingo; individual chapters, the contributors

The right of António Batarda Fernandes, Melissa Marshall, and Inés Domingo to be identified as the authors of the editorial material, and of the authors for their individual chapters, has been asserted in accordance with sections 77 and 78 of the Copyright, Designs and Patents Act 1988.

All rights reserved. No part of this book may be reprinted or reproduced or utilised in any form or by any electronic, mechanical, or other means, now known or hereafter invented, including photocopying and recording, or in any information storage or retrieval system, without permission in writing from the publishers.

Trademark notice: Product or corporate names may be trademarks or registered trademarks, and are used only for identification and explanation without intent to infringe.

British Library Cataloguing-in-Publication Data
A catalogue record for this book is available from the British Library

Library of Congress Cataloging-in-Publication Data
Names: Batarda Fernandes, António Pedro, editor. | Marshall, Melissa (Archaelogist), editor. | Domingo Sanz, Inés, editor.
Title: Global perspectives for the conservation and management of open-air rock art sites / edited by António Batarda Fernandes, Melissa Marshall, Inés Domingo.
Description: Abingdon, Oxon ; New York, NY : Routledge, 2023. | Includes bibliographical references and index.
Identifiers: LCCN 2022018327 (print) | LCCN 2022018328 (ebook) | ISBN 9780367376277 (hardback) | ISBN 9781032310039 (paperback) | ISBN 9780429355349 (ebook)
Subjects: LCSH: Rock paintings—Conservation and restoration. | Petroglyphs—Conservation and restoration. | Art, Prehistoric—Conservation and restoration. | Cultural property—Conservation and restoration.
Classification: LCC GN799.P4 G588 2023 (print) | LCC GN799.P4 (ebook) | DDC 709.01/13—dc23/eng/20220525
LC record available at https://lccn.loc.gov/2022018327
LC ebook record available at https://lccn.loc.gov/2022018328

ISBN: 978-0-367-37627-7 (hbk)
ISBN: 978-1-032-31003-9 (pbk)
ISBN: 978-0-429-35534-9 (ebk)

DOI: 10.4324/9780429355349

Typeset in Times New Roman
by codeMantra

Contents

List of figures ix
List of tables xv
List of acronyms xvii
List of contributors xxi
Preface and Acknowledgements xxix

Introduction: Global Perspectives for the Conservation and Management of Open-Air Rock Art Sites 1
ANTÓNIO BATARDA FERNANDES, MELISSA MARSHALL AND INÉS DOMINGO

SECTION I
Ethics, Community and Collaborative Approaches to the Conservation and Management of Open-Air Rock Art Sites 21

1 **Ethical and Political Matters in Open-Air Rock Art Conservation Practice** 23
ANTÓNIO BATARDA FERNANDES

2 **Murujuga: Managing an Archaeological and Sacred Landscape through Industry** 38
KEN MULVANEY

3 **Multidisciplinary and Integral Approaches to Rock Art as a Strategy for Rock Art Conservation: La Covatina Site as a Case Study** 55
INÉS DOMINGO, DÍDAC ROMAN, JOSÉ LUÍS LERMA, IRENE RODRÍGUEZ, M. ANTONIA ZALBIDEA MUÑOZ AND MARIUS VENDRELL

4 **Monitoring and Maintenance of Open-Air Rock Art Sites: Collaborating with Community in Northern Australia** 76
MELISSA MARSHALL AND PAUL S. C. TAÇON

SECTION II
Methodological Tools to Support Assessment and Monitoring of Open-Air Rock Art Sites 95

5 The Rock Art Stability Index: A Non-Invasive Rapid Field Assessment for Condition Evaluation 97
CASEY D. ALLEN, CAYLA D. KENNEDY, KAELIN M. GROOM, NICCOLE V. CERVENY, RONALD I. DORN AND DAVID S. WHITLEY

6 Confusion and Solution: Providing a Desk-Based Approach for the Management of Rock Art 117
GEORGE NASH

7 Rock Art Monitoring in the UK and Ireland: The CARE Toolkit – Going Online and Using Mobile Data 141
ARON D. MAZEL, MYRA J. GIESEN, MARK TURNER AND STEPHEN DOWSLAND

8 Rock Art and Geographical Information Technologies: SIPAAR and the Integral Management of Petroglyphs in Galicia 161
EMILIO ABAD VIDAL AND JOSE MANUEL REY GARCÍA

SECTION III
Scientific Examination and Interventions at Open-Air Rock Art Sites 175

9 Laser Cleaning vs. Chemical Cleaning for Removal of Lichen from Schist Surfaces in the Coa Valley (Portugal) and Siega Verde (Spain) Archaeological Sites 177
GRACIELA PAZ-BERMÚDEZ, BEATRIZ PRIETO AND JOSÉ SANTIAGO POZO-ANTONIO

10 *In-Situ* Rock Art Preservation in the Sabor Valley (Northwest Iberia) 194
SOFIA FIGUEIREDO, ANTÓNIO BATARDA FERNANDES, SUSANA LAINHO AND JOAQUIM GARCIA

11 Evaluating Thermal-Hygrometric Dynamics at a Levantine Rock Art Site: La Covatina (Vilafranca, Castelló) 214
IRENE RODRÍGUEZ AND INÉS DOMINGO

12 Calcium Hydroxide Nanoparticles Testing for the Consolidation of Prehistoric Paintings in Cova Remígia (Castelló, Spain) — 234
GEMMA BARREDA-USÓ, M. ANTONIA ZALBIDEA MUÑOZ AND JULIA OSCA PONS

13 Multi-Proxy Archaeometric Analyses on Rock Art Pigments in Different World Contexts — 252
HUGO GOMES, PIERLUIGI ROSINA, SARA GARCÊS AND CARMELA VACCARO

SECTION IV
Global Community and Collaborative Case Studies Innovating Methodologies for the Ongoing Monitoring and Management of Open-Air Rock Art Sites — 281

14 Rock Art in the Cerrado: Cultural and Natural Heritage Conservation Come Together at Serranopólis, Goiás, Brazil — 283
ANTÓNIO BATARDA FERNANDES, FERNANDA ELISA COSTA PAULINO E RESENDE, SERGIA MEIRE DA SILVA, UELDE FERREIRA DE SOUZA, JULIO CEZAR RUBIN DE RUBIN, MAIRA BARBERI, MARIA ELINA BICHUETTE, TAMIRES ZEPON AND JONAS EDUARDO GALLÃO

15 Community Engagement in Geologic Assessments of Thamudic Inscriptions and Petroglyphs in the Wadi Rum Protected Area, Jordan — 302
KAELIN M. GROOM, GEORGE BEVAN, SALEH AL-NOAIMAT, MOHAMMED AL-ZALABIAH AND CASEY D. ALLEN

16 Preservation of Endangered Bangudae Petroglyphs in Korea — 317
SANGMOG LEE

17 Rock Art Conservation in the Serra Branca Valley, Serra da Capivara National Park, Piauí, Brazil — 331
THALISON DOS SANTOS AND CRISTIANE DE ANDRADE BUCO

18 Trials and Tribulations of Artificial Silicone Driplines: A Case Study from Kakadu National Park, Australia — 352
MELISSA MARSHALL, KADEEM MAY, GABRIELLE O'LOUGHLIN AND JEFFREY LEE

Index — 375

Figures

1.1 Outcrop with no rock art intervened in 2004 at Canada do Inferno, Coa Valley. Note fracture filling. Photo: Jaime António   27

1.2 Unengraved outcrop relocated at the time of the dam's construction, to a not that *optimum* conservation environment, an open area of, mostly abandoned today, prefabricated administrative buildings supporting the project's construction. Photo by the author   30

1.3 Rock 2 at Ribeira de Piscos, as an example of a not yet intervened rock art surface at Coa Valley, although identified as in need of attention (Fernandes 2012). Photo by the author   33

2.1 Islands of the Dampier Archipelago including Burrup Peninsula (Dampier Is.) and population centres. Map by the author   39

2.2 Petroglyph depicting a macropod, situated within the rock slop of a rugged gully. Photo by the author   39

2.3 Rock-pools within the more protected areas within the sheltered dissected gullies provide a focus for past human activities including production of rock art. Photo by the author   45

2.4 Map showing the extent of developed land (white) within existing industrial leases (black), gazetted industrial land for future development (dark grey) and Murujuga National Park (hatched lines). Map by the author   48

3.1 Map showing the distribution of Levantine rock art and general view of La Covatina site both in winter and summer time. Photos and map by I. Domingo   56

3.2 *In situ* tests of various consolidants and pigments used in rock art conservation to evaluate their performance over time. Figure by I. Domingo   62

3.3 Images and digital reproductions of one of the figures at La Covatina. a. Image taken in 1972. Biblioteca Tomás Navarro Tomás - CCHS-CSIC. b. Image taken in 2014, prior to the conservation intervention. The figure is almost

x *Figures*

	invisible. c. Image taken in 2015, after the conservation intervention. d. Mesado's tracing showing a 'supposed' woman hunting a viper. e. Tracing produced in 2015 showing that the supposed viper is in fact the bottom part of a bundle of arrows. Figure by I. Domingo	64
3.4	Pathologies identified at La Covatina. a. Direct sun exposure. b. Dust. c. Graphite graffiti. d. Chalk Graffiti. e. Bird droppings. f. Insect nesting. g. Surface erosion. h. Black biopatina. Figure by I. Domingo	65
3.5	Building a 4D model of La Covatina. A. Data acquisition with a terrestrial laser scanner Leica ScanStation C10. B. Perspective view of 3D model. C. 3D model of the site visible in the virtual platform created to interact with the 4D model. D. 4D model of one motif. E. 3D model of one motif with tracings implemented. Figure by authors	69
4.1	Senior Traditional Owner Ronald Lamilami explaining the significance of paintings in the main Malarrak rock shelter. Photo by P. Taçon	80
4.2	Early Kakadu conservation efforts in the 1970s–1990s. Photos courtesy of Kakadu National Park	82
4.3	Early Kakadu conservation efforts in the 1970s–1990s. Photos courtesy of Kakadu National Park	83
4.4	Monitoring rock art in Kakadu as part of the annual and doctoral research programs. Photo by K. May	85
5.1	Location of RASI-assessed rock art sites on the Island of Grenada, West Indies (Caribbean), displaying their precarious locations next to the main ring road (Victoria and Waltham), the beach (Duquesne Bay), and interior rainforest in a perennial river (Mt. Rich). Map by K.M. Groom	103
5.2	The Victoria site hosts two panels on one boulder, each with a single face glyph. They rest next to the main road, adjacent storm drain and the Caribbean Sea – the latter two of which, during storms, partially inundates the boulder. Photo by C.D. Allen, 2015	105
5.3	(a) Panel 1 at the Victoria site displaying some splintering, particularly in the upper left of the image where the rock exhibits condensed linear cracks, as well as flaking and crumbling from perhaps continual abrasion (2015). (b) Comparative image of Panel 1 at the Victoria site displaying splintering, particularly in the upper left of the image where the rock exhibits condensed linear cracks, as well as flaking and crumbling from perhaps continual abrasion (2016). Photos by C.D. Kennedy	106
5.4	Waltham site setting (front view) consisting of four panels on two different boulders near the island's main road – with	

Figures xi

	the Caribbean Sea directly opposite – as well as a side street, houses, plant life/detritus, rubbish piles, and free-range livestock, pets, and people. Photo by C.D. Allen	108
5.5	Waltham site setting (rear view) of boulder hosting panels 2, 3, and 4 perched precariously the riverbank and near several houses, some of which contain both penned and free-roaming livestock, along with agricultural debris, rubbish, rubbish burning, and children using the boulder for fun activities such as climbing. Photo by C.D. Allen	108
6.1	Location of the two case study sites. Map by the author	125
6.2	Entrance to Cathole Cave. Image by the author	126
6.3	The engraved torso of a cervid, discovered in 2010. Image by the author	127
6.4	The insertion of a grille in 2014 that extends across the main gallery. Image by the author	128
6.5	View of the squared entrance to Merlin's Cave, looking north. Image by the author	134
7.1	Historical quarrying at We+G30st Lordenshaw 2c in central Northumberland. Photo by Aron Mazel	142
7.2	Whitsunbank 3 in north Northumberland. The original location of this panel is not known. Photo by Aron Mazel	143
7.3	Timeline of major UK rock art projects. Figure by Myra Giesen	146
7.4	A5 flyer to promote the CARE app. Flyer created by Eadington Graham	153
8.1	Distribution of petroglyphs in the region of Galicia, NW Spain. Map by the authors	162
8.2	Interface of the SIPAAR management application. Screen capture of the SIPAAR interface created by the authors	168
8.3	Location of the petroglyphs in the Rock Art Archaeological Park and its immediate surroundings. Map by the authors	169
9.1	(a) Location of the Coa Valley and Siega Verde archaeological areas. (b) and (c) Uncolonized schists from Coa and Siega Verde, respectively. (d) and (e) Two common lichen species on both archaeological sites; (d) Circinaria hoffmanniana, a species with a crustose thallus and (e) the foliose lichen Xanthoparmelia pulla. Photos by the authors	180
9.2	Micrographs of the samples from Coa cleaned of Circinaria hoffmanniana with Nd:YAG at 1064 nm and Er:YAG at 2940 nm. (a) and (b) images taken with stereomicroscopy. (c) and (d) SEM micrographs. Photos by the authors	183
9.3	Stereoscopic micrographs of the samples from Coa (a–d) and Siega Verde (e–h) cleaned by different procedures: an Nd:YAG laser operated at 1,064 nm (a, e), an Nd:YAG laser operated at 266 nm (b, f), Biotin T (c, g) and distilled water (d, h). Photographs by the authors.	185

xii *Figures*

9.4 Variations in colour 42 days after inoculation. IR (1064 nm wavelength) and UV (266 nm wavelength). Graphs by the authors 188

9.5 Bioreceptivity index for each lithotype and cleaning treatment. IR (1064 nm wavelength) and UV (266 nm wavelength). Graphs by the authors 189

10.1 Location of EP 621 with documentation work of its rock art. Photo and documentation work by the authors except ABF 198

10.2 Placing of successive layers of gauze, raw cloth and high-density geotextile blanket bond by aqueous acrylic resin at EP 215. Photo by the authors except ABF 204

10.3 Result of the implemented protection at EP 621. Photo by the authors except ABF 207

11.1 Top: Front view of La Covatina and the contiguous rock shelter where the thermo-hydrograph whose data has been used in this study was placed. Photos by I. Rodríguez. Centre: Location of the seven manual temperature and light exposure measurement points. The blue circles represent the location of rock art motifs (3D model made by GIFLE, LArcHer project). Bottom: Exact location of rock surface temperature measurement points A, B, E, F and G next to painted motifs (motifs 3, 6, 12, 26 and 34 respectively). Photos and tracings by I. Domingo (LArcHer project) 216

11.2 Top: Comparison between the reach of the line of the sun in the right-hand sector of the rock shelter at around 11:00 in February (left) and July (right). Bottom: View of the rock shelter on 26 February 2018. The dotted lines indicated the gradual descent of the shadow line between 9:53 and 14:55, when the whole rock shelter is protected from the sun. Figure by the authors 218

11.3 T and RH graphs recorded at La Covatina in periods in July (a) October (b) and February (c) and during particular days in July (d), October (e) and February (f). Graphics by I. Rodríguez 221

11.4 Graphs of the surface temperature of the rock (T in °C) and the illuminance received (E in lux x 100) at points A, B, C, D, E, F and G from 9:00 to 19:00 on three days from different times of year; and the graph showing the correlation between illuminance and surface temperature. Graphics by I. Rodríguez 223

11.5 Comparison between the illuminance range (left) and the thermal amplitude (right) of points A-G in the three periods measured. Graphic by I. Rodríguez 226

12.1 Geographic location of Cova Remigia rock shelter (top left: within the Iberian Peninsula; top right: within the

Valencian Community). Centre: View of the six cavities.
Bottom: Different views of the site. Photos by authors 235
12.2 Rock surface alterations of animal origin: polishing of
paintings, micro-scratches and small rock falls. Photos
by authors 238
12.3 Rock surface alterations: Top: Small detachments of
pictorial film. Centre: Small and micro-detachments of
pictorial film and calcareous neoformations on the surface.
Bottom: Graphite remnants used to outline the figures in
previous studies. Photos by authors 240
12.4 SEM images of different samples without and with
consolidating material. Bottom 4 images show that
CaLoSiL causes a greater concretion of the nanoparticulate
on the surface and, therefore, irregular carbonation. Photos
by authors 244
13.1 Sampling proceedings on different rock art painted sites.
Photos by the authors 257
13.2 Pigment samples (optical microscopy observations). Photos
by the authors 259
13.3 Pigment samples observed on SEM: (a) hematite;
(b) cinnabar. Photos by the authors 260
14.1 One of the most well-known rock art panels of the region,
belonging to GO-Ja.3 site at Pousada das Araras. Photo by
Fernanda Resende 284
14.2 The witness hill at Pousada das Araras that contains
GO-Ja.3. Photo by Nilo M. P. Resende 288
14.3 Cleaning of termite trails at GO-Ja.26. Photo by Fernanda
Resende 292
14.4 Graffiti removal at GO-Ja.13. Photo by Fernanda Resende 293
15.1 Dramatic landscape of the Hisma Desert with the stark red
sand, tall inselberg mountains and panoramic views. The
inset map shows the locations of Jordan within the Middle
East and the Wadi Rum Protected Area in the south. The
additional map showing the breadth of sites assessed as part
of the Rock Art Rangers Program including the three sites
highlighted in this chapter. Cartography by K. M. Groom 2018 303
15.2 Map of RASI panels at Ain Shallalah with colour
saturation indicating the RASI score and small inset
overlay showing Panel 8 with its location marking on the
map with a black square. Photography and cartography by
K.M. Groom 308
15.3 Map showing the location and RASI scores within Khazali
Canyon. The inset overlay is a photograph of Panel 33,
and its location is marked on the map with a black box.
Photography and Cartography by K.M. Groom 310

xiv *Figures*

15.4 Map showing the location and scores of RASI panels on the small outcrop of Alameleh. The primary panel is shown in the overlay and marked with a black box on the map. Photograph by C.D. Allen and Cartography by K.M. Groom 312
16.1 Documentation work of the total Bangudae rock art panel. Documentation work by Lee (2003) 323
16.2 Lines on whales at Bangudae rock art and inferred Makah Lines. Documentation work by Lee (2003) 325
17.1 Landscape and rock art of the four occupational movements at the Serra Branca Valley, Serra da Capivara National Park, Piauí, Brazil. A) Partial view of the Valley. B) Movement 1 "Grandes Animais" (cod. 53); C) Movement 2 "Povos de transição" (cod.54); D) Movement 3 "Povos de Passagem" (cod. 64); E) Movement 4 "Histórico" (cod.732). Credits: Buco, 2012 334
17.2 Physical, biological, chemical and anthropical damages in Rock-art of the Serra Branca Valley, Serra da Capivara National Park, Piauí, Brazil. A) Cracking lines, plaquette detachments and Maria pobre galleries (cod.235); B) Termite's galleries (cod.589); C). Fungi (cod.26); D) Rock peeling (cod.61); E) Rainwater and Lichens (cod.64); F) Saline (cod.49); G) Rainwater and human habitat (cod.425); H) Fire for cooking (cod.898). Credits: Buco, 2012 343
17.3 Most common damage agents in the rock art of the Serra Branca Valley 345
17.4 Rock-art curatorial intervention in Serra Branca Valley, Serra da Capivara National Park, Piauí, Brazil. A, B) Before and after cleaning of biological and chemical damage (cod.473); C, D, E) Process of collages of pictorial panel fragments (cod.54); F) Panel design – cod. 54 (Ignácio 2009); G, H) Tourist infrastructure (cod.33, cod.53) Credits: Buco, 2012 347
18.1 Application of artificial silicone driplines as illustrated by Gillespie (1983c, pp. 202–205) (Graphics by Jo Wilkins) 357
18.2 Perceived chemical reaction between silicone product and sandstone (Photograph M. Marshall) 361
18.3 Artificial dripline going around paintings individually with an unusual termination below. (Marshall 2020, p. 208) 363
18.4 Silicone dripline feeding algae prior to removal in July 2013 and re-photographed in August 2014 and August 2021 (Photographs M. Marshall) 364

Tables

2.1	Rock art density relating to five archaeological projects	45
9.1	Mineralogical composition (%) of the samples	179
9.2	Colorimetric differences (ΔL^*, Δa^*, Δb^*, ΔC^*_{ab}, ΔH^*, ΔE^*_{ab}) of the surfaces cleaned with laser a Nd:YAG at 1064 nm and 266 nm, Biotin T and distilled water taking as reference the colour of uncolonized schist from the same sites	186
11.1	Differences in maximum temperatures between the Covatina rock shelter and AEMET weather station (Vilafranca) at different times of the year	219
11.2	Days with the Maximum temperatures recorded at AEMET weather station (Vilafranca) in the different seasons and maximum temperatures recorded on the same date at Covatina rock shelter	219
11.3	Correlation between surface temperature and illuminance at the seven monitoring points used in this study at the three times of the year evaluated	229
13.1	Red pigment archaeometric analysis and results	262
13.2	Black, White, yellow and violet pigment archaeometry analysis and results	269
15.1	Comparison between average RASI scores and their respective category sums, displaying potential statistical differences between the overarching categories	306
17.1	Chronology of human occupation at the Serra Branca Valley	333

Acronyms

"0h"	zero hour
2D	Two-dimensional
3D	Three-dimensional
4D	Four-dimensional
ACOR	American Center of Oriental Research
AEI	Agencia Estatal de Investigación (Spanish State Research Agency)
AEMET	Agencia Estatal de Meteorología (Spanish State Meteorological Agency)
AHA	Aboriginal Heritage Act (1972)
AHRC	Arts and Humanities Research Council
AMS^{14}C	Accelerator Mass Spectrometry Carbon-14
ANU	Australian National University
ARC	Australian Research Council
ASEZA	Aqaba Special Economic Zone Authority
ATR-FTIR	Infrared Fourier Transform Spectroscopy
BBC	British Broadcasting Corporation
BC	Before Christ
BCE	Before the Common Era
BI	Bioreceptivity Index
BIC	(Spanish) Property of Cultural National Interest
BP	Before Present
CA	Conservation Agreement
Cadw	Welsh Government historic environment service
cal BP	calibrated years Before the Present
CARE (Chapter 5)	Condition Assessment and Risk Evaluation
CARE (Chapter 7)	Condition Assessment Risk Evaluation
CBA	Cost–Benefit Analysis
CE	Common Era
CEO	Chief Executive Officer
CESU	(United States National Park Service) Cooperative Ecosystem Study Unit
CIELAB	Commission Internationale de l'Eclairage
CIELCH	CIELAB Cylindrical model

CRA	Conzinc Riotinto of Australia Limited
CSIRM	Carved Stone Investigations: Rombalds Moor Project
CSIRO	Commonwealth Scientific and Industrial Research Organisation
CSSI	Cultural Stone Stability Index
CSW	Catalogue Service for the Web
DGPC	Direção-Geral do Património Cultural (Portuguese State Cultural Heritage Agency)
DSL	Dampier Salt Limited
E	Illuminance
EDP	Eletricidade de Portugal (Portuguese Power Company)
EDX	Energy Dispersive X-Ray
EP	Elemento Patrimonial (Heritage Element)
EPBC	Environment Protection and Biodiversity Conservation Act 1999 (EPBC)
ERA	England's Rock Art
ERDF	European Regional Development Fund
Er:YAG	Erbium-doped Yttrium Aluminium Garnet
EU	European Union
F0	Membrane sector
FCT	Fundação para a Ciência e Tecnologia (Portuguese State Research Agency)
FEDER	European Fund for Economic and Regional Development
FUMDHAM	Fundação Museu do Homem Americano
GIS	Geographic Information System
GPS	Global Positioning System
H_2O_2	Hydrogen Peroxide
HCL	Hydrochloric Acid
HE	English Heritage
HIPL	Hamersley Iron Proprietary Limited
HSP	(Lower Sabor Dam) Heritage Safeguard Plan
Hz	Hertz
IASGDCH	Inventory of Archaeological Sites of the General Directorate of Cultural Heritage
ICOMOS	International Council on Monuments and Sites
ICREA	Institució Catalana de Recerca i Estudis Avançats (Catalan Institution for Research and Advanced Studies)
ID	Identification
IFRAO	International Federation of Rock Art Organizations
INSPIRE	Infrastructure for Spatial Information in Europe

IPHAN	Instituto do Patrimônio Histórico e Artístico Nacional (Brazilian Government Cultural Heritage Agency)
IR	Infrared Radiation
J cm-2	Joules per square centimetre
KCHA	Korean Cultural Heritage Administration
KGP	Karratha Gas Plant
KOH	Potassium Hydroxide
kV	kilovolt
LGM	Last Glacial Maximum
LNEC	(Portuguese) Laboratório Nacional de Engenharia Civil (National Laboratory for Civil Engineering)
LNG	Liquefied Natural Gas
LRA	Levantine Rock Art
mA	microAmpere
MA	Motif Area
MAC	Murujuga Aboriginal Corporation
MAMSL	Metres Above Mean Sea Level
mm	millimetre
MS	Micro-Stratigraphic
NADRAP	Northumberland and Durham Rock Art Project
NAGPRA	Native American Graves Protection and Repatriation Act
Nd:YAG	Neodymium-doped Yttrium Aluminium Garnet
NEGP	National Estate Grants Programme
nm	nanometres
NOWTAG	Tynedale North of the Wall Archaeological Group
ns	nanosecond
NSF	(United States) National Science Foundation
OGC	Open Geospatial Consortium
OM	Optical Microscopy
PAAR	Rock Art Archaeological Park (Campo Lameiro, Galiza, Spain)
PDF	Portable Document Format
PEFO	Petrified Forest National Park (Arizona, USA)
pXRF	portable X-Ray Fluorescence
RAPP	Rock Art Pilot Project
RASI	Rock Art Stability Index
RH	Relative Humidity
RNTPBC	Registered Native Title Prescribed Body Corporates
RPPN	Reserva Particular do Patrimônio Natural (Private Natural Heritage Reserve)

RS	Raman Spectroscopy
SAM	Scheduled Ancient Monument
SCHEP	Sustainable Cultural Heritage through the Engagement of Local Communities Project
ScRAP	Scotland's Rock Art Project
SDI	Spatial Data Infrastructure
SEM	Scanning Electron Microscope
SHRA	Stone Heritage Research Alliance, Limited Liability Company
SIPAAR	Rock Art Archaeological Park Information System
SM	Stereo-Microscopic
SMR	Slope Mass Rating
SWOT	Strengths, Weaknesses, Opportunities, and Threats
T	Temperature
TAN plant	Technical Ammonium Nitrate Production Facility
UNESCO	United Nations Educational, Scientific and Cultural Organization
UK	United Kingdom
USAID	United States Agency for International Development
UV	Ultraviolet
XRFS	X-Ray Fluorescence Spectroscopy
XRM	X-Ray Microfluorescence
WCS	Web Coverage Service
WFS	Web Feature Service
WMS	Web Map Service
WRPA	Wadi Rum Protected Area
μm	micrometre
μs	microsecond

Contributors

Casey D. Allen is an award-winning geographer and educator with interests ranging from geomorphology to humanistic geography. He currently affiliates himself with The University of the West Indies, Cave Hill Campus in Barbados, and the Stone Heritage Research Alliance where he engages people of all ages in field-based learning experiences.

Saleh Al-Noaimat is committed to the conservation and management of Jordan's incredible natural and heritage resources as the director of the Wadi Rum Protected Area and government representative of the Aqaba Special Economic Zone Authority. He has a background in Economic and Management Sciences from United Arab Emirates University, Al-Ain, UAE, and extensive government experience.

Mohammed Al-Zalabiah was born and raised in Rum Village at the heart of Wadi Rum, Jordan. He is a dedicated environmental steward and advocate for responsible landscape management and sustainable tourism. He serves as a respected community liaison between the various indigenous tribes of southern Jordan and the Wadi Rum Protected Area officials.

Maira Barberi has a graduation and a Master's degree in Geology, and a PhD in Geosciences from the University of São Paulo, Brazil. She is a postdoctoral fellow at the University of Turku, Finland, and at the University of Brasilia. She is a Professor at the Pontifical Catholic University of Goiás. Her research interests are palaeontology, paleoecology, geoarchaeology, landscape and territory, and environmental analysis.

Gemma Barreda-Usó is an independent conservator-restorer. She has a PhD in Fine Arts from the Universitat Politècnica de Valencia, with an expertise in the conservation and restoration of Cultural Heritage. She was a Postdoctoral Researcher at the Universitat de Barcelona as part of the ERC Consolidator Grant 'LArcHer'. She carried out conservation interventions at rock art sites in Spain and France.

George Bevan is an Associate Professor in the Department of Geography and Planning at Queen's University, Canada, where he teaches GIS,

Photogrammetry, Cultural Heritage and Historical Geography. His current research interests involve the application of drones to document archaeological excavations, and of aerial photos and declassified satellite imagery to reconstruct past landscapes.

Maria Elina Bichuette has a degree in Biological Sciences from the University of São Paulo, Brazil, a Master, a PhD and Post-PhD in Zoology from, respectively, the University of São Paulo, the New Jersey Institute of Technology and the Chinese Academy of Sciences. She is currently an Associate Professor at the Federal University of São Carlos. Her research mainly focuses on the fauna of subterranean habitats.

Cristiane de Andrade Buco has a PhD in Archaeology from the University of Trás-os-Montes e Alto Douro, Portugal, with a thesis on the rock art of the Serra Branca Valley, Piauí, Brazil, and an MA in History from the Federal University of Pernambuco. She is currently a public archaeologist at the Instituto do Patrimônio Histórico e Artístico Nacional. Her interests include rock art, archeomusicology, art and heritage education.

Niccole V. Cerveny is a Professor of Geography at Mesa Community College, Arizona, USA, specializing in geosciences, conservation of cultural resources and undergraduate research. Her research ranges from studying climatic relationships through detrital quartz to the conservation of ancient rock art and inscriptions around the world. Her interests combine geoscience practices to cultural heritage challenges.

Inés Domingo is an ICREA Research Professor at the University of Barcelona and Vice-president of the World Archaeological Congress. Previously she taught at the Universities of Flinders (Australia) and Valencia (Spain). She currently leads the ERC Consolidator grant 'LArcHer' carrying out a multidisciplinary approach to bridge the gap between archaeological and heritage approaches to Levantine art.

Ronald I. Dorn, School of Geographical Sciences & Urban Planning, Arizona State University, USA. His research interests include desert geomorphology, the study of rock decay processes (focusing currently on processes that draw down atmospheric carbon dioxide) and how these two subjects connect with rock art.

Stephen Dowsland is a Senior Data Scientist at the National Innovation Centre for Data at Newcastle University. His research interests include Data Engineering, Cloud Computing and Machine Learning.

António Batarda Fernandes is an archaeologist heading the Division for Archaeology of DGPC, the Portuguese State institution for Cultural Heritage. With an MA from University College London, a PhD from Bournemouth University, and integrating the Centro de Estudos em Arqueologia, Artes e Ciências do Património of Coimbra University as an aggregated researcher, his interests evolve across all facets of rock art study.

Sofia Figueiredo has a degree in Archaeology from the University of Minho, Portugal, an MA from the University of Barcelona and a PhD from the University of Minho. From 2009 to 2015, she coordinated the rock art studies carried out in the frame of the Heritage Safeguard Plan motivated by the construction of the Baixo Sabor dam. Her research interests include rock art study, management and conservation.

Jonas Eduardo Gallão holds a degree in Biological Sciences from the Federal University of São Carlos (Brazil), an MA from the Graduate Program in Ecology and Natural Resources and a PhD from the University of São Paulo. In Ecology, his research interests include population ecology, functional and phylogenetic diversity; in Zoology, natural history, morphology, behaviour and taxonomy, namely of Arachnida.

Sara Garcês is a specialist in post-Palaeolithic rock art of the Iberian Peninsula with a PhD from the University of Trás-os-Montes e Alto Douro. She is a Guest Assistant Professor at Polytechnic Institute of Tomar, carrying out research in various fields of rock art such as pigment analyses, 2D and 3D documentation of paintings and engravings, or the prehistoric rock art of the Tagus River Basin.

Joaquim Garcia is a conservator-restorer who is managing partner of Arqueohoje, Lda., a company which devotes its efforts to the study, conservation, restoration, management, musealization and enhancement of cultural heritage, especially that of archaeological nature. His research interests include the theoretical-practical application of traditional techniques in conservation and restoration.

Jose Manuel Rey García is an archaeologist at the Directorate General for Cultural Heritage of the Xunta de Galicia (Spain), currently Director of the Pontevedra Museum. With a degree in Archaeology from the University of Santiago de Compostela and a PhD from the National University of Distance Education (UNED), where he also teaches, cultural heritage management and prehistoric rock art are his research interests.

Myra J. Giesen is a Research Associate at the School of Education, Communication & Language Sciences as well as a Visiting Fellow at the School of History, Classics & Archaeology, and at the School of Engineering at Newcastle University. She has a diverse background with experience in NAGPRA compliance and research in human osteology, digital heritage and social solutions to environmental dilemmas.

Hugo Gomes has a degree in Geology and an MA in Geosciences from the University of Coimbra, and a PhD in Geosciences from the University of Trás-os-Montes e Alto Douro. He is also a researcher at the Polytechnic

Institute of Tomar, the Geosciences Centre of the University of Coimbra, and the Earth and Memory Institute. He has been involved in research projects in Iberia, Italy, Brazil, Angola and Ethiopia.

Kaelin M. Groom is passionate about fieldwork, cultural stone decay and the profound intricacies that hold the world together. She is a professional researcher, instructor at Arizona State University, USA, and the founding director of the Stone Heritage Research Alliance LLC, a private consulting firm providing non-invasive geomorphologic and cultural stone decay research services and training.

Cayla D. Kennedy, U.S. Army Corps of Engineering, Portland District. Her current research interests include geoarchaeology field and laboratory methods, archaeological and geomorphological impacts of the Missoula Floods in Oregon, and indigenous archaeology and traditional ecological knowledge of the western United States.

Susana Lainho is a conservator-restorator who runs her own company dedicated to the conservation and restoration of cultural heritage, LAINHO – Conservação e Restauro. Her interests include the conservation of heritage, especially of that integrated into buildings.

Jeffrey Lee is the senior custodian/Traditional Owner of the Djok clan in Kakadu National Park. Jeffrey works as a ranger and is a member of the Park's governing management board and advocates for better protection of rock art at different forums. In 2012, he received a Member of the Order of Australia for his persistent advocacy on behalf of conserving his country.

Sangmog Lee is an archaeologist who has focused on the prehistory and rock art of Korea. He is a former Director of Ulsan Museum and Ulsan Petroglyphs Museum, Ulsan, South Korea. He studied archaeology and anthropology at Kyungpook University in Korea, and then he received his PhD in prehistory from the National Museum of Natural History, Paris, France.

José Luis Lerma is a Professor at the Universitat Politècnica de Valencia. He has a degree in Engineering and a PhD in Geodesy and Cartography, specializing in the documentation of cultural heritage. He has published extensively on subjects related to 2D/3D imaging, range-based and multispectral sensors in the field of cultural heritage, engineering and medicine.

Melissa Marshall is an archaeologist, GIS technician and Early Career Research Fellow based at the Nulungu Research Institute, the University of Notre Dame, Australia. With a focus on rock art research, conservation and management, she has worked extensively across northern Australia for more than 20 years with Traditional Owners and Indigenous ranger teams, specializing in cultural heritage management.

Kadeem May is a Larrakia man who has grown up on Country in Kakadu National Park and joined the Cultural Programs Unit as a Kakadu Indigenous Ranger Program trainee ranger in 2014 and as Cultural Programs Officer in 2015. Working alongside Traditional Owners and specialists, Kadeem is passionate about monitoring and management of rock art and likewise committed to cultural heritage management.

Aron D. Mazel is a Reader in Heritage Studies at Newcastle University, UK, and a Research Associate at the University of the Witwatersrand, South Africa. Aron has published on a range of topics, including museum and archaeological histories, the San hunter-gatherer past in the Thukela basin, South Africa, and rock art in the uKhahlamba-Drakensberg, South Africa, and Northumberland, UK.

Ken Mulvaney is an Adjunct Professor at the Centre for Rock Art Research and Management, working at Rio Tinto Iron Ore. Working with Traditional Owners, Ken's research has ranged from documenting totemic geographies and ritual associations, forensic analysis, recording strong quarrying technologies and rock art for the management and protection of Aboriginal cultural heritage.

George Nash is an Associate Professor at the Centro de Geociências da Universidade de Coimbra and Instituto Politécnico de Tomar, Portugal. Dr Nash is a specialist in Palaeolithic and Post-Palaeolithic rock art and has undertaken research in Chile, Malaysia, Mongolia, Norway and Wales. Currently, he is involved in the UAE Origins Project, to identify and record early prehistoric art on the Arabian Peninsula.

Gabrielle O'Loughlin lived and worked in Kakadu National Park, Australia, as the Senior Project Officer for cultural heritage programs in collaboration with Traditional Owners for the protection and management of their clan estates. Working closely with university and other institutions, she supported Owners in their custodial practice of looking after rock art sites, in conjunction with modern scientific research methods.

Graciela Paz-Bermúdez has been a Full Professor at the University of Vigo, Spain, since 2004. Her research interests include different topics in the study of lichens, mainly taxonomy and ecology. The study of lichen colonisation in cultural monuments, the environmental patterns that condition their distribution, as well as biodeterioration are fields in which she has been involved since the beginning of her career.

Julia Osca Pons is a Lecturer at the Department of Conservation and Restoration of Cultural Heritage, Universitat Politècnica de Valencia, and a member of the Instituto Universitario de Restauración del Patrimonio of the same University. She has a PhD in Fine Arts and devotes her teaching and research to the field of mural painting restoration. She has worked extensively across Spain for more than 25 years.

José Santiago Pozo-Antonio holds a PhD from University of Vigo (Spain) and is a senior researcher at the same university. His research is based on a multidisciplinary non-invasive approach to conservation, chemistry and physics of cultural heritage, addressing its characterization and mitigation regarding deterioration, its consolidation and protection, and green intervention alternative practices.

Beatriz Prieto is presently a Full Professor at the University of Santiago de Compostela, Spain, and coordinator of the Group of Environmental studies on Natural and Cultural Heritage. Her chief research interest is the interaction between environment and built heritage, namely biodeterioration and bioreceptivity of cultural heritage monuments, including development of innovative methodologies for conservation.

Fernanda Elisa Costa Paulino e Resende has a graduation in Archeology and Biomedical Sciences, a Master's in Cultural Heritage Management, both from the Pontifical Catholic University of Goiás, Brazil, and is a PhD candidate at the National University of the Center of the Buenos Aires Province, Argentina. She works in contract archaeology, devoting her efforts to cultural heritage conservation.

Irene Rodríguez has a Bachelor in Fine Arts, a Bachelor of Conservation and Restoration of Cultural Heritage, and an MA in Archaeology from the University of Barcelona. Between 2015 and 2018 she was a pre-doctoral researcher at the University of Barcelona, where she conducted research in the conservation and restoration of Levantine rock art.

Dídac Roman is a GenT Excellence Researcher at the University Jaume I of Castelló, Spain. He previously worked at the Universities of Barcelona, Valencia and Toulouse. He specializes in the study of the Palaeolithic and Mesolithic of Western Europe through material culture, having directed research projects in sites of that chronology throughout Mediterranean Iberia.

Pierluigi Rosina graduated in Geological Sciences from the University La Sapienza, Rome in 1997. He completed his DEA in Quaternary Geology in Perpignan, France, and obtained a PhD at the University of Ferrara, Italy. Since 1998, he has been an Assistant Professor at the Polytechnic Institute of Tomar, Portugal. He conducts research in geoarchaeology, archaeometry, heritage and landscape management.

Julio Cezar Rubin de Rubin has a degree in Geology from the University of Vale do Rio dos Sinos and a PhD in Geosciences from the Universidade Estadual Paulista Júlio de Mesquita Filho. He is a Professor at the Pontifical Catholic University of Goiás. He develops research in geoarchaeology, landscape and territory, and archaeological methods and excavation.

Thalison dos Santos is a public archaeologist at the Instituto do Patrimônio Histórico e Artístico Nacional, a department of the Brazilian Ministry of Tourism. He attained a PhD degree in 2019 following the Archaeology Graduate Program at Museu Nacional, Universidade Federal do Rio de Janeiro. His research focuses on rock art production techniques in Serra da Capivara, and other rock art sites in Ceará, Northeast Brazil.

Sergia Meire da Silva graduated in Archeology from the Pontifical Catholic University of Goiás, also having trained in Project Management at the Catholic University of Brasília. Her interests are geoarchaeology, lithic and ceramic analysis, archaeological sites and landscapes, and conservation of cultural heritage. Since 2015, she has been coordinating environmental licensing archaeological studies.

Uelde Ferreira de Souza graduated in Archeology from the Pontifical Catholic University of Goiás and is a PhD candidate in Archaeology at the National University of the Center of Buenos Aires Province, Argentina. His work experience includes Pre-Colonial, Colonial and Public Archeology, as well as archaeological heritage risk diagnosis and mitigation, and rock art studies.

Paul S. C. Taçon is a past ARC Australian Laureate Fellow (2016–2021), Chair in Rock Art Research and Distinguished Professor of Anthropology and Archaeology at Griffith University, Australia, where he also directs the Place, Evolution and Rock Art Heritage Unit. Since 1980, he has been conducting fieldwork across Australia, Southeast Asia and elsewhere, on rock art, material culture, colour, cultural evolution and identity.

Mark Turner leads the Research Software Engineering team in the Digital Institute at Newcastle University. The team focuses on delivering software engineering expertise for research projects across the university. Since joining the university in 2012, he has been designing and implementing software applications for several research projects, including gamification, rock art management and vector models applied to Newcastle City Centre.

Carmela Vaccaro is an Associate Professor at the University of Ferrara, Italy, where she coordinates the Petrology and Geochemistry Group of the Physics and Earth Sciences Department. Her research interests include water and soil geochemistry, microclimatic analysis, characterization of sites polluted by heavy metals, mineral surveys, geoarchaeology and archaeometry.

Marius Vendrell has a PhD in Geology from the University of Barcelona and is a lecturer of Crystallography and Mineralogy at the same University. He has been working in the study of heritage materials since 1984. He is the founding partner and scientific advisor of the company Patrimonio 2.0, born as a spin-off of a university research group, and at the same time acts as a cluster for the company through a collaboration agreement.

Emilio Abad Vidal is a professional archaeologist. He graduated in Applied Geography and in Prehistory and Archaeology from the University of Santiago de Compostela, where he also completed his PhD. Furthermore, he collaborates as a teacher-tutor in postgraduate and professional courses. His work focuses on data modelling for cultural heritage.

David S. Whitley lives in a blue oak forest high in the Tehachapi Mountains, California, USA. He digs holes in the ground for a living. His latest book is *Cognitive Archaeology: Mind, Ethnography and the Past in South Africa and Beyond* published in 2020 by Routledge.

M. Antonia Zalbidea Muñoz is a Lecturer at the Department of Conservation and Restoration of Cultural Heritage, Universitat Politècnica de Valencia. She has a PhD in Fine Arts, specializing in the study of consolidation materials for cultural heritage. She is in the Advisory Committee of the project Breaking Barriers between Science and Heritage – Levantine Rock Art through Archaeology, Heritage Science and IT (LarcHer).

Tamires Zepon has a graduation in Biological Sciences from the Federal University of São Carlos, Brazil, a master's degree and PhD from the Graduate Program in Ecology and Natural Resources at the same university. Her interests focus on terrestrial and aquatic subterranean faunal populations, regarding community ecology, diversity and preservation.

Preface and Acknowledgements

Close to a decade has passed since the publication of *Open-Air Rock-Art Conservation and Management: State of the Art and Future Perspectives* was co-edited by one of us. Importantly, the edition was dedicated to exploring the peculiarities of open-air rock art conservation and management, traditionally left on the periphery of rock art conservation science since the infancy of the discipline. This international volume was a starting point to raise awareness of the problems of caring for open-air rock art and the lack of consistent initiatives to understand and manage weathering effects, as well as to mitigate other impacts of natural and human-originated threats affecting preservation. It also illustrated how, at the time, there appeared to be a lack of communication between different stakeholders and especially with the public. Today in many countries around the world, engaging the public in conservation and management is deemed to be one of the best ways to preserve this open-air rock art, done so in a context that considers the challenges to protect such a dispersed and vulnerable heritage located in a wide variety of environments and thus exposed to diverse conditions.

In the years that followed the publication of this volume, there has been growing interest for the sustainable conservation of rock art heritage and increased awareness of the need to improve our conservation and management strategies globally. This has been particularly evident through the large participation of different international research teams in two sessions co-organised by us independently at two international congresses. In 2015, the session by A.P.B. Fernandes, T. Davill and H. Gomes on *Open-air Rock-art conservation and management: a further state of affairs,* was held at the *XIX International Rock Art Conference* IFRAO 2015. Celebrated in Cáceres (Spain), the session was attended by 17 international research teams. This was an indication that the previous year's publication was not the culmination but rather the beginning of a much-needed debate, which sought a balance between research, conservation and current uses of open-air rock art, and in which the contributions of all stakeholders (especially Traditional Owners, rock art Custodians and Local Communities) are essential.

Three years later, the session on *Conservation Issues and Preventive Measures in Open-air Rock Art Sites*, organized by I. Domingo, M. Marshall and

I. Rodríguez, at the *24th Annual Meeting of the European Association of Archaeologists* in Barcelona 2018: *Reflecting Futures,* also gathered international scholars to deepen multidisciplinary and multivocal approaches to rock art conservation. The two meetings opened new avenues of research and lead us to consider the need to join forces and put together a new volume to provide an updated global overview of the many issues involved in open-air rock art conservation: ethics, laws, informed policies, tested methodologies, sustainable practices, regular monitoring and public awareness. Moreover, there is a continued need to discuss the best approaches to fully understand the conservation history of the sites, identify pathologies, develop suitable protocols and resources to monitor and manage sites, recognize new threats and mitigate deterioration.

Co-editors of this volume wish to deeply thank all the authors participating in this volume for their sustained patience regarding the lengthy publication of this book, particularly during a time of global crisis caused by COVID-19. We would also like to acknowledge all of the First Nations people globally whose combined efforts have culminated in the rock art we collaborate to care for, sharing the creative inspirations, narratives, connections and cultural diversity for all of us here now and into the future.

Our research and participation in the congresses at the origin of this volume have been supported by different research grants and institutions: while A. Batarda Fernandes research has partially been funded by FCT – Fundação para a Ciência e a Tecnologia, acknowledgements are also due to his past and current employers, Fundação Coa Parque and Direção-Geral do Património Cultural respectively, for their steady support of ongoing research; M. Marshall's research was funded as part of an Australian Postgraduate Award for her doctoral studies at the Australian National University, with funding also provided through her position at the Nulungu Research Institute at the University of Notre Dame Australia and that invested by Kakadu National Park as part of the annual cultural programs; I. Domingo's research was funded by a 2018 ERC-Consolidator Grant, "Breaking barriers between Science and Heritage approaches to Levantine Rock art through Archaeology, Heritage Science and IT" (Acronym: LArcHer), funded by the European Research Council (ERC) under the European Union's Horizon 2020 research and innovation programme (grant agreement No 819404) and HAR2016–80693-P "Redefining Levantine art from an interdisciplinary perspective" funded by the Spanish Ministry of Science, Innovation and Universities. She also thanks her current employers ICREA and Universitat de Barcelona for providing the framework for ongoing research.

Introduction
Global Perspectives for the Conservation and Management of Open-Air Rock Art Sites

António Batarda Fernandes, Melissa Marshall and Inés Domingo

The current collection of experiences will be considered within four discrete parts that best reflect the worldwide scenario where contributions to the volume unfold, commencing with an examination of ethical, community and collaborative approaches to rock art conservation and management. The following section reports on developments in methodological frameworks and tools to support the ongoing monitoring and management of sites. An examination of several advancements taking shape within the conservation science discipline, in direct response to unique issues affecting open-air sites, ensues. The final part is dedicated to specific case studies representing attempts around the globe to monitor, maintain and manage rock imagery in different contexts. The diverse origin of contributions results in a holistic and interdisciplinary approach that conciliates perceived intervention necessity, community and stakeholders' interests, and rigorous scientific analysis regarding open-air rock art conservation and management.

Introduction

Ongoing research on open-air rock art management and conservation must engage in new avenues and resources to involve communities in rock art conservation, as well as the application of best practices to open rock art to the public for visitation. All these issues are classified by Agnew et al. (2015) as the four pillars of rock art conservation policy and practice: public and political awareness, effective management systems, physical and cultural conservation practice, and community involvement. It is argued these four pillars need to be sustained jointly to overcome the barriers that often exist between rock art research, preventive conservation and contemporary uses of this valuable heritage (Deacon 2006; Domingo and Bea 2016).

Building on contributions by researchers attending the IFRAO 2015 and EAA 2018 conferences referred to in the Preface, this new volume aims to further broaden horizons on the subject, presenting new research undertaken in recent years. Nevertheless, this is not a second instalment to a series. Rather, it is a different volume to that published in 2014. Indeed, *Open-Air*

Rock Art Conservation and Management: State of the Art and Future Perspectives (Darvill and Fernandes 2014) aimed to present diverse case-studies that could shed light on the road ahead regarding rock art conservation and management. Attention was mostly given to make known work been done in several areas of the world. Conversely, the present volume endeavours to consider presented case studies within a theoretical and ethical framework that values a holistic and multivocal approach to open-air rock art conservation and management practice.

A previous note on available theoretical frameworks that can frame debate around rock art conservation and management at this juncture is of interest. Particularly of note are the ongoing efforts to consider a decolonization approach regarding the study of the material and conceptual past (for instance Porr and Matthews 2017; Marshall 2020; Marshall et al. 2020). The first issue to consider is how to place present approaches to management and conservation in a context that celebrates what rock art could have originally represented to the artists (as described in May et al. 2019), and, in the cases where first-hand connection is still present with communities today (particularly of First Nations people as articulated in Mowaljarlai and Malnic 2001; Blundell and Woolagoodja 2005; Mangolamara et al. 2018). It is a case of arguing for contemporaneous decolonization of the past, i.e., how valid are our present constructs when attempting to conserve and manage rock art?

If in the aforementioned cases when rock art is still culturally and symbolically relevant for today communities, as with Aboriginal people in Australia, or San people in South Africa, the challenge is thus to conjugate cultural and traditional practice with scientific knowledge. Weathering, seen in western perspectives as a problem for rock art conservation, is seen by some cultures (like some Australian Aboriginal groups) as a natural process, and repainting (instead of preventive conservation) as the solution to preserve the values and significance of the rock art sites (Bowdler 1988; Mowaljarlai et al. 1988; Smith 2008).

When that is not the case, as happens with most rock art in the world, the issue is less clear-cut, although the ethnographic record can provide valuable accounts for the controlled, ethical and critical use of analogies to shed light into different aspects of the processes of creation and use of past rock art (Domingo et al. 2017; Domingo 2021). This point was articulated by Felton Bricker Sr., a Mojave People elder, who released a statement specifically discussing whether there is a need for graffiti removal: "conservation interferes directly with the history of the rock art and the place"; "Vandalism will have become a part of the place." (Bricker Sr., Holcomb and Dean 1999, p. 9). Indeed, not all instances require graffiti/vandalism removal, as suggested previously by one of the authors (Fernandes 2010). On that occasion, it was proposed that a case-by-case analysis should be employed when trying to discern between graffiti that may be of historical value, graffiti that is of no such significance, and pure acts of nihilistic vandalism. It was concluded that if most graffiti can be regarded only a form of pure vandalism, some might deserve to be retained due to their own specific merits (Fernandes 2010).

Graffiti aside, the fragile state of many stone surfaces presenting open-air rock art *per se*, will determine the need to consider conservation interventions at some point in time, if existing original rupestrian imagery is to be handed over in the best possible condition to subsequent generations. Where interventions are required, the process should always start from a prior understanding of the peculiarities and characteristics of the sites to be treated, as informed by research and adapted to the particularities of each site whilst considering the points of view of different stakeholders. As articulated by Agnew et al. (2015) traditional management methods should be recognized and respected encouraging dialogues with site custodians.

If at first glance the need for a post-colonialism approach may seem somewhat farfetched regarding open-air rock art conservation and management, the fashion in which the global prevalent media culture predominately engages with the archaeological record, rock art included, reveals that this effort is still needed. A recent example illustrates this, whereby previously identified and well-studied Colombian rock art was used to promote a TV series (Jungle Mystery: Lost Kingdoms of the Amazon 2020; Alberge 2020). The spectacular panels at the delicate conservation area of the Serrania La Lindosa were not known outside Colombia and a circle of rock art researchers and connoisseurs, primarily as images had not been available in English publications. Suddenly, images of the art become viral in the wake of the media campaign to promote the TV series. Previous work carried out by local researchers was not referenced and images from already known and studied sites were presented as new finds (Guillermo Muñoz, personal communication 2020). Moreover, as pointed out in one of the many worldwide publications regarding this apparent discovery (Finestre Sull'Arte 2020), was that due to the interests of the TV production, all of this was kept secret for one year, even from local Indigenous communities or archaeologists. Despite this difficult situation, the value of the rock art to the local community and their attempts to keep these ancient testimonies protected and out of sight from civil war, tourism, and land-grabbers was documented two decades ago (Calle 2020). Post-COVID, these challenges may increase once more.

The situation in Columbia likewise highlighted the use of language when conveying information such as this. One of the titles repeatedly used by newspapers (for instance, Alberge 2020) picked up an old-style comparison in rock art studies, but also in the media, which refers to Altamira, Lascaux, or other sites, depending on the sources[1], as the 'sistine Chapel' of rock art. As these are artistic events separated by hundreds of generations and cultural traditions, such comparisons should be made drawn with caution to avoid being misinterpreted as colonialist, both when referring to the past (for example when describing Altamira) – or to culturally and geographically distinct ancient rock art elsewhere. Even if the comparison is of a metaphorical nature and seeks to evoke that prehistoric art comprises masterpieces of similar quality and beauty to other recent artworks, there are certainly other artistic creations of humanity outside Europe with which they could be compared. By doing so, inadvertent and possibly inappropriate comparisons are avoided supporting a break away from the Eurocentric view that prevails in rock art studies whilst establishing alternative celebrations of artistic prowess across time, space and cultural diversity. Such renewed attitudes will certainly aid in managing and conserving sites that suddenly emerge in the spotlight, as media attention may trigger over-visitation and detrimental environmental changes, even before they have been properly studied, protected and prepared for public visits with permission of local Indigenous peoples and communities.

The recent discovery of sites with Levantine rock art in Castelló (Spain) between 2013 and 2016, awakened such national and international media interest (e.g. Archaeology 2014; Artribune 2014; Baltasar 2014; Europa Press 2014, 2016; Forssmann 2016; Kataloniji 2014; Ortega 2014; Pitarch 2017; The Heritage Trust 2014) that it generated a pressure to visit the newly discovered sites, even though people have shown little interest in visiting another site located in the same municipality and known since the 1970s. This pressure has had a serious impact on research of the rock art itself and the conservation issues affecting these sites, as the visits began even before the research team had been able to carry out all the necessary studies to make the discovery known under appropriate conditions. Moreover, in the digital era, it is difficult to control the distribution of images online when the site is still unpublished. This rush to visit the new finds is having a serious impact on research needs, timeframes and publications, as well as in the informed management, conservation and use of the sites.

Thus, digital media age and the production and consumption of immediate news through different sources are also opening new potential risks and challenges to rock art research and conservation that would have to be addressed in the near future to contribute to the protection of this fragile heritage. However, that is for consideration another day.

Volume overview

Our aim with this volume is to bring together different trends on open-air rock art research, monitoring, management, and conservation methodologies and practices, attempting to bridge gaps between purely scientific, curatorial, and managerial approaches. This volume brings together perspectives and experiences of different international research teams working across five continents. The 18 papers included in this book are divided into four discrete parts that best reflect the worldwide scenario where contributions to the volume unfold:

- ethics, community and collaborative approaches to the conservation and management of open-air rock art sites.
- methodological tools to support assessment and monitoring of open-air rock art sites.
- scientific examination and interventions at open-air rock art sites.

- global community and collaborative case studies innovating methodologies for the ongoing monitoring and management of open-air rock art sites.

The diverse origin of contributions results in a holistic and interdisciplinary approach that conciliates perceived intervention necessity, community and stakeholders' interests, and rigorous scientific analysis regarding open-air rock art conservation and management. Our ultimate goal was to unite the voices of the global community in tackling a significant challenge: to ensure a better future to open-air rock art.

Section I: Ethics, Community and Collaborative Approaches to the Conservation and Management of Open-Air Rock Art Sites

The volume starts with a series of papers and case studies dealing with ethical concerns while sharing community and collaborative approaches to rock art conservation and management. All chapters recall that today, approaches to rock art conservation must be interdisciplinary (conservation, archaeology, history, art, heritage sciences, architecture, legislation and so forth) and contemplate the different perceptions of the various stakeholders regarding time, values, interpretation, conservation, meanings and/or current uses, be they scientists, conservation specialists, management professionals, or communities.

In Chapter 1, Fernandes's paper on *Ethical and Political Matters in Open-Air Rock Art Conservation Practice,* opens this volume assessing current trends in the conservation of open rock art and exploring what he describes as the three main courses of action in rock art conservation practice: zero intervention, *in situ,* and *ex situ* conservation. Indeed, while some of the questions approached by chapters in this volume reflect the issue (Chapter 9 for instance), there has been limited debate on this matter. That is indeed fortunate, as instances when it has been needed to consider such options have been rare. Most of these episodes arise from industrial development projects, such as dams (again Chapter 9 but also 16), or mining and its transport from remote locations (Chapter 5). The potential benefits of building replicas of open-air rock art panels have not been contemplated either. Replicas can be helpful in minimizing the impact of over-visitation on the original sites, redirecting visitors to the replica to leave the original undisturbed (i.e., Chauvet and its replica). They can also be used to attract increasing numbers of tourists, as in the cases of cave sites such as Lascaux, (II and IV), Altamira, Tito Bustillo, or Ekain and Ekainberri, or simply to attract visitors. Thus, the worth of creating replicas of open-air rock art should also be considered. In the Coa Valley, for instance, six replicas of specific outcrops with rock art are included in the permanent exhibition at the Coa Museum. At Bangudae, Korea (Chapter 16), a replica of the rock art panel is on display nearby the site at the Petroglyph Museum. Whilst in the case of the Coa it has been possible to preserve much of the rock art *in situ* and available for visitors in addition to the replicas of some engraved outcrops, Chapter 9 points to a quite pragmatic case at Sabor in which a few prehistoric rock art outcrops where selected to be consolidated *in situ*. This occurred prior to submersion underwater and having in consideration earlier efforts at the Alqueva dam, where prehistoric rock art was also submerged, with no consolidation measures.

In Chapter 2, Mulvaney explains his experience of managing archaeological and sacred landscapes at Murujuga Aboriginal lands, located in the northwest coast of Australia, through industry, working with the Traditional Custodians and in partnership with academic institutions. As an employed academic to an industrial company exploring natural resources at the Dampier, Australia, he presents balanced analysis of how recent and ongoing development of this area does not offer a consistent outlook for one of the largest concentrations of petroglyphs anywhere in the world (an estimate of 30,000). Although this company presents a track record regarding involvement with Traditional Owners and archaeological knowledge input into corporate decisions since the end of the last century, recent events dictated the resignation of its CEO due to the destruction of two caves of sacred Aboriginal importance in the region (Khalil 2020). Despite efforts, so far inconclusive, to gauge the extent yet expanding industrial activity affects the condition of the rock art, the notion of conciliating both (industry and rock art conservation, management, and traditional ownership) seems "ludicrous", using Mulvaney's expression. Will the alluded resignation signal a change in fortune, in Australia as elsewhere since multinationals operate worldwide, when rock art sites are confronted with industrial development?

In Chapter 3, Domingo et al. reflect on the benefits of a multidisciplinary and integral approach to rock art conservation based on their experience at the Spanish site of la Covatina, one of the Levantine rock art sites listed in the UNESCO World Heritage List in 1998. The authors summarize the main challenges Levantine rock art faces today; as in other parts of the world, all sorts of natural and human threats. They also list the main types of preventive conservation interventions that have been undertaken in the region so far, introducing relevant discussions on the benefits and dangers of direct interventions. According to the authors, the lack of dialogue between heritage managers, mainly dealing with rock art conservation, and archaeologists, focusing on the study of art, have impacted some of the scientific values of this art: for example, calcium crusts have been removed disregarding whether they could be used for dating, as well as their protective nature (Domingo et al. 2021; Domingo and Barreda 2021). To fill the gap between archaeology and heritage approaches, the authors developed a pilot multidisciplinary and multistep project, bringing together archaeology, heritage science and cutting-edge digital technologies, to achieve a much-needed comprehensive understanding and recording of the art and the site. Their aim is to contribute to the long-term preservation of the site, both *in situ* and in digital formats, and to provide access to the scientific community and the public through different media (including a 4D reconstruction). The paper shows a new example of close collaboration with local administrations with the aim of increasing social awareness, which are key to ensuring a future for this fragile heritage. Along with the complete conservation assessment, another important result of this project has been the discovery of previously unseen figures, as well as new rock art sites, increasing the site values and the wealth of the region's heritage.

In Chapter 4, Marshall and Taçon discuss the importance of collaborating with Indigenous communities in the conservation and management of rock art in Australia. Framed in the context of the development of the discipline nationally in the past 40–50 years, the initial drive of the scientific community was to support Traditional Owners in the protection and preservation of sites through intervention. While considerate of culture, associated protocols and practice, the overwhelming assessment was one that inevitably gave primacy to scientific process over cultural and traditional maintenance. A serious challenge that is yet to be overcome was the little understanding of the specific long-term requirements of monitoring, maintenance and evaluation required for physical conservation work that included the trial of artificial silica sprays and installation of artificial silicon driplines; treatments of salts and minerals, cryptogamic growth; as well as dust removal. Indigenous people were at times present, but the longer-term implications of conservation and management programs were not always fully appreciated. Focusing on three case studies in the north of the continent, Marshall and Taçon have flipped the previous practice to one where western scientific processes walk beside or a step behind the cultural leaders who own, drive and control the introduction and/or continued use of conservation and management strategies moving forward. Their collective effort to work together with Indigenous communities, bringing knowledge from both worlds together to care for the rock art, implementing culturally based monitoring and maintenance programs in addition to the development of Conservation Management Plans to guide the processes, is having exceptional benefits for communities and preservation efforts alike.

Section II: Methodological Tools to Support Assessment and Monitoring of Open-Air Rock Art Sites

The development of methodological frameworks and tools to support the ongoing monitoring and management of open-air rock art sites is also needed to develop adequate conservation strategies and management plans, and it is the focus of this section in which papers discuss the benefits of using a variety of tools.

In Chapter 5, Allen et al. utilize Rock Art Stability Index (RASI), a non-invasive rapid field assessment tool created to evaluate geologic stability and rock weathering of rock art panels (as also described in Chapter 3) to evaluate recently discovered rock art in Grenada, Caribe. In this paper, they suggest a step further in the use of this research tool, by adding a Geographic Information System (GIS) component to the process. The sites, albeit popular with tourists, are quite understudied and their management is challenging as they are unprotected under national law. Moreover, most sites are privately owned. In spite of the risks, this situation might entail – for instance, the lack of management guidelines meant that a group of volunteers cleaned one of the sites without proper supervision resulting in the haphazard removal of protective rock coatings – there is also the opportunity to reach the local community and empower them with the tools to enhance both the safeguard and the touristic use of the rock art. Victoria, one of the sites in the public domain, has likely been affected by periodic 'refreshing' of the motifs, done by local inhabitants with the intention of rendering them more noticeable for tourists. Albeit Allen and fellow co-authors note that this is a typical practice worldwide at "unofficially protected" rock art sites; other instances have shown that at protected sites it was precisely management officials that engaged in the practice. The example here comes from painting and repainting in red engraved rock art, with the same goal of developing tourism to the sites, a practice which until recently was current in Scandinavia (Hygen 1996). They consider this further in the context of the current example and utilize RASI to assist in determining both the level of impact as well as a means for informed decision-making in response.

In Chapter 6, Nash explores another interesting tool for rock art management and conservation: the Strengths, Weaknesses, Opportunities, and Threats (SWOT) analysis model. Although the sites (Cathole and Merlin's Caves) in which the method was used are not located in the open-air (and in the case of rock art at Cathole Cave, the prehistoric chronology has been debated), the proposal's originality, hindsight and resulting information merits its inclusion in the present volume. SWOT analyses are helpful for a few reasons; perhaps the most significant one is that it potentially covers a range of issues with positive and negative outlooks. If it identifies risks and weak spots, it also allows the recognition of strong points and prospects for further amelioration. From a management point of view, it is important to put together a synthetic list of the most important issues to address, but also to build upon regarding planning and strategic options. Although more commonly used when planning for sustainable tourism at heritage sites (Hausmann 2007; Roslan, Ramli and Choy 2018), Nash offers an elucidative example of how rock art preservation and conservation practices can benefit from SWOT analysis. Indeed, when carried out with the involvement of multiple stakeholders, this analysis is a democratic process that engages, compromises, and conciliates diverse viewpoints when initiating the process of devising, through a Conservation Management Plan for instance, long term protection strategies, similarly to what occurs in nature conservation studies (Scolozzi et al. 2014).

In Chapter 7, direct community involvement in rock art conservation is discussed by Mazel et al. by utilizing a user-friendly monitoring toolkit in the form of the Condition Assessment and Risk Evaluation (CARE) app.

Further development in the app, building on what was reported before (Giesen et al. 2014), such as the creation of a portal, and the automatic sending via email of produced scorecards reporting on the condition of assessed rock art to heritage officials with the aim of informing decisions on management and conservation. Care was also given to wide-ranging promotion of the app, via personalized emails, flyers, press releases, some picked up by outlets such as the BBC, social media, or presentations to specialized audiences but also to the general public. Considering the importance of the project, notably when trying to engage communities in the conservation of 'their' rock art, authors put forward a relevant discussion of challenges lying ahead. Most consequential to the sustainability of the project are the needed upgrades to the app, in order to comply with mobile phones platforms upgrading. To date required alterations have been met by the generosity of CARE's software developers, however further funding must be secured to continue with the project. This raises an important issue regarding the necessity of funding organizations allowing the continuous maintenance of digital data and apps. Another noteworthy point is that of the persistence of such projects. CARE has been launched within academia, in Newcastle University. If individuals leading the project leave the University or are no longer able to devote efforts to its development, what happens to the large amount of data amassed, generously, by volunteer 'citizen scientists'? If the solution proposed by Mazel et al. is appealing (governmental heritage organizations should manage the project directly), the question remains as to why weren't those institutions the ones that first created and implemented the project?

In Chapter 8, Abad and Rey explain the potential of Rock Art Archaeological Park Information System (SIPAAR), as implemented by the Campo Lameiro Rock Art Park (Pontevedra, Spain), for the integral management of petroglyphs. The authors have used GIS to archive information on and geolocate the rock art sites existent in the Spanish region of Galicia. The advantages of using GIS are significant as it is possible to enhance research, management and conservation goals. In fact, it is possible to integrate in one system different cartographic series and produce digital terrain models to monitor and manage conservation of rock art at a regional scale. GIS tools can be powerful auxiliaries of integral management and conservation strategies for rock art. Abad and Rey also discuss the development and implementation of GIS tools taking into consideration interoperability, standardization, and sustainability of archived data, following EU's Infrastructure for Spatial Information in Europe (INSPIRE) directive. The project's development made it possible to create risk maps for the conservation of the rock art, namely when concerning forest fires, a significant threat for heritage sites in this area of the Iberian Peninsula. Another major outcome of the project concerns the possibility of carrying out effective planning of human activities that may impact the territory, or the rock art. Finally, as SIPAAR comprises records of rock art panels made over the years, it has been possible to monitor their degradation, thus better informing conservation intervention planning.

10   *António Batarda Fernandes et al.*

Section III: Scientific Examination and Interventions at Open-Air Rock Art Sites

Papers in this section examine several advancements taking shape within the conservation science discipline in direct response to unique issues affecting open-air sites. Papers discuss both monitoring techniques and research and practice on different direct conservation interventions.

In Chapter 9, Bermúdez et al. conduct a comparative assessment of different methods used to remove lichens from schists surfaces at the two World Heritage listed sites of the Coa Valley and Siega Verde: Laser cleaning *vs.* chemical. Lichens are one of the most common biofilms that cover rock art panels. Even if there is an ongoing debate regarding the need to remove them from rock art panels (see Fernandes 2012, pp. 80–82 and pp. 148–151), public presentation issues at different sites have led managers to promote cleaning actions. Hence, work presented in Chapter 9 on experimental research of diverse methods to avoid mechanical removal of lichens covering engraved panels at Coa (Portugal) and Siega Verde (Spain) rock art sites is highly relevant. A comparative study, implemented at rock surfaces possessing no rock art, was conducted involving several methods: distilled water aided by mechanical removal; application of biocides aided by mechanical removal (which is perhaps the most used method worldwide, mostly due to its effectiveness, albeit the disintegration of the rock material it can cause); and two different laser systems. A bioreceptivity study was then carried out on all surfaces subject to lichen removal to assess the durability of cleaning actions. Even if results point to lesser efficiency of laser removal vs. biocide cleaning, and that laser use increases bioreceptivity of cleaned surfaces, and may also promote surface rock disintegration, it is important that ongoing work by authors attempts to reverse these results, as the use of biocides in these situations should ideally be totally discontinued in the future. Besides what was noted above regarding damages it can cause to panel's surfaces, hence also to rock art, biocides are hazardous to the environment and pose challenges in their appliance due to their toxicity.

In Chapter 10, Figueiredo et al. explain *in situ* rock art preservation in the Sabor Valley (Northwest Iberia). The paper gives an example illustrating one of those cases in which intervention is the preferred course of action. It describes conservation work carried out in the scope of salvage archaeology in an area destined to be flooded by the construction of a dam reservoir on the Sabor River, Northern Portugal, not far from the World Heritage Coa Valley complex of rock art sites, addressed in Chapters 1 and 9. At Sabor, the rock supports of the most significant rock art imagery in the area to be submerged were selected to be consolidated (up to six) so as to withstand the forthcoming, now permanent, drastic environmental change. Selection options and applied conservation methodologies are discussed in the chapter. Of interest here, also considering Chapter 1, is to note that in the Sabor it was a question of *intervening* on the selected rock art outcrops as in most, less significant ones, zero intervention was followed. Hence, most occurrences were not intervened upon, while *ex situ* conservation was not considered in intervened ones; rather it was deliberately decided to consolidate *in situ*.

In Chapter 11, as part of the same project presented in Chapter 3, Rodríguez and Domingo explain in detail the aims and results of the thermal-hygrometric monitoring of la Covatina site in Spain. Temperature, humidity, and illuminance are climate variables that decisively influence the condition and degradation of rock art panels. This paper presents an evaluation of these dynamics regarding a site belonging to the Levantine rock art complex, La Covatina, with a view to inform recommendations to its conservation. The paper notes the importance of developing site-specific monitoring strategies considering the environmental changing nature of the locations of this open-air rock art tradition. The potential problems of the methods used are carefully discussed. Results point to significant annual and daily variations in temperature, humidity, and illuminance values negatively impacting the conservation of Levantine rock art, which mostly comprises painted motifs. Although the risk of gelifraction has been identified as low, recorded thermal amplitude on the coldest days of the year suggest the risk of thermoclasty. Another noteworthy conclusion is that, due to diverse factors such as shade, differences in temperature of the several measured points in the panel can reach up to 14 degrees. Hence, it is suggested that motifs at this site that are more exposed to solar radiation are the ones presenting worse condition.

In Chapter 12, Barreda, Zalbidea and Osca provide the results of a series of tests of calcium hydroxide nanoparticles used as consolidating materials, to identify their behaviour and benefits in open air rock art conservation. This is certainly another pioneering research field regarding open-air rock art conservation. At Cova Remígia site, another site with Levantine rock art, the application of calcium hydroxide nanoparticles consolidants was tested in instances where paint cohesion, fixation or consolidation issues occurred. Besides damage caused by climate conditions, public visitation to the shelter, in the form of touching and wetting the paintings for their perceived better viewing, and use as refuge by local shepherds and their goats, impacted negatively in the conservation of the rock art. Biodeterioration, fractures, and fissures are also present, further worsening the condition of the rock art. After careful examination of previous treatments using organic compounds such as Paraloid B72, it is praiseworthy to mention that inorganic materials were tested. Scanning Electron Microscope - Energy Dispersive X-Ray (SEM-EDX) analysis of treated samples revealed that both employed families of products, CaLoSiL and Nanorestore, achieved good results, at least in the short term.

In Chapter 13, Gomes et al. uses multiproxy archaeometric analysis to identify pigments used in rock art in different parts of the world. Their approach is of interest for both research on prehistoric practices as well as on conservation and monitoring of rock art paintings, since the composition and the environmental peculiarities of each site may influence conservation of pigments and substrates, and thus guide decision making regarding best practices for the preservation of the art. When considering painted open-air rock art conservation, it is essential to understand the matter that is the focus of intervention effort. Thus, characterization of pigments, as well as their preparation techniques, should be part of any conservation project. To that regard, Gomes et al. applied a range of archaeometry methods to study the pigments and natural ochre of several sites across three continents, in Iberia, Ethiopia, Angola, and Brazil. Chapter 13 presents the results of this project, also with a view to monitoring and management of the studied sites. Decisive in such a study is the correct identification of the binders used, as in these rests a possibility to attribute absolute dating to painted rock art. Moreover, the use of certain pigments and binders is often specific to certain periods or regions. Hence, this chapter presents a most timely state of the art on available archaeometric methods to characterize pigments used in rock art, from Optical Microscopy to Gas Chromatography. The main results from the sampled sites, located as noted above, indicates that raw materials used were procured locally and that hematite was the most used mineral. Authors suggest that this latter result may be explained by the great availability of the mineral on the Earth's crust; although the deliberate choice of the colour red found in hematite cannot also be disregarded. Another noteworthy find was the difficulty of fully identifying binders which suggests the need to further develop methods to characterize the composition of paints used in rock art. All in all, authors aptly exemplify how archaeometric techniques can be of use in long term planning of painted rock art conservation.

Section IV: Global Community and Collaborative Case Studies Innovating Methodologies for the Ongoing Monitoring and Management of Open-Air Rock Art Sites

The final section of this volume introduces specific case studies showing attempts around the globe to monitor, maintain and manage rock imagery in different contexts.

In Chapter 14, Fernandes et al. reflect on the need for and the benefits of carrying out the dual conservation of natural and cultural heritage, suggesting that both can mutually benefit when considered holistically together. Drawing on the significant Serranopólis, Goiás, Brazil, rock art complex, a case is put forward on how the preservation of the existent prehistoric imagery is utterly linked with the survival of the original vegetation cover, the Cerrado. In a country where original biomes are steadfastly disappearing, mostly due to agribusiness, the survival of rock art in pockets of still existing Cerrado points to the need to consider alternative land management strategies. Working example, the Pousada das Araras, a natural reserve where prehistoric rock art spanning over several millennia is kept and shown to visitors within the original Cerrado. It is argued that already on-going community outreach namely with the involvement of local and regional schools can prove instrumental to enhance awareness on the value of preserving both the Cerrado and the rock art. Moreover, there is the opportunity to use both in alternative land management strategies that expand sustainable tourism activities in the region. For these to produce long-term outcomes, local, regional, and federal government institutions, it is argued, must show the way forward by launching and supporting such projects, including the addition to the school curricula, at least on a state basis, of visits to the sites that can expound the importance of preserving the rock art and the Cerrado. Carried out conservation work at the sites presented in this Chapter is of no or minute consequence if local communities, namely future generations, are not engaged with the rock art in the medium and long-term when further conservation and maintenance work at the sites is again needed.

In Chapter 15, Groom et al. share their experience of community engagement in geologic assessments of Thamudic Inscriptions and Petroglyphs in the Wadi Rum Protected Area, Jordan. Considering debated colonialist attitude of successive academic expeditions to the region and continued ignorance of the wealth of information the local community can provide on the rock art and their rapport with it, the project presented in this Chapter sought to encourage community engagement in heritage condition assessment through the Wadi Rum Rock Art Rangers program. One of the final goals of the project was to help building local capacity and self-agency. Resorting to the established RASI methodology (see also Chapter 5; Dorn et al. 2008), aimed at facilitating public participation to monitor conservation at rock art sites, the program, incorporating both academics, government officials, and volunteers from the local community, recorded, over a one-year period, the condition of almost 1,200 rock art panels. One of the outcomes of the project was a wide-ranging debate among the whole team and the local community on best practices to avoid over-visitation at the most popular sites, and the problems it can cause, from tourists trying to carve their own motifs onto rock surfaces to the rubbish they left behind. Thus, through an organic, bottom up, engagement of the local community (guides, managers, users of the sites, volunteers, etc.), the fashion in which this project was conducted sheds light on the way forward to dispel colonialist approaches to rock art conservation and management practices.

In Chapter 16, with a focus on Korean rock art, Lee explains the conflicts involved in the preservation of Bangudae Petroglyphs, affected by a dam built in 1965, thus providing a new example of the fate of rock art subject to river damming. The Bangudae is a telling showcase of the detrimental effects of recurring drying and wetting episodes on the rock support due to shifting water levels of the Daegok dam, Ulsan, Korea. In fact, the discovery of the panel in 1971 was only made a few years after the dam was completed. Since then, particularly in the last two decades, encouraged by the echoes of the cancellation of the Coa Valley dam to safeguard existing rock art there (see Chapters

1 and 9; Baptista and Fernandes 2007), a vigorous debate has been occurring in South Korea, involving different levels of academia, national and local authorities, as well as the community, regarding what can/should be done to avoid damage to the rock art by rising waters. Throughout the years, many solutions, from dykes to completely emptying the reservoir, have been put forward, without reaching a compromise so far. All proposed solutions never contemplated *ex situ* conservation, in spite several replicas of the Bangudae panel have been commissioned and exhibited in different contexts. Hence, the only course of action for the Bangudae, after the dam's rising/lowering water levels issue has been resolved, is *in situ* conservation, as 50 plus years of such recurring episodes have left their toll, leaving the Bangudae panel badly requiring conservation work (Fitzner, Heinrichs and La Bouchardiere 2004).

In Chapter 17, a paper by Santos and Buco focus on the conservation of rock art in the Serra Branca valley, west side of the Serra da Capivara National Park, Piauí, Brazil, from a diachronic perspective. The Serra da Capivara area is a rock art complex included in United Nations Educational, Scientific and Cultural Organization (UNESCO)'s World Heritage List in 1991 (Nash 2009). Less well-known however is the adjacent Serra Branca valley rock art which is presented in this Chapter. As happens with other worldwide major rock art ensembles, the Serra Branca rock art spans a long diachronic evolution, up until the arrival of European settlers and even beyond. Accordingly, the condition of the rich variety of existing rock art (naturalistic *and* abstract motifs; paintings *and* engravings, for instance) varies significantly. Authors carried out a wide-ranging evaluation of factors affecting the conservation of the rock art. Consequential for this characterization is the concept that perhaps there has never been an 'optimal' condition of rock art. Freshly made rock art will have begun to degrade, the authors suggest, just after it was made, also because of coeval cultural use of the sites where it is present. This results, for instance, from ritual practices involving the use of fire inside shelters. Fire, it was ascertained, was used later, as a result of cultural evolution before post-Colombian times, inside rock art shelters in pottery producing processes. On the other hand, the use of fire in this productive activity may have triggered a rise in deforestation that could have led to climate patterns change which, in turn, also may be the driving factor affecting the rock art. Another interesting point is that the surface itself on which the rock art motifs are located, might have never been itself in an optimal condition (or at least as today a perfect canvas to receive artwork is considered to have to be): fractures and fissures, as other natural features may already have been present making the rocky support less than 'ideal' to host imagery for centuries and millennia.

This volume finishes with Chapter 18, a paper by Marshall, May, O'Loughlin and Lee, a collaborative team of Traditional Owners, Indigenous rangers, Park staff and academics who are investigating the benefits and limitations of artificial silicon driplines in Kakadu National Park, Australia. Since the late 1970s and subsequent inclusion of the area on the World Heritage List, the use of silicon to manage water flow to protect the vulnerable rock art within Kakadu has been applied extensively across the Park's

20,000km² landscape. Informed by scientific experiments at the time that involved camping in an area for three weeks during a Wet Season to observe water flow and install the silicon driplines in response to this. Nevertheless, changes in the operational management of cultural heritage in the proceeding decades meant that the technique was applied without the scientific rigor of the early trials. The team that is now conducting the project, is stepping back to monitor, observe and this time evaluate the effectiveness of the intervention technique, to reduce impact to affected sites while advancing scientific knowledge associated with the process. Through consideration of four specific examples at rock art sites across Kakadu, results are presented of one successful application, two failures and another that remains under assessment. Developing a strategy to manage and mitigate the challenges identified, the researchers argue that whilst of value at specific sites, there is a need to ensure the application of western science interventions is twofold – consistent with Indigenous cultural and traditional knowledges; and that the technique should only be applied under specific conditions that include ongoing evaluation and assessment processes.

Ways forward

The 18 international contributions assembled in this volume provide recent perspectives in the field of open-air rock art conservation and management, adding up new data, experiences and tools linked to different aspects of the four pillars of rock art conservation policy and practice: these include, questions and case studies dealing with public and political awareness and recalling the need for any sort of intervention to be guided by ethical principles; tested methodologies, tools and protocols to build more effective management systems; initiatives dealing with both physical and cultural conservation practices, and the need for community engagement and support to achieve better conservation outcomes. Each of these themes is discussed in depth as part of global initiatives framing opportunities and challenges alike and a range of contexts.

As a collective, the demand to move beyond the interests of a specific stakeholder, to embrace more integral and collaborative approaches to rock art conservation to meet the needs of all interested parties, is common to almost all chapters. They also illustrate the need for flexibility and dialogues to accommodate conservation protocols, strategies and practices to the various natural and cultural contexts in which open air rock art is located. Additionally, the development of monitoring tools and involvement of social agents in these tasks, considering how dispersed this heritage is, has also been pointed out in several chapters.

Whilst these valuable insights have been shared, importantly one of the key deficiencies that the different chapters in this book reveal is the lack of legal protection measures, in many parts of the world, to ensure the in situ and long-term preservation of this millenary art. While some countries have granted this heritage different types of legal protection, prioritizing in situ conservation and preventing destruction, removal, or relocation, others have not. Ultimately, this volume demonstrates that debates in this field have only just begun and that the role of communities will be instrumental to the success of long-term preservation which collectively, collaboratively and respectfully build a sustainable future to this delicate, diverse and unique heritage.

Note

1 For instance, a web browser search on "rock art Sistine Chapel before:2020" will produce bountiful results, both in the "General" or "News" sections. A Google Scholar search using the same expression will similarly produce interesting hits.

References

Agnew, N., Deacon, J., Hall, N., Little, T., Sullivan, Sh. and Taçon, P. (2015) *Rock Art. A Cultural Treasure at Risk*. Los Angeles: The Getty Conservation Institute.

Alberge, D. (2020) 'sistine Chapel of the ancients' rock art discovered in remote Amazon forest. *The Guardian*. Retrieved 6 December 2020, from https://www.theguardian.com/science/2020/nov/29/sistine-chapel-of-the-ancients-rock art-discovered-in-remote-amazon-forest?fbclid=IwAR1CyR9Dxuaz8F3EDI-fIpl1YlXA 11Cio55Q_1I_0X669AxUjQGNGtx0gwA\

Archaeology (2014) Cave Paintings Discovered in Spain. Retrieved 9 December 2021, from https://www.archaeology.org/news/2131-140522-vilafranca-cave-bull

Artribune (2014) Pitture del sito di arte rupestre di Vilafranca (Castellón). Retrieved 9 December 2021, from https://www.artribune.com/tribnews/2014/05/art-digest-hong-kong-patria-delle-nanogallerie-montpellier-baluardo-dei-settis-di-francia-non-vandalizzerei-ancora-il-rothko-ma-resto-yelliwist/attachment/pitture-del-sito-di-arte-rupestre-di-vilafranca-castellon/

Baltasar, M. (2014) Arte rupestre regresa después de 7000 años. Retrieved 9 December 2021, from https://origenoticias.com/arte-rupestre-regresa-despues-de-7-000-anos/

Baptista, A. M., and Fernandes, A. P. B. (2007) Rock art and the Côa Valley Archaeological Park: A case study in the preservation of Portugal's Prehistoric parietal heritage. In Pettit, P., Bahn, P. and Ripoll, S. (Eds.) *Palaeolithic Cave Art at Creswell Crags in European Context*. Oxford: Oxford University Press, pp.263–279.

Blundell, V. and Woolagoodja, D. (2005) *Keeping the Wanjinas Fresh: Sam Woolagoodja and the Enduring Power of Lalai*. Fremantle: Fremantle Arts Centre Press.

Bowdler, S. (1988) Repainting Australian rock art. *Antiquity*, 62, pp.517–523.

Bricker Sr., F., Holcomb, T. and Dean, C. A. (1999) Native American's thoughts on preservation and conservation of rock art. In Dean, C. (Coord.) *Rock Art Preservation and Conservation Symposium (1994: Flagstaff, Arizona). Images Past, Images Present: The Conservation and Preservation of Rock Art*. Tucson: American Rock Art Research Association, pp.7–9.

Calle, H. (2020) El polémico "descubrimiento" de pinturas rupestres en Guaviare. *El Espectador*. Retrieved 10 December 2020, from https://www.elespectador.com/noticias/medio-ambiente/el-polemico-descubrimiento-de-pinturas-rupestres-en-guaviare/?fbclid=IwAR3X9Mcltkmd-uwBCsCvpr3LHlQ v6BggaMVfzL5ctMqgtmIlI0-gcR46fs0

Darvill, T., Fernandes, A. P. and Batarda (Ed.) (2014) *Open-Air Rock art Conservation and Management. State of the Art and Future Perspectives.* New York: Routledge. https://doi.org/10.4324/9780203754177

Deacon, J. (2006) Rock art conservation and tourism. *Journal of Archaeological Method and Theory,* 13, pp.376–396.

Domingo, I. (2021) Shifting ontologies and the use of ethnographic data in prehistoric rock art research. In Moro, O. and Porr, M. (Eds.) *Ontologies of Rock Art Images, Relational Approaches and Indigenous knowledge.* Routledge: Taylor and Francis, pp.200–220.

Domingo, I. and Barreda, G. (2021) Knowledge-building in open-air rock art conservation: Sharing the history and experiences with Levantine Rock Art. *Studies in Conservation,* https://doi.org/10.1080/00393630.2021.1996092. https://www.tandfonline.com/action/showCitFormats?doi=10.1080%2F00393630.2021.1996092&area=0000000000000001

Domingo, I. and Bea, M. (2016) From science to heritage: New challenges for world heritage rock art sites in Mediterranean Spain in the twenty-first century. In Brady, L. and Taçon, P. (Eds.) *Relating to Rock Art in the Contemporary World.* Colorado: University press of Colorado, pp.213–244.

Domingo, I., Smith, C. and May, S. K. (2017) Etnoarqueologia y arte rupestre: potencial, perspectivas y ética. *Complutum,* 28(2), pp.285–305.

Domingo, I., Vendrell, M. and Chieli, A. (2021) A critical assessment of the potential and limitations of physicochemical analysis to advance knowledge on Levantine rock art. *Quaternary International,* 572, pp.24–40.

Dorn, R. I., Whitley, D. S., Cerveny, N. V., Gordon, S. J., Allen, C. D. and Gutbrod, E. (2008) The rock art stability index: A new strategy for maximizing the sustainability of rock art as a heritage resource. *Heritage Management,* 1(1), pp.37–70.

Europa Press (2014) Localizan un yacimiento con arte rupestre en Vilafranca con al menos 12 figuras de 7.000 años de antigüedad. Retrieved 9 December 2021, from https://www.europapress.es/comunitat-valenciana/noticia-cultura-localizan-yacimiento-arte-rupestre-vilafranca-menos-12-figuras-7000-anos-antiguedad-20140519180102.html

Europa Press (2016) Hallan pinturas rupestres "únicas" de hace 7.000 años en Villafranca del Cid. Retrieved 9 December 2021, from https://www.europapress.es/comunitat-valenciana/noticia-hallan-pinturas-rupestres-unicas-hace-7000-anos-villafranca-cid-20160726164922.html

Fernandes, A. P. B. (2010) Vandalism, graffiti or 'just' rock art? The case of a recent engraving in the Côa Valley rock art complex in Portugal. *FUMDHAmentos,* 9(III), pp.729–43.

Fernandes, A. P. B. (2012) *Natural Processes in the Degradation of Open-Air Rock art Sites: An Urgency Intervention Scale to Inform Conservation.* PhD diss., Bournemouth University.

Finestre Sull'Arte (2020) Colombia, scoperte migliaia di pitture rupestri con raffigurazioni di animali giganti. Retrieved 7 December 2020, from https://www.finestresullarte.info/arte-antica/colombia-scoperte-pitture-rupestri-con-animali-giganti?fbclid=IwAR00OA-_WhJCLU8U2FXx_5Lp8UGy4RT5rW9B46fczlr57gLYfkPYYR1g9pc

Fitzner, B., Heinrichs, K. and La Bouchardiere, D. (2004) The Bangudae Petroglyph in Ulsan, Korea: Studies on weathering damage and risk prognosis. *Environmental Geology,* 46, pp.504–26.

Forssmann, A. (2016) Descubren una escena de caza con jabalís en un abrigo rocoso de Vilafranca (Castellón). Retrieved 9 December 2021, from https://historia.nationalgeographic.com.es/a/descubren-escena-caza-jabalis-abrigo-rocoso-vilafranca-castellon_10573

Giesen, M. J., Mazel, A. D., Graham, D. W. and Warke, P. A. (2014) The preservation and care of rock art in changing environments: A view from Northeastern England, United Kingdom. In Darvill, T., Fernandes, A. P. B. (Eds.) *Open-Air Rock art Conservation and Management. State of the Art and Future Perspectives.* New York: Routledge, pp.38–52. https://doi.org/10.4324/9780203754177

Hausmann, A. (2007) Cultural tourism: Marketing challenges and opportunities for German cultural heritage. *International Journal of Heritage Studies,* 13(2), pp.170–184.

Hygen, A.-S. (1996) Conservation, intervention or destruction of rock art? Some Scandinavian experiences. *Rock Art Research,* 13(1), pp.49–52 (and comments pp.59–60).

Jungle Mystery: Lost Kingdoms of the Amazon (2020). Retrieved 6 December 2020, from https://www.channel4.com/programmes/jungle-mystery-lost-kingdoms-of-the-amazon

Kataloniji, N. (2014) V še eni španski jami odkrili prazgodovinske slikarije. Retrieved 9 December 2021, from https://www.rtvslo.si/kultura/drugo/v-se-eni-spanski-jami-odkrili-prazgodovinske-slikarije/337630

Khalil, S. (2020) Rio Tinto chief Jean-Sébastien Jacques to quit over Aboriginal cave destruction. *BBC.* Retrieved 13 December 2020, from https://www.bbc.com/news/world-australia-54112991?fbclid=IwAR0LVMGDiUN_n2jftN7pa2MkANbE8P2YNDw6XEqkVwWsVVnDKfdlF2vMU4I

Mangolamara, S., Karadada, L., Oobagooma, J., Woolagoodja, D., Karadada J. and Doohan, K. (2018) *Nyara pari kala niragu (Gaambera), gadawara ngyaran-gada (Wunambal), inganinja gubadjoongana (Woddordda) = We Are Coming to See You.* Derby: Dambimangari Aboriginal Corporation and Wunambal Gaambera Aboriginal Corporation.

Marshall, M. (2020) *Rock Art Conservation and Management: 21st Century Perspectives in Northern Australia.* PhD thesis, Canberra: Australian National University. doi:10.25911/5f969812a2f22.

Marshall, M., May, K., Dann, R. and Nulgit, L. (2020) Indigenous stewardship of decolonised rock art conservation processes in Australia. *Studies in Conservation,* 65, pp.205–212. DOI:10.1080/00393630.2020.1778264

May, S. K., Maralngurra, J. G., Johnston, I. G., Goldhahn, J., Lee, J., O'Loughlin, G., May, K., Nabobbob, C. N., Garde, M. and Taçon, P. S. C. (2019) 'This is my Father's Painting': A first-hand account of the creation of the most iconic rock art in Kakadu National Park. *Rock Art Research,* 36(2), pp.199–213.

Mowaljarlai, D. and Malnic, J. (2001) *Yorro Yorro: Everything Standing Up Alive. Rock Art and Stories from the Australian Kimberley.* Broome: Magabala Books Aboriginal Corporation.

Mowaljarlai, D., Vinnicombe, P., Ward, G. K. and Chippindale, C. (1988) Repainting of images on rock in Australia and the maintenance of Aboriginal culture. *Antiquity,* 62, pp.690–696.

Nash, G. (2009) Serra da Capivara. America's oldest art? *Current World Archaeology,* 37, pp.41–6.

Ortega, L. (2014) Localizado un yacimiento con arte rupestre de 7.000 años de antigüedad. Retrieved 9 December 2021, from https://elpais.com/cultura/2014/05/19/actualidad/1400518015_159619.html

Pitarch, M. (2017) Vilafranca desvela dos nuevos hitos para el arte rupestre levantino con 7.000 años de antigüedad. Retrieved 9 December 2021, from https://elpais.com/ccaa/2017/12/25/valencia/1514192832_612483.html

Porr, M. and Matthews, J. (2017) Post-colonialism, human origins and the paradox of modernity. *Antiquity*, 91(358), pp.1058–1068. doi:10.15184/aqy.2017.82

Roslan, Z., Ramli, Z. and Choy, E. A. (2018) The potential of heritage tourism development in Jugra, Selangor, Malaysia, using SWOT analysis. In Wahad, M. R. A., Zakaria, R. M. A., Hadrawi, M. and Ramli, Z. (Eds.) *Selected Topics on Archaeology, History and Culture in the Malay World*. Springer: Singapore, pp.159–170.

Scolozzi, R., Schirpke, U., Morri, E., D'Amato, D. and Santolini, R. (2014) Ecosystem services-based SWOT analysis of protected areas for conservation strategies. *Journal of Environmental Management*, 146, pp.543–551.

Smith, C. (2008) Panache and protocol in Australian Aboriginal art. In Domingo, I., Fiore, D. and May, S. M. (Eds.) *Archaeologies of Art: Time, Place and Identity*. Walnut Creek, CA: Left Coast Press, pp.215–241.

The Heritage Trust (2014) Prehistoric hunting scenes found in Spanish cave. Retrieved 9 December 2021, from https://theheritagetrust.wordpress.com/2014/05/22/prehistoric-hunting-scenes-found-in-spanish-cave/

Section I
Ethics, Community and Collaborative Approaches to the Conservation and Management of Open-Air Rock Art Sites

1 Ethical and Political Matters in Open-Air Rock Art Conservation Practice

António Batarda Fernandes

Introduction

Rock art is one of the most notable windows on the spiritual, social, or economic life of our ancestors providing a portal to their mindset, while there is dual value to ancient imagery engraved or painted in rock walls. On the one hand, rock art provides essential data that can be used in scientific attempts to characterize land-use, settlement patterns, migration waves, or religious and spiritual belief practices. On the other, rock art undeniably exhibits aesthetic attributes, making various motifs and compositions universal works of art. Although imagery can be divided, for consideration of management and conservation issues, and according to their location, in cave and open-air art, the current work considers only the latter.

Remarkable as it is, open-air rock art has survived despite various factors including unrelenting environmental conditions (Bahn 2016, pp. 170–197; Fernandes 2012; Tratebas, Cerveny and Dorn 2004; Walderhaug and Walderhaug 1998); human-induced damage, from vandalism to theft (Bauman 2005; Keenan 2000); in addition to environmental changes caused by human activities (Aberg, Stray and Dahlin 1999; Fitzner, Heinrichs and La Bouchardiere 2004; Hansen 1999). The present piece of work will attempt to briefly characterize the global situation concerning the condition of such sites, possible solutions, while considering ethical and political ramifications regarding relocation of rock art for conservation purposes.

Open-air rock art conservation: the need for interdisciplinary approaches

If cave art exists in environments that allowed the creation of natural cavities, open-air sites are quite more omnipresent and outnumber subterranean sites (Clottes 2008). Hence, open-air sites are as crucial as cave ones despite the latter being more popularly recognized. The threats open-air rock art faces vary according to particular locations, from desert to arctic environments. Hence, the task of conserving these sites poses demanding technical and methodological challenges.

DOI: 10.4324/9780429355349-3

From the repeated appeals for the conservation of rock art coming from different areas of the planet (see Anati, Wainwright and Lundy 1984; Silver 1989; Vidal 2001), the multiple menaces to the perpetuation of this significant heritage become apparent. While some authors reference physical weathering as the most pressing risk (Fitzner, Heinrichs and La Bouchardiere 2004; Meiklejohn, Hall and David 2009; Walderhaug and Walderhaug 1998), others invoke the adverse effects of Biodeterioration (Mottershead et al. 2003), notably regarding lichen colonisation (Tratebas 2004) or human agency (Deacon 2006; Hygen 1996). Different attributions of risk have, it is suggested, more to do with each researcher's specific area of expertise but, more importantly, with the diverse environments where rock art endures.

The global insufficiency of researchers interested in open-air conservation indicates that the matter has not yet received adequate attention (Silver 1989) as other archaeological hallmarks have drawn (for instance, Roman sites). The prospect is gradually improving as touristic growth is contributing to raising awareness, thus transforming some sites into attractions (Deacon 2006). Nonetheless, managers and conservators still have much to consider from more developed fields of research, namely weathering studies, Biodeterioration or cultural heritage conservation. However, regarding the latter, there is a crucial material difference to consider: fresh un-weathered stone more or less recently exposed to decay and paleo-weathered rock surfaces, out in the open for many millennia. Hence, conservation approaches, materials, and processes typically applied in building stone conservation have to undergo previous tests for later application in paleo-weathered rock faces possessing artistic motifs.

Doehne and Price remark that a conventional approach in building stone conservation tends to order weathering dynamics in confined areas of research. It is noteworthy to recognize the

> "important interrelationships between environmental, material, and historical variables. (...) a few key parameters often dominate each weathering process, and the result can be nonlinear and even chaotic, in contrast to previous assumptions about linear rates of erosion. (...)"
> (Doehne and Price 2010, p. 75)

To understand and tackle, in the most comprehensive fashion possible, interconnected weathering patterns, an interdisciplinary strategy is advisable. Conversely, and somewhat paradoxically, a quote provided by the same authors, intended to portray the general situation regarding build stone conservation, also applies to rock art conservation studies:

> "I (...) have the feeling that the general tendency among researchers is to remain confined to one's own specialty (...). Don't fail to see the wood for the trees! Before going into detail, an assessment of the whole is necessary."
> (Chamay, as quoted in Doehne and Price 2010, p. 69)

As Cerveny notes, "the application of stabilizing agents on rock art panels is not widely discussed in refereed publications, (although) proponents discuss active intervention on the stage of newsletters and similar forums" (2005, p. 8). The same author also "urge(s) treatment advocates to come out of the newsletters and short courses (and to) publish suggested treatments" (p. 38). Even though Cerveny's remarks refer only to the use of stabilizing agents on rock art panels, her critique accurately depicts the overall situation within (open-air) rock art conservation research. Indeed, studies are published less in peer-reviewed journals than in grey literature. This situation is unencouraging towards an interdisciplinary approach to rock art conservation and the advancement of this field of study.

Hence, not surprisingly, most methods used to categorize weathering in rock surfaces come from building stone conservation literature. Cerveny notes more than a dozen, ranging from Geographic Information System (GIS) data referencing to microscopic fractal analysis (2005, p. 102). Most of these are challenging to apply in the context of open-air rock art conservation due to ethical (for instance, sample collection directly from rock art motifs), logistical, or financial constraints.

A way to extend the scope of research is to investigate environmental studies which provide essential insights, data, and even methodological models of use in open-air rock art conservation. Bennie et al. (2008) investigated the role solar radiation plays in rock surface temperature and moisture, while Viles (2005) demonstrated how different solar exposures might determine distinct climate-induced weathering cadences. Other areas of interest are geomorphologic studies, including slope dynamics or aspect (Summerfield 1991, pp. 163–189; Yalcin and Bulut 2007). Finally, this author carried out a research project aimed at using diverse natural weathering phenomena or location attributes (such aspect and slope but also physical weathering or Biodeterioration) in the creation of an integrated urgency intervention scale for the Coa Valley open-air rock art complex (Fernandes 2012).

Considering this further, attempts to model the impacts of climate change on specific environmental systems may also assist. Kincey, Challis, and Howard (2008) point out that river basins are among the natural systems that are mostly influenced by climate change. As several open-air rock art sites are located in river valleys and quite near to or even on floodplains, it is of great importance to recognize the potential impact of climate change on fluvial systems. Generally speaking, an increase in rainfall and particularly in the occurrence and severity of flash flooding episodes is one of the likely primary consequences of climate change (IPCC 2007). These episodes will signify more river flooding incidents that will further intensify soil erosion (Kincey, Challis, and Howard 2008, p. 116) but also soil re-deposition dynamics. Moreover, climate change will not be a "smooth and progressive" process as available evidence strongly suggests that the "variability and clustering of events in time and space will be an important part of the geomorphic future" (Viles and Goudie 2003, p. 127).

Conservation interventions on open-air rock art

Devlet and Devlet (2002) present an enlightening description helpful in promoting informed rock art conservation: in the 1970s, interventions intended to stop surface deterioration of engraved schist rock art panels, including crack filling, surface impregnation with cement and other materials, were carried out in Siberia. These works instigated irreversible adverse impacts on existing rock art, complementing and advancing existing deterioration factors. Another case is the use of an acrylic resin (Paraloid B72) to strengthen rock art paintings in the Tadrart Acacus World Heritage site, Libya. The initial administration occurred some 30 years before Ponti and Persia investigated the affair. They concluded that the resin led to alterations in the colour of the paintings. Nevertheless, its application was still considered appropriate, albeit in a low concentration, despite admitting that, besides changes in tone, high temperatures can result in the resin's chemical bonds to break down thus becoming inefficient (2002, pp. 130–131).

Consequently, in the last few years, crack filling, reattachment, massif consolidation, and the impregnation of rock surfaces are being approached with prudence, notably given the range of involuntary but real harm emerging from past interventions (see above and Andersson 1986; Walderhaug and Walderhaug 1998). Against a background where conservation actions are of a complex and delicate nature, there is often little information on the long-term implications of using un-tested materials (Dean 1999) within largely unpredictable environments.

Avery offers an account on how laboratory testing might prove useful in avoiding ill-prepared interventions at rock art sites. It was the case when "a preservative with penetration of over one centimetre was introduced into a rock sample" (1978, p. 68). If following weathering tests were deemed to be adequate concerning the strengthening of the sample rock surface, it was not long before the protected exterior surfaces tidily cut off exactly "at the point of deepest penetration" (1978, p. 68). Avery hence warns: "success in simulated laboratory experiments may not necessarily indicate results which might be obtained over long periods of time under natural conditions in the field." (1978, p. 68).

Pilot tests have been carried out in outcrops with no imagery but of similar condition and active weathering patterns as those hosting rock art at the Coa Valley, Portugal, a United Nations Educational, Scientific and Cultural Organization (UNESCO)'s World Heritage Site. One of the aims of these was to begin establishing accounts on the behaviour of conservation materials in this specific environment. A discussion of these experiments, carried out in 2004, can be found in Fernandes and Rodrigues (2008). These experiments evidenced that it was possible to undertake tests in the 'real' environment. In fact, the intervened unengraved outcrops still subsist down at the slopes that border the Coa River, as applied materials, for more than a decade now. An updated but succinct examination of their condition reveals that cohesion of the outcrops has been reinforced and that used materials do not show weakness in strength (Figure 1.1).

Figure 1.1 Outcrop with no rock art intervened in 2004 at Canada do Inferno, Coa Valley. Note fracture filling. Photo: Jaime António.

Ethical and aesthetical issues regarding conservation work

Deliberating ethical and aesthetical issues, and particularly in the case of the Coa Valley, the present author suggested that it is the entire outcrop containing imagery that must be considered when planning and carrying out conservation interventions. It would be pointless to attempt only to tackle weathering dynamics that are active on individual panels, or specific areas of panels, comprising rock art without aiming to strengthen the whole outcrop. On the other hand, the total outcrop consists of a unique art object. Hence, conservation efforts must aim for the long-term endurance of this cultural landscape in its entirety, i.e., setting + outcrop + panel + existing rock art (Fernandes 2008a). However, not surprisingly, as described in Fernandes and Rodrigues (2008), the Portuguese building stone conservation specialists that carried out the Coa trials followed traditional methods and strategies to that area of expertise. These primarily consisted in the consolidation of outcrops, by filling up of fractures, gaps, and diaclase boxes. The materials used included different supplies, such as elastomeric membranes, or epoxy resins to test reattachment of small loose/detached pieces. However, the core element consisted of lime-based mortars combined in different gradations. These interventions were considered appropriate from a technical point of view, having in mind the objective of conferring greater stability to the outcrops, by a panel of specialists asked to appraise the tests (Fernandes

2008b). Nevertheless, these interventions can be seen as quite intrusive and even harmful to the authenticity of the rock art in its original context.

Available data at Coa appears to suggest hope for permanence by Prehistoric artists as many panels host superimposed motifs made to accumulate on the same surface for decades, centuries, or even millennia (Fernandes 2018). Nevertheless, it must be noted that there are instances where for original producing societies rock art was possibly never meant to last. That is the case with Australian rock art sites, where some authors (for instance, Edwards 1974; Hughes 1979) have pointed that it was the interruption caused by white colonization to the creative practice that has had the greatest impact on the survival of cultural traditions and narratives. Be as it may, truth is that motifs have indeed survived and require conservation attention (or not!), but in such a way in which intervention planning and implementation always tries to reach an accord with *all* involved stakeholders (see discussion below).

On the other hand, at Coa, as in other Upper Palaeolithic European rock art sites (Ogawa 2005), natural features of rock faces (namely fractures) were integrated into motifs or sometimes used to prompt or structure composition (Fernandes et al. 2017). So, the fractures filled and sealed during the Coa tests in unengraved outcrops in order to confer stability to the panels, may prove impossible to replicate on the engraved surfaces as evidence indicates it is likely that these fissures form an unequivocal part of the art motif in question.

The precise intentions and frame of mind of the original creators will always be unknown, and much (rock art) conservation work entails a degree of double-guessing. Furthermore, as with any other work of art (including contemporary ones), it may be considered, namely in a Western context, that, from the moment a rock art motif was completed, it no longer belongs to the artist but to everyone who views it. Today, only contemporary living beings, despite (personal) and group identities baggage, enjoy these ancient artistic motifs, and in this sense, rock art now belongs more to present-day admirers than it did to the original communities that produced it. At the other end of the spectre, when looking at locations such as in Australia, Africa, or the Americas where First Nation communities are still the undeniable linked to the rock art, it must be recognized that conservation work unfolds in an even more ethically and politically charged context than elsewhere (Anyon et al. 2000), not to speak of suggestions to relocate motifs, as addressed below.

Summing it up, when planning *in situ* conservation work, it would be a token of respect and modesty to original *art* motifs to try to take into consideration what the motivations and idiosyncrasies expressed through rock art may have been for original creators and viewers (Fernandes 2018; Fernandes et al. 2017), as still might be for current traditional custodians. The aim would be thus to intervene only when strictly unavoidable (and in the least intrusive form possible) to ensure the endurance of a rock art site. This should then be undertaken if agreed by stakeholders that panels should not be permitted to completely collapse due to weathering (or other natural or human-led processes).

Discussion: removal for conservation purposes, can it ever be justifiable?

On an ethical, policymaking but also practical level, the issue of removing rock art panels from original locations to place them in a specially designed conservation environment is a critical discussion that has up until now been feebly considered by the rock art conservation studies field. Indeed, besides technical accounts (Hollmann et al. 2017), initial considerations on the subject (Lee 1986), and vibrant pleas defending non-removal (Bednarik 2008a, 2008b), not much more can be found in the specialized literature. One of the factors that possibly blocks discussion is the profuse tradition of rock art removal by collectors and thieves in several parts of the world (Henry 2007; Keenan 2000). An evocative example forms part of Taliesin West, Frank Lloyd Wright's winter home in the outskirts of Phoenix, USA. Rock art panels located in the mountains belonging to the property have been relocated to the centre square of the building complex (Wright 2017). Today, this relocation would have been frowned upon quite harshly and attempts to prevent it would likely be undertaken as it is broadly believed that rock art only retains its full meaning if still placed in its original landscape. Nonetheless, the relocation made the rock art part of the present spirit of Taliesin West. Thus, suggestions to return these panels to their original standing would now arguably be discarded.

Nevertheless, removal has also been carried out for preservation purposes since human intervention on the landscape (during the construction of dams, roads, or mining activities, for instance), with many instances resulting in placing rock art panels in peril (Bednarik 2008a). When the Coa Valley rock art was discovered, a large dam was being built in the Coa River. Following intense discussion and international uproar, the Portuguese Government stopped its construction and created the Coa Valley Archaeological Park to manage, conserve and present the rock art to the public. When the debate on the destiny of the Coa was still unsettled, Eletricidade de Portugal (EDP), the power company that was building the dam, proposed to remove the most significant engraved outcrops in order to place them in some sort of conservation-controlled environment located outside of the area to be flooded. The removal of an unengraved outcrop was even carried out to prove such a proposal was technically achievable (Fernandes and Rodrigues 2008; Figure 1.2). Archaeologists and other experts refused the proposal as it would cause the loss of spatial information on the rapport between the engraved outcrops amongst themselves and with the broader landscape. Moreover, it would mean the loss of authenticity of the art in its landscape and, if the procedure implied damage during removal, transport, and relocation, it could have caused a loss of integrity. Finally, it was argued that *in situ* preservation allowed the comprehensive study of the rock art and the creation of a visitor attraction important to increase economic revenues in an undeveloped interior area of Portugal (Baptista and Fernandes 2007, Fernandes et al. 2008).

Figure 1.2 Unengraved outcrop relocated at the time of the dam's construction, to a not that *optimum* conservation environment, an open area of, mostly abandoned today, prefabricated administrative buildings supporting in the 1990s the dam project's construction. Photo by the author.

Hence, when the decision of the Portuguese government was in favour of the archaeological stance for the rock art panels to be preserved *in situ*, many believed that this would indicate a new ethical position for valuing, managing and preserving the world's rock art (Sundstrom and Hays-Gilpin 2011, p. 365). The removal of rock art for preservation reasons continues, being a recent case in point the Dampier Archipelago, Australia, where some of the rock art was relocated away from its natural setting because of industrial development (Bednarik 2008a) to the furore of First Nation people and archaeologists alike. Moreover, and unfortunately, vandalism, as reported by Joaquim Soler i Subils and Nick Brooks (as noted in Rush 2015, p. 171) in the most 'curious' of circumstances, or theft (for instance, Nikias 2012), continue to occur.

The main issue to address here is the ethical, policymaking but also practical issues regarding the removal of rock art outcrops or panels for purely conservation aims: can it be justified? When there is no direct or significant human menace to rock art surfaces and the most severe threats faced reside in natural processes, can it ever be reasonable to move rock art panels or outcrops to controlled optimum conservation conditions? Although this is a question that might arise more acutely regarding rock art imagery in poor condition, it can also be put (at least at a conceptual level) considering the entire corpus of open-air rock art. Would it make sense, if achievable in such a way that guarantees its full art object integrity (but not its authenticity, as discussed above), to remove panels from the open-air to artificial environments intended to offer 'optimum conservation conditions'?

Despite Prehistoric rock art having survived many millennia, all this ancient imagery will ultimately vanish. Removing and relocating endangered rock art panels or outcrops to an optimum conservation environment would arguably be the best solution to achieve its endurance, at least as long as there will be human management of the said environment. There are, of course, technical feasibility issues and financial questions connected with carrying out such endeavours to consider, notwithstanding future maintenance. However, the gist of the present debate is to consider if removal, even for conservation purposes, can be ethically justifiable.

Elsewhere this author has questioned whether we should let the art outcrops 'die' in their own due 'natural time' (Fernandes 2008a, p. 91) or do we directly intervene, with more or less impact, on rock art outcrops in peril? The above-referenced paper discussed the ethical and aesthetic implications of direct *in situ* intervention; that is, trying to consolidate and stabilize panels and outcrops in their original setting without considering removing them to another location. At the time, it was noted that *in situ* conservation is more readily accepted by those concerned with rock art conservation ethics than *ex situ* measures. Montelle noted that "a possible way out of the explicitly stated dilemma is to create a facsimile where reconstructed breakages and filled-in fractures could be presented in their natural texture while a zero-intervention policy be enforced on the original" (2009, p. 109). Implementing this suggestion would ease the predicament so far as *in situ* ethical issues are concerned, but "a zero-intervention policy (to) be enforced on the original" would not address the ongoing weathering impacts that threaten the endurance of *original* rock art. Another possible course of action would be to replace a removed (for conservation purposes) panel or outcrop by a replica, as faithful as possible, standing at precisely at the same locale.

These are issues that have barely been addressed by the rock art community because of the political, economic, and landscape management ramifications. Moreover, they have a sensitive nature as, first of all, agreeing to the need to displace rock art (or any other heritage value) because of natural threats would undermine worldwide efforts to preserve, in their meaningful standings, sites in danger due to human activities (Sundstrom and Hays-Gilpin 2011, pp. 364–365). For instance, had the dam been constructed, most of the identified rock art sites in 1994 at Coa would have become flooded. Nevertheless, the battle for preservation of the art in its original setting would have been severely impaired if removal would have been promoted by EDP, not as a way of having the best of two worlds (the dam and the engravings), but as the best solution to assure the long-term conservation of (at least a few) engraved outcrops. It is doubtful to envisage that the power company would finance the removal of all rock art outcrops identified, which, at the time, amounted to circa one hundred. Today, circa 1,200 engraved outcrops are known within this landscape (Reis 2014). If the dam existed today, the wealth of rock art imagery identified more recently would rest, unknown, below reservoir waters.

The author believes the issue deserves further debate since complex cases, such as the ones noted above, will continue to arise and it would be beneficial for the rock art and archaeological community to clarify positions and acceptable outcomes. It is point-worthy to quote a section from one of the most widely followed international guidance document regarding good practices in cultural heritage management, protection, and conservation, The Burra Charter:

> "contents, fixtures, and objects which contribute to the cultural significance of a place should be retained at that place. *Their removal is unacceptable unless it is the sole means of ensuring their security and preservation (...)*"
>
> (Australia/ICOMOS 1999, p. 5, emphasis by author)

Considering what has been discussed, three entirely distinct courses of action can be recognized when it comes to direct conservation interventions on rock art panels and outcrops. A summary can be presented as follows, noting that the last two can be applied together, before and/or after relocation:

1   *Zero intervention.* Considering that over (geological) time all rock surfaces possessing rock art will eventually be lost, and notwithstanding all the discussed above uncertainties surrounding conservation work in different natural environments, its ultimate disappearance should be serenely accepted. Therefore, as a last tribute to the art, and to fully respect its authenticity, these rock surfaces should be allowed to pass away in a dignified manner without any further meddling. If much of the art has survived until modern times, it is reasonable to assume that it will continue to exist for many years more if the environment in which it lies remains relatively unaltered (Figure 1.3).
2   *In situ conservation.* Geological time has a much grander scale than human time. Therefore, within human time scales, it makes sense, and it is worth trying to preserve panels in their landscape context where the art retains its full significance as evidence for the early nature of Human creative spirit. Many sites across the world are in a quite worrying condition concerning the non-anthropogenic threats they face. Hence, we should aim today at trying to offer rock art the conditions to last (at least) the years that it has already survived (Figure 1.1).
3   *Ex situ conservation.* Due to the same moral imperatives enunciated in the previous paragraph, this more alternative but roughly discussed course of action assumes that rock art must be preserved (almost) at any cost. However, instead of trying to preserve it in its natural setting, the goal of enduring existence legitimates relocation from its meaningful but hazardous context to a controlled and stabilized conservation environment (see Figure 1.2 regarding what would have probably happened to the most significant Coa rock art outcrops, known at the time, if the dam had been built).

Figure 1.3 Rock 2 at Ribeira de Piscos, as an example of a not yet intervened rock art surface at Coa Valley, although identified as in need of attention (Fernandes 2012). Photo by the author.

To carry on the debate, it is important to consider with whom the decisions to be taken ultimately rest, noting that while most times it wouldn't appear so, following a zero-intervention course is in itself a decision. But the point here is understanding that a resolution (or a set of resolutions over a period of time) should not rest solely upon the shoulders of experts. Rather, it has forcefully to be shared, by reason of the bestowed public mandate, by decision-makers, i.e., political officers. That is to say that while expert input is essential to correctly inform decision, there is a further level of validation and consideration that should be provided by elected or appointed state officials, placed at different ranks of hierarchy. This is a process where perceived intervention urgency is just one item to consider; others include budget availability; future maintenance and monitoring requirements and resources; the impact direct intervention might have on the publicly perceived authenticity or integrity of sites, or, more plainly, logistical issues in implementing interventions. Moreover, these are the kind of decisions that ideally would benefit greatly from broad public input. As such, monitoring and consulting groups involving a range of stakeholders (foremost, if applicable, First Nations, but also local interest groups, economic agents, school communities, and so forth) should be set up, so that, departing from expert input, and with state officials acting as facilitators/arbitrators, at any given moment a decision is taken, an ample consensus can be reached.

Conclusion

Intervention options on rock art panels and outcrops discussed above have a wide range of (expectable or not) consequences, so there is no simple answer as to which path to pursue. In the near future, mainly because of the political ramifications mentioned above, guidelines offering advice on the options available regarding open-air rock art conservation are unlikely to become available. Moreover, funds will not be widely available to intervene (or to do vital maintenance work on already undertaken interventions) at most rock art sites, also given their large numbers across the world. Therefore, zero-intervention is the most likely path to continue to be followed, which might not necessarily be a dire option (Allemand and Bahn 2005). Zero-intervention will also keep on being favoured not by choice but because it is difficult to consider either of the two remaining options, even if there is the political will to address the situation, not on cost grounds but because of the discussed uncomfortable ethical implications of *in situ*, and especially, *ex situ* conservation.

Acknowledgements

Research presented here has been partly funded by FCT (Fundação para a Ciência e a Tecnologia) towards the fulfilment of the PhD thesis "Natural Processes in the Degradation of Open-Air Rock art Sites: An Urgency Intervention Scale to Inform Conservation" completed by the author in 2012 at Bournemouth University. The author would like to thank the co-editor of this volume Melissa Marshall for valuable insights, namely regarding Australia, to the present discussion, and for revising the text.

References

Aberg, G., Stray, H. and Dahlin, E. (1999) Impact of pollution at a Stone Age Rock Art Site in Oslo, Norway, studied using lead and strontium isotopes. *Journal of Archaeological Science*, 26(12), pp.1483–1488. DOI:10.1006/jasc.1999.0445

Allemand, L. and Bahn, P. (2005) Best way to protect Rock Art is to leave it alone. *Nature*, 433(7028), pp.800. DOI:10.1038/433800

Anati, E., Wainwright, I. and Lundy, D. (1984) Rock art recording and conservation: A call for international effort. *Current Anthropology*, 25(2), pp.216–217. DOI:10.2307/2742823

Andersson, T. (1986) Preservation and restoration of rock carvings and rune-stones. In Brommelle, N. S. and Smith, P. (Eds.) *Case studies in the conservation of stone and wall paintings*. London: International Institute for Conservation of Historic and Artistic Works, pp.133–137.

Anyon, R., Ferguson, T. J. and Welch, J. R. (2000) Heritage management by American Indian Tribes in the Southwestern United States. In McManamon, F. P. and Hatton, A. (Eds.) *Cultural resources management in contemporary society. Perspectives on managing and presenting the past*. London: Routledge, pp.120–141.

Australia/ICOMOS (International Council on Monuments and Sites) (1999) *The Burra Charter: The Australia ICOMOS Charter for Places of Cultural Significance.* Sydney: Australia/ICOMOS.

Avery, G. (1978) Rock art conservation in South Africa. In Pearson, C. (Ed.) *Conservation of rock art. Proceedings of the International Workshop on the Conservation of rock art, Perth, September 1977.* Sydney: Institute for the Conservation of Cultural Material, pp.66–68.

Bahn, P. (2016) *Images of the Ice Age.* Oxford: Oxford University Press.

Baptista, A. M. and Fernandes, A. P. B. (2007) Rock Art and the Coa Valley Archaeological Park: A case study in the preservation of Portugal's Prehistoric parietal Heritage. In Pettitt, P., Bahn, P. and Ripoll, S. (Eds.) *Palaeolithic Cave Art at Creswell Crags in European Context.* Oxford: Oxford University Press, pp.263–279.

Bauman, J. (2005) Man charged with rock art vandalism. *AURA Newsletter,* 22(1), p.3.

Bednarik, R. (2008a) Removing rock art. *International Newsletter on Rock Art,* 50, pp.8–12.

Bednarik, R. (2008b) More on rock art removal. *South African Archaeological Bulletin,* 63(187), pp.82–84.

Bennie, J., Huntley, B., Wiltshire, A., Hill, M. and Baxter, R. (2008) Slope, aspect and climate: Spatially and implicit models of topographic microclimate in chalk grassland. *Ecological Modelling,* 216(1), pp.47–59. DOI:10.1016/j.ecolmodel.2008.04.010

Cerveny, N. (2005) *A weathering-based perspective on rock art conservation.* PhD diss., Arizona State University.

Clottes, J. (2008) UNESCO's World Heritage List and rock art. *Adoranten,* 2008, pp.5–12.

Deacon, J. (2006) Rock art conservation and tourism. *Journal of Archaeological Method and Theory,* 13(4), pp.376–396. DOI:10.1007/s10816-006-9024-y

Dean, C. (1999) Hardware store conservation: Why this week's "Best Buy" may not be such a bargain. In Dean, C. (Ed.) *Images past, images present: The conservation and preservation of rock art.* Tucson: American Rock Art Research Association, pp.21–26.

Devlet, E. and Devlet, M. (2002) Heritage protection and rock art regions in Russia. In Chalmin, E. (Ed.) *L'art avant l'histoire. La conservation de l'art préhistorique.* Champs-Sur-Marne: SFIIC, pp.87–94.

Doehne, E. and Price, C. (2010) *Stone conservation. An overview of current research.* 2nd edition. Los Angeles: Getty Conservation Institute.

Edwards, R. (1974) *Aboriginal rock paintings: Considerations for their future.* Sydney: Australian Museum.

Fernandes, A. P. B. (2008a) Aesthetics, ethics, and rock art conservation: How far can we go? The case of recent conservation tests carried out in un-engraved outcrops in the Coa Valley, Portugal. In Heyd, T. and Clegg, J. (Eds.) *Aesthetics and rock art III symposium.* Oxford: Archaeopress, pp.85–92.

Fernandes, A. P. B. (Ed.) (2008b) *A arte da conservação: Técnicas e métodos de conservação em arte rupestre. Actas das Sessões do 3º Congresso de Arqueologia de Trás-os-Montes, Alto Douro e Beira Interior. Volume 2.* Porto: ACDR de Freixo de Numão.

Fernandes, A. P. B. (2012) *Natural processes in the degradation of open-air rock art sites: An urgency intervention scale to inform conservation.* PhD diss., Bournemouth University.

Fernandes, A. P. B. (2018) The entrapment of art: Rock art, order, subversion, creativity, meaning, and the appeal of illusive imagery. *Open Archaeology*, 4(1), pp.280–298. DOI:10.1515/opar-2018-0017

Fernandes, A. P. B., Mendes, M., Aubry, T., Sampaio, J., Jardim, R., Correia, D., Junqueiro, A. Bazaréu, D., Dias, F. and Pinto, P. (2008) The evolving relationship between the Coa Valley Archaeological Park and the local community: An account of the first decade. *Conservation and Management of Archaeological Sites*, 10(4), pp.330–343. DOI:10.1179/135050308X12513845914462

Fernandes, A. P. B., Reis, M., Escudero Remirez, C. and Vázquez Marcos, C. (2017) Integration of stone features and conservation of the Coa Valley and Siega Verde open-air rock art, *Time & Mind*, 10(3), pp.293–319. DOI: 10.1080/1751696X.2017.1341246

Fernandes, A. P. B. and Rodrigues, J. D. (2008) Stone consolidation experiments in rock art outcrops at the Coa Valley Archaeological Park, Portugal. In Rodrigues, J. D. and Mimoso, J. (Eds.) *Stone consolidation in cultural heritage: Research and practice*. Lisbon: LNEC, pp.111–120.

Fitzner, B., Heinrichs, K. and La Bouchardiere, D. (2004) 'The Bangudae Petroglyph in Ulsan, Korea: Studies on weathering damage and risk prognosis'. *Environmental Geology*, 46(3–4), pp.504–526. DOI:10.1007/s00254-004-1052-x

Hansen, J. (1999) The state of rock art preservation and climate change: An example from the Central Sahara Desert. In Dean, C. (Ed.) *Images past, images present: The conservation and preservation of rock art*. Tucson: American Rock Art Research Association, pp.57–59.

Henry, L. (2007) A history of removing rock art in South Africa. *South African Archaeological Bulletin*, 62(185), pp.44–48.

Hollmann, J., Prinsloo, F., Fourie, W. and Hutton, M. (2017) Removal of rock art affected by the raising of the Clanwilliam dam wall, Western Cape Province, South Africa: Techniques and procedures. *Conservation and Management of Archaeological Sites*, 19(4), pp.244–268. DOI:10.1080/13505033.2017.1377029

Hughes, P. J. (1979) *The deterioration, conservation and management of rock art sites in the Kakadu National Park, NT*. Canberra: ANU.

Hygen, A. S. (1996) Conservation, intervention or destruction of rock art? Some Scandinavian experiences. *Rock Art Research*, 13(1), pp.49–52.

IPCC (2007) *Climate change 2007: Synthesis report. Contribution of working groups I, II and II to the fourth assessment report of the intergovernmental panel on climate change*. Geneva: IPPC.

Keenan, J. (2000) The theft of Saharan Rock Art. *Antiquity*, 74(284), pp.287–288.

Kincey, M., Challis, K. and Howard, A. (2008) Modelling selected implications of potential future climate change on the archaeological resource of river catchments: An application of Geographical Information Systems. *Conservation and Management of Archaeological Sites*, 10(2), pp.113–131. DOI:10.1179/175355209X435560

Lee, G. (1986) Problems in the conservation and preservation of rock art. *WAAC*, 8(1), pp.5–7.

Meiklejohn, K., Hall, K. and David, J. (2009) Weathering of rock art at two sites in the KwaZulu-Natal Drakensberg, Southern Africa. *Journal of Archaeological Science*, 36(4), pp.973–979. DOI:10.1016/j.jas.2008.11.020

Montelle, Y. P. (2009) Aesthetics and rock art III symposium. Review of aesthetics and rock art III symposium, edited by Thomas Heyd and John Clegg. *Rock Art Research*, 26(1), pp.108–110.

Mottershead, D., Baily, B., Collier, P. and Inkpen, R. (2003) Identification and quantification of weathering by plant roots. *Building and Environment*, 38(9–10), pp.1235–1241. doi:10.1016/S0360-1323(03)00080-5

Nikias, M. (2012) Native American rock carvings stolen in California Cliffs: Local Native Americans stunned. *ABC News*. Available from: https://abcnews.go.com/blogs/headlines/2012/11/ancient-petroglyphs-stolen-along-california-cliffs-local-native-americans-stunned [Accessed: 12 September 2019].

Ogawa, M. (2005) Integration in Franco-Cantabrian Parietal Art: A case study of Font-de- Gaume Cave, France. In Heyd, T. and Clegg, J. (Eds.) *Aesthetics and rock art*. Aldershot: Ashgate, pp.117–129.

Ponti, R. and Persia, F. (2002) The preservation of rock art in Lybia. In Chalmin, E. (Ed.) *L'art avant l'histoire. La conservation de l'art préhistorique*. Champs-Sur-Marne: SFIIC, pp.127–133.

Reis, M. (2014) 'Mil rochas e tal...!': Inventário dos sítios da arte rupestre do Vale do Coa (Conclusão). *Portvgalia* (Nova Série), 35, pp.17–59.

Rush, L. (2015) Military protection of cultural property. In Desmarais, F. (Ed.) *Countering illicit traffic in cultural goods. The global challenge of protecting the world's heritage*. Paris: ICOM, pp.163–174.

Silver, C. (1989) Rock art conservation in the United States: Wish or reality? In Crotty, H. (Ed.) *Preserving our rock art heritage. ARARA occasional paper 1*. San Miguel, CA: American Rock Art Research Association, pp.3–15.

Summerfield, M. (1991) *Global geomorphology: An introduction to the study of landforms*. Harlow, UK: Longman.

Sundstrom, L. and Hays-Gilpin, K. (2011) Rock art as cultural resource. In King, T. (Ed.) *A companion to cultural resource management*. Chichester: Wiley-Blackwell, pp.351–370.

Tratebas, A. (2004) Biodeterioration of prehistoric rock art and issues in site preservation. In St. Clair, L. and Seaward, M. (Eds.) *Biodeterioration of stone surfaces: Lichens and biofilms as weathering agents of rocks and cultural heritage*. Dordrecht: Kluwer Academic Publishers, pp.195–228.

Tratebas, A., Cerveny, N. and Dorn, R. (2004) The effects of fire on rock art: Microscopic evidence reveals the importance of weathering rinds. *Physical Geography*, 25(4), pp.313–333. DOI:10.2747/0272-3646.25.4.313

Vidal, P. (2001) *L'art rupestre en péril: Un patrimoine mondial a sauver*. Périgueux: Pilote.

Viles, H. (2005) Microclimate and weathering in the Central Namib Desert, Namibia. *Geomorphology*, 67(1–2), pp.189–209. DOI:10.1016/j.geomorph.2004.04.006

Viles, H., and Goudie, A. (2003) Interannual, decadal and multidecadal scale climatic variability and geomorphology. *Earth-Science Reviews*, 61(1–2), pp.105–131. DOI:10.1016/S0012-8252(02)00113-7

Walderhaug, O. and Walderhaug, E. (1998) Weathering of Norwegian rock art – a critical review. *Norwegian Archaeological Review*, 31(2), pp.119–139. DOI:10.1080/00293652.1998.9965626

Wright, A. (2017) *Petroglyphs at Taliesin West | Frank Lloyd Wright Foundation*. Available from: https://franklloydwright.org/petroglyphs/ [Accessed: 12 September 2019].

Yalcin, A. and Bulut, F. (2007) Landslide susceptibility mapping using GIS and digital photogrammetric techniques: A case study from Ardesen (NE-Turkey). *Natural Hazards*, 41(1), pp.201–226. DOI:10.1007/s11069-006-9030-0

2 Murujuga

Managing an Archaeological and Sacred Landscape through Industry

Ken Mulvaney

Introduction

Situated on the northwest coast of Australia, jutting out into the Indian Ocean is Murujuga: the Burrup Peninsula and the 42 islands of the Dampier Archipelago (Figure 2.1). This was a relatively remote area of the continent, with European settlement through wool and pearling operations commencing in the 1860s (De La Rue 1979; Withnell-Taylor 1980). There is now well documented evidence of a Pleistocene and Holocene occupation of this Pilbara region, extending back over 50,000 years (Morse et al. 2014; Veth et al. 2017). However, it remained a sparsely occupied district, dominated by its Aboriginal people until the mid-20th century when commercial development of iron ore deposits across the Pilbara commenced.

Murujuga is a rich cultural landscape, marked by its petroglyphs that occur on the rock surfaces of this rugged and impressive terrain (Figure 2.2). It is estimated that over 1 million images exist in this landscape, their production spanning tens of millennia, stopping only with the coming of European settlement (Mulvaney 2010, 2018). The scientific and aesthetic significance of the rock art was recognised in the National Heritage listing of the place in 2007 (McDonald and Veth 2009) and is currently being reviewed in preparation for nomination to United Nations Educational, Scientific and Cultural Organization (UNESCO) for its outstanding universal values.

This recent undertaking for World Heritage status comes decades after it was first proposed. In a report by a Joint Academies Committee and Australian Heritage Commission member, Professor D.J. Mulvaney stated:

> I have no hesitation in concluding that this is one of the richest and densest art provinces in Australia. It lacks the grandeur and colour of Kakadu paintings, but in the number of sites and motifs is equally great. ... There are numerous thylacine designs, while the total faunal species representation is surprisingly large. ... The most important known group of all is the 'Climbing Men' site. This deeply weathered yet excellently preserved panel is one of the great masterpieces of prehistoric

DOI: 10.4324/9780429355349-4

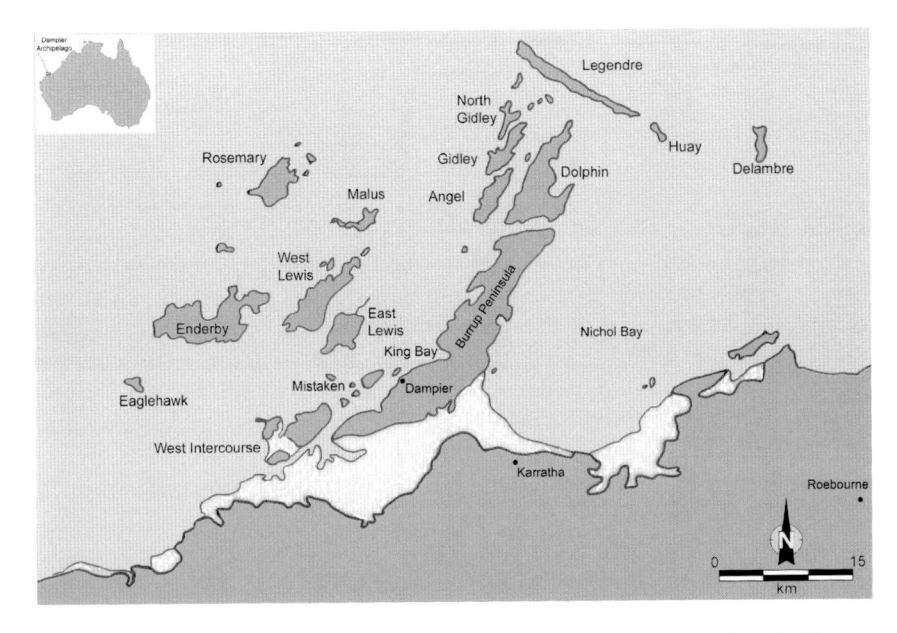

Figure 2.1 Islands of the Dampier Archipelago including Burrup Peninsula (Dampier Is.) and population centres. Map by the author.

Figure 2.2 Petroglyph depicting a macropod, situated within the rock slop of a rugged gully. Photo by the author.

art from any stone age gallery throughout the world. ... Without doubt, this region classes as one of the richest and most significant in Australia and of World Heritage nomination status

(Mulvaney 1980, p. 5)

When first proposed for industry, little was known of the Aboriginal cultural significance of Murujuga and it was assumed not to be of particular significance (Ride and Neumann 1964). So in 1964, the first port and rail facilities were constructed for the shipment of iron ore from inland mines. This was soon followed by the building of a sea-salt processing operation. In the establishment of both these resource industries, the natural landscape was changed and cultural heritage destroyed. It was only as a consequence of the then recent migrant workers to this location that awareness of the cultural values of Murujuga reached beyond that of its indigenous inhabitants (see Bednarik 1977, 2006; Virili 1974, 1977).

Now, in the 21st century, the industrial footprint has spread across 45.87 km^2 of Burrup Peninsula and adjacent islands, with an additional 31.28 km^2 earmarked for future infrastructure. This excludes the 104.9 km^2 of mangrove lined tidal mudflats which have been converted to sea-salt concentration ponds and the 1.64 km^2 that is the town of Dampier. There still remains nearly 225 km^2 of relatively untouched natural and cultural landscape of the Dampier Archipelago including the undeveloped portions of Burrup Peninsula. State and Commonwealth legislation now exists for the protection of heritage, and because of research sponsored by Rio Tinto, 32,445 petroglyphs have been subject to detailed *in-situ* recording, occurring within an area of 5.54 km^2 spread across Murujuga.

The area is one of the largest and most densely arranged open-air rock art landscapes in the world. That resource industries co-inhabit this place presents specific management issues with a range of potential adverse impacts. It is not just the footprint of infrastructure and the associated workforce activities, but the emissions that industry is adding into the environment that is concerning (Black et al. 2017). Understanding the issues, the impacts and management options are all important in guiding conservation options.

Heritage engagement

Rio Tinto, through its operating companies Hamersley Iron Proprietary Limited (HIPL) and Dampier Salt Limited (DSL), has been working in the Dampier Archipelago since 1965, with the first shipment of iron ore through the Parker Point terminal at King Bay in August 1966. For DSL, the construction and initial flooding of ponds began in 1969, officially opened in December 1971 and the first shipment of salt from the Mistaken Island jetty departed for Japan on 15th April 1972. HIPL and DSL are resource companies engaged with the production and export of minerals; nonetheless, their operations within Murujuga have a longstanding commitment to heritage management and limiting adverse impacts to this cultural asset. For example, in June 1973, staff of the

Western Australian Museum and the Surveyor-General, in the company of local employee Enzo Virili, visited sites within the DSL leases and surrounding areas for the purpose of registering Aboriginal sites (*Hamersley News* 28 June 1973:5). One year later, Virili was invited to present on the Dampier rock art at the Australian Institute of Aboriginal Studies in Canberra (*Hamersley News* 27 June 1974:7). This trip to Canberra and Virili's work with staff of the Western Australian Museum, lead to the engagement of French archaeologist and rock art specialist Michel Lorblanchet to assess the archaeological significance of several locations on the DSL Burrup lease (Lorblanchet 1977, 1983). These locations, known as Skew Valley and Gum Tree Valley, proved to have over 10,000 petroglyphs, extensive shell middens and provided Pleistocene and Holocene dates for occupation and rock art production in the area (Lorblanchet 2018).

In the mid-1990s, Leon Davis, then Managing Director and Chief Executive of Conzinc Riotinto of Australia Limited (CRA), is accredited with guiding the company into a cooperative approach and active partnership with Aboriginal people in all CRA exploration and mineral resource developments in Australia. Davis provided an awakening call to the mining industry and government that recognition of Native Title rights entailed significant shifts in the way resource companies operated and engaged with Aboriginal people. Many people within CRA were pivotal in the move toward Aboriginal engagement by Rio Tinto (see Holland-McNair 2018). It is clear from the activities within Murujuga in the early 1970s that it has not just been since the 1992 High Court of Australia ruling that the company has come together with Traditional Owners and concerned itself with heritage protection. However, much of the earlier engagement was a consequence of individuals employed within Rio Tinto and the localised influence they could muster, rather than the company wide policy which it became in the last two decades.

The fundamental change to the way the company worked with the Aboriginal community did follow on from implementation of the *Native Title Act* 1993 and Davis's 1995 'new directions' speech. It was from 1996, however, when Rio Tinto employed its first university trained archaeologist, Elizabeth Bradshaw, to develop and manage a heritage programme and set standards that created the real change to the company's cultural heritage practices (see Bradshaw 2000). These standards are by-in-large still in place today. The view of the Aboriginal community to Bradshaw's appointment was that of "having someone inside can only help" (Holland-McNair 2006). Bradshaw brought with her a legacy of previous engagement with Aboriginal people, a feature that remains at the forefront of all Rio Tinto heritage work. It was the first time an archaeologist was directly employed by an Australian mining company, or any mining company worldwide. Over the following years, the Rio Tinto Pilbara-based heritage team grew to be a large body of heritage professionals and Aboriginal advisors, at some stages employing over 40 people at the one time, reflecting levels of development activity. The team currently has 20 staff, with heritage consultants, Aboriginal organisations and Traditional Owner representatives undertaking most of the field work.

Rio Tinto continues the respectful engagement with Traditional Owners of this land over all new developments and expansions. Over the past ten years, Rio Tinto has developed Participation Agreements with the Pilbara Traditional Owner groups through their Native Title representative organisations. They provide both financial and non-monetary benefits to the groups, and ensure certainty for the Rio Tinto business. These Agreements formalised engagement and the heritage processes by giving control back to Aboriginal Traditional Owners. These aspects were reiterated in a recent speech made by Managing Director Joanne Farrell at the launch of a Kimberley art exhibition at the Art Gallery WA. Farrell stated that:

> We respect the connection Aboriginal people have to their land and actively collaborate on initiatives that preserve cultural heritage, and make our employees more culturally aware. Our engagement with Aboriginal people occurs at many levels – be it employment and training, heritage surveys and protection, business development and land use agreements. This engagement also includes initiatives that preserve, showcase and express the rich art and culture of Traditional Owners.
>
> (06/02/2019)

Employment of heritage professionals and the historic legacy of people like Virili and Lorblanchet have guided Rio Tinto in the management of the Murujuga leases and also in how the company engaged with the Commonwealth Government in relation to the listing of the Dampier Archipelago, including Burrup Peninsula, as a National Heritage Place in the mid-2000s. The culmination of the National Heritage consultation process and to achieve a better understanding of the Murujuga rock art assemblage is a Conservation Agreement (CA) signed by HIPL, DSL, and the Commonwealth Government. The CA was entered into by Rio Tinto as a mechanism for providing surety to its iron ore and salt operations as they occur on Burrup Peninsula (Part 14 of the *Environment Protection and Biodiversity Conservation Act 1999* (EPBC)). This agreement reflects the cooperative stance and in-house professional heritage management systems that Rio Tinto operates. In addition to the Federal Minister signing off on activities which Rio Tinto can conduct in their normal course of business without referral to the Minister (Approved Actions), there are obligations in relation to the National Heritage Values. These are identified as Net Benefit activities (section 5 of the CA) and are to:

i   identify all sites with National Heritage Values;
ii   present, and transmit information about, the National Heritage Values;
iii manage the National Heritage Values to ensure the values are conserved for future generations;
iv   research and monitor the National Heritage Values.

These Net Benefit activities are to be carried out within the National Heritage Place and particularly those areas that lie within the Rio Tinto managed leases, some 8.2 km² (36% of Rio Tinto's Burrup leases). Two significant projects in relation to Burrup leases have been the co-run University of Western Australia rock art recording field school and the Murujuga Aboriginal Corporation (MAC) site surveys. These activities have resulted in over 9,000 petroglyphs and several hundred other archaeological sites being recorded within the Rio Tinto leases.

Rio Tinto, through its employment of professional archaeologists and cultural heritage managers, along with their in-house procedures dealing with land disturbance activities, maintains a robust system to mitigate impact on cultural heritage. In the case of the Dampier Archipelago, apart from the historic developments (e.g., port, rail, and accommodation facilities), the company now limits ground disturbance to maintenance and activities on previously utilised land. Heritage site inspections and on-ground investigations with the MAC rangers are routinely conducted.

Murujuga, a rock art precinct

Since the early 1970s, all heritage sites have been protected by the *Heritage of Western Australia Act* 1990 and the Aboriginal Heritage Act (AHA) 1972, although it is only the latter which has relevance to Rio Tinto Dampier leases. In addition, after July 2007 when portions of Burrup Peninsula were afforded National Heritage listing, these places are also protected under the EPBC Act 1999. For the purposes of the AHA, an Aboriginal site is a place of importance and significance relating to Aboriginal practice, beliefs or activities, either material or intangible, that is situated within the State of Western Australia (section 5 AHA). Enacted in the early 1970s the AHA was a progressive and enlightened piece of heritage protection legislation. Unfortunately, administration of the act, coupled with low funding support, reduced the capabilities to ensure its appropriate application (Casey 2007; Herriman 2013). This is especially so when pressures of commercial developments and mining exploration escalated in the State from the mid-1990s.

When HIPL and DSL commenced their Murujuga operations no heritage legislation existed, nor did Aboriginal people have legal rights or citizenship recognition. Infrastructure development in the 1960s went on without regard to the destruction of cultural heritage or the impacts to their spiritual values. By the late 1970s heritage legislation existed and ten years of citizenship recognition for Aboriginal people, and as discussed above, there was a growing awareness of the significant cultural precinct that is Murujuga. Nonetheless, development for a petrochemical plant to process offshore gas fields (over 100 km away) on Burrup Peninsula went ahead with a Section 18 consent to destroy (as legislated through the AHA). Such provision of the AHA effectively exempts from prosecution the proponent when disturbing or destroying Aboriginal cultural property.

Even with the destruction associated with the building of the Karratha Gas Plant (KGP) facilities, a large amount of archaeological data was recorded, not least in documenting 9,244 petroglyphs and identification of 720 sites (DAS 1984). The results of this industry sponsored investigation, coupled with the earlier archaeological studies, unequivocally demonstrated the cultural richness and scientific values of this place, not just for Aboriginal people but as irreplaceable heritage to all. Murujuga is truly an integrated cultural landscape containing sites ranging from a single artefact to site complexes extending over thousands of square metres, and encompassing petroglyphs, stone arrangements, shell middens and flaked stone artefacts. Some of these locations hold over 10,000 images that represent tens of millennia of cultural production (Lorblanchet 2018; Mulvaney 2010).

The most comprehensive area survey is that associated with the KGP and covered some 13.4 km², indicating a density of 690 petroglyphs, 34 grinding patches, 15 stone artefact or shell scatters and 14 stone features per square kilometre (DAS 1984:48). Over a decade later, under the auspices of National Estate Grants Programme (NEGP), a survey was carried out over the northern section of Burrup Peninsula, comprising a series of 24 east/west running 100m wide transects covering a total area of 8.78 km² (Veth et al. 1993). This survey documented 498 sites, providing a density of 56.7 sites per square kilometre, comparatively similar to the results of the Karratha Gas Plant (KGP) survey at 53.7 sites per square kilometre. Rock art occurs at 156 sites, although not all sites were recorded in detail, a total of 2,581 motifs were recorded (Veth et al. 1993:102). A later survey for sites south of King Bay, that at the time was within the HIPL lease, revealed a density of 1349 petroglyphs, 100 grinding patches and 65 stone features per square kilometre (Gunn and Mulvaney 2008, p. 149). The density of archaeological features is, therefore, extremely high by any standard.

More recent detailed recording projects are those associated with Rio Tinto sponsored rock art field schools (2010–2018) and an Australian Research Council (ARC) Linkage project (Murujuga: Dynamics of the Dreaming 2016–2018). Both providing data used in undergraduate and post graduate university thesis (e.g., Clayton 2015; de Koning 2014). The field school investigated seven locations on Burrup Peninsula, resulting in the documenting of 18,463 petroglyphs as well as other cultural features within an area of just 1.73 km². While the ARC project focused on over 20 locations across the islands including Burrup Peninsula and recorded 13,982 petroglyphs, 845 grinding patches, and 459 stone features within a total area of 3.81 km². It is evident from these surveys that density of cultural features varies in association with the extent of landform types present (Table 2.1), in particular the presence of potable water and the nature of other resources.

Not surprisingly, the magnitude of rock surfaces predicates petroglyphs density and, with few exceptions, the places containing the densest concentrations of petroglyphs are those valley systems with massive block slopes and sheltered rock-pools (Figure 2.3).

Table 2.1 Rock art density relating to five archaeological projects

Survey	Area km²	Topographic Character	Density/ km²
NEGP	8.78	Foreshore; tidal inlet; undulating spinifex slopes; rocky knolls; ephemeral waterholes; rocky gullies	293
KGP	13.4	Foreshore; tidal inlet; undulating spinifex slopes; rocky knolls; ephemeral waterholes; rocky gullies	690
King Bay South	1.44	Foreshore; tidal inlet; undulating spinifex slopes; rocky knolls; ephemeral waterholes	1,349
ARC	3.81	Foreshore; tidal inlet; rocky knolls; ephemeral waterholes; rock-pool valleys	3,670
Field school	1.73	Rocky knolls; ephemeral waterholes; rocky gullies; valley slopes; rock-pool valleys	10,672

Figure 2.3 Rock-pools within the more protected areas within the sheltered dissected gullies provide a focus for past human activities including production of rock art. Photo by the author.

The archaeological pattern that has emerged from the various research and commercial surveys provides a wealth of cultural evidence. These include monumental stone structures; heaped stone arrangements, standing stones and foundation rings for dwellings, the later dated to some 8,000 years old (McDonald and Berry 2016). Rock has also been quarried for manufacture of artefacts; at one quarry site on Enderby Island worked material extends over 0.04 km². The habitation sites also contain flaked stone artefacts, along with grindstones, grinding patches and shell and bone remains.

Shellfish remains occur as isolated meal camps, with scatters extending over many 100m^2, or as midden-piles up to 3m thick. However, it is the rock art that is the most visually striking and ubiquitous across this landscape.

Murujuga petroglyphs spanning the Pleistocene and Holocene display spatial and temporal patterns in the style and subject of the images, some of which reflects the transformation of the environment from an inland series of hills and valleys over 100 km from the coast to islands in the Indian Ocean. This inscribed landscape reflects the cultural and social; the sacred and secular aspects of the people that experienced manifest climatic shifts and the inundation of their lands by the salt water.

A feature of the Murujuga petroglyphs is the inordinate diversity in subject, style and technique displayed (Lorblanchet 2018; McDonald and Veth 2009; Mulvaney 2010). Geometric designs, although many not visually striking, at 40% of the rock art repertoire, are numerically dominant; with human-like and animal-like images accounting for approximately 25% each; tracks, including human feet which comprise roughly 10% of the assemblage. Murujuga petroglyphs include depictions of extinct animals; the most recognisable is the thylacine (Tasmanian tiger), elaborate human face images that may well be the oldest portrayals in the world, and scenes illustrating ritual performances dating back over tens of millennia (Mulvaney 2015). Petroglyphs also reflect the shifting resource distribution associated within the changing environments brought on by the marine transgression. Consequently, with its extraordinarily high concentration and diversity of petroglyphs, Murujuga is one of the most significant rock art provinces in the world.

Question of impacts

As discussed, throughout the last 50 years, this location has become a major industrial hub and is now one of Australia's busiest ports. This development has irrevocably altered the sanctity of the place both from a cultural and natural perspective. It is clear that Murujuga petroglyphs have high scientific and aesthetic significance; they also have an extreme cultural importance and religious value to Aboriginal people (see MAC 2016). This rock art is in the domain of the Dreaming, the work of the creation beings, and is therefore imbued with spiritual power. Traditional Owners believe such disturbances to these places do have metaphysical repercussions and can result in harm to people, not just to themselves but throughout the wider community, including both Aboriginal and non-Aboriginal people alike. This is a situation that happens when sites are desecrated and country broken, such as with placement of industry, or simply with people being where they should not.

In the early 1980s the Committee for the Protection of Prehistoric Places of the four Australian Academies, Canberra, lobbied the Government of Western Australia and relevant Departmental managers with their concerns over the impact of industrial development and the way heritage surveys were being conducted at Murujuga. What had prompted this concern was that the archaeological recording programme associated with the KGP was a salvage operation occurring at the same time as the development itself, not as a timely and planned process well in advance. In addition, while little was known about the nature and extent of the cultural heritage of the Dampier Archipelago, land for future industrial expansion had already been gazetted. This disregard for heritage impact being what prompted the Joint Academies to call in the early 1980s for a comprehensive heritage survey. It was the Commonwealth, not State funding of the NEGP survey in early 1990s that went in part to address this call (Veth et al. 1993).

In 2002 as a response to public concern, the Western Australia government established the Burrup Rock Art Monitoring Management Committee (BRAMC). This committee commissioned several studies to investigate the possible industrial impact on the petroglyphs, including emissions air-dispersion modelling and likely ground-level concentrations and deposition rates; air-particulate and dust composition and deposition pattern; air quality, microclimate and microbiological analysis (CSIRO 2006, 2007; SKM 2003, 2009). The sampling studies ran intermittently from 2004 to 2008 at seven locations on Burrup Peninsula, two on the islands, and one site on the mainland, near Karratha. Additionally, accelerated weathering experiments were run to test erosion rates regarding physical and chemical change of rock under varying pollutant conditions. Annual monitoring of colour levels on rock surfaces, including petroglyphs, and spectral mineralogy were undertaken from 2004 on seven engraved surfaces, with three additional rock art blocks added in 2014 (CSIRO 2009, 2017a).

Based on results from these studies, the Burrup Rock Art Monitoring Management Committee concluded there was no scientific evidence of any measurable impact of industrial emissions on the rate of deterioration of Murujuga petroglyphs (BRAMC 2009, p. 3). These conclusions and the methodology of the monitoring studies have been contested (e.g. Black et al. 2017), which has led to the establishment of a new "Murujuga Rock Art Strategy" under the auspices of the Western Australia Department of Water and Environmental Regulations (DWER 2019) and additional weathering experiments (CSIRO 2017b). Uncertainty remains as to the extent and nature of any effect that industrial emissions have; it is hoped that the new strategy will bring a more acceptable scientific rigor and applicability to the circumstance of the Murujuga petroglyphs.

A press release (15/02/2019) by the Western Australia Minister for Environment Hon. Stephen Dawson MLC stated "[t]he McGowan Government is confident that the unique Aboriginal cultural and heritage values can continue to co-exist with well-regulated industry and new economic opportunities that deliver benefits to the local community". In this same media statement, MAC Chief Executive Officer (CEO) Peter Jeffries is cited as saying the "rock art is an integral part of our culture – it tells our history

48 *Ken Mulvaney*

and our stories, and we want to make sure that everything possible is done to protect it for future generations." This is the nub of the matter; 50,000 years of cultural creativity over-stamped by modern industrial output. Cultural safety protocols aside, it is not just the footprint of the commercial infrastructure that has impacted the Murujuga cultural and spiritual landscape; the added presence of people, industrial emissions and legislative weaknesses or non-enforcement are all taking their toll.

The existing physical area of impact, including buildings, tracks, borrow pits, service corridors and lay-down areas, is now over 25.7 km^2 of Burrup Peninsula and 1.4 km^2 of the adjacent islands (Figure 2.4). Currently 45.87 km^2 are held as leases by the various resource and service companies, the largest controlled by Rio Tinto and Woodside. In addition, 21.48 km^2 of Burrup Peninsula and 9.67 km^2 of near shore islands are gazetted for industrial development. Of Burrup Peninsula land, some 37.67 km^2 (~32%) have been subject to varying quality heritage surveys, in some cases multiple occasions and overlapping investigations conducted. Although much of the recorded archaeological features have been destroyed by industrial construction, tens of thousands of petroglyphs are still present within these commercial leases and hundreds of thousands occur in adjacent areas.

It is not just the physical footprint of existing resource companies and allied service providers that has impact; lighting and noise derived from this industry effects a much broader area. The natural ambiance of Murujuga

Figure 2.4 Map showing the extent of developed land (white) within existing industrial leases (black), gazetted industrial land for future development (dark grey) and Murujuga National Park (hatched lines). Map by the author.

has been altered by the pervasiveness of industrial noises; there is nowhere now on Burrup Peninsula that industry related sound is not heard. Such indirect impacts are only increasing with the development of more industrial facilities.

Concerns exist for the nesting turtles and other marine species because of artificial illumination derived from the industrial plants, as well potential impact from dredge work and ship strikes (see EPA 2007, p. 18).

The port of Dampier has one of the highest bulk carrier (iron ore) movements in Australia. In 2017, there were 1,293 vessels, these using high-sulphur fuels which resulted in Sulphur dioxide (SO_2) being released into the Dampier air-shed (Pilbara Ports Authority, pers. com. August 2018). The amount of iron ore now shipped out of Dampier port has raised from 80 million tons, when the Commonwealth Scientific and Industrial Research Organisation (CSIRO) studies where undertaken, to 250 million tonnes per year. With this throughput of iron ore is associated the increase in diesel-powered trains bringing the product to port, with each consisting of three locomotives hauling 25,000 tonnes in 236 ore cars (2.25 km in length). In accordance with Australian Government guidelines, Rio Tinto has undertaken to switch from high-sulphur to low-sulphur fuels in 2020. The company has also decommissioned the Hamersley Power Station, utilising a new gas fired power plant located on the mainland, further reducing the potential impact on Murujuga rock art.

Similar ramping up of production for the export market is present in the petrochemical facilities. Construction began in the late 1970s for Liquefied Natural Gas (LNG) processing; in addition to the commodities generated there is the release of emissions, both as a consequence of processing and the burning off of excess product. Since first shipment of product in 1984, there has been an increase in production through expansion of processing facilities and the development of a second plant went into production in 2012.

Although aware of the cultural and spiritual significance of the Murujuga petroglyphs, the petrochemical industry regards Burrup Peninsula's potential purely as an industrial estate. As Woodside's own promotional material states: "Burrup Hub could process more gas than the entire volume extracted from North West Shelf since start-up in 1984".[1] This proposal is for the processing through their Burrup facilities "of some 20 to 25 trillion cubic feet of gross dry gas resources", piping gas from the additional offshore fields (Scarborough ~430 km and Browse ~1033 km distance). Such developments will adversely impact Murujuga's cultural and natural landscape. It may suit Woodside commercially, however there are less environmentally and culturally contentious locations along the Western Australia coast which could be developed to process these offshore gas deposits.

Adding to the increase in emissions to the Dampier air-shed was the construction of a Technical Ammonium Nitrate Production Facility (TAN plant) which commenced operation in 2012. The predicted emissions outputs of nitrogen dioxide (NO_2) and ammonia (NH_3) are up to 163.7 and 19.5 tonnes per years, respectively under normal operating conditions. In addition, particulate matter as ammonium nitrate dust is up to 25.2 tons per year (EPA 2011:3). It is a requirement for the TAN plant operations that they adopt and implement best practice pollution control technology (EPA 2011, p. 36). However, on 29th April 2017 a member of the public photographed a NO_2 cloud drifting away from the TAN plant, on investigation it was identified that 73 such releases at over 1,000 parts per million (ppm) has occurred; concentrations >0.125 ppm are harmful to human health, but no data exists as to the levels dangerous to the petroglyphs (John Black, pers. com, March 2018). Despite this, in July 2018 the relevant State authority granted the company a permanent operating license.

The notion that industry and rock art can co-exist is ludicrous, as both landscape replacement by infrastructure and the probable deterioration of petroglyphs through acidic emission means it is a one-sided, short-lived co-existence, cultural heritage is destroyed. Despite the BRAMC sponsored CSIRO studies conducted since 2004, the exact levels of industrial emission nor their effects on the rock art remain unknown and unmitigated. What we do understand is that the recorded level of rock surface pH has shifted from mildly alkaline (>7.0) to acidic pH~4.2 (Ian MacLeod, pers. com. June 2018).

There are intentions through the State-sponsored (industry-funded) Burrup Rock Art Strategy to guide the development of a long-term framework in monitoring industrial emissions impacts and to protect the petroglyphs. Although the advisory body (Stakeholder Reference Group) has been meeting since September 2018, a formal strategy has not been forthcoming, and no monitoring or subsequent investigative studies have been implemented.

Conclusion

Murujuga, the Dampier Archipelago, contains a globally significant cultural resource that is spiritually linked to Aboriginal people and of heritage value to all. Outside of the Aboriginal community, recognition of this edifying cultural heritage began in the 1960s, reaching an appreciative and wider audience a few decades later. In 2007, in recognition of this cultural asset, especially its rock art, the area was placed on Australia's National Heritage List (CoA 2007). In extent and density, the Murujuga petroglyphs are unparalleled, the artistry and range in subjects depicted are superlative. Protection and management of such a cultural treasure would, elsewhere in the world, have been paramount. Unfortunately, emphasis has been placed in the commercial exploitation of the place and its industrial development.

Rio Tinto as managing both iron ore and sea salt processing and export facilities has been on Murujuga for some 50 years. Through its own workforce it became aware of the significant cultural heritage that surrounded its operations from a very early time. It became the first mining company to directly employ archaeologists, implement processes and procedures to mitigate impact on archaeological sites and to acknowledge the significance to the nation of Murujuga petroglyphs. Like other companies with facilities on Burrup Peninsula, Rio Tinto is engaged with the local Aboriginal corporations and ensures that people are aware of what is taking place on their traditional lands. A difference is that Rio Tinto directly employs heritage professionals and has for nearly two decades ensured that their commercial activities do not continue to have an impact on cultural sites. This is an important step in the direction of acknowledging the globally significant rock art and the responsibility to ensure its long-term survival.

In the words of Wonggotoo elder Wilfred Hicks:

> we, the Traditional Owners of the lands between the George and Maitland Rivers, have a special duty also for the country, as the holders of its spiritual energies ... alive in the thousands of rock engravings ... They were placed here by our ancestors, and we received from earlier generations the duty to protect them and must pass that on to our successors. ... It ties us to the land and the land to us. ... But you must realise that we cannot allow the spiritual side of our lands to be destroyed by building factories ... We cannot hand that disaster to our descendants
> (Hearson Cove rally speech 9th June 2002)

For some 50,000 years, the Dampier Archipelago has been home to both cultural and spiritual creativity. Industrial developments over the past five decades have replaced petroglyphs and standing stones for iron ore, salt and gas; scientific and aesthetic worth for steel and petrochemical. Spiritual energies and Dreaming values have been consumed by chemical plumes and emission fallout. This does not need to be the legacy of today's generation. Appropriate management and protection of this irreplaceable cultural heritage landscape is possible, but only if we acknowledge and rectify the impacts of industry.

Acknowledgements

Working from within a resource company, as a heritage professional, can seem daunting; however, I am gratified by Rio Tinto's progressive stance and in providing me the opportunity to work in this wonderful place. I acknowledge the Aboriginal custodians of the Dampier Archipelago, as well staff and rangers of the Murujuga Aboriginal Corporation, for their wisdom and friendship. R.G. (ben) Gunn and Elizabeth Bradshaw gave advice on an earlier version of this paper and to Mel Marshall for additional improvements. It also needs to be acknowledged that this conference presentation and subsequent article occurred prior to the Juukan rockshelter destruction.

Note

1 https://www.woodside.com.au/our-business/burrup-hub

References

Bednarik, R.G. (1977) A survey of prehistoric sites in the Tom Price Region, North Western Australia. *Archaeology and Physical Anthropology in Oceania*, 12(1), pp.51–76.

Bednarik, R.G. (2006) *Australian apocalypse: The story of Australia's greatest cultural monuments*, 14. Melbourne: Occasional AURA Publications.

Black, J.L., Macleod, I.D. and Smith, B.W. (2017) Theoretical effects of industrial emissions on colour change at rock art sites on Burrup Peninsula, Western Australia. *Journal of Archaeological Science: Reports,* 12(2017), pp.457–462.

Bradshaw, E. (2000) Mining and cultural heritage management: The Hamersley iron experience. In Lilley, I. (Ed.) *Native title and transformation of archaeology in the postcolonial world*. Oceania Monograph, 50. Sydney: Oceania Publications, University of Sydney, pp.10–23.

BRAMC (Burrup Rock Art Monitoring Management Committee) (2009) *Report and recommendations to the Minister for State Development.*

Casey, D. (2007) *Report of the review of the department of indigenous affairs*. Unpublished report to Department of the Premier and Cabinet, Perth.

Clayton, L. (2015) *From landscape to seascape: A spatial analysis of Murujuga rock art, Western Pilbara*. Unpublished MA thesis, University of Western Australia.

CoA (Commonwealth of Australia) (2007) Inclusion of a place in the National Heritage List. In E.A.W. Resources (Ed.) *Special gazette*. Canberra: Commonwealth of Australia.

CSIRO (Commonwealth Scientific and Industrial Research Organisation) (2006) *Burrup Peninsula air pollution study: Final report.* Unpublished report to Department of Industry and Resources, Perth.

CSIRO (2007) *Field studies of rock appearance – final report: Fumigation & dust deposition; - progress report: Colour change & spectral mineralogy.* Unpublished report to Department of Industry and Resources, Perth.

CSIRO (2009) *Burrup Peninsula Aboriginal petroglyphs 2004–8: Colour change and spectral mineralogy.* Unpublished report to Department of Industry and Resources, Perth.

CSIRO (2017a) *Burrup Peninsula Aboriginal petroglyphs: Colour change and spectral mineralogy 2004–2016*. Unpublished report to Department of Industry and Resources, Perth.

CSIRO (2017b) *Extreme weathering experiments on the Burrup Peninsula/Murujuga weathered gabbros and granophyres.* Unpublished report to Department of Industry and Resources, Perth.

DAS (Department of Aboriginal Sites) (1984) *Dampier archaeological project: Survey and salvage of aboriginal sites on portion of the Burrup Peninsula for Woodside Offshore Petroleum Pty Ltd. Catchment areas, geomorphic zones and tabulations.* Perth: Department of Aboriginal Sites, Western Australian Museum.

De Koning, S. (2014) *Thatharruga: A stylistic analysis of turtle engravings on the Dampier Archipelago, Western Australia*. Unpublished BA honors thesis, University of Western Australia.

De La Rue, K. (1979) *Pearl shell and pastures*. Karratha: Cossack Project Committee (Inc).

DWER (WA Department of Water and Environmental Regulations) (2019) *Murujuga rock art strategy.* Perth: WA Government.

EPA (Environmental Protection Authority) (2007) Pluto LNG development, Burrup Peninsula, Woodside Energy Ltd. *EPA Bulletin 1259*, Perth.

EPA (2011) Technical ammonium nitrate production facility, Burrup Peninsula, Burrup Nitrates Pty Ltd. *EPA Report 1379*, Perth.

Gunn, R.G. and Mulvaney, K. (2008) Of turtles in particular: A distributional study of an archaeological landscape in southern Murujuga. *Rock Art Research*, 25(2), pp.147–164.

Herriman, N. (2013) Western Australia's aboriginal heritage regime: Critiques of culture, ethnography, procedure and political economy. *Australian Aboriginal Studies*, 2013(1), pp.85–100.

Holland-McNair, L. (2006) *Breaking new ground*. Perth: Rio Tinto Iron Ore.

Holland-McNair, L. (2018) *Walking the land together: Pilbara conversations*. Perth: Agenda Publishing.

Lorblanchet, M. (1977) Summary report of fieldwork, Dampier, W.A. *Australian Institute of Aboriginal Studies Newsletter*, 77, pp.36–40.

Lorblanchet, M. (1983) Chronology of the rock engravings of Gum Tree Valley and Skew Valley near Dampier, WA. In Smith, M. (Ed.) *Archaeology at ANZAAS 1983*. Perth: Western Australian Museum, pp.39–59.

Lorblanchet, M. (2018) *Archaeology and petroglyphs of Dampier (Western Australia): An archaeological investigation of Skew Valley and Gum Tree Valley*. Technical reports of the Australian Museum, Online, number 27, 19 December 2018.

MAC (Murujuga Aboriginal Corporation) (2016) *Murujuga cultural management plan*. Karratha: Murujuga Aboriginal Corporation.

McDonald, J. and Berry, M. (2016) Murujuga, northwestern Australia when arid hunter-gatherers became coastal foragers. *The Journal of Island and Coastal Archaeology,* 12(1), pp.24–43.

McDonald, J. and Veth, P. (2009) Dampier Archipelago petroglyphs: Scientific values and National Heritage listing. *Archaeology in Oceania*, 44(supplement), pp.49–69.

Morse, K., Cameron, R. and Reynan, W. (2014) A tale of three caves: New dates for Pleistocene occupation in the inland Pilbara. *Australian Archaeology,* 79, pp.167–168.

Mulvaney, D.J. (1980) Protecting prehistoric places on the Burrup Peninsula: Comments following a visit 19–22 June 1980. Unpublished report to Western Australian Museum, Perth.

Mulvaney, K.J. (2010) *Murujuga Marni - dampier petroglyphs: Shadows in the landscape echoes across time*. Unpublished PhD thesis, University of New England, Armadale.

Mulvaney, K.J. (2015) *Murujuga Marni – Rock art of the macropod hunters and the Mollusc harvesters*. Perth: UWA Press.

Mulvaney, K.J. (2018) Murujuga at a crossroad: Considering the evidence of nineteenth century contact, Dampier Archipelago northwest Australia. *Australian Archaeology,* 84(3), pp.248–262.

Ride, W.D.L. and Neumann, A. (1964) *Depuch island*. Special Publication, 2. Perth: Western Australian Museum.

SKM (Sinclair Knight Merz) (2003) *Burrup rock art: Atmospheric modelling – concentrations and depositions*. Unpublished report to Department of Industry and Resources, Perth.

SKM (2009) *Burrup rock art monitoring program - summary report.* Unpublished report to the Burrup Rock Art Monitoring Management Committee, Perth

Veth, P., Bradshaw, E., Gara, T., Hall, N., Haydock, P. and Kendrick, P. (1993) *Burrup Peninsula aboriginal heritage project.* Unpublished report Department of Conservation and Land Management, Perth.

Veth, P., Ward, I., Manne, T., Ulm, S., Ditchfield, K., Dortch, J., Hook, F., Petchey, F., Hogg, A., Questiaux, D., Demuro, M., Arnold, L., Spooner, N., Levchenko, V., Skippington, J., Byrne, C., Basgall, M., Zeanah, D., Belton, D., Helmholz, P., Bajkan, S., Bailey, R., Placzek, C. and Kendrick, P. (2017) Early human occupation of a maritime desert, Barrow Island, North-West Australia. *Quaternary Science Reviews,* 168(2017), pp.19–29.

Virili, F.L. (1974) *A preliminary report on the Aboriginal sites and the rock art of the Dampier Archipelago, W.A.* Unpublished report Dampier Salt Ltd, Karratha.

Virili, F.L. (1977) Aboriginal sites and rock art of the Dampier Archipelago. In Ucko, P.J. (Ed.) *Form in indigenous art: Schematisation in the art of aboriginal Australia and prehistoric Europe.* Prehistory and Material Culture Series No 13. Canberra: Australian Institute of Aboriginal Studies, pp.439–451.

Withnell-Taylor, N.E. (1980) *A saga of the north-west Yeera-Muk-A-D00.* Fremantle: Fremantle Arts Centre Press.

3 Multidisciplinary and Integral Approaches to Rock Art as a Strategy for Rock Art Conservation
La Covatina Site as a Case Study

Inés Domingo, Dídac Roman, José Luís Lerma, Irene Rodríguez, M. Antonia Zalbidea Muñoz and Marius Vendrell

Introduction

Levantine rock art (LRA) is a prehistoric artistic tradition dating sometime around the transition from hunter-gatherers to farming societies in the eastern side of the Iberian Peninsula (around 7,500 years ago) (for an in-depth discussion of the complexities of dating this art see Villaverde et al. 2012 or Fernández 2014). However, the exact chronology and the living practices of the artists are still open to discussion. In all of Europe, there is no rock art tradition with the dynamism and narrative essence of this particular art. It includes thousands of extraordinary works of art (mainly paintings and only rarely very fine line engravings) reproducing, for the first time in prehistoric art in this part of the world, lively narrative scenes that to us today seem to be illustrating a variety of human activities and practices that we associate to hunting, violence, war, honey hunting, maternity and death, even though the real meaning is unreadable to us (Domingo 2021). The location in remote landscapes of the Mediterranean side of Iberia and the exposure to all sorts of natural and human threats (e.g., Ballester 2005; Alloza et al. 2009, 2012; Rodríguez and Domingo 2018) are some of the challenges menacing the long-term conservation of this heritage. Due to the vast geographical distribution (more than 600 km from the Pyrenees to the North-eastern part of Andalusia), in altitudes ranging from 100 m to more than 1,300 m above sea level, and at variable distances from the coast (barely 6 km from La Catxupa, Denia, to more than a 100 km of those located in inner Aragón, Cuenca or Albacete) it is subject to very diverse and complex environmental conditions (Figure 3.1). Furthermore, since LRA is located in open-air rock shelters and rock walls the art is often exposed to direct sunlight and solar radiation inducing daily and annual temperature variations on the rock surface and causing rock fatigue and weathering. This explains why, even though LRA

DOI: 10.4324/9780429355349-5

56 *Inés Domingo et al.*

is much younger than the Palaeolithic cave art found in Spain, the paintings are often more partially preserved and less visible (the colours are usually more faded, and the paintings are often covered by dirt, dust and/or translucent or opaque calcium carbonate and/or oxalate crusts hindering visualization). While there is a strong need to achieve a global understanding of this rock art tradition and the threats that endanger it, the widely varying conditions of the sites urged us to begin with a comprehensive study of each site and its peculiarities.

Despite the challenges, over the past 20 years, there has been a growing recognition of the singularity and uniqueness of this prehistoric rock art tradition, and the historic, cultural and artistic values, particularly after being awarded World Heritage Status in 1998. Moreover, in Spain, rock art is protected as Bien de Interés Cultural (*Property of Cultural National Interest*) under the 1985 Spanish Heritage Act, implying that both the art and the surrounding environment are protected and *in situ* preservation is mandatory. Thus, according to the law, rock art cannot be destroyed, damaged, removed or relocated. Unfortunately, though, vandalism continues today.

While the World Heritage declaration brought with it a growing recognition and more public investment, it also introduced additional challenges to archaeologists, authorities, heritage managers and consultants, landowners, and so forth, linked to the increasing interests of private

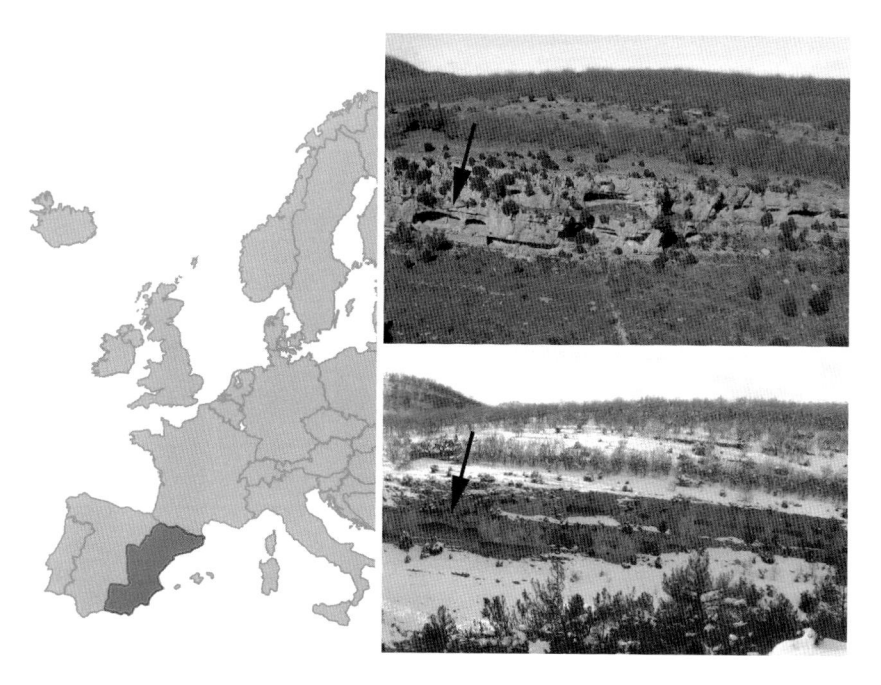

Figure 3.1 Map showing the distribution of Levantine rock art and general view of La Covatina site both in winter and summer time. Photos and map by I. Domingo.

archaeology consultants, regional and local authorities to access newly available funds and use this heritage in the marketing of rural areas subject to increasing depopulation as heritage destinations (Domingo and Bea 2016). Ever since, the number of preventive conservation interventions has significantly increased, including dust, dirt and crusts removal, consolidation of fragile and unstable bedrocks and crack filling (e.g. Ballester 2013a and b; Royo et al. 2013), occasional diversion of water flows using silicone driplines (Royo-Guillén 2001; Ballester 2003), mimetic chromatic retouching (imitating the colour of the bedrock patina) of bedrock or paintings loss using watercolours and mineral pigments to minimize visual impacts (e.g. Royo-Guillén 2001; Martínez 2001; Martínez et al. 2012; Ballester 2003, 2005, 2013a; Mateo-Saura 2017), graffiti removal (Guillamet 2000, 2005, 2012; Ballester 2003; Castells and Hernández 2009) or restitution of a partially removed figure (Miró 2019). Unfortunately, the impacts of some of these actions on archaeological research have not been fully considered and explored in parallel.

Today it seems unquestionable the need to find a balance between archaeology and heritage approaches to rock art (including conservation and restoration practices as well as any regulated contemporary uses of this heritage). While a few archaeological publications have shown an early concern on the fragility of this art, and even listed some of the natural and anthropic agents threatening it (e.g., Casanovas and Alonso 1984; Beltrán 1987; Rodríguez and Domingo 2018), archaeological research has mainly focused on its potential to inform on past human behaviour and practices, overlooking other research agendas concerning conservation and management. On the other hand, conservation practices have been mainly designed by heritage managers working for administrative bodies (e.g., Hernández and Castells 2000; San Nicolás 2014; Martínez 2015, Matamoros and López 2009; Miró 2019; etc.) and performed by consultants (e.g., Guillamet 2000, 2012; Martínez 2002; Martínez, Guillem and Ballester 2011). However, often once interventions have been conducted, no monitoring practices are designed to follow up their evolution through time or have been implemented. This is basically due to lack of resources and staff, as well as the geographic spread of this artistic phenomenon.

To fill the gap between archaeology and heritage approaches to LRA, we put together a multidisciplinary team to develop a pilot project bringing together archaeology, heritage science and cutting-edge digital technologies to transform the way we understand, care, use and manage this millenary legacy. This research was also conducted in close collaboration with the local administration (Vilafranca City Council), as they are directly responsible for the heritage located within the municipal boundaries. In particular, they were interested in better understanding the significance of the rock art located within their land, and in increasing the visibility of the only World Heritage site located in the municipality. This paper presents some preliminary results of this pilot project, developed at La Covatina del Tossalet del Mas de la Rambla site (Vilafranca, Castelló). The project is ongoing in order to continue monitoring the evolution of the site and the interventions over time.

The site

The LRA site of La Covatina del Tossalet del Mas de la Rambla is located at altitudes of 1126 m and 50 m above Carabasses ravine riverbed, which is part of the hydrographical network of the Ebro River. It sits at the base of a limestone cliff featuring many rock shelters, though only La Covatina has rock art preserved (Figure 3.1). It is composed of two contiguous cavities measuring 31 m long, 4 m deep and a maximum height of 4.8 m with rock art found only in the left one. Today the paintings are concentrated in four different parts of the panel (units 1 to 4), with the right area concentrating most of them. Nevertheless, the current state of preservation suggests that the site was once more complex than what we see today. The site faces SE, with the panels exposed to direct sunlight throughout the morning in the winter, while they are completely protected by the overhang of the rock shelter during summer (for more details, see Chapter 11 in this volume). A peripheral fence (stone wall imitating traditional shepherd's walls to minimize visual impact) to prevent unwanted and unregulated visitors was built in the 1980s.

The rock art was discovered by local schoolteacher Salvador Gómez Bellot sometime between 1968 and 1971 and it was mentioned in several publications. These publications were mostly partial (only listing a few motifs) and offered controversial interpretations of the art, reiterating the presence of a depiction of a bird of prey (Gómez 1971; Arasa 1977, 1982). While these animals are totally unusual in this art tradition, this interpretation has been perpetuated in archaeological literature and among public opinion. A few years later, Mesado added other debatable interpretations (1989). In his review of the site, including a more complete record of motifs (up to 26), he further reiterated the presence of a bird of prey, adding that it was being hunted with a sling (also unusual in LRA). In addition, he interpreted some other human figures as female viper hunters. As we will discuss in this paper, today all these interpretations can be refuted. New digital copies or tracings and a careful analysis of the integrity of the motifs and the rock reveal that current shapes, resembling a bird of prey or the supposed snakes identified by previous authors are fragments of figures originally representing something else. A careful analysis and comparison with other Levantine figures suggest alternative and more reliable interpretations, aligned with the characteristics and the subject matters depicted in LRA. The need to review the interpretation of this site, together with the interest of the city council to open the site to the public are the reasons that led us to select it to develop our pilot project.

La Covatina project: aims and methods

Considering the need to explore the scientific and heritage values of La Covatina collaboratively in order to retrieve as much scientific information as possible to achieve a comprehensive understanding of the art and the site, while ensuring all data is made available to the scientific community and the public through different media, we designed a medium-term (2013–2021) multidisciplinary and multistep approach including:

- An initial **archaeological study of the art and its archaeological and historical context**, to evaluate the scientific, historical, cultural and tourism potential of this site.
- A **comprehensive 2D and 3D digital recording** of the art and site of interest for research, conservation and public dissemination.
- A **comprehensive conservation assessment**, conducted by experts in rock art conservation and restoration, to identify degrading agents, perform a risk assessment, design a line of research in conservation, propose and conduct any conservation interventions deemed necessary, always based on a solid understanding of cross-sectoral needs (i.e. the needs of the different stakeholders involved, which in this case included Vilafranca city council and tourism information office, archaeologists and art conservators and restorers); and to design the protocols for the conservation and monitoring of the site in the long-term.
- **The preparation of a site management plan,** to promote a wider understanding of this heritage and make it accessible to the public in various formats.

The objectives and methodology of our multistep approach are described below.

Archaeological approach

Our archaeological analysis of the art and its context included review of previous literature (Gómez 1971; Arasa 1977, 1982; Mesado 1989) and detailed qualitative analysis of the art (motifs, styles and compositions) to evaluate prior interpretations, understand the sequence and verify the interest and the singularity of the site. We also conducted systematic archaeological surveys on the surroundings within Vilafranca municipality (in 2013 and 2016) looking for previously non-identified rock art sites, as well as human occupation sites dating between the end of the Palaeolithic and the beginning of the Neolithic (the periods when LRA was most likely produced). The aim was twofold: contextualize the art and understand how its authors lived while, in the event of further discoveries, increasing the number of heritage sites available in the area to advance research and as potential cultural and tourism products.

60 *Inés Domingo et al.*

An archival review in search of historical images that could inform of changes in the integrity of the site was also conducted. Of special interest were the images from the Gil Carles photographic archive produced in the 1970s (Cruz et al. 2005), with images taken soon after the discovery of this site (1972) and preserved at the Biblioteca Tomás Navarro Tomás CCHS-CSIC. Our aim was to evaluate potential changes in the art caused by the short-term impact of non-regulated visits to the site.

Digital recording techniques

The use of digital recording techniques is standard practice in rock art research today. As part of our first approach to this site we conducted a full 2D digital recording of the motifs using digital enhancement and colour selection tools (Adobe Photoshop and DStretch plugin to ImageJ) as described in Domingo et al. (2013). Given that restoration works conducted in 2015 and 2017 improved image viewing and led to the discovery of previously invisible figures or parts of figures (not even visible using digital enhancement techniques), we recorded the site twice, before and after the conservation interventions. These records were later implemented with the metric documentation of the site using photogrammetric and terrestrial scanning techniques (with time-of-flight Leica ScanStation C10). The goal was to capture the state of conservation of the site and the paintings at particular points in time by generating high-resolution three-dimensional (3D) photorealistic models for both the site and for each particular painting. For this latter product, we integrated high-end close-range photogrammetric solutions to improve both the resolution and the precision of the recording techniques.

Using historical photographs, we also implemented the current 3D models with old photographs taken by photographer Gil Carles in 1972 with the idea of building a 4D model of those figures recorded more than 40 years ago.[1] This virtual 4D model combines different sorts of documents: historical information and photographs, photorealistic 3D models of the site and the motifs, 3D models implemented with tracings, digital reconstructions of some partially preserved motifs (to facilitate public interpretation) and the evolution of the panel and the motifs through time. Importantly, this model can be updated and implemented over time.

Rock art conservation

Our conservation approach started in 2014 with a dedicated condition assessment. The first aim was to understand the characteristics of the bedrock and the whole spectrum of risks threatening the conservation of the art and the site. Several researchers (I. Rodríguez, Drs. M. Zalbidea and M. Vendrell) and conservation consultants (Drs. L. Ballester and G.

Barreda; and E. Guillamet) participated in this part of the project. *In situ* visual analysis and microscopic analysis (with a handheld digital microscope AM73915MZT Dino-Lite) were used together. Bedrock samples were also taken to characterize the nature and structure of the geosubstrate as well as to anticipate potential risks and develop protocols to mitigate those risks if they occur. In the following years two direct conservation interventions were undertaken (2015 and 2017). These included cleaning surface dust, dirt and organic remains as well as graffiti and herbaceous plants removal -plants, growing seasonally at the base of the rock shelter and in the immediate surroundings. The first intervention was conducted by restoration specialists and consultants L. Ballester and E. Guillamet, and the second by G. Barreda. In both cases a similar procedure was reported (Ballester and Guillamet 2015; Barreda 2017). They described mechanical removal of surface dirt and crusts using different sorts of brushes and diamond-tipped tools under magnifying lenses. Water was the only solvent used. The main difference between both interventions was that while in the first one, gaps and losses were mimetically restored with watercolours, in the second this procedure was no longer employed, as we will discuss below.

Systematic monitoring of thermal-hygrometric dynamics has been also performed, to understand the microclimatic conditions of the site and their potential correlations with weathering. These data are also valid to inform future conservation interventions planning the use of consolidating materials, since it might help to identify which materials are best suited to existing microclimatic conditions and at what time of the year the conditions are more appropriate for their use (for further details see Chapter 11 in this volume). In 2016, *in situ* tests of various consolidant materials (Nanorestore and CaLoSil IP5) and pigments (Winsor & Newton -Cotman®- watercolours and mineral pigments) used in rock art conservation were also prepared for surface and fissure application to evaluate their performance over time (Figure 3.2). The tests were set up in a rock shelter with no paintings located nearby, so that the microclimatic conditions were the same as those of the rock art site. Similar tests are also being conducted in the laboratory using aging and Ultraviolet cameras to accelerate deterioration processes. These tests are still in progress, so no consolidation interventions have been conducted to date.

Management plan and knowledge transfer

To elaborate a management plan, we followed Magar's scheme for managing sites (Identification of the site. Understanding the significance. Analysis of the site conditions. Defining policies or guiding principles. Defining goals for management. Design an action plan. Monitor, evaluation, review and correction of the action plan) (Magar 2012, pp. 539–542).

62 *Inés Domingo et al.*

Figure 3.2 *In situ* tests of various consolidants and pigments used in rock art conservation to evaluate their performance over time. Photo by I. Domingo.

Multidisciplinary and Integral Approaches 63

We started by evaluating the historical, ethnographic, cultural and tourism resources and capabilities of the town. We also explored if there was a system in place to visit the site, and evaluated site accessibility, distance to town, paintings visibility as well as the interpretive information available for visitors.

Surprisingly, while the site was one of the 758 sites included in the United Nations Educational, Scientific and Cultural Organization (UNESCO) World Heritage list in 1998, in 2013 visitor management was not implemented yet. Tourists could access the site on their own by getting the key and just leaving an identification. Moreover, there was no system in place to monitor potential impacts after the visits. According to the tourism information office they had enquiries about visiting the site only twice or three times a year and they had no information to offer visitors. Thus, the site was not one of the town's tourist attractions at the time, neither in terms of offer nor demand. Thus, as part of our project we: designed and demarcated a route to access the site setting up permanent information panels; prepared a visit and monitoring plan with guidelines to regulate and supervise the visits to the site and monitor site maintenance (that were provided to the city council); as well as prepared materials for printed and virtual dissemination.

Project results and discussion

Our archaeological approach to the site and its context has substantially improved understanding of this site and how it fits within LRA. Our systematic analysis and digital recording of the art using digital enhancement techniques resulted in a new interpretation of some of the motifs and the discovery of previously unseen figures (from 26 motifs published by Mesado in 1989 to up to 33 after our first study). In addition, other figures were found as a result of two conservation interventions, increasing the number of motifs and subject matters (from our initial 33 motifs recorded in 2014 to up to 40 after conservation). The previous interpretation of the two central and best-known figures of the site as a scene showing a sling hunter chasing a bird did not fit well within the Levantine repertoire.

This misinterpretation was constraint by poor conservation and a lack of in depth understanding of the deterioration processes that have modified the actual shape of the figures. Detailed analysis of the bedrock and the search for parallels show that the supposed bird of prey was in fact a partially preserved representation of a woman (a detachment of the rock caused the disappearance of her head). Similarly, the supposed sling hunter was an archer carrying the classic Levantine weaponry: a bow and a bundle of arrows. Other figures, previously interpreted as snake female hunters (a topic never depicted in LRA) are also archers, and the supposed snakes are rather part of the bundle of arrows partially preserved (Figure 3.3). Furthermore, the

64 *Inés Domingo et al.*

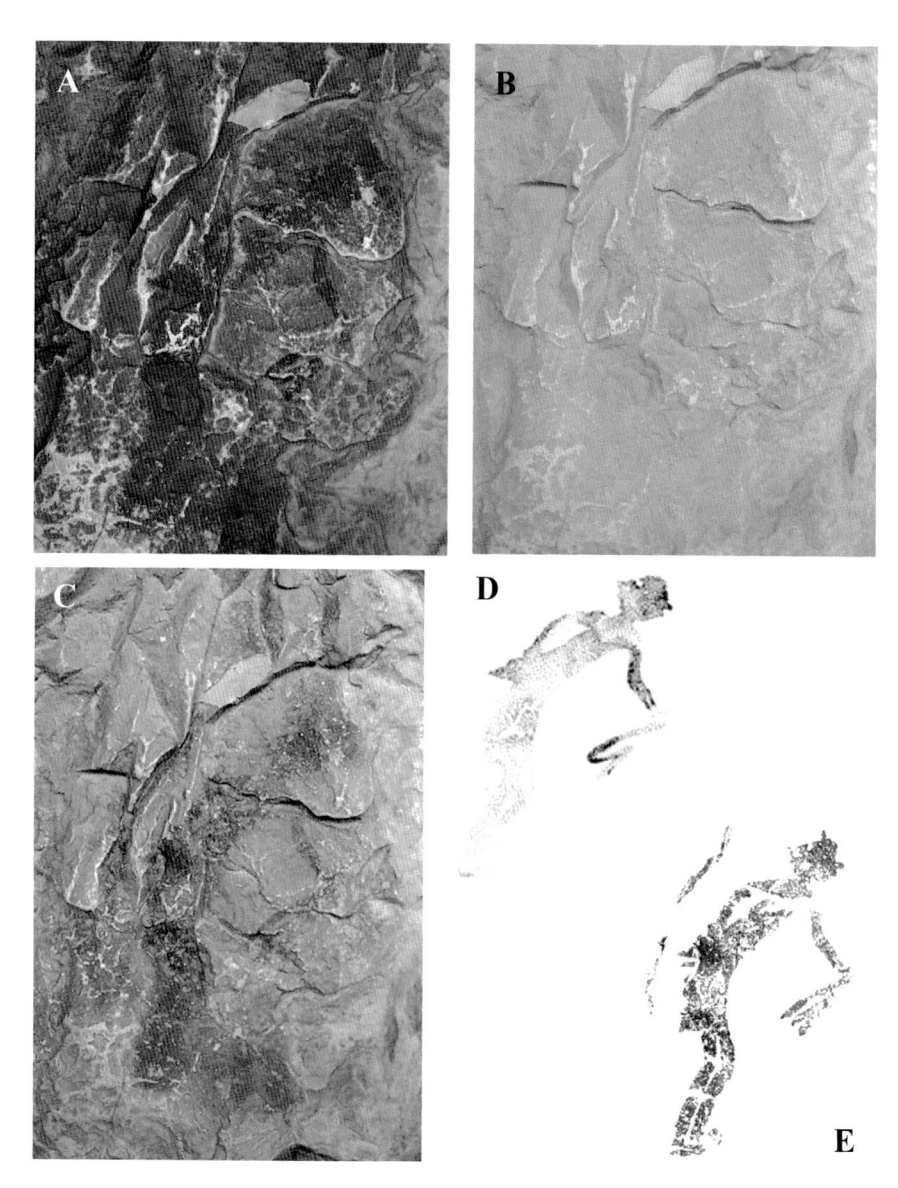

Figure 3.3 Images and digital reproductions of one of the figures at La Covatina. A. Image taken in 1972. Biblioteca Tomás Navarro Tomás -CCHS-CSIC. B. Image taken in 2014, prior to the conservation intervention. The figure is almost invisible. C. Image taken in 2015, after the conservation intervention. D. Mesado's tracing showing a 'supposed' woman hunting a viper. E. Tracing produced in 2015 showing that the supposed viper is in fact the bottom part of a bundle of arrows. Figure by I. Domingo.

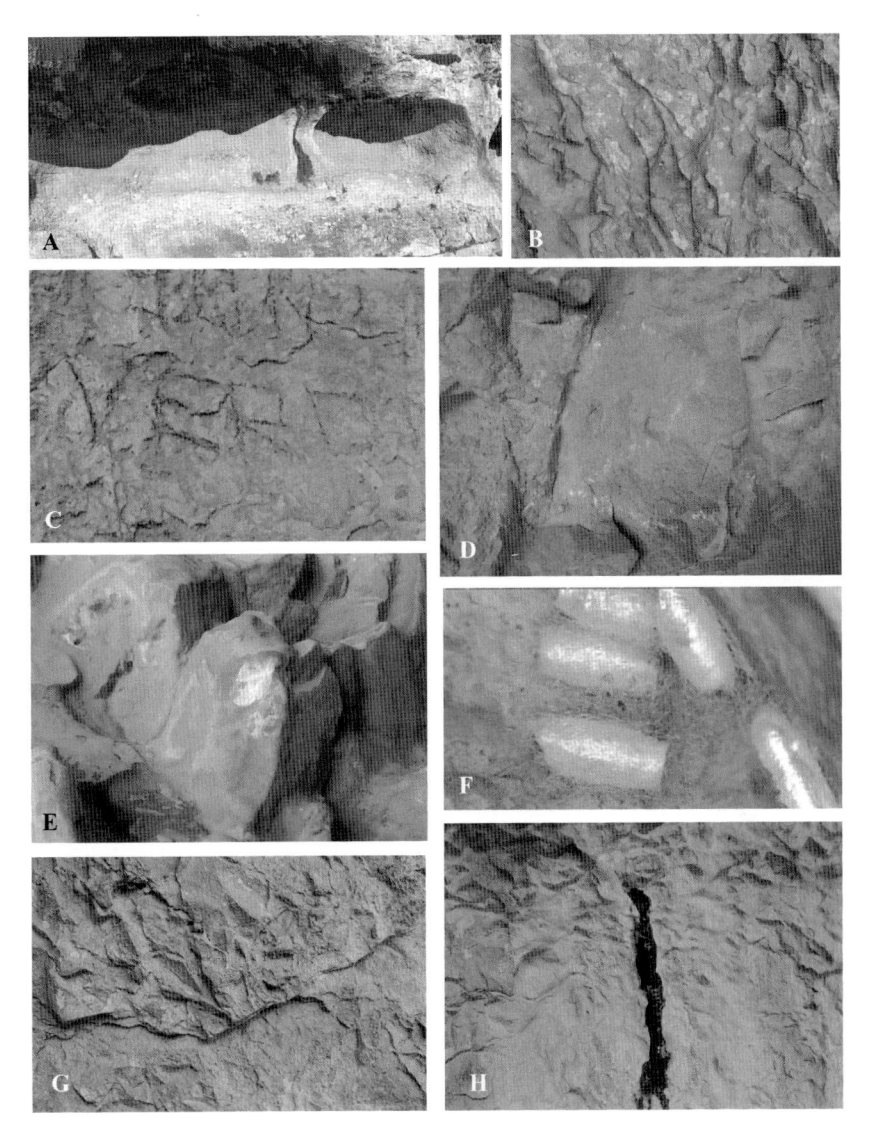

Figure 3.4 Pathologies identified at La Covatina. A. Direct sun exposure. B. Dust. C. Graphite graffiti. D. Chalk Graffiti. E. Bird droppings. F. Insect nesting. G. Surface erosion. H. Black biopatina. Figure by I. Domingo.

discovery of new figures added new subject matters to the site, significantly enriching this place both for research and the public. The site interpretation has now been enriched to include also a war-like scene, a hunting scene and a singular therianthropic figure, with very few parallels documented in LRA.

The archaeological surveys of the surrounding landscapes also resulted in the discovery of two new LRA sites, as well as a series of occupation sites, adding new heritage values to this municipality. The rock art finds attracted a great deal of media attention (both nationally and internationally), showing the potential of this heritage to generate interest in society, particularly when the public is properly informed. These newly identified sites have been also protected with a fence to regulate visits and they have been added to the cultural resources the town has to offer. These new sites are also important for archaeology, as they introduced new subject matters and fill a geographic gap in the distribution of this art.

The initial **conservation assessment** of the site identified significant deficiencies in motif visualization as well as rock weathering, biodeterioration and different sorts of animal and human threats (dust, insect nesting, bird droppings, calcium crusts, surface erosion, black bio-patina, direct sun exposure, changing temperatures and humidity, graffiti or shot marks with buckshot) (Figure 3.4). It was shocking to compare current photographs with those taken back in 1972 and see the rapid degradation they have undergone in barely three decades. In 2014 many of the paintings were covered by a white halo masking the art. While oxalate and calcium crusts are common natural formations affecting open-air rock art (Domingo, Vendrell and Chieli 2021), their higher concentration on the paintings was interpreted as a potential consequence of continuous wetting and rubbing to facilitate visualization, thus accelerating deterioration (Ballester 2014).

In addition, multiple unwanted graffiti text scratched or drawn (with graphite and chalk) on the walls since its discovery were seriously impacting the aesthetic integrity of this World Heritage site. Therefore, graffiti and crust removal were considered an immediate priority, while the monitoring of other pathologies and the completion of other types of direct intervention suggested by conservators (such as rock consolidation) were postponed and integrated into a more in-depth and medium-term study that is still ongoing. Since interventions were subject to sufficient funding to cover the costs of consultant conservators, they were divided into two phases. The first one, conducted in 2015 on two sides of the site, significantly improved the visualization of the art and led to the identification of previously unrecorded figures, as mentioned above. However, it also opened up important doubts or questions to be explored further as part of this/future research programs including:

- What is the impact of crust removal and surface cleaning on rock art conservation and dating?
- What is the potential impact of what has come to be called in the literature on LRA restorations as 'aesthetic resolution' (filling areas with material surface loss with watercolours or other mineral pigments or earths to cover them up) on archaeological approaches to past pigment technologies and recipes?

Surface cleaning and crust removal have been extensively applied in Levantine sites to improve visibility (Guillamet 2000; Ballester 2003; Guillamet 2012; Martínez et al. 2012; Ballester 2013a; Hernández and Royo 2013; Barreda 2016, etc.). While the benefits for the scientific study and for opening the sites to the public are evident (make the art visible again and discover new figures or parts of figures which would not otherwise be known), these are irreversible actions, the impact of which has not been properly assessed in the mid and long-term. As the painted walls are extremely irregular, mechanical cleaning may cause surface micro-erosions. These need to be seriously considered, not only for the loss of pigment but also because they can contribute a new source of deterioration. Furthermore, our analysis of the rock to understand the nature and potential risks showed that it was covered by a calcareous crust, similar to the patinas containing calcium oxalates identified at other Levantine sites (e.g., Hernanz et al. 2006, 2007, 2014; Mas-Cornellà et al. 2013; Pitarch et al. 2014, etc.). But the question to be further explored and discussed is whether this layer should be removed or reduced to facilitate motif visualization, since these crusts have also acted as a coat sealing the paint (Mas-Cornellá et al. 2013) and protecting the art from natural erosion, which therefor explains their conservation in the open-air over thousands of years. Thus, these layers are strategic for long term conservation (for an updated review and discussion on this sort of patinas see, Domingo, Vendrell and Chieli 2021). Interestingly, while the crusts are not opaque, they partially hide the paintings because of the diffusion of light scattered by the microscopic superficial roughness; therefore, once coated by water, the diffusion reduces, and the paintings can be better seen through the crust. In theory smoothing the surface would increase the visibility of the paints keeping part of the crust as a protective layer, but the risks of potential micro-erosions discussed above should be considered.

Additionally, as discussed previously by some researchers (Mateo 2013; Alonso and Grimal 2019), surface calcium oxalates could also be used as an alternative for dating this art using Accelerator Mass Spectrometry Carbon-14 AMS^{14}C) (e.g., Ruiz et al. 2006, 2012; Hernanz et al. 2007). And even though the results of this technique are still controversial (Bednarik 2002; Cole and Watchman 2005; Domingo 2008: 29; Ruiz et al. 2012, Domingo, Vendrell and Chieli 2021), crust removal or reduction can inhibit future attempts to date rock art with new techniques or refined versions of existing ones.

Aesthetic resolution or reintegration has been a recurrent practice for loss treatment at LRA sites (e.g., at Cavalls site in 1998; Mas d'en Josep and Civil sites 1999; La Sarga 2001–2005; Remígia 2005; La Roca dels Moros de Cogul in 2008, Capçanes 2015–2016, Cocó de la Gralla 2017; etc.) with no one questioning or analysing the extent to which the introduced materials may interfere with studies of past materials. Moreover, technical reports produced after the interventions are rarely published, so researchers are often unaware of which sites have been restored, and what materials have been introduced and where they have been applied. With this in mind, in the second phase of intervention, we excluded any possible reintegration, and we started a new line of research aimed at developing protocols to identify materials introduced in the past and monitor their evolution through time.

As part of the project, we also developed a **management plan** and we led various initiatives aimed at **transferring knowledge to society**, as social involvement is essential for the conservation of such a dispersed heritage. The proximity of the site to the town (only 5 km), a short and easy access (about five minutes' walk) suitable to everyone who can walk, and the relatively good visibility of the paintings (especially after the conservation interventions) make this site an ideal place for audiences of all ages to have a first contact with Levantine World Heritage rock art. To enrich the visit and enhance the understanding of the art and its context, we designed a circular access route with various stopovers to also contemplate the environmental diversity and the scenic beauty of the area where the site is located. At these points, informative panels were installed, providing information about the landscape and the animals inhabiting it around 7,500 years ago, as well as what is known regarding the lifestyles they lived. The idea is for visitors to understand not only the art but also how the authors lived and interacted with an environment that was different from today and to reflect on what might have been so special about this place for the artists to mark it with their paintings at various stages. These periodical visits are inferred from the presence of various styles of Levantine human figures.

We also proposed a series of measures to feasibly open the site to the public (appropriate use, different sorts of preventive and direct conservation interventions, regulated and guided visits with restricted number of visitors to minimize impacts and ensure the quality of the visitor experience, with proper and regular maintenance and monitoring measures, etc.) for the correct incorporation into the cultural offer of the municipality in a regulated and sustainable manner. These measures were guided by the need to preserve the values, authenticity and integrity of this cultural and artistic endangered legacy. Today, the site is included in the series of regular visits organized by the Valltorta Museum to LRA sites located outside the iconic Valltorta-Gasulla Cultural Park they manage. According to the Museum director P. Vidal, today this is the most visited site outside the Valltorta-Gasulla cultural park, demonstrating that global approaches to this heritage (including research, conservation and informed promotion) are needed to develop quality, regulated and sustainable cultural tourism offered for this fragile World Heritage.

Finally, to contribute to an understanding of the conservation history of the site over time, to make it accessible to a broad audience and to help build a digital future for this heritage, we used the graphic documentation produced for scientific purposes (2D and 3D models of the site and the motifs, and a 360° panoramic image of the site) to build the first real 4D interactive model of a LRA site (Figure 3.5). This model, available online,

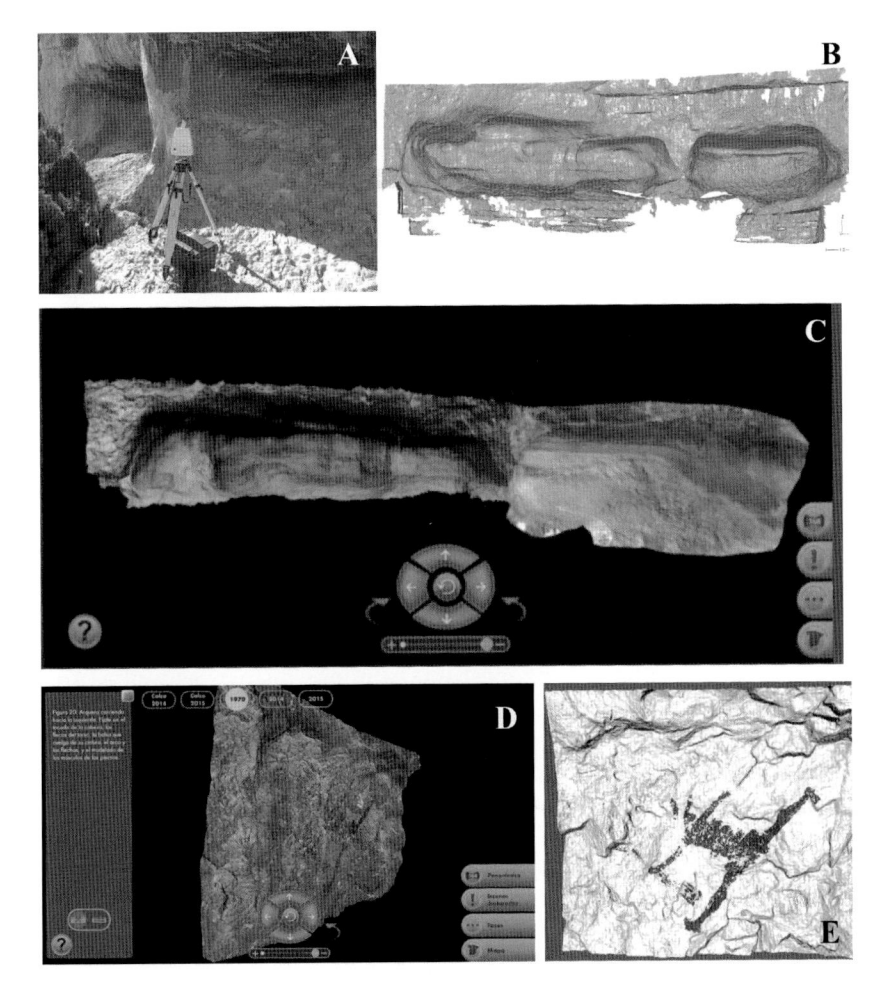

Figure 3.5 Building a 4D model of La Covatina. A. Data acquisition with a terrestrial laser scanner Leica ScanStation C10. B. Perspective view of 3D model. C. 3D model of the site visible in the virtual platform created to interact with the 4D model. D. 4D model of one motif. E. 3D model of one motif with tracings implemented. Figure by authors.

has multiple functions as an archaeological tool to explore the dynamics of rock art through time, while also serving for conservation and monitoring, and for public dissemination (http://turismevilafranca.es 4D/ and https://www.ub.edu/larcher/arte-rupestre-virtual/). Our idea was to offer a complete overview of the site through history; combining data of interest both to archaeologists and the general public, always informed by state-of-the-art scientific research, while providing some scientific tools for archaeologists interested in analysing either the motifs or the scenes.

The resulting model is not just a conventional photorealistic 3D model, which is something that has been done before, but a virtual window for users to interact with the site at different levels, from the overall site to the details of each motif.

Conclusion

Today, it is widely accepted that interdisciplinary and collaborative approaches are necessary to achieve a global understanding of the scientific, historical, artistic and heritage values of LRA and to contribute to the long-term conservation of this fragile and singular open-air heritage, both *in situ* and in digital formats. In this paper we demonstrate how interdisciplinary and collaborative approaches to a particular LRA site, La Covatina, has helped to:

- improve the interpretation of a previously overlooked and misinterpreted site, and place it in global debates regarding this art.
- discover new figures and themes, as well as new rock art sites, filling a geographic gap and attracting attention to this previously under-explored territory.
- understand the conservation history (the nature of the site, historical and new potential threats, past interventions history, as well as some of the agents contributing to the long-term preservation of the art) and how it has impacted our current perception of the motifs and the scenes.
- understand the need to contribute to rock art conservation through education and to reach a broad audience to help the public connect with this heritage through different interpretative materials in printed and virtual formats, engaging and benefitting from the results of cutting-edge research.
- contribute to building digital futures for this heritage, by introducing a step further in rock art recording and visualization, building the first real 4D model of a LRA site. This 4D model is of interest for research (motifs and scenes can be explored in detailed and be measured), for conservation and monitoring (to explore changes over time and to preserve this art for the future) as well as to bring this heritage to society in digital and appealing formats.

Working together with archaeologists and rock art conservators has helped us to better understand the benefits and dangers of direct conservation interventions and to open new debates and research questions that we will address in the near future in order to minimize our impact on this ancient legacy, always trying to find a balance between archaeology, conservation and use.

Working in collaboration with the Vilafranca City Council we have developed several initiatives aimed at increasing social awareness and interest in this endangered heritage as a key for the long-term conservation of this millenary legacy. We have also increased the number of cultural resources in the area, with the discovery of new rock art sites, and contributed to create protocols for sustainable and regulated use while urging for the necessary regular monitoring so often neglected. The results of this interdisciplinary and collaborative project bring together archaeology, heritage sciences and information technologies and are important for rock art research, documentation, conservation and education, following our commitment to change the way we understand, care, use and manage this particular prehistoric art.

Acknowledgements

Multiple public funding bodies provided funds over the years for different parts of this project under the direction of I. Domingo and D. Román. Research has been conducted as part of HAR2016-80693-P, funded by the Ministry of Economy, Industry, Competitiveness of Spain and cofounded by AEI/FEDER, EU; and the ERC CoG project LArcHer, funded by the European Research Council under the European Union's Horizon 2020 research and innovation programme – grant agreement No. 819404. Funds for archaeological surveying, 3D digital recording and conservation interventions were provided by Ministry of Education, Culture and Sports and Vilafranca City Council (2013–2014, 2014–2015, 2015–2016), and Excma. Diputació Provincial de Castelló (2016–2017).

We thank Biblioteca Tomás Navarro Tomás -CCHS-CSIC for providing digital copies of historical images of the Gil-Carles archive. We thank Pilar Vidal (director of the Valltorta Museum) for providing information about current visits to the site.

We thank all the people who have participated in the various campaigns, both hired (conservators L. Ballester, E. Guillamet, G. Barreda, archaeologists F. Duarte, R. Rubio, B. Rives, J. Palmer and surveyor M. Cabrelles) and collaborators (A. Chieli, A. Macarulla, F. Moya, I. Gil).

Note

1 http://turismevilafranca.es/4D/; https://www.ub.edu/larcher/arte-rupestre-virtual/

References

Alloza, R., Arranz, E., González, J.M., Baldellou, V., Resano, M., Marzo, P. and Vanhaekne, F. (2009) La conservación del arte rupestre: estudio de los factores de deterioro y de la composición química de los pigmentos. In *El arte rupestre del Arco Mediterráneo de la Península Ibérica. 10 años en la Lista del Patrimonio Mundial de la UNESCO*. Actas IV Congreso, Valencia: Generalitat Valenciana, pp.317–325.

Alloza, R., Royo, J.I., Recuenco, J.L., Lecina, M., Pérez, R. and Iglesias M.P. (2012) La conservación del arte rupestre al aire libre: Un desafío formidable. In *Jornadas Técnicas para la Gestión del Arte Rupestre, Patrimonio Mundial*. Parque

Cultural del Río Vero. Alquezar, Huesca: Comarca de Somontano de Barbastro, pp.89–106.
Alonso, A. and Grimal, A. (2019) Arte Levantino. Datar o restaurar. *Serie arqueológica,* 25, pp.129–196.
Arasa, F. (1977) Estudio arqueológico de Vilafranca del Cid (Castellón). *Cuadernos de Prehistoria y Arqueología Castellonense,* 4, pp.243–269.
Arasa, F. (1982) Arqueologia del terme municipal de Vilafranca. *Boletín de Amigos de Morella y su Comarca,* 1979–1982, pp.14–26.
Ballester, L. (2003) *Conservación de las pinturas rupestres del levante español* (PhD), València: Universitat Politècnica de València.
Ballester, L. (2005) Conservación de las pinturas rupestres del Levante español. In *Actas del Congreso de Arte rupestre de la España Mediterránea: Alicante, 25–28 de octubre de 2004,* pp.429–434.
Ballester, L. (2013a) Intervención de conservación del abrigo de las Monteses, Jalance. In Domingo, I., Rives, B., Román, D. and Rubio, R. (Eds) *Imágenes en la piedra. Arte rupestre en el abrigo de Las Monteses y su entorno (Jalance).* Jalance: Ayuntamiento de Jalance/Ministerio de Cultura, pp.41–42.
Ballester, L. (2013b) Intervención de conservación del abrigo del Barranco de los Robles, Jalance. Valencia. In Domingo, I., Rives, B., Román, D. and Rubio, R. (Eds) *Imágenes en la piedra. Arte rupestre en el abrigo de Las Monteses y su entorno (Jalance).* Jalance: Ayuntamiento de Jalance/Ministerio de Cultura, pp.55–56.
Ballester, L. (2014) *Estudio de conservación preventiva.* In *Project: Estudio, documentación integral y elaboración de un plan de gestión del abrigo de la Covatina del Tossalet del Mas de la Rambla (Vilafranca, Castelló).* Unpublished Technical Report.
Ballester, L. and Guillamet, E. (2015) *Pinturas Rupestres de La Covatina Del Tossalet del Mas de la Rambla o del Abrigo del Barranc de les Carabasses, Vilafranca, Castellón.* Unpublished Technical Report.
Barreda, G. (2016) *Consolidantes para soportes pétreos con manifestaciones de arte rupestre en la Comunidad Valenciana. Análisis prácticos en Cova Remígia (Barranc de Gassulla-Ares del Maestre)* (PhD) València: Universitat Politècnica de València.
Barreda, G. (2017) *Technical report for project Fase II de la intervención de conservación y restauración de las pinturas rupestres del abrigo de la Covatina del Tossalet del Mas de la Rambla o del Barranc de les Carabasses (Vilafranca-Castelló).* Unpublished Technical Report.
Bednarik, R.G. (2002) The dating of rock art: A critique. *Journal of Archaeological Science,* 29, pp.1213–1233.
Beltrán, A. (1987) La conservación del arte rupestre. *Cuadernos de prehistoria y arqueología castellonenses*, 13, pp.61–82.Casanovas, A. and Alonso, A. (1984) Problemática entorno a la conservación del arte rupestre en abrigos. In Sanz, R. (Ed) *Congreso de Historia de Albacete I: Arqueología y prehistoria.* Albacete: Instituto de Estudios Albacetenses, pp.67–76.
Castells, J. and Hernández, G. (2009) La gestión de los conjuntos con pinturas rupestres en Catalunya: estado de la cuestión. In *El arte rupestre del Arco Mediterráneo de la Península Ibérica. 10 Años en la Lista del Patrimonio Mundial de la UNESCO. Actas IV Congreso, 3–5 de diciembre de 2008,* Valencia, pp.197–204.
Cole, N. and Watchman, A. (2005) AMS dating of rock art in the Laura Region, Cape York Peninsula, Australia – protocols and results of recent research. *Antiquity,* 79–305, pp.661–678.

Cruz, M., Gil-Carles, J.M., Gil, M. and Martínez, Mª.I. (2005) Martín Almagro Basch, Fernando Gil Carles y el Corpus de Arte Rupestre Levantino. *Trabajos de Prehistoria*, 62(1), pp.27–45.

Domingo, I. (2008) Temporalidad y regionalización de las técnicas de representación en el Arte Rupestre Levantino. In *Proceedings of the IV Congreso del Neolítico en la Península Ibérica*. Alicante: MARQ, pp.22–30.

Domingo, I. (2021) New insights into the analysis of Levantine rock art scenes informed by observations on western Arnhem Land rock art. In Davidson, I. and Nowell, A. (Eds) *Making scenes: Global perspectives on scenes in rock art*. New York, Oxford: Berghahn Books.

Domingo, I. and Bea, M. (2016) From Science to Heritage: new challenges for World Heritage rock art sites in Mediterranean Spain in the twenty-first century. In Brady, L. and Taçon, P. (Eds) *Relating to rock art in the contemporary world. Navigating symbolism, meaning and significance*. Colorado: University Press of Colorado, pp.213–244.

Domingo, I., Vendrell, M. and Chieli, A. (2021) A critical assessment of the potential and limitations of physicochemical analysis to advance knowledge on Levantine rock art. *Quaternary International*, 572, pp.24–40. https://doi.org/10.1016/j.quaint.2020.09.020

Domingo, I., Villaverde, V., López, E., Lerma, J.L. and Cabrelles, M. (2013) Reflexiones sobre las técnicas de documentación del arte rupestre: la restitución bidimensional (2D) versus la tridimensional (3D). *Cuadernos de arte rupestre*, 6, pp.21–32.

Fernández, J. (2014) Traditions artistiques, interactions culturelles et contextes symboliques de la transition néolithique dans la region méditerranéenne espagnole. In Manen, C., Perrin, T. and Guilaine, J. (Eds) *La transition néolithique en Méditerranée. The Neolithic transition in the Mediterranean*. Errance – AEP.

Gómez, S. (1971) Nuevas pinturas rupestres en el Término de Villafranca del Cid. *Actas del I Congreso de Historia del País Valenciano*, II. Valencia, pp.185–188.

Guillamet, E. (2000) Intervencions de conservació-restauració en pintura rupestre. *Cota Zero*, 16, pp.111–119.

Guillamet, E. (2005) La conservación del arte rupestre en la Comunidad Valenciana. In Martínez Valle, R. (Ed.) *Arte rupestre en la Comunidad Valenciana*. València: Generalitat Valenciana, pp.393–403.

Guillamet, E. (2012) Intervenciones de conservación de arte rupestre al aire libre. En Juste Arruga, M.N. et al. (Eds) *Jornadas Técnicas para la gestión del arte rupestre, Patrimonio Mundial*. Alquézar (Huesca), 03 June 2012. Parque Cultural del Río Vero, pp.123–128.

Hernández, G. and Castells, J. (2000) Conservació i protecció dels conjunts amb pintures rupestres a l'aire lliure. *Cota Zero*, 16, pp.120–132.

Hernández, Mª.Á. and Royo, J.I. (2013) Actuaciones de conservación de arte rupestre en la Comunidad Autónoma de Aragón. In Junta de Castilla y León (Ed.) *Actas Jornadas Técnicas La Conservación del Arte Rupestre: Sostenibilidad e integración en el paisaje*. Salamanca: Consejería de Cultura y Turismo, pp.185–196.

Hernanz, A., Gavira-Vallejo, J.M. and Ruiz-López, J.F. (2006) Introduction to Raman microscopy of prehistoric rock paintings from the Sierra de las Cuerdas, Cuenca, Spain. *Journal of Raman Spectroscopy*, 37, pp.1054–1062.

Hernanz, A., Gavira-Vallejo, J.M. and Ruiz, J.F. (2007) Calcium oxalates and prehistoric paintings. The usefulness of these biomaterials. *Journal of Optoelectronics and Advanced Materials*, 9–3, pp.512–521.

Hernanz, A., Ruiz, J.F., Madariaga, J.M., Gavrilenko, E., Maguregui, M., Fdez-Ortiz de Vallejuelo, S., Martínez-Azkarazo, I., Alloza-Izquierdo, R., Baldellou-Martínez, V., Viñas-Vallverdú, R., Rubio i Mora, A., Pitarch, A. and Giakoumaki, A. (2014) Spectroscopic characterization of crusts interstratified with prehistoric paintings preserved in open-air rock shelters. *Journal of Raman Spectroscopy*, 45, pp.1236–1243.

Magar, V. (2012) Managing rock art sites. In McDonald, J. and Veth, P. (Eds) *A companion to rock art*. Blackwell Publishing Ltd, pp.532–545.

Martínez, R. (2001) Intervenciones preventivas, conservación y difusión del arte rupestre en la Comunidad Valenciana. *Panel*, 1, pp.70–83.

Martínez, R. (2002) La Sarga (Alcoy, Alicante), un proyecto para la conservación del yacimiento. In Hernández, M.S. and Segura, J.M. (Eds) *La Sarga. Arte rupestre y territorio*. Alcoi, Alacant: Ayuntamiento de Alcoi y Caja de Ahorros del Mediterráneo, pp.195–204.

Martínez, R. (2015) Conservación del Arte Rupestre en la Comunidad Valenciana. In *Actas Jornadas Técnicas La conservación del Arte rupestre: Sostenibilidad e integración en el paisaje. Salamanca/Siega Verde, 15–17 de octubre de 2013*. Salamanca: Junta de Castilla y León.

Martínez, R., Guillem, P.M. and Ballester, L. (2012) Los abrigos de Tortosilla. Una nueva visión tras los trabajos de conservación preventiva. In *Actas de las Jornadas Abrigo de Tortosilla 100 aniversario de su descubrimiento. Primer hallazgo de Arte Rupestre de la Comunidad Valenciana. Ayora 14–16 de octubre de 2011*, pp.79–86.

Mas-Cornellà, M., Jorge, A., Gavilán, B., Solís, M., Parra, E. and Pérez, P. (2013) Minateda rock shelters (Albacete) and post-palaeolithic art of the Mediterranean Basin in Spain: Pigments, surfaces and patinas. *Journal of Archaeological Science*, 40–12, pp.4635–4647.

Matamoros, C. and López, J.A. (2009) Gestión del arte rupestre de la Comunitat Valenciana. In López, J.A., Martínez, R. and Matamoros, C. (Eds) *El arte rupestre del Arco Mediterráneo de la Península Ibérica*. València: Generalitat Valenciana, pp.169–178.

Mateo, M.A. (2013) Estrategia de conservación de los conjuntos de arte rupestre de la región de Murcia: Sostenibilidad e integración en el paisaje. In Pr*eactas de las Jornadas técnicas La Conservación del Arte Rupestre. Sostenibilidad e integración en el paisaje, d*el 15 al 17 de octubre de 2013, Salamanca, pp.12–14.

Mateo, M.A. (2017) Los pilares de la gestión del arte prehistórico como elemento activo del patrimonio cultural. *Rev. MAHPAT*, 1, Julio–Diciembre 2017, pp.13–36.

Mesado, N. (1989) Las pinturas rupestres de la 'Covatina del Tossalet del Mas de la Rambla, Vilafranca, Castellón. *Lucentum*, VII–VIII, pp.35–56.

Miró, Mª T. (2019) Gestió i conservació de l'art rupestre a Catalunya. In Viñas, R. (coord.) *I Jornades Internacionals d'art rupestre de l'Arc Mediterrani de la Península Ibèrica. Montblanc, 2019*. Tarragona: MCCB, MAC, Ajuntament de Montblanc, pp.375–394.

Pitarch, A., Ruiz, J.F., Fdez-Ortiz de Vallejuelo, S., Hernanz, A., Maguregui, M. and Madariaga, J.M. (2014) In situ characterization by Raman and x-ray fluorescence spectroscopy of post-Palaeolithic blackish pictographs exposed to the open air in Los Chaparros shelter (Albalate del Arzobispo, Teruel, Spain). *Analytical Methods*, 6, pp.6641–6650.

Rodríguez, I.R. and Domingo, I. (2018) Los problemas de conservación del arte rupestre levantino: un estado de la cuestión. Levantine rock art conservation problems: state of the art. In *Proceedings of the 3rd international conference on best practices in world heritage: Integral actions Menorca, Spain, 2–5 May 2018*, pp.255–287.

Royo, J., Andrés, J.A., Royo, J.I. and Alloza, R. (2013) Trabajos de estabilización de urgencia en el soporte rocoso y estudio de patologías en el abrigo de "La Cañada de Marco" en Alcaine, Parque Cultural del Río Martín (Teruel). *Cuadernos de arte rupestre*, 6, pp.147–59.

Royo-Guillén, J.I. (2001) Arte rupestre Aragonés. Documentación, protección y difusión. *Panel*, 1, pp.44–53.

Ruiz, J.F., Hernanz, A., Armitage, R.A., Rowe, M.W., Viñas, R., Gavira-Vallejo, J.M. and Rubio, A. (2012) Calcium oxalate AMS 14C dating and chronology of post-Palaeolithic rock paintings in the Iberian Peninsula. Two dates from Abrigo de los Oculados (Henarejos, Cuenca, Spain). *Journal of Archaeological Science*, 39, pp.2655–2667.

Ruiz, J.F., Mas, M., Hernanz, A., Rowe, M.W., Steelman, K.L. and Gavira, J.M. (2006) First radiocarbon dating of oxalate crusts over Spanish prehistoric rock art. *International Newsletter On Rock Art* INORA, 46, pp.1–5.

San Nicolás, M. (2014) Gestión del Arte Rupestre del Arco Mediterráneo de la Península Ibérica. *Cuadernos de Arte Rupestre*, 7, pp.151–211.

Villaverde, V., Martínez, R., Guillem, P., López, E. and Domingo, I. (2012) What do we mean by Levantine rock art? In García, J.L., Collado, H. and Nash, G. (Eds) *The Levantine question: Post-Palaeolithic rock art in the Iberian Peninsula*. Budapest: Archaeolingua, pp.81–115.

4 Monitoring and Maintenance of Open-Air Rock Art Sites

Collaborating with Community in Northern Australia

Melissa Marshall and Paul S. C. Taçon

Introduction

Caring for, protecting, celebrating and sharing rock art globally is a concern that numerous communities and countries face. The enduring legacy past peoples shared through creative genius and collective wisdom is something that has been passed on across the generations over millennia and this is no more relevant than in Australia, where the oldest living culture not only survives but thrives. With rock artists such as Donny Woolagoodja (Blundell and Woolagoodja 2005) still alive and practicing today, as well as stories shared from artists who have passed on more recently (Doring 2000; Mowaljarlai and Malnic 2001) and their descendants (May et al. 2019; 2020), knowledge and narratives associated with rock art across Australia remain within these ancient, enduring and dynamic cultures (Mangolamara et al. 2018; Taçon 2019).

Given the unquestionable value of rock art, the challenge to preserve it for future generations remains. Whilst there have been numerous attempts to address this scientifically in the past through provision of scientific perspectives to Indigenous communities (CORLAB 1986; Gillespie 1983; Pearson 1978) as well as partnerships between Indigenous communities, rock art researchers and conservators (Mowaljarlai, Vinnicombe et al 1988 ; Mowaljarlai and Watchman 1989), recent collaborations are giving primacy to Indigenous stewardship (Brady and Kearney 2016; Brady et al. 2016; Huntley and Freeman 2016a, 2016b; Marshall et al. 2020; Taçon 2019; Taçon and Baker 2019).

Through equitable endeavours which give primacy to Indigenous ownership, cultural protocols and practices for looking after rock art, three communities in northern Australia have been developing and implementing projects to monitor and maintain rock art within broader cultural landscapes which are the focus for this discussion. The first involves the Traditional Owners of the Naminidjbuk Estate (Wellington Range, Arnhem Land, Northern Territory) where the emphasis has been placed on a two-way sharing of knowledge for rock-art research, site protection and conservation. Most importantly, there is community ownership of the conservation management plans developed for the site complexes. A second example is

DOI: 10.4324/9780429355349-6

that from Kakadu National Park and research associated with the monitoring and evaluation of scientific interventions conducted within the Park over the past 40 years. Techniques included an array of conservation practices such as the application of silica-based substances, studies of salt, dust and biological growth deposition and their subsequent removal, as well as the removal of termite and mud wasp nests. The final example is one from the Kimberley (in Western Australia) where Traditional Owners and Working on Country Aboriginal ranger teams are coming together to explore how scientific interventions can work alongside traditional caring for Country techniques. Ultimately, the goal is to provide the best possible protection and preservation for the iconic paintings of the region, using science primarily in response to human impacts whilst culturally based techniques are used more readily for the management of environmental impacts.

Background

Rock art conservation and management strategies in Australia developed over the past decades following recognition that Indigenous cultural protocols and practice had been unarguably interrupted due to colonisation (Marshall et al. in press). Initially developed to address impacts generated by environmental factors at play within sites (Gillespie 1983; Pearson 1978; Pearson and Pretty 1976; Rosenfeld 1985), these responses were also often part of rescue efforts to support the ongoing preservation of those impacted directly by human factors such as mining, development and tourism (Marshall and Taçon 2014; Taçon and Marshall 2014; Chapter 2). While this is a relatively short time in comparison to elsewhere in the world, the focus of most strategies and interventions trialled was specific for open-air rock art sites, as this has relevance to most sites across the country. To inform the practice, a series of workshops was initiated (Pearson 1978; Pearson and Pretty 1976; Rosenfeld et al. 1984) and early studies involved understanding deteriorating factors collectively (Hughes 1979) as well as the composition of pigments themselves (Clarke 1976). Deteriorating factors such as weathering from environmental conditions (Hughes and Watchman 1978), the behaviour of water and its associated impacts (Gillespie 1979), accretions from salt (Watchman 1985a; 1987) and lichen (Florian 1978) in addition to the protection afforded by silica skins (Watchman 1985b; 1989) were also examined to inform and improve practice to protect rock art for generations to come.

Many of these techniques were scientifically advanced and new for the discipline at the time they were developed. Early efforts focused on understanding how interventions implemented elsewhere in the world may have value in an Australian context. Foremost in the conservation trials conducted in the 1970s and 1980s were the application of consolidants to intervene in the deterioration process (CORLAB 1986, 1987, 1988, 1989). Across a three-year window in Kakadu, a pilot was established whereby assessments were made of the condition of approximately 20 sites prior to introduction of 18 different treatments (silicone modified vinyl acrylics, polyvinyl butyral [PVBs] and polyurethane) at eight trial locations. Evaluated 13 months later, their application and overall successful longevity is yet to be fully reviewed, evaluated and thus understood (Marshall et al. in press). This will be of immense value to the discipline to ensure that, where Traditional Owners have been informed of the opportunities and limitations of these intervention strategies, decisions can be made relating to the continued use of these strategies, advancing conservation practice through understanding and evidencing these options for further treatments or alternatives aligning with cultural values and community aspirations.

The formative scientific work of early conservators in Australia reached its pinnacle by the mid-1990s when there was a notable reduction in both academic literature and resourcing of initiatives to protect and preserve rock art sites (Marshall 2020, p. 126). Whilst rock art conservation as a discrete discipline was reviewed in the ensuing period (MacLeod 2000; Morwood and Smith 1994; Watchman 2005), a resurgence has since been observed in the past decade (Agnew et al. 2015; Marshall and Taçon 2014; Taçon and Marshall 2014). Thus, in addition to understanding these scientific interventions, and possibly more importantly, is the shift occurring with the involvement of Indigenous communities in conservation efforts. Initially, Indigenous people were consulted and, at times, present on site during interventionist rock art conservation works; however, explanations of these scientific applications and potential impacts were not always understood. At the time, many of these trials were designed to *preserve* the paintings as though the sites were static and part of an open-air museum and those applied were not always reversible. Recent times, however, have seen a move from consulting Indigenous groups to one where communities and researchers are working together to develop strategies jointly. This is not simply a practice of involving Indigenous people in the decision-making process but extends to ensure communities have an ownership of the strategies used. Techniques are now being developed utilising non-invasive scientific practices (including planning and documentation) alongside Indigenous caring for country methods (with activities such as traditional fire management – see Russell-Smith 1985; Steffensen 2020), in a holistic landscape approach that is undertaken with an understanding that sites are part of a dynamic and *living* culture. Several key projects using this cooperative approach are currently underway in northern Australia and are the focus of this paper.

Community collaborations in Northern Australia

One of the greatest challenges facing Indigenous communities, researchers and academics in collaborating to care for rock art sites, is the resourcing required to develop, implement, establish and continually evaluate and improve conservation and management mechanisms. The collaborations presented here utilised a range of opportunities afforded through Australian Research

Council grants, state-based government grants and doctoral research programs, each ensuring that communities were not simply consulted but engaged in the process from the start and each of these initiatives continues today. The first and northern-most area involves the Traditional Owners of the Naminidjbuk Estate (Traditional Owners of part of the Wellington Range, in Arnhem Land, in the Northern Territory). Here the emphasis has been placed on a two-way sharing of knowledge for rock art research, site protection and conservation. This has included the development of conservation management plans at two of the larger site complexes as part of a cultural tourism strategy. Most importantly, in this instance, the collaborations were initiated and driven by the community ensuring ownership of these plans developed to look after the sites as visitors are welcomed for a cultural experience.

The second example is that from the World Heritage area of Kakadu National Park that has more than 5,000 recorded rock art sites and potentially three-times this number (Chaloupka 1993; May and Taçon 2014). Here, a research project is underway associated with the monitoring and evaluation of scientific interventions that were conducted within the Park over the past 40 years (Marshall 2020; Marshall et al. in press). These techniques included an array of conservation practices such as the application of silica-based substances as both artificial driplines and surface sprays (CORLAB 1986, 1987, 1988, 1989; Gillespie 1979), studies of unique salts (Thorn 1993a; Watchman 1985a), dust deposition (Watchman 1999) and biological growth (Thorn 1993b), along with their subsequent treatments. Additionally, the treatment and removal of termite and mud wasp nests were common practice for many years (Madycki 2006) and, with new understanding of their usefulness, also were reviewed.

The final example is one from the Kimberley (in Western Australia) where Indigenous Traditional Owners and Working on Country ranger teams are coming together to explore how scientific interventions can work alongside traditional caring for Country techniques. Two ranger teams have been involved, the Wunggurr Rangers who are part of the Wanjina Wunggurr Wilinggin Native Title group, and the Nyikina Mangala Yimardoowarra Rangers who are part of the Nyikina and Mangala Native Title group (Marshall 2020). Each of these collaborations informs improvements to conservation practice nationally.

Naminidjbuk Estate (Wellington Range)

The Naminidjbuk Estate is in the north-west of Arnhem Land and extends from the picturesque northern coast that includes evidence of the Macassan trade, inland to the sandstone massifs of the Wellington Range. As part of an extensive Australian Research Council grant, the Picturing Change project looked at the contact rock art in the area between 2008 and 2011 as part of a nationwide study. During this time thousands of individual paintings were recorded in detail mainly within three site complexes located in the range, these being Malarrak, Maliwawa (Bald Rock) and Djulirri (May et al. 2010, 2013a, 2013b; Taçon et al. 2010a, 2010b, 2011, 2012). The latter of these, Djulirri, has 55 panels alone with more than 3,100 rock art images, both from ancient times and the recent past (or contact period as it is known in Australia indicating initially a period post-European colonisation; this term is now used to define the period after the outside world or international community made contact with Aboriginal and Torres Strait Islander peoples). The main gallery itself has over 1,100 images in a shelter just 51 metres long (May et al. 2010; Taçon 2010a, 2010b).

The Malarrak and Maliwawa complexes are also rich, although with a smaller number of images. At the main shelter at Malarrak, a total of 240 images were recorded in 17 superimposed layers of painting, complete with a shell midden near the entrance to the site (May et al. 2010, 2013a). The wealth and breadth of cultural heritage located in these two latter precincts has long been understood by the Traditional Owners, who refer to the sites as their history books. However, they found that assistance was needed with visitor management and sustainable tourism opportunities and that is how the subsequent project developed.

In 2013, at the behest of the Traditional Owners, the Lamilami family, and especially the late senior Traditional Owner Ronald Lamilami who had a life-long passion about his cultural heritage and especially rock art (Taçon et al. 2021), we developed and commenced the History Places: Wellington Range Rock Art project.

Figure 4.1 Senior Traditional Owner Ronald Lamilami explaining the significance of paintings in the main Malarrak rock shelter. Photo by P. Taçon.

Across the Wellington Range and Arnhem Land more generally pigs, termites, emerging tourism, vandalism, mining exploration and future development are the biggest risks to its rock art. Consequently, the History Places research project was designed to, among other things, develop a conservation and management model for use not only in this part of Arnhem Land but also nationally. A key long-term research objective was also to better understand chronological change in Wellington Range rock art and to record the contemporary cultural significance of these history places (Taçon 2018b, 2021).

While the 2013 component was designed as the first stage of a larger endeavour, the primary objectives were to continue the surveying and recording that had taken place across the Wellington Range as part of the initial Picturing Change project, as well as to develop a rock art conservation and management plan for the Malarrak and Maliwawa site complexes in preparation for a cultural tourism initiative (Marshall 2013a, 2013b). Central to this was also the need to link these plans with the Naminidjbuk Development Plan (Lamilami 2008), a guiding document that was developed through a participatory process to map out the community's needs regarding heritage conservation and tourism development. With involvement of the community, a decision was made to look at eight sites in the Malarrak complex and three in the Maliwawa Complex (Taçon 2013).

For the Malarrak Complex the focus was on the requirements for visitor access to the sites, those sites most appropriate to visit, as well as issues relating to unauthorised access and feral animal management. Walking trails for tourists as part of a guided visit were mapped (Taçon 2013, pp. 16–18), while options for fencing out unwanted feral animal guests were also proposed. As the massif is more than one kilometre in circumference, erecting a fence around it in its entirety is unlikely. The shorter fence is still approximately 300 metres in length; however, the goal for both is to remove from the area feral pigs, horses and other introduced animals that are damaging many of the archaeological deposits and paintings in the shelters (Taçon 2013, pp. 21–24).

The three sites reviewed in the Maliwawa Complex had less impact from both unauthorised access and feral animals, requiring minimal site management or intervention. This location would also be difficult to find without a guide and a loop trail was designed to assist the visit. In addition to these activities, current conditions of the sites were also determined, and additional environmental factors identified for future monitoring programs (Taçon 2013). Namunidjbuk Traditional Owners stated, "the best way to look after rock art from their perspective is through fire management, feral animal culling, vegetation monitoring, and managing access" (Taçon 2018b, p. 37). Working alongside the local Indigenous ranger team, information from our research was provided as part of a visual report via a PowerPoint display illustrating both the impacts and proposed mitigation strategies, in addition to the larger written plan to assist with site monitoring into the future. Driven by the Traditional Owners, Aboriginal guides and ranger team, this ongoing monitoring of site condition, maintenance of vegetation and regular visitation to sites also assists with efforts for the long-term protection of the rock art here. The outcomes of this project are now being replicated elsewhere across the country.

Kakadu National Park (World Heritage Area)

The second example is from Kakadu National Park, also in the Northern Territory. Inscribed on the World Heritage List initially in 1981 for its natural and cultural values (with further additions in 1987, 1992 and 2011), the Park has a wealth of rock art within its boundaries (e.g., see Chaloupka 1993; May and Taçon 2014). Being one of the first acknowledged and managed areas of rock art in Australia, much of the early research into rock art conservation and management in the country was initially trialled at the sites in the Park. As mentioned above, techniques focused on the conservation and management of tangible heritage and included an array of conservation practices such as the application of silica-based substances, studies of salt, dust and biological growth deposition and their subsequent removal, as well as the removal of termite and mud wasp nests. These became standard practice across the country and the ongoing review of the longevity and applicability of these techniques was often overlooked and underestimated. Over the past decade (Marshall et al. 2015; May et al.

Figure 4.2 Early Kakadu conservation efforts in the 1970s–1990s. Photo courtesy of Kakadu National Park.

Figure 4.3 Early Kakadu conservation efforts in the 1970s–1990s. Photo courtesy of Kakadu National Park.

2016; O'Loughlin et al. 2014), the collaborative team have been looking at some of these intervention activities and the techniques that were utilised to preserve and protect the paintings. We are just now beginning to understand some of the long-term impacts that can arise from their application (Marshall 2020).

Early interventions and related rock art research were undertaken originally in the 1970s. At this time uranium mining was proposed in the area and the National Park was developed out of this as a means to protect much of the area (although not all of it). With the creation of the Park and subsequent World Heritage nomination, visitors flocked to the sites and much of the early visitation management for open-air rock art sites was implemented, primarily at three rock art complexes – Ubirr, Nourlangie and Nanguluwurr. Additionally, researchers were employed directly by the Park and many of the recorded sites were initially documented at this time (including Chaloupka 1974, 1975, 1978, 1984; Sullivan and Haskovec 1985, 1986, 1987). Studies were undertaken into environmental factors at play, such as the identification of the Obiri salt that is not found elsewhere (CORLAB 1986), as well as the composition of the pigments used. A dedicated rock art team developed out of this and was operational until the 1990s. In amongst this, invasive and non-reversible intervention trials were also considered and applied at several sites in the 1980s and 1990s, with conservators indicating at the time that the important thing to know will be how they fail more than how they succeed. However, this review and evaluation has not been completed and will be the focus of upcoming research (Marshall et al. in press).

Much of this is due to the fact that the 1990s saw a shift from the protection and preservation of tangible heritage, to one that looked after intangible heritage. The cultural programs in the Park then focused on recording stories, songs, language and oral histories as many Traditional Owners were concerned that many of the old people were passing away, taking important traditional knowledge with them unless recorded beforehand. This continues today; however we are now trying to reconnect the methodologies to look after both the intangible values and narratives, as well as the tangible fabric which had formerly been the focus of preservation efforts.

Thus, since 2008 the approach has been modified to one of integrated management to support the maintenance of both the tangible and intangible heritage. A cultural database was developed in 2009 to hold archival information on sites within the Park, along with the recorded oral histories, photographs and other multimedia; an initial rock art conservation workshop was also conducted (May et al. 2009). In 2010, the Park brought together representatives of the clans with rock art specialists to develop An-garregen, a cultural heritage strategy to guide the cultural programs unit in their activities (Kakadu National Park 2011a, 2011b). Priorities were identified and targets set, of which the development of a specific program and supporting manual were two of these.

In 2014, the 'Looking after *Bim* (Rock Art)' manual (Director of National Parks 2014) and subsequent field manual (Director of National Parks 2015) were developed to provide information on the conservation history within the Park, the identification of environmental threats and human impacts to cultural heritage sites, the implementation of the monitoring and maintenance program, as well as on the use of the cultural database. The Rock Art Monitoring and Maintenance program itself was introduced in parallel to this in 2014 and supported professional development for rangers within the Park and those working in neighbouring Indigenous ranger teams. This has continued through an implementation phase (years 2–5 of the program running from 2015–2018) and into an establishment phase (years 6–10 of the program commencing in 2019). With the recent COVID-19 pandemic, the capacity of the program was reduced, so 2020–2021 have been combined as Year 7 of the program, with the ultimate embedding of the collaborative culturally based monitoring and maintenance program in Park practice now anticipated to be finalised in 2024. With an initial 40 sites visited in the first year, more than 300 are now being actively monitored and maintained annually. Participants in the program have also increased exponentially with back to Country trips for Traditional Owners and site custodians integrated into the program, ensuring that knowledge transfer is integrated facilitating opportunities between the generations.

Figure 4.4 Monitoring rock art in Kakadu as part of the annual and doctoral research programs. Photo by K. May.

Building on and supporting this work, broader research projects have been utilised to improve understanding of the durability and longevity of intervention strategies applied over the previous 30–40 years. This includes the development of cultural conservation management plans for Burrungkuy and Ubirr, as well as the *Pathways: people, landscape and rock art* which has included conservation as a core theme (May et al. 2020). Analysis continues of the impacts identified at sites from perishing, and at times unnecessary, artificial silicon driplines (see Chapter 18). Impacts have included the misdirection of water over paintings that is caused from holes in the old silicon (or original misplacement), as well as the feeding of algae over the paintings they were trying to protect. Additional, chemical leeching is also evident at many sites. Ongoing monitoring and evaluation are being undertaken to review each dripline individually – a massive task with thousands of them installed in the Park and at times incomplete records to relocate them (for details on this initiative, see Chapter 18).

Additional analysis continues with portable X-Ray Fluorescence (pXRF) of the consolidants used in the CORLAB trials (Marshall et al. in press; May et al. 2020). While there are limitations with pXRF compared to in lab techniques such as Scanning Electron Microscope (SEM), Traditional

Owners would like non-invasive techniques to be used in the first instance. This is being done with the understanding that the known chemical content of the sandstone of the Arnhem Land Plateau contains natural silicas and this may interfere with the results when looking for traces of the artificial silica spray residue. The results are being analysed and consideration will be given to sampling for future SEM analyses as directed and prioritised by Traditional Owners and Indigenous communities where results prove inconclusive.

Wanjina Wunggurr Wilinggin and Nyikina Mangala peoples in the Kimberley region

The third example is from the Kimberley region of Western Australia, where Indigenous Traditional Owners and Working on Country ranger teams are coming together to explore how scientific interventions can work alongside traditional caring for country techniques. Ultimately, the goal is to provide the best possible protection and preservation for the iconic paintings of the region, which has resulted in using science primarily in response to human impacts, whilst cultural protocols, knowledge and tradition are used on the whole for the management of environmental impacts. As part of a doctoral research program (Marshall 2020), rangers and researchers worked together in a two-way learning program that involved the sharing of scientific knowledge relating to the documentation, conservation and management of sites while utilising traditional methods to care for Country. This included activities such as vegetation removal, fire management and most importantly, following cultural protocols at sites. As with Kakadu, this also involved getting families and community members back out on country together to share stories and knowledge between the generations. This intangible heritage is seen as equal to, if not more important than, looking after the fabric of the paintings and the sites. It likewise involves utilising mechanisms to support the management of the rock art contextualised by the broader cultural landscapes, informing holistic improvements to rock art and the broader cultural landscape.

Both the Nyikina Mangala and Wunggurr Ranger teams are funded through the Working on Country program that is run by the Federal Government. At the time of Marshall's doctoral candidature, both were connected to the Kimberley Ranger Initiative of the Kimberley Land Council along with an additional 20 groups looking after Traditional Lands in an area larger than 420,000 km^2 (which is almost the same size as Spain). Whilst both are now managed by their Registered Native Title Prescribed Body Corporates (RNTPBCs), respectively the Walalakoo Aboriginal Corporation and Wilinggin Aboriginal Corporations, the ranger programs are designed to support caring for Country methods – both environmental and cultural. With healthy country plans guiding their work (Walalakoo Aboriginal Corporation 2016; Wilinggin Aboriginal Corporation

2012), activities include weed eradication programs; fire and feral animal management; threatened species and biodiversity studies; water resource management; and of course, the maintenance and management of cultural heritage places.

In particular, the latter task again supports the recording of both the physical attributes of sites (being the tangible heritage), as well as the stories and songs belonging there (thus the intangible values). Acknowledged as central to all of this is the opportunity to support other Traditional Owners to get out on country and visit remote places – often travelling for days through rugged terrain. The opportunity to welcome people to Country the right way, with knowledge sharing, cultural protocols and practices such as 'smoking' people with special wood leaves (to cleanse the spirits of visitors and the site alike), is intrinsic to this

Over the past 12 years, the Wunggurr Rangers have been working with researchers to look at a variety of issues associated with looking after rock art sites on their country. In 2009, at the invitation of the Dann family and the Windjingayr Community, a project began to assist with training the rangers in methods of documentation, monitoring, maintenance and management of the rock art sites on their country in the Napier Range. In addition to spectacular Wanjina paintings, this area contains a Devonian Reef, with in-situ fossils. The sites were recorded in detail and rangers participated in a variety of activities that included the development of site plans, recording characteristics and descriptions as well as capturing photographs of the paintings; in addition to condition assessments (Marshall 2020). Integrated within this project was capacity building for the Traditional Owners and rangers which resulted in the production of a conservation management plan for one of the sites (Dann and Dann 2017). What was most important for this group, however, was the transfer of knowledge through the sharing of stories, songs and culture between the generations, as well as assisting to get the old people back out on Country (cognisant that many Aboriginal people are centrally located in towns across the Kimberley region, it is often difficult for many to return to remote areas where they hold cultural authority and traditional connections).

The Nyikina Mangala Yimardoowarra Rangers were also involved in doctoral research (Marshall 2020) and two of the rock art sites on their country were recorded in detail in a similar way to that described above. One of these is on Aboriginal community land and can only be accessed this way. This has assisted in protecting the site from unauthorised access. Nevertheless, other human based impacts such as the spread of weeds (causing hotter fires) and issues with introduced feral animals have arisen. As part of their broader work plan, the rangers are looking at site protection methods and weed eradication programs. The second site is one that is on a pastoral lease and a fence was erected to protect the rock art as part of a statewide program many years ago. Unauthorised access by recreational users of the nearby river is an issue and interpretative signs have been developed to provide these visitors with information about the site, the Aboriginal people of the area and the protocols that should be followed when entering a special place. Contact details have been added to encourage visitors to obtain authorisation to access the site in the future.

Conclusion

The three initiatives discussed above highlight some of the current practices in Australia relating to the conservation and management of rock art sites – not simply the involvement of the respective Aboriginal Traditional Owners and custodians but ownership of the programs that are utilised to look after these places in a holistic way. Importantly, each exemplifies the integration of protection and preservation of intangible and tangible heritage. Whilst, from one viewpoint, each of these projects and programs may appear very different, comparisons and similarities were illustrated to showcase a universal method for the ongoing protection and preservation of open-air sites across Australia. While the initial management of rock art was informed only by cultural knowledges, and then shifted to one dominated by scientific interventions in consultation with Indigenous communities, today we increasingly see a positive transformation of the discipline to one that sees conservation methods driven by Indigenous stewardship informed by opportunities afforded through conservation mechanisms.

As we move further into the 21st century, management regimes in Australia are now often undertaken from a perspective of community-driven long-term monitoring and regular maintenance rather than invasive intervention that was the status quo four decades ago. Issues with resourcing and prioritising the evaluation of the earlier treatment programs are part of this. The need to ensure Indigenous people remain at the centre rather than on the periphery is likewise recognised as critical to the endurance of management programs. The review and evaluation of these early regimes now form the basis of developing research, looking at impacts arising from the overuse of artificial silicon driplines and maintenance concerns. The analysis of these mitigation strategies will contribute further understanding to the conservation and management of open-air rock art sites across the nation and further the conservation discipline as a whole. The continued drive and determination of Aboriginal people across Australia to care for their Country in their own way, using science to support these efforts where necessary, will be the key to future success in the longevity of this national treasure.

Acknowledgements

We would like to acknowledge all of the groups and organisations with whom we have worked on these projects and programs. Particularly we thank all of the Traditional Owners, Aboriginal communities and families who were involved in the research and have been mentioned previously, as well as Kakadu National Park for their support and openness about the journey they are on. We also thank the colleagues who have assisted us, particularly Dr. Sally K. May (Griffith University), Prof. Jo McDonald (UWA) and Prof. Laurajane Smith (ANU) for their doctoral supervision, as well as Nicholas Hall and Sharon Sullivan for their long-term support of rock art conservation and management programs in Australia.

The research for this paper relating to Kakadu and the Kimberley region was undertaken in the early stages as part of Marshall's doctoral candidature through the Australian National University (ANU) and funded through an Australian Postgraduate Award. Research conducted on the Naminidjbuk Estate was funded by a 2012 Northern Territory Government Heritage grant (38), a donation by John Kearney and Griffith University, and then in 2016 with an Australian Research Council grant for the *History Places: Wellington Range Rock Art Project* (DP160101832). The 2016 pXRF investigation was funded through the University of Notre Dame Australia's (UNDA) Research Incentive Scheme (RI17013); with the 2019 pXRF investigation as part of the *Pathways: people, landscape and rock art* project based at the Place, Evolution and Rock Art Heritage Unit, Griffith Centre for Social and Cultural Research at Griffith University, funded by the Australian Research Council grant *Australian rock art: history, conservation and Indigenous well-being*, as part of Paul S. C. Taçon's ARC Laureate Project (FL160100123).

References

Agnew, N., Deacon, J., Hall, N., Little, T., Sullivan, S. and Taçon, P. S. C. (2015) *Rock art: A cultural treasure at risk*. Los Angeles: The Getty Conservation Institute.

Blundell, V. and Woolagoodja, D. (2005) *Keeping the Wanjinas Fresh: Sam Woolagoodja and the enduring power of Lalai*. Fremantle: Fremantle Arts Centre Press.

Brady, L. M., Bradley, J. J. and Kearney, A. J. (2016) Negotiating Yanyuwa rock art relational and affectual experiences in the Southwest Gulf of Carpentaria, Northern Australia. *Current Anthropology,* 57(1), pp.28–52.

Brady, L. M. and Kearney, A. J. (2016) Sitting in the gap: Ethnoarchaeology, rock art and methodological openness. *World Archaeology,* 48(5), pp.642–655.

Chaloupka, G. (1974) *Report on site survey activities 1973–1974*. Unpublished report to Museums and Art Galleries of the Northern Territory, Darwin.

Chaloupka, G. (1975) *Report on site survey activities 1974–1975*. Unpublished report to Museums and Art Galleries of the Northern Territory, Darwin.

Chaloupka, G. (1978) *Djawumbu-Madjawarnja site complex*. Unpublished report for the Australian Heritage Commission, Canberra.

Chaloupka, G. (1984) *Rock Art of the Arnhem land plateau: Paintings of the dynamic figure style*. Darwin: Northern Territory Museum of Arts and Sciences.

Chaloupka, G. (1993) *Journey in time. The world's longest continuing art tradition*. Chatswood: Reed Books.

Clarke, J. (1976) Two Aboriginal rock pigments from Western Australia, their properties, use and durability. *Studies in Conservation*, 21, pp.134–142.

CORLAB (1986) *Conservation of post-estuarine period rock art in Kakadu National Park: Report on phase 1 study: Pigment identification.* Wilson: Australian Nature Conservation Agency.

CORLAB (1987) *Conservation of post-estuarine period rock art in Kakadu National Park: Final report on phase 2 study: Conservation treatment trials.* Wilson: Australian Nature Conservation Agency.

CORLAB (1988) *Conservation of post-estuarine period rock art in Kakadu National Park: Final report on phase 3 study: Conservation treatment trials.* Wilson: Australian Nature Conservation Agency.

CORLAB (1989) *Conservation of post-estuarine rock art in Kakadu National Park: Nourlangie gallery rock art restoration project.* Canberra: The International Centre for the Preservation and Restoration of Cultural Property and CORLAB Pty Ltd.

Dann, R. and Dann, K. (2017) *Barker river cultural heritage management plan.* Derby: Wunggurr Rangers.

Director of National Parks (2014) Looking After Bim: The Kakadu National Park Rock Art Monitoring and Maintenance Draft Manual. Prepared by M. Marshall for Kakadu National Park, Jabiru.

Director of National Parks (2015) Looking After Bim: Rock Art Field Manual. Prepared by M. Marshall for Kakadu National Park, Jabiru.

Doring, J. (2000) *Gwion Gwion Dulwan Mamaa: Secret and sacred pathways of the Ngarinyin Aboriginal People of Australia.* Köln: Könemann Verlagsgesellschaft mbH.

Florian, M. L. E. (1978) A review: The lichen role in rock art - Dating, deterioration and control. In Pearson, C. (Ed.) *Conservation of rock art: Proceedings of the international workshop on the conservation of rock art, Perth, September 1977.* Perth: The Institute for the Conservation of Cultural Material, pp.95–98.

Gillespie, D. (1979) *The rock art and archaeological sites of Ubirr, Kakadu National Park N.T: The beginning of a management strategy.* Unpublished report to Australian National Parks and Wildlife Service, Canberra.

Gillespie, D. (Ed.) (1983) *The rock art sites of Kakadu National Park - some preliminary research findings for their conservation and management.* Special Publication 10. Canberra: Australian National Parks and Wildlife Service.

Hughes, P. J. (1978) Weathering in sandstone shelters in the Sydney Basin and the survival of rock art. In Pearson, C. (Ed.) *Conservation of rock art: Proceedings of the international workshop on the conservation of rock art, Perth, September 1977.* Perth: The Institute for the Conservation of Cultural Material, pp.36–41.

Hughes, P. J. (1979) *The deterioration, conservation and management of rock art sites in the Kakadu National Park, NT.* Canberra: Australian National University.

Huntley, J. and C. Freeman Galamban (2016a). The material scientific investigation of rock art: contributions from non-invasive x-ray techniques. In R. Bednarik, D. Fiore, M. Basile, G. Kumar and T. Huisheng (Eds) *Palaeoart and materiality: The scientific study of rock art.* Oxford, Archaeopress Archaeology.

Huntley, J. and C. Freeman Galamban (2016b). "Wreck Bay Ochres: Rock art landscapes, continuing art practices and the western/scientific description of a traditional knowledge." Conference presentation at Interwoven: Indigenous and Western Knowledge in Archaeology and Heritage, AAA 2016. Terrigal, Australian Archaeological Association.

Kakadu National Park (2011a) *An-garregen: Land - language - culture. A strategy for cultural heritage management in Kakadu National Park. Volume 1: The strategy.* Canberra: Director of National Parks, Commonwealth Government.

Kakadu National Park (2011b) *An-garregen: Land - language - culture. A strategy for cultural heritage management in Kakadu National Park. Volume 2: The appendices.* Canberra: Director of National Parks, Commonwealth Government.

Lamilami, R. (2008) *Namunidjbuk development plan: A plan for heritage conservation and tourism development on Namunidjbuk Estate, West Arnhem Land.* Waminari Bay: Namunidjbuk Estate.

MacLeod, I. (2000) Rock art conservation and management: The past, present and future options. *Studies in Conservation,* 45(Suppl. 3), pp.32–45.

Madycki, Z. (2006) *Termite treatment at rock art sites.* Jabiru: Kakadu National Park.

Mangolamara, S., Karadada, L., Oobagooma, J., Woolagoodja, D., Karadada, J. and Doohan, K. (2018) *Nyara pari kala niragu (Gaambera), gadawara ngyarangada (Wunambal), inganinja gubadjoongana (Woddordda) = we are coming to see you.* Derby: Dambimangari Aboriginal Corporation and Wunambal Gaambera Aboriginal Corporation.

Marshall, M. (2013a) *Malarrak rock art site complex: Conservation management plan for the rock art sites at Malarrak, Wellington Range, Northern Territory.* Report to Griffith University and the people of the Naminidjbuk Estate, Derby.

Marshall, M. (2013b) *Maliwawa rock art site complex: Conservation management plan for the rock art sites at Malarrak, Wellington Range, Northern Territory.* Report to Griffith University and the people of the Naminidjbuk Estate, Derby.

Marshall, M. (2020) *Rock art conservation and management: 21st century perspectives in Northern Australia.* PhD thesis, Canberra: Australian National University. doi:10.25911/5f969812a2f22.

Marshall, M., Lee, J., O'Loughlin, G., May, K. and Huntley, J. (In Press) Preserving the rock art of Kakadu: Formative conservation trials during the 1980s. In Taçon, P. S. C., May, S. K., Frederick, U. and McDonald, J. (Eds.) *Histories of Australian rock art research.* Terra Australis#. Canberra, Australian National University.

Marshall, M., May, K., Dann, R. and Nulgit, L. (2020) Indigenous stewardship of decolonised rock art conservation processes in Australia. *Studies in Conservation,* 65, pp. 205–212. DOI:10.1080/00393630.2020.1778264

Marshall, M., O'Loughlin, G., May, K. and Whitehurst, K. (2015) *Kakadu's rock art monitoring and maintenance program: Merging science with society.* Unpublished paper presented at the Australian Archaeology Association (AAA) conference, 2–4 December 2015, Fremantle.

Marshall, M. and P. S. C. Taçon (2014). Past & present, traditional & scientific: the conservation and management of rock art sites in Australia. In T. Darvill and A. P. Batarda Fernandes (Eds) *Open-air rock-art conservation and management: state of the art and future perspectives.* London, Routledge, pp.214–228.

May, S. K., Huntley, J., Marshall, M., Miller, E., Hayward, J. A., Jalandoni, A., Goldhahn, J., Johnston, I. G., Lee, J., O'Loughlin, G., May, K., Domingo Sanz, I. and Taçon, P. S. C. (2020) New insights into the rock art of Anbangbang Gallery, Kakadu National Park. *Journal of Field Archaeology,* 45(2), pp.120–134. DOI: 10.1080/00934690.2019.1698883

May, S. K., Maralngurra, J. G., Johnston, I. G., Goldhahn, J., Lee, J., O'Loughlin, G., May, K., Nabobbob, C. N., Garde, M. and Taçon, P. S. C. (2019) 'This is my

Father's Painting': A first-hand account of the creation of the most iconic rock art in Kakadu National Park. *Rock Art Research,* 36(2), pp.199–213.

May, K., O'Loughlin, G., Marshall, M. and Lee, J. (2016) *Looking after bim: Two ways.* Unpublished paper presented at the Australian Archaeology Association (AAA) conference, 6–8 December 2016, Terrigal.

May, S. K. and Taçon, P. S. C. (2014) Kakadu national park: Rock art. In Smith, C. (Ed.) *Encyclopedia of global archaeology.* New York: Springer, pp.4235–4240.

May, S. K., Taçon, P. S. C. and Johnson, M. (2009) *An introduction to rock art conservation and management: Report on the June 15–17 training course for Kakadu National Park by the Institute for Professional Practice in Heritage and the Arts.* Unpublished report to the Director of National Parks. Canberra: Australian National University.

May, S. K., Taçon, P. S. C., Paterson, A. and Travers, M. (2013a) The world from Malarrak: Depictions of Southeast Asian and European subjects in rock art from the Wellington Range, Australia. *Australian Aboriginal Studies,* 2013(1), pp.45–56.

May, S. K., Taçon, P. S. C., Wesley, D. and Pearson, M. (2013b) Painted ships on a painted Arnhem Land landscape. *The Great Circle,* 35(2), pp.81–100.

May, S. K., Taçon, P. S. C., Wesley, D. and Travers, M. (2010) Painting history: Indigenous observations and depictions of the 'other' in northwestern Arnhem Land, Australia. *Australian Archaeology,* 71, pp.57–65.

Morwood, M. J. and Smith, C. E. (1994) Rock art research in Australia 1974–94. *Australian Archaeology,* 39, pp.19–38.

Mowaljarlai, D. and Malnic, J. (2001) *Yorro Yorro: Everything standing up alive. Rock art and stories from the Australian Kimberley.* Broome: Magabala Books.

Mowaljarlai, D., Vinnicombe, P., Ward, G. K. and Chippendale, C. (1988) Repainting of images on rock in Australia and the maintenance of Aboriginal culture. *Antiquity,* 62, pp.690–696.

Mowaljarlai, D. and Watchman, A. (1989) An Aboriginal view of rock art management. *Rock Art Research,* 6(2), pp.151–153.

O'Loughlin, G., Marshall, M. and Lee, J. (2014) *Kakadu National Park: Rock art monitoring and management.* Unpublished paper presented at the Getty Foundation: Rock Art Conservation, Management and Tourism, Southern Africa – Australia Exchange Program, 16 August 2014, Kakadu National Park, Northern Territory, Australia.

Pearson, C. (Ed.) (1978) *Conservation of rock art: Proceedings of the International Workshop on the Conservation of Rock Art, Perth, September 1977.* Perth: Institute for the Conservation of Cultural Material.

Pearson, C. and Pretty, G. L. (eds) 1976. *Proceedings of the national seminar on the conservation of cultural material, Perth 1973.* The Institute for the Conservation of Cultural Material, Perth.

Rosenfeld, A. (1985) *Rock art conservation in Australia.* Canberra: Australian Government Publishing Service.

Rosenfeld, A., Golson, J., Ambrose, W. R. and Hughes, P. J. (1984) Report of a meeting on rock art conservation. *Rock Art Research,* 1(1), pp.54–59.

Russell-Smith, J. (1985) Studies in the jungle: People, fire and monsoon forest. In R. Jones (Ed) *Archaeological Research in Kakadu National Park.* Canberra: Australian National Parks and Wildlife Service. Special Publication 13: 241–268.

Steffensen, V. (2020) *Fire country: How indigenous fire management could help save Australia.* Richmond: Hardie Grant Explore.

Sullivan, H. and Haskovec, I. P. (1985) *Annual report for the archaeological section of the Kakadu National Park Scientific Services.* Unpublished report to the Australian National Parks and Wildlife Service, Canberra.

Sullivan, H. and Haskovec, I. P. (1986) *Annual report for the cultural resource management section of the Kakadu National Park Scientific Services.* Unpublished report to the Australian National Parks and Wildlife Service, Canberra.

Sullivan, H. and Haskovec, I. P. (1987) *Annual report for the archaeological section of the Kakadu National Park Scientific Services.* Unpublished report to the Australian National Parks and Wildlife Service, Canberra.

Taçon, P. S. C. (2013) *History places: Wellington Range rock art: A report on Stage 1, 2013 (19 November 2013).* Gold Coast: PERAHU, Griffith University.

Taçon, P. S. C. (2018a) From rock art to contemporary art: Indigenous depictions of trains, planes and automobiles. *Australian Archaeology,* 84(3), pp. 281–293, doi: 10.1080/03122417.2018.1543095

Taçon, P. S. C. (2018b) Overview of Pillar IV: Community involvement and benefits. In Agnew, N., Deacon, J., Hall, N., McClintock, T., Sullivan, S. and Taçon, P. S. C. (Eds.) *Art on the rocks – engaging the public and professionals to network for rock art conservation. Abstracts from the Colloquium Namibia, 22–30 April 2017.* Los Angeles: The Getty Conservation Institute, pp.35–40.

Taçon, P. S. C. (2019) Connecting to the ancestors: Why rock art is important for Indigenous Australians and their well-being. *Rock Art Research,* 36(1), pp.5–14.

Taçon, P. S. C. (2021) 21st century innovation in conserving the rock art of northern Australia and Southeast Asia. In Gjerde, J. M. and Arntzen, M. S. (Eds.) *Perspectives on differences in rock art.* Sheffield: Equinox Publishing, pp.360–375.

Taçon, P. S. C. and Baker, S. (2019) New and emerging challenges to heritage and well-being: A critical review. *Heritage,* 2(2), pp.1300–1315. doi:10.3390/heritage2020084

Taçon, P. S. C., Brennan, W. and Lamilami, R. (2011) Rare and curious thylacine depictions from Wollemi National Park, New South Wales and Arnhem Land, Northern Territory, Australia. In Specht, J. and Torrence, R. (Eds.) *Changing perspectives in Australian archaeology. Technical reports of the Australian Museum, Online,* 23(11), pp.165–174 doi:10.3853/j.1835–4211.23.2011.1576

Taçon, P. S. C., Langley, M., May, S. K., Lamilami, R., Brennan, W. and Guse, D. (2010a) Ancient bird stencils in Arnhem Land, Northern Territory, Australia. *Antiquity,* 84(324), pp.416–427.

Taçon, P. S. C. and M. Marshall (2014). Conservation or crisis? The future of rock art management in Australia. In Y. Zhang (Ed) *A monograph of rock art research and protection.* Beijing, Zhong Guo Zang Xue Chu Ban She/ China Tibetology Publishing House, pp.119–133.

Taçon, P. S. C., May, S. K., Fallon, S. J., Travers, M., Wesley, D. and Lamilami, R. (2010b) A minimum age for early depictions of Southeast Asian praus in the rock art of Arnhem Land, Northern Territory. *Australian Archaeology,* 71, pp.1–10.

Taçon, P. S. C., Paterson, A., Ross, J. and May, S. K. (2012) Picturing change and changing pictures: Contact period rock art of Australia. In McDonald, J. and Veth, P. (Eds.) *A companion to rock art.* Chichester: Blackwell Publishing Ltd, pp.420–436.

Taçon, P. S. C., Wesley, D. and May, S. K. (2021) R. Lamilami, 1957–2021: Negotiating two worlds for cultural heritage. *Australian Archaeology,* 87(2), pp.220–225.

Thorn, A. (1993a) *The control of salts damaging to rock art.* Unpublished report for The Australian Institute of Aboriginal and Torres Strait Islander Studies, Hawthorn.

Thorn, A. (1993b) *Condition survey of four rock art sites in Kakadu National Park.* Unpublished report to the Director of National Parks, Hawthorn.

Walalakoo Aboriginal Corporation RNTBC (2016) *Walalakoo healthy country plan 2017–2027.* Derby: Walalakoo Aboriginal Corporation RNTBC.

Watchman, A. (1985a) *Geological investigations into the formation of salts at Aboriginal rock art sites in Kakadu National Park, Northern Territory.* Canberra: ANUTECH Pty Ltd.

Watchman, A. (1985b) Mineralogical analysis of silica skins covering rock art. In Jones, R. (Ed.) *Archaeological research in Kakadu National Park.* Special Publication 13. Canberra: Australian National Parks and Wildlife Service, pp. 281–290.

Watchman, A. (1987) Preliminary determinations of the age and composition on mineral salts on rock art surfaces in the Kakadu National Park. In Ambrose, W. R. and Mummery, J. M. J. (Eds.) *Archaeometry: Further Australasian Studies.* Canberra: Department of Prehistory. Research School of Pacific Studies, The Australian National University, pp.36–42.

Watchman, A. (1989) *Silica skins: Their composition, formation and role in conserving Aboriginal rock art.* Canberra: Australian Institute of Aboriginal Studies.

Watchman, A. (1999) Dust and the development of standards and monitoring methods to determine potential impacts from uranium mining at Jabiluka on the rock art of the surrounding area. Unpublished report to the Australian Heritage Commission, Canberra.

Watchman, A. (2005) Conservation of Australian Rock Art. *Coalition,* 10, pp.14–18.

Wilinggin Aboriginal Corporation (2012) *Wilinggin healthy country plan — looking after Ngarinyin Country 2012–2022.* Derby: Wilinggin Aboriginal Corporation.

Section II

Methodological Tools to Support Assessment and Monitoring of Open-Air Rock Art Sites

5 The Rock Art Stability Index

A Non-Invasive Rapid Field Assessment for Condition Evaluation

Casey D. Allen, Cayla D. Kennedy, Kaelin M. Groom, Niccole V. Cerveny, Ronald I. Dorn and David S. Whitley

Introduction

That rock art represents an interdisciplinary endeavour would most likely not be disputed. This is reflected in the number of different techniques used to evaluate these priceless heritage resources, which number perhaps close to 100, including this volume, its predecessor, and other multiple other studies (cf., Barnett et al. 2005; Darvill and Fernandes 2014; see also Fitzner, Heinrichs and La Bouchardiere 2002, 2004; Giesen et al. 2013; Hoerlé et al. 2016; Pineda et al. 1997; Pope 2000; Tratebas, Cerveny and Dorn 2004; Wasklewicz et al. 2005). Still, none of these truly offer a rapid, low-cost, easily accessible, non-invasive, field-based assessment of a host panel's inherent geologic characteristics. Even the recent Condition Assessment and Risk Evaluation (CARE) project (see https://rockartcare.ncl.ac.uk), though useful for documenting a panel's general *surrounding* conditions, has a lone, single opportunity to rate "erosion" (and in a yes/no fashion *only*), though stone deterioration mechanisms remain much more in-depth than "erosion" alone.

Gaining insight into a rock art panel's geologic and geomorphologic stability, therefore, represents a first step in managing this priceless component of cultural heritage for future generations. In fact, while perhaps not as flashy as other geo-heritage offerings, rock art nonetheless plays a role in tourism – in some places more than others. Most every country in the world hosts some type of rock art, and often even highly significant (and sacred) sites remain open to the casual tourist. A limited number of these rock art sites are well-funded enough to receive intense supervision and careful curation. Most, however, are left to the elements with perhaps a lone caretaker to watch them deteriorate. Being able to quickly and accurately assess a rock art host panel's geologic stability then remains an important aspect for many of these sites since rock art also represents an important tourism component.

DOI: 10.4324/9780429355349-8

More than a decade ago, Cerveny (2005) conceived an alternative technique to assess a rock art panel's geologic stability – giving researchers a way to quickly and effectively evaluate areas at-risk. This new technique focused on combatting the often costly and time-consuming assessments that centred more around built stone (e.g., architecture) and paid little attention to rock art specifically, let alone rock decay science (i.e., "weathering"[1]). The result of Cerveny's work, the Rock Art Stability Index (RASI, see Dorn et al. 2008), has since been used throughout the world to assess the geologic stability of thousands of rock art panels (cf., Allen and Groom 2013a, 2013b; Gharib 2020; Groom et al. 2019; Wright 2018). Even more importantly, RASI demonstrated not just replicability among trainees (Cerveny 2005; Dorn et al. 2008), but later showed that those trainees gained even deeper understanding of rock decay forms and processes, connecting their analyses to the larger landscape while gaining a greater sense of appreciation for rock art itself (Allen 2008, 2011; Allen and Lukinbeal 2011; Groom, Bevan and Allen 2018; 2020; in press). The technique has also been further validated using scanning electron microscopy (SEM), where observed decay forms correlated with SEM analyses (Cerveny et al. 2016), adding even more support to RASI's veracity. Additionally, since 2014, an adapted version of RASI has been developed, termed the Cultural Stone Stability Index (CSSI), and has been in use to assess historic buildings and monuments with similar success (Allen et al. 2018; Groom 2017; Hayes and Hayes 2019).

Though often conducted with pen-and-paper, RASI can still be completed quickly, and even on-the-fly *in situ* (Allen et al. 2011). With the addition of an electronic version of RASI currently using ESRI products, but with a specifically developed smart phone app currently being created by Stone Heritage Research Alliance (SHRA), field collection and data storage/analysis has been further enhanced. An example of this RASI e-version is highlighted in Chapter 3 of this volume. What this enhancement means, is that tying RASI into a Geographic Information System (GIS) can now be done without manually entering tabular data, allowing for correlation between rock art site/panel and specific decay forms/processes, as well as providing locational attributes more efficiently (e.g., Allen et al. 2011; Dorn et al. 2008). With more detailed analysis by a trained RASI analyst, specific problem areas (and their causes) on a host panel can also be pinpointed. Though not for specifically protecting rock art, with a short training period (e.g., weekend workshop) including an *in situ* component, RASI can be used by any rock art aficionado, irrespective of their previous background knowledge in rock decay science, archaeology, geology, or any other discipline. Even further, RASI's cost-effectiveness allows site managers to determine where best to spend their precious funds, and which panels may need more intensive and specialized treatment such as those noted by Viles et al. (1997) and Fitzner (2002). Based on sound principles of rock decay science – and much evaluation of validity and replicability (see Dorn et al. 2008 for full details) – RASI meets this perceived need, serving as a powerful technique in terms of open-air rock art management strategies, providing "triage" services for a site manager, and allowing for a quick snapshot of potentially endangered panels and sites.

To demonstrate the power of RASI as an open-air rock art management and conservation technique, consideration is now given to a broad overview of RASI, outlining its specific parameters and rating system. After highlighting RASI's successful uses around the world, a recent case study is offered as an example of how RASI might be used in a "wild" (i.e., unmanaged) open air setting. The case study focuses on two heritage sites on the Caribbean tri-island nation of Grenada where no regulation or official management strategy occurs. What monitoring is done in Grenada, aside from annual RASI assessments, remains haphazard at best, and there is not yet an official management plan. Drawing on the case study and its usage in different world locales, the final discussion in this chapter focuses on RASI's overall usefulness and applicability as an open-air rock art management technique, including potential implications its use may have for the rock art research, conservation, and sustainability communities.

Nuts and bolts of RASI

To classify the more than three-dozen distinct rock decay forms, RASI utilizes six overarching categories: site setting, impending/future loss, incremental erosional loss, large erosion events, rock coatings, highlighting vandalism and other issues. The first category, "Site Setting", evaluates a panel's basic geologic parameters (e.g., rock weakness and fissures/cracks). "Impending Loss," RASI's second category, assesses possible future forms (and potentially locations as well) of decay (e.g., scaling and undercutting). The third overarching category, "Large Break-off Events," focus specifically on meso-scale decay events that have already occurred (e.g., anthropogenic activities and fire). "Incremental Loss," RASI's fourth category, includes relatively small-in-size decay forms, such as lithobiont pitting (i.e., algae, lichen, and mosses) and granular disintegration. More than one-dozen rock decay forms are included in this fourth category, since rock decay forms at the micro scale (centimetre or millimetre) tend to be most abundant across all rock types. The fifth category, "Rock Coatings," represents an important concept often overlooked in other rock art assessment indices. In natural stone (as opposed to worked stone in architecture and building instances), rock coatings often serve to strengthen the overall rock, and RASI reflects this understanding by adding a negative value (i.e., 0, -1, -2, -3) to each of the respective forms, lowering the total score. A final, sixth category, "Vandalism and Other Issues," is also included in RASI. While its qualitative nature does not figure into the overall RASI score, it allows the researcher to highlight any other observations they may deem as affecting the host panel (e.g., graffiti and land use issues).

That RASI evaluates a wide range of forms (driven by their respective processes) means it can give the site manager and conservator a good handle on not just the intensity of a decay form, but potentially the specific cause of that decay. To recognize decay features and subsequently understand the processes behind their creation, however, requires training. The SHRA maintains an active website that offers a brief overview of RASI and its importance, as well as publications from SHRA members and collaborators[2]. In all cases, as with other specialized assessments across disciplines, parties interested in using RASI should always be trained appropriately by those with both experience conducting RASI assessments as well as expert knowledge related to rock decay processes and their subsequent forms. The SHRA represents the only entity to provide RASI certification at three levels: Basic, Analyst, and Trainer. Part of the SHRA's official RASI training is carried out *in situ*, whether in small groups or individually, as studies demonstrate hands-on practice with RASI in groups of fewer than 10 people results in the deepest understanding (Allen 2008, 2011; Allen and Lukinbeal 2011; Cerveny 2005; Dorn et al. 2008).

After completing specialized training then, potential RASI researchers gain practical experience in recognizing specific rock decay forms on a host panel associated with the first five categories, and rate each on a 0–3 severity-of-occurrence scale:

- Ranking of 0 ("Not Present"), where the rock decay form is not found on the host panel.
- Ranking of 1 ("Present"), where the rock decay form *is* found on the panel, but not specifically touching the rock art/glyphs/motifs.
- Ranking of 2 ("Obvious"), where the rock decay form is inflicting damage to the rock art/glyphs/motifs.
- Ranking of 3 ("Dominant"), where the rock decay forms are directly and dominantly impacting the rock art/glyph/motif.

After assessing the degree of each rock decay element individually, the rankings are tallied to create a "raw score", and then doubled for a panel's "final score". A RASI score ranges from 0 to 100 (a score of more than 100 is possible, but a panel would likely be unrecognizable as such with a score approaching 100), and when it comes to a panel's score, the lower an overall score, the more geologically stable a panel is. To enhance RASI's administrative function, overall score range classifications remain descriptive:

- 20: Excellent Condition.
- 20–29: Good Status.
- 30–39: Problem(s) that Could Cause Erosion.
- 40–49: Urgent Possibilities of Erosion.
- 50–59: Great Dangers of Erosion.
- 60: Severe Dangers of Erosion

As volunteers remain a staple for rock art awareness and assessment, one of RASI's main functions was to increase accessibility for non-specialists, irrespective of previous background. As illustrated above, the index therefore contains limited technical jargon, and where such verbiage must be used (e.g., "fissuresol"), even more time is spent explaining the form (and its precursory/resultant processes) during the training process. With a weekend workshop – one-three days spent in a classroom setting learning about rock decay forms and another day or two in the field practicing with a RASI professional – a person with no previous experience in archaeology, geology, geography, or rock decay science can be ready to fully utilize RASI. While these trainees may not necessarily have in-depth understanding of the process(es) behind each rock decay form's creation or petrologic significance, they learn to recognize specific forms that have potential to lead to a host panel's instability. Even though further training remains necessary to fully understand and interpret underlying decay processes – and the SHRA provides certification in this area – a basic RASI assessment provides a useful snapshot of a panel's overall geologic condition and stability in terms of decay. If a more in-depth analysis of the site in terms of its condition is required, a trained *rock decay scientist* (and/or trained RASI professional) can offer one, based on the specific scores of each category and decay element.

Cost also figures into rock art management plans, with a lack of monies usually inhibiting traditional research efforts. As RASI does not require long-term coursework, training, or laboratory-based apparatus or analyses, cost savings are significant. This allows managers to more appropriately allocate their (usually limited) funds. Obviously, when significant funds are available, more intense laboratory studies can help generate further benefits such as developing site-specific mitigation and/or management methods (c.f., Fitzner, Heinrich and La Bouchardiere 2002). Therefore, RASI provides a unique alternative that can immediately influence management and conservation efforts to both well-known and newly discovered sites. Additionally, RASI scores can be easily added to GIS, allowing for correlation and spatial analysis of not just site or panel distributional characteristics, but also specific decay patterns and phenomena even on the panel itself (Allen et al. 2011; Dorn et al. 2008).

Finally, unlike other rock art assessment techniques, RASI allows local communities to readily assist in the management of rock art. RASI has the potential to enhance local buy-in, cooperation, and personal investment. It also creates "Citizen Scientists", where individuals can gain experience utilizing and understanding science (geology and rock decay in this instance) in terms of resource management (Allen 2008; Allen et al. 2011; Allen and Lukinbeal 2011; Groom et al. chapter 15 in this volume). Ultimately, RASI represents an exemplary technique for open air rock art management by providing a rapid, non-invasive, and cost-effective way to engage local communities – helping to generate significant awareness about rock art, while also providing the site manager with timely, useful, and in-depth analyses of a host panel's overall and specific geologic stability.

Previous implementation of RASI and case study

From an applicability standpoint, RASI has been implemented in a myriad of locations, on different rock types, and by different (trained) research cadres. Since its inception, a few studies helped lay RASI's foundation as both a rock art assessment and a pedagogical tool. The technique's replicability (Cerveny 2005) and usefulness as a pedagogy (Allen 2008, 2011) were conducted in the Sonora Desert alongside another study that demonstrated how RASI aided non-rock decay specialists in connecting complex biophysical processes to the greater landscape (Allen and Lukinbeal 2011). Soon after the initial trials, RASI was applied to research undertaken by three universities (Arizona State University, Mesa Community College, and University of Colorado Denver) as part of a NSF grant and two CESU grants from 2008–2012. While these grants served both educational and research initiatives, each was focused on utilizing RASI to examine the thousands of Native American petroglyph panels found in PEFO while also (re)recording rock art panels' locations and motifs, and then evaluating them for geologic stability quickly (Allen et al. 2011). Indeed, over a four-year period (2008–2011) with only a few weeks in the field per year, approximately 100 trained volunteer researchers assessed nearly 3500 individual panels in that timeframe[3].

A year after the RASI assessments at Petrified Forest National Park (PEFO) in 2012, a small team of trained RASI researchers conducted the first stability assessment of Grenada's "Carib Stones" at two sites: Duquesne Bay and Mt. Rich (Allen and Groom 2013a, 2013b). Annual monitoring of these sites over the next several years revealed some interesting (and perhaps unknowingly, but potentially slightly detrimental) local management practices (Groom 2017). RASI has also been paired with historic repeat photography to yield an even richer analysis of (semi)protected sites in the Arkansan Ozarks (Groom 2016), as well as assessing the geologic stability of ancient inscriptions in Wadi Rum, Jordan (Chapter 15 in this volume). While RASI assessments were on-going in Grenada, during 2015 and 2016 specifically, a research team reassessed the Duquesne Bay and Mt. Rich sites, and two additional rock art sites, each situated immediately adjacent to the Island's main road in the villages of Victoria and Waltham (Figure 5.1).

The RASI's efficiency as an open-air rock art management technique aids site managers in not just basic recording of panel locations and motifs, but also provides a quick, non-invasive geologic assessment of these priceless heritage cultural resources, and these characteristics play critical roles in rock art management strategies. To showcase these abilities, a recent (but abbreviated) case study using RASI to evaluate two previously unassessed sites follows.

Figure 5.1 Location of RASI-assessed rock art sites on the Island of Grenada, West Indies (Caribbean), displaying their precarious locations next to the main ring road (Victoria and Waltham), the beach (Duquesne Bay), and interior rainforest in a perennial river (Mt. Rich). Map by K.M. Groom.

Grenada's "Carib Stones" at Waltham & Victoria

Located roughly at 12 degrees north latitude in the West Indies – approximately 150 km north of Venezuela – the tri-island nation of Grenada hosts a tropical, though monsoon-like climate. Classified as a Small Island Developing State, its economy relies heavily on tourism and agriculture. Known as "The Isle of Spice", this tiny nation produces fragrant spices such as cloves, allspice, and cinnamon, as well as roughly one-third of the world's nutmeg. Popular tourism sites include the Spice Market in St Georges, various waterfalls, the central rain forest, pristine white and black sand beaches, and the Amerindian rock art. Inhabited since pre-Columbian times by various peoples, both the Arawak and Carib Amerindians settled on Grenada for extended periods. Each followed the assumed south-to-north migratory path of Caribbean Amerindians, though dates of their occupations are mostly contextual and based on artefactual evidence

(Huckerby 1921; Martin 2013; Steele 2003). While Grenada's petroglyphs are known locally as the "Carib Stones", they are more likely the product of Arawak peoples rather than the Caribs, based on motif design (Dubelaar 1995; Hayward, Atkinson and Cinquino 2009; Marquet 2009). According to these authors, five or six main petroglyph sites have been located on Grenada, though at least one of these known sites hosts only grindstones/cupules, and locals also refer to these as Carib Stones. Still, Grenada's rock art sites host more than a hundred individual motifs, making them one of the richest concentrations of petroglyphs in the Lesser Antilles. Although unprotected and highly under-studied, Grenada's Carib Stones represent a priceless, cultural heritage resource which requires further immediate attention and management.

Without further awareness and condition assessment, Grenada's priceless heritage resources could be in danger of disappearing altogether. For example, despite good intentions, a local group of volunteers "cleaned" the Mt. Rich petroglyphs in mid-2015, unknowingly removing the various natural protective rock coatings, potentially destabilizing the site until a protective patina returns. Reassessing the site a year after the cleaning occurred demonstrates resilience of some panels, but less so on others (Groom 2017). The possibility for this well-meaning but inadvertent potential damage to happen at other sites – especially the Victoria and Waltham sites which sit next to the main road and in people's yards, respectively – puts the Carib Stones in a precarious management situation.

In Grenada, the Carib Stones are not yet protected officially by any entity. Subsequently, most sites are treated differently based on their location, leading to multiple management strategies depending on a site's location. While these sites have tourism potential – visitors to Grenada are often taken to a site or two by local tour companies – maintenance and upkeep represent key issues that need to be considered. Management of Grenada's Carib Stones is also a delicate endeavour, given their unofficial status as a heritage resource: they currently belong to the residents and local communities, not the tourists or government. Finding a balance between governmental and local management strategies and plans can be challenging.

Consideration is now given to both the examples in Victoria and Waltham, including implications to Grenadian tourism and subsequent informing of local management professionals of potential threats to these important heritage resources through the RASI examination. Simultaneously, these studies have also helped provide valuable insight into Grenada's history, as well as placing these little-known petroglyphs into the spotlight through potential sustainable tourism initiatives. While the Duquesne Bay and Mt. Rich sites were annually assessed with RASI from 2012 to 2016 (cf., Allen and Groom 2013a, 2013b), not until the summers of 2015 and 2016 was RASI employed at two other known petroglyph sites in Victoria and Waltham, both located on the island's western side.

Victoria site RASI assessment

Containing a single boulder with two panels, the Victoria site rests between the main road's retaining wall and the Caribbean Sea, and directly adjacent to a storm drain (Figure 5.2). In Grenada, all beaches are deemed public to the high tide mark. For the Victoria site, this means that, because it sits at the ocean's high tide mark on one side and the main road at the other, the site is technically on public land, creating unique challenges for conservation, as well as tourism. The host boulder was deemed too important to lose when the road was being reinforced, and it was partially cemented to the road's retaining wall, just above the storm drain. Locals will often tell tourists that another boulder with glyphs used to sit next to this one, but it was removed when the road was widened, and no one knows its current location. Although trash dumping is an illegal act on the island, the storm drain has been used for this purpose, as well as an impromptu shelter. The host boulder also rests just a few meters away from the ocean, leaving the panels open to storm surges and potential climate change-driven sea rise. Finally, because of its location on public land, stopping locals from washing and re-etching the art is a challenge. For example, during initial data collection in 2015 and follow-up assessment in 2016, a local picked up

Figure 5.2 The Victoria site hosts two panels on one boulder, each with a single face glyph. They rest next to the main road, adjacent storm drain and the Caribbean Sea – the latter two of which, during storms, partially inundate the boulder. Photo by C.D. Allen 2015.

a rock and began outlining the motifs, wanting to make them more visible for the "tourists", and perhaps earning a small tip for the effort. This type of behaviour remains typical for many unofficially protected rock art sites around the world, though researchers seem to differ on its appropriateness (Whitley 2001).

Panel one assessment

Splintering occurs on the face glyph (Figure 5.3a), including splintering bisecting the glyph's top left corner. The lithological differences and inconsistencies responsible for this decay form can become more apparent – and thus, more damaging – over time. Lithobiont growth is also obvious, growing on the glyph itself, as well as scaling at the glyph's base. Recent scratching from a local "caretaker" to make the glyph more visible for tourists was also visible in assessments both years. The splintering on the glyph's upper left corner remains consistent, though not as readily visible due to lighting and lack of rain in the 2016 image (Figure 5.3b). Scaling and lithobiont growth are also present with some of the lichen growth from 2015 being both desiccated and detached. Most notably, a termite trail runs through the glyph in the 2016 image (Figure 5.3b). While part of the boulder is held in place with retaining/seawall concrete, it remains susceptible to damage from water and

Figure 5.3 (a) Panel 1 at the Victoria site displaying some splintering, particularly in the upper left of the image where the rock exhibits condensed linear cracks, as well as flaking and crumbling from perhaps continual abrasion (2015). (b) Comparative image of Panel 1 at the Victoria site displaying splintering, particularly in the upper left of the image where the rock exhibits condensed linear cracks, as well as flaking and crumbling from perhaps continual abrasion (2016). Photos by C.D. Kennedy.

debris carried in the adjacent storm drain and storm surges during the rainy season. This panel earned RASI scores of 41 in 2015 and 44 in 2016 ("Urgent Possibility of Erosion").

Panel two assessment

Located on the north side of the boulder and difficult to see in direct sunlight like panel one, panel two consists of a simple face with eyes and a mouth. Compared to panel one, striations indicating splintering and subsequent scaling under the glyph remain more visible on panel two. Evidence of re-etching is evident in the scratch marks inside the grooves of the glyphs. As with panel one, this panel remains under perpetual threat from the storm drain and the Caribbean Sea. Panel two received RASI scores of 51 in 2015 and 53 in 2016 ("Great Danger of Erosion"), with the slight score change due to additional scratching present in 2016. In the RASI score sheet notes, suggestions were made that panel two could potentially be more contemporary – based on motif style – although the decay rate and aging signs seem similar to panel one.

Overall, averaging scores from both panels among several different researchers, the Victoria site scored 46 in 2015 and 48.5 in 2016 ("Urgent Possibility of Erosion"). Major concerns include the trash disposal in the storm drain adjacent to the boulder, proximity of the ocean, as well as residents re-etching the glyphs (which removes potentially protective patinas). Given these urgent factors, the one-point difference in RASI scores between 2015 and 2016 speaks to this rock type's resilience. The next scheduled RASI field visit to these sites is planned for 2020.

Waltham site RASI assessment

Just north of Victoria lies the village of Waltham, with two boulders located in the front and back yards of two separate residences (Figures 5.4 and 5.5). Along with the environmental concerns, how the landowners treat the Carib stones needs to be considered as well. For example, during data collection, one resident mentioned someone had suggested cleaning the boulder, but they were unsure if this was good for the motifs. A further consideration is that as the glyphs rest on private property, and the landowners can ask for compensation in return for seeing or studying the rock art. These challenges influence the way management efforts can be organized, especially where rock art on private land is concerned.

Panel one assessment

Facing almost due west and located a few steps from the main road panel one stretches over a large, flat-lying boulder. Three face glyphs were identified, one of which can be described as very simple, similar to the motif on panel

Figure 5.4 Waltham site setting (front view) consisting of four panels on two different boulders near the island's main road – with the Caribbean Sea directly opposite – as well as a side street, houses, plant life/detritus, rubbish piles, and free-range livestock, pets, and people. Photo by C.D. Allen.

Figure 5.5 Waltham site setting (rear view) of boulder hosting panels 2, 3, and 4 perched precariously the riverbank and near several houses, some of which contain both penned and free-roaming livestock, along with agricultural debris, rubbish, rubbish burning, and children using the boulder for fun activities such as climbing. Photo by C.D. Allen.

two at the Victoria site which was speculated to be more contemporary than historic. In 2015, this panel was assigned a RASI score of 36 ("Problems that Could Cause Erosion") and earned a score of 40 in 2016 – barely hitting the "Urgent Possibility of Erosion" score range. Reviewing the RASI score sheets in more depth suggests that the slight increase in score is due to more plant and animal activity at the time of the assessment in 2016 (it was raining during the 2015 assessment), as well as loss of rock coating.

Panel two assessment

The first of three panels hosted on a tri-facet boulder surrounded by foliage, trees, and a large rubbish heap, panel two faces southeast toward a small grouping of houses and local road. This panel contains multiple face glyphs, and what is thought to be a rudimentary body motif. The main decay features occurring on panel two include abrasion from the surrounding vegetation, lithobiont growth and release, and termite trails running over the boulder. In 2015, the panel was given a RASI score of 36, and assigned a score of 38 in 2016, with the slight score increase most likely due to more vegetation growth and lithobiont activity from a very active wet season (both scores still fall within RASI's "Problem(s) that Could Cause Erosion" score range).

Panel three assessment

Located on the western side of the boulder, and sloping downward toward the riverbed's south bank, panel three hosts multiple face glyphs, as well as what could be interpreted as a diamond-shaped kite. Dense foliage ("plant growth on/near panel") and proximity to the river (potentially leading to undercutting or even slope failure, landing the boulder *in* the riverbed) remain the primary concerns with panel three. Assigned a RASI score of 36 in 2015 ("Problem(s) that Could Cause Erosion"), it earned a RASI score of 26 ("Good Status") in 2016. Like all panels at the Waltham site, the difference in weather (it was raining heavily during 2015's assessment) could affect lighting, with decay features perhaps being clearer in the rain and corresponding low light, though there was noticeably less trash near the panel in 2016 and less lichen as well, each of which could contribute to this slight score change. This downward score movement also represents an example of why continued monitoring by a trained researcher remains necessary for a visual assessment technique such as RASI: so that data from panel can be analysed in-depth for specific change in RASI elements.

Panel four assessment

Facing north towards the riverbed, hosting multiple fissures and resting precariously on the riverbank, panel four at the Waltham site also remains continuously surrounded by vegetation (see Figures 5.5). The main glyph, a two-faceted face, can barely be seen even in the low light and rain. Termite trails on the boulder's underside serve to destabilize the rock matrix over time (biological decay), and scaling – impending, future, and existing – has influenced this panel's overall stability (light-coloured area of boulder, bottom right side of figure 12). In 2015, panel four earned a RASI score of 55 ("Great Danger of Erosion"), and a RASI score of 47 in 2016 (at the low-end of "Problem(s) that Could Cause Erosion"). Again, as with panel three, lighting played a role in the large scoring difference here, as did angle of assessment: in 2016, the amount of vegetation limited access to the same viewshed that was used in 2015. Continued and regular monitoring via RASI can help tease out the reasons behind the slight score change and, as with most scientific endeavours, additional data can lead to more refined analyses, providing greater detail and accuracy.

Taking each panel's average score, the Waltham site overall had a RASI score of 41 in 2015 (at the low-end of "Urgent Possibility of Erosion") and a 38 in 2016 ("Problem(s) that Could Cause Erosion"). The backyard boulder that hosts panels two-four is in danger from abrasion due to the trash heap, the dense undergrowth, in addition to the banana and palm trees very nearby, as well as the large lithification-independent fractures and undercutting that has occurred and will continue to occur in the near future. The lower score in 2016 occurred because vegetation and rubbish had been removed, meaning abrasion was no longer a top concern. Still, the major concerns facing the entire Waltham site include the land use, vegetation, and potential hazards due to the river's proximity. Another challenge here lies in the fact that the two boulders that have glyphs sit on private property, so any conservation efforts would have to go directly through the landowners, an increased challenge for protecting the sites.

As illustrated here, at a minimum, regular monitoring should occur for all Grenadian rock art sites, especially surrounding the potential erosional threats at each site: this includes examples from the case studies such as the ocean and adjacent dwellings at Victoria and Duquesne Bay, the proximity to free-range animals, dense vegetation, the nearby river and surrounding houses at the Waltham site, and the precarious location of the Mt. Rich site *in* the river also surrounded by dense vegetation. Indeed, since intuitively, rocks should decay over time instead of becoming more stable, data from continued RASI assessments are necessary to ultimately generate a more complete picture of each rock art panel and their decay parameters, which in turn can lead to specific management strategies.

Discussion and implications

The RASI not only addresses contextual differences, but also adapts to any environment or conservational/management challenge. For example, in harsh desert environments, intrinsic sandstone weaknesses are reflected in the RASI analyses with higher scores of flaking, splintering, and undercutting. These concerns were shared with the National Park Service though direct participation of park rangers and volunteers, allowing rapid implantation of alternative policies and tourism planning related to sites assessed at Petrified Forest National Park. Alternatively, the sites of Grenada's Carib Stones exhibited different threats from land-use, plant activity, and precarious locations. The challenges with applying strategic and integrated official management leave these sites vulnerable to both natural decay processes and unintentional impacts from unbridled tourism development – a necessary and dominant economic force in most developing nations.

Although there are many people who advocate that rock art could be more protected than it is, there appears to be a portion of the population in many locations that have little to no interest in preserving these sites for future generations. While this may relate to traditional belief systems, socioeconomic factors, or otherwise, a potential method to help garner interest would be to approach a management proposal from an economic perspective. For example, informing local communities that these sites can be used for financial gain may increase the desire to protect them. In any case, simply involving local communities in both data gathering and dissemination can be empowering for them, making it easier to include local populations in the overall management plan, especially since engagement with tangible cultural heritage has been shown to increase appreciation for management and preservation issues (cf., Allen 2011; Basu and Barton 2007; Tal and Morag 2007). Researchers can also share information with the community about how to conserve, manage, and protect rock art which may help inform local decisions about how to approach the management of the sites (cf., Groom et al., chapter 15, this volume). Specifically, information on preserving a specific rock art panel may be needed, as reports about well-intentioned "researchers" cleaning the surface of the boulders, re-etching/chalking the petroglyphs, and even removing entire panels have been discussed around the world (cf., Kivikäs 2001; Lee and Stasack 1999; Ritter 2010; Ziolkowski 1998). Though some of these actions may be well-intended to, for example, make the motifs more visible for the tourist and/or rock art aficionado or to better record the imagery, in most cases due to the host stone's geologic structure, those actions have the potential to damage the rock art and create new weaknesses that may lead to faster rock decay and glyph disappearance. Of course, this also depends on the reasons for chalking, (re)painting, and even re-etching, since sometimes these efforts represent the only means of continuing tradition or preserving the motifs (but such efforts should be part of any long-term management plan, cf., Swartz 1963; Walderhaug 2000; Ward 1987; Welsh 1995). Still, if time, money, and expertise are available, one remedy to such potentially invasive techniques rests in utilization of high-end equipment for visualization, recording, and assessment of rock art (Alexander, Pinzand and Reinbacher 2015; Domingo et al. 2013; Horn et al. 2018; Mark and Billo 2002; Simpson et al. 2004; Vogt 2007; Vogt and Edsall 2010; Wasklewicz et al. 2005). If funds and technological proficiency are lacking, however, RASI remains a viable alternative assessment to monitor deterioration rates of rock decay over time, while also providing a snapshot of current decay characteristics.

Many open-air rock art management challenges arise from the diversity of techniques used to create the images, as well as differing contextual landscapes in which the world's rock art exist – requiring flexibility and adaptability in their assessment. Rock art has been discovered in a myriad of different lithologies and environmental settings, each presenting its own conservation risks and benefits. Pecked petroglyphs on heavily varnished sandstone in a remote desert cannot be expected to decay the same as incised motifs on an algae-infested basalt boulder in the middle of a Caribbean village. Yet, this is an assumption often repeated by research and conservation methods too rigid in their application. The wide range of rock art locales and their different inherent characteristics necessitate the employment of flexible landscape-independent techniques like RASI, which can function in any environment, on any kind of host material, and still provide relevant case-specific information. Consistently employing rapid, low-cost assessments could be one way to instigate at least basic management approaches, as well as involve local stakeholders in longer-term monitoring and management strategies.

As a triage for rock art management, RASI can help alleviate some management pressure, satisfying the above criteria because, at its core, the technique focuses on assessing a host panel's geologic stability in a straightforward and accessible manner. With precise, yet not time-consuming training, the technique is readily available and applicable. Additionally, RASI offers the site manager a way to create community buy-in, while also providing a quantifiable, empirical assessment of their site that can be used to determine where to best spend their usually limited funds in terms of managing their priceless heritage resource: rock art.

Acknowledgements

This research was informed by NSF award numbers DUE 0837451, 0837051, and 0836812. Additionally, with the cooperation of PEFO, funding was procured through the Colorado Plateau and Rock Mountain Cooperative Ecosystem Units for related research endeavours. We profusely thank these agencies for their generous support. Allen and Groom would like to thank researchers from the *Sustainability in the Caribbean* field course (University of Colorado Denver) for assistance in gathering data over the years, as well as Dr. Angus Martin for his continued support. Kennedy extends her thanks to both the Undergraduate Research Opportunity Program and Department of Geography and Environmental Sciences at University of Colorado Denver for their support of her fieldwork on Grenada.

Notes

1 Like other researchers (e.g., Dorn et al., 2013), we support the term "rock decay" (or "stone decay") rather than "weathering" because, as Hall et al (2012, p. 9) note, "...we need a term that reflects the reality of what is happening more accurately."
2 https://www.shralliance.com/rasi
3 As evidenced in a short video of the 2011 research experience involving undergraduate students, Native American high school students, and K-12 teachers from Colorado and Arizona: http://www.youtube.com/watch?v=QbhRahgRzg4.

References

Alexander, C., Pinz, A. and Reinbacher, C. (2015) Multi-scale 3D rock-art recording. *Digital Applications in Archaeology and Cultural Heritage*, 2(2), pp.181–195.

Allen, C. D. (2008) *Using rock art as an alternative science pedagogy* (PhD Dissertation). Tempe, AZ: Arizona State University.

Allen, C. D. (2011) Concept mapping validates fieldwork's capacity to deepen students' cognitive linkages of complex processes. *Research in Geographic Education*, 13(2), pp.30–51.

Allen, C. D., Cutrell, A. K., Cerveny, N. V. and Theurer, J. (2011) Advances in rock art research. *La Pintura*, 37(1), pp.4–6, 13.

Allen, C. D., Ester, S., Groom, K. M., Schubert, R., Hagele, C., James, M. and Olof, D. (2018) A geologic assessment of historic St. Elizabeth of Hungary Church using the cultural stone stability index, Denver, Colorado. In Thornbush, M. J. and Allen, C. D. (eds.) *Urban geomorphology: Landforms and processes in cities.* Amsterdam, NL: Elsevier, pp.277–302.

Allen, C. D. and Groom, K. M. (2013a) Evaluation of Grenada's "Carib Stones" via the rock art stability index. *Applied Geography*, 42, pp.165–175.

Allen, C. D. and Groom, K. M. (2013b) A geologic assessment of Grenada's carib stones. *International Newsletter on Rock Art I.N.O.R.A.*, 65, pp.19–24.

Allen, C. D. and Lukinbeal, C. (2011) Practicing physical geography: An actor-network view of physical geography exemplified by the rock art stability index. *Progress in Physical Geography*, 35(2), pp.227–248. DOI:10.1177/0309133310364929

Barnett, T., Chalmers, A., Díaz-Andreu, M., Longhurst, P., Ellis, G., Sharpe, K. and Trinks, I. (2005) 3D laser scanning for recording and monitoring rock art erosion. *INORA*, 41, pp.25–29.

Basu, S. J. and Barton, A. C. (2007) Developing a sustained interest in science among urban minority youth. *Journal of Research in Science Teaching*, 44(3), pp.466–489.

Cerveny, N. (2005) *A weathering-based perspective on rock art conservation* (PhD Dissertation). Tempe, AZ: Arizona State University.

Cerveny, N. V., Dorn, R. I., Allen, C. D. and Whitley, D. S. (2016) Advances in rapid condition assessments of rock art sites: Rock Art Stability Index (RASI). *Journal of Archaeological Science: Reports*, 10, pp.871–877.

Darvill, T. and Fernandes, A. P. B. (2014) *Open-air rock-art conservation and management: State of the art and future perspectives.* London: Routledge.

Domingo, I., Villaverde, V., López-Montalvo, E., Lerma, J. L. and Cabrelles, M. (2013) Latest developments in rock art recording: towards an integral documentation of Levantine rock art sites combining 2D and 3D recording techniques. *Journal of Archaeological Science*, 40(4), pp.1879–1889.

Dorn, R. I., Gordon, S. J., Allen, C. D., Cerveny, N., Dixon, J. C., Groom, K. M., Hall, K., Harrison, E., Mol, L., Paradise, T. R., Sumner, P., Thompson, T. J. and Turkington, A. V. (2013) The role of fieldwork in rock-decay research: Case studies from the fringe. *Geomorphology,* 200, pp.59–74.

Dorn, R. I., Whitley, D. S., Cerveny, N. V., Gordon, S. J., Allen, C. D. and Gutbrod, E. (2008) The rock art stability index: A new strategy for maximizing the sustainability of rock art as a heritage resource. *Heritage Management,* 1(1), pp.37–70.

Dubelaar, C. N. (1995) *The petroglyphs of the Lesser Antilles, the Virgin Islands and Trinidad.* Amsterdam: Foundation for Scientific Research in the Caribbean Region, Publication 135.

Fitzner, B. (2002) Damage diagnosis on stone monuments - in situ investigations and laboratory studies. In *Proceedings of the international symposium of the conservation of the Bangudae Petroglyph, May 7, 2002, Ulsan City, Korea.* Seoul: Stone Conservation Laboratory, Seoul National University, pp.29–71.

Fitzner, B., Heinrichs, K. and La Bouchardiere, D. (2002) Damage index for stone monuments. In Galan, E. and Zezza, F. (eds.) *Protection and conservation of the cultural heritage of the Mediterranean Cities, proceedings of the 5th international symposium on the conservation of monuments in the Mediterranean Basin, Sevilla, Spain, 5–8 April 2000.* Lisse, The Netherlands: Swets & Zeitlinger, pp.315–326.

Fitzner, B., Heinrichs, K. and La Bouchardiere, D. (2004) The Bangudae Petroglyph in Ulsan, Korea: studies on weathering damage and risk prognosis. *Environmental Geology,* 46(3–4), pp.504–526.

Gharib, Z. (2020) Using the rock art stability index to facilitate management of rock art in Wadi Rum, Jordan. In *Inquiry@ Queen's Undergraduate Research Conference Proceedings.* DOI: https://doi.org/10.24908/iqurcp.14016

Giesen, M. J., Ung, A., Warke, P. A., Christgen, B., Mazel, A. D. and Graham, D. W. (2013) Condition assessment and preservation of open-air rock art panels during environmental change. *Journal of Cultural Heritage,* 15(1), pp.49–56.

Groom, K. M. (2016) Fading imagery: A mixed method analysis of rock art deterioration in the Arkansan Ozarks. *International Newsletter of Rock Art,* 74(1), pp.14–20.

Groom, K. M. (2017) *Rock art management and landscape change: Merits of rapid field assessment techniques for cultural stone decay* (PhD Dissertation). Fayetteville: University of Arkansas.

Groom, K. M., Allen, C. D. and Bevan, G. (In Press) The rock-art rangers program: Enhancing tourism and improving employment outcomes in Wadi Rum. *Studies in the History and Archaeology of Jordan, Volume XIII. Amman,* Jordan: Jordan Department of Antiquities.

Groom, K. M., Bevan, G. and Allen, C. D. (2020) Wadi Rum: Community-based rock art and epigraphic recording (2018–2019 season). *Archaeology in Jordan,* 2, pp.142–143.

Groom, K. M., Bevan, G. and Allen, C. D. (2018) Wadi Rum: Community-based rock art and epigraphic recording project (2016–17 season). *Archaeology in Jordan,* 1, pp.96–97.

Groom, K. M., Cerveny, N. V., Allen, C. D., Dorn, R. I. and Theurer, J. (2019) Protecting stone heritage in the painted desert: Employing the rock art stability index in the petrified forest national park. *Heritage,* 2(3), pp.2111–2123.

Hall, K., Thorn, C. and Sumner, P. (2012) On the persistence of 'weathering'. *Geomorphology,* 149–150(0), pp.1–10. DOI:http://dx.doi.org/10.1016/j.geomorph.2011.12.024.

Hayes, D. M. and Hayes, J. (2019) The Norman sicily project: A digital portal to Sicily's Norman past. *Digital Medievalist,* 12(1), p.3.

Hayward, M. H., Atkinson, L. G. and Cinquino, M. A. (2009) *Rock art of the Caribbean.* Tuscaloosa, AL: University of Alabama Press.

Hoerlé, S., Pearce, D., Bertrand, L., Sandt, C. and Menu, M. (2016) Imaging the layered fabric of paints from Nomansland rock art (South Africa). *Archaeometry,* 58, pp.182–199.

Horn, C., Ling, J., Bertilsson, U. and Potter, R. (2018) By all means necessary–2.5 D and 3D recording of surfaces in the study of southern Scandinavian rock art. *Open Archaeology,* 4(1), pp.81–96.

Huckerby, T. (1921) *Petroglyphs of Grenada and a recently discovered petroglyph in St. Vincent.* New York, NY: Museum of the American Indian, Heye Foundation.

Kivikäs, P. (2001) Rock paintings in Finland. *Folklore: Electronic Journal of Folklore,* 18–19, pp.137–161.

Lee, G. and Stasack, E. (1999) *Spirit of place: Petroglyphs of Hawaii* (Vol. 12). Los Osos, CA: Easter Island Foundation.

Mark, R. and Billo, E. (2002) Application of digital image enhancement in rock art recording. *American Indian Rock Art,* 28, pp.121–128.

Marquet, S. J. (2009) Contextual analysis of the lesser Antillean Windward islands Petroglyphs: Methods and results. In Hayward, M. H., Atkinson, L. G. and Cinquino, M. A. (eds.) *Rock art of the Caribbean.* Tuscaloosa, AL/USA: University of Alabama Press, pp.147–160.

Martin, J. A. (2013) *Island Caribs and French Settlers in Grenada: 1498–1763.* Grenada: National Museum Press.

Pineda, C., Martin, R., Hallbauer, D., Jacobson, L., Prozesky, V. and Przybylowicz, W. (1997) Geochemical microanalysis of patina layers on rock artefacts from the Central Karoo and Southern Free State, South Africa. *Nuclear Instruments and Methods in Physics Research Section B: Beam Interactions with Materials and Atoms,* 130(1), pp.628–635.

Pope, G. A. (2000) Weathering of petroglyphs: Direct assessment and implications for dating methods. *Antiquity,* 74(286), pp.833.

Ritter, E. (2010) An archaeological approach to the Rupestrian images at La Angostura, Central Baja California. *California Archaeology,* 2(2), pp.147–183.

Simpson, A., Clogg, P., Diaz-Andreu, M. and Larkman, B. (2004) Towards three-dimensional non-invasive recording of incised rock art. *Antiquity,* 78, pp.692–698.

Steele, B. A. (2003) *Grenada: A history of its people.* Oxford: Macmillan Education.

Swartz, B. (1963) Aluminum powder: A technique for photographically recording petroglyphs. *American Antiquity,* 28(3), pp.400–401.

Tal, T. and Morag, O. (2007) School visits to natural history museums: Teaching or enriching? *Journal of Research in Science Teaching,* 44(5), pp.747–769.

Tratebas, A. M., Cerveny, N. V. and Dorn, R. I. (2004) The effects of fire on rock art: Microscopic evidence reveals the importance of weathering rinds. *Physical Geography,* 25(4), pp.313–333.

Viles, H. A., Camuffo, D., Fitz, S., Fitzner, B., Lindqvist, O., Livingston, R. A. and Warscheid, T. (1997) Group report: What is the state of our knowledge of the mechanisms of deterioration and how good are our estimations of rates of deterioration? In Snethlage, R. (ed.) *Report of the Dahlem workshop on "Saving our architectural heritage: The conservation of historic stone structures", Berlin, March 3–8, 1996*. London: Wiley, pp.95–112.

Vogt, B. J. (2007) *A visual analytical approach to rock art panel condition assessment* (PhD Dissertation). Tempe, AZ: Arizona State University.

Vogt, B. and Edsall, R. (2010) Terrestrial laser scanning and exploratory spatial data analysis for the mapping of weathering forms on rock art panels. *Geocarto International*, 25(5), pp.347–367.

Walderhaug Saetersdal, E. M. (2000) Ethics, politics and practices in rock art conservation. *Public Archaeology*, 1(3), pp.163–180.

Ward, G. K. (1987) Retouch: An option to conservation? *Rock Art Research*, 5, p. 69.

Wasklewicz, T., Staley, D., Volker, H. and Whitley, D. S. (2005) Terrestrial 3D laser scanning: A new method for recording rock art. *INORA*, 41, pp.16–25.

Welsh, E. C. (1995) *Easy field guide to southwestern petroglyphs*. Phoenix, AZ: American Traveller Press.

Whitley, D. S. (2001) *Handbook of rock art research*. Oxford: Altamira Press.

Wright, A. M. (2018) Assessing the stability and sustainability of rock art sites: Insight from southwestern Arizona. *Journal of Archaeological Method and Theory*, 25(3), pp.911–952.

Ziolkowski, M. (1998) A study of the petroglyphs from Wadi al-Hayl, Fujairah, United Arab Emirates. *Arabian Archaeology and Epigraphy*, 9(1), pp.13–89.

6 Confusion and Solution

Providing a Desk-Based Approach for the Management of Rock Art

George Nash

Introduction

Complex strategies associated with rock art management are usually levelled at the United Nations Educational, Scientific and Cultural Organization (UNESCO) World Heritage Site (WHS) inscription. Inscribed onto the WHS list are a few designations specifically incorporating rock art and the landscapes in which they are located. Prior to designation, each area would have undergone rigorous evaluation and a set of criteria is followed so that World Heritage Site status can be attained. Preliminary documentation is usually in the form of a staged approach, incorporating the archaeology, historic significance and management proposals of the site. The information gathered allows the site to be placed on a tentative list. All sites on this list will undergo several evaluations with some being selected from the list to be placed on a Nomination List. Sites on the Nomination List are further evaluated by the International Council on Monuments and Sites (ICOMOS) and the World Conservation Union. These two bodies will make the necessary recommendations to the World Heritage Committee where the final decision is made to inscribe a site or not. It is within the various stages that the evaluation of the site is scrutinised, including its long-term management and site vulnerability. As part of the assessment to establish whether a potential site is worthy of World Heritage Site status, a set of generic and specific criteria is measured against it, usually in the form of a SWOT analysis (Strengths, Weaknesses, Opportunities and Threats). In a similar vein, a SWOT analysis is also be applied to Conservation Management Plans and the designation of archaeological sites and landscapes where threats from, [long- and short-term] natural changes, development, natural denudation, tourism, or anti-social behaviour may occur.

For this chapter, I discuss the history, development, and philosophy of the SWOT analysis and how it has been used in the management of archaeological sites/landscapes that have rock art as its focus. This is followed by two case studies undertaken where a SWOT analysis was employed following the discovery of Upper Palaeolithic rock art on the walls of two caves. Although both sites offer low tourism value, they have each been designated by their respective national heritage agencies as Scheduled Monuments.[1] Both

DOI: 10.4324/9780429355349-9

caves are under continuous threat of intentional and unintentional vandalism and require long-term strategies for conservation and protection either through direct (site enforcement) or indirect (education) actions.

Fieldwork at the two case study sites was undertaken by myself and the Welsh Rock Art Organisation (WRAO).

Background and definition of SWOT

A SWOT analysis (otherwise known as a SWOT matrix) is a strategic planning tool used to identify various aspects such as strengths, weaknesses, opportunities and threats that can be used in project managing of cultural heritage and archaeological sites/landscapes. However, as stated above, SWOT analysis is rarely used in cultural heritage and archaeological decision making at a strategic level. In many instances, alternative approaches are employed such as criteria within Environmental Impact Assessments and Environmental Statement using themes such as direct impacts, indirect impacts, impact on the setting, the magnitude of impact, the significance of effect and mitigation; nevertheless, these themes can also be seen in SWOTs.

Initially, SWOTs were intended to specify the aims and objectives within business-orientated projects. They identified the known and potential internal and external factors that influenced project objectives; be they favourable or unfavourable, the latter requiring some form of mitigation. The SWOT analysis was a process where meaningful subjective information for each of the four categories is listed, providing a useful tool to allow for a robust project to be initiated. As listed above, and as applied to cultural heritage management, SWOT comprises the following elements:

- Strengths: characteristic baseline of the project that provides the main benefits.
- Weaknesses: characteristics of the project that places it at a disadvantage relative to other project approaches.
- Opportunities: elements in the environment that the project could exploit to its advantage (i.e., increases or decreases in footfall to a particular site).
- Threats: elements of the project that could term the asset/project, such as adverse effects from conservation management or tourism (e.g., inappropriate heritage signage, routeways and development).

Argued applicability to cultural heritage contexts

As stated earlier, the SWOT analysis is one of several methods used in project planning. Over the past 20 years, the SWOT analysis has been used on high-profile projects including several by the author. It is sometimes convenient for the facilitator to undertake such a method without consultation, but for larger projects, they usually involve a multi-disciplinary approach that can involve many academic and professional concerns so that a range of other opinions are incorporated into the SWOT analysis. Overall, multi-agency involvement is the best way to facilitate the development of a SWOT analysis. Experience has shown that such an approach has been absent from many teams and sometimes training is advised prior to initiate the various elements that form a project design. This initial approach allows individuals within their respective teams to familiarise themselves with the protocols of SWOT analysis. The organising project team and invited stakeholders command diverse opinions. Regarding rock art within cave contexts (such as the two case studies discussed below), there was a requirement to engage in a dialogue with ecologists, in particular those dealing with bats and their hibernation sites. For the two case studies, access was time-limited due to winter hibernation (between October and April).

Initial planning for a SWOT analysis requires careful consideration in terms of finance, organisation, and resources. Outlined below are several prompts that assist in guiding a project to a successful outcome:

- Resources: For the two case studies outlined in detail below, a staged archaeological approach has been applied.
  - For Cathole Cave (Case Study No. 1), the site was surveyed using 3D laser scanning equipment to create point cloud images of much of the cave. This survey followed the discovery of a rock art panel located towards the rear section of the cave. The technology allowed the survey team to produce a definitive plan of the cave (Nash and Beardsley 2013). This work was followed by further geoprospection of the cave walls, resulting in new rock art discoveries (Nash 2015) and limited excavation within the main gallery (Walker et al. 2016).
  - For Merlin's Cave (Case Study No. 2), an archaeological staged approach was applied. Dialogue has been established between myself and Historic England (national heritage agency), and project design has been prepared to incorporate a SWOT analysis. It was during my initial visit in 2006 that potential painted prehistoric rock art was discovered.
- Past and present histories: Each cave site occupies similar landscape locations, and has been subjected to early investigations, involving excavation using available archaeological methods at the time. Both caves have also been investigated recently using up-to-date scientific methods. For both cave sites, there are still many opportunities to undertake further scientific research.
- Human resources: Scientists working within their specialised fields of research. In the case of the proposed work programme at Merlin's Cave, the project includes scientists who research the geochemistry of pigments and specialists in photogrammetric surveys.

- Financial constraints: For any proposed project organised by the Welsh Rock Art Organisation, available grants, funding agencies and other sources of income are applied for. Usually, much of the funding required for potential projects such as the one for Merlin's Cave relies sometimes on the in-kind support of university departments and the supply of specialised equipment. In the case of a proposed programme for Merlin's Cave, the University of Coimbra provided the use of X-Ray Fluorescense (XRF) and Raman spectrometer equipment. Much of the financial resourcing was organised prior to project design; the golden rule is no money, no project!
- Funding sources: Can a SWOT analysis identify potential funding sources? Indeed, due to the statutory designation of each cave site, funding can derive directly from each of the two national heritage agencies?
- Visitor intentions: Curious visitors, academics? Local, national or international? One can also include (for the wrong reasons) those individuals who intend to cause harm to a rock art site.
- The physical environment: Does the location of each cave site decrease or increase the risk of harm and are there ways of mitigating this and other constraints?
- Legislation: Does current guidance and legislation restrict an organisation's ability, such as the WRAO to achieve a long-term conservation plan for each of the two caves?
- Monitoring: All Scheduled Monument sites in the UK are monitored by national heritage inspectors. To undertake any work within a scheduling boundary of a protected site, an initial dialogue is imperative. From such a meeting, the researcher will produce a detailed project design, along with a health and safety risk assessment. At Cathole Cave and Merlin's Cave, there are many issues concerning health and safety, such as access, irregular floor levels and possible rockfall. As a result, full Personal Protection Equipment must be worn. Whilst fieldwork is ongoing, the monitoring authority should undertake regular visits in order to gain a full understanding of the archaeological resource (i.e., context). As part of the initial process, several preliminary documents were produced and as a result a desk-based assessment was initiated. This document summarised the cave's archaeological history, ecology, geology/geomorphology, along with a series of field investigations between 2010 and 2015. By understanding the recovered archaeological finds from previous excavations, in particular diagnostic flint and faunal remains,[2] an understanding of the chronological sequence and contextual archaeology of the cave was gained. Not surprisingly, the style of the engraved cervid had chronological associations with archaeology recovered from previous excavations, much of it Late Upper Palaeolithic (LUP) in date.

Implementation of a SWOT

A SWOT analysis is usually implemented when ideas and concepts are still free-flowing around and within an organisation. It can also occur at a time when the various stakeholders are together and collective decisions are made, facilitating a series of general aims and objectives for the project. This democratic process has been installed in all the decision-making prior to any project executed by WRAO, a not-for-profit organisation. Since 2004, this research body has undertaken five major field projects involving research specifically aimed at promoting a baseline between prehistoric rock art and associated Neolithic and Bronze Age monumentality. Within the ethos of the organisation is a desire to include public engagement. As a result, there has been the successful completion of four excavation projects linked to rock art (Trefael 2010–2013; Perthi Duon 2012–2014; Llwydiarth Esgob Stone; Trellyffaint 2014–Present) and a long-term project of recording engraved art within the Neolithic passage grave of Barclodiad y Gawres, Ynys Môn, North Wales.

At the initial stage, for each of the WRAO projects a SWOT analysis was undertaken. Decisions on research and field programme protocols were discussed, usually through a brainstorming session. This would occur before any dialogue with the heritage agency – Cadw. All five projects comprise sites that are designated as scheduled monuments and all require Scheduled Monument Consent as well as permission from the various landowners.

Internal and external factors

A SWOT analysis identifies key internal and external factors fundamental to achieving an objective. These can be visitor numbers and their effect on the rock art site. Based on this and other elements, such as environment stabilisation of rock surfaces or chemical reaction to airborne pollutants, a SWOT analysis would group key pieces of information into two main categories:

- Internal factors — the strengths and weaknesses internal to the organisation undertaking monitoring, and short and long-term conservation of rock art sites.
- External factors — the opportunities and threats presented by the environment external to the organisation such as the requirements of other conservation agencies (protected flora and fauna and their potential impact on rock art and other archaeological resources).

An example of where significant changes have occurred to a World Heritage Site due to footfall and environmental damage is the Lascaux cave system. The cave was discovered in 1940 and has been subjected to many thousands of unsolicited visitors each week for at least the next 45 years. As a result of significant changes in the cave's microclimate, the paintings were threatened by bacteria and fungi that were considered harmful to the fragile pigments, in particular the soil-based fungus Fusarium solani. In 1963, the general public was denied access due to further infestations of green algae and introduced fungi which were flourishing due to the chemical changes occurring in response to large numbers of visitors. Following closure of the cave, scientists of the French heritage agencies (with support from leading rock art specialists) devised a scheme to replicate a millimetre-accurate plan of the cave system and construct a facsimile, and by 1984, Lascaux II was opened to the public. The success of Lascaux II prompted a travelling exhibition promoting the cave's riches – Lascaux III. The current Lascaux facsimile with attached museum and workshop – Lascaux IV was opened to the public in 2016 at a cost of nearly 60 million Euros.[3]

Based on the Conservation Management Plan for Stonehenge and nearby Avebury[4] it was becoming clear that the old facilities such as the small gift shop, cafe and washrooms were woefully inadequate for the number of visitors. Using a SWOT analysis many of the internal factors considered as strengths or as weaknesses were dependent upon their effect on the objectives English Heritage had set in their long-term strategy. However, what may represent strength concerning one objective may be weaknesses for another (i.e., how much disruption would be created by decommissioning a road that cut through the prehistoric avenue to the north of the henge?).

As we are now witnessing, external factors such as the construction of a short or long tunnel to form a bypass south of Stonehenge has extended far beyond the SWOT analysis for cultural heritage and is currently being considered by the national government; the main factor being of a financial nature: is a tunnel worth the investment from substantial public funding?

When can a SWOT analysis be applied?

A SWOT analysis is usually incorporated into documentation before a project is initiated. It organises and compartmentalises information into various headings. In doing so, it allows organisers to discuss and debate the various issues and trajectory the SWOT analysis should take; above all identifying the strengths and opportunities the project offers and at the same time being aware of the weaknesses and threats.

Generally, a SWOT analysis can be used to:

- Explore solutions to mitigate problems.
- Identify those barriers that will limit the long-term aims/objectives of the project.
- Organise a brainstorming event in order to implement a general plan of action.
- Decide on the direction that will provide the most effective outcome.
- Identify possibilities and limitations for modification to the project design.
- Incorporate plans for revision should changes be required midway through a project (making the project fluid and dynamic).

- Enhance the credibility and interpretation that will be used in presenting a trajectory to project organisers and the various stakeholder organisations.
- Introduce transparency into the decision-making process.

Specifics: environmental considerations

A SWOT analysis needs to include an assessment of the current state of the site's archaeological knowledge, heritage status and significance, management situation and proposals for ongoing conservation. It could be the case that some of the protocols for its conservation are already in place. However, these may require substantial updating and the SWOT process should identify this as a particular need. It is prudent, however, that any conservation management plan should be reviewed, appraised, and updated regularly. For the two case studies, periodic visits by Cadw and Historic England are made, and their observations recorded. For Cathole Cave (Case Study No. 1), which had wide public access due to its location, Cadw inspectors recorded serious damage to the fabric of the main gallery, (attributed in part to campfires and graffitiing the walls). At Merlin's Cave (Case Study No. 2) such damage was not recorded; again, this was probably due to its difficult access.

Environmental considerations should not be aimed at archaeology and cultural heritage. Both inside and outside each of the caves a unique fauna and flora are protected under particular guidance, legislation and policy.[5]

Heritage benefits

The SWOT analysis comprising any given site social context is beneficial because it helps organisations decide whether an objective is obtainable and therefore enables organisations to set achievable goals, objectives, and steps which help develop social change or community involvement. This approach, albeit not in a SWOT format, is used by public organisations applying for National Heritage Lottery Fund (NHLF) funding. Although the questions asked by the NHLF achieve the same outcomes as using a SWOT analysis, NHLF criteria employed was aimed towards small-scale funding projects which have a relatively short duration (up to three years). Usually, there is a determined project termination with limited long-term outcomes.

This was exemplified by the research conducted following the discovery of Upper Palaeolithic rock art at Cathole Cave in 2010, whereby Welsh heritage agency Cadw awarded several grants to address certain research aims including a SWOT. The first of these funding tranches was to initiate a 3D laser scan of the cave (Nash and Beardsley 2013). In the short term, the aims of the digital survey were met with the production of a sub-millimetre plan of the cave. From this data, the 3D plan could be manipulated to create a 2D plan of the cave thus assisting in the long-term by illustrating the original floor level before the first archaeological excavations when most of the deposits within the main galley were unceremoniously removed. The second tranche of funding financed the excavation programme undertaken by the National Museum of Wales (Walker et al. 2014). Again, this was a short-term funded project that had long-term outcomes, providing the necessary trenching for the installation of a steel grille for the protection of the main gallery and rear section of the cave. The grille would provide the much needed protection of undisturbed archaeological deposits that were dispersed across much of the rear section of the cave.

Limitations to SWOT

It should be noted that the SWOT analysis is a basic starting point for any project discussion and therefore cannot, in itself, be considered as a means of how to fully implement a project design. It does, however, alert the various heritage agencies to the significance of a site and the potential threats and advantages a site might have. The SWOT analysis requires constant updating, usually through regular monitoring and amendments. In the case of the two examples I have used, change may be witnessed through visitor numbers, changes in landscape management or threats from vandalism.

Disadvantages to SWOT can be seen in those projects that only use certain recognised criteria within the analysis and disregard criteria of opportunities and threats sections. Of course, these omissions may be the results of changes in management strategy, diminishing interest in the project, changes in the politics of the project management or simply, a lack of funding (e.g., Hill and Westbrook 1997; Novicevic et al. 2004). Other researchers, using a business model also relevant to cultural heritage management have critiqued the abuse of SWOT as a tool that can be constructed with little critical thought consideration – i.e., a simple means to an end. This sometimes ad-hoc approach can distort and misrepresent the outcome of SWOT analysis. Any such approach can be easily identified by monitoring agencies or funding groups and result in rejection or serious delays to a project.

Other limitations to achieve a successful SWOT analysis can include the reuse of previously decided aims and objectives. This sometimes complex and outdated practice can lead to limitations on brainstorming opportunities, especially when a project and its management system is fluid. For example, in my chosen Case Study of Cathole Cave, I could not allow my original aims and objectives in respect of recording, publication and securing of the site to be changed, irrespective of any succeeding event or change. This was since I have produced and submitted a project design, outlining my project rationale to Cadw. I took similar approaches in the excavation of four megalithic sites in Wales where the aims and objectives of the original SWOT had to be strictly adhered to. I will likely adopt similar approaches when researching the potential cave art in Merlin's Cave, South Herefordshire (Case Study No. 2) (see Figure 6.1).

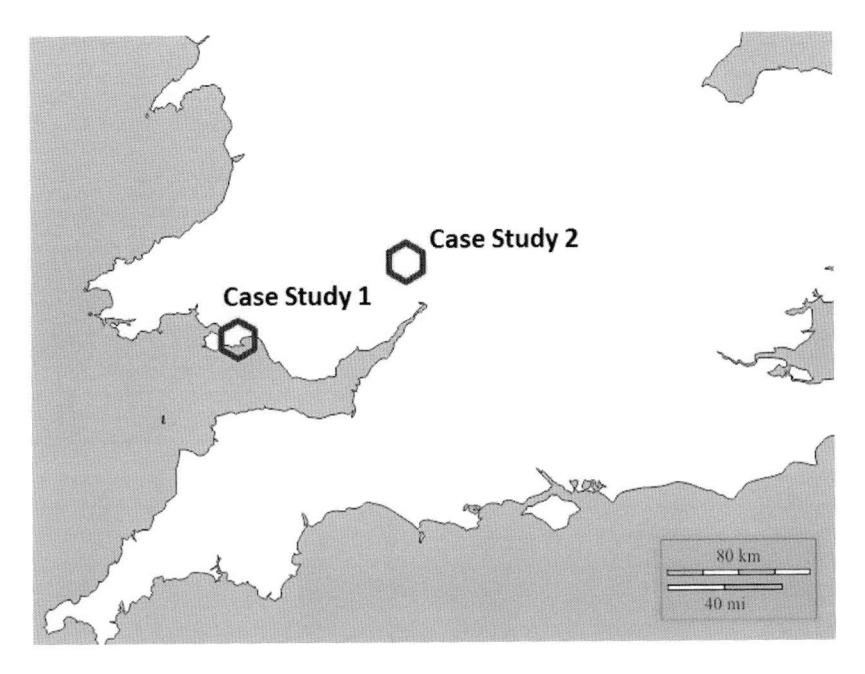

Figure 6.1 Location of the two case study sites. Map by the author.

Case study no. 1: Cathole Cave

So far, I have described and discussed the role of the SWOT analysis in terms of its potential use in rock art conservation management. I have also highlighted, albeit briefly where a SWOT analysis has been used. I now wish to turn to a rock art discovery I made in 2010 in a cave in South Wales. Cathole Cave is located on the Gower Peninsula and is naturally formed in a limestone outcrop that has been eroded from water action and freeze-thaw processes (see Figure 6.2). At the time of discovery, most areas of the cave were publicly accessible. Indeed, the cave has been subjected, over the past 200 years, to systematic and accidental vandalism, usually through archaeological and antiquarian investigations, campfires and graffiti. The cave site stands within an area still frequented by many thousands of visitors each year (including the Scout Movement), usually during the summer months. The long-term damage of the site probably started with an archaeological excavation in the main gallery of the cave by Colonel Woods in 1864. During this excavation over c. 1m of deposits was removed (reported in Garrod 1926 and Roberts 1887). Later excavations were undertaken by McBurney in 1958–1959 (McBurney 1959), Campbell in 1975–1976 (Campbell 1977) and Walker (Walker et al. 2014); each project arguably took its toll on the long-term conservation outcomes for this cave.

(*Continued*)

Figure 6.2 Entrance to Cathole Cave. Image by the author.

Prior to the Walker excavation, I made a significant discovery in the rear section of the cave (Nash et al. 2012). Located within a narrow niche, the clear engraving of a cervid (possibly a reindeer) was etched into a botryoidal calcite flowstone (Figure 6.3). The result of this discovery as described above led to a digital 3D mapping survey of the cave (Nash and Beardsley 2013), geo-prospection of the cave walls (Nash 2015) and further sampling of the geochemistry for the potential of applied pigments within the main gallery, as well as followed by limited excavations by the National Museum of Wales (Walker et al. 2014).

Figure 6.3 The engraved torso of a cervid, discovered in 2010. Image by the author.

Regarded by many, including national heritage agency Cadw, Cathole is considered a significant early prehistoric designated heritage asset. This is based on what has been revealed from previous excavations including a unique assemblage of faunal remains and a large lithic assemblage that probably dates to the Early Upper Palaeolithic (Campbell 1977; Garrod 1926; McBurney 1959).

Although the initial archaeological investigations were limited to specific areas within the cave, recent investigations by Walker and her team

(*Continued*)

resulted in most artefacts dating to the LUP. However, deposits that contained evidence of human activity to around 35,500 + 650 cal. BP (Walker et al. 2014) were also uncovered, pushing back evidence of human occupation to the transition period between the Upper and Middle Palaeolithic. In addition, Garrod (1926, p. 65) identified a Font Robert point or tanged point, a diagnostic tool form now attributed to the early Gravettian and dated to around 28,000 BP (Jacobi and Higham 2011a, p. 210). She also recorded a Cheddar point, a burin and an assemblage of end-scrapers (Garrod 1926, pp. 65–66). These latter tools are now generally attributed to the Late Upper Palaeolithic period in Britain, around 12,600 BP (Jacobi and Higham 2011b, p. 229).

A research team from the Natural Environment Research Council Open University Uranium Series Dating Facility extracted four samples for uranium-series disequilibrium dating. One sample was taken from the surface on which the engraving is placed and two from younger speleothem deposits which partly covered the engraving. Another sample, close to the nose of the carving gave a minimum date range of 12,572 ± 660 cal. BP (GN-10 GHS2; Nash et al. 2012). A further date obtained from flowstone to the left of the engraved muzzle provided a minimum date range of 14,505 ± 560 cal. BP (CAT 11#4; Nash 2012, p. 113). Given the significance of the discovery, the results of this dating programme and aspects of the project were widely reported over 12 months through national and international media outlets including the BBC.

Figure 6.4 The insertion of a grille in 2014 that extends across the main gallery. Image by the author.

> Unfortunately, part of this engraving was subsequently vandalised in late August or early September 2011 and as a result, Cadw decided to construct a grille across the outer gallery section of the cave (Plate 3). Despite the vandalism undertaken just before the insertion of a steel grille, the cave was surveyed using a variety of techniques that ranged from tape and off-set methods to 3D laser [point-cloud] survey (Nash and Beardsley 2013).

SWOT analysis for Cathole Cave

Universal value

Strengths

The site is located within a secluded valley that stands close to the Bristol Channel. Cathole Cave has been excavated four times, most recently in 2014. Since 2010 the cave has been thoroughly surveyed and sampled for the presence of potential prehistoric rock art, in particular LUP rock art. It is considered by national heritage agency Cadw to be the best example of Upper Palaeolithic cave assemblage in Wales.

Weaknesses

The cave had until relatively recently been open to the public and as a result had suffered sporadic episodes of vandalism and neglect, even though the site is a scheduled monument (GM349). The hidden nature of this and other cave sites within the valley allows acts of vandalism to go unnoticed.

Opportunities

Ironically, the most recent vandalism incident occurred in 2011 which resulted in the heritage agencies installing a steel grille across the main gallery of the cave and to clear and manage vegetation along the west-facing slopes that stand in front of the cave entrance. The grille has also afforded protection to several endangered bat species who use the cave as a hibernaculum.

Threats

By opening up the landscape, the cave entrance is visible from the valley floor and, therefore, increasing the footfall and the potential for antisocial behaviour. Exposure from social media also has the potential for increased footfall and antisocial behaviour.

Archaeological value

Strengths

Much of the cultural heritage comprises well-defined archaeological features, associated with cave archaeology. Indeed, the site has been the focus for antiquarian and later, archaeological investigations. The cave stratigraphy, especially within the side chambers and the northeast gallery is generally in a good state of preservation and has the potential for further archaeological and speleological research.

Weaknesses

Historically, the cave has been the focus for antiquarian and archaeological activity which has resulted in much of the main galley floor being excavated and removed during the late 19th century. Furthermore, the immediate landscape has also been the focus for archaeological investigations (e.g., McBurney 1959). This and later investigations were undertaken without the use of modern scientific excavation techniques.

Opportunities

There is an opportunity to enhance the known archaeological heritage through dedicated educational display boards and to update the Regional Historic Environment Record; additionally to collate all archaeological literature and publish it as a dedicated monograph. The monograph will place the archaeological, geomorphology, and speleology into a wider context (especially with other caves within the valley and along the limestone outcropping of the south Gower Coast).

Threats

Despite the significance of the site (and its interconnection with a lower cave), there are a number of potential threats that include systematic attempts to enter the cave from vandalising the steel grille. There is also a potential threat from untrained consultants who monitor the bat colony that roosts within the rear section of the cave where the most sensitive archaeology is located.

Contextual value

Strengths

Cathole Cave is a designated scheduled monument (GM349) and stands close to several other scheduled monuments: Llethrid Tooth Cave (GM284) and Parc Le Breos Cwm Neolithic burial chamber (GM122). The cave is also near Church Hill Romano-British enclosure (GM603), Trinity Well and Remains of a chapel (GM158) and Parc Le Breos Limekilns (GM536). These sites, along with many non-designated heritage assets (including historic woodland and field boundaries) constitute a complex archaeological and cultural heritage landscape that dates between the Upper Palaeolithic (40 to 10 ka cal. BP) to the post-medieval period.

Weaknesses

The heritage assets identified within the site boundary are of national importance but have varying degrees of public access. Although Cathole Cave (and the adjacent Lower Cathole Cave) and Llethrid Tooth Cave are protected by steel grilled entrances there have been attempts to vandalise these grilles and gain access. Although both sites are visible from footpaths, the entrances to both are concealed and therefore prone to antisocial behaviour.

Opportunities

Between 2010 and 2016 Cathole was thoroughly surveyed and geoprospected for rock art (Nash, Calsteron et al. 2012; Nash and Beardsley 2013; Nash 2015), and the floor partially excavated (Walker et al. 2014). The geo-prospection undertaken by Nash (2015) revealed the potential of further rock art of LUP date. The mapping of the cave by Nash and Beardsley (2013) also revealed the extent of the northern section of the cave and the largely undisturbed floor deposits present. There are areas in the cave and within the current entrance area that offer an opportunity to archaeologically investigate the sub-surface remains (e.g., similar to those undertaken by Campbell (1977) and McBurney (1959). In summary, the archaeological potential for the cave and its immediate landscape is considered high.

Threats

Potential sub-surface archaeological remains would be lost following any future excavation programme.

Public appreciation and realm value

Strengths

Cathole Cave contains a significant archaeological and historic resource that contributes to our understanding of the early prehistory and later archaeology of the site. Currently, Cadw and Natural Resources Wales administer the site and the surrounding landscape. As part of the public realm, Cadw and Natural Resources Wales have erected several display boards providing a general introduction to the site and its archaeology and ecology. In addition, academic papers covering fieldwork and research since 2010 are widely available via the internet and the University of Bristol Speleological Society (UBSS).

Weaknesses

Historically, there has been an issue with access to the cave. Prior to the installation of a steel grille in 2014, all accessible areas of the cave were prone to periodic vandalism. Conversely, the grille has done much to impinge on the visitor experience, with only part of the main gallery and entrance made accessible.

Opportunities

Despite the installation of a steel grille, visitors can still experience the various cave sections that are within the western section of the cave, suggesting that the present access arrangements are a compromise between full access and complete closure. Cathole Cave is one of six Scheduled Monuments within the valley that provide the visitor with a view to a complex past: from Upper Palaeolithic settlement and ritual cave sites to a Neolithic burial-ritual site and post-medieval limekilns.

Threats

There are concerns that future illegal attempts to enter the cave could result in acts of vandalism. There are also concerns from archaeologists that bat specialists (who have their own research objectives) may inadvertently damage the walls and panels of the main gallery and side chambers. These threats are ongoing despite the fact that the cave and other archaeological sites with the valley (Green Cwm) are periodically monitored by the heritage agency Cadw.

Case study no. 2: Merlin's Cave

I now wish to turn my attention to another cave site and its surrounding landscape that houses probable rock art which is yet to be scientifically verified. The site, Merlin's Cave, is a scheduled monument[6] and was first excavated during the early to mid-1920s by T.F. Hewer and is one of several that occupy the steep limestone outcrops of the

River Wye around the village of Symond's Yat (Hewer 1924, 1925). Although Cathole Cave and Merlin's Cave occupy similar topographic locations and geological bedrock, each poses different issues to their protection and long-term conservation. Merlin's Cave is sited on the south-eastern side of the Great Doward, overlooking the River Wye (NGR SO 55 15). The site is on a steep-sided slope with an entrance facing south (Figure 6.5).

On approach, the cave's rectangular entrance appears to have been remodelled, probably during a time when limestone extraction extended across much of the Great Doward. The entrance is initially approached by a near-vertical climb from the sloped floor to a narrow ledge. The cave is shaped by a large north-south rift that extends 18m northwards to the rear of the cave. Located on the eastern side of the entrance is a small rock cavity that may connect to the main cave; however, this is yet to be verified. The cave was scientifically discovered by speleologists during the early 19th century when iron-ore prospection and subsequent mining was in operation. The Hewer excavations of the mid-1920s identified substantial deposits including human remains from Late Glacial contexts below a stal [speleothem] floor. Also recovered from the same deposit were drilled ornaments of shell and animal teeth; these items were considered to be associated with the burials and are probably Late Upper Palaeolithic or Early Mesolithic in date. Faunal remains recovered from the excavation were later radiocarbon dated to about 10,000 cal. BP and confirm the cave was in use during the last major Glacial period (Barton 1996).[7] Substantial traces of these deposits, as well as the stal floor, are still visible, along with potential undated painted rock art. It is this latter discovery, made in 2006 that highlights major issues for the long-term protection and conservation of the cave and its immediate surroundings.

The SWOT analysis was undertaken in 2018 when I was reviewing potential rock art projects within this area of the British Isles. Images of the potential rock art, the cave and its immediate landscape were considered by a multi-disciplinary team that included pigment specialists and geomorphologists from the Geosciences Centre, University of Coimbra, Portugal. It was from the various meetings held that a formal process to investigate the cave walls was made to Historic England (to apply for a Section 42 Licence). As a result of a formal application, permission was granted in May 2019 to investigate the walls of the cave and cliff-face below the entrance allowed the team to consider adopting a SWOT analysis which will form part of the documentation process for this project.

(Continued)

Figure 6.5 View of the squared entrance to Merlin's Cave, looking north. Image by the author.

Swot analysis for Merlin's Cave

Universal value

Strengths

The site is located on the western slopes of a secluded valley overlooking the River Wye, south of Symonds Yat. Merlin's Cave is within the vicinity of several other prehistoric sites including King Arthur's Cave (List Entry

No. 1010289) and the Little Doward Camp (List Entry No. 1001766). There are also several non-designated heritage assets including historic woodland, later prehistoric field boundaries, several burials and a small number of prehistoric find spots and lithic scatters. Based on the graffiti present, access had until relatively recently been made by determined individuals who had the technical ability to climb a 4m vertical rock-face and navigate a narrow ledge before entering the cave. As a result, the cave remains in a good state of preservation. In terms of damage to the archaeological resource (i.e., the cave floor deposits), much of this occurred during the Hewer and Phillips excavation programmes of the early 20th century and, therefore, does not apply to the current potential Conservation issues of the site.

Weaknesses

The cave has limited access and is approached by a narrow woodland track before negotiating a difficult climb to the cave entrance; gaining access for research purposes is therefore difficult. The cave is frequented by specialists who have little knowledge of the archaeological significance including those dealing with bats and cavers.

Opportunities

Apart from the excavations that were undertaken by Hewer, and Phillips and, more recently, a survey and test-pit programme by Barton (1996), limited research has been undertaken using, up-to-date surveying methods (e.g., 3D point cloud technology and environmental sampling strategies). There is, therefore, an opportunity to enhance and update previous studies that are specific to this cave site. In late 2019, I gained a Section 42 License from Historic England to record and digitally-sample the cave walls using various photogrammetric methods, portable XRF and Raman portable spectrometry. This work was undertaken in June 2020 (avoiding the [UK] bat hibernation season October to April). The data from this programme of work will allow a better understanding of the cave and its early prehistory.

Threats

By releasing scientific information either through conventional publishing or via the internet there is a concern that the more accessible areas of the cave may lend themselves to increased footfall and possible antisocial behaviour.

Contextual value

Strengths

Merlin's Cave stands close to several designated and non-designated heritage assets and is within an Area of Outstanding Natural Beauty.

This cave and nearby King Arthur's Cave, along with numerous other caves along the Great Doward have yielded significant early prehistoric archaeological records (see Barton 1996; Walters 1992). Several excavations occurred at King Arthur's Cave in the late 19th and early 20th centuries. Further investigations at this and other cave sites and rock shelters nearby were undertaken by Barton during the early- to mid-1990s. Merlin's Cave stands within a complex multilayered archaeological landscape that has its origins in the Middle and Upper Palaeolithic.

Weaknesses

The immediate landscape to the south of the cave entrance has been investigated by Herefordshire Council's Archaeology Service (Hoverd 2012). As a result, the area has been cleared of vegetation and the cave entrance is more prominent (however, over time shrubbery and tree saplings will re-colonise the area, thus affording a visual screen that will conceal the cave from the south).[8]

Opportunities

Over its archaeological history, Merlin's Cave has been subjected to limited archaeological investigations (Barton 1996; Hewer 1924, 1925; Phillips 1931). Hewer and Phillips undertook a series of excavations that did not use up-to-date archaeological field methods for that time. However, Barton produced a definitive plan of the cave, along with an assessment of the finds and stratigraphic contexts from the previous excavations. The current fieldwork will focus on the potential for painted and engraved rock art. Incorporated into this project will be a long-term conservation strategy, especially if the rock art is verified as being Late Upper Palaeolithic in date.

Threats

Potential sub-surface archaeological remains could be lost due to limited footfall and long-term erosion on the northern slopes outside the cave.

Archaeological value

Strengths

Merlin's Cave has been investigated four times: by Bate (1901); Hewer (1924, 1925); Phillips (1931) and Barton (1996). Barton produced within his publication a detailed floor plan which supersedes one made by Hewer in 1924. Since the initial excavations made by Hewer, the cave has been thoroughly investigated. In 2006, an exploratory examination revealed the potential presence of painted rock art of LUP date (yet unpublished). The rock art cannot be viewed from outside the entrance of the cave nor can it be seen without the scrutiny of the cave walls.

Weaknesses

Despite difficult access to the cave, determined individuals/groups can enter the monument. The known rock art resource is protected due to its deep location within the cave; however, rock art is considered fragile if direct contact is made.

Opportunities

Due to its access and difficult approach the cave has few visitors. The research aims include a Project Design incorporates an initial three-phased programme of fieldwork including a photogrammetric survey of the cave walls, portable XRF and Raman portable spectrometry programme. The photogrammetric survey will incorporate a desk-based colour algorithm that will assist in establishing whether human agency is involved in the application of haematite onto the eastern wall of the cave. Portable XRF and Raman portable spectrometry will assist in understanding the geochemical make-up of the pigmentation.

Threats

Despite the significance of the site and its immediate landscape, there are several potential threats that include systematic vandalism and footfall.

Public appreciation and realm value

Strengths

Merlin's Cave contains a potentially significant archaeological and historic resource and, given future scientific research will contribute to the understanding of the early prehistoric archaeology of the site and the surrounding landscape. Currently, Historic England administers the site. Concerning public realm and given the sensitivity of the site, the cave site is largely inaccessible; however, nearby King Arthur's Cave has open access, including its large spoil heap which stands immediately south of the cave's entrance. In addition to its archaeological sensitivity, Merlin's Cave is also regarded as an important bat hibernation site and has prohibited access to it between October and April. There is good digital information provided by Historic England[9] and other heritage agencies and society websites including the University of Bristol Speleological Society (UBSS).[10]

Weaknesses

There will always be a potential threat concerning access to this cave by determined individuals/groups who may wish to cause harm to the cave and its archaeological resource.

Opportunities

Determined and responsible visitors can experience the internal architecture of the cave. The cave does offer researchers a unique opportunity to study various aspects using a variety of scientific approaches (see above).

Threats

There are concerns that future attempts to enter the cave could result in acts of vandalism. There is also concern that bat specialists (who have their own research objectives) may inadvertently damage the walls and panels of the main gallery. Note, the haematite-covered cave walls are fragile.

Summary

In this paper, I have shown that a SWOT analysis can provide archaeologists and conservation specialists with an ideal 'thinking process' which can assist in the long-term protection, enhancement and conservation of rock art sites. I am not advocating that a SWOT analysis should be applied to every potential rock art project. What I do promote though is that for those projects where there is the likelihood of long-term conservation issues, planning using a SWOT analysis can provide a systematic way to achieve particular aims and objectives. Once initiated, a SWOT analysis can be amended and updated (this allows dialogue between the various stakeholders). I would further argue (as advocated in this chapter) that a SWOT analysis is also beneficial for those projects that involve multiple stakeholders (landowners, multidisciplinary groups, local, regional and national heritage agencies, and interested societies) and for those sites that are statutory protected such as Cathole Cave and Merlin's Cave. For both sites, I applied a SWOT analysis, initially to construct a long-term strategy for applying an archaeological staged approach to further investigate each site. From the initial SWOT analysis, I instigated the verification process and funding from Cadw to undertake a further programme of archaeological and conservation work at Cathole. For the verification process, I invited the Senior Inspector of Monuments for South Wales, the Principal Curator for Collections & Access to Palaeolithic & Mesolithic Archaeology at the Department of History and Archaeology within the National Museum Wales, three senior academics in Palaeolithic archaeology from the University of Oxford and an Emeritus professor in anthropology from the University of Durham.

Also invited during the verification process were the editor and case officer from the University of Bristol Speleological Society and a Senior lecturer in karst geomorphology from the University of Ulster.

The SWOT analysis for Cathole Cave proved to be a successful way of organising and initiating a project such as this. Using similar criteria for Cathole, I have applied a SWOT analysis for Merlin's Cave; however, for this site I have installed a scientific committee, thus establishing a more democratic and measured approach to understanding the potential Strengths, weaknesses, opportunities and threats; and providing a more holistic view, from project inception to the initiation of a Conservation Management Plan that will offer a measured response to the long-term protection of a rock art site.

Notes

1 As referred to in Department for Communities and Local Government *National Planning Policy Guidance* (National Planning Policy Framework, Chapter 16) 2019 and the Welsh Government's *Planning Policy Wales* (December 2018) [Chapter 6].
2 Published by Garrod (1926).
3 https://www.theguardian.com/travel/2016/dec/15/prehistoric-cave-art-lascaux-dordogne-france-grotto-replica
4 Stonehenge and Avebury World Heritage Site Management Plan (2015)
5 For example, Wildlife and Countryside Act of 1981 (amended) and the National Planning Policy Framework, Chapter 15, Conserving and enhancing the natural environment (February 2019).
6 List Entry Number: 1012448
7 Originally examined by Kennard & Woodward (1924) and Newton (1924)
8 It should be noted that at the time of the Hewer excavations in 1924 and 1925 much of the slopes of the Great Doward were largely cleared of trees.
9 https://historicengland.org.uk/listing/the-list/list-entry/1012448
10 http://caveburial.ubss.org.uk/midlands/merlinscave.htm

References

Barton, R. N. E. (1996) Fourth interim report on the survey and excavations in the Wye Valley, 1996. *Proceedings of the University of Bristol Speleological Society*, 20 (3), pp.263–273.
Bate, D. M. A. (1901) A short account of a bone cave in the Carboniferous Limestone of the Wye Valley. *Geological Magazine*, 8, pp.101–106.
Campbell, J. B. (1977) *The Upper Palaeolithic of Britain. A Study of Man and Nature in the Late Ice Age.* Oxford: Clarendon Press.
Garrod, D. A. E. (1926) *The Upper Palaeolithic Age in Britain.* Oxford: Clarendon Press.
Hewer, T. F. (1924) First report on excavations in the Wye Valley. *Proceedings of the University of Bristol Speleological Society,* 2(2), pp.147–155.
Hewer, T. F. (1925) Second report on excavations in the Wye Valley. *Proceedings of the University of Bristol Speleological Society,* 2(3), pp.216–228.
Hill, T. and Westbrook, R. (1997) SWOT analysis: It's time for a product recall. *Long Range Planning,* 30(1), pp. 46–52.

Hoverd, T. (2012) *Further investigations at Merlin's Cave, Symond's Yat West, Herefordshire.* Herefordshire Archaeology Report No. 299. Herefordshire Archaeology.

Jacobi, R.M. & Higham, T.F.G. (2011). The British earlier upper palaeolithic: Settlement and chronology. In Ashton, N.M., Lewis, S.G. & Stringer, C.B. (Eds.) *The ancient human occupation of Britain.* Volume 14 (Developments in Quaternary Science), 181–222 & 229. Amsterdam: Elsevier Science.

Kennard, A. S. and Woodward, B. B. (1924) Report on the non-marine mollusca of Merlin's Cave. *Proceedings of the University of Bristol Speleological Society,* 2(2), p.162.

McBurney, C. B. M. (1959) Report on the first season's fieldwork on British Upper Palaeolithic cave deposits. *Proceedings of the Prehistoric Society,* 25, pp.260–269.

Nash, G. H. (2012) Brief note on the recent discovery of Upper Palaeolithic rock art at Cathole Cave on the Gower Peninsula, SS 5377 9002. *Archaeology in Wales,* 51, pp.111–114.

Nash, G. H. (2015) Further possible discoveries of engravings within Cathole Cave, Gower, Swansea. *Proceedings of the University of Bristol Speleological Society,* 26(3), pp. 27–39.

Nash, G. H. and Beardsley, A. (2013) A Mapping Survey of Cathole Cave, Gower Peninsula, South Wales. *Proceedings of the University of Bristol Spelaeological Society,* 26(1), pp.73–83.

Nash, G. N., Calsteren, P. van, Thomas, L. and Simms, M. J. (2012) A discovery of possible Upper Palaeolithic parietal art in Cathole Cave, Gower peninsula, South Wales. *Proceedings of the University Bristol Spelaeological Society,* 25(3), pp.327–336.

Novicevic, M., Harvey, M., Autry, C. and Bond, E. (2004) Dual-perspective SWOT: a synthesis of marketing intelligence and planning, *Marketing Intelligence & Planning,* 22(1), pp. 84–94.

Newton, E. T. (1924) Note on birds' bones from Merlin's Cave. *Proceedings of the University of Bristol Speleological Society,* 2(2), pp.159–161.

Phillips, C. W. (1931) Final report on the excavations at Merlin's Cave, Symonds Yat. *Proceedings of the University of Bristol Speleological Society,* 4(1), pp.11–33.

Roberts, S. J. (1887). Cats Hole Cave. Annual report and Transactions of the Swansea. *Scientific Society,* pp. 15–23.

Walker, E. A., Case, D., Ingrem, C., Jones, J. R. and Mourne, R. (2014) Excavations at Cathole Cave, Gower, Swansea. *Proceedings of the University of Bristol Speleological Society,* 26(2), pp.131–169.

Walters, B. (1992) *The Archaeology and History of Ancient Dean and the Wye Valley.* Cheltenham, UK: Thornhill Press Ltd.

7 Rock Art Monitoring in the UK and Ireland

The CARE Toolkit – Going Online and Using Mobile Data

Aron D. Mazel, Myra J. Giesen, Mark Turner and Stephen Dowsland

Introduction

Ever since people started making rock art, it has experienced change brought on by both natural phenomena and human engagement. Indeed, erosional forces were well underway before the rock was selected to be painted, engraved, or carved; however, these phenomena are being intensified, particularly during the last few hundred years with growing population densities and, more recently, accelerated climate change through human activities (e.g., Fernandes 2012; Giesen et al. 2014a).

Threats to UK and Irish open-air rock art are, therefore, not new; for example, almost 20% of panels in Northumberland show signs of historical quarrying (Giesen et al. 2014a: Figure 7.1). Growing population densities and extensive agricultural practices have in recent times intensified the risk to rock art (Barnett and Díaz-Andreu 2005; Sharpe et al. 2008; Giesen et al. 2011, 2014a, 2014b; Mazel et al. 2013; Mazel and Giesen 2019). This is reflected, for example, in rock art panels being driven on; trampled and scratched by livestock; and cleared from fields and then dumped on field edges (Figure 7.2), used as building material, or relocated to be displaced elsewhere, often being lost. These tangible threats are heightened through "warming temperatures, added seasonally variable precipitation, and increased wind speeds in the future, which would encourage the intensification of stone deterioration resulting from enhanced physiochemical weathering" (Mazel and Giesen 2019, pp. 162–163; see also Giesen et al. 2014a, 2014b). Combined, these factors signify increased risk to panels today, suggesting this concern needs to be addressed through multiple strategies sooner rather than later.

In the UK, rock art is legally protected when it is designated as a Scheduled Ancient Monument (SAM), with only a small percentage of rock art being allocated SAM status (Mazel and Giesen 2019). Legislation and policy frameworks were enacted to protect SAMs from deliberate harm or actions that might cause harm and to 'encourage owners and occupiers to maintain their scheduled monuments in good condition so that the remains

DOI: 10.4324/9780429355349-10

Figure 7.1 Historical quarrying at West Lordenshaw 2c in central Northumberland. Photo by Aron Mazel.

survive for future generations' (Historic England 2014, p. 6). Theses conventions do not, however, necessitate landowners/managers/tenants (hereafter, managing stakeholders) to proactively manage the rock art on their land.

The extent of the rock art in the UK and Ireland is not always appreciated. Although it extends back to the Upper Palaeolithic over 10,000 years ago (Bahn and Pettitt 2009; Nash et al. 2012), it would be fair to comment that the vast majority was made during the Neolithic and Early Bronze Age periods dating to around 6,000 and 3,800 years ago. This art is largely curvilinear with intermittent square-shaped designs. The overwhelming number of carvings was made on open-air outcrops and boulders; although, some

Figure 7.2 Whitsunbank 3 in north Northumberland. The original location of this panel is not known. Photo by Aron Mazel.

have been found in ceremonial monuments, burial cairns, and rock shelters (Mazel 2007). Around 7,500 rock art panels are known in the UK and Ireland, located primarily in England (ca. 3,500 panels) and Scotland (ca. 2,500 panels) (Sharpe 2012; Mazel and Giesen 2019).

Acknowledging the threats to UK and Irish rock art, the 'Heritage and Science: Working Together in the Condition Assessment Risk Evaluation (CARE) of Rock Art' project (hereafter CARE project) was established with the primary goal to "co-produce a user-friendly, non-invasive condition assessment risk evaluation toolkit for gathering and organising information essential for the long-term preservation of open-air rock art" (CARE 2012). This included developing a CARE toolkit, which we initially envisioned to include management guidance to enable the monitoring and prioritisation of rock art panels, along with producing user-friendly monitoring reports (and definitions) for use by non-specialists. Complementing these goals, we gathered environmental and rock art data from locations in Northumberland (England), Donegal (Ireland), and Dumfries and Galloway (Scotland) to validate the scientific core of our CARE approach (Giesen et al. forthcoming) and created a "how-to-guide" on management interventions for stakeholders (CARE n.d.-a). A critical issue underpinning the CARE project was the need to establish baseline knowledge about the rock art that combined the complementary assessments of condition and risks to inform proactive custodianship and management. By establishing this baseline dataset, we would then be able to compare future reports against previous ones, allowing us to monitor changes and impacts over time.

The aim of this chapter is to show how the user-friendly CARE toolkit uses online and mobile data to monitor rock art and create a valuable baseline dataset of its condition and risks, with specific reference to the CARE app, which to the best of our knowledge is the first bespoke mobile app developed for rock art monitoring. We begin with an international perspective of rock art monitoring efforts, followed by a chronology of monitoring in Ireland and the UK. Next, we present the route to creating the CARE toolkit and the realisation that some tools were best achieved online or through mobile data options. We finish by discussing some of the challenges regarding the sustainability and use of the app, concluding with some thoughts about the ways forward.

Monitoring, an international perspective

Although the recognition and recording of rock art has a long history – for example, dating back to the late 1,600s in Ireland (O'Kelly 1982) – this is not the case with monitoring. The monitoring of open-air rock art, including shallow rock shelters, was only recognised in the 1970s, in the United States and Australia, as a fundamental mechanism through which open-air rock art should be protected (Sullivan 1973). Particularly, it was observed that it is necessary to identify changes in the art that may require a management response. Loubser (2017, our emphasis) has framed the relationship between management and monitoring as "A reasonable compromise between accepting the status quo versus proactive management is to implement minimal, compatible, repeatable, sustainable, and distinguishable management and conservation actions at rock art sites with *regular monitoring* and an appropriate interpretative context" or that "Regular monitoring does not necessarily imply intervention, but rather assessing signs of deterioration and the need for various degrees of intervention" (Loubser 2001, p. 107).

Despite the recognition of the importance of monitoring as a conservation and management tool, it has generally not received a high level of attention in published academic literature about open-air rock art. Progress has, however, been made on this issue as shown in reviews about monitoring by, for example, Fernandes (2012), Loubser (2001, 2017), and Marshall (2019). Little has been published about the frequencies with which rock art should be monitored; although, it is appreciated that this information is likely to be contained in grey literature and internal documents (e.g., management plans) for rock art places. One exception to this is the uKhahlamba-Drakensberg, in the eastern part of South Africa, where proposed patrolling frequencies were published in the early 1980s (Mazel 1982) and then updated in the late 1990s (Wahl et al. 1998). In this scenario, site ranking, and monitoring frequencies was informed by "the quality and quantity of the art, the presence of archaeological deposits, ease of access to the site, evidence of vandalism, and evidence of modem usage" (Wahl et al. 1998, p. 163). A checklist was provided about what should be monitored, such as evidence of people using the site and interfering with the paintings, signs of burning, and vegetation and animals rubbing up against the paintings. More recently, the Rock Art Stability Index (RASI), "a rapid, quantitative approach to rock art condition assessment" has been developed and applied in the United States but also used more widely, ranging from small islands in the Caribbean to the harsh deserts of the Middle East (Chapters 5 and 15). RASI was "designed for use by college students, volunteers and archaeologists, following a minimum amount of training" (Cerveny et al. 2016, p. 871; see also Wright 2018). RASI includes a range of criteria with the main headings of 'Site setting (geological factors)'; 'Weaknesses of the rock art panel', 'Evidence of large erosion events on and below the panel'; 'Evidence on small erosion events on the panel'; 'Rock coatings on the panel'; 'Highlighting vandalism and other issues'; 'Notations on rock coatings less difficult to identify in the field'; and 'More difficult coatings to identify in the field' (Cerveny et al. 2016, pp. 872–873).

Monitoring in the UK and Ireland, a chronology

Like elsewhere in the world, the development of rock art monitoring in the UK and Ireland is informed by a rich tradition of recording. It is fair to say that sustained rock art monitoring has received little attention in the UK and Ireland, despite funding from UK Research Councils (e.g., Mazel and Ayestaran 2010; Mazel et al. 2013; ScRAP n.d.-a) and Historic England (HE, e.g., Barnett 2010; Darvill 2014) to record and research rock art.

Figure 7.3 provides a timeline of key UK rock art projects that included elements around condition assessment of panels. This is not to say that monitoring is absent in Ireland, however, Twohig and Williams (2014, p. 79) have commented, "condition assessment and risk evaluation investigations need to be undertaken more extensively."

In 1999, English Heritage (EH, now HE) commissioned Rock Art Pilot Project (RAPP), to synthesise existing rock art studies, including summarising methodologies and available data, with the aspiration of setting recommendations for future work. RAPP (Darvill et al. 2000, p. 9) found "very little investigation" had been conducted at or near rock art sites, but when it was done, the methods used were variable including accuracy and completeness of record. While the focus was on examining recording and documentation methods, RAPP commented that "[v]ery little has been done to systematically record rock art in a way that is useful in conservation studies or to monitor change in England." Nevertheless, RAPP (Darvill et al. 2000, p. 122) states the main threats posed to panels are issues of weathering (chemical, physical and biological) and human damage. One of the report's conclusions was that "an urgent need for further work on British rock art

UK ROCK ART PROJECTS with Condition Assessment ROADMAP

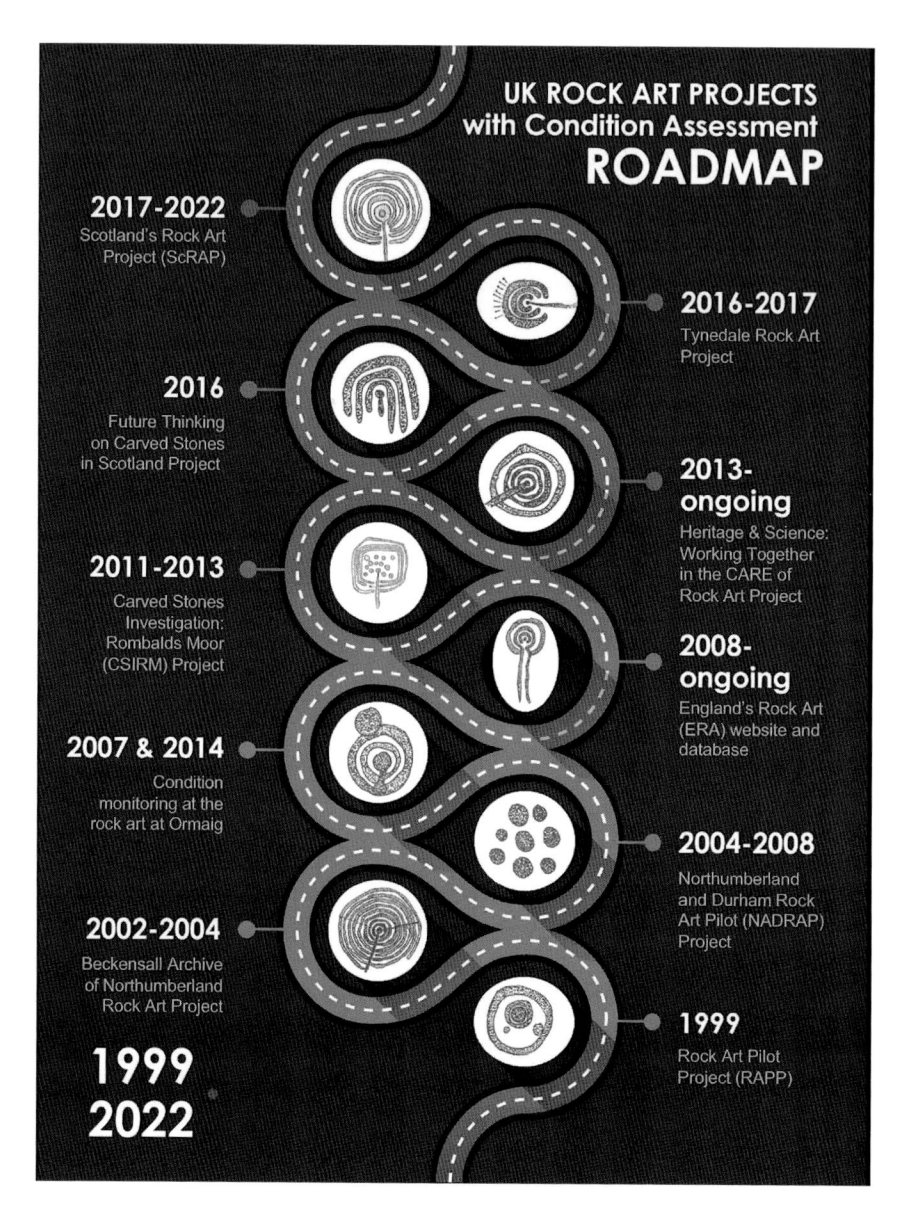

- **2017-2022** — Scotland's Rock Art Project (ScRAP)
- **2016-2017** — Tynedale Rock Art Project
- **2016** — Future Thinking on Carved Stones in Scotland Project
- **2013-ongoing** — Heritage & Science: Working Together in the CARE of Rock Art Project
- **2011-2013** — Carved Stones Investigation: Rombalds Moor (CSIRM) Project
- **2008-ongoing** — England's Rock Art (ERA) website and database
- **2007 & 2014** — Condition monitoring at the rock art at Ormaig
- **2004-2008** — Northumberland and Durham Rock Art Pilot (NADRAP) Project
- **2002-2004** — Beckensall Archive of Northumberland Rock Art Project
- **1999** — Rock Art Pilot Project (RAPP)

1999 – 2022

Figure 7.3 Timeline of major UK rock art projects. Figure by Myra Giesen.

[is needed] as it is under considerable threat and is a relatively understudied and undervalued component of the historic environment (Darvill et al. 2000, p. 10)." The report goes on to say that, "the future conservation of rock art in the [UK] will be the effective monitoring of rock art sites" (Darvill et al. 2000, p. 127).

The Beckensall Archive of Northumberland Rock Art Project (2002–2004) addressed many of RAPP's recommendations (Mazel and Ayestaran 2010). Its primary goal was to create a website to host Beckensall's rock art archive as a basis for future research, educational outreach, and wider public access to rock art. Two of its subsidiary objectives were to (1) improve the understanding around the vulnerability of and threats to rock art, and (2) develop an appreciation for conservation and management requirements. Five hundred and sixty panels were evaluated during fieldwork with the recording of information related to environmental setting, panel surface, panel type, type of motifs, and additional variables related to management and conservation. These data were added to the rich information from Beckensall's records to produce panel specific information on the website, with the expectation that managing stakeholders could use the information to make informed decisions about the protection, presentation, and management of the rock art. The resulting website held information on 1,060 panels supported by 6,000 images. This website is no longer active; however, the information has been incorporated into England's Rock Art (ERA) website and database (ERA n.d.-a), The theme of management was promoted to all website visitors in the audience development plan, with the term "management" being identified as a search term. Mazel and Ayestaran (2010, p. 146) reported that the Management section, along with the Location, Archaeology, and Environment sections of the individual panel reports received a substantial number of visits on the website.

RAPP (Darvill et al. 2000) formed the basis of EH's 'Rock Art Management, Access, Study and Education Strategy', which provided a framework for their future work on rock art (Sharpe et al. 2008). It prompted EH to commission and fund Northumberland and Durham Rock Art Project (NADRAP), which was managed by the Northumberland and Durham County Councils (Sharpe et al. 2008). NADRAP ran from 2004 to 2008, with the goal of developing a recording strategy along with the creation of a larger rock art archive, focusing on Northumberland and Durham in the first instance. Over 1,500 rock art panels were evaluated by NADRAP volunteers, resulting in a national standard for recording rock art. Predictably, this project too reiterated the need for accurate records for conducting research as well as conserving and managing rock art. From this work came the ERA website and database (ERA n.d.-a), which built on and incorporated the Beckensall Archive and the NADRAP data. ERA is successful in providing online information and a popular publication about the challenges of protecting rock art (Sharpe et al. 2008), calling for visitors to treat it with respect, noting the responsibility for its safeguarding lies with each of us. The ERA website has a dedicated section on management and conservation that addresses threats to rock art; protection and presentation measures; the Rock Art Code; information for manager stakeholders; and two case studies (ERA n.d.-b).

In 2007 and again in 2014, the AOC Archaeology Group used high resolution sub-millimetre terrestrial laser scanning to record rock art at Ormaig in

Argyll and Bute, Scotland. The project goal was to establish whether a comparison between datasets collected several years apart would allow stone weathering and erosion to be detected and accurately monitored over time (Ritchie 2016). The research team found significant changes to the site, with moss and lichen growth, caused by the removal of the surrounding conifer plantation that previously had provided a protective canopy. Unfortunately, this resulted in many data voids in the comparative analysis reducing their comparisons to only a few areas. Overall, the changes they detected were obvious to the naked eye, suggesting the specialist kit was not necessary in this instance, but emphasising the need for ongoing repeat visits.

NADRAP

The Carved Stone Investigations: Rombalds Moor Project (CSIRM) Project (2010–2013) in the South Pennines (England) expanded the methodology developed by NADRAP (CSI: Rombalds Moor 2010). It was, however, primarily a recording endeavour, capturing around 500 rock art panels. Importantly, the project results were added to the ERA website and database, providing invaluable benchmark assessments for monitoring change and help to inform on future management. CSIRM in conjunction with the West Yorkshire Archaeology Advisory Service encouraged rock art monitoring through a Rock Art Monitoring form, which includes the following information: name of recorder, their email address, date of report, location, grid reference, panel id, damage (choose from a list), and notes, with a request for supporting images. The form is available as a Word document or can be completed online (watershed\landscape n.d.).

The Heritage and Science: Working Together in the CARE of Rock Art (CARE) project was initiated in 2013 with the explicit aim to create an open-air rock art monitoring tool for its long-term conservation (CARE 2012). Today, this toolkit consists of six elements (a report, report definitions, scorecard, management guidance, a web portal, and an online dataset) to encourage greater public involvement in collection information so managing stakeholders can prioritise rock art panels for management and intervention. See below for an overview of the CARE toolkit.

The Future Thinking on Carved Stones in Scotland (Foster et al. 2016, p. 10) was a collective effort to develop a "more strategic approach to the opportunities and challenges carved stone monuments present," with the outcome of this effort manifesting in a thematic section in the Scottish Archaeology Research Framework. The aim of this part of the framework was to "link, inspire, mobilize and direct the efforts of anyone with an interest in carved stone monuments in Scotland" (Foster et al. 2016, p. 20). It is noted that research into conservation needs of rock art is negligible in Scotland, where information is gained through individual projects, like the abovementioned Ormaig example. Foster et al. (2016, pp. 90–105) discuss protective measured for securing carved stone for the future, which sits nicely with Carved Stones: Scottish Executive Policy and Guidance (Historic Scotland 2005).

As a part of the 2016–2017, Beyond the Wall: Edges Green Project, Tynedale North Of The Wall Archaeology Group (NOWTAG) managed the Tynedale Rock Art Project in Northumberland (Bowyer and Curtis 2017). The project aims included (1) recording rock art using the CARE app; (2) adding to and update data on the ERA database; (3) carrying out photogrammetric imaging and generate rotatable 3D models; and (4) compiling a gazetteer of rock art sites in Tynedale. In total, 43 rock art panels were assessed at Bellshiel Law, Carr Hill, Cleughfoot, Hartleyburn Common, Heavenfield, Howden Hill, Padon Hill, and Wallridge (Bowyer and Curtis 2017).

Starting in 2017, the five-year Scotland's Rock Art Project (ScRAP) is the first major research project focusing on rock art in Scotland. The main aim of the project is "to enhance understanding and awareness of Scotland's prehistoric rock art through community co-production and research" (ScRAP n.d.-a). As a major recording project, previously undocumented panels are being recorded with consistent data gathered, which will establish vital baseline information from which to monitor panels. Additionally, a 'caring for rock art' section on the ScRAP website identifies how individuals can help safeguard rock art, referencing ScRAP Guidance on Risks to Rock Art and a Rock Art Code. Furthermore, they promote the CARE project and support the use of the CARE app in monitoring rock art.

Route to the CARE toolkit

The CARE project and its ground-breaking toolkit have been described in detail elsewhere (Mazel and Giesen 2019). In short, a key project goal was to co-produce a user-friendly, non-invasive condition assessment, risk evaluation toolkit, which gathers and organises information required for long-term conservation of open-air rock art in the UK and Ireland. To achieve this, we built on our original appeal to create a management tool to prioritise ancient stone monuments (Giesen et al. 2011) and the subsequent creation of the Motif Area (MA) method using condition assessment for open-air rock art (Giesen et al. 2014b).

Moving forward, it was important that our approach be grounded through underpinning science, incorporating community input, and integrating risk evaluation into our application. In 2013, we investigated 78 carved panels in 18 different places in England, Scotland, and Ireland through completing paper-based forms to monitor the condition of each panel and took about 180 soil samples and 800 portable X-ray fluorescence readings to investigate weathering and the source rock (Giesen et al. forthcoming). We also gathered information on hazards or risks known to influence the condition of a rock art panel. Additionally, in that year, we held specialist-based advisory board meetings and public consultations via two focus groups, and interviewed seven managing stakeholders with responsibilities for safeguarding rock art.

The outcome of these efforts was the creation of a one-page report supported by accompanying definitions. The report considers 24 data entry categories: four specific to the panel being monitored; three associated with the recorder; five related to the environment around the panel; ten connected to the panel's condition; one related to image captures of the panel; and one open comment field. Concurrently, we sought effective, low-cost mitigation solutions on how to minimise or resolve particular risks to be included in our management guidance (Mazel and Giesen 2019, pp. 175–176).

At this point, the toolkit included a report, report definitions, and a good portion of the guidance complete. When we started contemplating how to approach the remaining tools, it became evident that an online solution was the most appropriate pathway. This seemed especially true for (1) integrating risk data with our existing MA method (Giesen et al. 2014b); (2) prioritising mitigation; (3) disseminating reports and guidance to heritage officials, members of the public, and managing stakeholders; and (4) consolidating and curating results in one place.

As part of this realisation, ADM and MJG began working closely with MT and SD (software engineers) to transform the report and definitions into a mobile app, anticipating that the rapid proliferation of mobile devices in everyday life would help us reach a diverse audience and encourage them to assist in monitoring rock art. Going online also solved the gateway issue for collecting reports; contacting relevant interested parties; and curating reports for making comparisons over time.

The CARE app allows users to gather essential data whilst working offline – as rock art generally is in the countryside with low or no internet connectivity. The app mirrors the paper-based report, including help sections made up from the report definitions. It has built in sensors that aid in the collection of certain types of data, e.g., location is achieved with a Global Positioning System (GPS) sensor, panel slope with an accelerometer, and a visual record using the device's camera. Once the report is complete, the user either can upload it to our web application (i.e., the CARE portal (CARE n.d.-b) immediately if network connectivity exists, or later once it is available.

The web application (CARE portal) is a webserver that acts as a gateway for storing, sending, accessing, mapping, and creating reports (Turner et al. 2018). Reports are sent to the portal from the CARE app. To interact with existing reports or create new ones within the portal, a user must register for an account and have a valid session. As a default, the user can only view reports they have created. Once a report is submitted, it and a scorecard (see below) are emailed to specific heritage officials in Ireland and the UK, with only a few known managing stakeholders included in the notification cycle at this time due to the extensive size of this group together with data protection issues. The portal accepts reports from non-UK and Ireland locations; however, it does not have the capacity to forward notices to relevant authorities within these locations. Nevertheless, individuals can use the portal to produce downloadable scorecards, map their reports, and use it at a local level regardless of their geographic location.

Guidance and some other documentation are available publicly from the portal. The portal has additional functionality if the logged-in user has administration security privileges, as they can edit and delete reports, modify the access rights of other users, and control the mailing list that decides where to send new reports when they arrive on the system. Stakeholder users, such as heritage officials or managing stakeholders, can view and edit reports about rock art in their jurisdiction. Importantly, the portal curates all the reports, creating baseline data required to meet a monitoring paradigm of measuring change over time.

A scorecard tool was created to aid in prioritising interventions. The specific details of the scorecard calculations are detailed in Mazel and Giesen (2019) and, to a lesser extent, in Turner et al. (2018). Using ten of the 24 data entry categories, mentioned above, the app automatically generates a scorecard for a panel. The scores convert information to a traffic light rating system, which informs management decisions. This triage approach indicates when a panel is at serious risk (red), at risk (amber), or not at risk (green); consequently, a red signal indicating immediate intervention is required, while an amber signal raises concern, with the possible need for management intervention. No action is required for a green signal.

The scorecard's overall assessment signal is calculated by weighted values for (1) direct risk (either human or animal impacts on panels) and (2) non-direct risks (current land use, local impact, cracks, potential for standing water, maximum height, surface stability, and motif angle) filtered against motif condition. Direct risks can signal red, amber, or green, while non-direct risks with stage 2 and stage 3 motifs will always signal at risk (amber) or seriously at risk (red). The overall assessment signal (or final mark) results from combining the direct risk and non-direct risks signals, where the signal with the greater risk takes precedence. In other words, green + amber = amber; green + red = red; and amber + red = red.

Following an alpha test of the CARE app and portal by the software team, we asked 12 individuals to beta test it during the month of July 2015. One individual had to withdraw from the testing, so we were left with 11 testers. We received 71 comments during the testing period; many were positive observations requiring no adjustments or actions. Thirteen points were technical in nature and were resolved by the software team, while 17 were related to the online help, requiring some modifications by the CARE team.

In conclusion, the CARE toolkit consists of six elements (a report, report definitions, scorecard, management guidance, a web portal, and an online dataset) to encourage greater public involvement in collection information so managing stakeholders can prioritise rock art panels for management and intervention. The toolkit is accessible online through the CARE portal. The report, report definitions, and guidance are downloadable as hardcopies, however, we recommend using the app that integrates the report and definitions. The CARE portal brings everything together allowing users to see reports and make management decisions.

Promotion of the CARE toolkit

From the outset of the CARE project, we appreciated that it was imperative to promote the toolkit outside the purely academic route of professional peer viewed publications. Therefore, we utilised several popular media outlets to promote the toolkit and monitoring more generally. These included Facebook, press releases, The Conversation and other newsletter articles, targeted emailing, a flyer, and mentions on prominent UK rock art webpages.

Two Newcastle University press releases were issued; one entitled "Ancient rock art at risk, warn experts" (Newcastle University 2013) and the other "Preserving rock art at the touch of a button" (Newcastle University 2017). Both press releases were picked up by a range of news outlets, including the BBC, who responded with articles entitled "Climate change threat to Northumberland rock art" (BBC 2013) and "Northumberland ancient rock art protected by modern app" (BBC 2017) respectively. The latter press release was done in conjunction with an article in The Conversation (Mazel and Giesen 2017a), which by 27 November 2019, had been read by 6,056 people. Two other articles were used to promote the CARE toolkit: one in the online Rock Articles newsletter (Mazel and Giesen 2017b) and the other in the International Newsletter on Rock Art (Mazel and Giesen 2018). The former article was aimed at a UK and Irish audience, while the latter article was for an international audience. The toolkit, but more specifically the app, was included in a regional newspaper article (Henderson 2018) at the request of the CARE team.

In August 2016, we sent personalised emails to a range of UK and Ireland potential rock art stakeholders, including organisations, societies and clubs, which introducing them to the CARE project, and requesting that they or their members download and use the CARE app. Emails were sent to local, regional, and national archaeological, antiquarian and historical societies or groups (n=241); leads for the Young Archaeologist Clubs (n=35); university archaeology student organisations (n=37); CARE stakeholders (n=106); rambler organisations (n=3); and other miscellaneous individuals (n=33). Some emails bounced and several organisations and societies reported that they had sadly disbanded. Unfortunately, we were unable to confirm how this email appeal translated into specific downloads of the app, visits to the portal, or general engagement with the CARE toolkit as a concept.

Additionally, we have given presentations at both professional meetings and local archaeological groups on different aspects of the toolkit. These have ranged from highly technical talks to more general presentations about the need for monitoring and how to use the CARE app as a member of the public.

Another initiative aimed at promoting the CARE toolkit was the creation a flyer (Figure 7.4); 928 of these were distributed to archaeological and antiquarian societies, visitor information centres, and museums in the

Figure 7.4 A5 flyer to promote the CARE app. Flyer created by Eadington Graham.

north of England and Ireland. Moreover, the flyer was published in Rock Articles (Mazel and Giesen 2017b). The app has been highlighted on websites, such as Scotland's Rock Art Project (ScRAP n.d.-b) and the Cumberland and Westmoreland Antiquarian and Archaeological Society (Cumbria Past 2018).

Challenges and lessons learnt

Despite the success of adding the app to the toolkit, it has raised several challenges that merit sharing; and as we reflect on them, their value to future rock art projects and/or monitoring apps is apparent. Here we identify and discuss three key challenges.

The first of these relates to the sustainability of the app. It is well known that versions of apps have limited lives, and, after a matter of time, they will become unusable if not upgraded together with the fact that various platforms will not support previous versions of them. We recently experienced this with the CARE app in relation to the updated version of the android platform, which now only supports those from version 4.4 onwards (October 2013), while previously they had supported from version 2.3 (December 2010). Certain parts of the CARE app were upgraded, and alternatives found for dependencies that have since moved or no longer exist. The updated app was tested, in September 2019, on Android versions 5, 8.1, 9 and 10 (10 being the latest) and appeared to work as expected. The updating of the app was done through the generosity of the software developers (MT and SD), as the project funds have long ended. Such work for future upgrades cannot continue at no cost. It is possible that personal research funds may be used for future upgrades, however, the sustainability of the app based on either ground cannot be guaranteed, requiring further consideration.

In the context of Arts and Humanities Research Council (AHRC) research funded projects in the UK, such as CARE, these do not generally have the option to apply for follow up funding to sustain web related outputs after the completion of the project. This is irrespective of whether the output is a project website or a ground-breaking app, such as the CARE app (released in September 2016), which, as mentioned above, has begun to encounter issues regarding its sustainability. This is not a new or novel issue regarding UK and Irish rock art, as roughly at the same time as the CARE app was being finalised, the Beckensall Archive of Northumberland Rock Art website (Mazel and Ayestaran 2010) was deemed to be a security risk by Newcastle University, as the software had not been updated since its launch in January 2005. Funds were unavailable from within the university to update it, while the AHRC's, 'Follow-on Funding for Impact and Engagement Scheme' states that it "Cannot be used to support resource enhancement activities or to develop or extend an existing website or resource" (AHRC 2019, p. 28).

Faced with this situation, one of the most extensive and successful regional rock art websites internationally (Mazel and Ayestaran 2010) was closed with limited prospects of it being relaunched. Obviating this issue is that NADRAP's ERA website (ERA n.d.-a), drew extensively on the Northumberland data contained within the Beckensall website and, therefore, updated information about the panels is available. There is, however, some data from the initial Beckensall website, including his original descriptions of most of the Northumberland panels, which are not currently available on the ERA website. As already mentioned, the CARE app faces a similar fate, as three years after its launch issues have emerged relating to its ongoing maintenance. To date, this has been managed with the goodwill of the software developers; however, its long-term sustainability remains in jeopardy. Lessons learnt from these experiences are two-fold. Firstly, researchers need to pressurise funding bodies to make greater provision for the maintenance of digital outputs for a reasonable amount of time. Secondly, aligned to the first point, researchers need to include funding in grant applications for the maintenance of digital outputs, although it is unclear whether this will be funded by agencies with the UK and Ireland.

The second challenge is the issue of succession planning with projects that are intended to collect data from the public over an extended time-period. Particularly, as the CARE project is a university-based research council funded project driven by individuals concerned about the protection on UK and Ireland's rock art. What happens to the data generated by projects, such as CARE, when large contributions are made through citizen science? Or, if alternatively, people leading the projects leave their posts and/or are no longer able to work on it? It is unlikely that this situation is unique, emphasising the need for succession planning, especially if the project is lodged in an institution that does not have statutory responsibility for the resource in question. More generally, it needs to be asked whether archaeologists and rock art scholars need to consider what happens to monitoring information generated by citizen scientists to ensure that it is sustained in the long-term. On reflection, it could be suggested that the location of the CARE project might have been better served by embedding the project in relevant statutory heritage organisations, such as HE or Cadw.

The final challenge regards the uptake of the CARE toolkit, more specifically the app tool. As indicated above, a sizeable effort was made to promote the app among stakeholders and communities interested in heritage and archaeology generally and rock art specifically. A measure of this success happened when NOWTAG elected to use the CARE app as part of their 'Beyond the Wall' project, where a "programme of volunteer visits to selected rock art sites in Tynedale to record various aspects of the decorated stones and their contexts" (Bowyer and Curtis 2017, p. 2). As already mentioned, 43 panels were visited as part of this project. Apart from NOWTAG's use of the CARE app, the uptake of the app has been disappointing, with only 71 completed panel reports being uploaded.

This would suggest that the publicity generated for the CARE project and the app was not effective in encouraging people to make use of the app. During the last decade, several UK rock art projects have benefitted immensely from the support of volunteers within a co-ordinated programme (e.g., Barnett 2010; Bowyer and Curtis 2017; CSI: Rombalds Moor 2010). The challenge is to translate the goodwill of these volunteers (and others) into completing the CARE app outside of a formal project, and for them to do it on an individual or shared basis. It is suggested that following the launch of the app, it would have been beneficial to have run workshops or focus groups with archaeology and heritage groups to formally introduce the app to them and to encourage them to monitor rock art using it and to inspire others to do so.

Conclusion and way forward

Despite the identified challenges, we believe that the CARE toolkit is fit for purpose, representing the best available option for user-friendly rock art monitoring that is suitable for use by non-specialists in the UK and Ireland and, with adjustments, elsewhere in the world. As a universal assessment tool, the results are consistent and powerful, allowing informed choices to be made regarding management interventions. To this end, we will continue to actively promote the CARE toolkit; seek funds to cover upgrades into the near future; and workout a succession plan to allow it to continue. Our call to action for the readers of this chapter is to visit the CARE portal and download the app. The CARE app and more generally the CARE toolkit is more likely to reach its potential once individuals active in recording rock art engage with it; thereby, allowing them to endorse it and integrate it into their recording strategies.

Acknowledgements

Our thanks are due to Professor David Graham, Peter Lewis, Dr Patricia Warke for their significant contribution to the CARE project; the members of the Advisory Board (Chris Burgess, John Hughes, Chris Jones, David Manning and Kate Wilson); colleagues who contributed to the fieldwork (Beate Christgen, Rebecca Enlander, David Graham, Peter Lewis, Jen Roberts and Patricia Warke); the manager stakeholders who we interviewed; and, members of the public who participated in the focus groups. We want to acknowledge the motif images used in Figure 3 derive from original line drawings made by Stan Beckensall and scanned during Beckensall Archive of Northumberland Rock Art Project. Additionally, we want to acknowledge Eadington Graham for the design of the flyer represented as Figure 4. Thanks are also due to the AHRC Science and Heritage Research Development Awards for funding the CARE project (AHRC Reference: AH/K006320/1).

References

AHRC (Arts and Humanities Research Council) (2019) *Research funding guide, Version 4.7.* Accessed 4 October 2019. https://ahrc.ukri.org/documents/guides/research-funding-guide1/.

Bahn, P. and Pettitt, P. (2009) *Britain's oldest art: The ice age cave art of Creswell Crags.* London: English Heritage.

Barnett, T. (2010) Putting people in the picture: Community involvement in rock art recording. In Barnett, T. F. and Sharpe, K. E. (Eds.) *Carving a future for British rock art: New approaches to research, management and presentation.* Oxford: Oxbow Books, pp.25–36.

Barnett, T., and Diaz-Andreu, M. (2005) Knowledge capture and transfer in rock art studies: Results of a questionnaire on rock art decay in Britain. *Conservation and Management of Archaeological Sites,* 7, pp.35–48. https://doi.org/10.1179/135050305793137567.

BBC (2013) Climate change threat to Northumberland rock art. *BBC,* 14 March 2013. https://www.bbc.co.uk/news/uk-england-tyne-21789329.

BBC (2017) Northumberland ancient rock art protected by modern app. *BBC,* 25 November 2017. https://www.bbc.co.uk/news/uk-england-tyne-42123939.

Bowyer, P. and Curtis, A. (2017) *Tynedale rock art project, part of the beyond the wall: Edges green project.* Accessed 2 January 2020. http://tynedalearchaeology.org.uk/rockartreport.html.

CARE (2012) *Heritage and science: Working together in the CARE of rock art.* Arts and Humanities Council Science and Heritage Research Development Awards. AHRC Reference: AH/K006320/1.

CARE (n.d.-a) Rock Art CARE management guidance. Accessed 20 December 2019. https://rockartcare.ncl.ac.uk/#!/guidance/.

CARE (n.d.-b) Welcome to the Rock Art CARE Portal! Accessed 20 December 2019. https://rockartcare.ncl.ac.uk/#!/.

Cerveny, N. V., Dorn, R. I., Allen, C. D. and Whitley, D. S. (2016) Advances in rapid condition assessments of rock art sites: Rock Art Stability Index (RASI). *Journal of Archaeological Science: Reports,* 10, pp.871–877. https://doi.org/10.1016/j.jasrep.2016.06.032.

CSI: Rombalds Moor (2010) About. Accessed 29 November 2019. https://csirm.wordpress.com/about-2/.

Cumbria Past (2018) *Activities: Monitoring ancient rock art.* Accessed 20 December 2019. https://cumbriapast.com/cgi-bin/cwaas/cp_main.pl/.

Darvill, T. (2014) Approaches to the conservation and management of open-air rock-art panels in England. In Darvill, T. and Fernandes, A. P. B. (Eds.) *Open-air rock-art conservation and management: State of the art and future perspectives.* New York: Routledge, pp.17–37.

Darvill, T., Eklund, J., Fulton, A., Hentula, H., Kleinitz, C., O'Connor, B., Price, C., Stanley-Price, N. and Ucko, P. (2000) *Rock art pilot project. Main report.* Bournemouth and London: School of Conservation Sciences Bournemouth University and Institute of Archaeology University College London for English Heritage. Limited-circulation printed report. Accessed 2 January 2020. http://eprints.bournemouth.ac.uk/9602/.

ERA (English Rock Art) (n.d.-a) Welcome. Accessed 20 December 2019. https://archaeologydataservice.ac.uk/era/.

ERA (n.d.-b) Managing rock art. Accessed 20 December 2019. https://archaeologydataservice.ac.uk/era/section/record_manage/rm_manage_home.jsf/.

Fernandes, A. P. B. (2012) *Natural processes in the degradation of open-air rock-art sites: an urgency intervention scale to inform conservation.* PhD Dissertation, Bournemouth, UK: Bournemouth University.

Foster, S., Forsyth, K., Buckham, S. and Jeffrey, S. (2016) *Future thinking on carved stones in Scotland.* Accessed 8 July 2019. http://eprints.gla.ac.uk/129968/1/129968.pdf/.

Giesen, M. J., Mazel, A. D., Graham, D. W. and Warke, P. A. (2011) Care and management of ancient stone monuments during environmental change. *International Journal of Heritage and Sustainable Development,* 1(1), pp.60–71. http://ijhsd.greenlines-institute.org/volumes/2011/IJHSD_2011_V01_01_Giesen_60_71.pdf

Giesen, M. J., Mazel, A. D., Graham, D. W. and Warke, P. A. (2014a) The Preservation and care of rock-art in changing environments: A view from Northeastern England, United Kingdom. In Darvill, T. and Fernandes, A. P. B. (Eds.) *Open-Air Rock-Art Conservation and Management: State of the Art and Future Perspectives,* New York: Routledge, pp.38–52.

Giesen, M. J., Mazel, A. D., Warke, P. A., Lewis, P. And Graham, D. W. (Forthcoming) Caring for open-air rock art in the UK and Ireland: integrating environmental and management parameters.

Giesen, M. J., Ung, A., Warke, P. A., Christgen, B., Mazel, A. D. and Graham, D. W. (2014b) Condition assessment and preservation of open-air rock art panels during environmental change. *Journal of Cultural Heritage,* 15(1), pp.49–56. https://doi.org/10.1016/j.culher.2013.01.013.

Henderson, T. (2018) Mysteries carved in stone. *The Journal,* 15 August 2018, p. 8.

Historic England (2014) *Scheduled monuments: A guide for owners and occupiers.* Historic England. https://historicengland.org.uk/images-books/publications/scheduled-monuments-guide-for-ownersand-occupiers/guideforownersofscheduledmonuments/.

Historic Scotland (2005) *Carved stones: Scottish executive policy and guidance.* Edinburgh: Historic Scotland. http://www.carvedstones.scot/uploads/4/4/0/3/44032535/_carved-stones-scottish-executive-policy.pdf

Loubser, J. (2001) Management planning for conservation. In Whitley, D. (Ed.) *Handbook of Rock Art Research.* Walnut Creek: Altamira, pp.80–115.

Loubser, J. (2017) The conservation and management of rock art: An integrated approach. In David, B. and McNiven, I. J. (Eds.) *The Oxford handbook of the archaeology and anthropology of rock art,* Oxford: Oxford University Press, pp.993–1020.

Marshall, M. R. (2019) Rock art conservation and management: 21st century perspectives from Northern Australia. PhD dissertation. The Australian National University.

Mazel, A. D. (1982) Principles for conserving the archaeological resources of the Natal Drakensberg. *South African Archaeological Bulletin,* 37, pp.7–15. DOI: 10.2307/3888576

Mazel, A. D. (2007) On the fells and beyond: Exploring aspects of Northumberland rock-art. In Mazel, A. D., Nash, G. and Waddington, C. (Eds.) *Art as metaphor: The prehistoric rock-art of Britain.* Oxford: Archaeopress, pp.231–256.

Mazel, A. D. and Ayestaran, H. (2010) Visiting Northumberland rock art virtually: The Beckensall archive analysed. In Barnett, T. F. and Sharpe, K. E. (Eds.) *Carving a future for British rock art: New approaches to research, management and presentation.* Oxford: Oxbow Books, pp.140–150.

Mazel, A. D. and Giesen, M. J. (2017a) What Neolithic rock art can tell us about the way our ancestors lived 6,000 years ago? *The Conversation*. 20 December 2017. https://theconversation.com/what-neolithic-rock-art-can-tell-us-about-the-way-our-ancestors-lived-6-000-years-ago-84865.

Mazel, A. and Giesen, M. (2017b) Safeguarding rock art: Using a mobile app to get the job done. *Rock Articles,* 18, p.9. https://www.scribd.com/document/362396560/Rockarticles-18.

Mazel, A. D. and Giesen, M. J. (2018) Mobile app developed to support the protection of UK and Irish rock art. *International Newsletter on Rock Art,* 82, pp.22–25.

Mazel, A. D. and Giesen, M. J. (2019) Engagement and management: Developing a monitoring system for open-air rock art in the UK and Ireland. *Conservation and Management of Archaeological Sites,* 21(3), pp.160–183. https://doi.org/10.1080/13505033.2019.1662228.

Mazel, A. D., Graham, D., Giesen, M., Lewis, P. and Warke, P. (2013) A responsibility of CARE: Heritage and science in the service of safeguarding threatened ancient rock art. In Cassar, M. and Williams, D. (Eds.) *Sustaining the impact of UK science and heritage research: Contributions to the AHRC/EPSRC science and heritage programme conference.* AHRC/EPSRC Science and Heritage Programme, pp.46–47. http://issuu.com/heritagescience/docs/sustaining_the_impact_of_uk_science/13?e=6573787/5553610.

Nash, G. H., Simms, M. J., Thomas, L. and van Calsteren, P. (2012) A discovery of possible Upper Palaeolithic parietal art in Cathole Cave, Gower Peninsula, south Wales. *Proceedings of the University of Bristol Spelaeological Society,* 25(3), pp.327–336.

Newcastle University (2013) Ancient rock art at risk, warn experts. *Newcastle University Press Release,* 13 November 2013. https://www.ncl.ac.uk/press/articles/archive/2013/03/ancientrockartatriskwarnexperts.html/.

Newcastle University (2017) Preserving rock art at the touch of a button. *Newcastle University Press Release,* 23 November 2017. https://www.ncl.ac.uk/press/articles/archive/2017/11/rockartapp/.

O'Kelly, M. J. (1982) *Newgrange: Archaeology, art and legend.* London: Thames and Hudson.

Ritchie, M. (2016) Case Study 37 Condition monitoring at the rock art at Ormaig. In Foster, S., Forsyth, K., Buckham, S. and Jeffrey, S. (Eds) *Future thinking on carved stones in Scotland,* https://www.scottishheritagehub.com/content/case-study-condition-monitoring-rock-art-ormaig.

ScRAP (Scotland's Rock Art Project) (n.d.-a) About the Project. Accessed 20 December 2019. https://www.rockart.scot/index.cfm/about-us/about-the-project/.

ScRAP (n.d.-b) Caring for Rock Art. Accessed 19 December 2019. https://www.rockart.scot/about-rock-art/caring-for-rock-art/.

Sharpe, K. (2012) Reading between the grooves. Regional variations in the style and deployment of 'cup and ring' marked stones across Britain and Ireland. In Cochrane, A. and Jones, A. M. (Eds.) *Visualising the neolithic (neolithic studies group seminar papers).* Oxford: Oxbow Books, pp.47–63.

Sharpe, K., Barnett, T. and Rushton, S. (2008) *The prehistoric rock art of England: Recording, managing and enjoying our carved heritage.* English Heritage, Northumberland County Council and Durham County Council. https://archaeologydataservice.ac.uk/catalogue/era-836/dissemination/pdf/ERA_Brochure.pdf

Stone Heritage Research Alliance, LLC. (n.d.) Rock Art Stability Index (RASI). Accessed 20 December 2019. https://www.shralliance.com/rasi/.

Sullivan, S. (1973) *Report of a tour of the United States, to study management and protection procedures for prehistoric and historic sites. June–September, 1973*. Sydney: National Park and Wildlife Service of New South Wales.

Turner, M., Dowsland, S., Mazel, A. and Giesen, M. (2018) Rock art CARE: A cross-platform mobile application for crowdsourcing heritage conservation data for the safeguarding of open-air rock art. *Journal of Cultural Heritage Management and Sustainable Development,* 8(4), pp.420–433, https://doi.org/10.1108/JCHMSD-09-2017-0064.

Twohig, E. S. and Williams, K. (2014) Irish open-air rock-art: Issues of erosion and management. In Darvill, T. and Fernandes, A. P. B. (Eds.) *Open-air rock-art conservation and management: state of the art and future perspectives.* New York: Routledge, pp.70–81.

Wahl, E. J., Mazel, A. D. and Roberts, S. E. (1998) Participation and education: Developing a cultural resource plan for the Natal Drakensberg Park, KwaZulu-Natal, South Africa. *Natal Museum Journal of Humanities*, 10, pp.151–170.

Watershed\Landscape (n.d.) Rock art monitoring. Accessed 20 December 2019. https://www.watershedlandscape.co.uk/heritage-landscape/rock-art-monitoring/.

Wright, A. M. (2018) Assessing the stability and sustainability of rock art sites: Insight from Southwestern Arizona. *Journal of Archaeological Method and Theory,* 25, pp.911–952. https://doi.org/10.1007/s10816-017-9363-x.

8 Rock Art and Geographical Information Technologies

SIPAAR and the Integral Management of Petroglyphs in Galicia

Emilio Abad Vidal and
Jose Manuel Rey García

Introduction

Galicia, a region on the north-west Atlantic coast of the Iberian Peninsula, contains one of the most important collections of open-air rock art in Europe. Although the first publications on this phenomenon date back to the end of the 19th century, and although there is a consolidated research tradition, we are still far from achieving a detailed knowledge on determinant issues, such as its irregular distribution throughout the region of Galicia, the identification of local styles or variants, the associations between figures, or the total number of carvings. This does not mean that these questions have not been of interest to researchers. Rather, they have been studied from a limited and reductionist perspective, either because of an excessive generalization, or reduced territorial scope. Only recently have these questions been approached from a different perspective, in which the scope of analysis extends to the entire Galician territory also resorting to the incorporation of GIS tools in information management, and statistical methods for data processing (Vázquez Rozas 2006; Vázquez Martínez et al. 2016; Rodríguez Rellán et al. 2018).

From the pioneering work of Sobrino Buhigas in the preparation of his famous Corpus (1935), perhaps the first catalogue of Galician petroglyphs, to the present day, the number of rock surfaces with carvings known in Galicia has increased exponentially. The last count (Rodríguez Rellán et al. 2018) puts the number at 3,374 sites, also offering a current overview of the situation, albeit not significantly different from what other researchers have suggested over the last few decades (Peña Santos and Vázquez Varela 1979; Peña Santos and Rey García 2001; Fábregas Valcarce 2010). In essence, that we are dealing with geometric motifs, with the highest concentration in the province of Pontevedra, especially in the central valley of the River Lérez (Campo Lameiro and Cotobade), and in the territories bordering the most southerly Galician estuaries. However, this study has brought a series of evidence to light that has so far only been approached from a local

DOI: 10.4324/9780429355349-11

perspective. Large numbers of newly discovered engraved rocks in areas where not much rock art was known previously, especially in Baixo Miño (Martínez Soto et al. 2017) or in Barbanza (Fábregas Valcarce et al. 2012) is one of the most evident, meaning that areas initially considered peripheral or of minor interest have now achieved greater notoriety (Rodríguez Rellán et al. 2008, p. 115). Another factor is the increasingly frequent observation of the existence of regional variations, which are manifested in the absence or presence of different motifs, in a special way of outlining the figures, and in the reiteration of gestures that give the composition a stereotyped character. This can be most clearly seen in the Baixo Miño region and its extension to the other side of the Portuguese border, as the number of complex hunting scenes found has multiplied in recent years in which, frequently, human figures and horsemen on horseback catching other equine species are identified, helped by dogs that are chasing the animal, and certain types of geometric designs that are usually considered to be traps (Vázquez Martínez et al. 2016).

However, despite these improvements in the understanding of the rock art phenomenon, the chronological debate regarding this artistic tradition remains open, and although a significant number of researchers coincide in situating it within a time span that runs from the Late Neolithic through to

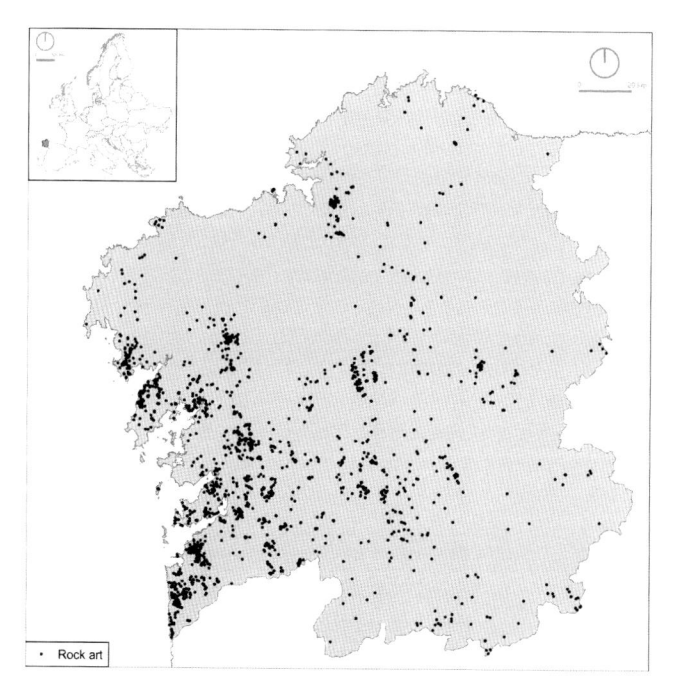

Figure 8.1 Distribution of petroglyphs in the region of Galicia, NW Spain. Map by the authors.

later moments of the Bronze Age (Peña Santos and Rey García 2001; Fábregas Valcarce and Rodríguez Rellán 2012), other authors persist in ascribing it to the Iron Age (Santos Estévez 2013).

Currently, the main source of information for studying Galician petroglyphs from a merely numerical and territorial perspective is the Inventory of Archaeological Sites of the General Directorate of Cultural Heritage (IASGDCH) of the Regional Government of Galicia. This inventory is being carried out, at a certainly unequal pace, since responsibilities in the field of culture were transferred from the central government in the mid-1980s. Admittedly, the work is still unfinished, and its current state is far from ideal. In spite unquestionable value, a series of hurdles limit its real value, mainly the existence of notable differences in the quality of carried out work. In addition to the participation in field surveys of professionals with different degrees of familiarity with rock art, this is largely related to the difficult legibility of the figures, the lack of uniform criteria for documenting motifs, their support, and context, and the past absence of now widespread tools, such as Global Positioning System (GPS) and online access to aerial photos, and thematic maps. In practice, these limitations have resulted in the existence of vague and imprecise descriptions for many of the petroglyphs included in the inventory, the difficulty in establishing today correlations and concordances between petroglyphs documented in the past, and the uncertainty surrounding the approximate number of existing petroglyphs, probably greater than the currently estimated number.

The rock art archaeological park and the integrated management of information

Despite the new data regarding the spatial distribution of Galician petroglyphs, even today, the territories intersected by the central valley of the River Lérez, coinciding to a large extent with the municipalities of Campo Lameiro and Cerdedo-Cotobade, still contain the largest number of carved rocks, the greatest diversity of figures, and some of the largest and most complex compositions. The singularity of this collection of petroglyphs made possible that a large part of the studies on Galician petroglyphs concentrated here between the end of the 19th and the beginning of the 20th century. It also allows us to understand why the first projects aimed at restoring areas with petroglyphs for public enjoyment were carried out in this area. The slow process of recovering rock art for social purposes culminated with the opening in 2011 of the Rock Art Archaeological Park in Campo Lameiro (PAAR), an ambitious cultural facility created with the aim of providing a public service, with the intention of becoming a reference centre for the integrated management of Galician rock art, advocating a balance between conservation, research, and dissemination (Rey García et al. 2004). Throughout its creation and during its still short life, the PAAR generated a great deal of expert knowledge and accumulated a large volume of archaeological information, in very different media, which called for the development of a tool that would allow for its efficient and multipurpose management. The answer was Rock Art Archaeological Park Information System (SIPAAR), an Spatial Data Infrastructure (SDI) that integrates a wide range of resources to store, manage, and disseminate the large amount of documentation available.

In recent years, the use of georeferenced information management tools has become common, namely in cultural heritage studies and archaeology in particular (Fraguas et al. 2010; Parcero-Oubiña et al. 2013; Fernández Freire et al. 2014), although its application to rock art is still punctual and limited. However, some examples are known, such as the Rock Engravings on the Web initiative, led by the Soprintendenza per i Beni Archeologici della Lombardia (Poggiani Keller et al. 2009) or, regarding rock art conservation (Fernandes 2013). In comparison to these tools, SDIs represent an important leap forward, as technological solutions that are based on and take advantage of the Internet, allowing for globalized intercommunication and interoperability between systems that handle geographical information. As a result, the power of spatial data infrastructures is not their ability to access or store data in our PCs, but instead their interoperability and the possibility of linking different geographic information services releasing us from the need to accumulate and maintain both data and processes in our own systems. At the same time, they allow us to access different types of thematic information and spatial data through Open Geospatial Consortium (OGC) services (Catalogue Service for the Web, Web Map Service, Web Feature Service, Web Coverage Service), provided by the Open Geospatial Consortium,[1] an international non-profit organization committed to generating open and interoperable standards for the global geospatial community. For this reason, one of the cross-cutting concepts of heritage SDI development is knowledge transfer.

The emphasis on interoperability and standardization in the exchange of data has its raison d'être in the European Union's Infrastructure for Spatial Information in Europe (INSPIRE) Directive, proposed with the aim of making geographic information available in a standard, quality format accessible via the Internet.[2] Therefore, structuring the information about the graphic rock art register on the basis of the criteria established by INSPIRE has provided the conceptual support necessary to design a project for the collection, storage, analysis, and presentation of relevant information about Galician petroglyphs, and for the geospatial and rock art-related data to be accessible by means of various types of clients, either lightweight web browsers or viewers, or by means of more heavyweight clients such as the different Geographic Information Systems (GIS) that support OGC standards.

A multi-layered architecture for SIPAAR

SIPAAR was designed based on geographic information standards and Esri's Geodatabase format,[3] with the information organized at three different levels: the data storage layer, which brings together information of geospatial nature stored in a database; the web services layer, which meets the protocols and information access standards for data interoperability; and the web interface layer (geographical viewer) for end users. This structure can be recognized in other similar works (Fraguas et al. 2010) that are technologically implemented through service-oriented architectures that aim to optimize resources, based on criteria of simplicity, efficiency, scalability and availability.

Integration of archaeological information

In order to integrate the results derived from the different studies previously carried out at PAAR in a spatial GIS-managed database, it was necessary to compile them in a common repository and develop the necessary tools for their edition and use. In order to satisfy this objective, several interrelated actions were designed:

- Definition of a data model that would permit the integration of existing information, considering location and their administrative and identifying information, based on official codes.
- Adaptation of the different existing inventories to a defined data model that integrated and summarized available heterogeneous information.
- Conversion of digital cartographic formats to GIS format.
- Integration of heritage elements within a GIS project that allows to produce thematic cartographies at different scales, as well as of other official layers, such as land use, aerial photographs or digital terrain models, which facilitates multipurpose analysis.

As a result, the process of integrating the information on rock art from the Archaeological Park and its surrounding area was based on the different cataloguing procedures carried out to date, which obeyed different criteria and objectives and which, consequently, resulted in dissimilar results. Specifically, we had to go through seven different past instances of data gathering carried out by several teams of archaeologists, framed by the IASGDCH. The disparity between these studies is considerable, such as the number of rocks documented by the different teams, their location or the computer formats and projection systems used. This diversity of situations highlighted the need to dedicate considerable efforts to the systematization and unification of the different existing sources, and to ensure that the incorporation of new elements documented in future work was done in a more precise and efficient way.

Two layers of information were created in order to standardize data. The first layer stores the individual aspects of all the rocks identified in the different versions available, represented by the point geometry as the basic unit. This allows access to the complete set of rocks and to select the most precise locations one by one. The identification process also made possible to ungroup rocks that were assembled under the same code, which involved creating new identification codes that make it easier to recognize each individual case. This selection process also unified data on each rock while documenting the original source that was used, meaning that in the future this information can be corrected and reinterpreted in later evaluations.

The second data layer records the contour of each individualized rock using polygon geometry. The degree of precision depends on the source, whose details are stored as attributes of the layer. When carrying out work in the future, the delimitation of the contour of the rock is preferable, since in addition to providing information on the geometry of the support, it helps to locate it in the field, something that in a region like Galicia is often difficult, due to the large amount of plant cover and the horizontality of most panels.

Structure of the database

The SIPAAR container is based on a relational database that stores each of the rocks with carvings and their spatial information. Its structure is based on a set of tables in which each stored element has a unique key that allows it to be uniquely identified within the overall structure. There are three types of tables:

- Main tables. These collect individualized and descriptive data from different elements such as rock art sites, carved rocks, photographs, text documents, etc. The relationships between the objects are made through the combination of primary elements and external elements, making it possible to solve these relationships on a one-to-one or one-to-many basis. Their combination allows us to solve questions such as the name of a particular rock, or which rocks belong to a given site.
- Secondary tables. These group together the existing relationships between the different elements of the various types. By using these tables, we can know which documents are related to a rock, such as photographs or texts, but also which rocks have been referred to in a publication.
- Domain tables or value lists. These store possible values of a given field in the main and secondary tables. Some of these tables store the different figures represented on the rocks, administrative codes, or chronological ascriptions. They are therefore lists of ordered and coded values, making it possible to have control over particular attributes.

The general structure of the database is organized around the Rocks table, which individually details all engraved surfaces. Attributes allow identification, main name and description, geographical coordinates, and source documentation. In turn, the 'Stations' table groups the rocks into sets that are near to each other and form a clear aggrupation of petroglyphs.

The different motifs or individualized figures on each of the rocks are included in the 'Motifs' table, making possible to evaluate their greater or lesser presence, analyse spatial distribution at a local or regional level, or link them with the landscape in which they are located. In addition, the table structure also documents the associations and superimpositions between different types of figures, which opens new possibilities in readability, interpretation, and ascertaining relative chronology to each other. All motifs are individualized using a list of values in which the figures documented to date are collected in the iconographic repertoire of the rock art of the Archaeological Park and its immediate surroundings. This is a list that can be modified and enlarged as a result of the appearance of new sites, something that is bound to happen, especially if its application is extended to the rest of Galicia.

With the aim of being able to organize the wide variety of cases, the list has been organized into three descriptive levels, resulting in the creation of a code with a fixed length of eight characters. The first level identifies the basic recognizable motifs, such as circles, zoomorphs, or weapons. In a second level, the variations observed for each of the above motifs are included. If we use the zoomorphs as an example, this level would include the different animals that have been identified, such as cervids, bovids or equids. Finally, the third level incorporates particularities derived from their morphological structure, or the interpretations that can be suggested. Continuing with the previous example, this could be a deer with branched antlers. Therefore, the code of this specific figure would be 09.02.01, where 09 are the digits that identify the zoomorphs, 09.02 the cervids, and the complete code indicating the type of antler representation.

The 'Documents' tables make it possible to interconnect the existing documentation for each rock, such as photographs, tracings, or reports, as well as the metadata for each of them. 'Location' incorporates the set of tables that facilitate the spatial referencing of rocks, such as their delimitation in the form of polygons, administrative references or those relating to ownership. Finally, 'Support and Conservation' bring together the information that makes it possible to characterize the substrate on which the figures were carved and determine their state of conservation. All this description is made from controlled lists of variables that give uniformity to the data set.

Forms for producing and editing data

The creation of a repository that includes the rock art within a given area requires the integration of a large volume of data. Hence, the management of this information must be carried out efficiently and optimally by controlling the processes of data generation and editing. Several methods are used to organize the information within the database. So, for each rock, an initial form is produced that provides access to general information, such as name and site, identifying codes, geographical coordinates and administrative identifiers, description, existing figures, and chrono-cultural affiliation.

By using a second form we can access the documentation of the motifs represented on each of the rocks, identifying the number of existing figures, or their associations and superimpositions. Finally, a form was created that allows each rock to be associated with the existing documentation, such as photographs, drawings, text documents, etc. This selection will filter the different

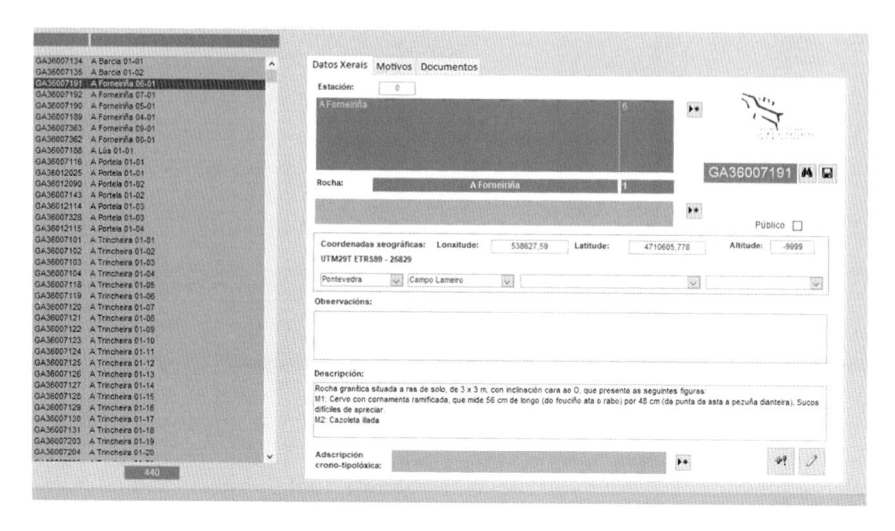

168 Emilio Abad Vidal and Jose Manuel Rey García

Figure 8.2 Interface of the SIPAAR management application. Screen capture of the SIPAAR interface created by the authors.

types of file formats in a file explorer, which allows choosing the document to be linked, storing in the database the paths that contain the files, as well as other relevant information, such as the author, date, or annotations.

Forms also perform quality control of the stored data, so that the integrity of the information is automatically controlled, performing the tasks of adding, removing or updating the data through the creation of triggers, which are activated when any of the above actions are carried out.

In addition, functions have been included within the information management system presenting standardized records for the presentation of data for one or more rocks. This task is performed automatically through predesigned templates that are activated when requested by the user. In this way, the process of converting tabular data into query-oriented Portable Document Format (PDF) documents is carried out simply and quickly.

Petroglyphs: markers in the social landscape

Although the SIPAAR implementation process has not been completed, its use has led to a more efficient management of the enormous flow of information generated in the area now occupied by the Archaeological Park and, at the same time, allows us to suggest some basic ideas regarding the characterization of petroglyphs and their relationship with the social landscape of which they are part.

In recent decades, Galicia has undergone a marked improvement in the understanding of land occupation strategies during Late Prehistory. Generally, settlements from the period tend to be linked to wetlands in which reserves of fresh grass were produced for livestock during the summer, and over which light and well-drained soils formed, capable of supporting hoe-based agriculture that was compatible with used light ploughs (Méndez Fernández 1994, p. 86). These areas would have had intermittent human occupation, spanning several millennia, often starting in the Neolithic and reaching the Bronze Age. These spaces of preferential use are often delimited by petroglyphs, which would have served as territorial markers, as the most conspicuous elements of the landscape appropriation strategy of past human groups (Peña Santos and Rey García 1993, 2001; Méndez Fernández and Rey García 2005; Fábregas Valcarce 2010).

The basic characteristics of this model can be recognized in the PAAR area and its immediate surroundings. This space is configured as a small convex ridge that stretches in a north-south direction, delimited by small river courses to the north and west. It covers an area of approximately 143 hectares and is characterized by a gentle, undulating relief of granite ridges and small basins in which sedimentary deposits accumulate (Costa and Martínez 2013). In recent years, the PAAR has been the focus of several surveys and inventories of rock art, as well as intense archaeological and paleo-environmental research, which allowed the precise characterization of the evolution and transformation of this area over the last 10,000 years (Criado et al. 2013).

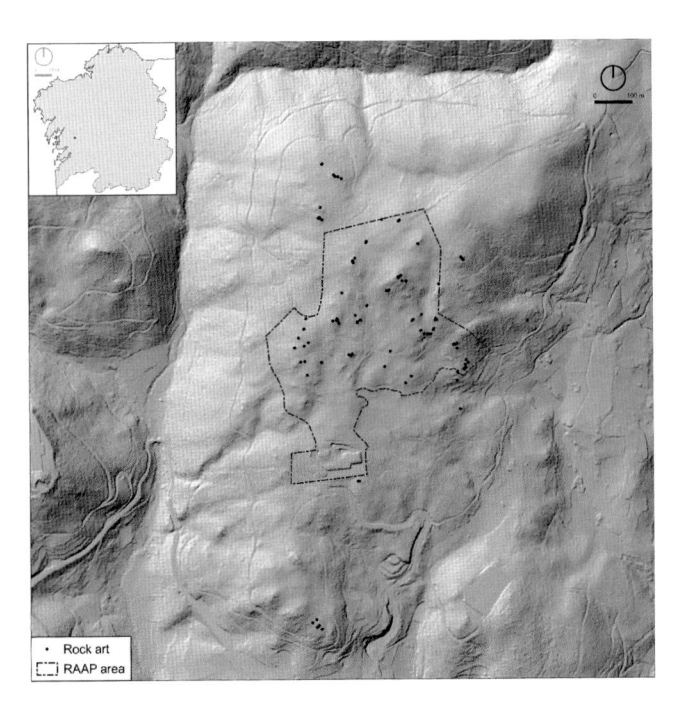

Figure 8.3 Location of the petroglyphs in the Rock Art Archaeological Park and its immediate surroundings. Map by the authors.

Within this territory, 103 rocks have been identified so far, with engravings containing more than a thousand different figures, which are quite representative of the petroglyphs of Galicia. The vast majority can be ascribed to different moments of Late Prehistory, although others provide a more recent chronology which, in some cases, dates back to modern or contemporary times, such as crosses, letters, and numbers. Unlike the situation in other European areas with rock art, such as the Alpine region, superposition of figures is infrequent, and the panels seem to have been composed gradually from the successive addition of carvings, from the centre to the outer edge of the rocks, without the 'story' appearing to be altered as new figures are incorporated. This makes it considerably more difficult to study and establish a precise chronological sequence.

The analysis of its spatial distribution helps in a better understanding of the patterns followed by prehistoric communities in selecting locations to make rock art. An initial observation suggests that the engraved rocks are not found on steep slopes that delimit the ridge to the north and west and that, on the contrary, the highest concentrations of petroglyphs are found in the central sector. Within this area, the carvings are arranged mainly within a limited altimetric range between 320 and 240 metres above sea level, with the figures engraved on the granite crests surrounding the basins in which the sedimentary deposits are confined. On the lower platform giving access to this central sector, several signs of intense construction activity have been identified, at least during the IV-III millennia cal BC (Bonilla Rodríguez and César Vila 2013; Méndez Fernández and López Alonso 2013), in the form of differently sized pits, ditches, post holes, and even a silo, which may well have been built by the authors of the petroglyphs.

In the area of the PAAR, motifs are arranged in a monotonous and repetitive manner, leaving little room for surprise. The typical elements of the Atlantic tradition – cupmarks – and simple or concentric circles – are the most frequent. But unlike the situation in other Atlantic rock art groups, the stock of images available to the artists was relatively large and not limited to geometric designs. In this sense, there is also a considerable presence of animal figures in the sample. Adult male deer and horses are easily recognizable, but many other quadrupeds lack distinctive anatomical features, making it difficult to identify them, although they may well be young specimens or females of different deer sub-species. In a relevant example, around 20 of these animals are associated with several anthropomorphs and a large sword. The considerable presence of simple or multiple lines should be considered with caution, bearing in mind that they most certainly correspond to the remains of partially lost figures, which today we are unable to fully identify.

The variability in the organization of the panels with carved figures is extraordinarily high, ranging from very simple panels, made up of a small grouping of cupmarks or a simple circle with an inner cupmark carved on a small rock, to large, highly complex panels containing dozens of geometric designs, often complemented by figurative motifs. In this sense, most of the petroglyphs could be considered as non-complex accumulations, as they include fewer than ten figures and a limited variety of themes. On the contrary, apart from a boundary petroglyph (Ferro Couselo 1952) containing around 20 cruciforms, only four panels exceed this number of figures in a very particular manner. Laxe da Forneiriña 1.R1, Outeiro dos Cogoludos 1.R1, Coto da Chan da Isca and, above all, Laxe dos Carballos account for just over 40% of the total number of individualized figures. These are rocks that stand out for their large size and for the accumulation of a wide variety of motifs, making them especially relevant. Furthermore, their location seems to reveal a marked centrality in the social landscape. The presence of other smaller rock art carvings in the vicinity, their connection to the areas that concentrate the main evidence of human occupation throughout the different moments of Recent Prehistory, would seem to underline the significance of these petroglyphs in the appropriation of the landscape by these human groups.

From risk management to dissemination

A tool such as SIPAAR, which incorporates georeferenced archaeological information obtained at different times and integrates it with other thematic maps and digital terrain models, facilitates the efficient management of risks that threaten the conservation of rock art, makes it possible to monitor it over time, and makes it accessible to users for different purposes.

In this sense, in addition to being a tool for improving the management of the extraordinary volume of information available, one of the main advantages of SIPAAR is that it can be configured as a preventive tool. As it contains the geolocalized inventory of rock carvings and other data of a spatial nature, it is possible to draw up risk maps and areas of special vulnerability for this type of heritage asset, which often appears on small stone supports that are difficult to perceive in the landscape. In this respect, it is likely that a wide range of possibilities will be open in the future with the development of algorithms that can automatically audit existing vulnerability and impact reports that allow us to anticipate possible risks to rock carvings, and even to the cultural landscapes that contain them.

By including these vulnerable areas in the different land use planning instruments, it is possible for them to be considered in projects that have a potential capacity to alter the territory and to introduce, where appropriate, corrective measures to mitigate these impacts. In addition, the interoperable nature of geoservices makes it possible for any agent to evaluate, prior to the planning of an activity, its possible effects on rock carvings and their landscape, thereby avoiding damage arising from possible unawareness of their existence or location errors. This is especially relevant for forestry work as it often leads to very aggressive practices with the subsoil or rocky outcrops, especially those related to preparing the ground by deep subsoiling or processing the offcuts, tasks that are carried out with heavy machinery that can cause irreversible damage to the supports with carvings and their possible archaeological context.

Access to this type of data is also vital for the agents intervening in emergency situations arising from forest fire extinction (Rey García 2019). It should be noted in this regard that in Galicia there are a large number of forest fires every year and that fire consumes thousands of hectares of forest that seriously compromise the preservation of rock art. In all likelihood, climate change will worsen this problem, as demonstrated by the increased number of wildfires, which have already become responsible for the most serious environmental catastrophes in Galicia. Including the geospatial data contained in SIPAAR in an emergency and risk management plan for areas with high concentrations of rock art would ensure a better response to the effects derived from waves of forest fires and, at the same time, would make it possible to minimize the damage resulting from fires, extinguishing tasks, or even subsequent restoration work.

Conclusion

Thanks to its multipurpose nature, SIPAAR is also a tool capable of satisfying other needs. Beyond its essentially archaeological use, the information can also be oriented towards conservation, including a diagnosis of the alteration agents and factors identified in each of the rocks. As SIPAAR contains records made in different years, it is possible to monitor their state, recognize the extent of each of the alterations, observe their evolution over time, and facilitate decision-making processes when intervening to ensure their preservation.

Finally, the tool also facilitates the dissemination of contents for information purposes. As it gathers all the documentation related to the rock carvings in the Rock Art Archaeological Park and its immediate surroundings, it is a resource that provides access to a diverse list of contents, such as distribution maps, descriptions, images, or tracings of the carvings. Although it is intended to be the management tool for the Park, a considerable amount of this information will be openly accessible to the public.

Notes

1 http://www.opengeospatial.org/
2 INSPIRE (Infrastructure for Spatial Information in Europe): http://inspire.jrc.ec.europa.eu. INSPIRE Directive 2007/2/EC https://eur-lex.europa.eu/legal-content/EN/TXT/PDF/?uri=CELEX:32007L0002&from=EN
3 Despite the fact that this software was used for organisational purposes, SIPAAR is prepared to easily migrate to Open Source software.

References

Bonilla Rodríguez, A. and César Vila, M. (2013) Excavación de un posible yacimiento relacionado con los petroglifos en la zona de Chan das Pozas. Campaña de 2005. In Criado Boado, F., Martínez Cortizas, A. and García Quintela, M. V. (Eds.) *Petroglifos, paleoambiente y paisaje. Estudios interdisciplinares del arte rupestre de Campo Lameiro (Pontevedra)*. TAPA 42. Madrid: Consejo Superior de Investigaciones Científicas, pp.124–129.

Costa Casais, M. and Martínez Cortizas, A. (2013) Dinámica geomorfológica del área de estudio y su relevancia en la transformación del paisaje. In Criado Boado, F., Martínez Cortizas, A. and García Quintela, M. V. (Eds.) *Petroglifos, paleoambiente y paisaje. Estudios interdisciplinares del arte rupestre de Campo Lameiro (Pontevedra)*. TAPA 42. Madrid: Consejo Superior de Investigaciones Científicas, pp.65–80.

Criado Boado, F.; Martínez Cortizas, A. and García Quintela, M. V. (Eds.) (2013) *Petroglifos, paleoambiente y paisaje. Estudios interdisciplinares del arte rupestre de Campo Lameiro (Pontevedra)*. TAPA 42. Santiago de Compostela: Consejo Superior de Investigaciones Científicas.

Fábregas Valcarce, R. (2010) *Los petroglifos y su contexto: un ejemplo de la Galicia meridional*. Vigo: Instituto de Estudios Vigueses.

Fábregas Valcarce, R. and Rodríguez Rellán, C. (Eds.) (2012) *A Arte Rupestre no Norte do Barbanza*. Santiago de Compostela: Andavira.

Fernandes, A. P. B. (2013) GIS use in open-air rock art conservation: The case of the Côa Valley, Portugal. In Contreras, F., Farjas, M. and Melero, F. J. (Eds.) *CAA2010. Fusion of cultures. Proceedings of the 38th annual conference on computer applications and quantitative methods in archaeology*. Oxford: Archaeopress, pp.209–212.

Fernández Freire, C., Parcero-Oubiña, C. and Uriarte González, A. (Eds.) (2014) *A data model for cultural heritage within INSPIRE*. CAPA 35. Santiago de Compostela: Instituto de Ciencias del Patrimonio (Inicipit).

Ferro Couselo, J. (1952) *Los petroglifos de término y las insculturas rupestres de Galicia*. Ourense: Museo Arqueológico.

Fraguas, A., Menchero, A., Uriarte, A., Vicente, J., Consuegra, S., Díaz-del-Río, P., Castañeda, N., Criado, C., Capdevila, E. and Capote, M. (2010) Infraestructuras de datos espaciales y datos de excavación arqueológica: Sílex, la IDE de la mina neolítica de sílex de Casa Montero (Madrid). *Cuadernos de Prehistoria y Arqueología de la Universidad de Granada*, 20, pp.65–95.

Martínez Soto, E., Verde Andrés, C., Álvarez, X., Centelles García, B., Manso de la Torre, X., Vilar Pedreira, X. L. and Ledo Bernárdez, M. (2017) O Proxecto Equus: un novo paradigma nas escenas de caza da arte rupestre galega e do norte de Portugal. *Revista de EstudosMiñoráns*, 16–17, pp.23–75.

Méndez Fernández, F. (1994) La domesticación del paisaje durante la edad del bronce gallego. *Trabajos de Prehistoria*, 51(1), pp.79–94

Méndez Fernández, F. and López Alonso, F. (2013) Excavación del yacimiento de Chan das Pozas, Campaña de 2008. In Criado Boado, F., Martínez Cortizas, A. and García Quintela, M. V. (Eds.) *Petroglifos, paleoambiente y paisaje. Estudios interdisciplinares del arte rupestre de Campo Lameiro (Pontevedra)*. TAPA 42. Madrid: Consejo Superior de Investigaciones Científicas, pp.130–137.

Méndez Fernández, F. and Rey García, J. M. (2005) De conxuntosmateriais a poboados: patróns de asentamento en O Morrazo durante a Prehistoria Recente. In Criado, F. and Cabrejas, E. (Coord.) *Obras Públicas e Patrimonio: estudo arqueolóxico do corredos do Morrazo.* TAPA, 35. Santiago de Compostela: Instituto de Estudos Galegos Padre Sarmiento, pp.95–105.

Parcero-Oubiña, C., Fábrega-Álvarez, P., Vicent-García, J. M., Uriarte-González, A., Fraguas-Bravo, A., del-Bosque-González, I., Fernández-Freire, C. and Pérez-Asensio, E.(2013) Conceptual basis for a cultural heritage data model for INSPIRE. *Revue Internationale de Géomatique*, 23(3–4), pp.445–467.

Peña Santos, A. de la and Rey García, J. M. (1993) El espacio de la representación. El arte rupestre galaico desde una perspectiva territorial. *Pontevedra. Revista de Estudios Provinciais*, 10, pp.11–50

Peña Santos, A. de la and Rey García, J. M. (2001) *Petroglifos de Galicia.* Oleiros/A Coruña: Vía Láctea Editorial.

Peña Santos, A. de la and Vázquez Varela, J. M. (1979) *Los petroglifos gallegos. Grabados rupestres prehistóricos al aire libre en Galicia.* Sada/A Coruña. Cuadernos del Seminarios de Estudios Cerámicos de Sargadelos, 30.

Poggiani Keller, R., Liborio, C. and Ruggiero, M. G. (2009) Valle Camonica (Italy). The rock art database by the ministry of cultural heritage and activities-Soprintendenza for Archaeological Heritage of Lombardía: From IR project to IRWEB. In Poggiani-Keller, R., Dimitradis, G., Coimbra, F., Liborio, C. and Ruggiero, M. G. (Eds.) *Rock Art database. New methods and guidelines in archiving and cataloguing.* BAR International Series 1996. Oxford: Archaeopress, pp.13–24.

Rey García, J. M. (2019) Paisaje, petroglifos e incendios forestales: hacia una gestión preventiva de los paisajes rupestres. *Proceedings of Congreso Internacional Patrimonio Cultural y catástrofes: Lorca como referencia,* Lorca, Spain 2018. Madrid: Ministerio de Cultura y Deporte, pp.345–351.

Rey García, J. M., Infante Roura, F., Rodríguez Puentes, E. and Tallón Nieto, Mª. J. (2004) *El Parque Arqueológico del Arte Rupestre. Ideas, estrategias y acciones para una gestión integral de los petroglifos gallegos.* RGPA Cuadernos, 3. Santiago de Compostela: Xunta de Galicia.

Rodríguez Rellán, C., Vázquez Martínez, A. and Fábregas Valcarce, R. (2018) Cifras e imágenes: una aproximación cuantitativa a los petroglifos gallegos. *Trabajos de Prehistoria*, 75(1), pp.109–127.

Santos Estévez, M. (2013) Una propuesta de periodización para el arte rupestre atlántico. In Criado-Boado, F., Martínez-Cortizas, A. and García Quintela, M. V. (Eds.) *Petroglifos, paleoambiente y paisaje. Estudios interdisciplinares del arte rupestre de Campo Lameiro (Pontevedra).* TAPA, 42. Santiago de Compostela: Instituto de Estudos Galegos Padre Sarmiento, pp.283–289.

Sobrino Buhigas, R. (1935) *Corpus Petroglyphorum Gallaeciae.* Santiago de Compostela: Edicións do Seminario d'Estudos Galegos.

Vázquez Rozas, R. (2006) Aproximación estadística a los petroglifos gallegos. *Minius*, 14, pp.349–364.

Vázquez Martínez, A., FábregasValcarce, R. and Rodríguez Rellán, C. (2016) Going by the numbers: A quantitative approach to Galician prehistoric petroglyphs. In Fábregas Valcarce, R. and Rodríguez Rellán, C. (Eds.) *Public images, private readings. Multi-perspective approaches to the Post-Palaeolithic Rock art. Proceedings of the XVII UISPP world congress,* Burgos Spain 2014. Oxford: Archaeopress Archaeology, pp.63–69.

Section III
Scientific Examination and Interventions at Open-Air Rock Art Sites

9 Laser Cleaning vs. Chemical Cleaning for Removal of Lichen from Schist Surfaces in the Coa Valley (Portugal) and Siega Verde (Spain) Archaeological Sites

Graciela Paz-Bermúdez, Beatriz Prieto and José Santiago Pozo-Antonio

Introduction

Lichens are some of the most frequent colonizers of stone surfaces in archaeological sites. In rock art sites, the presence of lichen colonies may obscure motifs and carvings and may also lead to biodeterioration processes which can damage rock art imagery (De los Ríos et al. 2004; Piervittori et al. 2004; Seaward et al. 2001). It is therefore argued that the removal of lichens should be contemplated.

The choice of removal method must be made carefully, as (1) lichens are expected to recolonize the surfaces if the original causes of colonization are not halted and preventive conservation measures are not carried out (Lisci et al. 2003; Nimis 2001) and (2) the cleaning procedure itself may alter the stone and enhance its bioreceptivity (Sanmartín et al. 2019).

Different methods can be used to remove colonization from stone monuments (Pozo-Antonio et al. 2016c). Application of biocides followed by mechanical removal is one of the most common cleaning techniques used in prehistoric rock art in different archaeological sites worldwide (Tratebas 2004; Tretiach at al. 2007). However, the use of biocides has decreased in recent years because of the potential risks to human health and to the environment (Tratebas 2004). Moreover, mechanical removal may induce the removal of minerals and the appearance of fissures, thus increasing deterioration of the surface (Pozo-Antonio et al. 2016a–c). Hence, new methods such as thermal shock (Tretiach et al. 2012) and laser cleaning (Pozo-Antonio et al. 2016c; Speranza et al. 2013) have recently been used to remove lichens from stone surfaces in different monuments.

Laser-based treatments were first used to clean stones in cultural heritage monuments in 1972 (Asmus et al. 1972), specifically to remove incrustations

DOI: 10.4324/9780429355349-13

from Venetian marble. Since then, there has been a gradual increase in research focused on the optimization of lasers to maximize cleaning while minimizing damage to forming minerals (Barreiro et al. 2020). This type of treatment is considered eco-friendly as it reduces the hazards to conservators, visitors and the environment (Tratebas 2004). It also minimizes the risk of physical damage to the stone as it only uses radiant energy and does not involve the use of abrasive particles or chemicals (Gemeda et al. 2018).

The Coa Valley (Guarda, NE Portugal) and Siega Verde (Salamanca, NW Spain) Archaeological Parks (Figure 9.1a) are home to some of the most remarkable open-air prehistoric rock art in Western Europe (Baptista 2009). Although these archaeological sites are located in different countries and are separated by a distance of around 80 km, they are located within the same geographical region. Both are included in the World Heritage Site World Heritage List and comprise hundreds of panels with Upper Palaeolithic rock art, engraved in the faces of joints in differently graded schists and greywackes in the Coa Valley and Siega Verde (Fernandes et al. 2017). Lichen colonization on granite rock art panels, only existing in the Portuguese site (Fernandes 2014), was not considered for the purposes of the present study.

Removal of lichens from some engraved panels from Siega Verde and the Coa was first done when the archaeological areas were created, in the 1990s. Great care was taken not to damage the treated surfaces during the cleaning procedure, which usually involved careful washing with water and soft brush (Cristina Escudero, pers. comm.; Fernandes 2007). Writing on the situation more than a decade after these interventions Fernandes (2007) stated that removal of lichens in the Coa site might be repeated in the future, but only after meticulous analysis of the benefits and harms of such action in each specific outcrop.

The present study was conducted in three stages in order to establish the best method for removing lichens at both sites:

- Two different laser systems, i.e. a Q-switched Neodymium-doped Yttrium Aluminium Garnet (Nd:YAG) and an Erbium-doped Yttrium Aluminum Garnet (Er:YAG) operated at wavelengths in the infrared region (1,064 and 2,940 nm respectively), were applied to samples collected from the Coa valley (Canada do Inferno site) to determine which laser performed best.
- Samples cleaned with the most effective laser treatment (the Nd:YAG or the Er:YAG) were compared with those cleaned with either a commercial biocide or distilled water.
- A bioreceptivity study was applied to the cleaned surfaces (with laser, biocide or water) to determine the duration of the cleaning results.

Here, we consider the results of these case studies in relation to the type of material treated, method of application, and the outcome regarding the optimization of lichen removal.

Materials and methods

Samples

One sample block (ca. 30cm × 30cm × 20cm) was obtained from schist outcrops (with no rock art) colonized by lichens in each archaeological site (Figure 9.1a); both blocks were profusely covered with crustose and foliose lichens. The blocks were cut into five samples of approximate dimensions 6cm × 6cm × 6cm with at least one face colonized. Uncolonized samples with the natural weathering patina were also obtained in from each site, again from panels with no rock art (Figure 9.1b and c).

Petrographic characterization of the schist samples collected at both sites has previously been reported (Sanmartín et al. 2019). The mineralogical composition is summarized in Table 9.1.

Macroscopically, depending on the site, the schists showed differences in terms of colour and texture. In the Coa site, the stone is brown and schistosity planes are sub-perpendicular to surfaces (Figure 9.1b), while in Siega Verde, the tone is green-bluish, and the schistosity planes are parallel to the surfaces (Figure 9.1c).

Samples were colonized by lichen species corresponding to a typical community found on these rock surfaces (Marques et al. 2014; Paz-Bermúdez et al. 2018), dominated by crustose taxa, mainly *Caloplaca pellodella* (Nyl.) Hasse, *Candelariella vitellina* (Hoffm.) Müll. Arg., *Circinaria hoffmanniana* (S. Ekman & Froberg ex R. Sant.) A. Nordin (Figure 9.1d), *Diploschistes actinostomus* (Ach.) Zahlbr, *Lecidea fuscoatra* (L.) Ach., and some foliose species, such as *Parmelina tiliacea* (Hoffm.) Ach., *Xanthoparmelia conspersa* (Ehrh.) Hale (Figure 9.1e) and *X. pulla* (Ach.) O. Blanco, A. Crespo, Elix, D. Hawksw. & Lumbsch. One of the crustose lichen species most commonly found in both sites is *Circinaria hoffmanniana*. The thallus is areolate, light brown and pruinose (Figure 9.1d); it is composed by angular, flat and smooth areolas, of diameter less than 1 mm, with distinct light greyish green edges.

Cleaning methods

Two different lasers operated at wavelengths in the infrared region were compared in order to select the best performing type. The aim was to

Table 9.1 Mineralogical composition (%) of the samples (Sanmartín et al. 2019)

Minerals	Coa	Siega Verde
Quartz	53%	60%
Biotite	7%	10%
Muscovite-sericite	22%	21%
Chlorites	17%	8%

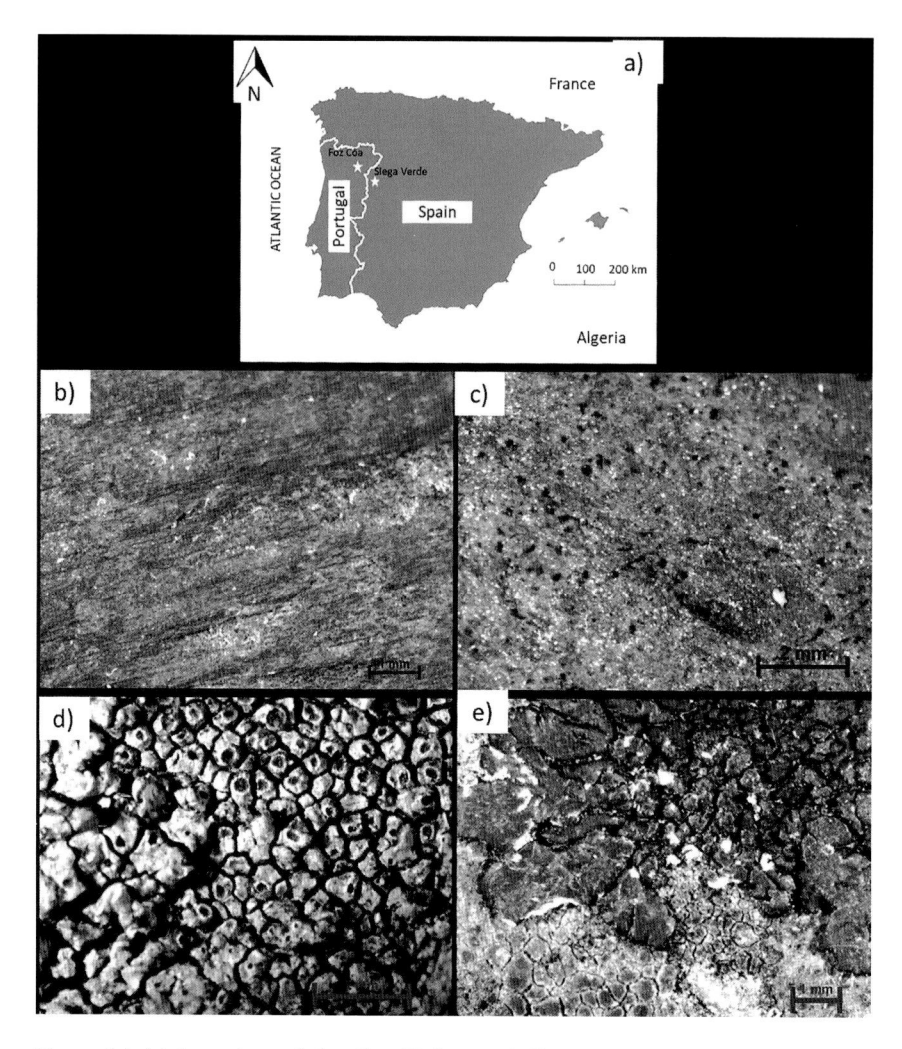

Figure 9.1 (a) Location of the Coa Valley and Siega Verde archaeological areas; (b) and (c) Uncolonized schists from Coa and Siega Verde, respectively; (d) and (e) two common lichen species in both archaeological sites, *Circinaria hoffmanniana* (d), a species with a crustose thallus and the foliose lichen *Xanthoparmelia pulla* (e). Photographs by the authors.

remove the greatest amount of lichen while causing minimum damage to the substrates in a single scan. With this aim, both lasers were applied to Coa samples colonized by *Circinaria hoffmanniana* because this common crustose lichen adhered strongly to the substrate. The characteristics of the laser systems are summarized as follows:

- Q-switched Nd:YAG laser (Quanta Ray, INDI), operated at a wavelength of 1,064 nm with a pulse duration of 6 ns at a constant repetition

rate of 10 Hz. The beam was focused at normal incidence by a spherical plane-convex lens with a focal length of 250 mm. Fluences applied ranged from 1 J.cm^{-2} to 25 J.cm^{-2}. This laser can also be operated at 266 nm (ultraviolet radiation).
- Er:YAG laser (emission wavelength: 2,940 nm), with a pulse duration of 250 μs applied at a constant repetition rate of 10 Hz. Fluences between 1 J.cm^{-2} and 10 J.cm^{-2} were applied.

Preliminary cleaning tests were evaluated by stereomicroscopy (SMZ800 NIKON®). The most satisfactory cleaning was yielded by fluences of 25 J.cm^{-2} for the Nd:YAG and 10 J.cm^{-2} for the Er:YAG.

Once the best laser system for removing *Circinaria hoffmanniana* from the Coa samples was established, this system was applied to samples colonized by lichen communities affecting stones in both sites. The system was compared with chemical cleaning with a commercial biocide, specifically Biotin T® at 3% (v/v in distilled water) supplied by CTS (Italy). Biotin T is commonly used to clean phototrophs from stones (Sanmartín et al. 2011). It is based on N-Octyl Isothiazolinone and quaternary ammonium salt (cationic surfactant). After application by brushing on the surface of the 6cm × 6cm × 6cm sample from each site, the samples were covered by black plastic for three hours to prevent evaporation of the product. The surfaces were then rinsed with distilled water and brushed vigorously for three minutes. The surfaces were then neutralized with a solution of 50% ethanol (v/v in distilled water), used to prevent chemical contamination by chloride salts.

The areas cleaned with laser and Biotin T were also compared with those cleaned by brushing with distilled water for three minutes. Cleaning with Biotin T and water was repeated after 24 hours.

Evaluation of cleaning performance

The Coa samples in which *Circinaria hoffmanniana* was removed with the Nd:YAG and the Er:YAG laser treatments were examined by stereomicroscopy (SMZ800 NIKON®), to detect any lichen remains and surface damage. Scanning Electron Microscope (SEM) in secondary electron and Backscattered Electron modes with Energy Dispersive X-Ray (EDX) spectroscopy (Philips XL30 equipment) was used to detect lichen remains and any damage to the schist forming minerals. C-coated samples of the cleaned surfaces were visualized under an accelerating potential of 15–20 kV, with a working distance of 9–11 mm and a specimen current of approximately 60 mA.

After selection of the best-performing laser, the samples cleaned by that laser and those cleaned with the biocide and distilled water were examined to determine the cleaning efficacy and bioreceptivity. The cleaning efficacy was assessed by stereomicroscopy (SMZ800 NIKON®) and colour spectrophotometry. The colour of the samples was characterized in Commission Internationale de l'Eclairage (CIELAB) and Commission Internationale de l'Eclairage Cylindrical Model (CIELCH) colour spaces (CIE S014-4/E,

182 *Graciela Paz-Bermúdez et al.*

2007) by means of a Minolta CM-700d spectrophotometer. The L* coordinate represents the lightness, ranging from 0 (black) to 100 (white), and the a* and b* coordinates express the colour wheel, with values ranging from +60 (red) to −60 (green) for a* and from +60* (yellow) to −60* (blue) for b*. The chroma or colour saturation (C^*_{ab}), which expresses the relative strength of a colour, was also computed, as $C^*_{ab} = [(a^*)^2+(b^*)^2]^{1/2}$, along with the hue (tone), as $h_{ab} = \tan [1 - (a^*/b^*)]$. The measurements were made by excluding the specular component with a spot diameter of 8 mm, illuminant D65 and an observation angle of 10°. Twenty colour measurements were made at random in each area to yield statistically representative results (Prieto et al. 2010b).

Considering the colour measurements of the uncolonized surfaces as the reference values (Figure 9.1b and c), the colour differences after cleaning were computed as follows:

$$\Delta L^* = L^*_2 - L^*_1;$$
$$\Delta a^* = a^*_2 - a^*_1;$$
$$\Delta b^* = b^*_2 - b^*_1;$$
$$\Delta C^*ab = C^*_{ab,2} - C^*_{ab,1}$$
$$\Delta h = h^*_2 - h^*_1;$$

where the subscript 2 denotes the colour parameter of a cleaned area and the subscript 1 denotes the colour parameter of the uncolonized surface.

The global colour change (ΔE^*_{ab}) was computed as follows:

$$\Delta E^*_{ab} = [(\Delta L^*)^2 + (\Delta a^*)^2 + (\Delta b^*)^2]^{1/2}$$

It is therefore expected that a lower ΔE^*_{ab} will indicate more effective removal of biological colonization because the colour of the cleaned surface will be similar to that of the uncolonized schist.

Bioreceptivity study

After evaluation of the cleaning efficacy of the different methods, samples were inoculated with a phototrophic multispecies culture (described in Vázquez-Nion et al. 2016). To promote biofilm development (Vázquez-Nion et al. 2017), the sample blocks were held in an INCUDIGIT incubator for 6 weeks (42 days) at a temperature of between 22°C and 27°C, relative humidity of 95% and with 12 h light (~25 μmol photon m^{-2} s^{-1})/12 h darkness cycles. Biofilm development was monitored for 42 days by the non-destructive colour measurement and Pulse Amplitude Modulated fluorometry techniques (Vázquez-Nion et al. 2018a; 2018b). Finally, the Bioreceptivity Index (BI) was calculated for each sample following the method proposed by Vázquez-Nion et al. (2018a).

Results and discussion

Considering the colonized surfaces of the Coa samples cleaned with the laser treatments (Figure 9.2), the sample cleaned with Nd:YAG (Figure 9.2a) showed white fungal remains, specifically from the medulla of the lichen, as the upper cortex and the algal layer were totally removed. The surface cleaned with Er:YAG (Figure 9.2b) showed organic tissues with a darker coloration (Figure 9.2b), and the different layers of the lichen structure were completely indistinguishable.

SEM analysis revealed the presence of organic matter on the surfaces (Figure 9.2c and d) as reported in previous studies involving other laser systems (wavelength, pulse duration and fluence), lichens and stone types (Rivas et al. 2018; Sanz et al. 2017; Speranza et al. 2013).

Regarding damage caused to the substrate, SEM observation revealed that, despite a considerably higher fluence, the Nd:YAG laser caused less intense morphological changes (Figure 9.2c) than the Er:YAG laser, which induced intense melting of the biotite grains (Figure 9.2d).

The best results were obtained with Nd:YAG, and this laser was therefore selected for treating the stones (from both sites) colonized by the most common lichen species. As this laser can also be operated using Ultraviolet

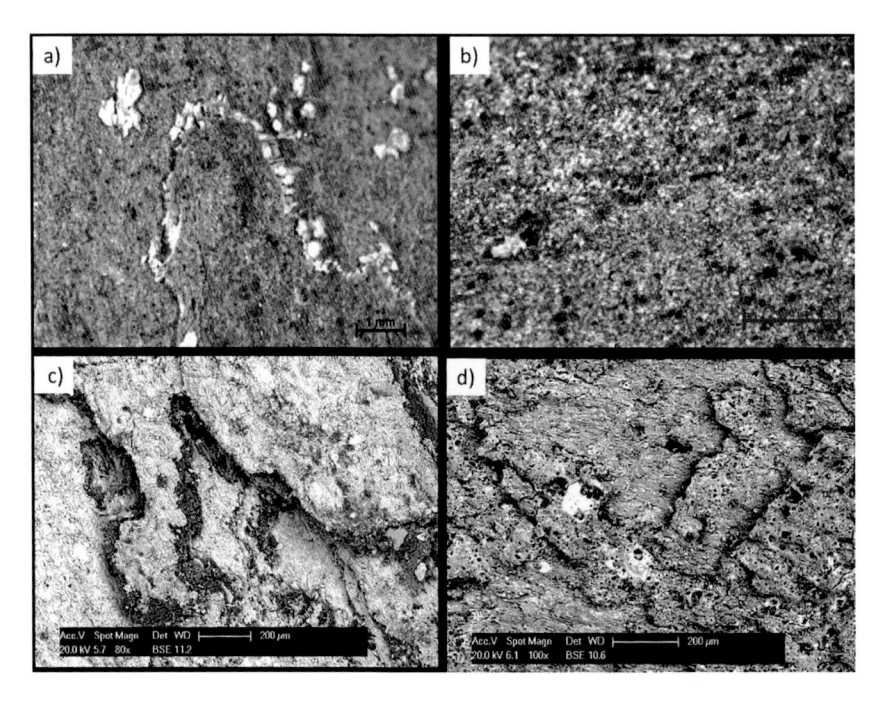

Figure 9.2 Micrographs of the Coa samples colonized by *Circinaria hoffmanniana* cleaned with a Nd:YAG laser operated at 1,064 nm (a, c) and a Er:YAG laser operated at 2,940 nm (b, d). (a) and (b) are stereoscopic images, and (c) and (d) are SEM micrographs. Photographs by the authors.

(UV) radiation (266 nm), this wavelength was used for comparative purposes. Considering the results of preliminary cleaning trials, Infrared Radiation (IR) was applied at a fluence of 25 $J.cm^{-2}$ to the Coa sample and a fluence of 23 $J.cm^{-2}$ to the Siega Verde sample. For samples from both locations, UV irradiation was conducted at a wavelength of 0.66 $J.cm^{-2}$.

Stereomicroscopic analysis (Figure 9.3) enabled identification of lichen remains on the treated surfaces. Removal of the colonization was more efficient at the 1,064 nm wavelength (Figure 9.3a and e) than at the 266 nm (Figure 9.3b and f). On the 266 nm-cleaned surfaces, remains of the entire lichens (including the upper cortex) were detected on the surfaces. Thus, although the lichens underwent morphological and physiological changes (colour changes and decrease in the maximum quantum yield), they were not detached from the substrate.

On the samples irradiated at 1,064 nm (Figure 9.3a and e), the level of removal was higher in the Coa sample than in the Siega Verde sample (Figure 9.3e), because green algal remains were detected on the latter. Considering the effects of the laser, the surfaces irradiated at 1,064 nm (Figure 9.3a and e) were slightly paler than the reference surfaces (Figure 9.1b and d).

Considering the chemical cleaning with Biotin T, better results were obtained for the Siega Verde sample, because the lichen thalli were almost completely removed (Figure 9.3g). However, some lichen thallus remains (medulla) were detected on the Coa sample cleaned with Biotin T (Figure 9.3c).

The water-based cleaning produced different results considering the provenance of the blocks (Figure 9.3d and h). The method performed best with the Siega Verde sample (Figure 9.3h), as the surface of the Coa sample (Figure 9.3d) had lichen remains covered by earth originating from the fractures associated with the schistosity planes of the stone. During cleaning, large amounts of earth originating from the fractures were observed in the Coa sample. However, the Siega Verde sample showed white lichen remains and an intense dark orange coloration corresponding to remains of the lichen thalli, specifically the algal layer and the medulla (Figure 9.3h).

Considering the colour measurements (Table 9.2), the parameter most affected by the different cleaning treatments was L*, except in the Siega Verde sample cleaned with distilled water, in which b* was the parameter most affected, with a decrease of −5.29 CIELAB units. This decrease in b* represents the dark orange colouration observed on this surface relative to the uncolonized surface (compare Figure 9.3h with 9.2b) and which was associated with the algal layer and the medulla remains on the surface (Rivas et al. 2018).

Increases in L* were detected on all cleaned surfaces, except those irradiated at 266 nm (both sites). The surfaces irradiated at 1,064 nm showed the greatest increases in L*, which were much higher for the Siega Verde sample (ΔL*=10.58 CIELAB units). Stereomicroscopic analysis revealed that for the surfaces irradiated at 1,064 nm, few lichen remains were observed on the Siega Verde sample (Figure 9.3e) and an almost total absence of organic remains on the Coa sample (Figure 9.3a). Therefore, although it was expected that the colour changes would be lowest on surfaces on which lichen removal was

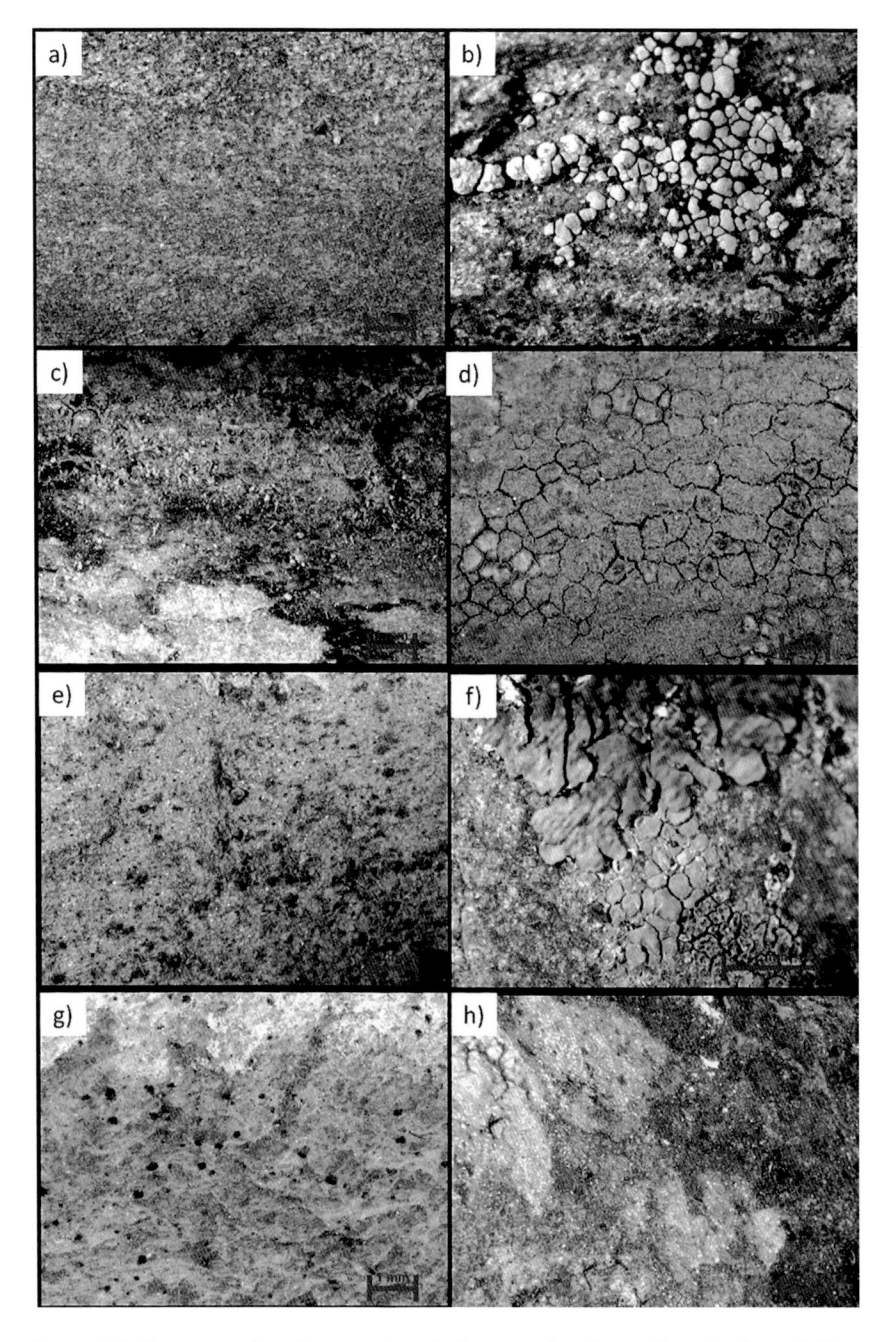

Figure 9.3 Stereoscopic micrographs of the samples from Coa (a–d) and Siega Verde (e–h) cleaned by different procedures: an Nd:YAG laser operated at 1,064 nm (a, e), an Nd:YAG laser operated at 266 nm (b, f), Biotin T (c, g) and distilled water (d, h). Photographs by the authors.

Table 9.2 Colorimetric differences (ΔL*, Δa*, Δb*, ΔC*$_{ab}$, ΔH*, ΔE*$_{ab}$) of the surfaces treated with an Nd:YAG laser operated at wavelengths of 1,064 nm and 266 nm, Biotin T and distilled water, expressed relative to the colour of uncolonized schist from the same sites

Sampling Site	Cleaning Method	ΔL*	Δa*	Δb*	ΔC*$_{ab}$	ΔH*	ΔE*$_{ab}$
Coa	Nd:YAG at 1,064 nm	5.75	−0.68	−2.72	−2.78	0.36	6.40
	Nd:YAG at 266 nm	−3.40	−0.55	−2.01	−2.06	0.37	3.99
	Biotin T	4.75	−3.76	−2.25	−3.24	3.00	6.47
	Distilled water	3.18	−1.01	−2.68	−2.83	0.45	4.28
Siega Verde	Nd:YAG at 1,064 nm	10.58	0.91	−0.34	−0.41	−0.94	10.63
	Nd:YAG at 266 nm	−7.54	1.75	1.52	1.46	−1.81	7.88
	Biotin T	3.68	0.04	−1.96	−1.90	0.46	4.17
	Distilled water	1.52	−2.59	−5.29	−5.73	1.15	6.08

most efficient (as the colour changes were determined relative to the colour of the uncolonized schists), the highest ΔL* values detected on the surfaces cleaned with 1,064 nm were associated with the colour changes in the stone caused by the laser and not by removal of the lichen. In previous research on the cleaning of lichen from schist with a Nd:YAG operated at 1,064 nm, the increase in L* was found to be due to physical and mechanical changes in the forming minerals, such as melting and fissuring (Pozo-Antonio et al. 2019). Such changes will slightly increase the roughness of the surface.

On the other hand, water-based cleaning induced the lowest ΔL*, suggesting that the L* measured on the cleaned surface was similar to that measured on the uncolonized schist surfaces. However, as observed by stereomicroscopy, in the Coa sample cleaned with water the surface was almost entirely covered by lichens and earth originating from the fissures in the stone (Figure 9.3d), and the Siega Verde sample showed a dark orange coloration and white lichen remains (Figure 9.3h). Therefore, as previously concluded (Pozo-Antonio et al. 2016b; Rivas et al. 2018), colour measurements must be interpreted with caution when this technique is used to assess cleaning effectiveness regardless of the patina, crust or coating being extracted.

The decrease in L* on the 266 nm-cleaned surfaces was related to the extensive lichen remains detected on the surfaces, which could even be seen with the naked eye (Figure 9.3b).

The ΔL* values were higher for Siega Verde samples than for Coa samples. As the ΔL* for the surfaces irradiated at 1,064 nm was conditioned by the damage to the stone, the Siega Verde sample was more affected than the Coa sample. However, Biotin T and water in the Coa samples induced higher ΔL* than in the Siega Verde samples, because in the former, the cleaning was less efficient. This may be related to the texture of the stone; the Siega Verde samples showed schistosity planes parallel to the irradiated surfaces, and the laser beam thus affected the entire surface at the same intensity, while the levels of extraction and damage were not homogeneous, because of the fissures on the surface of the Coa stones (caused by the sub-perpendicular schistosity planes). Moreover, as the fissures enable the lichens to adhere better to the surfaces, brushing with Biotin T or water did not weaken the adhesion of the lichen to the fractures. The effectiveness of each method therefore mainly depended on the texture of the stone.

In the Coa samples, the decrease in a* was related to a brownish coloration caused by the cleaning procedure, while in the Siega Verde samples, the increase in a* detected on the surfaces cleaned with laser and Biotin T were related to the greenish colouration associated with phototrophic pigments, including chlorophyll a, phycocyanin and carotenoid (Sanmartín et al. 2010). The decrease in b* observed on all surfaces, except the Siega Verde sample irradiated at 266 nm, suggests loss of the bluish coloration and an increase in brownish tones. For the Coa samples, a decrease in b* of around 2 CIELAB units was observed, while for the Siega Verde samples, the b* showed different trends, with the greatest decrease in b* (−5.73 CIELAB units) observed on the surface cleaned with distilled water.

As result of these observed variations, the chroma and the hue also underwent some changes. The chroma decreased (except in the Siega Verde sample irradiated at 266 nm) suggesting paler surfaces than in the uncolonized samples. The hue underwent negligible increases, except in the Siega Verde samples treated with laser (at both wavelengths).

In all surfaces, the ΔE^*_{ab} was higher than 3 CIELAB units, considered the upper limit of rigorous colour tolerance or perceptible change in colour (Prieto et al. 2010a, b; Wyszecki and Stiles 1982). Moreover, despite the high extraction levels observed on the 1,064 nm-treated surfaces, the ΔE^*_{ab} was higher than 5 CIELAB units. These findings indicate a high risk of incompatibility of the treatment with the conservation strategies for cultural heritage (Rodrigues and Grossi 2007).

The bioreceptivity tests revealed differences in the growth of the biofilm in relation to the treatment applied. Figure 9.4 shows ΔE^*_{ab} and the in vivo fluorescence (F0) of the inoculated surfaces at the end of the experiment. Both parameters have been widely used for monitoring biofilm-forming microorganism on rocky surfaces (Prieto et al. 2005, 2006; Vázquez-Nion et al. 2018a, b). In relation to total colour variation, for each lithotype, samples cleaned with biocide yielded the lowest values (which in the context of the bioreceptivity tests indicates least biofilm development), while samples irradiated at 1,064 nm yielded the highest value (greatest biofilm development). Total colour variation was similar for water and 266 nm laser treatments.

There was a large difference in ΔE^*_{ab} values obtained for the two lithotypes. In the treated Siega Verde samples, except those cleaned with biocide, the ΔE^*_{ab} values were higher than 3 CIELAB units (Prieto et al. 2010a, b; Wyszecki and Stiles 1982). By contrast, the values for the treated Coa samples, except those irradiated at 1,064 nm, were below that threshold.

188 *Graciela Paz-Bermúdez et al.*

Nevertheless, the total colour variation was not higher than 7 CIELAB units in either case: this is not very high relative to those obtained in previous bioreceptivity tests with Coa schist (Marques et al. 2015).

In relation to the F0 of dark-adapted cells, which can be used to estimate the biomass of the culture used as the inoculum in this study (Vázquez-Nion

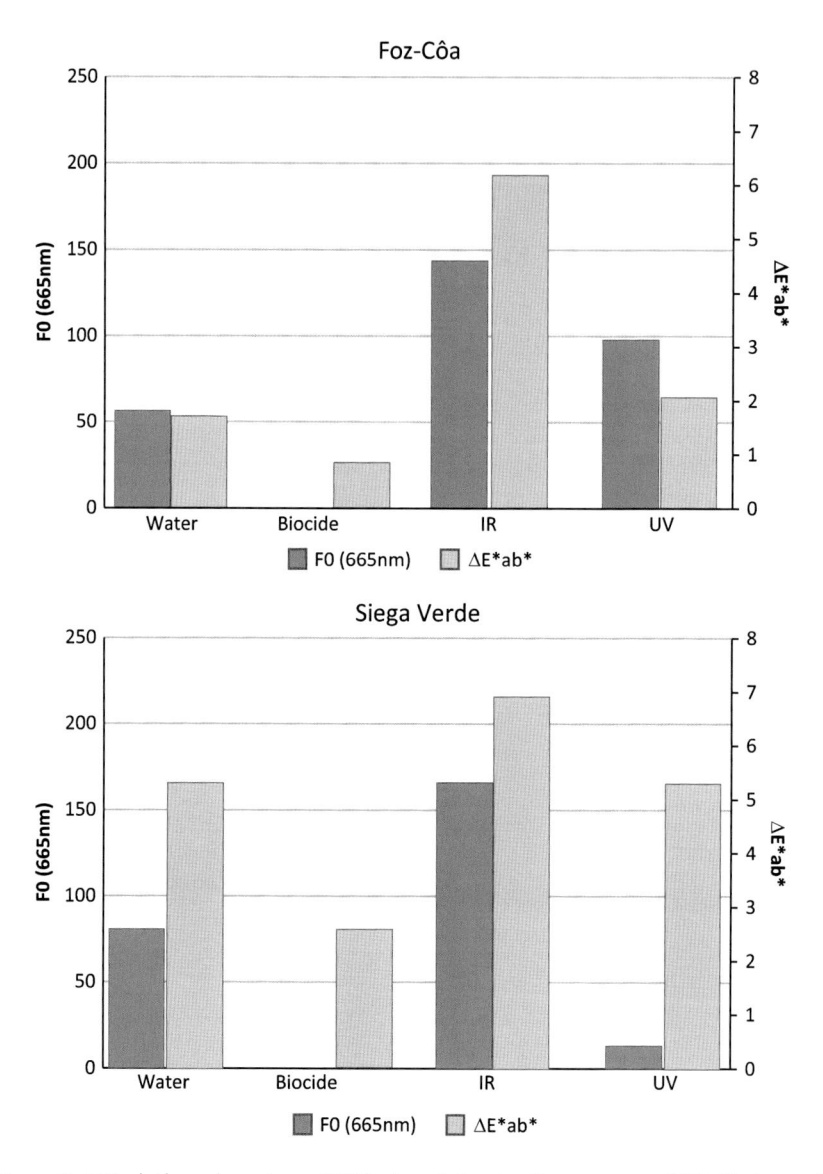

Figure 9.4 Variations in colour (DE*$_{ab}$) and *in vivo* fluorescence (F0) 42 days after inoculation. IR (1,064 nm wavelength) and UV (266 nm wavelength). Graphs by the authors.

et al. 2018a), the signal was similar in both lithotypes. The strongest signal (more biomass) corresponded to the samples irradiated at 1,064 nm, while no signal (no biomass) was detected in samples cleaned with biocide. F0 values for water and 1,064 nm were similar in Coa samples, but a very weak signal was obtained in Siega Verde samples irradiated at 266 nm.

Considering that water-based treatment is the minimal cleaning treatment that can be used to remove biocolonization, this treatment was used as a control for interpreting the results of the bioreceptivity tests. Thus, there were important differences, in terms of biomass (F0 values), between samples from both Coa and Siega Verde cleaned with water and those cleaned by the other three treatments. However, while biocide cleaning caused a decrease in the biomass, relative to the water-based treatment, irradiation at 1,064 nm led to an increase in the same parameter. Nevertheless, the biomass on the samples irradiated at 266 nm depended on the lithotype and was greater in the Coa samples than in the Siega Verde samples. The BI was calculated for each lithotype and cleaning treatment (Figure 9.5).

The Siega Verde samples yielded higher BI values than the Coa samples, except for the 266 nm-treated surface. Relative to the control water-based treatment, which is theoretically the most innocuous of the treatments tested, the application of Biotin T greatly reduced the bioreceptivity by preventing further biofilm formation. By contrast, the laser treatments caused an increase in bioreceptivity. This increase is related to the mechanical

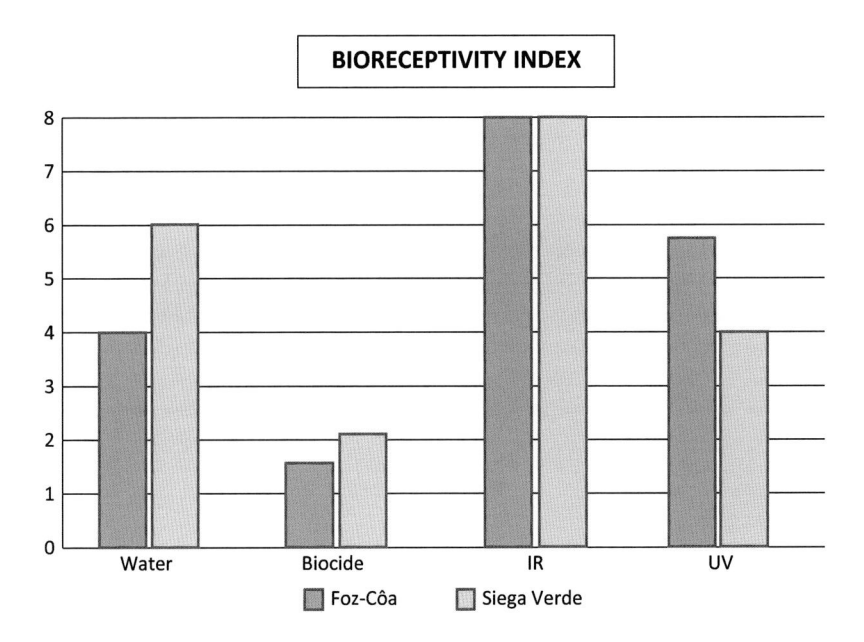

Figure 9.5 BI determined for each lithotype and cleaning treatment. IR (wavelength, 1,064 nm) and UV (wavelength, 266 nm). Graph by the authors.

and physical changes assigned to the melting and cracking in the forming minerals induced by the laser treatment and which facilitates adherence of microorganisms.

Conclusion

Considering the performance of the Nd:YAG laser, UV radiation (266 nm) did not induce satisfactory results, while IR radiation (1,064 nm) produced satisfactory results in terms of lichen removal. However, the mechanical and physical changes induced on the schist surfaces preclude use of this procedure for cleaning cultural heritage objects. Further studies will be carried out in order to optimize laser-based cleaning methods. Biotin T and water yielded different results considering the sample provenance: better results were obtained with the Siega Verde samples than with the Coa samples.

The duration of the treatments, as assessed by bioreceptivity analysis, was quite limited. Application of the biocide was the only treatment that reduced the bioreceptivity of the rocks and hence prevented recolonization. Conversely, the laser treatment induced an increase in the bioreceptivity of the schist. This finding must be considered in developing cleaning methods, as the increase in bioreceptivity will probably lead to rapid recolonization of the stone.

Overall, Biotin T yielded satisfactory results in terms of lichen extraction and the duration of the treatment effects regarding removal of lichen mosaics from schists in the Siega Verde archaeological site. The cleaning efficacy was greatly influenced by the orientation of the schistosity planes, with those planes parallel to the surface facilitating lichen removal.

Acknowledgements

The authors are grateful to staff at the Coa Valley and Siega Verde Archaeological Parks for permission to collect lichen specimens and rock samples. Special thanks are given to archaeologist António Batarda Fernandes and conservator-restorer Cristina Escudero for providing valuable information. J.S. Pozo-Antonio was supported by the Ministry of Science and Innovation, Government of Spain through grant number RYC2020-028902-I. This research was partly financed by the ERDF through the Spanish Ministry of Science and Innovation (project CGL2011-22789) and Xunta de Galicia (project ED431C 2018/32).

References

Asmus, J., Munk, W. H. and Wuerker, R. F. (1972) Lasers and holography in art preservation and restoration. In *Proceedings of the IEEE Northeast Electronics Research and Engineering Meeting*, Boston, FL, USA, 5–9.

Baptista, A. M. (2009) *O paradigma perdido: O vale do Côa e a arte Palaeolitica de ar livre em Portugal.* Porto, Portugal: Edições Afrontamento.

Barreiro, P., Andreotti, A., Colombini, M. P., González, P. and Pozo-Antonio, J. S. (2020) Influence of the laser wavelength on harmful effects on granite due to biofilm removal. *Coatings,* 10, pp.196–213. DOI: 10.3390/coatings10030196

CIE S014-4/E. (2007) Colorimetry—Part 4: CIE 1976 L*a*b* Colour space; Technical Report, Commission Internationale de l'Eclairage. Vienna, Austria: CIE Central Bureau.

De los Ríos, A., Galvan, V. and Ascaso, C. (2004) In situ microscopical diagnosis of biodeterioration processes occurring in the Convent of Santa Cruz la Real Segovia, Spain. *Int. Biodeterior. Biodegrad.,* 54, pp.113–120. DOI: 10.1016/j.ibiod.2004.03.020

Fernandes, A. B. (2007) The conservation programme of the Coa Valley Archaeological Park: Philosophy, objectives and action. *Conserv. Manage. Archa.,* 9, pp.71–96. DOI: 10.1179/175355208X381822

Fernandes, A. P. B. (2014) *Natural processes in the degradation of open-air rock-art sites: An urgency intervention scale to inform conservation.* Oxford: Archaeopress.

Fernandes, A. B., Reis, M., Escudero Remirez, C., and Vázquez Marcos, C. (2017) Integration of stone features and conservation of the Coa Valley and Siega Verde open-air Rock-Art. *Time&Mind,* 10(3), pp.293–319. DOI: 10.1080/1751696X.2017.1341246

Gemeda, B. T., Lahoz, ·R., Caldeira, A. T. and Schiavon. N. (2018) Efficacy of laser cleaning in the removal of biological patina on the volcanic scoria of the rock hewn churches of Lalibela, Ethiopia. *Environ. Earth Sci.,* 77, pp.35–47. DOI: 10.1007/s12665-017-7223-3

Lisci, M., Monte, M. and Pacini, E. (2003) Lichens and higher plants on stone: A review. *Int Biodeterior Biodegrad,* 51, pp.1–17. DOI: 10.1016/S0964-8305(02)00071-9

Marques, J., Hespanhol, H., Paz-Bermúdez, G. and Almeida, R. (2014) Choosing between sides in the battle for pioneer colonization of schist in the Coa Valley Archaeological Park: A community ecology perspective. *J. Archaeol. Sci.,* 45, pp.196–206. DOI: 10.1016/j.jas.2014.02.021

Marques, J., Vázquez-Nion, D., Paz-Bermúdez, G. and Prieto, B. (2015) The susceptibility of weathered versus unweathered schist to biological colonization in the Coa Valley Archaeological Park (north-east Portugal). *Environ. Microbiol.,* 17, pp.1805–1816. DOI: 10.1111/1462-2920.12642

Nimis, P. L. (2001) Artistic and historical monuments: Threatened ecosystems. In *Frontiers of life, part 2: Discovery and spoliation of the biosphere, sect. 2: Man and the environment.* S. Diego, CA: Academic Press, pp.557–569

Paz-Bermúdez, G., Carballal, R., Marques, J. and López de Silanes, M. E. (2018) Catálogo de los líquenes saxícolas (Ascomycota) del área arqueológica de Siega Verde (Salamanca, España). *An. Jardín Bot. Madrid,* 75, pp.e076. DOI: 10.3989/ajbm.2465

Piervittori, R., Salvadori, O. and Isocrono, D. (2004) Literature on lichens and biodeterioration of stonework. IV. *Lichenologist,* 36, pp.145–157. DOI: 10.1017/S0024282904014136

Pozo-Antonio, J. S., Barreiro, P., González, P. and Paz-Bermúdez, G. (2019) Nd:YAG and Er:YAG laser cleaning to remove Circinaria hoffmanniana (Lichenes, Ascomycota) from schist located in the Côa Valley Archaeological Park. *Int. Biodeterior. Biodegrad.,* 144, pp.104748. DOI: 10.1016/j.ibiod.2019.104748

Pozo-Antonio, J. S., Ramil, A., Rivas, T., López, A. J. and Fiorucci, M. P. (2016a) Effectiveness of chemical, mechanical and laser cleaning methods of sulphated black crusts developed on granite. *Constr. Build. Mater.*, 112: 682–690. DOI: 10.1016/j.conbuildmat.2016.02.195

Pozo-Antonio, J. S., Rivas, T., Fiorucci, M. P., López, A. J. and Ramil, A. (2016b) Effectiveness and harmfulness evaluation of graffiti cleaning by mechanical, chemical and laser procedures on granite. *Microchem. J.*, 125, pp.1–9. DOI: 10.1016/j.microc.2015.10.040

Pozo-Antonio, J. S., Rivas, T., Fiorucci, M. P., Ramil, A. and López, A. J. (2016c) Effectiveness of granite cleaning procedures in cultural heritage: A review. *Sci. Total Environ.*, 571, pp.1017–1028. DOI: 10.1016/j.scitotenv.2016.07.090

Prieto, B., Sanmartín, P., Aira, N. and Silva, B. (2010a) Color of cyanobacteria: Some methodological aspects. *Appl. Opt.*, 49, pp.2022–2029. DOI: 10.1364/AO.49.002022

Prieto, B., Sanmartín, P., Silva, B. and Martínez-Verdú, F. (2010b) Measuring the color of granite rocks. A proposed procedure. *Color Res. Appl.*, 35, pp.368–375. DOI: 10.1002/col.20579

Prieto, B., Silva, B., Aira, N. and Álvarez, L. (2006) Toward a definition of a bioreceptivity index for granitic rocks: Perception of the change in appearance of the rock. *Int. Biodeterior. Biodegrad.*, 58, pp.150–154. DOI: 10.1016/j.ibiod.2006.06.015

Prieto, B., Silva, B., Aira, N. and Laiz, L. (2005) Induction of biofilms on quartz surfaces as a means of reducing the visual impact of quartz quarries. *Biofouling*, 21, pp.237–246. DOI: 10.1080/08927010500421294

Rivas, T., Pozo-Antonio, J. S., López de Silanes, M. E., Ramil, A. and López, A. J. (2018) Laser versus scalpel cleaning of crustose lichen on granite. *Appl. Surf. Sci.*, 440, pp.467–476. DOI: 10.1016/j.apsusc.2018.01.167

Rodrigues, J. D. and Grossi, A. (2007) Indicators and ratings for the compatibility assessment of conservation actions. *J. Cult. Herit.*, 8, pp.32–43. DOI: 10.1016/j.culher.2006.04.007

Sanmartín, P., Aira, N., Devesa-Rey, R., Silva, B. and Prieto, B. (2010) Relationship between color and pigment production in two stone biofilm-forming cyanobacteria (Nostoc sp PCC 9104 and Nostoc sp PCC 9025). *Biofouling*, 26, pp.499–509. DOI: 10.1080/08927011003774221

Sanmartín, P., Fuentes, E., Montojo, C., Barreiro, P., Paz-Bermúdez, G. and Prieto, B. (2019) Tertiary bioreceptivity of schists from prehistoric rock art sites in the Côa Valley (Portugal) and Siega Verde (Spain) archaeological parks: Effects of cleaning. *Int. Biodeterior. Biodegrad.*, 142, pp.151–159. DOI: 10.1016/j.ibiod.2019.05.011

Sanmartín, P., Villa, F., Silva, B., Cappitelli, F. and Prieto, B. (2011) Color measurements as a reliable method for estimating chlorophyll degradation to phaeopigments. *Biodegradation*, 22, pp.763–771. DOI: 10.1007/s10532-010-9402-8

Sanz, M., Oujja, M., Ascaso, C., Pérez-Ortega, S., Souza-Egipsy, V., Fort, R., de los Rios, A., Wierzchos, J., Cañamares, M.V., and Castillejo, M. (2017) Influence of wavelength on the laser removal of lichens colonizing heritage stone. *Appl. Surf. Sci.* 399, 758–768.

Seaward, M. R. D., Giacobini, C., Giuliani, M. R., and Roccardi, A. (2001) The role of lichens in the biodeterioration of ancient monuments with particular reference to Central Italy. *Int. Biodeterior. Biodegrad.*, 48, pp.202–208. DOI: 10.1016/0265-3036(89)90028-6

Speranza, M., Sanz, M., Oujja, M., de los Rios, A., Wierzchos, J., Pérez-Ortega, S., Castillejo, M. and Ascaso, C. (2013) Nd-YAG laser irradiation damages to Verrucaria nigrescens. *Int. Biodeterior. Biodegrad.*, 84, pp.281–290. DOI: 10.1016/j.ibiod.2012.02.010

Tratebas, A.M. (2004) Biodeterioration of prehistoric rock art and issues in site preservation. Biodeterioration of prehistoric rock art and issues in site preservation. In Clair, L. St. and Seaward, M. (eds.) *Biodeterioration of stone surfaces. Lichens and biofilms as weathering agents of rocks and cultural heritage.* Dordrecht: Springer Science, pp.195–228.

Tretiach, M., Crisafulli, P., Imai, N., Kashiwadani, H., Hee Moon, K., Wada, H. and Salvadori, O. (2007) Efficacy of a biocide tested on selected lichens and its effects on their substrata. *Int. Biodeterior. Biodegrad.* 59, pp.44–54.

Tretiach, M., Bertuzzi, S. and Candotto Carniel, F. (2012) Heat shock treatments: A new safe approach against lichen growth on outdoor stone surfaces. *Environ. Sci. Technol.*, 46, pp.6851–6859. DOI: 10.1021/es3006755

Vázquez-Nion, D., Rodríguez-Castro, J., López-Rodríguez, M. C., Fernández-Silva, I. and Prieto, B. (2016) Subaerial biofilms on granitic historic buildings: Microbial diversity and development of phototrophic multi-species cultures. *Biofouling*, 32, pp.657–669. DOI: 10.1080/08927014.2016.1183121

Vázquez-Nion, D., Silva, B. and Prieto, B. (2018a) Bioreceptivity index for granitic rocks used as construction material. *Sci. Total Environ.*, 633, pp.112–121. DOI: 10.1016/j.scitotenv.2018.03.17

Vázquez-Nion, D., Silva, B. and Prieto, B. (2018b) Influence of the properties of granitic rocks on their bioreceptivity to subaerial phototrophic biofilms. *Sci. Total Environ.*, 610–611, pp.44–54. DOI: 10.1016/j.scitotenv.2017.08.015

Vázquez-Nion, D., Silva, B., Troiano, F. and Prieto, B. (2017) Laboratory grown subaerial biofilms on granite: Application to the study of bioreceptivity. *Biofouling*, 33, pp.24–35. DOI: 10.1080/08927014.2016.1261120

Wyszecki, G. and Stiles, W. S. (1982) *Color science. Concepts and methods, quantitative data and formulae.* New York: John Wiley and Sons.

10 *In-Situ* Rock Art Preservation in the Sabor Valley (Northwest Iberia)

Sofia Figueiredo, António Batarda Fernandes, Susana Lainho and Joaquim Garcia

Introduction

In 1996, the discovery of a wealth of prehistoric open-air rock art, notably from the Ice Age, later included in United Nations Educational, Scientific and Cultural Organization (UNESCO)'s World Heritage List, led to the cancellation of the construction of a large dam in the Coa River (Baptista and Fernandes 2007). Those who regarded this outcome as an achievement that would signal shifts in the usual rapport between heritage preservation and dam building, in Portugal but also elsewhere, must have been disappointed with the following decades. Indeed, large dams carried on being built, with major effects on the preservation of archaeological sites (see, for instance, Kitchen and Ronayne 2001; Flad and Chen 2013, pp. 43–70; Ribeiro 2015). Portugal was no exception, and after the Coa episode, major hydroelectric infrastructures have been built, namely the Alqueva dam on the Guadiana River, the largest artificial reservoir in Europe (Dias-Sardinha, Ross and Calapez Gomes 2018; ERN 2020), the Foz Tua dam, fortunately not directly affecting any rock art site (Teixeira et al. 2016), and the Lower Sabor, the case presented in this chapter.

Prior to the Coa affair, other dams, built within the frame of a global Portuguese hydroelectrical plan being implemented since the 1950s, have resulted in the submersion of rock art. Such was the case of Fratel in the Tagus (Serrão et al. 1972), finished in 1973, or Pocinho in the Douro (Baptista 1983), finished in 1984. The construction of the latter even resulted in the submersion of rock art outcrops in the margins of both the Douro and the Coa rivers that later have integrated the area of the Coa Valley Archaeological Park and are recognized today as belonging to the different chronological periods that form the legally protected National Monument, the Coa rock art ensemble.

Nevertheless, there were non-neglectable positive outcomes arising from the cancellation of the Coa dam, besides the obvious and remarkable gain that the *in-situ* preservation of the Coa rock art represented per se. One was the establishment of stricter regulatory guidelines regarding the need to include archaeology in prior environmental impact studies and safeguarding compensation measures, as the Sabor case exemplifies. Another was the creation of a

DOI: 10.4324/9780429355349-14

government body to oversee Portuguese archaeology (Baptista and Fernandes 2007; Marques and Neto 2018). Overall, even if affected sites became flooded, the Lower Sabor Dam Heritage Safeguard Plan (HSP) allowed to amass diverse and multidisciplinary scientific information, namely on rock art of different eras (Figueiredo et al. 2016a). Other areas in the regional study of human occupation periods also benefited in knowledge, as the excavation of an Iron Age fortified storage facility at Castelinho illustrates (Seabra et al. 2020).

As defined by the HSP (see Dordio et al. 2017 for a summary of results), work at the rock art sites started in early 2010 and ended in April 2015. Contrary to most studies included in the HSP, which had delimited timelines, rock art tasks sought to examine an heterogenous materiality, the "rock art", covering a span ranging from the Palaeolithic era to the contemporary period, across the entire area impacted by the construction of the dam.

Some 40 outcrops bearing rock art in the Sabor Valley were known before the beginning of the project. The same methodology for data recording was to be adopted in all cases, materialized through graphic, photographic, topographic and 3D surveying. These constituted the initial universe to be considered for *in-situ* preservation. However, after two initial intense seasons (2010/2011), the number of rock art sites more than quadrupled. In fact, at the end of 2011, it was already anticipated a major increase in the identification of new rock art sites. In five years, more than 200 rock art panels were studied both in the open-air and inside shelters or sheltered surfaces, and over 750 carved blocks located in over 80 built structures were examined. Furthermore, 2,000 portable rock art plaques, from distinct periods, were recovered in the safeguard excavations that occurred at several sites in the area of the reservoir. A noteworthy case is the Upper Palaeolithic portable art pieces recovered at Foz do Medal (Figueiredo et al. 2016b), a site that also yielded an abundance of Ice Age lithic assemblages (Gaspar et al. 2016).

With the number of rock art sites increasing and considering both the technical and chronological variability observed in the material, which included Upper Palaeolithic pecked motifs, painted motifs from recent prehistory and fainted engravings from historical periods, there was the need to redefine which outcrops were to be preserved *in-situ* for the project to be carried out as scheduled, i.e., before the end of the dam's construction. In this chapter, our aim is to describe the methodology adopted up to the completion of these interventions, designed for the rock art to resist any potential damage caused by submersion but also to prepare it to be appreciated again in the future, if the reservoir ever gets emptied.

Selection of rock art heritage sites

Given the large number and the diversity of sites existing in the Sabor Valley, there was the need to develop sorting criteria; occurrences were divided as having either high, medium or low heritage value. A classification of this type is always problematic and complex, notwithstanding subjective issues, but necessary for the purposes of the HSP. Under these circumstances, and attempting to minimize as much as possible the subjectivity inherent to assigning a heritage value to each rock art site, we took into consideration the following criteria, which should be understood as having been employed together to order the relevance of each rock art testimony:

- Chronology. Older material, remnant of periods from which the likelihood of vestiges, rock art included, to have been preserved until the present decreases, constitutes an unequal source of information for Archaeology. This was the baseline notion regarding chronology that was followed, to the contrary of what some suggest, notwithstanding precise value judgements that might be applied in different world contexts (Bednarik 2004, p. 165).
- Originality of figures. Despite inherent subjectivity to this sort of analysis, it is recognized that, when considering any given chronologically cohesive rock art corpus, motifs or compositions can be classified as more significant than others (see for instance Fernandes et al. 2017). Criteria included rarity of portrayed themes or aesthetic value.
- Depiction of scenes. It is suggested that identified evidence of association of motifs constituting scenes, (see Santos, 2017 regarding the nearby Coa Valley Upper Palaeolithic art, a period also represented at Sabor) are significant in enhancing current debates on rock art interpretation.
- Superimposed motifs. Besides suggesting that what was noted in the previous point is also valid here, superimpositions are important in establishing relative chronology of panels, particularly in the case of regional open-air rock art (see, again for the Coa Valley, Baptista 1999 or Aubry, Santos and Luís 2014).
- Location and rapport with other sites. The location of a site or its relationship to other heritage elements, whether other decorated rocks, human occupation sites or archaeological/historical buildings, can provide to data to inform more comprehensive analysis in the structuration of the art ensemble. At the Coa Valley patterns of distribution, creating pilgrimage paths across the landscape, e.g., associated to waterways mouths', or deliberate choice of panels to place rock art, often forming palimpsestic accumulation of motifs, have been argued as indicating complex original art drives, namely in what respects social use of symbols (see Fernandes 2017; Santos 2017). Isolated finds provide less such information.
- Condition of outcrops/surfaces/motifs. Considering the sheer number of identified rock art sites/panels, the option to not invest resources in the preservation of deteriorated panels as these would be submerged could have been a factor. Rather, the precise opposite stance has been followed: always considering previous points, if significant outcrops and panels were in delicate condition, that factor weighted in the choice of intervention sites (see Fernandes 2014 regarding condition susceptibility ranking at the Coa Valley).

- Position relative to the reservoir water level. The fact that outcrops positioned just below the maximum water level could undergo repeated harmful wetting and drying episodes due to changes in the water level, as it happens at Coa (Fernandes 2014, pp. 189–190), but also better located for monitoring action during potential drought events, were considered factors in the choice of outcrops.

After the selection of outcrops was completed and approved by concerned institutions, Eletricidade de Portugal (EDP) and Direção-Geral do Património Cultural (DGPC), the final list was reduced to six from a total of circa 200 rock art outcrops that became submerged by the reservoir:

- EP153 – Schist outcrop featuring a panel where a figure depicting an aurochs was engraved in a quite regular pecking technique. This is the only outcrop, in the area affected by the Sabor dam reservoir, in which an Upper Palaeolithic chronology was attributed to existent rock art (Baptista 2009).
- EP215 – Large schist outcrop where in a sub-horizontal surface several motifs, achieved resorting to the abrasion technique, were engraved. Besides linear motifs, other geometric compositions, as an internally segmented square, have been identified. All motifs are believed to be of Iron Age chronology (Xavier et al. 2014).
- EP221 – Relatively large shelter located in a schist outcrop, where eight rock art panels have been identified. Among cup marks, fusiform incisions, and pecked ensembles, six zoomorphic figures are observable, such as goats and deer. To these latter motifs, an Epipaleolithic chronology was attributed (Teixeira 2016, p. 58).
- EP504 – Schist outcrop with two vertical panels with bearable visible fine line incisions. Nevertheless, two deer, an anthropomorphic figure, and a horse are noticeable. Chronology is believed to correspond to the Iron Age.
- EP621 – In this vertical large-sized outcrop, six engraved panels have been identified. Motifs include zoomorphic figures, interpreted as representing deer, cup marks, and scattered pecked depictions, and are believed to range from the Epipalaeolithic to the Chalcolithic (see Figure 10.1; Figueiredo et al. 2016a).
- EP954 – The outcrop where this panel is located stood out in the landscape due to its pronounced verticality and reddish tone. The panel comprises a pecked deer, with the body totally filled in. It is believed that chronology of this motif can be attributed to a period ranging from the Epipalaeolithic to the Chalcolithic (Figueiredo et al. 2016a).

The complete characterization of the rocky outcrops to be preserved *in-situ* preceded the development of each respective intervention. To this end, a set of technical-scientific studies was carried out, including comprehensive photographic, topographic and 3D surveys, as well as the collection of samples and their handling through examination methods and laboratorial

198 *Sofia Figueiredo et al.*

Figure 10.1 Location of EP621 with documentation work of its rock art. Photo and documentation work by the authors except ABF.

analysis, described in the next section. It was therefore possible to generate in-depth data with regards to each site, to later develop the methodology more appropriate to the specificities of each intervened outcrop.

Geological characterization of the outcrops

From a scientific standpoint, the analysis of the outcrops allowed their geological and geo-mechanical characterization, alongside the identification of potential instabilities, thus enabling the anticipation of possible weakened areas. The rocky outcrops containing rock art are located along the banks of the Sabor River within autochthonous, sedimentary and metamorphic formations from the Cambric and Siluric periods deformed during the Hercynian Orogeny.

Further characterization was provided by LNEC which conducted petrographic examinations and studied the mineralogical composition and textural features of the outcrops. The goal was to get in-depth characterization of the bedrock containing rock art engravings to be submerged. Collected samples were observed with the naked eye and binocular magnifying glasses, but also resorting to petrographic characterization by Optical Microscopy (OM) and Scanning Electron Microscopy (SEM), semi-quantitative chemical analysis of primary composition by Wavelength Dispersive X-Ray Fluorescence Spectrometry, and chemical-mineralogical characterization by X-Ray Diffractometry.

The obtained results revealed that the macroscopic features of the materials collected from the six outcrops to be intervened were very similar in all the samples: dark grey, sometimes greenish, fine-grained material, generally anisotropic with foliation marked by the presence of lighter coloured layers. Observation under binocular magnifying glasses of all the samples collected demonstrated the presence of a mafic component, consisting of dark minerals of varying colour and size distributed around a matrix of whitish crystals. At this magnifying level, it was therefore possible to conclude that these materials possessed different granularities. Further analysis demonstrated the asymmetry of the samples and led to the conclusion that despite the macroscopic similarity of the studied materials, they present different mineralogical and chemical features. These mostly consisted of fine-grained pelitic sediments with coarser intercalations and lenticular quartz levels, in addition to coarser detrital rocks, metamorphosed into the schist facies. Only one of the samples (corresponding to EP220) presented a metamorphic paragenesis indicating an igneous rock of basic composition to be at its source.

Still in 2012, the Laboratório de Geotecnia e Materiais de Construção at Centro de Formação Profissional da Indústria da Construção Civil e Obras Públicas do Norte carried out abrasion tests in wet storage in order to better determine durability quotients, alongside tests to determine the degradability coefficient of the outcrops. The analyses were performed on samples from all six rocks to be preserved, and the results were quite encouraging:

the degradability coefficient in all was 1 and the durability percentage ranged from 98.7% to 99.47% (AFNOR 1992), further suggesting that the outcrops possessed enough resilience to undergo submersion.

Condition of intervened outcrops

Overall, it can be said that the constraints which affected the condition of the Sabor rock art outcrops were similar to those that had been identified and studied at the Coa Valley (Fernandes 2014).

The project presented here allowed for careful observation of Sabor outcrops with rock art motifs, resulting in the identification of several damages and anomalies, both on the surface and on its bulk. The studied outcrops referred to small and isolated schist masses that were surrounded by arable land. In 2006, a first macro-scale study carried out by LNEC classified the outcrops as being extremely resistant to dissolution phenomena, which supports the theory that the engravings were preserved for thousands of years not only in the Sabor Valley but also in the neighbouring similar case of the Coa Valley (see Rodrigues 2003). The presence of sharp edges was considered as one of the most significant signs of their resistance to chemical weathering, thus leading to the belief that submersion would not affect the rocks by dissolution (ASTM 2016).

The strong anisotropy of schist rocks and structural weaknesses contributed, however, to exfoliation, namely with breakage lines causing the separation of masses. This phenomenon, together with other natural ongoing degradation dynamics, weakens the overall structure fostering its gradual break-up. Regional diaclase families of unvarying alignment, as in Coa (see Fernandes 2014, pp. 133–138), further contribute to the general weakening of outcrops and, in certain cases, cause them to break apart.

Throughout existent crevices, especially on those located near the soil, chemical degradation has had a higher impact as fractures were widened by sediment filling coming from arable lands above. The presence of soil allowed the seeding of vegetation, which in turn contributed to the progressive widening of fractures and, in the longer term, to the instability of the outcrop itself. Diaclases existing on many of the outcrops were studied, mapped and characterized according to their depth, length, width, roughness, filling and alteration. All the collected information was analysed and handled according to a set of potential instabilities, in order to adequately adapt the preservation proposals.

The rock massifs exhibited geo-mechanical behaviour that was studied for its merits through the comparison of several parameters. An analysis of the outcrops to be intervened upon under the Rock Mass Rating ranking system (Bieniawski 1989) concluded these ranged from Good (level II; EP153, 504, 621 and 954) to Reasonable (level III; EP215 and 221). Further analysis using SMR (Romana 1985) classified EP153 as stable, EP504, 621 and 954 as partially unstable, EP215 as completely unstable, while EP221 was not possible to rank according to this rating system.

Gathered data was critically examined with the aim of determining the damage biological constraints could cause to surfaces when submerged. Biodeterioration assessment also comprised the inventory of lichen colonization. The study identified 79 taxa of lichen, three of which were present on all the surfaces with colonization, but most of the species were only present on a small part of the surface and mainly concentrated either on small pits or along fissures. A more in-depth study of the dominant species, those playing a more active role in the deterioration of the bedrock, was conducted. Considering the percentage of the area occupied by crustacean lichens, it was concluded that rocks EP153 (50%), EP221 (60% and 80%, depending on the section) and EP954 (50%) were the most affected.[1]

Assessment of expected conditions after submersion

Affected outcrops in the Sabor Valley would be submerged by the dam reservoir, a circumstance implicating an abrupt change in the environmental conditions where they have subsisted previously. Thereby, it was also necessary to anticipate detrimental submersion effects, in order to better assess resulting potential damage to the rock art outcrops.

The rocks selected for *in-situ* preservation, under normal dam operation conditions, are submerged by over 40 meters of water. The only exception was outcrop EP215 which stands 18 meters below surface. Schist outcrops are relatively stable regarding dissolution and even chemical damage but are relatively fragile when subjected to wetness and dryness episodes, especially if recurring (see Fernandes 2014, pp. 143–144). Nevertheless, if being underwater causes the total saturation of outcrops, permanent submersion will make them subject to water flow and tidal regimes, even if the expected outcome is the progressive covering of outcrops by the accumulation of successive sediment layers (Brandt 2000).

At the Sabor, outcrops were fractured and had significant soil presence along diaclases and gaping areas, hence were very susceptible to lose their support system and become unstable. Considering an early stage after submersion characterized by initiating, thus incipient, sediment accumulation processes, water flow within the reservoir could lead to the erosion of the soil filling the outcrops' gaps. Reports on submerged rock art resulting from the construction of the Alqueva dam suggest that in the precise case of surveyed outcrops no major incidences affect their conservation. It was also noted that a layer of silt deposited after submersion, reaching a thickness of a 30 cm in some instances, may act as a protective layer (Figueiredo and Monteiro 2012).

Siltation at Sabor is also likely to deposit a layer of sediments on the outcrops, which will eventually bury them. This potential concealment has not been considered a problem in terms of the surfaces' preservation, but in the case of preserved outcrops measures in the form of concrete bollards have been adopted to facilitate their later location.

Finally, attention was also given to the fact that lichens detected on engraved surfaces prior to submersion would disappear entirely, given that all identified species were exclusively land based. Freshwater lichens (see Thüs,

Aptroot and Seaward 2014), or even microorganisms native to freshwater environments (Stranghoener et al. 2018), may begin colonizing the outcrops, but only within a discrete time frame prior to the eventual covering of the outcrops by sediments.[2]

The precise situation in which these outcrops will endure will only be known when monitoring is possible, either by the lowering of the dam reservoir, or eventually by diving inspections, similarly to what occurred in the Alqueva case noted above. However, due to expectable high-dynamic reservoir deposition processes,[3] the time window in which such inspections would be possible, without removing accumulated sediments, is reasonably short. The exception to these constraints is the six intervened upon and protected rock art outcrops that, at least for quite some time, will not be affected by freshwater biological colonization. Moreover, before sediments cover them, the only possible inspection procedure in the case of these six outcrops, either with the aid of diving gear or when drought events occur, is, without removing them, to the sturdiness of the added protective covering layers.

In-situ preservation work

Interventions were set with the aim of preserving engraved surfaces as well as conferring stability to the outcrops. *In-situ* preservation work followed a strategic methodological approach comprising cleaning, stabilization, and monitoring. A team of specialists from several areas of knowledge, particularly Geology, Conservation and Restoration, Engineering and Archaeology, took part in the interventions given the quite rare challenge of wet environment preservation. The establishment of intervention measures for the outcrops considered all the analyses and background studies performed for each rock art outcrop.

Considering the above-described selection criteria, particular attention was focused on outcrops with significant degradation levels where gaps, large fractures and soil were present, namely along diaclases/joints. The outcrops structural stability was key in avoiding future damages, such as the loss of sections of outcrops and eventual detachment processes.

The preparation/sealing of outcrops was designed to allow physical/chemical equilibrium after submersion also supplying resistance to mechanical erosion effects. Considering that at the time of submersion, the effects of erosion would be accentuated by water rise and flow and an expectable increase of suspended materials, the construction of an outer barrier assembled with large inert blocks made of local granite was designed. This structure acts as a defence mechanism against the effects of water flow, while simultaneously allowing the cohesion of the entire structure.

Land geometry where intervened outcrops stand was also studied as some were located on areas with steep slopes and high up from the existing riverbed before dam construction. This situation, coupled with the large amount of inert material needed to smooth slopes, led to a solution of compromise considering the envisioned standard conditions at the reservoir, where the effects of downfall are believed to be low; it is expected that slopes will withstand the damage caused by mechanical erosion. The subsequent precipitation of surface salts was also considered, although it will only occur when reservoir waters lower, which can occur due to dam maintenance work or during already mentioned drought episodes. Finally, size and composition of outcrops' protective layers considered the best adaptation and stabilization of the engraved surfaces during the rising of waters, thus enabling them to maintain a more stable inner environment, namely when considering temperature and humidity.

The stabilization, preparation and sealing works conceived for the rock art outcrops complied with international guidelines regarding conservation and restoration of cultural heritage (such as ICOMOS 2003), and all intervention processes have been guided by the principles of minimum intervention, compatibility of materials, and reversibility in their application, while acknowledging, regarding the latter, the conceptual but also practical debate put forward, for instance, by Oddy and Carroll (1999).

Project implementation

The preserved rock outcrops, in a total of six, were studied and intervened upon between November 2013 and April 2014. They are all currently underwater. Work began by vegetation cleaning in the surrounding area and in the rock massif itself. Higher plants were eliminated through the application of herbicide; manual, and at times mechanical, removal of weeds ensued. The soil and roots present inside the fractures, fissures and gaps were manually removed. The comprehensive removal of mosses and wider biological contamination material was carried out with nylon spatulas and brushes. Finally, and with the aim of thoroughly cleaning the engraved surfaces, nylon brushes and occasionally wooden spatulas and brooms were also used.

Structural stabilization of the rocks to be preserved continued by filling existing gaps, thus making the massif more homogeneous, whilst also consolidating and subsequently concealing fractures. This operation was performed by applying traditional lime and sand mortar in the areas to be filled and, whenever necessary, introducing properly sized stone elements consisting of granite from quarries in the region to fill gaps. In the case of shelters, namely in EP215 and 221, and after engraved surfaces were protected, as described below, the shelter itself was filled, with stone masonry and mortar in part of EP215, and with dry stone masonry in its entirety in the case of EP221.

One of the most important phases in the *in-situ* preservation process was the protection of the engraved surfaces, as motifs are the reason why these massifs are important. These were all located at vertically oriented panels, except for EP215 where the engraved surface is sub-horizontal. Hence, covering operations started from the bottom up: gradual layers of the beneath detailed compatible materials were applied shielding the engravings, thus preparing them for subsequent layers to be placed as outer shells. First, a thick layer of clay and sand was applied to the surfaces, over which schist stones were glued with Paraloid B-72 to reinforce protection. In the case of the sub-horizontal EP215, this protection consisted in the bonding of

Figure 10.2 Placing of successive layers of gauze, raw cloth and high-density geotextile blanket bond by aqueous acrylic resin at EP215. Photo by the authors except ABF.

successive layers of gauze, raw cloth and high-density geotextile blanket bond by aqueous acrylic resin (see Figure 10.2). Considering reversibility, it is believed that, not without effort, especially if they are still underwater, these successive layers can be dismantled to again reveal, most presumably intact, protected rock art motifs.

The final stage included the sealing of outcrops and comprised the placement of several filling layers composed of sand, gravel of various sizes, high density geotextile fabric, geogrid and large stone blocks that were all sequentially placed according to what was defined in each specific case.

Discussion

The Sabor dam was defended by its promoters as the best alternative to the non-construction of the Coa, although when the decision was taken there were other options on the table. At the time (2003/2004), one of the authors (ABF), when working at the Coa Valley Archaeological Park, took part in a governmental evaluation commission aimed at deciding amongst two options to replace the perceived hydroelectrical and flood control potential of the cancelled Coa dam: still in the Coa, but upstream to the area of the Park, or in the Lower Sabor. Within this commission, not constructing any dam (the so-called zero option) was also considered, although it became apparent that most participating institutional stakeholders did not favour this choice, or indeed the upstream Coa hypothesis, believed to be too intrusive and more expensive to build than the Sabor. Opposing views to the Sabor alternative were shared by a coalition of environment protection Non-Governmental Organizations, under the motto "Sabor: the last wild River in Europe" (see, for an account of the affair, PAeM 2016).

Looking back with the benefit of time passed, it is believed that if the political hydroelectric development goals set by successive Portuguese governments would have been allowed to run their due course, undisturbed by the Coa find, the Sabor would have been built after the Coa's completion. Indeed, both dams, as others, were already included in a national major hydroelectrical plan devised from the 1950's onwards to take advantage of suitable locations to build this kind of infrastructures, namely in the Douro basin (Luís 2003, p. 110; Moura 2015). Gradually, the plan is being implemented and just a few of suitable identified locations have not been intervened, with the Coa being the most notable exception, as already discussed.

Still, there is an important point to make here: as the relatively low number of intervened upon rock art outcrops in the course of the works presented here denotes, while the area affected by the Sabor reservoir possesses circa 200 outcrops bearing rock art, the current estimates at Coa point to over 1,200. While at Sabor just one outcrop with Ice Age rock art was in the area to become flooded (EP153), at Coa almost half of the above-mentioned number of outcrops have motifs from the Upper Palaeolithic ranging from the Gravettian/Solutrean on to the Magdalenian (Reis 2014), and perhaps even to the Azilian (Aubry et al. 2017). Moreover, not considering the exceptional collection of portable rock art that was recovered from different sites with diverse chronologies (and if it wasn't for the construction of the Sabor dam, chances were that significant sites such as Foz do Medal or Castelinho would remain unidentified and/or excavated for many years onwards),[4] it is widely perceived that rock art at Coa has an exceedingly quality that ultimately led to the classification of the ensemble of pre-historic motifs as World Heritage. Subjective as the stance may be, it was believed that the less exuberant Sabor rock art could not, on its own, be considered for such a status.

It may judiciously be suggested that just one affected rock art panel is one too many. Such a stance, yet again illustrates how unparalleled, and justified, was the decision not to build the Coa dam. As detailed here, that wasn't the case in Sabor (or Alqueva and other instances). Hence, described work devoted its main efforts to attempt assuring that affected rock art outcrops were prepared, as befittingly as current knowledge can ensure, to properly withstand submersion. Regarding available courses of action (see Fernandes, Chapter 1), the decision to construct the Sabor dam led to choose the *in-situ* conservation of the most significant rock art outcrops as the preferred option (see Figure 10.3). It is worthwhile to note that, albeit the extensive documentation work conducted will assure the survival of flooded imagery in the form of archived tracings or photos, the execution of replicas was not considered, perhaps as a result of the 'lower' perceived value of Sabor rock art. Nevertheless, it is suggested that at least EP153 could have been selected for such an action. Nonetheless 3D documentation that can be used to produce replicas was carried out in the case of 16 submerged rock art outcrops.

During the unfolding of the Coa affair, EDP proposed the removal of the most important rock art outcrops to a location outside the area to be flooded, accompanied by a vague promise to create some sort of visitor centre to welcome them. This was an attempt to conciliate the best of two worlds, i. e. constructing the dam and preserve at least some rock art out of the reservoir area. The same company that rescued some of the archaeological assets removed and rebuilt elsewhere during the construction of the Assuam Dam in Egypt was hired to cut and relocate outcrops akin to engraved ones but with no rock art to prove it was technically feasible to do so without endangering the cohesion of rock masses (see Chapter 1; Fernandes and Rodrigues 2008).

Nevertheless, archaeology and heritage conservation practitioners (authors included) and those in other scientific or artistic areas believed, within the public debate arena at the time in Portugal, that Coa rock art should be maintained in its original place of execution and context so that it could today be studied and shown to the public within its full remnant original landscape (for instance, Fernandes 2004, 2008, 2010; Jorge 1995 or Zilhão 1998).

Hence, when the Alqueva and the Sabor dams were later built, the somewhat tacit consensus pointed to *in-situ* preservation of rock art, even if it was to become flooded: in this case with six outcrops protected at Sabor and the remaining unprotected outcrops covered with reservoir sediments at the same location, as the entirety of those at Alqueva. Conceivably, an underlying semiconscious determination to keep safeguarding the Coa as

Figure 10.3 Result of the implemented protection at EP 621. Photo by the authors except ABF.

the crown jewel endures; such an unexpected and unprecedented decision to stop the dam's construction is somehow not completely reassuring regarding the perpetuation of its present unsubmerged condition. It is suggested that this fact largely explains why relocating the outcrops, or producing replicas, hasn't been considered when planning safeguard measures put in place regarding Sabor rock art, as it could provide arguments for those still invoking purely economic development gains from dam building, thus possibly undermining all that was and has been achieved at Coa, both at a public archaeology level (for instance Fernandes et al. 2008), or in the scientific inquiry realm (for instance Zilhão et al. 1997, Aubry 2009 or Aubry et al. 2020).

Conclusion

Interventions planned and carried out within the Sabor dam construction HSP regarding rock art had the objective of documenting the totality of identified motifs as well as preserving *in-situ* the six most significant outcrops bearing rupestrian imagery. To that end, prior examination of each outcrops comprising the characterization analyses described here were instrumental in the definition and subsequent execution of preservation work implemented in each case. Each completed measure can be divided into four groups according to the nature of the procedure: cleaning, structural stabilization, surface protection and structural protection. It is argued that established objectives have been achieved and that the work developed during the HSP have strengthen the capacity of intervened rock art outcrops to resist impacts resulting from submersion. Hopefully, it may one day be possible to ascertain the condition of the rock art and how it has adapted to conditions it faces since the filling up of the reservoir.

With the launch of the national hydroelectrical plan back in the 1950s, the history of rock art research, preservation, and conservation in Portugal has developed hand in hand with river damming. Indeed, if it wasn't for the construction of these infrastructures, probably most if not all rock art sites discovered in Portugal in the last half-century would have remained unnoticed by Archaeology. Hence, an important question arises: why hasn't this common history not resulted in improved legal protection measures for this kind of heritage? This is even a most pressing issue if we consider that in 1985, Portugal's neighbour Spain automatically attributed to all caves, shelters and sites containing rock art the utmost legal heritage protection status (BOE 1985). By contrast, the most recent version of the Portuguese Cultural Heritage Law (DR 2001) does not mention rock art at all, with its protection falling under the rules set for the protection of overall archaeological properties. Inevitably, the momentous issue of a quite longer tradition of consolidated rock art studies in Spain, inaugurated with the 19th century discovery of Altamira, must be considered.

Nonetheless, following what was discussed above, it is further proposed that the answer rests amongst the interstices amid Portuguese Archaeology, and its struggle to attain a fully recognized position both as a discipline and stakeholder, namely when considering public policies, development strategies, and regional or national political dynamics. All these have been utterly interconnected in the past decades in relation to rock art preservation but also to heritage protection in general, when the prospect of artificially rising river levels looms.

Notes

1 See Marques (2013) for a regional (Upper Douro) assessment of the susceptibility of schist surfaces to lichen-induced weathering.
2 A window which is suggested to span diversely according to the specific conditions of each outcrop and, more importantly, to the specific geometry of outcrops and the rapport of their different faces with slope angles.
3 At the Coa Valley, as a result of the construction of the Pocinho dam in the Douro River in 1984, archaeological excavations have shown that a circa one meter thick layer has accumulated on the river bed of the area affected by this reservoir, spanning some 6 kms upstream of the Coa's confluence with the Douro (Aubry, Santos and Luís 2014).
4 See Gameiro (2018) for an account on the gains in knowledge for Upper Paleolithic studies in Portugal the construction of dams in the last decades signified.

References

AFNOR (1992) *Sols: Reconnaissance et Essais. Coefficient de Dégradabilité des matériaux Rocheux*. NF P 94-067, Association Française de Normalisation.

ASTM (2016) *Standard test method for slake durability of shales and other similar weak rocks*. ASTM International.

Aubry, T. (ed.) (2009) *200 séculos da história do Vale do Côa: Incursões na vida quotidiana dos caçadores artistas do Paleolítico*. Lisboa: IGESPAR.

Aubry, T., Santos, A. T., Luís, L. (2014) Stratigraphies du panneau 1 de Fariseu: analyse structurelle d'un système graphique paléolithique à l'air libre de la vallée du Coa (Portugal). In Paillet, P. (Ed.) *Les Arts de la Préhistoire: Micro-analyses, Mise en Contexte et Conservation: Actes du Colloque "Micro-analyses et Datations de l'art Préhistorique dans son Contexte Archéologique", MADAPCA (Paris, 16–18 Novembre 2011)*. Les Eyzies-de-Tayac: Société des Amis du Musée National de Préhistoire et de la Recherche Archéologique (Paléo, numéro spécial), pp.259–270.

Aubry, T., Gameiro, C., Santos, A., Luís, L. (2017) Existe Azilense em Portugal? Novos dados sobre o tardiglaciar e o pré-boreal no Vale do Côa. In Arnaud, J. and Martins, A. (Eds.) *Arqueologia em Portugal 2017- Estado da Questão. Actas do II Congresso da Associação de Arqueólogos Portugueses*. Lisboa: Associação de Arqueólogos Portugueses, pp.403–418.

Aubry, T., Dimuccio, L. A., Barbosa, A. F., Luís, L., Santos, A. T., Silvestre, M., Thomsen, K. J., Rades, E., Autzen, M. and Murray, A. S. (2020) Timing of the middle-to-upper Palaeolithic transition in the Iberian inland (Cardina-Salto do Boi, Côa Valley, Portugal). *Quaternary Research*, 98, pp.81–101. https://doi.org/10.1017/qua.2020.43

Baptista, A. M. (1983) O complexo de gravuras rupestre do Vale da Casa – (Vila Nova de Foz Côa). *Arqueologia*, 8, pp.57–69.

Baptista, A. M. (1999) *No tempo sem tempo: A arte dos caçadores paleolíticos do Vale do Coa. Com uma perspectiva dos ciclos rupestres pós-glaciares.* Vila Nova de Foz Coa: Parque Arqueológico do Vale do Coa; Centro Nacional de Arte Rupestre.

Baptista, A. M. and Fernandes, A. P. B. (2007) Rock art and the Coa Valley archaeological park: A case study in the preservation of Portugal's Prehistoric parietal heritage. In Pettitt, P., Bahn, P. and Ripoll, S. (Eds.) *Palaeolithic cave art at Creswell Crags in European context.* Oxford: Oxford University Press, pp.263–279.

Baptista, A. M. (2009) *O Paradigma Perdido: O Vale do Coa e a Arte Paleolítica de Ar Livre em Portugal.* Edições Afrontamento e Parque Arqueológico do Vale do Coa.

Bednarik, R. G. (2004) Public archaeology and political dynamics in Portugal. *Public Archaeology*, 3(3), pp.162–166. doi:10.1179/pua.2004.3.3.162

Bieniawski, Z. T. (1989) *Engineering rock mass classifications.* New York: Wiley.

BOE – Boletín Oficial del Estado. 1985. Ley 16/1985, de 25 de junio, del Patrimonio Histórico Español. https://www.boe.es/eli/es/l/1985/06/25/16/con. Accessed 23 August 2020.

Brandt, S. A. (2000) Classification of geomorphological effects downstream of dams. *Catena*, 40(4), pp.375–401. https://doi.org/10.1016/S0341-8162(00)00093-X.

Dias-Sardinha, I., Ross, D., and Calapez Gomes, A. (2018) The clustering conditions for managing creative tourism destinations: The Alqueva region case, Portugal. *Journal of Environmental Planning and Management*, 61(4), pp.635–655.

Dordio, P., Gaspar, R., Sastre, J., Pereira, S., Santos, F., Figueiredo, S. S., and Lainho, S. (2017) O Plano de Salvaguarda do Património do Aproveitamento Hidroeléctrico do Baixo Sabor, 2010–2015. *Côavisão*, 2017, pp.123–169.

DR – Diário da República. 2001. Lei n.º 107/2001. https://dre.pt/pesquisa/-/search/629790/details/maximized. Accessed 23 August 2020.

ERN - European Rivers Network 2020 Dam Watch. https://www.ern.org/en/damwatch/ Accessed 08 May 2020.

Fernandes, A. P. B. (2004) Visitor management and the preservation of rock art: Two case studies of open-air rock art sites in Northeastern Portugal: Côa Valley and Mazouco. *Conservation and Management of Archaeological Sites*, 6(2), pp.95–111.

Fernandes, A. P. B. (2008) Aesthetics, ethics, and rock art conservation: How far can we go? The case of recent conservation tests carried out in un-engraved outcrops in the Côa Valley, Portugal. In Heyd, T. and Clegg, J. (Eds.) *Aesthetics and Rock Art III symposium. Proceedings of the XV UISPP world congress (Lisbonne, 4–9 Septembre 2006)*, Vol. 10, Session C73. Oxford: Archaeopress, pp.85–92.

Fernandes, A. P. B. (2010) Vandalism, graffiti or 'just' rock art? The case of a recent engraving in the Côa Valley rock art complex in Portugal. *FUMDHAmentos*, 9(III), pp.729–43.

Fernandes, A. P. B. (2014) *Natural processes in the degradation of open-air rock-art sites: An urgency intervention scale to inform conservation.* Oxford: Archaeopress.

Fernandes, A. P. B. (2017) Isto não é um afloramento! É uma rocha de arte rupestre... Factores potenciais de escolha de superfícies de arte rupestre na fase antiga paleolítica da Arte do Coa. In Arnaud, J. and Martins, A. (Eds.) *Arqueologia em Portugal 2017- Estado da Questão. Actas do II Congresso da Associação de Arqueólogos Portugueses*, 901–1001. Lisboa: Associação de Arqueólogos Portugueses, pp.991–1001.

Fernandes, A. P. B. and Rodrigues, J. (2008) Stone consolidation experiments in rock art outcrops at the Côa Valley Archaeological Park, Portugal. In Rodrigues, J. and Mimoso, J. M. (Eds.) *Stone consolidation in cultural heritage: Research and practice* (Proceedings of the International Symposium). Lisbon: Laboratório Nacional de Engenharia Civil, pp.111–20.

Fernandes, A. P. B., Mendes, M., Aubry, T., Sampaio, J., Jardim, R., Correia, D., Junqueiro, A., Bazaréu, D., Dias, F., and Pinto, P. (2008) The evolving relationship between the Côa Valley Archaeological Park and the local community: An account of the first decade. *Conservation and Management of Archaeological Sites,* 10(4), pp.330–43.

Fernandes, A. B., Reis, M., Escudero Remirez, C., and Vázquez Marcos, C. (2017) Integration of stone features and conservation of the Coa Valley and Siega Verde open-air Rock-Art. *Time&Mind,* 10(3), pp.293–319. DOI: 10.1080/1751696X.2017.1341246

Figueiredo, A. and Monteiro, C. (2012) A Arte Rupestre do Alqueva (revisitada): Projecto de estudo do estado de conservação. *Almadan, II série,* n° 17, pp.159–161. https://issuu.com/almadan/docs/almadan_online_17_1/5

Figueiredo, S. S., Nobre, L. Xavier, P. Gaspar, R. and Carrondo, J. (2016b) First approach to the chronological sequence of the engraved stone plaques of the Foz do Medal alluvial terrace in Trás-os-Montes, Portugal. *ARPI, 04 Extra (Homenaje a Rodrigo de Balbín Behrmann),* Universidade de Alcalá: Alcalá de Henares, pp.64–77.

Figueiredo, S. S., Xavier, P., Neves, D., Maciel, J., Nobre, L. and Domínguez-García, I. (2016a) Illustrating the Sabor Valley (Trás-os-Montes, Portugal): Rock art and its long-term diachrony since the Upper Palaeolithic until the Iron Age. In Fábregas Valcarce, R. and Rodríguez-Rellán, C. (Eds.) *Public images, private readings: Multi-perspective approaches to the Post-Palaeolithic Rock Art: Proceedings of the XVII UISPP world congress (1–7 September 2014, Burgos, Spain),* Volume 5/Session A11e. Oxford: Archaeopress Archaeology, pp.17–28.

Flad, R. K. and Chen, P. (2013) *Ancient Central China: Centers and peripheries along the Yangzi river.* Cambridge: Cambridge University Press.

Gameiro, C. (2018) Upper Paleolithic and preventive Archaeology in Portugal: Challenges and opportunities. *Raport,* 13, pp.203–207.

Gaspar, R., Ferreira, J., Carrondo, J., Silva, M. J. and García-Vadillo, F. J. (2016) Open-air Gravettian lithic assemblages from Northeast Portugal: The Foz do Medal site (Sabor valley). *Quaternary International,* 406, pp.44–64. doi:10.1016/j.quaint.2015.12.054

ICOMOS (2003) ICOMOS CHARTER - Principles for the analysis, conservation and structural restoration of architectural heritage. *Ratified by the ICOMOS 14th General Assembly in Victoria Falls, Zimbabwe.* https://www.icomos.org/charters/structures_e.pdf

Jorge, V. O. (Ed.) (1995) *Dossier Côa.* Porto: Sociedade Portuguesa de Antropologia e Etnologia.

Kitchen, W. and Ronayne, M. (2001) The Ilisu Dam in Southeast Turkey: Archaeology at risk. *Antiquity,* 75(287), pp.37–38. doi:10.1017/S0003598X00052674

Luís, L. (2003) Sauvegarde, conservation et valorisation du patrimoine de la Vallée de la Côa (Portugal). In *Vestiges Archéologiques En Milieu Extrême,* Paris: Institut National du Patrimoine; Monum, Éditions du Patrimoine, pp.110–119. https://www.inp.fr/Recherche-colloques-et-editions/Editions/Monographies/Vestiges-archeologiques-en-milieu-extreme

Marques, J. M. (2013) *A framework for assessing the vulnerability of exposed schist surfaces to lichen-induced weathering in the Upper Douro region (NE Portugal).* PhD thesis. Porto University. https://repositorio-aberto.up.pt/bitstream/10216/71524/2/24395.pdf

Marques, J. and Neto, F. (2018) Steps towards public engagement with archaeological heritage - some Portuguese examples, *Internet Archaeology*, 49. https://doi.org/10.11141/ia.49.13

Moura, A. M. (2015) Aproveitamento hidroelétrico da bacia do Douro: Um olhar crítico. *Neutro à Terra*, 15, pp.5–14. https://recipp.ipp.pt/bitstream/10400.22/6501/1/RevistaNeutroATerra_N15_2015_ART_3.pdf

Oddy, W. A. and Carroll, S. (1999) *Reversibility, does it exist?* London: British museum.

Ribeiro, L. (2015) Development projects, violation of human rights, and the silence of archaeology in Brazil. *International Journal of Historical Archaeology*, 19(4), pp.810–821.

Romana, M. (1985) New adjustment ratings for application of Bieniawski classification to slopes. In *Proceedings of the international symposium on the role of rock mechanics in excavations for mining and civil works*. Zacatecas: International Society of Rock Mechanics, pp.49–53.

PAeM (Portugal Ambiente em Movimento) (2016) *Sabor ameaçado: o último rio selvagem da Europa!* https://www.ambientemovimento.org/baixo-sabor. Accessed 31 May 2020.

Reis, M. (2014) Mil rochas e tal...: Inventário dos sítios da arte rupestre do Vale do Côa (3a parte). *Portvgalia*, Nova Série, 35, pp.17–59.

Rodrigues, J. D. (2003) Histórias com água e pedras. Nem sempre mole, nem sempre duras. In Ferreira, M. (Ed.) *A geologia de engenharia e os recursos geológicos*. Vol. II Coimbra: Imprensa da Universidade, pp.419–436.

Santos, A. T. (2017) *A arte paleolítica ao ar livre da bacia do Douro à margem direita do Tejo: uma visão de conjunto*. PhD thesis. Porto: Universidade do Porto. https://repositorio-aberto.up.pt/handle/10216/109327

Seabra, L., Santos, F., Vaz, F. C., Leite, J. and Tereso, J. P. (2020) Crops behind closed walls: Fortified storage at Castelinho in the Late Iron Age of NW Iberia. *Journal of Archaeological Science: Reports*, 30. https://doi.org/10.1016/j.jasrep.2020.102200.

Serrão, E. C., Lemos, F. S., Monteiro, J. P., Querol, M. A., Jorge, S. O. and Jorge, V. O. (1972) O complexo de arte rupestre do Vale do Tejo (V.ª V.ª de Ródão - Nisa): primeiras hipóteses e programa de trabalhos. *O Arqueólogo Português*, 3ª Série, 6, pp.63–77.

Stranghoener, M., Schippers, A., Dultz, S. and Behrens, H. (2018) Experimental microbial alteration and Fe mobilization from basaltic rocks of the ICDP HSDP2 Drill Core, Hilo, Hawaii. *Frontiers in Microbiology*, 9. 10.3389/fmicb.2018.01252

Teixeira, J. C. (2016) O Abrigo de Parada, um sítio de arte rupestre do Vale do Sabor (Alfândega da Fé, Bragança, Trás-os-Montes). In Sanches, M. J. and Cruz, D. J. (Eds.) *Estudos Pré-Históricos* Vol. XVIII. Actas da II Mesa Redonda. Artes Rupestres da Pré-história e da Proto-história: Estudo, Conservação e Musealização de Maciços Rochosos e Monumentos Funerários. Viseu: Centro de Estudos Pré-Históricos da Beira Alta, pp.41–70.

Teixeira, J. C., Valdez-Tullet, J. and Sanches, M. J. (2016) O abrigo da Foz do Rio Tua-Alijó (Trás-os-Montes, Portugal). identificação e estudo preliminar. In Sanches, M. J. and Cruz, D. J. (Eds.) *Estudos Pré-Históricos*, Vol. XVIII. Actas da II Mesa Redonda. Artes Rupestres da Pré-história e da Proto-história: Estudo, Conservação e Musealização de Maciços Rochosos e Monumentos Funerários. Viseu: Centro de Estudos Pré-Históricos da Beira Alta, pp.131–140.

Thüs, H., Aptroot, A. and Seaward, M. R. D. (2014) Freshwater lichens. In Jones, E. B. G., Hyde, K. D. and Pang, K.-L. (Eds.) *Freshwater fungi and fungal-like organisms.* Berlin: Walter de Gruyter, pp.333–358.

Xavier, P., Cristo Ropero, A., Maciel, J. and Figueiredo, S. S. (2014) Do ver ao compreender as as gravuras "fusiformes" do vale do Sabor. In Honardo Castro, J., Brezmes Ecribano, M. A., Tejeiro Pizarro, A. and Rodríguez Monterrubio, O. (Eds.) *II Jornadas de Jóvenes Investigadores del Valle del Duero: Del Neolítico a la Antiguedad Tardía.* Glyphos Publicaciones, pp.87–98.

Zilhão, J., Aubry, T., Carvalho, A. F., Baptista, A. M., Gomes, M. V., and Meireles, J. (1997) The rock art of the Côa Valley (Portugal) and its archaeological context: First results of current research. *Journal of European Archaeology,* 5(1), pp.7–49.

Zilhão, J. (1998) The rock art of the Côa Valley, Portugal: Significance, conservation and management. *Conservation and Management of Archaeological Sites,* 2(4), pp.193–206.

11 Evaluating Thermal-Hygrometric Dynamics at a Levantine Rock Art Site
La Covatina (Vilafranca, Castelló)

Irene Rodríguez and Inés Domingo

Introduction

Levantine rock art (LRA) is a prehistoric rock art tradition located in Mediterranean Iberia. It includes different sorts of figurative motifs (humans and animals), both painted and more rarely engraved, interacting in narrative scenes. The significance of this rock art tradition has been globally acknowledged with the nomination as World Heritage in 1998. The wide geographical distribution of this millenary art explains the variety of outdoor locations in which it has been preserved. They range from well-protected rock shelters to vertical walls with nearly no overhang to protect the art from weather conditions. These diverse locations involve direct exposure to a variety of degrading agents, including both natural (physical, chemical and biological) and anthropogenic deterioration (Rodríguez and Domingo 2018). As such, LRA sites are an extremely vulnerable and fragile heritage needing urgent attention to identify deterioration mechanisms and, when possible, minimize potential impacts threatening both their aesthetic and physical integrity.

Since LRA sites are located across the Mediterranean Iberia, with altitudes ranging between 200 and more than 1,000 Metres Above Mean Sea Level (MAMSL), at various distances from the coast and facing different orientations, significant variations and microclimates among the different sites are to be expected. Thus, more than universal protocols for LRA conservation, we need to develop site-specific strategies to understand the peculiarities of each local environment. Only then we will be able to adapt conservation intervention to the specificities of each site and minimize the loss of values.

It is well known that steep and fluctuating changes in daily and seasonal climatic parameters (temperature, humidity and illuminance) cause material stress or fatigue. These changes can eventually cause instability and deterioration to the physical and visual properties of the materials involved in rock art (bedrock and pigments), such as colour change and fading, or changes in shape, hardness and mass of the bedrock. To mitigate or at least anticipate the impacts of such changes, appropriate understanding and monitoring of the local environmental conditions is necessary. Microclimatic monitoring

DOI: 10.4324/9780429355349-15

is more common in Palaeolithic caves where alterations of microenvironmental conditions, especially when opening caves for tourism, impacts the natural dynamic equilibrium of cave systems (see, for example, Sánchez et al. 2014). Similar analyses have been less often conducted in open air sites (Hoerlé 2006; Meiklejohn et al. 2009; Fernandes 2012), with only a few examples in Levantine rock art (Alloza 2013; Alloza et al. 2012, 2016; Hernández and Royo 2013; Barreda 2016; Barreda and Zalbidea 2018).

This paper uses La Covatina del Tossalet del Mas de la Rambla site (Vilafranca, Castelló, Spain) as a case study. The site is located 1,126 MAMSL facing south-east. While it is only 60 km away from the Mediterranean Sea, it is located at a supramediterranean bioclimatic area, with cold winters and temperate summers due to its altitude (for more information on this site, see also Chapter 3 in this volume). The paper presents the results of a medium-term monitoring of yearly and daily environmental deterioration agents such as light exposure, temperature and relative humidity, using different environmental control systems. The potential and problems of the methods used are also discussed. The results are used to develop a series of recommendations for the preventive conservation of this site considering the specificities of the natural environment.

Methodology

In order to record the environmental parameters affecting the processes of deterioration of rock art in the open-air Temperature (T), Relative Humidity (RH), Illuminance (E) were measured at La Covatina using various devices. Temperature and relative humidity were monitored uninterruptedly throughout the year. Alongside this, in planned visits at different seasons, the surface temperature of the rock and the light to which various points of the rock shelter were exposed were measured manually throughout the day. The whole process was recorded photographically.

Monitoring

In July 2016, two portable Data Logger LOG32 thermo-hygrographs were installed at La Covatina rock shelter and another contiguous one with no art but with similar orientation and characteristics to the painted shelter. The idea was not to depend on a single device and verify whether both behaved in the same way. However, the thermo-hygrograph installed at La Covatina disappeared and it was impossible to recover it. The ambient temperature data presented in this study therefore comes exclusively from the contiguous rock shelter (Figure 11.1 top), although its validity was confirmed by comparing the measurements from the rock shelter with those provided by the local meteorologist, Ignasi Llopis, who used to gather several meteorological parameters at the Spanish State Meteorological Agency (AEMET) weather station placed in Vilafranca del Cid. The correlation between the

Figure 11.1 Top: Front view of La Covatina and the contiguous rock shelter where the thermo-hydrograph whose data has been used in this study was placed. Photos by I. Rodríguez. Centre: Location of the seven manual temperature and light exposure measurement points. The blue circles represent the location of rock art motifs (3D model made by GIFLE, LArcHer project). Bottom: Exact location of rock surface temperature measurement points A, B, E, F and G next to painted motifs (motifs 3, 6, 12, 26 and 34, respectively). Photos and tracings by I. Domingo (LArcHer project).

temperature and relative humidity registered there and the ones registered at La Covatina site is very high.

The thermo-hygrograph was programmed to record data every two hours, following previous criteria (Barreda 2016) so the results may be eventually compared if needed, and it was placed in a part of the rock shelter that was not very visible to prevent possible theft. However, it was daily exposed both to shadow and to direct sunlight to emulate the conditions of various paintings in La Covatina.

One of our aims was to analyse seasonal changes. To do this, we selected dates in three specific periods: from 21 June to 21 July 2017 representing the warm season; from 17 October to 16 November 2017, representing the intermediate seasons, and from 1 to 28 February 2018, as a representative of the ambient parameters in the cold seasons. To simplify reading, we will refer to these periods as July, October and February, although the first two periods include dates in June and November respectively.

Temperature measurements and light exposure on the rocky surface

The rock surface temperature and light exposure measurements were taken manually with a Testo 905-T2 contact thermometer and a Milwaukee SM700 luxmeter. As it is a relatively large rock shelter, seven points at different heights and positions were chosen to observe whether there were significant differences between them based on their orientation and level of exposure (Figure 11.1 centre).

Some of the points were selected next to rock art figures (points A-B-E-F-G) so that collected data represented the conditions paintings are subjected to (Figure 11.1 centre and bottom). In these cases, direct contact with the motifs was avoided when making the measurements. Point A is next to archer 3; B is next to a series of pigment splashes (motif 6); points E and F are next to female figure 12 and a human figure decorated with a deer's antler (motif 26); and point G is next to archer 34. Points C and D are not near rock art motifs but were selected as reference points to find out what happens in intermediate areas of the rock shelter.

The measurements analysed correspond, as ambient measurements, to specific dates in July and October 2017 and February 2018. They were taken at 11 different times of day between 9:00 and 19:00. The measurements were made at one-hour intervals, except for the period between 11:30 and 16:40, when they were taken every half hour. As these were the times of most sunlight, we wanted to check whether changes could be appreciated at shorter time intervals.

Notes were taken concerning the incidence of sunlight on the point analysed to know whether, at the time of measurement, the point selected was in the sun or the shade. The general weather conditions of the day, such as wind or the presence of clouds, which might interfere in the comparison of data between one session or another, were also noted.

This whole process was documented photographically, allowing us to show the extent of the incidence of sunlight at different times of day, as well as areas remaining in the shade at different times of year (Figure 11.2).

218 *Irene Rodríguez and Inés Domingo*

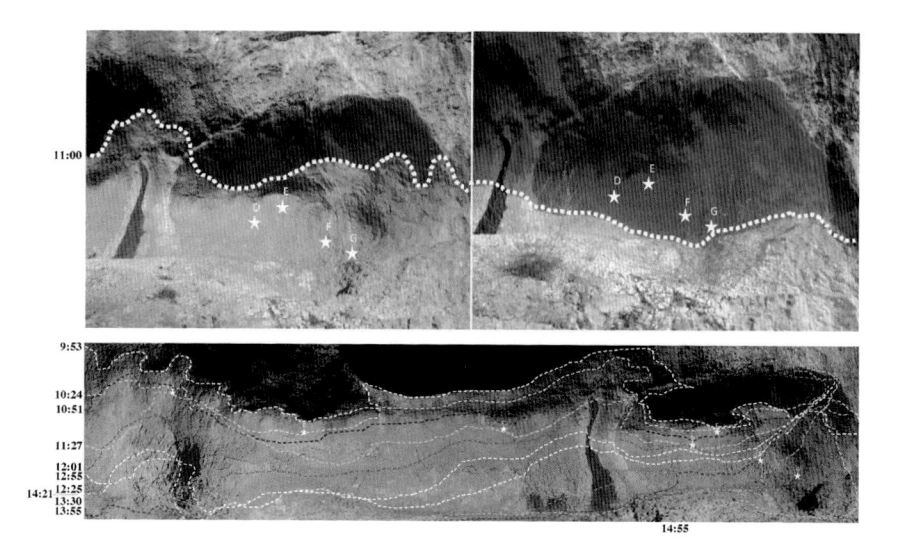

Figure 11.2 Top: Comparison between the reach of the line of the sun in the right-hand sector of the rock shelter at around 11:00 in February (left) and July (right). Bottom: View of the rock shelter on 26 February 2018. The dotted lines indicated the gradual descent of the shadow line between 9:53 and 14:55, when the whole rock shelter is protected from the sun. Figure by the authors.

Finally, all data obtained were processed using Microsoft Excel® spreadsheets obtaining graphs of development curves designed with the time variable on the x axis and the numerical values for T, RH or E on the y axis.

Results

Environmental data analysis in monthly time bands

Below we analyse the temperature and ambient humidity graphs relating to different months of the year.

In July 2017 (Figure 11.3a) it is observed that the minimum and maximum temperature showed small variations throughout the month, marking a development curve showing no drastic changes. RH data is also quite coherent, marking parallel lines, although the minimum RH is conditioned by the increase in temperature, as would be expected.

In October 2017 (Figure 11.3b), by contrast, a significant difference between a stable minimum temperature and a fluctuating maximum temperature can be seen, particularly in the second half of the period. The greater daytime temperature variation is, in turn, translated into inverse correlation with the minimum RH, which falls to its lowest values on the days when the maximum temperature reaches its highest ones.

In February 2018 (Figure 11.3c) the behaviour of the maximum and minimum temperatures already seen in October is maintained, and, in fact, the sharp rises and falls are accentuated. The minimum temperature remains relatively stable by contrast with a maximum T showing great fluctuations from one day to another, in turn influencing the minimum RH, which stands out once again for its notably negative correlation with the maximum temperature.

As the site is in an inland geographical area where distance from the sea and altitude lead to greater thermal amplitude between day and night, more dramatic temperature changes would have been expected during the summer. However, the data shows the opposite phenomenon: July turned out to be a month with significantly less pronounced variation than in February, while in October the transition process between seasons could be seen as the month went on.

In fact, while the maximum temperature value for July at the rock shelter does not exceed 28.6°C on the 22nd, the data records a maximum T of up to 41.7°C on 10 October and up to 33°C on 26 February. For these same dates, the environmental data collected at the AEMET weather station indicated that Vilafranca achieved a maximum temperature of 32.5°C on 12 July 2017, 25.5°C on 26 October 2017 and 11°C on 26 February 2018 (Tables 11.1 and 11.2).

Table 11.1 Differences in maximum temperatures between the Covatina rock shelter and AEMET weather station (Vilafranca) at different times of the year

Season	Date	Maximum T at La Covatina Site	Maximum T at AEMET Weather Station (Vilafranca)
June–July 2017	12 July	28.6°C	32.5°C
October–November 2017	26 October	41.7°C	25.5°C
February 2018	26 February	33°C	11°C

Table 11.2 Days with the maximum temperatures recorded at AEMET weather station (Vilafranca) in the different seasons and maximum temperatures recorded on the same date at Covatina rock shelter

Season	Date	Maximum T at AEMET Weather Station (Vilafranca)	Maximum T at La Covatina Site
June–July 2017	12 July	32.5°C	28.6°C
October–November 2017	26 October	25.5°C	41.7°C
February 2018	15 February	18.5°C	29.2°C

Carrying out the opposite exercise based on the maximum monthly T recorded at Vilafranca and checking the maximum temperature recorded at the rock shelter on these same dates, it can be seen (Tables 11.1 and 11.2) that in the June–July and October–November periods, the day of the highest ambient temperature in Vilafranca is also the day of highest ambient temperature at the rock shelter. By contrast, in February 2018 the day with the highest ambient temperature recorded at Vilafranca corresponds to the day when the second highest ambient temperature was recorded at the rock shelter.

This data shows that the temperature recorded at Vilafranca runs parallel to that recorded at the rock shelter, although higher temperatures were recorded at the rock shelter in the colder months than in the warmer ones. This apparent anomaly is directly related to the incidence of direct sunlight in the rock shelter. As the year goes on, the inclination of sunlight hitting the Earth changes, so that in the summer, as the sun remains higher, the overhang of the rock shelter projects shade into it, while when winter approaches the sun is lower in the sky, fully lighting up the inside of La Covatina. This also explains why in February 2018 we find dramatic contrasts between one day and another depending on whether it is a cloudy or clear day.

Other important data observed on the graphs is that the minimum temperature at La Covatina hardly dropped below 0°C (just once, in February 2018, on the 9th, when −0.1°C was recorded at around 8:00), while in Vilafranca the data collected by Ignasi Llopis did show frequent falls below 0°C in winter. Checking the data obtained the previous year (2017), it could be seen that the data logger recorded an annual minimum of −4.3°C on 18 January 2017. For this date at Vilafranca a significant minimum of −9.7°C was also recorded. However, in general, although in Vilafranca there are often temperatures below 0 in the winter, at La Covatina this only happens on exceptionally cold days. This would imply that the rock shelter is really a shelter, with milder temperatures inside, even in the early hours of the morning.

Ambient data analysis in daily time bands

We will now analyse the T and RH data obtained over 24 h on the same days as T and light exposure measurements were taken on the rock surface.

As suggested in the monthly data (Figure 11.3d), we see that the thermal amplitude for a day in July is by no means dramatic. There is just 5.8°C difference between the maximum and minimum values recorded: 23.6°C at 10:23 and 17.8°C at 00:23, respectively.

In October (Figure 11.3e), on the other hand, in mid-morning the temperature rises sharply, moving from 12°C recorded at 7:22 to 34.2°C at 12:22, so the value for the thermal amplitude for that day would be 22.2°C, almost four times as high as in July.

Finally, the graph from February (Figure 11.3f) is similar to that for October concerning temperatures: the minimum is recorded at dawn, with 6.1°C at 7:22 and the maximum at 12:22 with 33°C, with a thermal amplitude of 26.9°C. The fact that such high temperatures can be reached inside the rock shelter in February is attributed precisely to the fact that these geological formations, because of their characteristics, are sheltered from the wind, retaining the heat generated by exposure to the sun.

Analysis of temperature and incidence of light on the rock surface at points A–G

Once the behaviour of the monthly and daily parameters had been analysed, we moved on to check whether there was a clear correlation between the temperature and level of light exposure recorded on the rock surface.

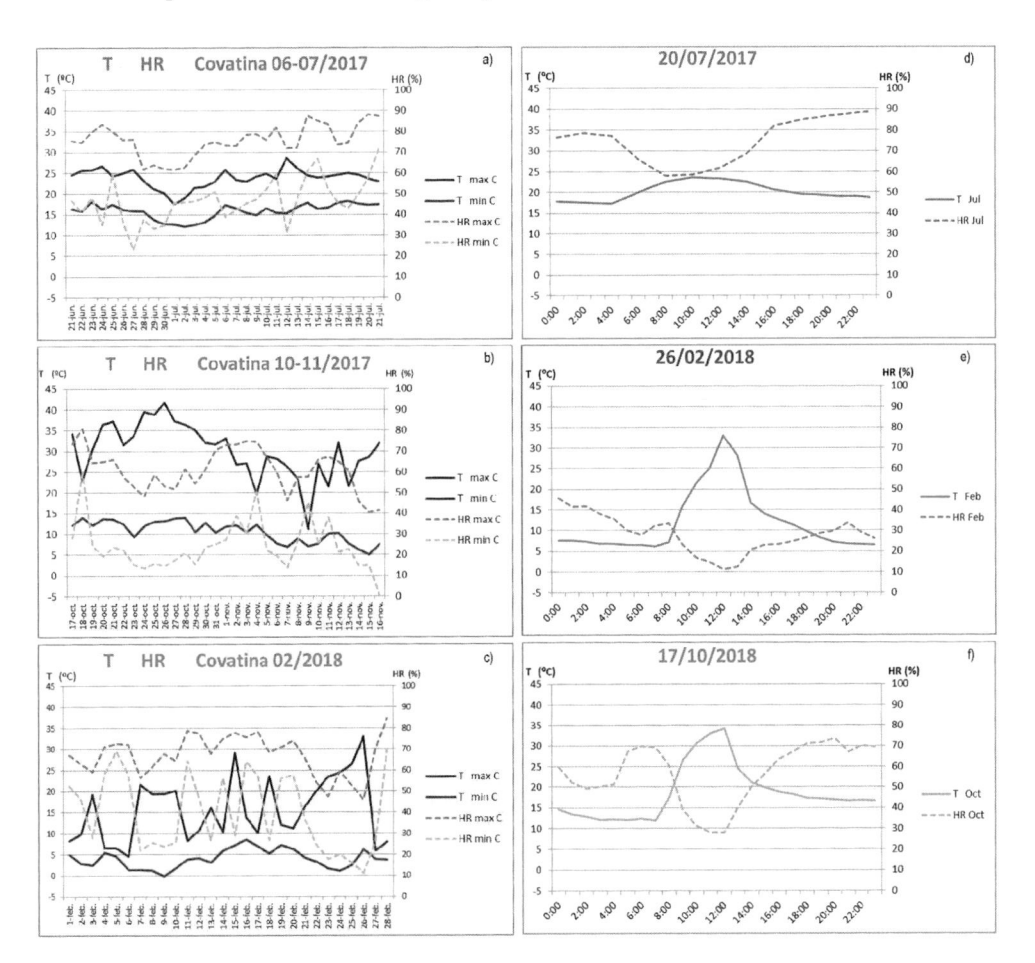

Figure 11.3 T and RH graphs recorded at La Covatina in periods in July (a) October (b) and February (c) and during particular days in July (d), October (e) and February (f). Graphs by I. Rodríguez.

Considering the characteristics of the site in terms of dimensions, orientation and layout of the overhang, the degree of direct incidence of sunlight on the 40 preserved rock paintings varies. This variation was observed both between different seasons of the year (due to variations in the angle of the light because of changes in the position of the sun on the horizon) and between the different motifs. Depending on their position with respect to the floor, the extent of the overhang protecting them and their orientation, each motif has different levels of exposure.

Taking direct measurements at different points of the panel allows us to analyse the degree of exposure of the motifs depending on their location (Figure 11.1 centre).

The following graphs include the measurements taken manually throughout a whole day in three different months, except at night. However, the data provided by the data logger in the exterior cavity shows a relatively stable ambient temperature between 7 in the evening and 9 in the morning (time band when no manual measurements were taken). The variation during this time band is between 2 and 5 degrees depending on the month analysed, but in no case were sharp temperature changes observed, just a gradual fall. That variation is greater in October (4.9°C) than in February (2.1°C) or July (2.1°C). The absence of sunlight in both cavities at this time (both in the exterior cavity and in the rock shelter with paintings) suggests that this variation observed outside the rock shelter could be extrapolated to the rock shelter with paintings and, therefore, there would be a correlative fall in temperature of the painted medium during the night.

Measurements at point A

This point is several centimetres to the right of Archer 3, who is drawn in a bow shooting position (Figure 11.1a). Its state of preservation is poor, with considerable losses of pictorial material, and it is difficult to see.

At this point of the panel, the overhang offers little protection – compared with other areas inside the cavity – and the rock surface, which is significantly high off the ground, is quite exposed.

As can be seen in the graph (Figure 11.4), it receives high levels of light first thing in the morning and more so in February and October, months when exposure to the sun continues until after 10:00 (Figure 11.2 bottom).

The temperature of the rock surface rises as exposure to the sun goes on and afterwards falls once it remains in the shade.

Measurements at point B

This point is at the base of a niche containing splashes of paint (Figure 11.1.B) inside the rock shelter and particularly protected by the overhang.

In this case, the dotted lines indicated a slightly different light pattern, with little incidence of direct sunlight (Figure 11.4): in July, the radiation does not hit after 9:00. In February and October, it hits until only one hour afterwards.

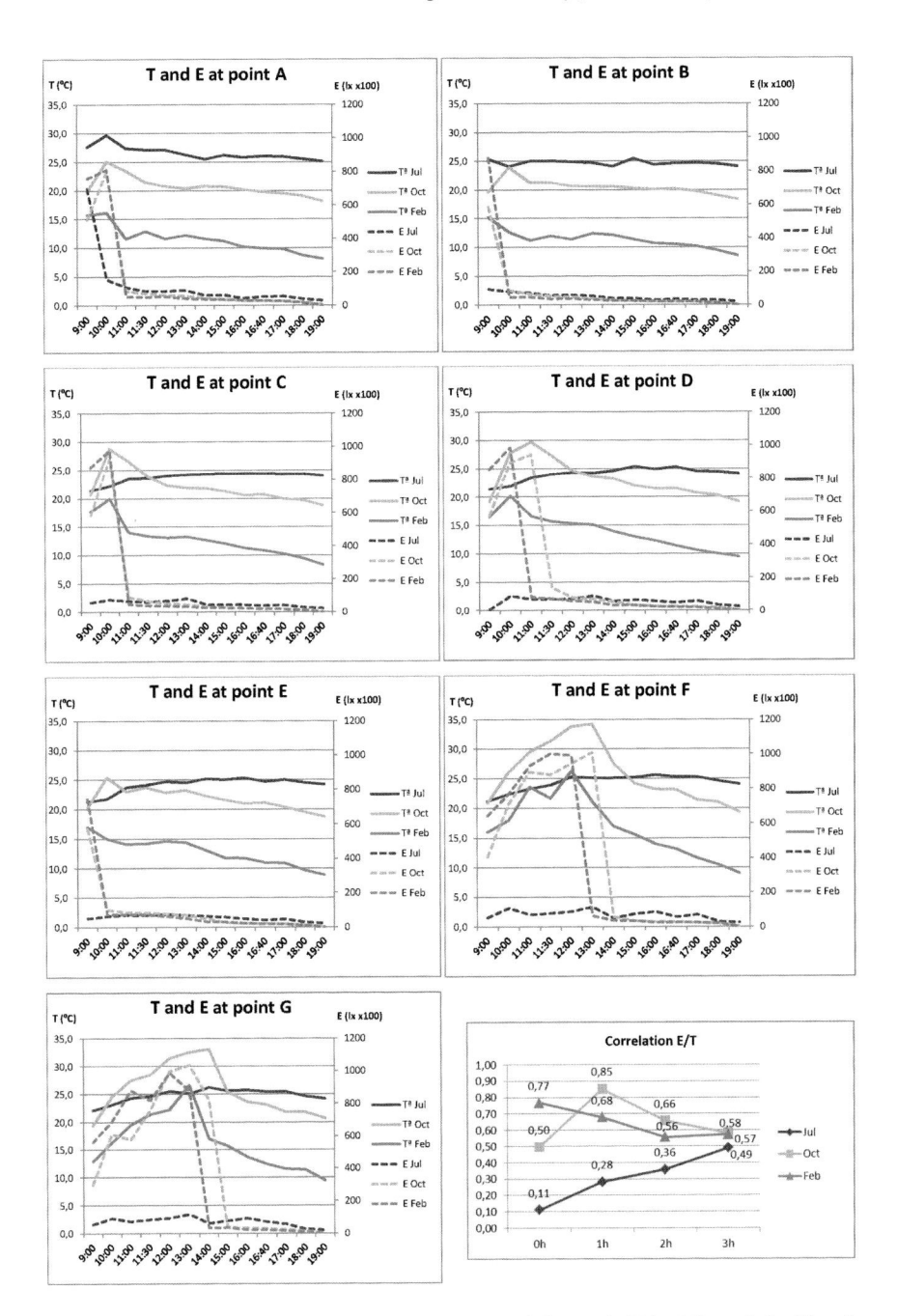

Figure 11.4 Graphs of the surface temperature of the rock (T in °C) and the illuminance received (E in lux x 100) at points A, B, C, D, E, F and G from 9:00 to 19:00 on three days from different times of the year; and graph showing the correlation between illuminance and surface temperature. Graphics by I. Rodríguez.

Temperatures remain stable in July, with a small peak of 25.5°C after midday which is slightly lower than the 26°C recorded at 9:00. In October and February, it showed a downward tendency after the early morning. Only in October did it retain heat on the surface after 10:00.

Measurements at point C

Point C is not close to any preserved painting, but it is representative of the exposure conditions of the rock surface in a central area of the rock shelter (Figure 11.1c). It is slightly nearer the floor than point B, but the characteristics are similar: a small cavity in a deep area of the rock shelter where the overhang provides good protection.

In July it does not receive sunlight at the earliest measurement time (9:00) (Figure 11.4), however it does in October and February until after 10:00.

Alongside the July temperature, which is not altered by direct incidence of the sun in the early morning, it shows a gentle, stable rising curve attributable to the increase in the ambient temperature. It does not begin to fall until the end of the day.

Measurements at point D

Point D does not have rock paintings nearby either, but it is in a shallower area of the rock shelter, midway between point C and the next ones and at an intermediate height from the floor between point E, and points F and G (Figure 11.1d).

As in the previous case, at warm times of the year the light does not directly hit the surface at the first measurement time, although this does happen in February until after 10:00 and in October until after 11:00 – times when the dotted lines of illuminance fall sharply (Figure 11.4).

Surface temperatures in July also reproduce the behaviour of point C: a gradual rise from the first hour measured and not beginning to fall until late in the afternoon. The surface temperature lines from February and October have certain parallels between one another and they follow the illuminance data: the rock surface temperatures are higher in the first measurements taken in the morning and they decrease when direct exposure to the sun ends.

It must be pointed out that the surface temperature at 10:00 in October is 27.8°C, 21.9°C in July and 20.2°C in February. It is surprising to see that at this point D, in the transition seasons, the rock heats up more than at warmer periods, and even in the middle of winter the maximum temperature is close to the values obtained in July.

Measurements at point E

Point E measures the conditions of the female figure (Figure 11.1e), which is in excellent state of preservation except for the loss of pictorial material in the upper segment. The figure is one of the highest from the floor and is quite deep into the shelter, so it has the protection of the overhang.

The lux values remain virtually stable in July, when sunlight does not directly hit the motif. At this point, the almost perpendicular position of the sun in summer allows the rock shelter overhang to protect the painted motifs throughout the day (Figure 11.2 top). However, in both October and February (when the change of angle in the position of the sun leads to the direct exposure of the motif), the lux value shows the following pattern: high values first thing in the morning (even more so in February) and a dramatic fall between 9:00 and 10:00, when the figures overlap with those for July (Figure 11.4).

In this case, on the day in October the temperature rose 5.1°C in barely an hour, reaching the maximum temperature of 25.4°C at 10:00, and then fell, with smaller peaks in the middle of the day. By contrast, on the chosen date in July, temperatures gradually increased, reaching their highest levels after midday.

Meanwhile, in February, the surface temperature continued to fall after the first hour measured. In fact, when calculating the thermal amplitude, we obtain values of 8.1°C in February, 6.6°C in October and 4°C in July.

Measurements at point F

Point F corresponds to the human figure wearing a headdress consisting of a deer's antler (Figure 11.1f). The state of preservation is deficient with poorly defined edges. This figure is in the right-hand segment of the rock shelter, near a flow of water and quite near the floor, where the level of exposure is greater.

The measurements from point F show a similar behaviour to that observed in previous graphs as the rock surface temperatures are closely linked to the illuminance received.

So, the lux and the temperature recorded in July vary little, as shown by an almost horizontal line. As in the previous figure, this is explained by the lack of direct exposure to sunlight thanks to the higher position of the sun on summer days.

By contrast, both in October and in February the temperature rises significantly through the morning until the point when the incidence of direct sunlight falls with the consequent drop in temperature (Figure 11.4). The thermal amplitudes on this graph are 17.2°C in February, 14.8°C in October and 4.4°C in July.

Measurements at point G

Point G is near the remains of a poorly preserved archer (Figure 11.1g) located to the right of point F.

The measurements show patterns similar to the previous point: the lux and temperature for July remain stable, while in October and February the temperature rises throughout the morning until the incidence of direct sunlight falls, then the surface temperatures also drop. In addition, the data shows that exposure to the sun goes on for an hour longer in October than in February (Figure 11.4). The thermal amplitudes in this figure were 17.1°C in February, 13.7°C in October and 4.9°C in July.

When comparing the results with other measurement points, it is observed that, as it is located at the lower part of the panel, in February it receives almost 3.5 hours of sunlight more than point E (female figure), although in July almost all the points are in the shade at around 11:00 (Figure 11.2 top).

Illuminance range and thermal amplitude

We will now analyse the illuminance range (difference between the maximum and minimum value) and the thermal amplitude (difference between the maximum and minimum temperature values) for each season of the year at each of the points measured. The aim is to numerically examine the point in which the changes registered at surface level are abrupt, as sharp changes have a greater effect on the state of preservation of materials than gradual ones.

When combining the analysis of the two graphs (Figure 11.5), we see that in July the illuminance level is high only at points A and B, which are the ones that receive direct sunlight first thing in the morning at this time of the year. However, looking at the thermal amplitude it is clear the figure for point A is notably higher than at point B. This is explained by the fact that sunlight shines for longer at point A (it continues until after 9:00) so the rock retains heat for longer, whereas point B goes into the shade before 9:00).

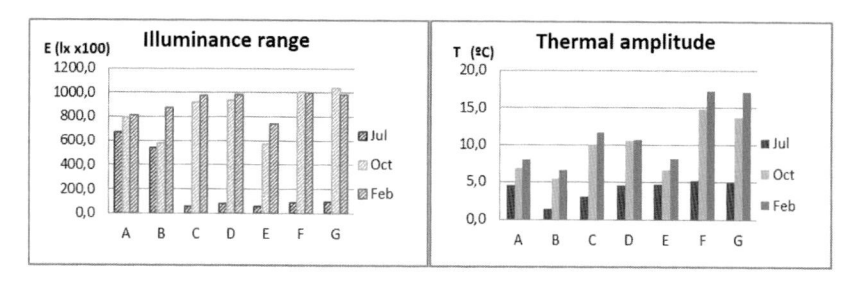

Figure 11.5 Comparison between the illuminance range (left) and the thermal amplitude (right) of points A-G in the three periods measured. Graphic by I. Rodríguez.

It is also noticeable that the thermal amplitude at point B is the lowest for all the points measured and is even lower than those that do not receive direct sunlight in July. This is probably because of the impact of ambient temperature on the temperature of the rock surface. The cool ambient temperatures in the morning have less effect on the surface temperature at point A, because the direct sunlight strikes for longer and has greater capacity to increase it. On the contrary, at point B the sun barely heats the rock long enough as to warm it up a little and compensates the cool ambient temperature, so the surface temperature remains stable and stays there once point B is in the shade. By contrast, at the other points the sun does not hit, it is only the ambient temperature that affects the thermal amplitude. So, the thermal amplitudes in July for this time band (from 9:00 to 19:00) are higher the longer the rock surface is exposed to the sun, but they remain average when they depend only on the ambient temperature, and low when the short early sun exposure can only just compensate for the cool of the morning.

As for the differences in thermal amplitude between points C-G, it can be seen that C (in a high, deep cavity) is the one showing least variation; that points D–E (highest from the floor and with similar protection from the overhang) show similar values; and that points F and G are the ones which, even when they remain in the shade, achieve the greatest temperature difference, perhaps conditioned by their location (further out and closer to the floor).

As for October and February, it can be seen that there is a correlation between the range of illuminance and the thermal amplitude at all points measured.

Points A and B also receive plenty of direct light first thing in the morning, but, as they are high up in the rock shelter, they are soon protected by the shadow, so their thermal amplitudes are kept relatively low, as they do not accumulate heat for hours.

Something similar happens with point E, corresponding to the female figure, which is at a significant height above the floor and is therefore one of the first to be covered by the shadow. This figure is the one receiving least direct light at both times of year and one of those showing the least difference between maximum and minimum temperatures.

Points C and D show average values because, although the level of light exposure is high, the fact that they are in deeper sectors of the rock shelter means there is a considerable overhang, and they are protected relatively early by the shadow.

Meanwhile, points F and G (at the extreme right of the rock shelter, with least protection from the overhang and greatest level of exposure) are those receiving greatest illuminance for the longest period (until after midday) (Figure 11.2 bottom), so their thermal amplitudes are notably greater, particularly in February. As it is a colder month, when the shadow reaches the figures, the surface temperature comes to be influenced only by the ambient temperature, which is much colder than when there is direct incidence of the sun.

Correlation between surface temperature and illuminance

The surface temperature of the rock depends on several variables: the illuminance received, and the ambient temperature are particularly important. The above graphs point to the direct incidence of the sun having greater capacity to condition the surface temperature of the rock than the ambient temperature of the rock shelter. To quantify this phenomenon, we now conduct an analysis of the correlations in order to show the relationship between the surface temperature and level of illuminance.

To do this, at each of the seven points the correlations between the two variables have been calculated at the same time. The aim was to measure the strength of the correlation between the variables every time measurements were taken. This is what from now on we will call "0h". In addition, apart from the correlation between the surface temperature and the illuminance at the same time ("0h"), the correlation is shown between the temperature and the illuminance received an hour earlier ("1h"), two hours earlier ("2h") and three hours earlier ("3h"). The aim is to show how the irradiation received at a given point has effects on the temperatures recorded in the subsequent hours. An average has been obtained with this data reflecting the behaviour of this parameter at the three times of year evaluated.

The values for the correlation coefficients may be between −1 and 1. A positive value shows that there is correlation between the variables, and this is higher the closer the values move to 1.

The data for February shows very high correlation (0.77) between the two variables because of the effect of illuminance received on temperature (Figure 11.4). This correlation becomes weaker as time goes on due to the effect of the low ambient temperatures of winter on the temperature of the rock.

By contrast, in October the figures show that the highest correlation (0.85) corresponds to the relationship between the temperature at a given time and the illuminance received an hour before (Figure 11.4), which seems to indicate that the surface heat is retained for longer than in February, as the ambient temperature is not so cold.

Finally, in July, there are no apparent significant correlations between the two variables, at least at "0h" and "1h" (less than 0.28). As explained, during July the devices yielded the maximum illuminance in the early morning measurements, when the temperatures are coolest. It is only after several hours when moderately important correlation values appear. However, it is difficult to attribute causality to this data as during this month the points measured were mostly in the shade, so the variable most affecting the surface temperature of the rock was simply the ambient temperature.

In any case, there are differences between the individual correlations of the different points, as can be seen in the data breakdown in Table 11.3.

Table 11.3 Correlation between surface temperature and illuminance at the seven monitoring points used in this study at the three times of the year evaluated

Correlation between Surface Temperature and Illuminance

Point		July	October	February
A	r T E(0h)	0.43	0.62	0.85
	r T E(h−1)	0.89	0.82	0.60
	r T E(h−2)	0.65	0.68	0.54
	r T E(h−3)	0.67	0.55	0.57
B	r T E(0h)	0.42	−0.03	0.74
	r T E(h−1)	0.02	0.85	0.44
	r T E(h−2)	0.49	0.51	0.11
	r T E(h−3)	0.49	0.58	0.35
C	r T E(0h)	−0.42	0.61	0.87
	r T E(h−1)	−0.26	0.84	0.72
	r T E(h−2)	−0.26	0.76	0.56
	r T E(h−3)	0.07	0.67	0.55
D	r T E(0h)	0.17	0.62	0.71
	r T E(h−1)	0.47	0.90	0.73
	r T E(h−2)	0.56	0.77	0.66
	r T E(h−3)	0.42	0.72	0.68
E	r T E(0h)	−0.09	0.85	0.64
	r T E(h−1)	0.13	0.91	0.49
	r T E(h−2)	0.44	0.75	0.41
	r T E(h−3)	0.71	0.55	0.46
F	r T E(0h)	0.05	−0.03	0.77
	r T E(h−1)	0.14	0.73	0.89
	r T E(h−2)	0.10	0.46	0.83
	r T E(h−3)	0.60	0.63	0.73
G	r T E(0h)	0.21	0.86	0.81
	r T E(h−1)	0.59	0.92	0.89
	r T E(h−2)	0.52	0.67	0.78
	r T E(h−3)	0.46	0.37	0.66
Average	r T E(0h)	0.11	0.50	0.77
	r T E(h−1)	0.28	0.85	0.68
	r T E(h−2)	0.36	0.66	0.56
	r T E(h−3)	0.49	0.58	0.57

Discussion/Conclusions

The quantitative analysis of the effect of direct solar radiation on the bedrock and Levantine rock paintings at La Covantina rock shelter, using thermo-hygrographs, a contact thermometer and a manual luxmeter, show significant annual and daily variations in temperature, humidity and illuminance that negatively affect its state of preservation. Although the negative impact of sunlight on the bedrock and the pigment is known, the fact is that the level of exposure of each site and even, as we have been able to show in this work, of each motif, varies depending on the location, altitude, orientation, or level of protection, among others. Knowing the specific impact on each site, and even on each figure, is fundamental to be able to adopt protective measures suitable for the characteristics both of the site and the figure, depending on its level of exposure.

One interesting aspect of this study has been to see that it is at cold times of year, and especially in winter, when the rock shelter records more dramatic monthly and daily changes in temperature. On the coldest days the thermal amplitude shoots up to as much as 17 degrees. These drastic changes can lead to weathering by thermoclasty. By contrast, it is also seen that, even though the ambient temperature usually goes below 0 in winter, the shelter temperatures rarely drop below 0 thanks to maintenance of the heat received during the day, so the risk of weathering through gelifraction is low.

Another curious fact is that, considering the characteristics of this site, inside the rock shelter higher ambient temperatures are recorded in winter and autumn than in July. This is attributed to the direct incidence of the sun in the colder seasons due to seasonal changes in the angle of declination of the sun.

It was also recorded that the increase in temperature on the surface of the rock depends more on the direct incidence of the sun than on the ambient temperature, as reflected in the correlations graph, which shows how surface temperature is related to the illuminance received at the time and the previous hours.

The same conclusion can be drawn from the individual graphs in which it is curious to see how at the same time (13:00) in February there are temperature differences of up to 14 degrees between different points on the panel as a result of their level of exposure to the sun. So, for example, if we compare the graphs of points E and F, separated from one another by barely 1.1 metres but at different heights (74 cm difference) we see that the level of illuminance in winter falls at E earlier than it does at F. This is because, as it is lower, point F does not receive the same protection from the overhang, so it receives more hours of sun, and its surface temperature is maintained for longer. In this way, at 13:00, these two points show a difference of 11 degrees (point E: 23.2°C and F: 34.2°C).

On the other hand, if we compare points F and G, separated by 80 cm but nearer in height (difference of just 15.7 cm), they show more similarities. The barely 4 degrees of difference at 13:00 are not due to differences in the level of protection offered by the overhang, but possibly changes in orientation with respect to the sun.

In addition, when analysing the graph for point E and comparing it to the daily ambient temperatures for February, we see that, although the maximum ambient temperature recorded that day was 33°C at 12:00, at that time the surface temperature of the rock at that point, which is in the shade, was 14.4°C. By contrast, the highest surface temperature recorded that day was 17°C at 9:00, despite that fact that the ambient temperature at that time was 7.5°C. This is since, at the time, it was receiving direct radiation.

It is therefore clear that the heat generated by solar radiation on the rock contributes more actively to generating thermal stress on the surface of the panels than the actual ambient heat. So, in summer, when the ambient temperature is higher, the paintings remain in the shade, moderating surface temperatures. By contrast, in winter the paintings receive sunlight for between three and seven hours, depending on their location (Figure 11.1 top). This leads to an increase in surface temperature during exposure and a subsequent fall when they are left in the shade. At La Covatina, therefore, there is not always an evident correlation between the surface and the ambient temperature, as observed at other Levantine sites (Alloza et al. 2016). Instead, at times of direct radiation we see inverse behaviour between the two temperatures.

From these observations it can be deduced that the state of preservation of painted open-air rock art depends to a certain degree on their level of exposure to solar radiation, and they are more likely to be preserved when located in less exposed areas. Undoubtedly, in this specific rock shelter, the best-preserved figures are the ones that are highest up, more protected from radiation by the overhang. It would be interesting to study whether this pattern is repeated at other rock shelters and to cross-reference the data obtained with other deterioration factors that can actively interfere in each case.

These results might suggest the need to prevent direct radiation as a preventive preservation measure. However, as the paintings are in an open space exposed to many natural deterioration factors, which cannot therefore be controlled, any measure intended to alter the micro-environmental parameters could be damaging for the conservation of the site. In fact, the study of the individual thermal amplitudes reveals that point B is the one with the least pronounced temperature changes (Figure 11.5) because, although it receives more radiation than other points, that illuminance occurs precisely at the time when the ambient temperature is lowest (first thing in the morning) so that the brief period when it receives sunlight helps to moderate the surface temperature, preventing thermal amplitude from soaring. It is therefore essential to acquire a deep knowledge of the operation of the micro-ecosystem of each panel and each figure before proposing measures intended to change the current sunlight regime, or any other, for that matter.

Finally, this data is of interest both to find out the effect of the factors analysed on the conservation of the art and when it comes to determining which conservation materials are best suited to the microclimatic characteristics of the site and the times when the conditions are most favourable for them to be applied. As Barreda (2016) concluded in her experimental analysis of different consolidating products applied to the rock of a Levantine rock art site, the materials selected for consolidating are as important as the environmental conditions in which they are applied, since these products behave differently depending on temperature and humidity. In her study, both Nanorestore® and CaLoSiL® behaved differently when applied in different environmental conditions: while high moisture contributed to faster and better carbonation, dry environmental conditions and wind reduced the penetration capacity of the products and the material cohesion was less satisfactory (Barreda 2016, p. 536).

Acknowledgements

This research has been conducted as part of the research projects HAR2016-80693-P (Spanish Ministry of Science, Innovation and Universities) and LArcHer project (ErC Consolidator Grant, Grant agreement 819404), led by I. Domingo. Research by I. Rodríguez was funded by an APIF-UB pre-doctoral grant (University of Barcelona).

We thank Dr. M. Antonia Zalbidea Muñoz and Dr. Dídac Roman for advice and collaboration in the field, and Ignasi Llopis for kindly providing meteorological data recorded at the AEMET Vilafranca weather station.

References

Alloza, R., Royo, J. I., Recuenco, J. L., Lecina, M., Pérez, R. and Iglesias, Mª. P. (2012) La conservación del arte rupestre al aire libre: Un desafío formidable. In Juste, Mº. N., Hernández, Mª. A., Pereta, A., Royo, J. I. and Andrés, J. A. (Eds.) *Jornadas Técnicas para la Gestión del Arte Rupestre, Patrimonio Mundial. Parque Cultural del Río Vero (28 al 31 de mayo de 2012).* Alquézar, Huesca: Comarca de Somontano, pp.89–105.

Alloza, R. (2013) Caracterización del soporte rocoso del arte rupestre. *Cuadernos de Arte Rupestre,* 6, pp. 69–75.

Alloza, R., Royo, J. I. and Latorre, B. (2016) La conservación de un bien declarado Patrimonio Mundial y el proyecto de monitorización del arte rupestre en Aragón. In Lorenzo, J. L. and Rodanés, J.Mª. (Eds.) *Actas del I Congreso de Arqueología y Patrimonio Aragonés (CAPA).* Zaragoza: Colegio Oficial de Doctores y Licenciados en Filosofía y Letras y en Ciencias de Aragón (24 y 25 de novembre de 2015), pp.635–642.

Barreda, G. (2016) *Consolidantes para soportes pétreos con manifestacions de arte rupestre en la Comunidad Valenciana. Análisis práctico en Cova Remigia (Barranc de la Gasulla, Ares del Maestre).* PhD Thesis. Valencia: Universitat Politécnica de Valencia.

Barreda, G. and Zalbidea, M. A. (2018) Estudio de conservación del abric de Pinos (Benissa, Alacant): patologies i causes de deterioració d'un jaciment amb art rupestre llevantí. *Pyrenae,* 49(1), pp.155–183.

Fernandes, A. (2012) *Natural processes in the degradation of open-air rock-art sites: An urgency intervention scale to inform conservation.* PhD Thesis. Bournemouth University.

Hernández, Mª.Á. and Royo, J.I. (2013) Actuaciones de conservación de arte rupestre en la Comunidad Autónoma de Aragón. In *Actas Jornadas Técnicas La Conservación del Arte Rupestre: Sostenibilidad e integración en el paisaje,* Barbastro: Comarca de Somontano de Barbastro, pp.185–196.

Hoerlé, S. (2006) Rock temperatures as an indicator of weathering processes affecting rock art. *Earth Surface Processes and Landforms,* 31(3), pp.383–389.

Meiklejohn, K. I., Hall, K. and Davis, J. K. (2009) Weathering of rock art at two sites in the KwaZulu-Natal Drakensberg, southern Africa. *Journal of Archaeological Science,* 36(4), pp.973–979.

Rodríguez, I. and Domingo, I. (2018) Los problemas de conservación del arte rupestre Levantino: un estado de la cuestión. In *Proceedings of the 3rd international conference on best practices in world heritage: Integral actions Menorca, Spain, 2–5 May 2018,* pp.255–287.

Sánchez, S., Cuezva, S., García-Anton, E., Fernández-Cortes, A., Elez, J., Benavente, D., Cañaveras, J. C., Jurado, V., Rogerio-Candelera, M. A. and Saiz-Jimenez, C. (2014) Microclimatic monitoring in Altamira Cave: Two decades of scientific projects for its conservation. In Saiz-Jimenez, C. (Ed.) *The conservation of subterranean cultural heritage.* London: Taylor & Francis Group, pp.139–144.

12 Calcium Hydroxide Nanoparticles Testing for the Consolidation of Prehistoric Paintings in Cova Remígia (Castelló, Spain)

Gemma Barreda-Usó, M. Antonia Zalbidea Muñoz and Julia Osca Pons

Introduction

Cova Remígia is one of the 757 examples of Levantine rock art included in the United States Agency for International Development (UNESCO) World Heritage List in 1998. This art is considered a unique artistic expression in prehistoric Europe, for the exceptional narrative scenes and the naturalism of the depictions reproduced (Sanz 2012; Utrilla et al. 2012; Domingo 2015; López-Montalvo 2018). This site is located in the northern part of the province of Castelló, within the township of Ares del Maestrat, a mountainous area of the Mediterranean pre-coastal area in the Iberian Peninsula. The shelter is located at a slope of the Gasulla ravine, in the region known as Maestrat, a landscape formed by flat mountain peaks known as muelas (tablelands) and very steep mountain ranges.

Cova Remígia was purchased by the Provincial Council of Castelló in 1957 (Martínez and Guillem 2002). Since then, custody and protection of Cova Remígia belongs to the Provincial Council of Castelló. Since 1994, it is managed by the Valltorta-Gasulla Museum, located in the township of Tírig (Castelló). The Valltorta-Gasulla territory is considered among the most important areas of Levantine rock art, because of the great density and high-quality prehistoric rock art within a limited territorial scope.

Currently it is possible to visit Cova Remígia upon prior appointment, since it is closed with a stone wall and a wire fence to protect the paintings. The shelter is approx. 20m long, a maximum of 9m deep and 7m high. It is formed by six cavities (see Figure 12.1) where highly dynamic hunting scenes are depicted. Original documentation of this shelter was conducted by Porcar et al. (1936), which published an essential reference for current studies. Deer, goats and wild boars are depicted among other animals. Bees surrounding honeycombs are represented too. Depiction of female figures is rare and, in fact, only three have been recorded. Five scenes where human sacrifices are represented can be observed too, which has sparked great

Figure 12.1 Geographic location of Cova Remigia rock shelter (Top left: within the Iberian Peninsula. Top right: within the Valencian Community). Center: view of the six cavities. Bottom: different views of the site. Photos by authors.

interest within research forums (Viñas and Rubio 1988; Sarriá 1989), as an expression of an act of dominance and control of human behaviour within a certain social organization.

The Cova Remígia paintings fall within the artistic tradition known as Levantine rock art, although some representations could fall within Schematic art (Sarriá 1989, p. 32). Chronologically both traditions belong to the post-Paleolithic period. In the absence of direct dating, some authors suggest that Levantine art was produced in the Mesolithic (Alonso and Grimal 1999; Mateo Saura 2005), while others support more recent chronologies in a fully Neolithic context (second half of the 6th millennium cal BC) (Fortea and Aura 1987; Martínez and Guillem 2005; Villaverde et al. 2006, 2012).

Cova Remígia

Modesto Fabregat, owner of the "Mas Modesto" farmhouse, which is located only a few metres away from the shelter (Sarriá 1989), was first aware of the existence of the paintings in Cova Remígia. He did not pay much attention to the paintings, and it was only later in 1934 that Gonzalo G. Espresati revealed the paintings to Eduardo Codina Armengot and Juan Bautista Porcar (Porcar et al. 1936, p. 7). Porcar started research but stopped on the onset of the Spanish Civil War, only resuming, nearly on his own, in the 1940s. From 1970 to 1982, several research projects regarding prehistoric rock art took place in the area, carried out by Ramón Viñas and Eduardo Ripoll. Viñas brought the research back to Valltorta through the Catalan school of archaeology, along with the creation of the Archaeological and Prehistoric Research Service (SIAP) of the Provincial Council of Castelló in 1975 (Olària 1997; Martínez 2000; Román and Domingo 2017). Francesc Gusi (SIAP director) and Carme Olària resumed excavation of new sites such as Cingle de l'Ermita (Albocàsser, Castelló) (Gusi 1975).

E. Ripoll (1963) resumed research on chronology and styles in the Cova Remígia, establishing four stages of execution (Ripoll 1968). A. Beltrán (1985) identified five stages instead, and several differences in chronology in comparison to Ripoll (1966, 1983). Yet Sarriá Boscovich (1989) identified six different stages in the chronology of the shelter, based on chromatic overlapping. Reexamination of preceding research and updating of documentation work by Sarriá Boscovich (1989) resulted in the recognition of 285 previously unidentified figures which, added to those already known, reach the total amount of 759 pictorial units, making Cova Remígia one of the most important sites of Spanish Levantine rock art. Research on the shelter and its compositional sequences continued (Domingo 2005; López-Montalvo 2009). In 2005, preservation and restoration[1] actions took place (Guillamet 2012). Several research groups continued to study the paintings and their preservation from different scientific fields, such as archaeology, conservation and restoration, physics and chemistry, and so forth. These different approaches include spectral analysis of pigment aging with microfading spectrometry (MFS) (Hoyo-Meléndez et al. 2015); in situ study of the elemental physicochemical composition of pigments, patinas and bedrocks using portable X-ray fluorescence spectrometry (e.g. López-Montalvo et al. 2014) and mineralogical characterization of the rock, environmental studies with the installation of Data Loggers and research on new nanometric inorganic materials for bedrock consolidation (Barreda-Usó 2016; Barreda-Usó et al. 2017b; Barreda-Usó and Zalbidea 2014 and 2020). State of the art digital recording techniques, including terrestrial laser scanning and photogrammetry, and digital augmented reality (AR) have been also used for research and dissemination (Domingo et al. 2013; Carrión-Ruiz et al. 2017).

Purpose

The singularity of this study is reflected by the interest in establishing working patterns in consolidation and stabilization of the stone support in Cova Remígia, in order to contribute to preventive conservation and selection criteria for the appropriate materials and restoration treatment in this and other shelters with similar characteristics.

This paper is focused on the study of any issues related to paint consolidation (cohesion) and its support, since consolidation is one of the most complex phases in the conservation and restoration process, due to the circumstances that result in multiple intervention alternatives.

It is aimed to avoid the use of synthetic organic products with a composition difference that leads to differential behaviors that accelerate deterioration, as well as opting for products that are completely compatible with the physical-chemical nature of the original material.

Methodology

Different work stages have been established to achieve goals set in this study:

- Characterization of the stone material in Cova Remígia,[2] using a Zeiss Axioskop 40® Polarized Light Optical Microscope. The research took place at the Scuola Universitaria Professionale della Svizzera Italiana (SUPSI), Dipartimento Ambiente Costruzioni e Design, Istituto Materiali e Costruzione.
- Selection of the consolidant materials: Nanorestore® and CaLoSiL® (CaLoSiL E5®, CaLoSiL E25 grey®, CaLoSiL IP5®, CaLoSiL NP5®).
- Sample preparation: elaborated with stone material from fragments collected around the shelter, always keeping the painted panels intact.
- Consolidants were applied to the stone surface of the samples with a brush, all at a concentration of 5g/L. They were never tested in situ at the site.
- These have been analysed and studied through: Leica® DM 750 Optical Microscope, Leica® S8 APO Stereoscopic Microscope and SEM-EDX Hitachi S-4800 Scanning Electron Microscope with XR detector, with a spotlight of field emission (FEG) with a resolution of 1.4nm at 1KV. This equipment has a backscattered detector of RX BRuker, transmission detector and QUANTAX 400 for microanalysis. Research took place at the Central Service for Experimental Research (SCSIE), Universitat de València (UV).

53 samples were used, divided into two groups. Group A with a polished surface[3] and group B (1, 2), which preserves the original surface patina. Subsequently they were subject to further tests and analyses, such as:
- Water absorption by capillarity test under the UNE-EN 15801 regulation: Conservation of cultural property-Test methods-Determination of water absorption by capillarity.
- Accelerated aging test with temperature and humidity variations, following the guidelines by ASTM International at the D1183-03

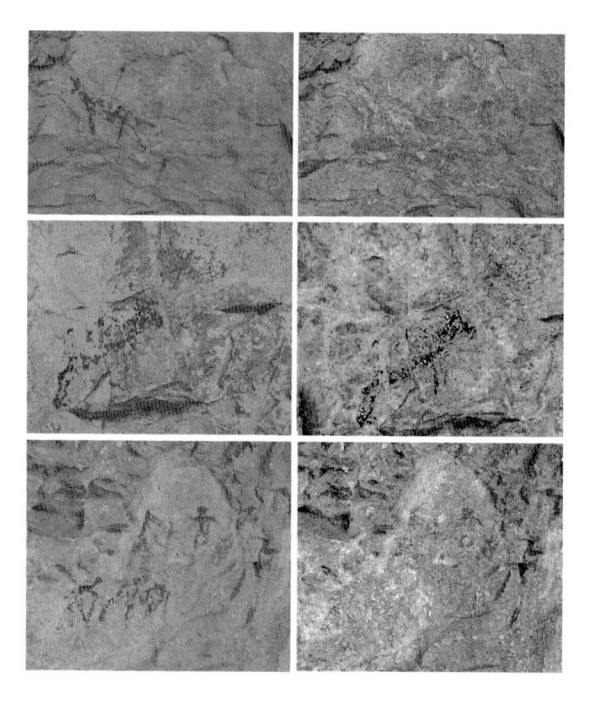

Figure 12.2 Rock surface alterations of animal origin: polishing of paintings, micro-scratches and small rock falls. Photos by authors.

trial: Standard Practices for Resistance of Adhesives to Cyclic Laboratory Aging Conditions. The Dycometal CCK-25/300 climatic chamber from the University Research Institute (Institute for the Heritage Restoration-Universitat Politècnica de València) was used to carry out this test.
- Control of colour variations, through the CIELab* system, under the UNE-EN 15886 regulation: Conservation of cultural property-Test methods-Colour measurement of surfaces. The Eye-One Defined X-Rite spectrophotometer from the Institute for the Heritage Restoration (Universitat Politècnica de València) was used for the measurements.

State of conservation of Cova Remígia

The state of conservation of Cova Remígia was thoroughly documented by Barreda-Usó (2016) with damage charts and maps where different kinds of deterioration factors were identified, including loss of material generated by polishing, peeling, biopatinas, concretions and calcareous washing, surface dirt (dust and particulate), microfissures, fissures, fractures, and graphite remains that outlined some figures left behind by previous documentation work (Beltrán 1987b; Guillamet 2000; Barreda-Usó 2016).

In general, Cova Remígia, like all the shelters discovered in this area during the early 20th century, suffered damage mainly caused by the climatic conditions to which it is exposed. In addition, the shelter underwent numerous uncontrolled visits by curious visitors encouraged by the presence of foreign researchers in the 1930s, and the paintings were affected because they were touched and wet with different liquids (Beltrán 1987b) so they could be easily appreciated, generating polishing and accelerating surface carbonations that worsened over time. Along with these visits, the shelter has been used as a refuge by local shepherds and their livestock for many years. By rubbing the rock surfaces animals have generated structural alterations such as polishing of paintings, scratches and small rock detachments (see Figures 12.2 and 12.3).

Nearly the entire surface of the shelter has an orange appearance typical of oxalate patinas.[4] Calcium carbonate scab formations that mainly affect the upper part of the shelter, bordering the ledge where water circulation is abundant, are also present.

Biological alteration was detected (Barreda-Usó 2016) due to insect nests, among them arachnids, which generated aesthetic and chemical alteration (Northup and Lavoie 2001) due to the corrosive substances they contain, in addition to mechanical alteration due to the friction and degradation they may generate during the construction of their nests, thus inducing deterioration processes (Cañaveras et al. 2001; Northup et al. 2001, 2003). In addition to biological deterioration, fractures and fissures were detected on the entire surface of the shelter (Barreda-Usó 2016), as well as scaling and decohesion in the pictorial film. They affect both the surface of the background and the figures, giving these areas great fragility and sensitivity to the action of atmospheric agents, such as freeze-thawing periods very frequent in the Maestrat region. These cycles can cause alteration by mechanical action, resulting in decohesion and microdetachments. Likewise, fractures and fissures are areas prone to accumulate organic matter, capable of offering sufficient substrate for germination of seeds deposited by wind or other transport, causing additional damage.

Almost all the figures presented small detachments of the pictorial film (Barreda-Usó 2016), due to sudden changes in temperature-humidity, during long periods of sunstroke.

Therefore, Cova Remígia presents a diverse state of conservation depending on the location of the panel studied. The most deteriorated cavities are those that are not protected by the upper ledge, which acts as a natural protection. Thus, cavities I, II, III and VI are those that suffer the greatest degree of degradation in the form of flaking with the danger of detachment (see Figures 12.2 and 12.3). Instead, cavities IV and V, located in the central and deepest part of the shelter, are better preserved.

Figure 12.3 Rock surface alterations: Top: Small detachments of pictorial film; Center: Small and micro-detachments of pictorial film and calcareous neoformations on the surface; Bottom: Graphite remnants used to outline the figures in previous studies. Photos by authors.

Proposed treatments

In anticipation of future intervention, studies were carried out in order to determine the proper material to treat decohesion (Barreda-Usó 2012, 2016; Barreda-Usó and Zalbidea 2017, 2018, 2020; Barreda-Usó et al. 2017b). But before that, it is necessary to specify concepts and working methods directly related to this topic. On the one hand, the consolidation by filling and adhesion that takes place when there are two separate surfaces. On the other hand, the consolidation achieved through the cohesion of a fine structure that has lost its solidity (Fort et al. 2005; Osca 2005; Pierce 1996). The first case is used to attach scales or flakes that threaten detachment, while in the second case, consolidation is achieved through the cohesion of a fine structure that has lost its solidity (Pierce 1996) and is used to restore the force of attraction between adjacent particles within the same solid body.

Different materials have been used to adhere and consolidate weak painted areas in rock art shelters. Ballester (2003, p. 141) used Paraloid B72® diluted at 3% in Xylene during the intervention in Cueva de La Serreta (Cieza, Murcia). The same action was taken in Cova dels Cavalls (Tírig,

Castelló) (Ballester, 2003, p. 159), but in both cases there were no exact references to where it was applied (figure or panel).

Martínez Valle, Guillem and Ballester (2012, p. 84) mentioned the use of an acrylic resin to consolidate powdery spots of disintegrated paint at a shelter in Tortosilla, without determining what type of resin or where it was applied. On the same shelter, "…mortars of slaked lime and washed and sifted sand from the shelter itself or very resistant volcanic pozzolans[5]" (Martínez-Valle et al. 2012, p. 84[6]) were used for the adhesion of flakes, filled with fissures and cracks. Unfortunately, we do not know the painting area or the panel where it was applied, the proportions between aggregate and lime or the type of fat lime used. Consolidation was implemented with pozzolans and slaked lime also in Coves del Civil (Tírig, Castelló), La Joquera (Borriol, Castelló), in La Serreta (Cieza, Murcia) and in the shelters of Cañaíca del Calar (Moratalla, Murcia), (Guillamet 2012). In the Barranco de los Robles shelter (Jalance, Valencia), "…traditional slaked lime mortars and pozzolan sand or roman mortar"[7] (Ballester 2013, pp. 41, 56) were used for the adhesion of surfaces with risk of detachment.

We are unaware of the location of the panel area where the mortar was applied in this intervention. In the La Serradeta shelter in Vistabella (Castelló), "… ethyl silicate at very low concentration in acetone"[8] was used (Ballester 2003, p. 143). In Val del Charco del Agua Amarga, Alcañiz (Teruel) this Roman mortar is used with addition of white cement (Ballester 2003, p. 150), although cement is totally unadvised in wall restoration interventions (Mora et al. 2001). Another product used for consolidation by injection and adhesion is the PLM® commercial mortar (Ballester 2003, p. 146), although neither the specific type of PLM®[9] mortar used nor the shelter of use were specified. Royo-Lasarte et al. (2013) remarked that NHL 3.5 hydraulic lime was used to consolidate the peeling in the shelter of La Cañada de Marco in Alcaine, Parque Cultural del Río Martín (Teruel), although there is no graphic reference of the specific location where the intervention took place.

The materials used for consolidation of rock art paintings match with the materials regularly used in consolidation of wall painting, and there are many studies regarding the latest in scientific publications. Synthetic products have many defenders in the specialized literature, because the first studies carried out by Torraca and Mora (1965) provided satisfactory results regarding aging tests, such as the case of the Paraloid B72® synthetic polymer compared to natural organic polymers traditionally used. However, subsequent studies have shown that its stability is limited. In the short-medium term they generate cross-linking in the material which, in practice, results in irreversibility, as well as a visible chromatic alteration and high acidity at approximately pH 4.7 (Borgioli and Cremonesi 2005; Osca 2005; Bensi 2006; Finozzi 2006). An example of chromatic alteration caused using Paraloid B72® for consolidating was detected in the Tadrart Acacus rock paintings in Libya (Fernandes 2012, p. 71). Studies such as Amoroso (2002) proved dubious resistance and stability before the presence of microorganisms. In further recent studies on the behavior of these types of synthetic consolidants applied on limestone stone support, such as Barreda-Usó (2012), it was established that there was irregular accumulation and distribution of the resin on the surfaces treated with Paraloid B72®. Thus, excessive deposition of the product was formed in some areas, producing alterations in the water vapour permeability of the rocky support and causing uneven aging in these areas over time with respect to the rest of the surface.

Synthetic polymers such as Paraloid B72® have been used on inorganic materials due to their easy injection and handling. Besides, they also generate rapid adhesion compared to inorganics whose setting time is much slower and therefore consolidating effects are not immediately visible. Studies such as David (2008) dismissed the use of the Primal AC33® polymer due to its obvious colour change after application. Other studies such as Barreda-Usó (2012) dismissed Paraloid B72® too, not only because of the colour change, but also due to a clear change in the permeability of the rock and its irreversibility, as already mentioned.

Therefore, this research took into consideration:

- The products tested in previous research, both organic and inorganic, and the recommendations regarding their use.
- The type of consolidation intended to achieve, that is, the application of a product to the pictorial surface with either a purely adhesive purpose or a cohesive purpose with limited action.

After discarding organic products to consolidate scales and give cohesion to the paint, specific products for future use in rock art shelter such as Cova Remígia were selected. The consolidants chosen in this research were the Nanorestore® together with some products from the CaLoSiL® range (CaLoSiL E5®, CaLoSiL E25 gray®, CaLoSiL IP5®, CaLoSiL NP5®) for surface consolidation, de-cohesion or powdery treatments. From a compatibility point of view, inorganic substances are the best options for Cova Remígia because of the chemical similarity with the substrate to consolidate. Inorganic substances and more specifically nanoparticles are used only to reinforce and enable cohesion of powdery and decohesive areas.

With the development of nanoscience and nanotechnology, the synthesis of different materials with brand new functional and structural characteristics has been achieved (Hansen et al. 2003; Gómez-Villalba et al. 2012a,b; Sierra-Fernández et al. 2014; López-Arce and Zornoza-Indart 2015). These consolidants consist of nanostructured particles based on calcium hydroxide Ca $(OH)_2$ dispersed in different types of alcohols, Dei and Salvadori (2006) and Ziegenbalds (2008). Alcohol guarantees optimum penetration in the porous matrix, leaving the nanoparticles inserted in the interstices and in the porous network to consolidate. Once transformed into calcium carbonate by the action of atmospheric carbon dioxide, they originate a network of calcite microcrystals that confer high mechanical properties without introducing foreign materials to the chemical nature of the rock. The particles, at a nanometric scale, give these products a different behaviour compared to traditional materials (Gómez-Villalba et al. 2012b).

The application of nanoparticles (Daniele et al. 2008; López-Arce et al. 2010; Gómez-Villalba et al. 2010, 2011, 2012b) enables the use of protective treatments, by improving the degree of coating (Gómez-Villalba et al. 2012b), penetration, application methods (Gómez-Villalba et al. 2013) and the effectiveness of hydrofugation treatments (Facio and Mosquera 2013), allowing the development of new hydrorepellent products (Gómez-Villalba et al. 2011).

Dispersions of 5g of calcium hydroxide per litre of alcohols were used in this study, which favour penetration and prevent re-adhesion between the same nanoparticles of Ca $(OH)_2$, since in highly concentrated dispersions, conglomerations are created that hinder penetration through the porous structure and remain retained on the surface, generating whitish veils or patinas (Dei et al. 2007).

Results and conclusions

The results obtained through the observation and analyses of samples through the SEM-EDX allow determining certain variations between the products: CaLoSiL® and Nanorestore®. Especially the difference is in the shape of the nanoparticles, being those of Nanorestore® much thinner, laminar and smaller than those of the CaLoSiL® range. In addition, the latter tend to generate small clusters on the treated surface, detecting more opaque whitish veils compared to the Nanorestore®. This effect is clearly verified in the CaLoSiL E25 grey® and in the CaLoSiL E5®, where nano and microcracks were shown in areas where consolidating material has accumulated. Probably, the fact that the two products (CaLoSiL E25 grey® and CaLoSiL E5®) are dispersed in ethanol, caused the fast evaporation of the solvent to generate a greater concretion of the nanoparticulate on the surface and thus an irregular carbonation of the same (see Figure 12.4). Besides, it was detected in the samples made with CaLoSiL E5® that the product originated a network of micropores that extended along the entire surface of the sample.

Another conclusion reached throughout this study is the fact that the application of both Nanorestore® and CaLoSiL® in atmospheres with high moisture (more than 60%), lead to a greater and faster carbonation, generating more regular calcium carbonate crystals. On the contrary, the application of these products in dry environments and in areas with air flows induces the fast evaporation of alcohols, so that the penetration of the material is significantly reduced. This fast evaporation not only affects the depth of the consolidating action, but also the morphology of the calcium carbonate crystals that form on the treated surfaces. Larger crystals are

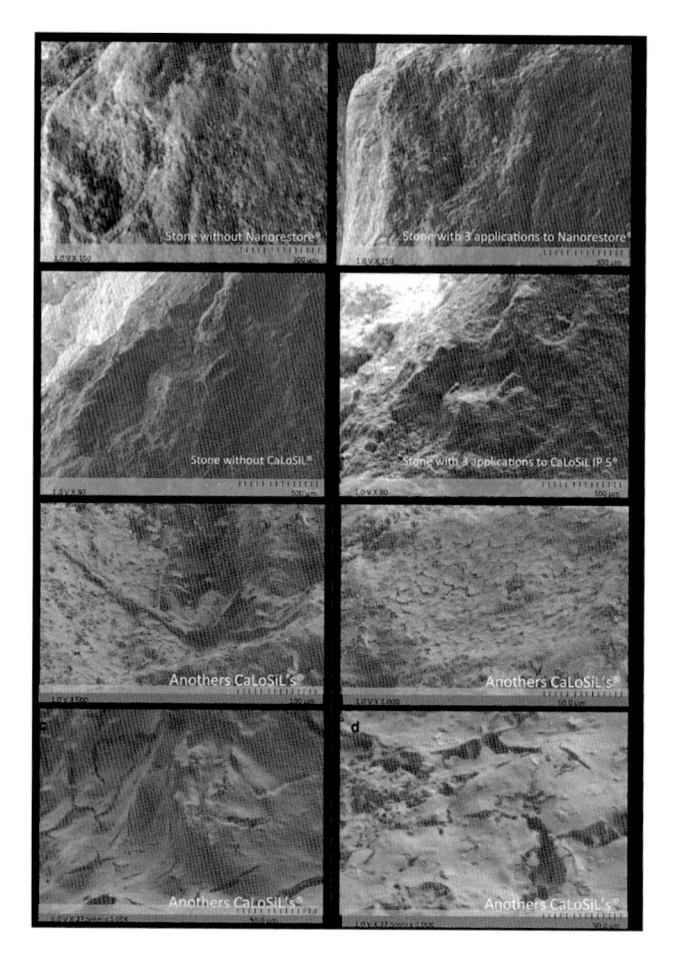

Figure 12.4 SEM images of different samples without and with consolidating material. Bottom 4 images show that CaLoSiL causes a greater concretion of the nanoparticulate on the surface and, therefore, irregular carbonation. Photos by authors.

formed; the consolidating action concentrates on surface layers and does not satisfactorily merge the disintegrated support.

The colorimetric analysis carried out on the different samples detected slight variations in the L*, a* and b* values according to the CIELab* system. In general, these variations were invisible to the human eye. Only the sample treated with CaLoSiL NP® belonging to group B (samples with unpolished surface), experienced a very noticeable darkening during treatment and after accelerated aging with a ΔL^* value of (-8,30). These results are important and should be considered when planning to use this consolidant because the human eye perceives colorimetric changes from values only greater than 2,5 (Melgosa et al. 2001).

The consolidants that achieved the best colorimetric results were Nanorestore® and CaLoSiL IP® (see Figure 12.4), since the changes detected in both products are insignificant for samples belonging to either group A or group B. It should be noted that the conclusions reached after the completion of the experimental part and the behavioural assessment of the tested consolidating products have been decisive in establishing the criteria for selecting the appropriate treatment for the consolidation of unattached flaked areas in Cova Remígia. Specifically, the use of Nanorestore® and CaLoSiL IP® is recommended (among the four products tested from the CaLoSil® range, only the latter presented satisfactory results), based on its chemical affinity with the support, the absence of whitish veils, the lack of obstruction of the porous network and the lack of scabs that could obstruct the free circulation of water. Therefore, it is proposed to continue the study of these materials in rocky support with pictorial layers. The behavior of these products within areas that contain pigments can be very different; not only because of their different chemical composition with respect to the rock, but also because of their different absorbing properties. Iron oxide-based pigments tend to be more absorbent than carbon black pigments or black smoke pigments, which can interfere in the results and therefore in the consolidating efficacy of the products tested.

One final conclusion of this study is that the effectiveness of both nanoconsolidants still needs to be fully understood when applied to weathered substrates. This study provides more information regarding the behavior of different products on limestone areas. The results of this research could be the key to determine the selection of a consolidant product to strengthen weathered substrates. Further research will focus on the achievement of long-term performance in terms of mechanical and physical properties, as well as the influence of different environmental conditions on both nanoconsolidants.

Acknowledgements

Part of the work present here was accomplished when carrying out Barreda-Usós's 2016 PhD thesis: "Consolidantes para soportes pétreos con manifestaciones de arte rupestre en la Comunidad Valenciana. Análisis prácticos en Cova Remígia (Barranc de Gasulla-Ares del Maestrat)". Directed by M. Antonia Zalbidea Muñoz and Julia Osca Pons. Polytechnic University of Valencia. Department of Conservation and Restoration of Cultural Heritage.

Notes

1 Made by specialists in rock painting conservation and restoration E. Guillamet, L. Ballester, G. Barreda-Usó and M. Domènech, under the *Dirección General del Patrimonio Cultural Valenciano* and the coordination of the *Museu de la Valltorta* (Tírig, Castellón).
2 Commissioned to be undertaken by researcher G. Cavallo.

3 Two types of samples were tested in this investigation. *Group A*, including samples following the UNE-EN 15801 standard, which require samples to be prepared with all surfaces polished to carry out the "*Conservation of cultural property-Test methods-Determination of water absorption by capillarity*" test. And the samples of *Group B*, which are made following the same regulations as the previous ones, but with the variant of keeping a face unpolished. So that one side of the sample retains the original external patina where the products will be applied. This patina has the same characteristics as the surface where the paintings are located. Reason why, it was considered important to carry out the test with this variation, with the objective of being able to evaluate with more precision the operation of these consolidants when applied in real treatments.

4 Some authors (Edwards 1991) stated that the precipitation of calcium oxalate is due to the action of oxalic acid secreted by microorganisms such as lichen or blue algae that colonize the monuments. Oxalic acid interacts with calcium carbonate precipitates as calcium oxalate (monohydrated whewellite and dehydrated weddelite). In these studies, it is concluded that calcium oxalate produced by some lichens can naturally act as a means of protecting the stones against acid attack. In crystalline microlayers that form naturally, the thin membrane formed over centuries is very compact and can obstruct the free diffusion of soluble salts, although calcium oxalate itself is hydrophilic (Matteini et al. 1994).

5 Pozzolans are materials of volcanic origin consisting essentially of silica and alumina (with lesser amounts of iron oxides). Due to their origin they are very reactive. The reactivity of pozzolans is mainly manifested when mixed with lime or cement, materials that interact forming hydraulic compounds and that have a very high mechanical resistance. For more information see Zalbidea (2007) and Moropoulou and Anagnostopoulou (2005).

6 The original text written in Spanish states: "*...se han utilizado morteros de cal apagada y arena. La arena perteneciente al propio abrigo lavada y tamizada o pozzolana de naturaleza volcánica y muy resistente.*" (Translation note).

7 The original text in Spanish states: "*...morteros tradicionales de cal apagada y arena puzolana o mortero romano*".

8 The original text in Spanish states: "*...silicato de etilo a muy baja concentración en acetona*".

9 *PLM®* is the commercial name of a range of injection mortars for the restoration of murals and mosaics, from the Italian Company CTS. The *PLM* line consists of 6 varieties: *PLM-A, PLM-AL, PLM-I, PLM-M, PLM-S and PLM-SM®*, and each of them is used for a certain consolidation procedure.

References

Alonso, A. and Grimal, A. (1999) Cultura artística y cultura material inslavable?. *Bolskan*, 16, pp.71–107.

Amoroso, G. (2002) *Trattato di scienza della conservazione dei monumenti. Etica della conservazione, degrado dei monumenti, interventi conservativi, consolidanti e protettivi*. Firenze: Alinea.

Ballester Casañ, L. (2003) *Conservación de las pinturas rupestres del Levante Español*. Unpublished PhD. Valencia: Universidad Politécnica de Valencia.

Ballester Casañ, L. (2013) Intervención de conservación del abrigo del Barranco de los Robles, Jalance. Valencia. In Domingo, I., Rives, B., Román, D. and Rubio, R. (Eds) *Imágenes en la piedra. Arte rupestre en el Abrigo de Las Monteses y su*

entorno (Jalance). Jalance: Ministerio de Cultura de España, Ayuntamiento de Jalance.
Barreda-Usó, G. (2012) *Investigación de tratamientos de consolidación del soporte rocoso en el Abric de Pinos (Benissa-Alicante)*. (Unpublished Diploma de Estudis Avançats [DEA]). València: Universitat Politècnica de València.
Barreda-Usó, G. (2016) *Consolidantes para soportes pétreos con manifestaciones de arte rupestre en la Comunidad Valenciana. Análisis prácticos en Cova Remígia (Barranc de Gassulla-Ares del Maestre)*. PhD Thesis. València: Universitat Politècnica de València. https://doi.org/10.4995/Thesis/10251/63280
Barreda-Usó, G. and Zalbidea Muñoz, M. A. (2014) Estudio comparativo entre consolidantes para soporte pétreo con manifestación de arte rupestre mediante ensayos de penetración por tinción. In Vivancos, M. T., Domènech, M. T., Sánchez, M. and Osca, J. (Eds) *EMERGE 2014-Jornadas de Investigación Emergente en Conservación y Restauración de Patrimonio*. València: Universitat Politècnica de València, pp.13–20.
Barreda-Usó, G. and Zalbidea, M. A. (2018) Estudi de conservació de l'Abric de Pinos (Benissa, Alacant): patologies i causes de deterioració d'un jaciment amb art rupestre llevantí. *Pyrenae*, 49(1), pp.155–183.
Barreda-Usó, G. and Zalbidea Muñoz, M. A. (2017) Tratamientos de consolidación de soporte rocoso con manifestaciones de arte rupestre. Abric de Pinos (Benissa-Alicante). In *III Congreso Internacional de Investigación en Artes Visuales. Aniav 2017 Glocal [codificar, mediar, transformar, vivir]*. Editorial Universitat Politècnica de València. https://dx.doi.org/10.4995/ANIAV.2017.5861
Barreda-Usó, G. and Zalbidea Muñoz, M. A. (2020) Luminescent staining with Rhodamine B to study the penetration of calcium hydroxide-based (Ca (OH)$_2$) nanoparticulated consolidants to preserve rock art. In Fuster-López, L., Stols-Witlox, M. and Picollo, M. (Eds) *UV-Vis luminiscence imaging techniques, conservation 3600*. València, España: Editorial Universitat Politècnica de València. https://doi.org/10.4995/360_2019.110002
Barreda-Usó, G., Zalbidea Muñoz, M. A. and Osca Pons, J. (2017b) Comparativa entre distintos consolidantes inorgánicos nanoparticulados a base de hidróxido cálcico. Editorial Universitat Politècnica de València. In *III Congreso Internacional de Investigación en Artes Visuales. Aniav 2017 Glocal [codificar, mediar, transformar, vivir]*. Editorial Universitat Politècnica de València. http://dx.doi.org/10.4995/ANIAV.2017.5702
Beltrán Martínez, A. (1985) Problemas del arte rupestre levantino en la provincia de Castellón. *Cuadernos de Prehistoria y Arqueología Castellonenses*, 11, pp.111–140.
Beltrán Martínez, A. (1987) La conservación del arte rupestre. *Cuadernos de Prehistoria y Arqueología Castellonense*, 13, pp.61–81.
Bensi, P. (2006) Le resine acriliche sulle pitture murali. In Finozzi, A. (Ed.) *Seminario Esperienze e Materiali di Restauro. Le Resine Acriliche Sulle Pitture Murali: Thiene (VI), Villa Fabris (11 giugno 2005)*. Padova: Il Prato, pp.81–84.
Borgioli, L. and Cremonesi, P. (2005) *Le resine sintetiche usate nel trattamento di opere policrome*. Padova: Il Prato.
Cañaveras, J. C., Sánchez-Moral, S., Soler, V. and Saiz-Jiménez, C. (2001) Microorganisms and microbially induced fabrics in cave walls. *Geomicrobiology Journal*, 18, pp.223–240.
Carrión-Ruiz, B., Pons, S. B., Lerma, J. L. and Montalvo, E. L. (2017) Técnicas multivariantes y de realidad aumentada aplicadas a la difusión de arte rupestre.

In *La ciencia y el arte VI. Ciencias experimentales y conservación del patrimonio*. España: Subdirección General de Documentación y Publicaciones, pp.194–207.

Daniele, V., Taglieri, G. and Quaresima, R. (2008) The nanolimes in cultural heritage conservation: Characterisation and analysis of the carbonatation process. *Journal of Cultural Heritage*, 9(3), pp.294–301. https://doi.org/10.1016/j.culher.2007.10.007

David, H. (2008) *Contribución a la conservación del arte rupestre prehistórico*. PhD thesis. València, Universitat Politècnica de València. https://doi.org/10.4995/Thesis/10251/3789

Dei, L., Bandini, F., Felici, A., Lanfranchi, M. R., Lanterna, G., Macherelli, A. and Salvatori, B. (2007) Pre-consolidation of pictorial layers in frescoes: The high performance of CSGI's method based on nanolime evaluated by opd team in agnolo gaddi's Leggenda della Vera Croce Paintings, Santa Croce. *Scienza e Beni Culturali*, XXIII, pp.217–223.

Dei, L. and Salvadori, B. (2006) Nanotechnology in cultural heritage conservation: Nanometric slaked lime saves architectonic and artistic surfaces from decay. *Journal of Cultural Heritage*, 7, pp.110–115. https://doi.org/10.1016/j.culher.2006.02.001

Domingo Sanz, I. (2005) *Técnica y ejecución de la figura en el arte rupestre levantino: hacia una definición actualizada del concepto de estilo: validez y limitaciones*, PhD Thesis. Valencia: Servei de Publicacions de la Universitat de València.

Domingo Sanz, I. (2015) LRA (Levantine Rock Art). *Expression*, 8, pp.44–50.

Domingo Sanz, I., Villaverde, V., López-Montalvo, E., Lerma, J. L. and Cabrelles, M. (2013) Latest developments in rock art recording: Towards an integral documentation of Levantine rock art sites combining 2D and 3D recording techniques. *Journal of Archaeological Science*, 40(4), pp.1879–1889.

Edwards, H. G. M. (1991) Raman spectra of oxalates in lichen encrustations on Renaissance frescoes. *Spectrochimica Acta*, Part A, (47A), pp.1531–1539.

Facio, D. S. and Mosquera, M. J. (2013) Simple strategy for producing superhydrophobic coatings in situ on a building substrate. *Materiales e interfaces aplicados por ACS*, 5(15), pp.7517–7526. https://doi.org/10.1021/am401826g

Fernandes, A. P. B. (2012) *Natural processes in the degradation of open-air rock art sites: An urgency intervention scale to inform conservation*. PhD thesis. Bournemouth, Bournemouth University.

Finozzi, A. (2006) *Esperienze e materiali di restauro. Villa Fabris, Thiene (VI)-11 giugno 2005. Le resine acriliche sulle pitture murali. Atti del seminario*.

Fort, R., Álvarez de Buergo, M., Varas, M. J. and Vázquez, M. C. (2005) Valoración de tratamientos con polímeros sintéticos para la conservación de materiales pétreos del patrimonio. *Revista de Plásticos Modernos*, 89(583), 83–89.

Fortea, F. J. and Aura, E. (1987) Una escena de vareo en La Sarga (Alcoy). Aportaciones a los problemas del Arte Levantino. *Archivo de Prehistoria Levantina*, XVII, pp.97–120.

Gómez-Villalba, L. S., López-Arce, P., Álvarez de Buergo, M. and Fort, R. (2012a) Atomic defects and their relationship to aragonite-calcite transformation in portlandite nanocrystal carbonation. *Crystal Growth & Design*, 12(10), pp.4844–4852.

Gómez-Villalba, L. S., López-Arce, P., de Buergo, M. A., Zornoza-Indart, A. and Fort, R. (2013) Mineralogical and textural considerations in the assessment of aesthetic changes in dolostones by effect of treatments with Ca(OH)2 nanoparticles. In Rogerio-Candelera, M. A., Lazzari, M. and Cano, E. (Eds.) *Science and technology for the conservation of cultural heritage*. London: CRC Press, pp.235–329.

Gómez-Villalba, L. S., López-Arce, P., Fort González, R. and Álvarez de Buergo, M. (2010) La aportación de la nanociencia a la conservación de bienes del patrimonio cultural. *Patrimonio Cultural de España*, 4, pp.43–56.
Gómez-Villalba, L. S., López-Arce, P., Fort González, R., Álvarez de Buergo, M. and Zornoza-Indart, A. (2011) Aplicación de nanopartículas a la consolidación de patrimonio pétreo. In Del Egido, M. and Juanes, D. (Eds.) *La ciencia y el arte III: Ciencias experimentales y conservación del patrimonio*. Madrid: Ministerio de Cultura de España, Subdirección General de Publicaciones, Información y Documentación, pp.39–58.
Gómez-Villalba, L. S., López-Arce, P., Zornoza-Indart, A., Álvarez de Buergo, M. and Fort, R. (2012b) Modern restoration products based on nanoparticles: The case of the Nano-Lime, interaction and compatibility with limestone and dolostones surfaces, advantages and limitations. *EGU General Assembly Conference Abstracts*, 14, pp.2418.
Guillamet, E. (2000) Intervencions de conservació-restauració en pintura rupestre. *Cota Zero: revista d'arqueologia i ciència*, 16, pp.111–119.
Guillamet, E. (2012) Intervenciones de conservación de arte rupestre al aire libre. In *Jornadas Técnicas para la gestión del arte rupestre, Patrimonio Mundial (Alquezar)*, pp.123–128.
Gusi Jener, F. (1975) Un taller de sílex bajo abrigo en la 2a cavidad de Cingle de la Ermita (Albocácer). *Cuadernos de Prehistoria y Arqueología Castellonense*, 2, pp.39–64.
Hansen, E., Doehne, E., Fidler, J., Larson, J., Martin, B., Matteini, M., Rodríguez-Navarro, C., Sebastian Pardo, E., Price, C., de Tagle, A., Teutonico, J. M. and Weiss, N. R. (2003) A review of selected inorganic consolidants and protective treatments for porous calcareous materials. *Reviews in Conservation*, 4, pp.13–25. https://doi.org/10.1179/sic.2003.48.Suppplement-1.13
Hoyo-Meléndez, J. M., Lerma, J. L., López-Montalvo, E. and Villaverde, V. (2015) Documenting the light sensitivity of spanish levantine rock art paintings. *ISPRS Annals of the Photogrammetry, Remote Sensing and Spatial Information Sciences*, 2(3), pp.53–59. doi:10.5194/isprsannals-II-5-W3-53-2015
López-Arce, P., Gómez-Villalba, L. S., Pinho, L., Fernandez-Valle, M. E., de Buergo, M. Á. and Fort, R. (2010) Influence of porosity and relative humidity on consolidation of dolostone with calcium hydroxide nanoparticles: Effectiveness assessment with non-destructive techniques. *Materials Characterization*, 61(2), pp.168–184. https://doi.org/10.1016/j.matchar.2009.11.007
López-Arce, P. and Zornoza-Indart, A. (2015) Aceleración de la carbonatación de las nanopartículas de hidróxido de calcio: inducidas por fermentación de levadura. *Física Aplicada A*, 120(4), pp.1475–1495.
López-Montalvo, E. (2009) Caracterización de la secuencia levantina a partir de la composición y el espacio gráfico: el núcleo Valltorta-Gassulla como modelo de estudio. In *Actas del IV Congreso del arte rupestre del Arco Mediterráneo de la Península Ibérica (Valencia, 3, 4 y 5 de diciembre de 2008)*. Valencia: Generalitat Valenciana, pp.81–94.
López-Montalvo, E. (2018) Hunting scenes in Spanish Levantine rock art: An unequivocal chrono-cultural marker of Epipalaeolithic and Mesolithic Iberian societies?. *Quaternary International*, 472, pp.205–220.
López-Montalvo, E., Villaverde, V., Roldán, C., Murcia, S. and Badal, E. (2014) An approximation to the study of black pigments in Cova Remígia (Castellón, Spain): Technical and cultural assessments of the use of carbon-based black

pigments in Spanish Levantine Rock Art. *Journal of Archaeological Science,* 52(0), pp.535–545.

Martínez Valle. R. (2000) El Parque Cultural de Valltorta-Gasulla (Castellón). *Trabajos de Prehistoria,* 57(2), pp.65–76.

Martínez Valle, R. and Guillem Calatayud, P. M. (2002) Dossier: El Parque Cultural de Valltorta-Gasulla. *Penyagolosa. Revista de la Excma. Diputació de Castelló,* IV (3), pp.73–86.

Martínez Valle, R. and Guillem Calatayud, P. M. (2005) Arte rupestre de l'Alt Maestrat: las cuencas de la Valltorta y de la Rambla Carbonera. In Hernández Pérez, M. S. and Soler Díaz, J. A. (Eds) *Arte rupestre en la España mediterránea.* Alicante: Instituto Alicantino de Cultural "Juan Gil-Albert", pp.71–88.

Martínez Valle, R., Guillem Calatayud, P. M. and Ballester Castañ, L. (2012) Los abrigos de Tortosilla. Una nueva visión tras los trabajos de conservación preventiva. In Domingo, I., Rubio, R. and Rives, R. (Coord.) *Actas de las Jornadas: Abrigo de Tortosilla 100 aniversario de su descubrimiento. Primer hallazgo de Arte Rupestre de la Comunidad Valenciana.* Ayora 14–16 de Octubre de 2011. Ayora: Ayuntamiento de Ayora.

Mateo Saura, M. Á. (2005) En la controversia de la cronología del arte rupestre levantino. *Cuadernos de Arte Rupestre,* 2, pp.127–156.

Matteini, M., Moles, A. and Giovannoni, S. (1994) Calcium oxalate as a protective mineral system for Wall paintings: Methodology and analyses. In Fassina, V., Ott, H. and Zezza, F. (Eds) *Conservation of monuments in the Mediterranean basin: Stone monuments, methodologies for the analysis of weathering and conservation.* Procedings of the 3rd International Symposium, Venice, 22–25 June 1994, pp.155–162.

Melgosa, M., Gómez, M. D. M. P., Yebra, A., Huertas, R. and Villaverde, E. H. (2001) Algunas reflexiones y recientes recomendaciones internacionales sobre evaluación de diferencias de color. *Óptica pura y aplicada,* 34(1), pp.1–10.

Mora, P., Mora, L. and Philippot, P. (2001) *La conservazione delle pitture murali.* Bologna: Editrice Compositori.Northup, D. E., Barns, S. M., Yu, L. E., Spilde, M. N., Schelble, R. T., Dano, K. E. and Dahm, C. N. (2003) Diverse microbial communities inhabiting ferromanganese deposits in Lechuguilla and Spider Caves. *Environmental Microbiology,* 5(11), pp.1071–1086.

Northup, D. E. and Lavoie, K. H. (2001) Geomicrobiology of caves: A review. *Geomicrobiology Journal,* 18, pp.199–222.

Olària Puyoles, C. (1997) La investigación arqueológica y prehistórica en las comarcas de Castelló. Millars. *Espai i Història,* 6(20), pp.7–9.

Osca, J. (2005) El empleo de consolidantes inorgánicos y organosilíceos como alternativa a los consolidantes orgánicos. In *Actas del Seminario sobre restauración de pinturas murales. Tratamientos y metodologías de conservación de pinturas murales,* Aguilar de Campoo (Palencia), 20–22 de julio 2005. Aguilar de Campoo (Palencia): ed. Fundación Santa María la Real-C.E.R., pp.10–47.

Pierce, C. A. (1996) *Stone Conservation: An Overview of Current Research (16–17).* Santa Mónica, CA.: The Getty Conservation Institute.

Porcar, J. B., Obermaier, H. and Breuil, H. (1936) *Las pinturas rupestres de la Cueva Remígia (Castellón).* Madrid, Junta Superior de Excavac. y Antigüedades.

Ripoll Perelló, E. (1963) *Pinturas rupestres de la Gasulla (Castellón).* Monografías de Arte Rupestre. Arte Levantino, (2).

Ripoll Perelló, E. (1966) Cuestiones en torno a la cronología del arte rupestre postpaleolítico en la Península Ibérica. *Simposio Internacional de Arte Rupestre, IPA,* Barcelona, pp.165–192.

Ripoll Perelló, E. (1968) *The Painted Shelters of La Gassulla (Castellón),* Monographs on Cave Art, 2, Barcelona.

Ripoll Perelló, E. (1983) Cronología y periodización del esquematismo prehistórico en la Península Ibérica. *Zephyrus,* 36, pp.27–35.

Román, D. and Domingo, I. (2017) El final del Paleolítico superior en Castellón: un territorio clave para la comprensión del final del Pleistoceno en el Mediterráneo ibérico. *Pyrenae,* 48(1), pp.47–70.

Royo-Lasarte, J., Moreno, J. A. A., Guillén, J. I. R. and Izquierdo, R. A. (2013) Trabajos de estabilización de urgencia en el soporte rocoso y estudio de patologías en el abrigo de "La Cañada de Marco" en Alcaine, Parque Cultural del Río Martín (Teruel). *Cuadernos de arte rupestre,* 6, pp.147–159.

Sanz, N. (2012) Arte rupestre y la lista del patrimonio mundial de la UNESCO. Un compañero del arte rupestre, pp.491–514.

Sarriá Boscovich, E (1989) Las pinturas rupestres de Cova Remígia (Ares del Maestre, Castellón). *Lucentum VII, VIII* (1988/-89), pp.7–33.

Sierra-Fernández, A., Gómez-Villalba, L. S., Milosevic, O., Fort, R. and Rabanal, M. E. (2014) Synthesis and morpho-structural characterization of nanostructured magnesium hydroxide obtained by a hydrothermal method. *Ceramics International,* 40(8), pp.12285–12292. https://doi.org/10.1016/j.ceramint.2014.04.073

Torraca, G. and Mora, P. (1965) Fissativi per pitture murali. *Bollettino dell'Istituto Centrale del Restauro,* Roma, pp.109–132.

Utrilla, P., Baldellou, V. and Bea, M. (2012) Aragon and Spanish Levantine Art: A territorial study. In García, J., Collado, H. and Nash, G. (Eds) *The Levantine question: Post-Palaeolithic rock art in the Iberian Peninsula.* Budapest: Archaeolingua, pp.263–282.

Villaverde, V., Guillem, P. M. and Martínez, R. (2006) El horizonte gráfico Centelles y su posición en la secuencia del arte Levantino del Maestrazgo. *Zephyrus.* Homenaje a Francisco Jordá Cerdá, 59, pp.191–198.

Villaverde, V., Martínez, R., Guillem, P., López-Montalvo, E. and Domingo, I. (2012) What do we mean by Levantine rock art? In García, J., Collado, H. and Nash, G. (Eds) *The Levantine question: Post-Palaeolithic rock art in the Iberian Peninsula.* Budapest: Archaeolingua, pp.81–116.

Viñas, R. and Rubio, A. (1988) Un nuevo ejemplo de figura humana flechada en el conjunto de la Valltorta (Castellón). *Cuadernos de Prehistoria y Arqueología Castellonense,* 13, pp.83–93.

Zalbidea Muñoz, M. A. (2007) La cal, aglomerante en los morteros tradicionales. *EcoHabitar,* V, pp.28–30.

Ziegenbalds, G. (2008) Colloidal calcium hydroxide: A new material for consolidation and conservation of carbonate stone. In *11th International congress on deterioration and conservation of stone III.* Poland: Nicolaus Copernicus University Press, pp.1109–1115.

13 Multi-Proxy Archaeometric Analyses on Rock Art Pigments in Different World Contexts

Hugo Gomes, Pierluigi Rosina, Sara Garcês and Carmela Vaccaro

Introduction

The study of pigments is one of the most active fields of research within the field of Art History. Considering that several studies have been published on the analysis of pigments, the application of these techniques has been extended to other types of artefacts and to rock art panels. In recent decades an innovative and multi-disciplined oriented line of research in Archaeology has developed. Together, the close collaboration between various disciplines has become a new working formula providing new points of view in the scientific discourse.

The multi-interdisciplinarity is intended to measure human occupation and paleo-environmental dynamics more effectively, crossing the crucial information developed by specific research, thus achieving better results. These are achieved through constant integration and collaboration by disciplines such as rock art and archaeometry, with studies of all types of rock art representations and the development and application of specific scientific methods and analysis techniques for the detailed characterization of the paintings and engravings. Archaeometric studies aim at the characterization of pictorial materials, raw materials and the monitoring and conservation of rock art panels (Gomes and Martins 2013; Gomes et al. 2013a, b, c, d; Rosina et al. 2013, 2014a, b; Gomes et al. 2015; Garcês et al. 2019).

Pigments and natural ochre from several sites of western Iberia (Portugal and Spain), Africa (Ethiopia and Angola) and Brazil were examined under the Rupsciense project (FCT: PTDC/HIS-ARQ/101299/2008), developed between 2010 and 2014 (Gomes and Martins 2013; Gomes 2015). This project focused on the characterization of prehistoric rock art paintings and the identification of preparation techniques for prehistoric pigments. Research was developed in an interdisciplinary manner and the prehistoric pigments were chemically and mineralogically characterized and analysed using archaeometric techniques. All samples were analysed by Raman Spectroscopy (RS), in order to determine the mineralogical components of the paintings, the technology used for the preparation, and identification

DOI: 10.4324/9780429355349-17

of the material for possible dating. Also, Optical Microscopy (OM), X-Ray Microfluorescence (XRM), Scanning Electron Microscopy (SEM) and SM/MS analyses were applied for selected samples.

Red pigments, essentially consisting of iron oxides or hydroxides, are the most common materials used in the production of painted prehistoric rock art. The recurrence of these materials points to local raw materials use as these pigments are abundant in the earth's surface, and do not suffer rapid processes of alteration. In the Iberian Peninsula (in agro-pastoral societies) there is a very clear tendency for the use of red being effectively the most represented in all artistic styles. Pigments of other colours (such as black and white) are very sporadically.

However, in other contexts with Archaeometric studies (like Angola, Ethiopia and Brazil), the colour variation of the pigments is much higher, the use of red being clearly recognized, but white and black are more frequently identified the use of dichromatic figures. In Brazil, the use of white pigments is more recurrent, but other colours are also recognized as a result of mixtures, composing of red pigments and various shades, grey, brown, among others. In Palaeolithic paintings in Europe (primarily in cave environments) the colour is more varied (red, black, yellow, brown and violet). The preservation conditions in cave environments are more favourable, due to minimal microclimatic variations. In Post-Palaeolithic periods (mainly painted open-air shelters) pigments use is mostly monochromatic, and most likely using red.

Additional consideration needs to be given to the question of the colour tone and pigment brilliance that may have had an association with the symbolic nature of the painting and the artist. In various areas of the Iberian Peninsula various shades of red have been used in the making of paintings to create perspectives, shadows and movement, some in association with black and white pigments, as example in Altamira.

Despite this knowledge of pigments, the detection of organic binders has been low. However, the recognition of organic substances may be associated with poor preservation of the sites. Based on ethnographic evidence and bibliographies of the speciality, the binders are mainly composed of organic substances normally inserted in the pigment preparation (Rudner 1982, 1983). In a recent study, organic binders were identified in association with white pigments in Ethiopia (Gomes et al. 2013a). The question arises whether this result is derived from the recent chronology of the paintings (Rosina et al. 2014a), or from questions related to the preservation of these components.

Pigment analysis objectives

The goal of our research was to provide an alternative approach to the chemical and mineralogical characterization of prehistoric pigments and rocky supports to better understand the origin of the raw materials, the processes of preparation of prehistoric pigments and the conservation measures to be adopted to the sites (Gomes et al. 2019). Raw materials used for prehistoric rock art paintings pass through various transformations along time (before and after preparation), due to scraping or grinding processes. Binders were often added in order to achieve certain physical characteristics, probably as constituency of the paste and thickness (López-Montalvo et al. 2017; Rosina et al. 2019).

The different types of pigments and their use demonstrate a certain level of land exploitation as well as the notwithstanding symbolic thought, and thus their study also helps to better understand the societies that created rock art (Gomes et al. 2019). In many cases, the identification of binders is essential to confirm the composition and identification of the raw material used and even to certify the authenticity (or not) of certain panels. On the other hand, it is often possible to find similarities between the specific use of the pigments throughout a period, region or culture, information about the chronology of the paintings and even the recipes applied in certain periods or in certain artistic "styles".

Pigments and raw materials

The preferential or basic colours in the prehistoric European palette are red and black, applied with different shades. White pigments and other shades such as oranges or browns are less common in Iberian Peninsula (Ruiz et al 2013). Red pigments used in prehistoric paintings are essentially constituted by minerals, especially oxides or iron hydroxides (Hradil et al. 2003). The first prehistoric pigments used by humankind were ochre, which in Greek literally means "yellow". Ochre is extracted from the goethite-iron oxide monohydrate. A yellow powder is produced through grinding, while other colours can be obtained by heating (Barnett et al. 2006).

Black pigments are usually of organic origins such as charcoal and are prepared through the burning of wood. This type of pigment is used in one of the most common ways to date prehistoric paintings (Valladas et al. 1999; Bonneau et al. 2011; Pettit and Bahn 2015; Troncoso et al. 2017).

In the distant past, in addition to charcoal, the process of calcination of bones and ivory has also been used to produce black colour (Cabrera 1979). On other occasions, manganese oxides have also been identified as the source of black pigments (Fortea and Hoyos 1999; Guineau et al. 2001), together with mixtures of this oxide and charcoal (Menu and Walter 1996). One can consider a material to be a pigment when it has the following characteristics: finely ground, not losing colour when mixed with other substances, resistant to heat, light and chemically stable.

The word ochre has been used primarily as a synonym of yellow ochre (Elias et al. 2006). However, there are clays with greater or lesser presence of different iron oxy hydroxides that give different tonalities. Hematite (Fe_2O_3) has high iron content (70%), and its name is derived from the Greek word "blood", in allusion to its red colour. When mixed with clay, the hematite forms the so-called "red ochre". It is the mineral most used as pigment, even today (Elias et al 2006).

However, it is difficult to know the origin of ochres since they are very abundant in nature and have a great mineralogical variability. In Europe, American continent and Africa, the presence of ochre in many rock art painted sites is believed to be symbolic (Watts 1999, 2002, 2009; Cavalcante et al. 2011), although evidence for this is limited. This symbolism would justify the systematic manipulation of this material in remote territories (Watts 2010, Bonjean et al. 2015), as well as the deliberate heating to modify the colour (Pomiès et al. 1999a, b; Pomiès and Menu 1999; d'Errico et al. 2010). There are examples of presence of ochre in funerary rituals (Aldhouse-Green and Pettitt 1998; Zilhão and d'Errico 1999a, b; Pettitt 2000; Duarte 2002; Pettitt et al. 2002; Zilhão and Trinkaus 2002) body decoration (Loubser 1992; Erlandson et al. 1999; Taçon et al. 2003; Petru 2006), and also associated with antiseptic functions (Bates and White 1985; Wadley et al. 2004, 2009; Wadley 2005; Aubert 2012; Huntley 2012).

The technology of painted prehistoric rock art

Studies on the complete operative chain of painted rock art are still not very developed but a few recent studies have addressed this gap (Santos da Rosa 2019a). In many art studies, researchers suggest that pigments would be grounded and mixed with different binding substances such as animal fat, blood, water, urine, honey, milk, egg or products of vegetable origin that were used to enhance the adhesion of the pigment to the support (Barnett et al. 2006) such as in Australia (Gillespie 1983; Loy et al. 1990; Huntley 2012). However, the determination of the binders in rock art pigments is a quite difficult task due to scarcity of remnants of organic substances conserved within the archaeological record (Vandenabeele et al. 2000). There is evidence to suggest that some of the red pigments used in prehistoric paintings were prepared by calcination or heating of yellow ochre (Hradil et al. 2003; Iriarte et al. 2009, 2013) and by crushing, mixing and heating processes (Marshall et al. 2005; Chalmin et al. 2006). However, they could also have been applied dry or with pieces of stones directly on the surface of the rock.

These mixtures could have been made in baskets or shells like the *Pecten jacobaeus* found in Altamira (Lasheras 2003; Montes-Barquin et al. 2004). At the Blombos cave in South Africa, shells have been found with ochre residues in their interior and quartzite tools that appear to have been used to grind the ochre, although no evidence of carbon or organic elements added to the mixture was identified (Salomon et al. 2011, 2012). Bone could also have been used to mix and apply the pigments, but application with brushes made of vegetable or animal fibres, feathers, spatulas, skin, fingers have also been documented (Cole and Watchman 1992; López-Montalvo 2017). Additionally, in the case of stencils, pigments have been either blown or airbrushed (Santos da Rosa, 2019a, b, c).

Archaeometric research methodology on rock art

Analytical studies of painted prehistoric rock art pigments have been carried out since the 1970s, but their integration in archaeological research is recent, especially since the beginning of the 21st century (Wadley 2005; d'Errico et al. 2010, 2012; Zilhão et al. 2010; Henshilwood and d'Errico 2011a; Henshilwood et al. 2011ab; Baldellou and Alloza 2012; Rifkin 2012; Roebroeks et al. 2012; Salomon et al. 2012, etc.). Until the 1980s, the use of iron oxide, manganese or carbon had not been scientifically confirmed. Its use was based on theory, and the first studies that identified recipes and pigments were not made until the 1990s (Gomes 2015). This was because the methodology required extraction of large samples of pigments, a very invasive process. But little by little the methodology of analysis was perfected and nowadays the methods and devices that are used have non-invasive characteristics and some of them work with non-destructive analysis. It is these advancements that are now specifically considered as we examine archaeometric methods for pigment sampling and analysis.

Archaeometry methods

Sampling

For the analysis of pigments, it is necessary to acquire microsamples, less than 1mm^2, which are collected according to international standards related to preservation ethics (AIC 2015). A sterilized tungsten scalpel is used, and when the samples are removed, they are stored in Eppendorf tubes. Before the removal, the samples are selected from a discreet location in the painting. To protect the integrity of the motifs, the pigment is scraped from cracks in the rock or thicker layers. In total, the collected pigment cannot exceed 2 micrograms; hence, no visible damage to the painting is caused. The whole sampling process is photographed with macro and microphotographs.

Pigment archaeometry analysis techniques

From the outset, the most appropriate analytical method must be chosen, because the techniques must be carried out within certain parameters. For this, the following factors must be considered: the type of information to be obtained; the amount of sample available; the accuracy and precision of the analytical method; analytical interferences and their control; difficulties with possible contamination; time necessary to analyse each sample; or price of the analysis per sample. A range of techniques were trialled as part of this research and consideration will now be given to the abilities, results and overall effectiveness in meeting the overarching objectives of archaeometric pigment analysis.

Figure 13.1 Sampling proceedings on different rock-art painted sites. Photos by the authors.

Optical microscopy

The use of this technique is essential for the detailed study of the extracted samples and establishing the stratigraphy of painted panels. Through the microscopic, microphotographic observation of stratigraphic sections of the painting samples can be conducted. This allows for the various characteristics of the samples to be seen, such as the thickness and sequence of the layers, the colour, the texture and the distribution of the pigments in the samples' layers. In this way, photographs with a large increase of the samples and the layers with which they are formed can be produced. These stratigraphic sections can be used for other studies such as SEM. It is necessary to complement the observations from the OM with the Stereoscopic Microscope. This allows the detailed study of fragments and 3D viewing, while also providing the option to zoom in 16 to 40 times the size of the sample. It is thus possible to observe colour, texture, arrangement of the painting, and type of application, plus the strokes, which can suggest the instrument that was used (brushes, fingers, twigs, etc.). It is also possible to visualize the size of the pigment particles and evidence of alterations to the panels.

Scanning electron microscopy

SEM works through a fine electron probe directly on the outer layer of a sample making it possible to observe the topography of the surface with a lateral resolution of up to several nanometres. The images produced by electrons allow the quantitative determination of the atomic concentrations in the micrometre range. It is based on the dispersion of electrons that impinges on the surface of the sample and its composition, showing only the morphology of the samples in 3D images while allowing for the analysis of many samples. The sample preparation is thus a slow process, yet the sample is not destroyed through the analysis.

A complement of the electron microscopy is SEM EDX, which is performed with x-rays and helps to determine the elementary composition of the elements. While this process can produce high resolution images of the surface of a sample, the sample is destroyed.

Raman spectroscopy

This is a high-resolution technique that can provide chemical and structural information of any material – organic or inorganic – within a few seconds, allowing for its rapid identification. This analysis is based on the monochromatic light of a certain frequency that when influencing the study material behaves differently depending on the type of material. There are two primarily two types of dispersion – Rayleigh and Raman. The light that maintains the same frequency does not reveal any information about the material is the Rayleigh dispersion. This phenomenon was observed experimentally in

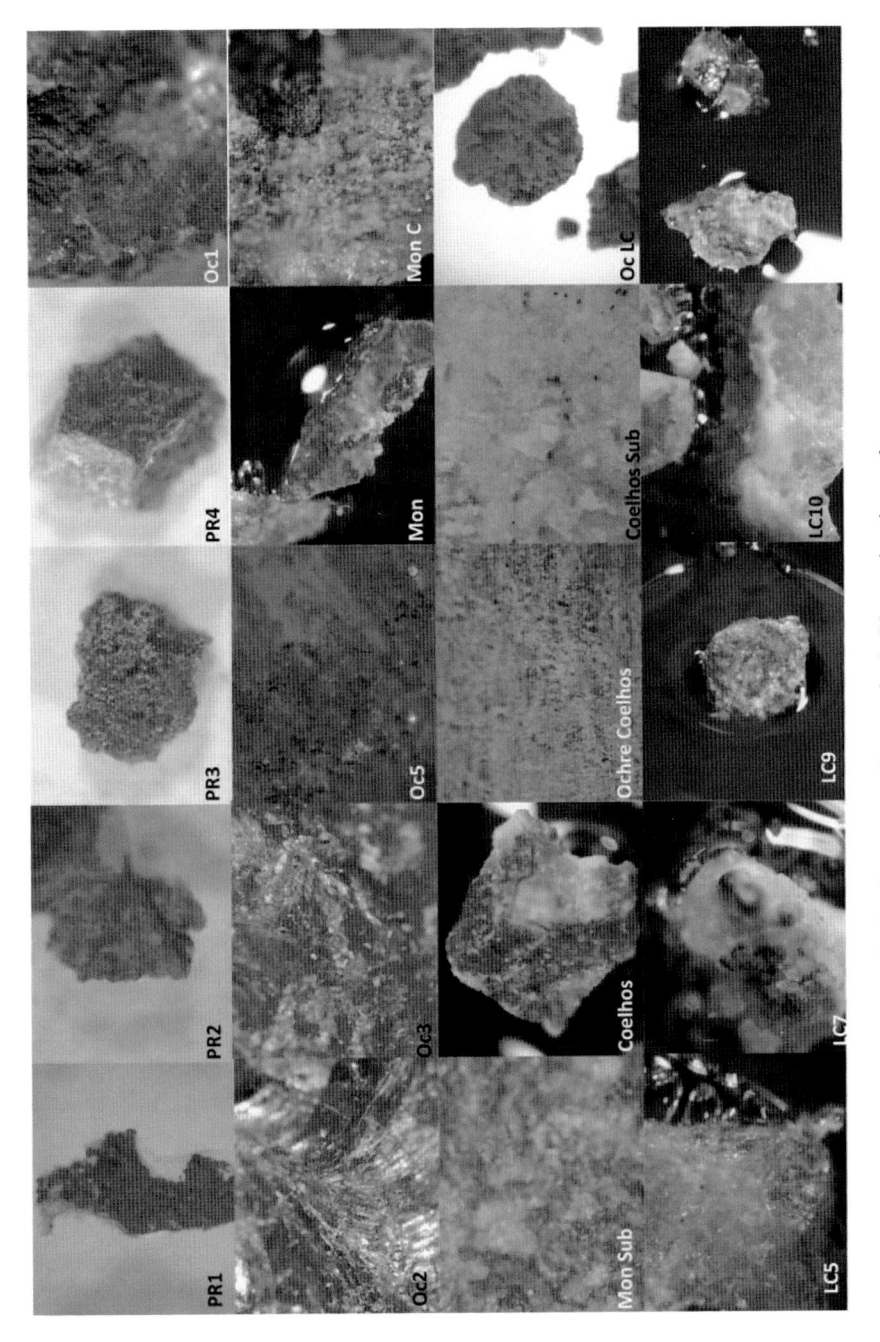

Figure 13.2 Pigment samples (Optical Microscopy observation). Photos by the authors.

Figure 13.3 Pigment samples observed on SEM: (a) hematite; (b) cinnabar. Photos by the authors.

1928 by Chandrasekhara Venkata Raman in India (Singh 2002) and, for that reason, was named after him. Raman microscopy allows for the study of areas up to 1 μm in diameter. A laser coupled to the optical microscope is used and there are several types of lasers available depending on the pigment: the green lasers are more suitable for blue and green pigments, while the red lasers are more suitable for red and yellow pigments. This technique is applied directly on the sample without requiring special preparation of the material. Moreover, it is a non-destructive technique, so that the same sample can be studied by other techniques after having been subjected to Raman analysis. Each chemical species, be it a pigment, dye, substrate, binder, etc., offers a different spectrum. This spectrum is like a digital impression that allows its unambiguous identification also in addition to the detection of chemical alterations caused by its interaction with other substances or the environment. RS also permits the differentiation of polymorphs (substance that has different structures) and therefore different properties including those that, despite having the same chemical formula, have different crystalline structures. Therefore, it serves to examine the complex chemical reactions that occur over time, helping to determine the degradation processes. Due to the success of RS in analysing prehistoric materials, it has been possible to make an accurate description of the chemical-mineralogical composition of pigments and to reach a better understanding of past production processes.

Infrared spectroscopy by Fourier transforms

ATR-FTIR is a type of absorption spectroscopy that uses the infrared region of the electromagnetic spectrum. The infrared radiation is guided through an interferometer that produces a signal when it passes through the sample. This signal achieves a spectrum identical to that of conventional spectroscopy, although in a more rapid way because the information of all frequencies is collected simultaneously. This allows multiple readings of the same sample which can be measured, increasing the sensitivity of the analysis. Due to all these advantages, all current infrared spectrophotometers are ATR-FTIR. Organic materials can be detected by this method.

X-ray fluorescence spectroscopy

This technique applies X-rays to electrons to alter their orbit. This change is registered in a spectrum constituted by peaks of energy characteristic of these elements. Therefore, this technique allows the multi-element analysis of the chemical composition of pigments. XRFS is a non-destructive technique that has been widely used in various rock art studies. While organic materials cannot be detected with this method, the results may indicate large amounts of sulphur and phosphorus that represent probable organic origins. At present, portable XRFS systems are being used to carry out measurements in situ.

Table 13.1 Red pigment archaeometric analysis and results

Main Components	Other Elements	Methods	Chronology	Location	Site	Bibliographic References
Hematite		SEM/EDX	Paleolithic	Asturias (Spain)	Tito Bustillo	Fortea y Hoyos, 1999
Hematite			Paleolithic	Asturias (Spain)	El Pindal	Balbín y González, 1999; Fortea 2000
Hematite	Fatty acids	Análisis de fosfatos	Paleolithic	Asturias (Spain)	La Lloseta	Navarro Gascón, 2002
Hematite		DRX	Paleolithic	Asturias (Spain)	Tito Bustillo	Fortea y Hoyos, 1999; Balbín et al., 2003
Hematite and Manganese	Wustite, amorphous carbon	Raman, SEM, EDX	Paleolithic	Asturias (Spain)	Tito Bustillo y El Buxu	Hernanz et al., 2011
Hematite and Goethite	Quartz	Raman, EDxrf	Paleolithic	Asturias (Spain)	Peña Candamo	Olivares et al., 2013
Iron Oxides	Clays and animal fat	DRX, CG	Paleolithic	Asturias (Spain)	Tito Bustillo	Fortea y Hoyos, 1999; Balbín et al., 2003
Hematite	Carbonates	Raman	Paleolithic	Cáceres (Spain)	Maltravieso	Martínez-Ramírez et al., 2015
Hematite			Paleolithic	Cantabria (Spain)	Altamira	Cabrera, 1978
Hematite		SEM/EDX	Paleolithic	Cantabria (Spain)	El Pendo	Lasheras et al., 1979; García Díez, 2001; González Sainz et al. 2003
Hematite		Raman	Paleolithic	Cantabria (Spain)	Altamira y El Soplao	Gázquez et al., 2014; Rull et al., 2014
Hematite		Raman, IR	Paleolithic/Post-paleolithic	Córdoba (Spain)	Los Murciélagos	Hernanz et al., 2006b

Hematite	Gypsum and Whewellite	Raman, SEM, EDX	Paleolithic/Post-paleolithic		Hoz de Vicente Minglanilla Cuenca (Spain)	Hernanz et al., 2010
Iron Oxides		Raman, EDxrf, DRX, PIXE	Paleolithic	France and Spain	Several paleolithic sites	Menu et al., 2009
Hematite		Raman, IR	Paleolithic	Málaga (Spain)	Ardales	Ferrón et al., e.p.
Hematite and Goethite		FT-Raman	Paleolithic	Málaga (Spain)	Ardales	Hernández et al., 2014
Hematite			Paleolithic	Basque Country (Spain)	Altxerri	Apellanz, 1982
Hematite			Paleolithic	Basque Country (Spain)	Santimamiñé	Hoyos, 1993
Iron	Quartz and Clays	SEM	Paleolithic	Basque Country (Spain)	Ekain	Chalmin et al., 2002
Hematite and Manganese			Paleolithic	Basque Country (Spain)	Arenaza	Garate et al., 2004
Hematite	Clays		Paleolithic	Basque Country (Spain)	Ekain	Chalmin et al., 2002
Hematite	Clay, Calcite, Calcium sulphate, Clay, Calcite, Calcium sulphate	SEM/EDX	Paleolithic	Basque Country (Spain)	Arenaza	Garate et al., 2010
Iron Oxides	Clay and Apatite	SEM/EDX	Paleolithic	Basque Country (Spain)	Arenaza	Garate et al., 2013

(*Continued*)

Main Components	Other Elements	Methods	Chronology	Location	Site	Bibliographic References
Iron Oxides		SEM/EDX, DRX	Paleolithic	Basque Country and Cantabria (Spain)	Ekain, Arenaza, Garma, Tito Bustillo	Pradeau et al., 2014
Hematite and Goethite		Raman, SEM, Edxrf	Paleolithic	Region of Murcia (Spain)	Cueva de los Aviones	Zilhão et al., 2010
Hematite and Goethite	Fatty acids, oxalates, Calcium, carbonates, Potassium and feldspars	Microfotografía, SEM/EDX, EDxrf, Raman, CG, Espectrocopia de Masa	Post-Paleolithic	Albacete (Spain)	Minateda, Abrigo del Barranco de la Mortaja	Mas et al., 2014
Iron Oxides		Espectroscopía de Masa	Post-Paleolithic	Aragón (Spain)		Baldellou y Alloza, 2012
Haematitis	Carbonates	Raman, EDxrf	Post-Paleolithic	Mediterranean Arc	Minateda, Mediodía, Buen Aire, Canaica del Calar I, Solana Covalachas	Ruiz et al., 2013 (proyecto 4D)
Hematite and Goethite	Quartz and Magnetite	Raman	Post-Paleolithic	Badajoz (Spain)	La Calderita	García et al., 2015; Gomes 2015
Hematite		FTIR	Post-Paleolithic	Cáceres (Spain)	Monfragüe	Ballester, 2006
Hematite		Raman, EDxrf	Post-Paleolithic	Cáceres (Spain)	Monfragüe	Collado et al., 2014
Hematite	Charcoal	Raman, LA-ICPMS	Post-Paleolithic	Cáceres (Spain)	Monfragüe	Collado et al., 2014

Hematite	Charcoal	Raman, EDxrf	Post-Paleolithic	Cáceres (Spain)	Monfragüe	Gomes 2015; Gomes et al., 2015
Iron Oxides	Bacteria, Methyl esters, fatty acids		Post-Paleolithic	Cádiz (Spain)	Atlanterra	González et al., 1999
Iron Oxides	Animal fat?		Post-Paleolithic	Cádiz (Spain)	Tajo de las Figuras	Carreras y Caballero, 1999
Hematite	Other elements	EDxrf portátil	Post-Paleolithic	Castelló (Spain)	La Saltadora	Roldán et al., 2010
Hematite and Manganese		Raman, SEM, EDxrf	Post-Paleolithic	Castelló (Spain)	Cova de Rossegadors and Saltadora	Hernanz et al., 2012
Hematite	Other oxides	Varias técnicas	Post-Paleolithic	Castilla la Mancha (Spain)	Several sites	Gismero et al., 2013
Hematite and cinnabar	Quartz	TXRF, DRX	Post-Paleolithic	Comunidad Valenciana (Spain)	Cova de l'Or	García y Borja et al., 2007
Óxidos de hierro	Cinnabar	EDxrf, TXRF, DRX	Post-Paleolithic	Comunidad Valenciana (Spain)	Cova de l'Or, Cova de la Sarsa y Cova Foscá	Roldán et al., 2007, 2010
Hematite	Quartz, calcite and clays	TXRF, DRX, FTIR, CG	Post-Paleolithic	Comunidad Valenciana (Spain)	Cova de la Sarsa y Cova Foscá	García y Borja et al., 2007
Hematites y Cinabrio		SEM-EDX, TXRF, DRX, FTIR, CG	Post-Paleolithic	Comunidad Valenciana (Spain)	Cova de l'Or, Cova de la Sarsa y Cova Foscá	Domingo et al., 2012
Hematite	Whewellite, Weddellite and amorphous coal	Raman	Post-Paleolithic	Cuenca (Spain)	Tío Modesto	Hernanz et al., 2006b

(Continued)

Main Components	Other Elements	Methods	Chronology	Location	Site	Bibliographic References
Hematite	Whewellite and weddellite	SEM, DRX, Raman, IR	Post-Paleolithic	Cuenca (Spain)	Sierra de las Cuerdas	Hernanz et al., 2007. 2008
Ocre	Manganese, Potassium and Phosphorus	DRX	Post-Paleolithic	Spain		Harneau, 2011
Hematite		Raman, SEM LA-ICPMS	Post-Paleolithic	Huesca (Spain)	Rio Vero	Resano et al., 2009
Hematite y Magnetita	Gypsum, coal and phosphates	Raman, Microscopía Óptica, EDxrf, SEM/EDX, Estereomicroscopía, Microestratigrafía.	Post-Paleolithic	Portugal	Abrigo do Lapedo 1	Gomes e Martins, 2013; Gomes, 2015
Iron	Other elements	EDxrf	Post-Paleolithic	Portugal	Abrigo de Nossa Senhora da Esperança	Nuevo et al., 2011
Hematite y Magnetita	Heated ochre and charcoal	Raman, Microscopía Óptica, EDxrf, SEM/EDX, Estereomicroscopía, Microestratigrafía.	Post-Paleolithic	Portugal	Pego da Rainha	Gomes, 2015
Hematite		Raman, Microscopía Óptica, EDxrf, SEM/EDX, Estereomicroscopía, Microestratigrafía.	Post-Paleolithic	Portugal	Abrigo do Ribeiro das Casas	Gomes, 2015

Hematite					Gomes, 2015
Hematite	Raman, Microscopía Óptica, EDxrf, SEM/EDX, Estereomicroscopía, Microestratigrafía.	Post-Paleolithic	Portugal	Abrigo de Segura	
Iron	EDxrf	Post-Paleolithic	Región de Murcia (Spain)	Abrigo Riquelme	Medina-Ruiz et al., 2010
Iron	Calcite	Raman	Post-Paleolithic	Región de Murcia (Spain)	Abrigo Riquelme	Ruiz et al., 2012
Hematite		Raman	Post-Paleolithic	Segovia (Spain)	Abrigo Remacha	Iriarte et al., 2013
Hematite	Organics?	Raman, LA-ICPMS	Post-Paleolithic	Teruel (Spain)	Río Martín	Baldellou y Alloza, 2012
Hematite	DNA? Organics?	LA-ICP/MS	Post-Paleolithic	Teruel (Spain)	Barranco de las Olivanas	Bea, 2012
Hematite		SEM/EDX, IR, Raman, EDxrf	Post-Paleolithic	Teruel (Spain)	Val del Charco del Agua Amarga	Izquierdo, 2013
Hematite	Manganese oxide	Raman, EDxrf, DRX	Post-Paleolithic	Teruel (Spain)	Los Chaparros	Pitarch et al., 2014

Gas chromatography

This is a physical-chemical method of separation of mixtures, to identify and quantify the relevant components. Once the elements of a mixture are determined, it is possible to identify and quantify them. This technique is applied with the objective of detection of fatty acids, terpenes and amino acids. Therefore, it is a good technique to identify organic binders. However, many of the organic materials are perceived as concretions that could be the result of other microorganisms, increasing the difficulty with their identification. ATR-FTIR spectroscopic analysis and RS are applied as complementary tools to avoid these problems.

Results of pigments analysis on prehistoric rock art

It is evident from the above review that these techniques have the potential to develop the study of painted rock art. In recent years, techniques favoured the identification of pigments (organic and inorganic), grounds, and binders. However, it is important to be aware that different techniques provide diverse information. For example, some techniques, such as RS, will identify materials but for more detailed information on components further analysis is required, such as with chromatographic analysis, which separates and detects organic components of a mixture. In order to gain a better understanding of materials used in painted rock art, it is crucial to understand the capabilities of instruments, including their limits of detection as well as depth and spatial limits.

Non-invasive spectroscopy has been used in the identification and characterization of paints and pigments for around 80 years. As it requires little material to produce a result, it is ideal for identifying tiny quantities of pigments and dyes. As well as being non-invasive its advantage is that it is relatively portable allowing the object to be examined in-situ.

As explained earlier in this chapter, the techniques of production and application of pigments are not directly related to chronology or pictographic style, although in many cases they show a stylistic homogeneity. The extraction of the pigment, choice of colour and its preparation must be, in part, the result of the availability of the raw material. The results gathered on the different production techniques are quite relevant. Therefore, results from Rupscience project analyses (Gomes et al. 2015) suggest that red pigments have been made from different minerals or prepared with different techniques: through grinding, heat treatment or inclusion of corrosives elements or binders.

The alteration of the raw material, by grinding or heating, reveals that these two actions were carried out by someone in a certain context. It implies an intention and previous planning. Thus, the preparation of pigments must be the result of a choice of raw material but also the adopted techniques, so the decisive factor for selection would be the desired colour, obtained directly from the mineral components or after their manipulation.

Table 13.2 Black, White, yellow and violet pigment archaeometry analysis and results

Black Pigments Main Components	Other Elements	Methods	Chronology	Location	Site	Bibliographic references
Charcoal			Paleolithic	Asturias	Tito Bustillo	Fortea y Hoyos, 1999; Balbín et al., 2003
Charcoal and Manganese		SEM/EDXS, DRX	Paleolithic	Asturias/ Cantabria/ País Vasco	Gargás, Ekain, Arenaza, La Garma, Tito Bustillo	Pradeau et al., 2014
Charcoal			Paleolithic	Cantabria	Altamira	Cabrera et al., 1978
Charcoal and Manganese		EDxrf, SEM/EDX	Paleolithic/Post Paleolithic	Castelló	Cova Remigia	López-Montalvo et al., 2014
Hematite and Manganese		Raman, SEM, EDxrf	Post-Palaeolithic	Castelló	Cova de Rossegadors y Saltadora	Hernanz et al., 2012
Manganese and Iron	Other elements	Portable EDxrf	Post-Palaeolithic	Castelló	La Saltadora	Roldán et al., 2007, 2010
Charcoal		Raman, IR	Palaeolithic/Post Palaeolithic	Córdoba	Los Murciélagos	Hernanz et al., 2006
Charcoal	Gypsum, Whewellite	Raman, SEM/EDX	Palaeolithic/Post Palaeolithic	Cuenca	Sierra de las Cuerdas	Hernanz et al., 2010
Charcoal		DRX	Post-Palaeolithic	Galicia	Pedra da Moura, Pedra Cuberta, Arca da Piosa, Casota do Páramo, Dombate, Forno dos Mouros	Martínez-Ramírez et al., 2008
Charcoal	Manganese oxide	SEM	Paleolithic	Málaga	Cueva de Nerja	Sanchidrián, 2001
Charcoal			Paleolithic	País Vasco	Ekain	Chalmin et al., 2002, 2004, 2006
Pyrolusite (manganese dioxide)	Calcite	Raman	Post-Palaeolithic	Murcia region	Abrigo Riquelme	Ruiz et al., 2012
Paracoquimbita	Charcoal	Raman	Post-Palaeolithic	Segovia	Abrigo Remacha	Iriarte et al., 2013

(Continued)

Main Components	Other Elements	Methods	Chronology	Location	Site	Bibliographic references
Black Pigments						
Charcoal	Organics?	Raman, LA-ICPMS	Post-Palaeolithic	Teruel	Río Martín	Alloza et al., 2009
Manganese Oxide		Raman, EDxrf	Post-Palaeolithic	Teruel	Los Chaparros, Albalate del Arzobispo	Pitarch et al., 2014
Manganese Oxide		Raman, DRX	Post Palaeolithic	Teruel	Los Chaparros	Pitarch et al., 2014
White Pigments						
Calcium phosphates, carbonates		Raman	Paleolithic	Cáceres	Maltravieso	Martínez-Ramírez et al., 2014
Calcium sulphate, gypsum		EDxrf, TXRF, DRX	Post Palaeolithic	Valencia	Cova de l'Or, Cova de la Sarsa y Cova Foscá	Roldán et al., 2007
Yellow Pigments	Other elements					
	Hematite	DRX	Paleolithic	Asturias	Tito Bustillo	Fortea y Hoyos, 1999
Violet Pigments	Other elements					
	Hematite, manganese		Paleolithic	Asturias	Tito Bustillo	Fortea y Hoyos, 1999

Final remarks

Archaeometric research of prehistoric pigments is a complex task, and only the application of different techniques can help in the specific resolution of archaeological questions. Different techniques used for the characterization of pigments demonstrate the effectiveness of these methods to identify the mineralogical components of the pigments and their preparation techniques (Brunet et al. 1995, 1997; Wainwright et al. 2002; Fiore et al. 2008; Cavalcante et al. 2009, 2011, 2012). The advantages of a complex methodological approach together with a complementarity of archaeometric techniques and certain adaptations in instrumental parameters lead to the identification of pigment mineralogical components and their preparation techniques. This approach also helps in the development of appropriate monitoring and conservation measures for rock art sites.

Pigment analysis has the main objective of characterizing the chemical-mineralogical composition, the identification of the preparation processes as well as the choices and selection of the materials used in the pigment production. This work aimed to establish the mineralogical characterization of the schematic art paintings of the southwest of the Iberian Peninsula and to raise questions about the preparation, production and conservation of prehistoric pigments in world contexts. The obtained data show that raw materials used for the pigment preparation have local origin and hematite was unsurprisingly the most common mineral identified, indicating that this homogeneity in pigment composition, may be the result of an obvious cultural choice (the preference for the use of red) and/or related to the availability of raw materials (iron oxides which are widely disseminated throughout the world). Whereas the poor recognition of organic components may be related to site preservation and/or methodological issues used to identify the organic compounds. To characterize the organic components, it will be necessary to perform complementary analyses and compare the resulting chromatograms to those of the known organic components (blood, milk, saliva, among others).

These techniques, in addition to identifying the composition and the methods of preparation of the pigments, also help with the management of measures of monitoring and conservation of sites with rock art paintings. Each rock art site has a unique microclimate that influences the conservation of pigments and substrates, so it is necessary to perform Archaeometric studies at a local level in order to help decision-making regarding its preservation. Pigments analysis is useful inasmuch that it provides this essential information for conservation and management practices for the long-term preservation of the site (e.g., Alloza et al. 2009). A long-term monitoring of the figures backgrounded by chemical analyses is useful not only in determining the chemical composition of pigments but also to determine any change in this same chemical composition over time. Preventive conservation actions can and should be taken through these results. In this sense, we argue that decisions regarding the conservation of rock art sites should consider results from analyses of the paintings. For example, previous studies from the Main Caves at Giant's Castle and at Battle Cave at Injisuthi, in the uKhahlamba/Drakensberg Park, South Africa, show that the rock surface onto which San art is painted, the preparation of this surface and the nature of the paints themselves influence pigment response to the ambient environment (Hall et al. 2007). In some cases, pigments are also known to alter the albedo, porosity, chemistry and thermal properties of the surface.

This influence on thermal properties can lead to pigment-to-pigment as well as pigment-to-rock stresses, negatively influencing the preservation status. Additionally, thermal infrared data has shown that the rock and both the white and ochre pigments have quite different responses to solar heating (Buzgar et al. 2009), which can be explained by the different thermal properties of the materials. When exposed to solar radiation, the materials comprising the paintings and painting–rock associations may well experience shearing forces that cause cracking (Scott and Hyder 1993) and ultimately failure. Considering results such as these, it was requested that an evaluation of any change in the environmental conditions at the art site (e.g., removal of vegetation to improve touristic view) be documented for San rock art sites (Arocena, Hall and Meiklejohn 2008) because such changes might significantly increase thermal fluctuations in pigments and promote crack formation and hence the decay of the rock art panels.

Another example, applicable to some paintings (but not all) found in the Drakensberg area, is that the surface on which a painting (or paintings) was created had been both smoothed, possibly with a water-polished stone (such stones were observed on the floor at all the sites investigated) and covered with a (white) clay-based ground (Mazel and Watchman 1997; Prinsloo et al. 2008, 2013). Application of a ground mineral (huntite) underneath paintings has also been reported from Australia, where such application was found to be predisposed to advanced deterioration, especially under damp or humid conditions (Ford, MacLeod and Haydock 1994). It is reported that both the smoothing and the clay-based ground mineral significantly modified the physical and chemical characteristics of the surface. Smoothing of the rock changes surface porosity and increases strength (Katz, Reches and Roegiers 2000) and serves to remove any weakened, weathered surface that would otherwise be beneath the painting. In this instance it is argued that it is the application of a clay-based mineral however, that is perhaps more significant to the longevity of the paintings. The clay-based ground acts as an impermeable barrier for moisture flow, both into the rock and from the rock to the air; it also greatly changes thermal properties (Hall, Meiklejohn and Arocena 2007).

Furthermore, observations suggest that in many instances what was interpreted as weathering of rock is, in fact, loss of the clay attachment to the rock and this has ramifications for remediation or preservation (Hall et al. 2007). Some authors suggest that pigments, at least where there is a clay base, do not penetrate the rock but occur as discrete layers on the rock (Hall, Meiklejohn and Arocena 2007). In terms of weathering and conservation, consideration must be given to maintaining the clay–rock link otherwise the painting deteriorates; not through weathering of the rock but as a result of separation of the clay from the rock. Due to this, changes in environmental conditions, notably of moisture and temperature, are suggested to affect the stability of the pigment–clay–rock bonds (Spagnolo et al. 1997; Hall et al. 2007).

It is further argued (Hall et al. 2007; Hall, Meiklejohn and Arocena 2007) that both climatic change and local, human-induced environmental changes may cause loss of stability of the rock–clay and clay–pigment bonds also affect San paintings that are not on a clay base. Other reports about south African rock art suggest, in respect of human-induced changes (Hall, Meiklejohn and Arocena 2007) that the removal (or loss) of trees, largely for visitor purposes, at sites such as Giant's Castle Main Caves, has influenced ambient thermal and humidity conditions, thereby affecting the paintings and possibly resulting in accelerated deterioration. Global climatic changes, particularly those leading to increased precipitation and humidity, would serve to exacerbate the situation.

Understanding how rock art paintings interacts with threats and other processes that result in damage helps researchers to create long-term protective strategies for the site in question. For example, identification of salts, microbial communities, fats, binders, other minerals and components are being used in many different sites (Zoppi et al. 2002; Laiz, Gonzalez and Saiz-Jimenez 2003; Arocena, Hall, and Meiklejohn 2008; Prinsloo et al. 2008). The technology involved on these types of analyses can also be used to study the microclimatic conditions at sites.

According to some authors (Hall et al. 2007) the challenge now is to evaluate and use all the analytical data to undertake real-time modelling of the surface conditions affecting rock art and, hence, suggest possible protective or remedial actions that will not, by default, worsen the situation.

In places such as Zimbabwe, limited research has been undertaken despite the many different damages made to rock art sites in the last few decades (Nhamo 2018). The necessity of using advanced archaeometry technologies in site analyses is increasingly evidenced, providing an understanding that pigment characteristics are influenced by the geological sources, binders, and preparation methods (Hall, Meiklejohn and Arocena 2007; Bonneau, Pearce and Pollard 2012). These differ from place to place but it is important to study diagenesis processes that are taking place on both the rock paintings and engravings of endangered places in order to create conservation protocols that will include not only mitigatory measures and general maintenance but also conservation research and training, conservation policy and short-term and long-term protection solutions for rock art sites (Nhamo 2018).

The identification of diverse processes of transformation and preparation of the pigments reveals that this would be an activity that needed specific time and knowledge within the community. The action of transforming natural matter implies an initial conceptual approach where the final objective would already be predefined. Archaeometric multiproxy approaches can, in this sense, be considered a very powerful tool for creating a protective intervention and for long-term planning.

References

AIC (2015) *American Institute for Conservation - Code of Ethics and Guidelines for Practice.* AIC.

Aldhouse-Green, S. H. R. and Pettitt, P. B. (1998) Paviland cave: Contextualizing the Red Lady. *Antiquity,* 72, pp.756–772.

Alloza, I. R., Arranz, E., González, J. M. G., Baldellou, M., Resano, V., Marzo, M. P. and Vanhaecke, F. (2009) La Conservación del Arte Rupestre: estudio de los factores de deterioro y de la composición química de los pigmentos. In *El Arte Rupestre del Arco Mediterráneo de la Península Ibérica, 10 años en la Lista del Patrimonio Mundial de la UNESCO. Actas IV Congreso.* Valencia: Generalitat Valenciana, pp.317–325.

Arocena, J. M., Hall, K. and Meiklejohn, I. (2008) Minerals provide tints and possible binder/extender in pigments in San Rock Paintings (South Africa). *Geoarchaeology,* 23(2), pp.293–304.

Aubert, M. (2012) A review of rock art dating in the Kimberley, Western Australia. *Journal of Archaeological Science,* 39, pp.573–577.

Baldellou, V. and Alloza, R. (2012) El análisis de pigmentos en Aragón. Otra forma de documentar el arte rupestre. In Juste, N., Hernández, M. A., Pereta, A., Royo, J. I. and Andrés, J. A. (Eds.) *Jornadas técnicas para la gestión del arte rupestre Patrimonio Mundial.* Barbastro: Comarca de Somontano de Barbastro, pp.73–83.

Barnett, J. R., Miller, S. and Pearce, E. (2006) Colour and art: A brief history of pigments. *Optics Laser Technology,* 38(4–6), pp.445–453.

Bates, D. and White, I. (1985) *The Native Tribes of Western Australia/Daisy Bates.* Edited by I. White. Canberra: National Library of Australia.

Bonjean, D., Vanbrabant, Y., Abrams, G., Pirson, S., Burlet, C., Di-Modica, K., Otte, M., Vander-Auwera, J., Golitko, M., McMillan, R. and Goemaere, E. (2015) A new Cambrian black pigment used during the late Middle Palaeolithic discovered at Scladina Cave (Andenne, Belgium). *Journal of Archaeological Science,* 55, pp.253–265.

Bonneau, A., Brock, F., Higham, T., Pearce, D. G. and Pollard, A. M. (2011) An improved pretreatment protocol for radiocarbon dating black pigments in San Rock Art. *Radiocarbon,* 53(3), pp.419–428. https://doi.org/10.1017/S003382220003455X

Bonneau, A., Pearce, D. G. and Pollard, A. M. (2012). A multi-technique characterization and provenance study of the pigments used in San Rock Art, South Africa. *Journal of Archaeological Science,* 39(2), pp.287–294. doi:10.1016/j.jas.2011.09.011.

Brunet, J., Vouvé, J., Vidal, P., Malaurent, P. and Lacezedieu, G. (1995) Theories and practice of the conservation of our heritage of rock art: Concrete examples of interventions in natural climatic environment. In Thorn, A. and Brunet, J. (Eds.) *Preservation of Rock Art.* Occasional AURA Publication 9. Melbourne: Australian Rock Art Research Association Inc., pp.1–12.

Brunet, J., Vouvé, J. and Malaurent, P. (1997) Conservation of subterranean historic and prehistoric monuments: The importance of the environment and microclimate. In Agnew, N. (Ed.) *Conservation of Ancient Sites on the Silk Road: Proceedings of an International Conference on the Conservation of Grotto Sites: Mogao Grottoes, Dunhuang, The People's République of China, 3–8 Octobre 1993.* Los Angeles: Getty Conservation Institute, pp.259–269.

Buzgar N., Buzatu A. and Sanislav I.V. 2009. The Raman study on certain sulfates. *Analele Stiintifice ale Universitatii "Al. I. Cuza",* 55, pp.5–23.

Cabrera, J. M. (1979) Les matériaux de peinture de la caverne d'Altamira. *Actes de la cinquième réunion triennale du comité de conservation de l'ICOM.* Zagreb, pp.1–9.

Cavalcante, L. C. D., Lage, M. C. S. M., Fabris, J. D. and Etchevarne, C. A. (2009) Análise Arqueométrica de Pintura Rupestre do Sítio Poções, Bahia, Brasil. *Revista de Arqueologia,* 22(2), pp.95–103.

Cavalcante, L. C. D., Luz, M. F., Guidon, N., Fabris, J. D. and Ardisson, E. D. J. (2011) Ochres from rituals of prehistoric human funerals at the Toca do Enoque site, Piauí, Brazil. *Hyperfine Interactions,* 203(1–3), pp.39–45.

Cavalcante, L. C. D., Silva, H. K. S., Lima, O. G. and Alves, Y. R. V. (2012) Arqueometria aplicada à conservação do património arqueológico: o caso do sítio de arte rupestre Letreiro da Pedra Riscada. In *Congresso Internacional de História e Património.* EDUFPI 3. pp.1–11.

Chalmin, E., Vignaud, C., Salomon, H., Farges, F., Susini, J. and Menu, M. (2006) Minerals discovered in Paleolithic black pigments by transmission electron microscopy and micro-x-ray absorption near-edge structure. *Journal of Applied Physics,* A.83, pp.213–18.

Cole, N. and Watchman, A. (1992) Paintings with plants: Investigating fibres in Aboriginal rock paintings at Laura, north Queensland. *Rock Art Research,* 9(1), pp.27–36.

d'Errico, F., Salomon, H., Vignaud, C. and Stringer, C. B. (2010) Pigments from the Middle Palaeolithic levels of Es-Skhul. *Journal of Archaeological Science,* 37, pp.3099–3110.

d'Errico, F., García-Moreno, R. and Rifkin, R. F. (2012) Technological, elemental and colorimetric analysis of an engraved ochre fragment from the Middle Stone Age levels of Klasies River Cave 1, South Africa. *Journal of Archaeological Science,* 39(4), pp.942–952.

Duarte, C. (2002) The Burial Taphonomy and Ritual. In Zilhão, J. and Trinkaus, E. (Eds.) *Portrait of the Artist as a Child. The Gravettian Human Skeleton from the Abrigo do Lagar Velho and its Archaeological Context.* Trabalhos de Arqueologia, 22. Lisboa: Instituto Português de Arqueologia, pp.187–201.

Elias, M., Chartier, C., Prévot, G., Garay, H. and Vignaud, C. (2006) The colour of ochres explained by their composition. *Materials Science and Engineering,* B. 127, pp. 70–80.

Erlandson, J. M., Robertson, J. and Descantes, C. (1999) Geochemical analysis of eight red ochres from western North America. *American Antiquity,* 64, pp. 517–526.

Fiore, D., Maier, M., Parera, S. D., Orquera, L. and Piana, E. (2008) Chemical analyses of the earliest pigment residues from the uttermost part of the planet (Beagle Channel region, Tierra del Fuego, Southern South America). *Journal of Archaeological Science,* 35, pp. 3047–3056.

Ford, B., MacLeod, I. and Haydock, P. (1994) Rock Art Pigments from Kimberley Region of Western Australia: Identification of the minerals and conversion mechanisms. *Studies in Conservation*, 39(1), pp. 57–69. www.jstor.org/stable/1506491.

Fortea, J. and Hoyos, M. (1999) La Table Ronde de Colombres et les études de protection et conservation en Asturies réalises de 1992 à 1996. *Bulletin de la Société Préhistorique Ariège-Pyrénées*, 54, pp.235–242.

Garcês, S., Gomes, H., Haddab, L., Cura, P. and Rosina, P. (2019) Experimentation of rock art pigments with re-created prehistoric rock art figures from Central Sahara in order to increase the m-FTIR spectrum databases of organic and inorganic paintings material. *Rock Art Research*, 36(2), pp.182–188.

Gillespie, D. A. (1983) The practice of rock art conservation and site management in Kakadu National Park. In Gillespie, D. A. (Ed.) *The rock art sites of Kakadu National Park*. Canberra: Australian National Parks and Wildlife Service.

Gomes, H. (2015) Arqueometria de Pigmentos da Arte Rupestre. Caracterização mineralógica e técnicas de produção na arte esquemática da Península Ibérica ocidental. [Ph.D. Thesis] in Quaternário, Materiais e Culturas. Vila Real: Universidade de Trás-os-Montes e Alto Douro, 322p.

Gomes, H., Collado, H., Martins, A., Nash, G., Rosina, P., Vaccaro, C. and Volpe, L. (2015) Pigment in Western Iberian schematic rock art: An analytical approach. *Mediterranean Archaeology and Archaeometry*, 15(1), pp.163–175.

Gomes, H. and Martins, A. (2013) Pintura Rupestre Esquemática em Portugal: uma abordagem arqueométrica. *JIA - Jornadas de Jovens Investigadores em Arqueologia 7 a 11 Maio 2013*, Barcelona.

Gomes, H., Rosina, P., Holakooei, P., Solomon, T. and Vaccaro, C. (2013a) Identification of pigments used in rock art paintings in Gode Roriso-Ethiopia using micro-Raman spectroscopy. *Journal of Archaeological Science*, 40, pp. 4073–4082.

Gomes, H., Rosina, P., Martins, A. and Oosterbeek, L. (2013b) Pinturas Rupestres: Matérias Primas, Técnicas e Gestão do Território. *Estudos do Quaternário*. Apeq, Braga. 9, pp.45–55.

Gomes, H., Rosina, P. and Oosterbeek, L. (2013c) Pigmentos pré-históricos na Península Ibérica: caracterização e técnicas de produção. In *Arqueologia em Portugal-150 anos*. Lisboa: Associação dos arqueólogos portugueses. (CD-Artigo61).

Gomes, H., Rosina, P., Guidon, N., Buco, C., Santos, T., Volpe, L., Vaccaro, C., Nash, G. and Garcês, S. (2019) Identification of organic binders in Prehistoric pigments through multiproxy archaeometry analyses from the Toca do Paraguaio and the Boqueirão da Pedra Furada shelters (Capivara Sierra, Piauí, Brazil). *Rock Art Research*, 36(2), pp.214–221.

Guineau, B., Lorblanchet, M., Gratuze, B., Dulin, L., Roger, P., Akrich, R. and Muller, F. (2001) Manganese black pigments in prehistoric paintings: The case of Black Frieze of Pech Merle (France). *Archaeometry*, 4, pp.211–225.

Hall, K., Meiklejohn, I. and Arocena, J. (2007) The thermal responses of rock art pigments: Implications for rock art weathering in southern Africa. *Geomorphology*, 91, pp.132–145.

Hall, K., Meiklejohn, I., Arocena, J., Prinsloo, L., Summer, P., Hall, L. (2007) Deterioration of San rock art: New findings, new challenges. *South African Journal of Science*, 103, pp.361–362.

Henshilwood, C. S. and d'Errico, F. (2011) Middle Stone Age engravings and their significance to the debate on the emergence of symbolic material culture. In

Henshilwood, C. S. and d'Errico, F. (Eds.) *Homo Symbolicus: The Dawn of Language, Imagination and Spirituality.* John Benjamins Publishing Company, pp. 75–96.

Henshilwood, C. S., d'Errico, F., van Niekerk, K. L., Coquinot, Y., Jacobs, Z., Lauritzen, S.-E., Menu, M. and García-Moreno, R. (2011b) A 100,000-year-old ochre processing workshop at Blombos Cave, South Africa. *Science,* 334, pp.219–222.

Hodgskiss, T. (2010) Identifying grinding, scoring and rubbing use-wear on experimental ochre pieces. *Journal of Archaeological Science,* 37(12), pp.3344–3358.

Hradil, D., Grygar, T., Hradilova, J. and Bezdic, P. (2003) Clay and iron oxide pigments in the history of painting. *Clay Science,* 22, pp. 223–236.

Iriarte, E., Foyo, A., Sánchez, M. A. and Tomillo, C. (2009) The origin and geochemical characterization of Red Ochres from the Tito Bustillo and Monte Castillo Caves (Northern Spain). *Archaeometry,* 51(2), pp.231–251.

Iriarte, M., Hernanz, A., Ruiz-López, J. F. and Martín, S. (2013) μ-Raman spectroscopy of prehistoric paintings from the Abrigo Remacha rock shelter (Villaseca, Segovia, Spain). *Journal of Raman Spectroscopy,* 44, pp.1557–1562.

Katz, O., Reches, Z. and Roegiers, J. C. (2000) Evaluation of mechanical rock properties using a Schmidt Hammer. *International Journal of Rock Mechanics and Mining Sciences,* 37(4), pp.723–728.

Laiz, L., Gonzalez, J. M. and Saiz-Jimenez, C. (2003) Microbial communities in caves: Ecology, physiology, and effects on palaeolithic paintings. In Koestler, R. J., Koestler, V. R., Carola, A. E. and Nieto-Fernández, F. E. (Eds.) *Art, Biology, and Conservation: Biodeterioration of Works of Art.* New York: The Metropolitan Museum of Art, pp.210–225.

Lasheras, J. A. (2003) El Arte Paleolítico de Altamira. In Lasheras, J. A. (Ed.) *Redescubrir Altamira.* Madrid: Turner Ediciones, pp.65–91.

López-Montalvo, E., Roldán, C., Badal, E., Murcia-Mascarós, S. and Villaverde, V. (2017) Identification of plant cells in black pigments of prehistoric Spanish Levantine rock art by means of a multi-Analytical approach. A new method for social identity materialization using chaine operatoire. *PLoS ONE.* https://doi.org/10.1371/journal.pone.0172225

Loubser, J. H. N. (1992) Materials used by Bushmen to make rock paintings. *Culna,* 42, pp.16–17.

Loy, T. H., Jones, R., Nelson, D. E., Meehan, B., Vogel, J., Southon, J. and Cosgrove, R. (1990) Accelerator radiocarbon dating of human blood proteins in pigments from Late Pleistocene art sites in Australia. *Antiquity,* 64, pp.110–116.

Marshall, L. J. R., Williams, J. R., Almond, M. J., Atkinson, S. D. M., Cook, S. R., Matthews, W. and Mortimore, J. L. (2005) Analysis of ochres from Clearwell Caves: The role of particle size in determining colour. *Acta Spectrochimica,* Part A, 61, pp.233–241.

Mazel, A. D. and Watchman, A. L. (1997) Accelerator radiocarbon dating of Natal Drakensberg paintings: Results and implications. *Antiquity,* 71, pp.445–49.

Menu, M. and Walter, P. 1996. Matières picturales et techniques de peinture. In Brunet, J. and Vouvé, J. (Eds.) *La Conservation des Grottes Ornées.* Paris: CNRS, pp. 31–41.

Montes-Barquín, R., Munos, E., Lasheras, J. A., De Las Heras, C., Rasines, P. and Fatás, P. (2004) The association between deer/hind and mountain goat in the rock art assemblages of the lower/middle Magdalenian of the centre Cantabrian region: New discoveries and some interpretations. *Prehistoric and Tribal Art: New*

Discoveries, New Interpretations and New Methods of Research. *XXI International Valcamonica Symposium.*

Nhamo, A. (2018) Burning images: A critical review of rock art conservation in Zimbabwe. *Conservation and Management of Archaeological Sites,* 20(2), 58–75. doi:10.1080/13505033.2018.1453725

Petru, S. (2006) Red, black or white? The dawn of color symbolism. *Documenta Praehistorica,* 33, pp.203–208.

Pettitt, P. (2000) Radiocarbon chronology, faunal turnover and human occupation at the Goat's Hole, Paviland. In Aldhouse-Green, S. (Ed.) *Paviland Cave and the Red Lady: Definitive Report.* Bristol: Western Academic and Specialist Press, pp.63–71.

Pettitt, P., Van der Plicht, H., Ramsey, C. B., Soares, A. M. M. and Zilhão, J. (2002) The radiocarbon chronology. In Zilhão, J. and Trinkaus, E. (Eds.) *Portrait of the Artist as a Child. The Gravettian Human Skeleton from the Abrigo do Lagar Velho and its Archaeological Context.* Trabalhos de Arqueologia, 22. Lisboa: Instituto Português de Arqueologia, pp.132–138.

Pettitt, P. and Bahn, P. (2015). An alternative chronology for the art of Chauvet cave *Antiquity,* 89: 542–553. https://doi.org/10.15184/aqy.2015.21

Pomiès, M. P., Barbaza, M., Menu, M. and Vignaud, C. (1999a) Préparation des pigments rouges préhistoriques par chauffage. *L'Anthropologie,* 103(4), pp. 503–518.

Pomiès, M. P. and Menu, M. (1999) Red palaeolithic pigments: Natural hematite or heated goethite? *Archaeometry,* 41(2), pp.275–285.

Pomiès, M. P., Menu, M. and Vignaud, C. (1999b) TEM observations of goethite dehydration: Application to archaeological samples. *Journal of the European Ceramic Society,* 19, pp.1605–1614.

Prinsloo, L. C. (2007) Rock hyraces: A cause of San rock art deterioration? *Journal of Raman Spectroscopy,* 38, pp.496–503.

Prinsloo, L., Barnard, W., Meiklejohn, I. and Hall, K. (2008) The first Raman spectroscopic study of San rock art in the Ukhahlamba Drakensberg Park, South África, *Journal of Raman Spectroscopy,* 39, pp.646–654. doi:10.1002/jrs.1901.

Prinsloo, L. C., Tournié, A., Colomban, P., Paris, C. and Bassett, S. T. (2013) In search of the optimum Raman/IR signatures of potential ingredients used in San/Bushman rock art paint. *Journal of Archaeological Science,* 40, pp. 2981–2990.

Rifkin, R. F. (2012) Processing ochre in the Middle Stone Age: Testing the inference of prehistoric behaviours from actualistically derived experimental data. *Journal of Anthropological Archaeology,* 31(2), pp.174–195.

Roebroeks, W., Sier, M. J., Kellberg Nielsen, T., De Loecker, D., Parés, J. M. and Arps, E. S. (2012) Use of red ochre by early Neanderthals. *Proceedings of the National Academy of Sciences of the United States of America,* 109, pp.1889–1894.

Rosina, P., Gomes, H., Martins, A. and Oosterbeek, L. (2013) Caracterização de Pigmentos em Arte Rupestre. Arkeos 34. CEIPHAR, Tomar. pp.255–262.

Rosina, P., Gomes, H., Nash, G. H. and Salomon, T. (2014a) Dating beeswax pictograms from Gode Roriso in Ethiopia. *Journal of Archaeological Science,* 49, pp.206–212.

Rosina, P., Gomes, H., Salomon, T., Oosterbeek, L. and Collado, H. (2014b) O Tratamento Térmico do Ocre para a Produção de Pigmentos Vermelhos na Arte Rupestre. *Actas IX Jornada de Arqueologia Ibero-Americana. I Jornada de Arqueologia Transatlântica, 2013. Criciúma, SC, Brasil.* Brasil: Habilis Press, pp.129–146.

Rosina, P., Collado, H., Garcês, S., Gomes, H., Eftekhari, N., Nicoli, M. and Vaccaro, C. (2019) Benquerencia (La Serena - Spain) rock art: An integrated spectroscopy analysis with FTIR and Raman. *Helyon*, 5(10), e02561. https://doi.org/10.1016/j.heliyon.2019.e02561

Rudner, I. (1982) Khoisan pigments and paints and their relationship to rock paintings. *Annals of the South African Museum*, 87, pp.1–281.

Rudner, I. (1983) Paints of the Khoisan rock artists. *South African Archaeological Society Goodwin Series*, 4, pp.14–20.

Ruiz, J., Sebasatian, M., Quesada, E., Pereira, J., Fernandez, S., Martinéz, I., Maguregui, M., Madariaga, J. M., Pitarch, A., Lorente, J. C. and Dólera, A. (2013) *Memoria final proyecto 4D Arte Rupestre*. Ayuntamiento de Jumilla. Secretaria de Estado de Cultura, Ministerio de Educação, Cultura e Despostos, pp.367.

Salomon, H., d'Errico, F., van Niekerk, K. L., Coquinot, Y., Jacobs, Z. Lauritzen, S. E. Menu, M. and García-Moreno, R. A. (2011) 100,000-year-old Ochre-processing workshop at Blombos Cave, South Africa. *Science*, 334, pp.219–222.

Salomon, H., Vignaud, C., Coquinot, Y., Beck, L., Stringer, C., Strivay, D. and d'Errico, F. (2012) Selection and heating of colouring materials in the Mousterian level of EsSkhul (100 000 YearsBp), Mount Carmel, Israel. *Science*, 334, pp. 219–222.

Santos da Rosa, N. (2019a) La Tecnología Del Arte Rupestre Levantino. *Cuadernos de Arte Prehistórico*, 7, pp.120–146.

Santos da Rosa, N. (2019b) Tecnología rupestre: una perspectiva teórico-metodológica para el estudio del arte levantino. *I Jornades Internacionals d'Art Rupestre de l'Arc Mediterrani de La Península Ibèrica*, pp.481–496.

Santos da Rosa, N. (2019c) *La Tecnología del Arte Rupestre Levantino: aproximación experimental para el estúdio de sus cadenas operativas* [Ph.D. Thesis]. Tarragona: Universitat Rovira i Virgili, pp.604.

Scott, David A. and Hyder, William D. (1993) A study of some Californian Indian Rock art pigments. *Studies in Conservation*, 38(3), pp.155–173.

Singh, R. C. V. (2002) Raman and the discovery of the Raman effect. *Physics in Perspective*, 4, pp.399–420. https://doi.org/10.1007/s000160200002

Spagnolo, G. S., Paoletti, D., Ambrosini, D. and Guattari, G. (1997) Electro-optic correlation for in situ diagnostics in mural frescoes. *Pure and Applied Optics: Journal of the European Optical Society*, Part A, 6(5), pp.557–563. doi:10.1088/0963-9659/6/5/007

Taçon, P., Mulvaney, K., Ouzman, S., Fullagar, R. L., Head, L. M. and Carlton, P. (2003) Changing ecological concerns in: Rock-art subject matter of North Australia's keep river region. *Before Farming*, 3(4), pp.1–14.

Troncoso, A., Moya, F., Sepúlveda, M. and Carcamo, J. J. (2017) First absolute dating of Andean hunter-gatherer rock art paintings from North Central Chile. *Archaeological and Anthropological Sciences*, 9(2), 223–232. https://doi.org/10.1007/s12520-015-0282-z

Valladas, H., Tisnerat, N., Cachier, H. and Maurice, A. (1999) Datation directe des peintures prehistoriques par la methode du carbone 14 en spectrometrie de masse par accelerateur. *Mémoires de la Société préhistorique française*, 26, pp.39–44.

Vandenabeele, P., Wehling, B., Moens, L., Edwards, H., Reu, M. and Hooydonk, G. (2000) Analysis with micro-Raman spectroscopy of natural organic binding media and varnishes used in art. *Analytical Chemistry*, 407, pp.261–274.

Wadley, L., Williamson, B. and Lombard, M. (2004) Ochre in hafting in Middle Stone Age Southern África: A pratical role. *Antiquity,* 78, pp.661–675.

Wadley, L. (2005) Putting ochre to the test: Replication studies of adhesives that may have been used for hafting tools in the Middle Stone Age. *Journal Human Evolution,* 49, pp.587–601.

Wadley, L., Hodgskiss, T. and Grant, M. (2009) Implications for complex cognition from the hafting of tools with compound adhesives in the Middle Stone Age, South Africa. *Proceedings of the National Academy of Science,* 106(24), pp.9590–9594.

Wainwright, I. N. M., Helwig, K., Rolandi, D. S., Gradin, C., Podestá, M. M., Onetto, M. and Achero, C. A. (2002) Rock paintings conservation and pigment analysis at Cueva de las Manos and Cerro de los Indios, Santa Cruz (Patagonia). In Vontobel, R. (Ed.) *ICOM Committee for Conservation, 13th Triennial Meeting, Rio de Janeiro, 22–27 September 2002.* London: James and James. Science Publishers, pp. 582–589.

Watts, I. (1999) The origin of symbolic culture. In Dunbar, R., Knight, C. and Power, C. (Eds.) *The Evolution of Culture.* Edinburgh: Edinburgh University Press, pp. 113–146.

Watts, I. (2002) Ochre in the Middle Stone Age of southern Africa: Ritualized display or hide preparation? *South African Archaeological Bulletin,* 57, pp.1–14.

Watts, I. (2009) Red ochre, bodypainting, and language: Interpreting the Blombos ochre. In Botha, R. and Knight, C. (Eds.) *The Cradle of Language.* Oxford: Oxford University Press, pp.62–92.

Watts, I. (2010) The pigments from Pinnacle point cave 13B, Western Cape, South Africa. *Journal of Human Evolution,* 59, pp.392–411.

Zilhão, J. and d'Errico, F. (1999a) The chronology and taphonomy of the earliest Aurignacian and its implications for the understanding of Neanderthal extinction. *Journal of World Prehistory,* 13(1), pp.1–68.

Zilhão, j. and d'Errico, F. (1999b) Reply, in The Neanderthal problem continued. *Current Anthropology,* 40(3), pp.355–364.

Zilhão, J. and Trinkaus, E. (2002) *Portrait of the Artist as a Child. The Gravettian Human Skeleton from the Abrigo do Lagar Velho and its Archaeological Context.* Trabalhos de Arqueologia, 22. Lisboa: Instituto Português de Arqueologia.

Zilhão, J., Angelucci, D., Badal-García, E., d'Errico, F., Daniel, F., Daynet, L., Douka, K., Highman, T., Martínez-Sánchez, M. J., Montes-Bernández, R., Murcia-Mascarós, S., Pérez-Sirvent, C., Roldán-García, C., Vanhaeren, M., Villaverde, V., Wood, R. and Zapata, J. (2010). Symbolic use of marine shells and mineral pigments by Iberian Neanderthals. *Proceedings of the National Academy of Sciences,* 17(3), pp.1023–1028.

Zoppi, A., Signorini, G. F., Lucarelli, F. and Bachechi, L. (2002) Characterisation of painting materials from Eritrea Rock art sites with non-destructive spectroscopic techniques. *Journal of Cultural Heritage,* 3, pp.299–308. doi:10.1016/S1296-2074(02)01234-7.

Section IV

Global Community and Collaborative Case Studies Innovating Methodologies for the Ongoing Monitoring and Management of Open-Air Rock Art Sites

14 Rock Art in the Cerrado

Cultural and Natural Heritage Conservation Come Together at Serranopólis, Goiás, Brazil

António Batarda Fernandes, Fernanda Elisa Costa Paulino e Resende, Sergia Meire da Silva, Uelde Ferreira de Souza, Julio Cezar Rubin de Rubin, Maira Barberi, Maria Elina Bichuette, Tamires Zepon and Jonas Eduardo Gallão

Introduction

Situated in Central Brazil, notably encompassing areas in the states of Goiás, Mato Grosso, and Mato Grosso do Sul, the Cerrado consisted of the typical ecosystem of roughly 20% of the area of the country until a few decades ago. By now, it is estimated that more than half of this original cover has been lost to agriculture and livestock with only 2.2% of its total area protected under federal laws (Ratter, Ribeiro and Bridgewater 1997; Klink and Machado 2005). The municipality of Serranópolis accumulates the presence of reasonably well-preserved Cerrado areas with a significant archaeological complex encompassing rock art and human occupation sites. Just over 30 sites are known, featuring prehistoric art, and archaeological layers, the latter reaching back to 11,000 BP. The archaeological ensemble was originally identified, excavated, and researched in the 1970s by teams lead by Pedro Ignácio Schmitz (Schmitz et al. 1989, 1997, 2004).

With the publication of these reference works for the study of this archaeological complex, this first chapter of research ended, and the sites were almost forgotten. This was in spite of the efforts of the local community, namely tour companies or lodging facilities that established tourism ventures focused on the rock art. Local guides and property owners of touristic accommodations, namely the Pousada das Araras (see Figure 14.1) or the Pousada do Guardião, together with researchers that work in the area, namely Julio Rubin (Rubin et al. 2017) or Fernanda Resende (2013), co-authors of this chapter, remained vigilant to alerting authorities and the community on the worsening condition of the rock art sites. Ultimately, by 2019, the insistence paid off, as the Goiás Superintendency of Instituto do Patrimônio Histórico e Artístico Nacional (IPHAN; Brazilian government Cultural Heritage agency) commissioned conservation work at the rock art sites.

DOI: 10.4324/9780429355349-19

284 António Batarda Fernandes et al.

Figure 14.1 One of the most well-known rock art panels of the region, belonging to GO-Ja.3 site at Pousada das Araras. Photo by Fernanda Resende.

Work was carried out by MRS Estudos Ambientais Ltda., with the participation of several specialists.[1] The first stage of interventions at Serranopólis consisted of emergency work aimed at mitigating and consideration of methods to eliminate negative impact of Biodeterioration at the sites. The main issues identified and addressed were vegetation growth, termite infestation, and bee and wasp colonies. Further conservation work will be aimed at examining and devising preventive measures to counter weathering and erosion processes, active both at the scale of the rock shelters and of the engraved and painted panels; removal of the fortunately few painted vandalism inscriptions present at sites; or substitution of degraded wooden catwalks and protective rails.

From a management point of view, other actions are also deemed as important in the near future. This includes installing signage describing the rock art and its context, and addressing the conservation issues it faces, while also warning about hazardous micro-fauna that dwells in the shelters walls. Further study is also deserved of the environmental factors that may contribute to the expanding number of ticks, Africanized bees, or toxic venom hematophagous mosquitoes in the region; the need to remove introduced exotic plants; as well as restraining cattle and limit farming in the areas surrounding sites.

In the following sections, the condition of the sites as well as the methodology of carried out conservation work will be presented. These interventions will be discussed considering the synergies that can be created between rock art conservation and environmental concerns. Finally, a way forward encompassing both dimensions will be discussed with a view of valuing the endogenous original resources of the region, while seeking to establish a paradigmatic case study regarding the combined preservation of cultural and natural values in Brazil and elsewhere. Furthermore, consideration is given to the relevant role comprehensive environment educational programs can fulfil.

Context and condition of the sites

Although the number of known sites has increased in the last few years, namely during the activities presently addressed (MRS 2019), work carried out in the 1970s initially identified 26 archaeological sites in the Serranópolis area, along both margins of the Rio Verde (Schmitz et al. 1989, 1997, 2004). In a region geomorphologically characterized by tabular and convex forms, the latter correspond to witness hills illustrating episodes of differential erosion and as such are commonly designated as "testimonies". The sites are predominately located in sandstone shelters, associated with these hills, and in large stone walls found in tabular forms. Besides an important collection of painted and engraved rock art, the sites yielded considerable amounts of lithic and ceramic materials, associated to different occupation periods: the Paranaíba (hunter-gatherers), the Serranópolis (transition between hunter-gathering and ceramic producing societies), and the Jataí (farming and ceramic producing societies) phases. The oldest date obtained for human occupation in the region consists of 10.740 ± 85 BP for the site GO-Ja.1 (Schmitz et al. 1989, 2004).

Despite the importance of the dates for human occupation that were possible to obtain from the excavations, rock art is arguably the most prominent archaeological feature in the region. Indeed, these artistic works provide valuable insights, such as the profuse superposition of motifs, which can be used to characterize the evolution of human occupation in the area, in addition to prehistoric regional ties across the central Brazilian plateau. Several motifs bear stylistic resemblances with rock art present in other sites of the macro-region, and the identification of major artistic themes can contribute to greater understanding of the prehistoric symbolic expression in the area. Indeed, two main types or traditions were identified in the rock art: a naturalist and a geometric one (Schmitz et al. 1989).

Naturalist motifs include images of humans and of animals such as deer, cingulates, lizards, fish, birds, as well as human, feline or bird tracks, feet, and plants. Geometric motifs include straight and curved lines arranged in different ensembles (stars, crosses, dots, squares, rectangles, triangles, lozenges, circles, ellipses, oval, or head-shaped), and what has been interpreted as objects such as throwers, masks, baskets, besides other undetermined motifs. As originally recorded by Schmitz et al. (1989), engraved motifs (just over 4,000) vastly outnumber painted motifs (just over 1,150). When considering geometric motifs vs. naturalist ones, the latter account for only a fifth of the total of painted motifs and even less regarding engraved imagery. Insights provided by the work coordinated by Schmitz include the fact that shelters with a higher amount of rock art correspond to those with the longest sequence of human occupation; judging from tools and flakes with traces of paint recovered during excavation, painted rock art can be traced back to the origins of human occupation in the area; depicted zoomorphic figures do not coincide with the majority of animal remains found in the archaeological layers; and superposition of motifs indicate that naturalist depictions increased with the passage of the millennia, suggesting increasing cultural diversity (Schmitz et al. 1989, pp. 152–180, 1997).

Of known sites, ten (distributed along three different clusters) presented a more fragile condition and were chosen for intervention at this stage. The following account describes these sites and emergency intervention work carried out.

Cluster A

This cluster, known as Complexo do Diogo, is located on the left margin of the Rio Verde and five different rock art sites have been identified. Despite other significant sites, namely GO-Ja.8 and GO-Ja.8a with their deeply pecked footsteps motifs, it was only possible to conduct these initial emergency conservation interventions at GO-Ja.1 and GO-Ja.2. These two sites are located at the base of a large sandstone cliff-face about 40 meters high surrounded by pasture for cattle, with a few traces of the original Cerrado still present. Hence, the owner of the ranch containing these sites was previously notified by IPHAN to prevent livestock from entering the shelters. Regrettably, the fence that was initially installed has failed and the site is today trampled by cattle. The site is visited by tourists led by local guides, but access is made through an adjacent ranch via the plateau on top of the sites. Therefore, according to the federal legislation that protects registered archaeological sites, permission needs to be sought from the landowner who, together with local guides, control the number of tourists allowed at the site in order to keep impacts of public visitation in check.

Both GO-Ja.1 and GO-Ja.2 present a variety of rock art motifs, either painted or engraved, inside small caves on large and high walls and, in the case of GO-Ja.1, an unknown before upper quite difficult to access natural terrace, covered by vegetation prior to the cleaning interventions described herein. If Schmitz documented over 100 painted motifs (1997, pp. 34–36), work carried out in the frame of these emergency interventions allowed for the identification of previously unrecorded figures restricted to the area of the external terrace. It is noteworthy to mention that it was in GO-Ja.1 that the human burials were excavated from which the early dates for human presence in the region mentioned above were quantified (Schmitz 1989, pp. 33–40). Vestiges of human prehistoric presence in the form of lithic tools were also abundant in the deposit, evidencing this further. The sites were both affected by the continuous presence of cattle, with resulting faeces and urine penetrating the sandy soil. This is in addition to vegetation growth, namely of creeper roots that partially covered the mouth of the shelter. Bats, bees and termites and other micro-fauna were also present. Significant quantities of guano, originating mainly from bats but also other animals were also present at both shelters. While painted rock art is generally quite faded, engraved motifs have fared relatively well.

Cluster D

Known as Pousada das Araras, this area constitutes the most significant collection of sites in the Serranópolis region, due not only to the quantity of motifs, but primarily because of the aesthetical, scientific, and current economic importance of existing rock art. Six sites have been identified by Schmitz et al on the right margin of the Rio Verde (1997, pp. 41–49), although the recent work as described here identified a handful more (MRS 2019, p. 154). Located on a 175 ha property (Fazenda Bonito), the site was scheduled in 1998 as a Reserva Particular do Patrimônio Natural (RPPN; Private Natural Heritage Reserve) (IBAMA 1998) following the initiative of the proprietors (who remain the same). The owners chose to maintain the original Cerrado cover in the whole property, founding an Inn (the *Pousada das Araras*), offering visitors tours of the rock art in a preserved area where reasonably abundant endemic natural resources can still be found. Indeed, besides medicinal plants and fruits, fauna abounds including macaws (which give the name to the property), endangered deer or anteater species, together with a spring of crystalline waters. All this subsists in a relatively pristine setting, comparative to the high percentage of land in the surrounding region used for intensive crops – soya, sugar cane or corn – and cattle grazing.

The six sites originally identified by Schmitz's team were all subject to conservation intervention work as part of the current initiative: GO-Ja.3, GO-Ja.4, GO-Ja.25, GO-Ja.26, GO-Ja.27, and GO-Ja.28. Of these, the first two are the largest with the remaining sites possessing much less rock art. GO-Ja.3 is without a doubt the most important rock art site in the region and arguably the state of Goiás, due to several hundred painted (including polychromous) and engraved motifs over an 80-meter-long wall located at the foot of large and high-standing hill that dominates the surrounding landscape (see Figure 14.2). Schmitz et al. excavated the site, finding vestiges of human occupation reaching back some 10,000 BP, besides two more recent (Jataí phase) children's burials (1989, pp. 87–89, 2004, pp. 19–44). During the current intervention, a previously unexplored upper terrace was identified, and rock art documented in detail, together with the original deposition of lithic tools in rock orifices. GO-Ja.4 also presents interesting rock art, more so considering that it does not completely follow the distinctive traits found at GO-Ja.3. Indeed, while the latter possesses primarily painted motifs, at the former site distribution between the two types is more even.

Figure 14.2 The witness hill at Pousada das Araras that contains GO-Ja.3. Photo by Nilo M. P. Resende.

Likewise, rock art at GO-Ja.4 is constituted by a higher percentage of geometric motifs than in GO-Ja.3, with new categories identified during presently described work. The latter, together with GO-Ja.26, are the only sites shown to the public during tourist visits at Pousada das Araras. At GO-Ja.3, human intervention in the form of wooden walkways and rails, aimed at protecting the archaeological deposit and the existing rock art from tourism activities, introduced complementary conservation issues. Indeed, decaying wood constitutes a complementary food resource for termites. Moreover, the degraded condition of the structures threatens the security of visitors. All sites at this cluster are affected by the presence of micro-fauna (termites, bees, spiders or wasps); by weathering, notably the precipitation of elements at surface level forming horizontal 'dark lines' that cross the wall at certain locations; by erosion, as fallen blocks indicate; and by vigorous vegetation cover. Besides gripping roots, in some cases mature trees grow near the rock art on the surface. As in other sites, lichens are present but do not, except for a very limited number of cases, constitute large colonies that might prove hazardous for the conservation of rock art. Bats do not dwell in these shelters apart from a few cases where inner cave-like niches occur. Other animals dwell in the Reserve, namely quite a number of species of birds, monkeys, deer, snakes, some especially poisonous, or wild pigs.

Cluster E

This cluster is located on the right margin of the Rio Verde. Earlier work carried out in 1970s originally identified six sites. Present emergency interventions allowed for the discovery of a dozen previously unrecorded rock art sites. GO-Ja.13 and GO-Ja.13C were the sole sites at this cluster to be intervened upon. As described by Rubin et al. (2017), all the sites are surrounded by pasture whereby the erosive effects of cattle farming on intervened sites are quite visible. The resulting replacement of original vegetation by pasture has in the last few years led to a significant increase of erosion (Almeida Filho 2004). These processes resulted in the deposition of a large volume of sediments inside the shelter. These were primarily brought in by the flow of a water course that has been altered upstream due to the seasonality of rainfall, deforestation, or cattle trampling. In turn, the subsequent changes in water flow and volume constitute a further structural instability factor for the preservation of the shelter. As with the sites at Complexo do Diogo, the landowner allows visits to GO-Ja.13 only if carried out by professional guides.

GO-Ja.13, known as Véu do Muquém, consists of a sandstone shelter containing paintings and engravings on its ceiling, with a waterline pouring down as a waterfall in its frontal area (Schmitz et al. 1997, pp. 49–51). Nearby there is a small shelter also containing rock art, categorized by Schmitz as GO-Ja.13C, where three human burials were excavated, all from the Serranopólis phase (1997, p. 51). Contrary to other sites, where painted rock art is more profuse, at GO-Ja.13 the number of painted versus engraved motifs is relatively similar. Regarding the former, polychromous motifs were documented along with carved depictions of several small-sized feet. The different rock art styles present at the shelter point to different occupation horizons during prehistory. Motifs at GO-Ja.13 are in reasonable condition, contrary to those in GO-Ja.13C where erosive and weathering processes have taken their toll. Unfortunately, the ceiling at GO-Ja.13 has been vandalized in the last 30 years by several sprayed inscriptions, purple in colour. Some of these inscriptions directly affect rock art motifs. On the other hand, cattle do not wander through the shelter due to difficulty of access. Likewise, bat presence was not identified, contrary to termites, recluse spiders and the omnipresent tick. Although not as serious as at other intervened sites, vegetation also poses conservation problems for the rock art and its support.

Methodology and undertaken actions

Due to the state of neglect the sites reached, priority was given to the cleaning of vegetation and micro-fauna, as well as the testing of modern graffiti removal agents in this initial stage of intervention. A comprehensive approach to the protection, management, and tourism-use of the sites should be implemented in further stages. Without such an approach, work carried out will stand as a make-do and ephemeral intervention. In the long run, it would be ideal to limit scheduled future interventions to every two or three decades assisted by reaching the scenario that would allow current owners (with municipal, state or federal assistance) to carry out seasonal supervised cleaning of the sites. Hence, this initial stage prioritized development of a research, management and conservation program for the rock art sites at Serranopólis.

During this phase, the methodological approach aimed at assuring the least-possible invasive techniques and materials were used. The main concern was to avoid intervening upon panels with rock art. However, that was not always possible, such as when removing termite nests. Details of interventions carried out at sites are discussed below, alongside an analysis of ethical and methodological constraints when relevant, followed by identification of further work that is still needed.

Cleaning of extensive termite trails that directly impacted rock art

Termites constitute the single most significant issue currently affecting the rock art here and the elimination or mitigation of its impact the most challenging Biodeterioration concern. This is why it is of the upmost importance to establish a management program that includes: the periodic cleaning of the sites; contemplating the removal of dead wood; the maintenance of a small band in front of painted panels free of vegetation, and ideally removal of plants directly above panels when feasible; as well as the substitution of degraded walkways at GO-Ja.3 (and even the installation of new ones at other sites) by structures made of ideally termite-proof, neutral tested conservation materials. During these intervention works, termite galleries were removed mechanically with the help of wooden and plastic spatulas and soft bristle brushes, taking care to avoid direct contact with painted and engraved art. Monitoring occurred during the subsequent three months, resulting in a body of evidence that the termites and their nests will again return after cleaning. Therefore, other solutions had to be considered. One possible solution that was tested successfully could be found in traditional country knowledge regarding controlling termite infestation in stables, houses and other wooden constructions: this involved spraying water mixed with salt at the end of removed trails and in the remnants that lingered, always avoiding painted areas. At GO-Ja.25, it was observed that the application of the saline solution would prevent termites restoring and reconstructing nests. Through monitoring the effectiveness of this treatment and any resultant impact due to the potential need of periodical applications, the intervention strategies can be modified accordingly. For example, if it is ascertained that repeated application may further contribute to the degradation of the geo-substrate even if avoiding rock art directly, then this is a method that must be cautiously applied in future.

Testing of different compounds to clean the remnants left on the rock surfaces after removal of termite trails, and other microbiome elements such as lichens

If an initial assessment of painted motifs using a 50× magnifier revealed that the paint continues to adhere quite well to the rock, (generally presenting itself in quite good condition), focus was less on the removal of galleries than the elimination of older remnants and removed trails on top of painted and engraved rock art. This poses the most pressing ethical and technical questions, hence the approach undertaken at this stage was to perform tests in areas where trails did not cover rock art and this was completed at just one site, GO-Ja.26. Different materials which have proven effective previously were employed (Resende et al. 2014a, 2014b): Potassium Hydroxide (KOH), Hydrochloric Acid (HCL), Hydrogen Peroxiide (H_2O_2), a surfactant agent (alkyl dimethyl benzylammonium chloride at a concentration of 24%), and mineral water as a test control. Windows, also comprising information on used materials, were established as controls for the application of each, ensuring that those undertaking the work wore protective gear to apply these toxic solutions. Of the used compounds, only KOH, at a concentration of 5%, was effective in clearing the dark-brown line left behind by termite galleries, although total removal of the remnants tarnish was not achieved (see Figure 14.3). KOH, at a concentration of 10%, was effective in removing lichens. All other compounds were not effective in sequestrating organic material left by trails, but also removing lichens. At this stage, as tests occurred at non-painted or engraved areas of panels, ethical issues are straightforward to consider, as application was done with the utmost care not to sully tested panels. It is believed that vigilant monitoring of the tested areas, as well as further testing in more panels, is needed to ascertain the evolution, impact, and validity of such methodology regarding its potential future application directly on galleries covering parts of rock art motifs. On the other hand, lichen removal is a controversial issue within rock art conservation, with some authors advocating caution while others are in favour of removal (see Fernandes 2014, pp. 87–88). Moreover, at other locations, such as the Iberian Peninsula, less invasive and potentially toxic methods are being tested, namely laser cleaning for lichen removal (see Chapter 9). As observed in the field, it is believed that lichens are not the most pressing Biodeterioration issue present at the sites, although from a management and tourism perspective they sometimes prevent a comprehensive reading and observation of motifs by visitors but to a lesser degree than termite galleries. It is considered that the observations above regarding the use of chemical solutions for eradicating termite nests are not only valid for lichens, but also potentially for removal of soot or other existent rock varnishes (if deemed adequate). Lastly, it should be noted that lichen samples were collected for

292 *António Batarda Fernandes et al.*

Figure 14.3 Cleaning of termite trails at GO-Ja.26. Photo by Fernanda Resende.

identification of species. Photos taken before and after cleaning will help in future monitoring of the progression of recolonization by different species.

Testing of compounds regarding posterior elimination of graffiti over or near rock art motifs

Auspiciously, vandalism in the form of graffiti over or very near the rock art was only identified at GO-Ja.13. Although it takes only one of these actions to significantly affect the significance of a rock art motif, and at this site a few graffiti are present, it is indeed fortunate that in a region with such a wealth of prehistoric art only one site was vandalized. It was apparent at the site that most graffiti were applied sometime in the last 30–40 years using the same type of 'paint': a bright dark violet pigment present in Lepecid, the commercial name of a widely used larvicide spray to treat cutaneous myiasis (botflies) in cattle wounds. On site observation using a 50x magnifier revealed that the pigment, or at least its superficial cover, hasn't mineralized, making it possible to attempt to sequestrate it using a solvent. To signal that these incidents will not be further tolerated, it was decided to begin considering methods to remove these abusive inscriptions. Hence, tests were carried out on graffiti that was not directly over rock art. Two commercially available solvents were used in the tests, both fabricated by the Sherwin-Williams Company: Thinner 454 and Thinner 500. These compounds are made of aromatic hydrocarbons, esters, glycols, alcohol and ketones, which adhere to polymer or polyester matter by sequestrating molecules, thus making it possible to remove superficial pigments. Testing began by selecting 5×5 cm areas to constitute application windows, followed by use of alcohol at a 70%

concentration for a period of ten minutes. This application did not remove any pigment. Hence, tests proceeded with the use of Thinner compounds, which were applied with gauze and covered with plastic so that the product stuck to the ceiling surface. Tests were repeated at five-minute intervals, for better control of undergoing reaction of the pigment to the solvents. In between tests, as used compounds are water-soluble, water and surfactant soap were applied to interrupt the chemical reaction so that the base rock would not be affected. Unsurprisingly considering the way these solvents work, results of the tests indicated that thicker pigment surface layers can effectively be removed, similarly to what happens in the case of termite nest remnants where a 'stained' area remains on the rock (see Figure 14.4). Moreover, in older graffiti presenting a less bright tone, the above-described treatment was less effective. Hence, it should be highlighted that it is possible to greatly decrease the impact of intervened upon graffiti to the site and its rock art, but it is unattainable to completely remove all the traces left by the seepage of the product into the rock from the initial act of vandalism.

Removal of vegetation, beehives, and debris

Except for those located in Cluster A (which is surrounded by the Cerrado 'savannah' sub-biome type), intervened sites are located well within the so-called Cerradão. This is a type of forest with moderately sparse and willowy trees, a mainly constant canopy, with individuals reaching an average height of 8–15 metres (Gomes et al. 2004). Nevertheless, all intervened sites have copious vegetation presence in the form of roots and residues of trees, vines, bushes and cactus – foliage, fallen branches, and stumps – as well as other debris. As previously reported (Fernandes 2014, pp. 86–90), biological

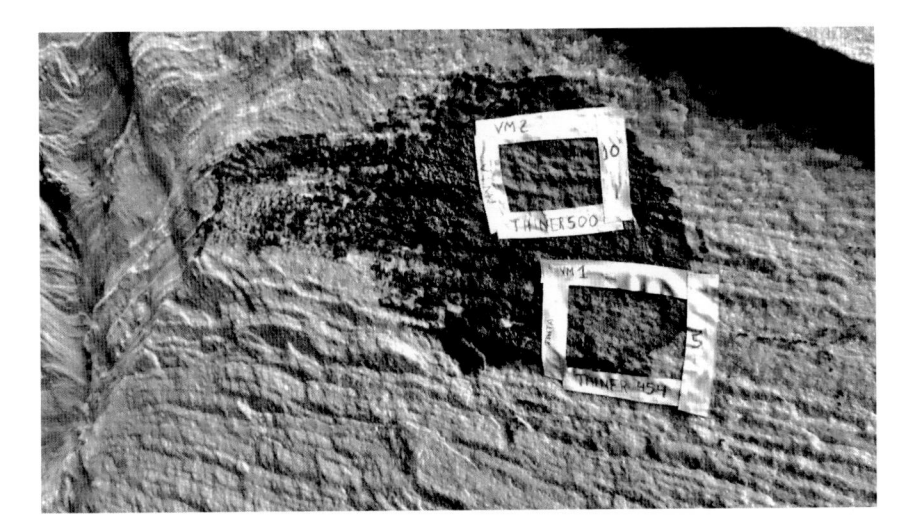

Figure 14.4 Graffiti removal at GO-Ja.13. Photo by Fernanda Resende.

cover impacts rock art and its support, and hence should be subject to regular monitoring and cleaning actions as needed. Since the discovery of the sites, limited vegetation management has taken place apart from sporadic monitoring by owners, guides and researchers. Sites needed thorough vegetation clearing, as well as cleaning of animal remains such spider webs or ant colonies, in addition to animal faeces and bones. Care was taken so that rock art motifs were not touched during these interventions. Worthy of a detailed note is the situation regarding hyper-defensive feral African honeybees (Michener 1975) which were present and proved dangerous for anyone visiting the sites (be it visitors or the team that carried out the emergency conservation work, with some integrants suffering a few painful stings). Hence, a beekeeper was called in to relocate beehives established near or at the intervened sites. At this point, it wasn't necessary to remove any wasp nests from sites.

Assessment of micro-fauna present at rock art shelters

Considering the ecological diversity present inside the shelters and in rock art panels, and the impact of micro-fauna in the conservation of existing rock art, a team specialized in subterranean biology took part in the interventions. The team focused on shelter inhabitant species which may pose an imperceptible hazard to visitors at sites, such as poisonous spiders (namely the brown recluse). Hence, several species were collected which will be subjected to further analysis with a view towards a complete portrayal of present micro-fauna and ecologic diversity, in addition to an opportunity for the discovery of new species as it occurred in similar environments (Monte and Bichuette 2020). Indeed, all the rock art clusters at Serranopólis possess inner cavities, some with aphotic characteristics where bat colonies of different species reside. These significant locations should be also protected as bats, besides being part of existing biodiversity, have an important role in the endurance of the Cerrado as pollinators and seed dispersers. Finally, it should be noted that a blind species of brown recluse has been identified inside these inner caves. Further characterization of the find will be subsequently published in a specialized journal.

Other tasks undertaken at this stage included the assessment of rock art and shelters versus what was described by Schmitz's team in the 1970s; geo-structural and environmental assessment; identification and cartography of caves inside shelters, and video and photographic documentation.[2] All records will be instrumental in further conservation, management and education programs which have the potential to unfold if these initial interventions are to be followed. It would be regretful to waste this opportunity to initiate a comprehensive plan that has begun to balance touristic potential, preservation of rock art and the Cerrado, and integrate community involvement.

Future work

Establishing a wide-ranging research programme will be vital not only for any future candidature or grant application, but also to further available data on the importance of the Serranópolis archaeological complex. Some of the issues that such a programme would attempt to tackle include:

- Ascertaining the possibility of direct dating painted rock by carrying out pigment analysis.
- Excavation of shelters non-intervened during the 1970s research programmes, or extension of previously excavated areas adjacent to the earlier ones.
- Comprehensive archaeological survey of the region to accurately identify, and map new sites – which local inhabitants have known about and weren't worked on by Schmitz et al. –, which will prove important to analyse rock art and human occupation at the local and regional level.
- Systematic revision of the data gathered by Schmitz et al., including re-documenting and re-mapping motifs and shelters with modern technologies (photogrammetry, laser scanning, GIS, etc.), and incorporating recently discovered rock art and habitat sites in the Serranópolis archaeological complex corpus.
- Building a finer chronology of human presence in the area to help to characterize shifts and permanencies in cultural, social, and economic land use throughout the ages.

Complementing archaeology, other disciplines should be part of an inclusive future research programme. Such is the case with both geology, which is of use in the characterization of the structural stability of shelters; and biology, which is important to broaden knowledge on biota occupying shelters, monitoring their behaviours in the process as some pose security risks for visitors. Geology input is also important if conservation intervention is needed in areas of the shelters where mineral precipitation formed speleothems, subject to protective measures under Brazilian law. Biology subdisciplines are also of use to characterize existing vegetation, including the out-of-control expansion of invasive introduced species such as signal or Guinea grass.

Regarding rock art preservation, management, and awareness-raising issues, the following priorities have been identified:

- Fencing rock art sites located in grazing areas to prevent cattle entry.
- Heritage and environmental education actions aimed at the local community but also agriculture companies, the major polluters and environmental threat in the region, to combat their use of pesticides and on-going deforestation activities.

- Supporting owners in setting up management plans for each site, proposing alternative land use (namely sustainable tourism), and supplying accurate site mapping.
- Use of rock art documentation to produce information and promotion materials.
- Installation of protection rails, as well as considering artificial driplines made from tested materials to divert running water on rock faces with art where needed, walkways, sightseeing areas, well-signalized trails, and increased planting of native species at sites.

Discussion: rock art and Cerrado conservation

The background of these interventions dictates that a deeper and interconnected discussion should be engaged that could launch ambitious partnerships in the development of a management, research, and conservation strategy for (at least some) sites at Serranopólis. Recent data indicates that "deforestation is leading to a process of mass extinction of the biome" (CicloVivo 2020; translation by the authors). This is easily observable in the state of Goiás, and particularly in the Serranopólis region, where ongoing deforestation has extensively erased the original Cerrado and left only 175ha of the RPPN Pousada das Araras as one of the few small green islands lost among vast corn, sugar cane, soya, and cattle fields. At this point, the disappearance of the Cerrado seems sadly inevitable and places as the RPPN must be valued as precious 'reserves' where future generations will be able to learn about nature and heritage preservation. Hopefully this dire situation may still be reversed, whereby RPPN sites constitute another kind of reserve – one that stores ecological diversity for future rewilding flora and fauna projects, akin to what is being considered and implemented elsewhere (Foreman 2004; Pereira and Navarro 2015). Indeed, a comprehensive approach to management and conservation should consider the two dimensions more than complementary, rather as the core of future efforts. Since heritage preservation targets seem more accomplishable in the short or medium term, it is argued that such an approach is the ideal opportunity to lay the basis for the future survival of the Cerrado in the region.

If rock art sites can be presented in good shape; if an extensive research plan that continues the work initiated by Schmitz in the 1970s and continued today is established; if visitors to the sites increase in a sustainable and conservation-friendly fashion; if current education activities are extended to form part of regular curricular activities; and if the community is engaged in preservation efforts, then broadening the scope towards Cerrado conservation will be more likely to result in encouraging outcomes. This project in its many required interdisciplinary iterations, can also be of use in the preparation of a UNESCO World Heritage Site candidature dossier, or other applications (recognitions, funding, etc.) as local, state, or federal authorities see fit. It is believed that the conjugation of rock art and Cerrado preservation could be a strong candidate for World Heritage status. Hence, presenting a mixed site candidacy that highlights combined value, its conservation and social use would be the holistic target.

In 2008, Rios et al. discussed the Pousada das Araras RPPN as a case study in ecotourism and economics employing Cost – Benefit Analysis (CBA) (Mishan and Quah 2007). The main objective was to ascertain if preserving natural areas would be more advantageous for owners relating strictly to economic benefits as opposed to agriculture land use. This study revealed that in the state of Goiás out of 44 existing RPPNs in 2008, only 21 had interest in developing an ecotourism offer (Rios et al. 2008, p. 3). Of five CBA employed simulations over an 18-year period, three indicated financially advantage for owners from preserving the environment and not swifting to agrobusiness while two were prejudicial.

While the authors present their conclusions in the light of the necessity of designing and putting in to place environmental strategies to encourage the creation of these reserves, even suggesting the implementation of levies on agriculture activities near to reserves and taxes incentives for landowners that decide to create RPPN's, truth is that both (other) financial and non-financial benefits have not been considered in the analysis. The latter, referred to as the monetary incommensurability of certain values, is appropriately one of the major critiques addressed to CBA (Hwang 2016, p. 76). Indeed, in the specific case of the Pousada das Araras RPPN, it is impossible to give a monetary value to the conservation per se of rock art and biodiversity, or to the use of both in awareness-raising education strategies.

Be as it may, today the relevant values deriving from nature conservation can be subject to monetary appraisal. Such is the case with carbon sequestration as Kerdan et al suggest regarding Brazil: "a reforestation-only scenario projects that (…) by 2050 the country's carbon stock would have been increased (…), mainly supported by natural vegetation regeneration in the Cerrado biome" versus sugarcane driven-expansion that would result in a lesser increase (2019, p. 9). Regarding this comparison, and the fact that all plants do capture CO_2, it is worth emphasizing that restoration of the Cerrado has more potential for sequestration than crops such as sugarcane, particularly when considering the following point. In a current world-wide scenario where carbon emissions licenses are increasingly being traded (Belfiori 2017), if it is possible to calculate how much carbon a forested area can sequestrate (Zald et al. 2016) then a monetary value can be attributed to each tree in the Cerrado, exclusively due to its sequestration action.

Such an approach must be analysed in conjunction with landowners and communities' interests, considering also the need of further maintenance of the sites. As the current situation in this region of Brazil is one in which deforestation sharply progresses and agriculture land use increases at the expense of the Cerrado, it is extremely unlikely that an inversion of the situation could be achieved in the short or even medium term. Therefore, it is vital to sustain projects in the area (such as the Pousada das Araras RPPN) as examples of Cerrado and rock art conservation, and further as a significant place for environmental education that may be able to foster a more deeply engaged community that recognizes the importance of conserving an area rich with cultural and natural values.

Taking in to account the fortunately few vandalism incidents that occurred so far at sites (see above GO-Ja.13), it is vital to implement education and engagement programs that may prevent future incidents. In the case of Pousada das Araras RPPN, the Rios et al. study (2008) concluded that most simulations point to financial benefits for owners as a result of the reserve's creation, using these resources as the core of its touristic activities. Hence, the example of a Reserve that preserves both the Cerrado and the rock art also in a strictly economically sustainable manner should be promoted more intensively by municipal, state and national official institutions in addition to ONGs and other organizations. On the local and regional scale which is currently a frontline for the battle of nature's preservation in Brazil, after measuring the range of views and opinions entrenched within the community, one cannot help but have the sense these issues are largely ignored and need to be extensively debated. However, the greatest concern rests with local, state, and federal authorities, unable to lead the way in preventing the disappearance of the Cerrado, and only now investing in the preservation of the rock art sites in a remedial manner. Hopefully, further conservation work, holistic management, and divulgation of the sites, can be carried out in a regular basis with financial support from different levels of government but also from other doners (ONGs or even agriculture, transformation and distribution companies).

Lastly, considering the range of biodiversity present in the Cerrado and particularly at the rock art shelters, paired with the need to undertake regular maintenance, attention should be given to the ethical issues surrounding conservation work. On the one hand, it is suggested that suppression of life forms (be it insects, plants, fungus or lichens), with a Biodeterioration effect on the rock art should not be carried out to such a magnitude that would negatively impact the preservation of existent biodiversity. Nevertheless, it is important to possess ample knowledge of what is present in order to pay special attention to any existing vulnerable endemic species. On the other hand, the approach followed in the described emergency conservation work, which authors assert needs to continue to be implemented in further interventions, attempted to minimize its potential hazardous effects. Such is the case regarding the utilization of salt to counter termite nest expansion, or the methodology employed in undertaking tests with chemical agents to treat graffiti or remove biological material, whilst using upmost caution on a few precisely defined and minute test windows. Looking forward, it would be ideal to utilize this knowledge to develop a kit specific for cleaning interventions concerning Biodeterioration hazards, defining mitigation strategies further and the application of associated materials to use in this part of the world.

Conclusion

It is argued in this chapter that the above emergency conservation work at Serranopólis created the opportunity for establishing a far-reaching project devoted to the research, management, conservation, and public involvement of the quite forgotten, neglected, and threatened cultural and natural heritage values in the region: the rock art and the Cerrado. After presenting work carried out, a policymaking, economic, social, but above all, political discussion was engaged. Indeed, this is a foremost political discussion, comprising much broader issues than just the conservation of the rock art and the Cerrado in just this region of the state of Goiás, Brazil. It would be naïve to assume that the conservation of these features solely rests in the technical or academic sphere. Rather, notably considering the Pousada das Araras case study, it is advocated that these can be the fields that might draw attention to the importance of what is still needed to protect the natural and cultural values in the area. Conclusively, it is believed that, given the current worldwide situation regarding resource sustainability, climate change, and the 'business as usual' policies that continue to be employed, the motto "Think globally, act locally" has never been so true as in the case of Serranopólis. Can local action here, based on the unique and endogenous natural and cultural riches of the area contribute to shape a more ecological sound and heritage respecting global development model? The time for action is upon us...

Notes

1 Specifically, FECPR and ABF (Archaeologists) managed the overall project with the former coordinating all interventions and the latter acting as a consultant in rock art conservation; SMS (Archaeologist) coordinated field work; UFS (Archaeologist) carried out archaeology field work; JCRR and MB (Geologists) identified active erosion processes; MEB, TZ and JEG (Biologists) carried out invasive micro-fauna identification, sample collection, and removal.
2 Some of the produced documentation videos can be found at https://vimeo.com/search?q=Complexo+Arqueol%C3%B3gico+de+Serran%C3%B3polis.

References

Almeida Filho, G. S. (2004) *Noções básicas para controle e prevenção de erosão em áreas urbanas e rurais.* São Paulo: IPT.

Belfiori, M. E. (2017) Carbon pricing, carbon sequestration and social discounting. *European Economic Review*, 96, pp.1–17. https://doi.org/10.1016/j.euroecorev.2017.03.015

CicloVivo (2020) Cerrado perde uma cidade de São Paulo a cada três meses. https://ciclovivo.com.br/planeta/meio-ambiente/cerrado-perde-cidade-sao-paulo/?fbclid=IwAR0XbBR6SQ5fUi9MCIP5yW-D7PzUjIbskrMNLbocW4g6bBSdIGA_CA-YmUE [Accessed 23 Jan. 2020].

Fernandes, A. P. B. (2014) *Natural processes in the degradation of open-air rock art sites. An urgency intervention scale to inform conservation. The case of the Côa Valley world heritage site, Portugal.* Oxford: Archaeopress.

Foreman, D. (2004) *Rewilding North America: A vision for conservation in the 21st century.* Washington, DC: Island Press.

Gomes, B. Z., Martins, F. R. and Tamashiro, J. Y. (2004) Estrutura do Cerradão e da transição entre Cerradão e floresta paludícola num fragmento da International Paper do Brasil Ltda., em Brotas, SP. *Revista Brasileira de Botânica*, 27(2), pp.249–262.

Hwang, K. (2016) Cost-benefit analysis: Its usage and critiques. *Journal of Public Affairs*, 16(1), pp.75–80.

IBAMA (1998) Portaria 173, de 24 de dezembro de 1998. https://www.ibama.gov.br/component/legislacao/?view=legislacao&legislacao=103179 [Accessed 10 Jan. 2020].

Kerdan, I. G., Giarola, S., Jalil-Vega, F. and Hawkes, A. (2019) Carbon sequestration potential from large-scale reforestation and sugarcane expansion on abandoned agricultural lands in Brazil. *Polytechnica*, 2(1–2), pp.9–25. https://doi.org/10.1007/s41050-019-00012-3

Klink, C. A. and Machado, R. B. (2005) Conservation of the Brazilian Cerrado. *Conservation Biology*, 19(3), pp.707–713.

Michener, C. C. (1975) The Brazilian bee problem. *Annual Review of Entomology*, 20, pp.399–416.

Mishan, E. J. and Quah, E. (2007) *Cost-benefit analysis.* New York: Routledge.

Monte, B. G. O. and Bichuette, M. E. (2020) Taxonomic distinctness of the subterranean fauna from Peruaçu Caves National Park, state of Minas Gerais, eastern Brazil. *Biota Neotropica*, 20(1), e20190810. https://doi.org/10.1590/1676-0611-BN-2019-0810

MRS (2019) Relatório parcial II - Eliminação da microfauna e limpeza da Vegetação - Realização de ações emergenciais de conservação das pinturas e gravuras rupestres nos sítios de abrigos do complexo Arqueológico de Serranópolis – GO. MRS Estudos Ambientais Ltda. Unpublished report presented to IPHAN (Instituto do Patrimônio Histórico e Artístico Nacional).

Pereira, H. M. and Navarro, L. M. (Eds.) (2015) *Rewilding European landscapes.* New York: Springer International Publishing.

Ratter, J. A., Ribeiro, J. F. and Bridgewater, S. (1997) The Brazilian Cerrado vegetation and threats to its biodiversity. *Annals of Botany*, 80(3), pp.223–230.

Resende, F. E. C. P. (2013) *Arte rupestre – Estudo comparativo entre imagens do passado e do presente nos abrigos de Palestina de Goiás e Serranópolis. Resgate de pinturas e gravuras invisibilizadas pela ação do tempo.* Goiânia: Instituto de Pré-História e Antropologia, Pontifícia Universidade Católica de Goiás.

Resende, F. E. C. P., Souza, U. F. and Barberi, M. (2014a) Relatório de Salvamento do Sítio Arqueológico Lapa do Chupador – Registro, Documentação e Conservação da Arte Rupestre. In Cardoso, J. F. (Ed.) *Projeto de Aproveitamento Múltiplo de Irrigação de Jequitaí – MG – CODEVAS.* Belo Horizonte: IPHAN.

Resende, F. E. C. P., Souza, U. F. and Barberi, M. (2014b) Relatório de Salvamento do Abrigo Cachoeirão. In Cardoso, J. F. (Ed.) *Projeto de Aproveitamento Múltiplo de Irrigação de Jequitaí – MG – CODEVAS.* Belo Horizonte: IPHAN.

Rios, R. M., Nogueira, J. M. and Imbroisi, D. (2008) Ecoturismo e conservação da diversidade biológica: uma avaliação econômica de potenciais complementaridades. In *XLVI Congresso da Sociedade Brasileira de Economia, Administração e Sociologia Rural.* Rio Branco, Acre, Brasil.

Rubin, J., Lorenzo, F., Silva, R. and Correa, D. (2017) Efeitos da erosão em sítios arqueológicos no Estado de Goiás. Casos de Serranópolis e Palestina de Goiás. *Clio Arqueológica,* 32(1), pp.37–67.

Schmitz, P. I., Barbosa, A. S., Jacobus, A. L. and Ribeiro, M. B. (1989) *Arqueologia nos cerrados do Brasil Central. Serranopólis I.* Antropologia 44. Instituto Anchietano de Pesquisas.

Schmitz, P. I., Rosa, A. O. and Bitencourt, A. L. V. (2004) *Arqueologia nos cerrados do Brasil Central. Serranopólis III.* Antropologia 60. São Leopoldo: Instituto Anchietano de Pesquisas - UNISINOS.

Schmitz, P. I., Silva, F. A. and Beber, M. V. (1997) *Arqueologia nos cerrados do Brasil Central. Serranopólis II. As Pinturas e Gravuras dos Abrigos.* Publicações Avulsas nº 11. São Leopoldo: Instituto Anchietano de Pesquisas/UNISINOS.

Zald, H. S. J., Spies, T. A., Harmon, M. E. and Twery, M. J. (2016) Forest carbon calculators: A review for managers, policymakers, and educators. *Journal of Forestry,* 114(2), pp.134–143. https://doi.org/10.5849/jof.15-019

15 Community Engagement in Geologic Assessments of Thamudic Inscriptions and Petroglyphs in the Wadi Rum Protected Area, Jordan

Kaelin M. Groom, George Bevan, Saleh Al-Noaimat, Mohammed Al-Zalabiah and Casey D. Allen

Introduction

Carved on the slopes of monolithic mountains surrounded by rolling sands, the numerous petroglyphs and inscriptions of the hyper-arid Hisma region epitomize the intricate and tenacious connection between humans and the desert. Straddling the Kingdoms of Jordan and Saudi Arabia and covering much of the southwestern edge of the Arabian Peninsula, the Hisma Desert houses some of the most dramatic and iconic desert landscapes in the world (Figure 15.1), features which are showcased and conserved in the Wadi Rum Protected Area (WRPA) in southern Jordan. The stark uniqueness of the reserve's landforms has inspired substantial literature on desert geomorphology (e.g., Rahman 1985; Goudie 2013), but hidden within the textbook-esque inselbergs, pediments, valleys, and ergs is an entirely different aspect of the region's complicated human-environment interaction: expansive networks of intricate, overlapping, and multi-lingual petroglyphs and inscriptions. The mere existence of this rock imagery proves a long and rich occupational history in this harsh and desolate desert. However, their content also provides significant archaeological and climatological information. Depicting scenes of large camel trains, hunting prey no longer found in the region, the domestication of livestock the current climate could not support, the rock imagery throughout the Hismaic area provide scholars a myriad of tantalizing research questions and glimpses into what ancient life may have been like in the past (Borzatti von Lowenstern and Masseti 1995; Corbett 2012)—they are even listed twice among the outstanding universal values of the WRPA's inclusion in the UNESCO World Heritage program as one of the programs rare Natural and Cultural World Heritage Sites (WHC 2011).

Despite the immense scientific and cultural value of the region's rock art and inscriptions, very little research has been conducted to assess their physical geological condition. As is common with rock art sites around the

DOI: 10.4324/9780429355349-20

world, various archaeologists and epigraphers have conducted field surveys to document and interpret the content of the region's inscriptions and carvings (e.g., Fares-Drappeau 1997; Ruben and Nasser 1999), but usually dismiss or neglect assessing their tangible context and overall stability, which is vital to instituting effective long-term conservation policies and planning (Dorn et al. 2013a; Groom 2017). Of course, while such epigraphic and rock art documentation projects provide profound knowledge and insight into the history of the region and the indigenous people who lived there, they tend to focus on a single aspect of an extremely complex and dynamic stone heritage resource.

Additionally, and unfortunately frequent with rock art sites, the local community who have lived in the region for generations—possible descendants of the ancient people who marked the stones in the first place—along with local site managers responsible for protecting the cultural resources, are completely segregated from nearly all academic explorations in the valley. Aptly described by a local community leader in Rum Village: "They come, they do research, they leave, and we learn nothing." Not only does this dissonance understandably frustrate local communities but it also robs academia of the immense wealth of local

Figure 15.1 Dramatic landscape of the Hisma Desert with the stark red sand, tall inselberg mountains and panoramic views. Inset map shows the locations of Jordan within the Middle East and the WPPA in the south. Additional map showing the breadth of sites assessed as part of the Rock Art Rangers Program including the 3 sites highlighted in this chapter. Cartography by K. M. Groom 2018.

knowledge and inherent familiarity with the valley's vast carved heritage and long-standing occupational history. Proposing a new integrated approach to research, the primary purpose of this chapter is to showcase the benefits, both scientific and social, of promoting community engagement in heritage assessment analyses using the Wadi Rum Rock Art Rangers program as a case study.

Supporting existing WRPA conservation and research efforts, the authors conducted an interdisciplinary stability analysis throughout the Protected Area employing several members of WRPA staff, volunteer participants of the USAID-funded Sustainable Cultural Heritage through the Engagement of Local Communities Project (SCHEP), and multiple international and Jordanian scholars to provide a complementary geological perspective to Wadi Rum's expansive stone imagery inventory. After a brief overview of the SCHEP program and explanation of methods employed, site analyses and results of the study are outlined, followed by a discussion of project implications and conclusions, as well as the potential—and necessity—for subsequent research on the geologic stability and the bolstering of community involvement in future management of petroglyphs and inscription across the wider Hismaic Region.

SCHEP recruitment

Working with nine heritage sites across Jordan, SCHEP is a collaborative service and research program run through American Center of Oriental Research (ACOR) and funded by USAID focused on building local capacity and self-agency to help manage and protect Jordan's vast cultural heritage resources. Both Jordanian and foreign scholars manage each SCHEP project with an emphasis on encouraging a unique community-first approach and hands-on style of teaching and engaging local communities.[1]

Specific to Wadi Rum, SCHEP's leadership—many of whom served with the Jordanian Department of Antiquities for several years—aided in establishing working relationships with the director of WRPA, as well as larger overseeing governmental bodies, such as Aqaba Special Economic Zone Authority (ASEZA). A core team consisting of Jordanian and international scholars, local community leaders, and key personnel from the WRPA was created to test methods and lead the Wadi Rum SCHEP program. The local core team members were instrumental in facilitating research outings in the protected area as well as recruiting participants for the Rock Art Rangers and Rock Art Stability Index (RASI) documentation programs.

Methods

Primary stability assessments were collected using RASI, a rapid non-invasive field survey designed to provide detailed geologic stability information without requiring complicated, and often cost-prohibitive technical training in rock decay and geomorphological sciences (Cerveny et al. 2016;

Groom et al. 2019). Individually rating over three-dozen specific rock decay forms and processes, RASI is organized into five thematic categories, each addressing a different aspect of geologic stability and, inversely, weaknesses (Dorn et al. 2008). These categories range from general, such and "Site Setting" and "Large Erosion Events" looking at the host stone as a whole, to the very specific "Incremental Loss" gaging minute and consistent micro-scale decay processes. The index also incorporates a section dedicated to indicators of future decay potential ("Impending loss") where researchers identify evidence of building vulnerability or the beginning stages of larger deterioration issues. The fifth category of the index addresses the complicated relationship between stone imagery and different rock coatings and biofilms. Since some rock coatings are considered stabilizing agents for rock art (Dorn 1998), they are scored differently than those known to promote decay.

Once a researcher is trained to accurately identify the various rock decay elements analysed in RASI, they then complete the survey by rating each individual feature on a pre-defined scale of 0 (non-existent) to 3 (dominant)–thereby providing management with not only a numerical "RASI score" to aid conservation prioritization but also give an indication of which decay processes pose the most risk to each site. More information on RASI is available on Stone Heritage Research Alliance, Limited Liability Company (SHRA) website: www.shralliance.com. This organization owns the index copyrights and the only agency in the world currently offering professional RASI training services, as well as its sister index: the Cultural Stone Stability Index (CSSI) designed for historic buildings, archaeological sites, monuments, and many other forms of heritage stone (e.g., Allen et al. 2018).

For ease of use and application, each panel was assessed using a custom-built interface within Esri's Survey123™ and Collector™ apps on smartphones/tablets—the results of which are stored in an online geo-database now administered by ASEZA (the Jordanian governmental body overseeing the WRPA). Essentially, for each panel, a single Global Positioning System (GPS) location was recorded within the app and then researchers proceeded to complete a RASI assessment and take anywhere from two to five photographs of the rock art panel and its geologic context. Both the completed RASI score, and photographs are inherently tied to the collected GPS point, so each panel collection was uploaded as a grouped dataset to the project's dedicated online Geographic Information System (GIS) database. If data collection took place in a region with decent cell reception, each panel submission was uploaded immediately; however, since most sites assessed in the project were too remote, the data was simply saved to the collecting device (i.e., individual smartphones and/or tablets). Once back within cell range or connected to the internet, the whole batch of collected data points would be uploaded at once. Despite the region's remote location and limited reception, field GIS techniques have been successfully utilized in the past (see Corbett 2012) and since the WRPA is home to tens of thousands of petroglyphs and inscriptions, collecting data digitally helped ensure each data "package" (i.e., GPS with corresponding RASI score and photographs) remained intact within the larger database.

Results

RASI fieldwork and data collection took place during multiple two-to-three-week intensive field seasons. This was supplemented by minimal, but continuous, research done by a handful of dedicated WRPA staff and volunteer participants. With the project spanning slightly over a year, a running total of 1179 individual panels (discrete rock faces with a shared aspect housing one or more inscription/image) spread across more than 85 different sites (groupings of panels within a definable location) have been assessed—each dataset included a dedicated RASI score, photograph, and geographic location stored in the project's online geo-database. These collected RASI scores can now be analysed geospatially within the online framework to visualize the broad distribution of primary decay threats within the WRPA and determine which sites may be suitable for tourism development depending on panel stability.

A few useful over-arching stability observations can also be inferred based on the fairly comprehensive compilation of data collected throughout the WRPA--although various autocorrelations and statistical limitations do exist in such assessments. For example, when comparing average scores and category sums across the five main RASI categories (Table 15.1), the "site setting and geologic context" category appears significantly more influential than expected, especially when compared to other categories with considerably more recorded features. Of course, categories with more decay features may have a higher count of "not present (0)" scores, which would inherently lower averages. That said, comparing these values can still provide useful insight into which decay patterns and behaviours are present in the WRPA. For instance, the negative average score for the "Rock Coatings" category indicates, in general, the stabilizing influences of many rock coatings found in the region—such as mature desert varnishes and case hardening (Dorn et al. 2012; Dorn et al. 2013b), which outweigh the negative impacts of salts and anthropogenic activities in the study area.

Table 15.1 Comparison between average RASI scores and their respective category sums, displaying potential statistical differences between the overarching categories

	Site Setting	Impending Loss	Large Erosion Events	Small Erosion Events	Rock Coatings
Average score	0.82	0.56	0.29	0.56	−0.26
Mode	0.75	0.50	0.20	0.64	−0.25
Category sum averages	971.00	663.60	343.00	665.75	−305.25

Beyond average category scores, specific averages for each assessed rock decay feature can help quickly identify which processes are most prominent within the study area. It is important to note that with over 1,000 panels recorded in this study and many decay features scoring "not present (0)", most average feature scores are decimals, indicating any decay feature with an average score of 1 or above is a widespread or significant concern. For Wadi Rum, these threats include scaling and flaking of the rock surface in both impending (1.26 points) and active decay categories (1.08 points), rounding and blurring of petroglyph edges leading to loss of clarity (1.30 points), and general intrinsic weaknesses within the lithology itself (1.46 points).

Generic assessments such as these can be useful for park management, but the benefit and applicability of the RASI geo-database is more apparent when used to analyse specific sites and smaller clusters of panels. To demonstrate this, RASI data and score interpretations for three key sites within the WRPA are presented: Ain Shallalah—a spring on the eastern face of Jabel Rum just above Rum Village; Siq al-Khazali—a slot canyon on the northern tip of Jabel Khazali and the primary rock art tourism site of Wadi Rum; and Alameleh—an archeologically significant site depicting various ancient technologies and cultural events, also a popular destination for tours originating from the neighbouring Disi Village (See Figure 15.1). These three sites exemplify regional decay patterns, lithologies, as well as heritage management challenges—both anthropogenic and natural—influencing the long-term sustainability of Wadi Rum's irreplaceable rock art and inscriptions.

Ain Shallalah

Straddling the contact between the region's dark volcanic basement rock and the hardened Umm Ishrin sandstone, Ain Shallalah is a unique site nestled in a small crook of the mountain "Jabel Rum", directly west of Rum Village in the very centre of the WRPA. This site not only houses the protected area's most complete Nabataean shrines and inscriptions, but these panels have also developed a thick calcrete coating unlike anywhere else in the surrounding region. The pleasant atmosphere created by the perennial trickling of spring water, protection from the harsh desert sun, and the smell of wild spearmint growing nearby—all within an easy hike from the village below— has made Ain Shallalah a popular destination for tourists and locals alike.

Unfortunately, RASI analyses revealed several human-driven decay processes and negative impacts of the site's high foot traffic and relatively unrestricted visitation. Including several panels along the trail leading to the spring itself, 21 individual RASI assessments were recorded for this site. Final RASI scores ranged from 36 (Panel 1) to 68 points (Panel 9) with a site average of 53.2 points—well above the total project average (32.2 points) (Figure 15.2). As might be expected, the panels nearest the spring and flat picnic area exhibited the most anthropogenic decay, mostly modern carving, paint, and chiselling sections of Nabataean inscriptions. The site's

Figure 15.2 Map of RASI panels at Ain Shallalah with colour saturation indicating RASI score and small inset overlay showing Panel 8 with its location marking on the map with a black square. Photography and cartography by K.M. Groom.

primary natural decay processes identified via RASI are interesting, as they are also commonly found in limestone—possibly reflecting the high calcrete and carboniferous characteristics of the Umm Ishrin sandstone on which most of Wadi Rum's petroglyphs are located (Rahman 1985). Specific RASI elements with consistently higher scores at Ain Shallalah include the development of tafoni (pitting), textural anomalies either inhibiting or enhancing surface deterioration, widespread flaking (typically of the calcrete coating taking subsurface material with it), and polygenetic decay explicitly leading to loss of detail and/or clarity of motifs.

Serving as an appropriate representative of stone stability—or more aptly instability—currently exhibited at Ain Shallalah, Panel 8, near the spring, showcases the site's uniqueness as well as visible examples of all the above-mentioned conditional challenges. Among the most academically significant panels at the spring, the centre of Panel 8 displays what has been interpreted as a Nabataean shrine with two distinctive Nabataean inscriptions on either side (Dudley and Reeves 2007; Hayajneh 2009). Additionally, there is the possibility of an additional item in the upper left corner where a large section of the stone face has been crudely removed. The thick calcrete layer covering much of the panel's surface has obscured some of the writing, but the removal of this coating has caused more damage to the inscriptions—as seen along the lower sections of Panel 8 where the texture of the stone is dominated by small flakes and scales preparing to detach. In areas where the rock coating is more secure, the surface has begun developing networks of cavities and pitting, known as tafoni (Groom et al. 2015), along the upper right corner of the panel—also dramatically changing the overall texture of the stone surface. Consistently higher scores in the "Impending Loss" RASI category—for Panel 8 and most others at Ain Shallalah—indicate the site's rock art and inscriptions will only continue to deteriorate, especially if human interaction and land-use remain unregulated.

As a site commonly utilized by the Rum community, Ain Shallalah also prompted excellent discussions among the program volunteers, exemplifying inherent necessity to include local stakeholders in stability research. Many, if not all, of the program participants already voiced concerns regarding trash and rubbish found at the site, admitting they could do better about promoting clean-ups or better land-use practice; but once they started collecting RASI scores, they were surprised to learn just how fragile these panels actually were. In the middle of data collection, local site managers and WRPA staff began talking with local guides and community leaders about ideas for better protecting the site, with some even trying to identify the individuals responsible for the more invasive vandalism so they could be held accountable. RASI analyses with higher scores at Ain Shallalah not only provided credence to existing concerns about the site, but by including community members in the data collection process, also allowed for a more organic, and potentially effective, response to these issues. Rather than an external power trying to enforce new rules, program participants can promote change from within the community, teaching by example to respect the site for future generations.

Siq al-Khazali

Arguably, the most famous rock art site in the whole Hisma Desert, Siq al-Khazali—commonly known as "Khazali Canyon"—features numerous petroglyphs, overlapping inscriptions, and singularly unique motifs within a dramatic slot canyon at prominent location near the centre of the WRPA. The site's easy accessibility, interesting setting, and high concentration of engravings have made it a key-stone tourist attraction within the protected area—so much so that the site is included on nearly every tour itinerary and also featured heavily on promotional material for the park. Reflecting the prolific occupational history of Wadi Rum, Khazali's RASI analysis included 38 individual panels, with petroglyph ages spanning from Neolithic (>3000 BCE) to Thamudic (~300 BCE–400 CE) and Early Islamic (~600–800 CE) (Ruben and Nasser 1999). In fact, several inscriptions within the canyon are cited as some of the earliest known examples of written modern Arabic (Hayajneh 2009)—adding to the site's interest, as well as its historical and epigraphic value. With the canyon itself being quite narrow (2–3 meters at the widest), the daily influx of large tour groups and visitors has certainly had a profound influence on the site. This is reflected in the site's RASI results, but the canyon's unique lithological variances seem even more significant regarding panel stability and decay.

The final RASI scores for Khazali varied dramatically from a mere 12 points (Panel 18—a nearly perfect score) up to 80 points (Panel 33—practically falling apart), making the site average of 33.4 points a relatively poor representative for the site as a whole, even though it aligns well with the WRPA's total average (32.2 points). That said, when viewed geographically, a few spatial patterns emerge. For instance, panels exhibiting the inner canyon's higher RASI scores (42–50, Average: 45.6) are located above the opening and along the upper ledges out of hands reach (Figure 15.3). Primary decay threats for these panels, as identified via the index, include typical sandstone vulnerabilities such as rampant flaking and splintering (i.e., disintegration of stone matrices along weakened layers of concentrated bedding planes (Goudie et al. 1994)), and the ever-present threat of graffiti and vandalism, particularly along the outer edges of the canyon opening.

Alternatively, and somewhat counter-intuitively, the panels with the lowest scores (14–32, Average: 26.2–indicating higher stability and resilience), are located directly alongside the path leading into the canyon and experience regular human interaction, as most visitors use the panels as handholds to safely move through the narrow canyon. Human contact is usually considered damaging to rock art (Whitley 2005), so finding such low RASI scores within arm's reach in Khazali was surprising, but not entirely inexplicable: each of the "stable" panels are contained within a single meter-thick geologic strata with an unusually thick silica coating, which has, over time,

Figure 15.3 Map showing the location and RASI scores within Khazali Canyon. The inset overlay is a photograph of Panel 33 and its location is marked on the map with a black box. Photography and Cartography by K.M. Groom.

effectively encased the rock art and inscriptions under a shiny, and highly resilient, epoxy-like outer layer. Further research is necessary to determine the relationship between nearly constant human contact, periodic flooding, and the development of this coating, but its presence has certainly been a stabilizing agent for Khazali's inner panels, at least for now. While the surfaces are currently relatively solid, sub-surface deterioration leading to the complete detachment of entire panels in a single devastating event remains a concern. This type of low-frequency high-impact decay is demonstrated along the lower portion of the site's highest scoring panel (Panel 33 - RASI score: 80), where large sections of inscriptions and petroglyphs have detached, exposing the extremely friable and brittle subsurface, which now threatens the rest of the panel's overall stability.

Contrary to Ain Shallalah, which is popular with locals and visitors alike, nearly all foot traffic in and around Khazali canyon is tourist related, making tour guide inclusion in stability assessments immensely important. Most of the local volunteers in the Rock Art Rangers program are seasoned guides in the area with years of experience working around Khazali. However, many guides in the area would simply drop visitors off at the mouth of the canyon to explore the crevice unsupervised, leaving the area vulnerable to graffiti and vandalism (one of the site's main problems identified via RASI). Armed with a greater understanding of rock decay, as well as basic epigraphic and historical knowledge of the canyon, program participant guides now regularly lead groups through the canyon to discuss the rich heritage and importance of the site, both enriching the visitor experience as well as more closely monitoring their behaviour and discouraging vandalism.

Additionally, local engagement in research and stability assessment at such a prominent site in the park has been very effective in raising awareness among tour guide associations from various villages. For example, one of the participating tour guides caught a tourist attempting to carve their name in the outer canyon wall. Not only did the guide immediately alert proper authorities but was also able to provide the offender accurate information regarding the devastating impact their action could have on the stability of the stone. Similarly, by promoting from within the community, the attitude towards and willingness to participate in protective activities has also increased at Khazali. During a preliminary workshop to remove graffiti in the outer canyon, several local guides (not officially part of the program) openly helped and happily joined the efforts lead by WRPA staff and foreign scholars—such as the successful removal of the black spray paint on Panel 33 shown in Figure 15.4 by WRPA staff and local volunteers.

Alameleh

Differing slightly from the other sites explored in this paper, Alameleh houses a single large and complex panel with only a few outliers on either

Figure 15.4 Map showing the location and scores of RASI panels on the small outcrop of Alameleh. The primary panel is shown in the overlay and marked with a black box on the map. Photograph by C.D. Allen and Cartography by K.M. Groom.

side. Despite the site's limited number of panels, the concentration, diversity, and clarity of motifs and inscriptions on this small outcrop make Alameleh a prime tourist destination, an invaluable epigraph and academic resource. The site's unique features include large depictions of camel trains, hunting scenes, herding activities, texts and inscriptions of multiple styles—representing the relatively high literacy rate among Thamudic peoples (Stein 2009)—and an interesting visualization of technological evolutions in the region (i.e., moving from spears, bows and arrows to swords to firearms and rifles). On top of the site's profound historical value, it also demonstrates the effective application of RASI as a practical conservation and/or "emergency response" research tool: less than two years ago, the main panel at Alameleh was vandalized with latex paints. ASEZA and the WRPA responded quickly by contracting a professional conservator to clean the site. However, as with even the best restoration applications, faint evidence of both the vandalism event and subsequent restoration remains--evidence that can be recorded and monitored via repeated RASI analysis as the panel continues to recover.

Officially, there are five panels at Alameleh (a cluster of four along the northern ridge and a single panel on the outcrop's southern tip)—all five were analysed, but this discussion will focus primarily on the site's key panel (appropriately designated Panel 1), as it dwarfs the rest in both size and complexity (Figure 15.4). With a final RASI score of 42 (only slightly over the project average), the geology substrate of the main Alameleh panel is fortunately quite stable, especially when considering its complicated history with human interaction. The most prevalent decay features include the development of cavernous decay (tafoni), impending scaling and flaking of the stone surface, and decay related to numerous fissures (cracks) independent of the outcrop's bedding plane. Residue from the site's vandalism is still present and scored high in the "anthropogenic rock coating", as did "abrasion" and "[natural] rock coating detachment", both being common side effects of conservation efforts when cleaning a panel of this size. Additionally, the panel is housed on a relatively uniform section of sandstone meaning the site does not contain the various textural and superficial anomalies exacerbating decay elsewhere in the WRPA.

Nearing the outer border of the official protected area, Alamaleh is a popular rock art destination for tours originating from Disi Village--one of the largest villages in the area. With both Khazali and Ain Shallalah squarely within park boundaries, the inclusion of border sites such as Alameleh is vital in encouraging cross-tribal engagement in stone heritage conservation. Program volunteers from multiple different tribes and villages participated in site visitation, discussion, and stability assessment at Alameleh to showcase shared heritage, as well as collective challenges facing the entire region, which include vandalism and other common sandstone decay features (e.g., splintering, flaking, and rock coating detachment). While the social relations among Wadi Rum's Bedouin tribes remain somewhat complicated, gaining equal knowledge of stone decay and rock art assessment may encourage more cross-tribal efforts to protect the area's universal cultural and natural heritage, such as those exhibited at Alameleh. Including what is generally considered a "Disi site" in this geographically comprehensive stability assessment both validates the site's universal value for all tribes but also, potentially, helps foster a more collaborative attitude in relation to protecting ALL rock art and inscription sites within the protected area, and beyond.

Discussion and conclusion

Arguably, one of the key strengths of RASI is that the index forces the scorer to slow down and see the rock art for what it is: vulnerable. The perception that all rock is hard or invincible is, unfortunately, relatively common, much to the detriment of stone heritage sites across the world--especially open-air rock art sites. In many cases, the casual sentiment of "It's lasted this long so it's fine" often leads to misdiagnosing stability concerns, disregarding major issues, or simple indifference regarding long-term site sustainability. By engaging local tour guides and community members alongside site management professionals in rock art stability assessments in the Wadi Rum Protected Area of southern Jordan, the Rock Art Rangers program illustrates how community collaboration in scientific research can have a profound influence on promoting effective site management. This study has not only provided numerical values to help guide site management in the creation of new protective policies under the purview of the WRPA but also fostered support and understanding in the local community, who helped gather those values, which in turn help promote beneficial social change to uphold those policies. Rather than relying on data collected by an outside entity, the communal structure of SCHEP and the Rock Art Rangers programs provides local community members social agency and the opportunity to actively participant and contribute to the protection of their shared heritage.

While tourism has been proven to put considerable physical strain on fragile stone heritage resources (Archer et al. 2005; Brandt 2011; Caletrío 2011), such as the rock art and inscriptions of the Hisma, these activities are often a financial necessity to provide the resources and personnel required to effectively manage them. With such a complicated relationship between conservation, tourism, and sustainable development, collaboration between official management agencies and local communities becomes even more vital to the long-term stability of heritage sites. The SCHEP-model's ability to foster this type of cooperation is, arguably, the program's greatest success—as is evident in the Wadi Rum Protected Area. Of course, future research is still required to complete a truly comprehensive rock art and inscription database of the entire region, but the fact that local tribes people are still working alongside WRPA staff and government employees is testament to the lasting influence of community engagement efforts and collaborative research.

Acknowledgements

This work would not have been possible without (continued and sustained) support from the WRPA and ASEZA, both of which provided in-kind funding that helped with training, lodging, and transport, and without whom projects like this would not be as beneficial to the local community. A very special thank you and sincerest appreciation also goes to the amazing people of Wadi Rum for their continued interest in RASI, their unwavering support of this project, and sincere desire to help people learn about their fascinating history. Funding for this project was made available from the SCHEP, housed at ACOR in Amman, Jordan, and sponsored by USAID.

Note

1 More information about SCHEP and the individual projects can be found on their website: www.usaidschep.org.

References

Allen, C. D., Ester, S., Groom, K. M., Schubert, R., Hagele, C., Olof, D. and James, M. (2018) A Geologic Assessment of Historic Saint Elizabeth of Hungary Church Using the Cultural Stone Stability Index, Denver, Colorado. In Thornbush, M. and Allen, C. (Eds.) *Urban Geomorphology.* Oxford: Elsevier, pp. 277–302.

Archer, B., Cooper, C. and Ruhanen, L. (2005) The Positive and Negative Impacts of Tourism. In Theobald, W. F. (Ed.) *Global Tourism.* Oxford: Elsevier, pp.79–102.

Borzatti von Lowenstern, E. and Masseti, M. (1995) Rock carvings of cattle in the Hisma Basin, Southern Jordan. *Studi per l'Ecologia del Quaternario,* 17, pp.10–19

Brandt, J. (2011) Carrying capacity-how much tourism can protected areas cope with? In Fiefer, S. & Ostermann, O. (Eds.) *Parks & Benefits: Guide to Sustainable Tourism in Protected Areas.* Rostock, Germany: Baltic Sea Region Programme, pp. 26–37.

Caletrío, J. (2011) Tourism, landscape change and critical thresholds. *Annals of Tourism Research,* 38(1), pp.313–316.

Cerveny, N. V., Dorn, R. I., Allen, C. D. and Whitley, D. S. (2016) Advances in rapid condition assessments of rock art sites: Rock Art Stability Index (RASI). *Journal of Archaeological Science: Reports,* 10, pp.871–877.

Corbett, G. J. (2012) The signs that bind: Identifying individuals, families and friends in hismaic inscriptions. *Arabian Archaeology and Epigraphy,* 23(2), pp.174–190.

Dorn, R. I. (1998). *Rock Coatings* (1st ed. Vol. 6). Amsterdam: Elsevier.

Dorn, R. I., Dorn, J., Harrison, E., Gutbrod, E., Gibson, S., Larson, P. and Allen, C. D. (2012) Case Hardening Vignettes from the Western USA: Convergence of Form by a Divergence of Hardening Processes. *Association of Pacific Coast Geographers Yearbook,* 74, pp.53–75.

Dorn, R. I., Gordon, S. J., Allen, C. D., Cerveny, N., Dixon, J. C. and Groom, K. M., Turkington, A. V. (2013a) The role of fieldwork in rock-decay research: Case studies from the Fringe. *Geomorphology,* 200, pp.59–74.

Dorn, R. I., Krinsley, D. H., Langworthy, K. A., Ditto, J. and Thompson, T. J. (2013b) The influence of mineral detritus on rock varnish formation. *Aeolian Research,* 10, pp.61–76.

Dorn, R. I., Whitley, D. S., Cerveny, N. V., Gordon, S. J., Allen, C. D. and Gutbrod, E. (2008) The rock art stability index: A new strategy for maximizing the sustainability of rock art as a heritage resource. *Heritage Management,* 1(1), pp.37–70.

Dudley, D. and Reeves, M. B. (2007) Luxury in the desert: A Nabataean Palatial residence at Wadi Ramm. In Levy, T. E., Daviau, P. M. M., Younker, R. W. and Shaer, M. (Eds.) *Crossing Jordan: North American Contributions to the Archaeology of Jordan.* London: Equinox Publishing Ltd, pp.401–407.

Fares-Drappeau, S. (1997) Epigraphic survey in Wadi Rum 1996. *Annual of the Department of Antiquities Jordan,* 41, pp.37–44.

Goudie, A. S. (2013) *Arid and Semi-Arid Geomorphology.* Cambridge: Cambridge University Press.

Goudie, A., Atkinson, B., Gregory, K., Simmons, I., Stoddart, D. and Sugden, D. (1994) *The Encylopedic Dictionary of Physical Geography.* Oxford: Blackwell.

Groom, K. M. (2017, April 2013). Assessment and Preservation of Rock Art: Analysis and Technologies for Petroglyphic Conservation in Wadi Rum. In *Paper*

Presented at the Man and the Desert 2nd Annual Conference on Wadi Rum, 2013, Amman, Jordan.

Groom, K. M., Allen, C. D., Mol, L., Paradise, T. R. and Hall, K. (2015) Defining tafoni: Re-examining terminological ambiguity for cavernous rock decay phenomena. *Progress in Physical Geography,* 39(6), pp.775–793.

Groom, K. M., Villa Cerveny, N., Allen, C. D., Dorn, R. I. and Theuer, J. (2019) Protecting stone heritage in the painted desert: Employing the rock art stability index in the Petrified Forest National Park, Arizona. *Heritage,* 2(3), pp.2111–2123.

Hayajneh, H. (2009) Ancient North Arabian-Nabataean Bilingual Inscriptions from Southern Jordan. In *Proceedings of the Seminar for Arabian Studies 39, London, 24–26 July 2008.* Oxford: Archaeopress, pp. 203–222.

Rahman, A. A. Abd El (1985) The deserts of the Arabian Peninsula. In Evenari, M., Noy-Meir, I. and Goodall, D.W. (Eds.) *Hot Deserts and Arid Shrublands* (Vol. Ecosystems of the World, 12B). Amsterdam: Elsevier, pp. 29–54.

Ruben, I. and Nasser, G. (1999) *Review of the Archaeology of the Wadi Rum Protected Area.* Jordania: American Center of Oriental Research.

Stein, P. (2009) Literacy in Pre-Islamic Arabia: An Analysis of the Epigraphic Evidence. In *The Qur'ān in Context. Historical and Literary Investigations into the Qur'ānic Milieu.* Leiden, The Netherlands: Brill, pp. 255–280. https://doi.org/10.1163/ej.9789004176881.i-864.58

Whitley, D. S. (2005) *Introduction to Rock Art Research.* Walnut Creek, CA: Left Coast Press.

World Heritage Committee, WHC (2011, June 19–29) Decisions Adopted by the World Heritage Committee at its 35th Session. In *Paper Presented at the UNESCO Conventions Concerning the Protection of the World Cultural and Natural Heritage,* UNESCO Headquarters, Paris.

16 Preservation of Endangered Bangudae Petroglyphs in Korea

Sangmog Lee

Introduction: discovery of the petroglyphs

The existence of petroglyphs in Korea first became known when Dongguk University Museum Investigation Team, exploring ancient Buddhist relics in the Ulsan region of southern Korea, accidentally discovered the Cheonjeon-ri Petroglyphs in the Bangudae valley (Mung-Dae Moon 1984). The valley is one of the most popular scenic spots in southern Korea, and it is thought that the name of Bangudae (盤龜臺 in Chinese characters) originated from the shape of the mountain slopes and valleys adorned with oddly formed rocks which look like a turtle lying face down. A connection has been made between the name Bangudae as it is related to Ban-go-sa, an ancient Buddhist temple. It was here that Wonhyo, one of the most eminent scholar-monks in Korean history, is said to have practiced asceticism and authored books during the 7th century.

The Investigation Team's leader Professor Myung-Dae Moon first visited this location on December 24, 1970 (Mung-Dae Moon 1984). Unfortunately, at this time the downstream area of the Bangudae Valley was already submerged by the dam. But an old local resident named Gyung-Hwan Choi told the disappointed team that they would see a broken stone pagoda in the upper reaches of the Bangudae Valley. In response to this information, the team travelled upstream and accidently discovered the Cheonjeon-ri Petroglyphs. Located about 1.7km upstream from Bangudae, on a wide and flat rock about 10m wide and 3m high, the site contained a large accumulation of motifs from different historic and prehistoric times. At that time, however, the team focused on the inscriptions written in Chinese characters and motifs from historical periods that are found on the lower part of the rock rather than on the prehistoric petroglyphs. An epigraph on the lower part of the panel read "On the morning of June 18, AD 525, Galmunwang, brother of King Beopheung (the 23rd monarch of the Silla Dynasty) visited here to see the valley." This epigraph was valued as the oldest written record ever found in Korea and, in 1973, was designated as a National Treasure (Lee 2011). However, the fact that the Bangudae petroglyphs found in 1971 were designated as a National Treasure only 24 years after its discovery denotes

DOI: 10.4324/9780429355349-21

low interest by Korean academia in prehistoric petroglyphs at that time. The archaeological community was also focused on the historical period, and a limited number of researchers studied prehistory (Lee 2011).

The first discovery in Korea of a site from the Palaeolithic was dated in1964 at Seokjang-ri, South Chungcheong Province. Bo-gi Sohn, the former Yonsei University professor of history who led a team excavating the Seokjang-ri site, was one of the first academics in Korea to focus on studying the Palaeolithic Era. Since then, many of his students become interested in prehistory, with some travelling to foreign countries to pursue further studies. In this sense, the Seokjang-ri Palaeolithic sites can be said to have served as the cradle of prehistoric studies in Korea (Pow-Key Son 1974).

Research on the Cheonjeon-ri Petroglyphs was undertaken between April 10 and May 2, 1971, and the investigation techniques included drawing, rubbings (making an impression using traditional Korean paper and ink), and photo documentation. While conducting investigations in Cheonjeon-ri, Prof. Myung-Dae Moon was told by local residents that they had seen animal figures like tigers on the cliffs submerged by a dam on the downstream area of the Bangudae Valley. Prof. Moon presented the results of his investigations in Cheonjeon-ri in a seminar held by the Korean Historical Association in October in Seoul. Upon hearing his presentation with interest, Professor Jung-Bae Kim, ancient historian and archaeologist, and the archaeologist Professor Yung-Jo Lee suggested to Prof. Moon they visit the site together. On December 25, 1971, they visited the site. A drought had fortunately lowered the water level and they borrowed a boat to approach the cliffs seasonally submerged by the dam. At last, in a huge cliff, they discovered engravings of turtles, human figures and whales (Mung-Dae Moon 1984, Lee 2011).

Documentation work on the Bangudae Petroglyphs was subsequently undertaken for ten days from March 16 to 26, 1972. In 1973, the Yonsei University Museum Team led by Prof. Bo-Gi Sohn also conducted research at the site. Material documented by the team were kept at the Seokjang-ri Museum until part of the collection was moved to the Ulsan Petroglyph Museum at Bangudae, where they are now used as the foundation materials to study rock art. Prof. Moon never overlooked the aesthetic values of the Petroglyphs, and continued to organize the related drawings and materials for about a decade to finally publish the report titled "Bangudae Petroglyphs in Ulju" (Mung-Dae Moon 1984).

This report was published following efforts by an amateur rock art researcher who with limited experience in the field of petroglyphs analysis. The rock art was recorded using rubbings techniques which included the use of Korean traditional paper used for documenting epigraphs; drawings completed by installing grids on the rock surface; and comprehensive photos. Until 2010 when the Ulsan Petroglyph Museum of Bangudae began to regularly publish investigative reports on the petroglyphs in Korea, the report served as the only reference material researchers could rely on for the study of rock art in Korea. Although the original report often caused misinterpretations of the engravings among researchers, it also stimulated a renewed interest in the study of petroglyphs and more sites began to be located.

On May 30, 2008, the Ulsan Petroglyph Museum of Bangudae was opened as Korea's single research institution and museum dedicated to rock art, with rock art research produced since 2009 (Lee 2011). Inappropriate techniques such as rubbing have subsequently been excluded, and a new methodological approach applied. This includes drawing on transparent vinyl, night-time photographing, and 3D digital scanning. To sufficiently reflect diverse archaeological and contextual attributes of the rock art, research has also been conducted using technologically advanced archaeological science procedures. Reports published annually and distributed to researchers and research institutions home and abroad have contributed to establish a wide network of institutions devoted to Korean rock art. As these have experienced difficulties in writing research reports, most of them contact the Ulsan Petroglyph Museum when new rock art sites are located. Through this network, the Museum undertakes research regarding these sites in a prompt manner, also collecting and organizing related archaeological materials that have been scattered across different institutions (Ulsan Petroglyphs Museum 2013).

Environment

Geography

The Bangudae Petroglyphs are located near Ulsan, southeastern Korea. The Daegok stream, forms a typical entrenched valley, which was moulded by extended erosion processes during the Cretaceous Period, with the sediments deposited due to the overflowing of the lakes and rivers. The areas surrounding the stream possess uniquely beautiful scenery featuring river cliffs, river terraces, precipices, winding streams and wetlands. This attractive scenery may have served as a major attraction point to this area from prehistoric times. The submerged downstream reaches remain inaccessible at this time; however, except for the Cheonjeon-ri engraved panel, no prehistoric sites of particular significance have been located along the upper reaches of the stream. Therefore, it is presumed that, while living in coastal areas, the Neolithic communities who engraved the Bangudae Petroglyphs came to the valley with a specific purpose. The Bangudae Valley is also believed to have been of particular spatial significance during historical periods, as the Cheonjeon-ri Petroglyphs, feature inscriptions and drawings engraved by the royal families of the Silla Dynasty. It is also reported that Jeong Mong-Ju (1337–1392), a noted Confucian scholar and diplomat of the Goryeo Dynasty, comforted himself during his time exiled in the valley, with a memorial stone built to pay tribute to his achievements. The paintings by

Jeong Seon (1676–1759), one of the most famous landscape painters of the Joseon Dynasty, as well as hundreds of poems composed by classical scholars, describe the beautiful natural scenery of the Bangudae Valley (Ulsan Petroglyphs Museum 2013).

Paleoenvironment

After the Last Glacial Maximum (LGM) in the northern hemisphere, temperatures began to gradually rise until the beginning of the Holocene about 10,000 years ago. This global climate phenomenon made animals that used to live under the cold climate of the Pleistocene gradually disappear, significantly affecting the activities of human beings. Available data on pollen analysis on the southern part of the Korean Peninsula suggests, besides other changes in vegetation cover from the LGM until the present, that 2,000 ago, Pinus began to gradually expand, a growth believed to be related to human deforestation activities (Sang-Il Hwang and Soon-Ok Yoon 2014).

The most ancient motifs at Bangudae, the oldest petroglyphs found in the Korean Peninsula until now, are presumed to date to the early Neolithic, about 7,000 years BP. The changes in sea level in the post-glacial age are very important to characterize the way of life and chronology of the communities who engraved the Bangudae Petroglyphs. Sang-Il Hwang and Soon-Ok Yoon (2014, pp. 97–101) inferred sea level, on the rise after final glacial times, reached the innermost inland areas about 7,000 years BP. Judging it would have been technically difficult at that time to hunt whales in open sea, they suggest whaling may have begun then given the optimal environmental conditions to drive whales on seasonal migration to Ulsan Bay. Hence, the oldest maximum chronology for the Bangudae Petroglyphs was estimated to be 7,000 years BP. Ulsan Bay at that time expanded inland, with the distance between the Bangudae Petroglyphs and the coast at that time being less than 10 km, far shorter than the current 20 km. The fact that Ulsan Bay became narrower due to river sediments deposition between 2,800- and 2,700-years BP and whaling declined due to the spread of agriculture in the Ulsan region, suggests this is the lowest chronological range for the Bangudae Petroglyphs (Sang-Il Hwang and Soon-Ok Yoon 2014).

Archaeological context

Judging from sea level during the Upper Palaeolithic, the Korean Peninsula is presumed to have been connected with the Japanese Islands, forming a large lake in the current East Sea (Mou-Chang Choi 1987). Since Bangudae was then some distance from the sea, it is plausible to suggest it unlikely that petroglyphs depicting whaling activities have a Palaeolithic chronology. While it is difficult to determine when humans first began hunting whales in the region, whaling activities have been evidenced in archaeological strata (approximately 2m below the current sea level) at the coastal

Hwangeong-dong Neolithic site, situated about 20 km from Bangudae (Sang-Il Hwang and Soon-Ok Yoon 2014).

Traces of human settlement in the Korean Peninsula go back as early as circa 12,000 years BP. The time of the first emergence of pottery, which Korean archaeologists suggest as evidence of settlement, has been suggested as the beginning of the Neolithic. However, except for the Gosan-ri site on Jeju (12,000 to 10,000 years BP) where the most ancient pottery was found in Korea (Lee 2007), no other traces corresponding to the Neolithic-like agriculture, livestock farming and inhabited settlements - have been identified to date. Pottery found at Gosan-ri is made of soft clay containing plant fibres with no decorative patterns, thus significantly different from the standard Neolithic pottery excavated elsewhere: usually made of earth mixed with shell powder or soft sand and with geometric patterns on the surface. Flake stone tools like scrapers or burins, microliths such as stone blades, and arrowheads are characteristic of the transition period between the end of the Palaeolithic and the Mesolithic. Regarding the establishment of sea-oriented cultures, French social anthropologist Alain Testart, has summed up current debate when he noted that:

> "Sea level during the glacial epoch was by far lower than the current level, and coasts of the epoch are now under water. The first archaeological evidence of an ocean-oriented culture only points to the time when sea level began to stabilize rather than to the beginning of an oceanic culture."
>
> (Testart 1982, p. 186, translated from the French; see also Laming-Emperaire and Baudez 1968, pp. 219–220)

In the southern part of the Korean Peninsula, the evidence of Neolithic style pottery, polished stone tools, and traces of settlements and villages are found in the Osan-ri site (about 8,000 years BP). Korean Peninsula Neolithic period is significantly different from that of Europe and the Near East in that the traces of agriculture are not found until the Middle Neolithic (Lee 2007). Most of the Neolithic sites are found in the coast and river margins. Shell mounds scattered along the coast maintain vestiges relatively intact, allowing to reconstruct everyday life of that time. For example, in the bottom layer of the Bibong-ri shell mound (circa 8,000 years BP) a 4m-long wood boat in an excellent condition and pine logs, acorn storage pit, stone mound containing deer bones, seeds of nuts, stone axes, comb-pattern pottery, reed bag, and farming tools were found (Joowon Shin 2020).

It is believed that communities living in the Korean Peninsula during the Neolithic hunted sea mammals like whale and seals, in addition to the collection of clams in the coast from winter to spring (Lee 2007). In the autumn they collected acorns and nuts and hunted animals like deer, maintaining settlements with no farming. Pottery was mostly used for cooking and storing food acquired from hunting and gathering. Most shell mounds date from between 8,000 years BP and 3,500 years BP, and gradually disappear by the Bronze Age (3,500 to 2,300 years BP). As an exceptional case, traces of farming (rice, barley, wheat, and millet) were found in the Daecheon-ri site (3,500 BC to 3,000 BC), but farming remained secondary to hunting and gathering. Traces of farming gradually increase from the Middle Neolithic, and, entering the Bronze Age (1,500 BC–300 BC), drastic changes occur as evident in the appearance of tombs, dwellings, and complex settlements. It remains unproven whether the advent of agrarian society and Iron Age culture comes from immigrants to the Korean Peninsula, or alternatively that the local Korean populations adapted to outside influences. Nevertheless, there are few signs of conflict between farming and hunting groups. (Lee 2011).

The Bangudae Petroglyphs

General situation

Having presented information on the location and environment surrounding the Banguade Petroglyphs, we will now turn our attention to the content of the rock art assemblage itself.

About 300 engravings have been recorded on a flat rock face (8m wide × 5m high); a few other petroglyphs are also found nearby on about ten rock faces around the cliff. The rock is composed of shale and hornfels, and the petroglyphs are engraved at the base of the cliff in a panel located at an elevation between 52m and 58m. Research conducted by the Korean National Research Institute of Cultural Heritage in 2013 shows that the bottom of the old river channel is at an altitude between 45m and 47m, demonstrating that the river bottom rose several meters due to sediments deposited since the construction of the dam (Ulsan Metropolitan City 2003). The rock is oriented towards the north and receives full sun at sunset during about half of the year but is mostly in the shade between November and March. The top of the steep vertical cliff has the structure of a rock shelter, protecting the petroglyphs engraved below from erosion. However, due to the construction of the dam, the rock face bearing the petroglyphs now becomes submerged for about eight months per year. The construction of another dam in 2005 in the upper reaches of the Daegok stream allowed an artificial control of the water level, significantly reducing the period when the petroglyphs are submerged to just one month. The Korean government and the Ulsan City continue to consider alternative measures to allow for the complete protection the site from submerging waters.

Themes

The first report on the Bangudae published by the Dongguk University Press in 1984 identified a total of 191 engravings; research undertaken by the Ulsan Petroglyph Museum in 2012 revealed a total of 307 engravings. Themes of the rock art assemblage can be largely divided into anthropomorphic figures

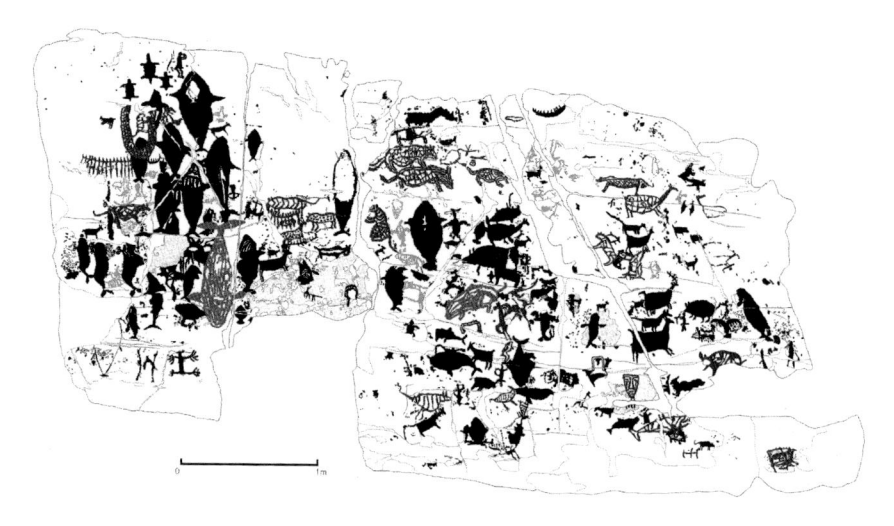

Figure 16.1 Documentation work of the total Bangudae rock art panel. Documentation work by Lee (2003).

that depict human bodies or faces; sea and land animals; tools, equipment and material culture used for hunting and fishing like boats, floats, nets and arrows; and undetermined motifs. Animals (n=169) account for 55% with whales (n=53) accounting for 17.2% of the entire total. There are also 14 anthropomorphic figures (4.5%), 16 tools (5.2%), and 180 undetermined figures (35.1%). Most of the sea animals are engraved on the left side of the frieze as if the ocean world is intentionally separated from the terrestrial world. There are about 20 species of animals whose species could be identified including large cetaceans, other sea animals like seals, fish, and seabirds; and land animals such as deer, or felines (Ulsan Petroglyphs Museum 2013).

Anthropomorphic figures

Anthropomorphic motifs recorded at the site comprise two faces and ten full-bodied figures, phallic and in profile. One exception is a motif on the lower left area of the panel with a unique form featuring stretched hands and legs, and no phallus. Some anthropomorphic motifs are engaged in scenes along with animals, like the one hunting deer with an arrow, or the figure holding an upside-down whale with one hand. The motif blowing a long stick, a masked face, and a naked figure with an exaggerated phallus all seem to represent special types of individuals, connected with symbolic/religious meaning.

Zoomorphic figures

Whale-species represented at Bangudae include sei, humpback, right, blue, and sperm whales, which are historically the ones caught in traditional whaling. Most are shown from above; those depicted in profile or horizontally are invariably rendered in a semi-twisted drawing technique. Particular species can be identified from anatomical details depicted in the motifs, such as skin folds, breathing, as well as form and location of the dorsal fin. Other details include head shape, or pectoral, dorsal, and caudal fins. Motifs in which these mammals are depicted upside down, with lines on their body perhaps represent dead animals. These lines could represent cutting lines, as known among the Makah (Lee 2011) (Figure 16.2).

Artiodactyls

Manchurian wapiti, Pekin sika, elk, roe deer and musk deer are native species to the Korean Peninsula and are also depicted at Bangudae. Generally thought as representing deer species, antlers are seen only among bucks of Manchurian wapiti, pekin sika and roe deer. Types of animals without antlers can be identified by the body shape, length of the tail, comparative lengths of the forelegs and hind legs.

Carnivores

Felines at Bangudae include tigers, leopards, lynx, and wildcats while canids include foxes, wolves, raccoons, and Asian wild dogs. Felines can be identified based on fur patterns, as in the case of tigers which have black lines all over the body; while leopards, lynx, and wildcats have black spots on the back. Felines also have a round head, slender body and long tail. By contrast, canids have long legs, thicker tail, sharp muzzle, and large triangular ears. Raccoons have a short head, sharp muzzle, thick and short tail, and thin legs.

Other animals

While whales, artiodactyls and carnivores account for most of the petroglyphs depicting animals, there are also other species including tortoises, fish and birds. Tortoises are mostly shown on the top or bottom of the rock face. There are also sharks, which look like whales but have slender head and body, and single fins. Noticeably at Bangudae, birds are always depicted close to whales. These scenes evoke how birds gather around feeding whales, providing an avenue for detection of whales from a distance. There are also two pinnipeds, either seals or sea lions, and two rabbits with pricked ears.

Fishing and hunting

Judging from the fact that the several hunting scenes depicted at Bangudae are very detailed, featuring boats, harpoons, floats, and nets, or even fishing traps, it is possible to infer that whale hunting seems to have thrived at

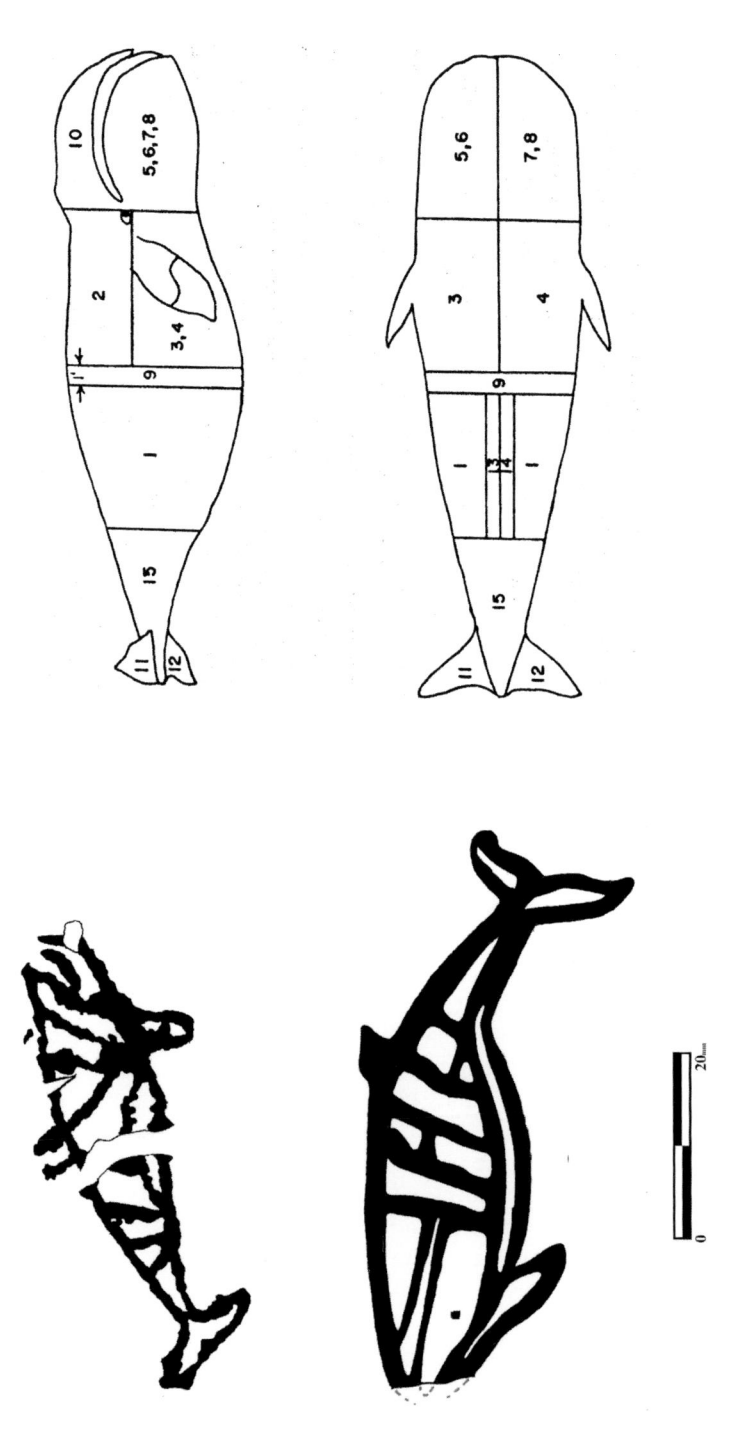

Figure 16.2 Lines on whales at Bangudae rock art and inferred Makah Lines. Documentation work by Lee (2003).

the time the rock art was made. Traditional whale hunting techniques seen across diverse ethnic groups include the use of boats and harpoons (Inuits), boats, floats and poison-applied harpoons (Aleuts), boats, and harpoons and nets (Ainous) (Lee 2011). As depicted at the panel, one of the major hunting targets during the Neolithic was deer, but tigers, otters, and foxes were also hunted, perhaps for food but mostly for their fur.

Chronology

The discovery of the Bangudae Petroglyphs puzzled the nation's archaeological researchers over the unexpected whaling hunting scenes. Nevertheless, many subsequently inferred their respective opinions on the chronology of the rock-art, ranging from the Palaeolithic Era to the Iron Age. The excavation of the Hwanseong-dong shell midden in the Ulsan shoreline in 2000, yielded remains of animals such as whales, wild boars, deer, seals, and sea lions along with materials typical of the Neolithic period. Dendrochronologic analysis of the layer where whale bones were found generated a date of 6,240±50 BP (Choi 2020). In the 2004 excavation of the Bibong-ri shell midden in Changnyeong, about 60km west of Ulsan, several artefacts were identified including net bags, wooden knives, pottery depicting boars and deer, acorn storage, and a wooden boat. Made of singed pine trees, 310–400cm long, 80cm width and about 20cm deep, the wooden boat was made using sharp stone tools, and is estimated to be about 8,000 years old. The results of paleoenvironmental studies suggest that the Bibong-ri site, current 30km inland, was located on the shoreline during this time (Joowon Shin 2020). In 2010, further research in Hwangseong-dong shell midden was conducted leading to the discovery of important vestiges (Eun-ah Choi 2020). The animal remains found in this site include those of whales, boars, elks, deer, sea lions, brown bears, raccoons, foxes, dogs, and tigers. Excluding brown bears, all these animal species can be found at the Bangudae rock-art panel. Of note are the three whale bones with piercing harpoon heads recovered, further supporting theories relating to the occurrence of whale hunting in the area during the Neolithic Age. The layer where these bones were identified produced a date of 5,410±50 BP to 5,090±50 BP (Eun-ah Choi 2020). Harpoons and whale bones were also found in lower layers, but the exact date could not be ascertained. However, the artefacts like pottery identified in these same layers indicate an Early Neolithic date. Since the Hwangseong-dong shell midden is located some 20 km from Bangudae, and many whale bones were found in the different layers dating back from 7,200 years to 3,500 years ago, the site is believed to be the place where whale hunters settled for thousands of years from the Early to the Middle Neolithic (Lee 2011). This site is believed to the most reliable archaeological evidence that supports a Neolithic dating for the Bangudae Petroglyphs, from 7,200 years BP to 3,500 years BP. It can thus be inferred that Bangudae features the oldest depictions of whale hunting.

Preservation of the Bangudae Petroglyphs

Since the identification of the Bangudae Petroglyphs site in 1971, researchers have recognized the need to keep rock art out of submerged water to improve preservation of its fabric (Ulsan Metropolitan City 2003), but unfortunately the matter has not been seriously considered until recently. This is due to the numerous archaeological and cultural heritage sites that have been submerged in recent decades in the process of constructing dams in South Korea to improve access to water storage for the population. This loss was accepted as inevitable in relation to the existing strength of national economic development policies. All archaeological researchers could achieve when large scale dam construction plans were in progress, was to carry out emergency excavations prior to submersion of the sites and/or to relocate cultural heritage assets in peril. As Bangudae was designated as a Korean National Treasure in 1995, calls on saving the petroglyphs began to rise, and preservation of these petroglyphs became a major issue at the academic seminar held in 2000 to celebrate the 30th anniversary of the discovery of Bangudae Petroglyphs. The local government of Ulsan City started seeking mitigation strategies to preserve Bangudae and avoid the negative effects of submersion by the waters of the dam. In 2003, assisted by the Stone Conservation Science Laboratory of Seoul University, Ulsan City proposed three ways to preserve the Bangudae: (1) Building a small barrier wall in front of the cliff where the petroglyphs are located; (2) Diverting the waterway; (3) Lowering the water level of the dam (Ulsan Metropolitan City 2003). Lowering the water level was selected following consultation with Korean Cultural Heritage Administration (KCHA), but a way to countermeasure water loss resulting from lowering the level was not considered at the time. The preservation of Bangudae Petroglyphs eventually became a political issue beyond the domain of science due to the differences of opinion between Ulsan City and KCHA (Ulsan Metropolitan City 2003).

In order to fully preserve the rock art, the most ideal solution is indeed to lower the water level of Sayeon Dam and both parties agreed on this. However, a solution for the resulting loss of water was a matter that was beyond the scope of heritage conservation policies, which typically do not deal with such matters. Eventually, the Minister's office at the central government pushed to mediate the differences between the two and proposed a new solution called 'Kinetic Dam'. The Kinetic Dam Project offered a long-term commitment by the central government to install an alternative anti-flood structure in front of the cliff as a temporary measure until other sources of water can compensate the loss of water if the level of Sayeon Dam is lowered. Professor Yoon-Seon Ham, proponent of this plan, believes this metal structure, mainly produced ex situ and then transferred to the site for assembly, can be easily dismantled in the future (Chegal et al. 2014). In the end, this proposal was accepted as ideal to solve the conflict between Ulsan City and KCHA by June 2013. However, following several unsuccessful trials with indoor experiments between December 2015 and July 2016, it was found that there were serious defects such as leakage of the structure (see newspaper articles https://www.donga.com/en/article/all/20160727/616908/1). Hence, the Technical Advisory Committee at the KCHA advised that, after all, this was not a feasible solution. Therefore, plans for the preservation of the Bangudae Petroglyphs had to be reviewed again. Subsequently, the Korean government is reviewing two alternative methods for preserving the Bangudae Petroglyphs:

- The first is to install floodgates in Sayeon Dam to lower the water level below 52m. In this case, it is expected that water storage of Sayeon Dam, currently at 19,510,000m^3, will be reduced to 6,660,000m^3. Drinking water would be supplied to the citizens of Ulsan by procuring a replacement resource elsewhere. To do this, a political process must be initiated including receiving agreement from the local government and residents; and not neglecting construction costs that must be secured at an estimated 232.5 billion wons (approximately 185,790,000 euros). Regarding this solution, what concerns the Korean government primarily is that it is difficult to reach the end of this whole process, including the construction of the alternative dam, in a short period of time; even if everything runs smoothly, namely building a national consensus supporting this course of action, since the Bangudae Petroglyphs cannot be left flooded for a long term (Ulsan Metropolitan City 20109).
- The second proposal is to install an embankment in front of the cliff of Bangudae Petroglyphs. While maintaining the water level at Sayeon Dam this solution would avoid flooding of the Bangudae Petroglyphs. This approach was suggested by Ulsan City in 2003 but KCHA raised the concern that the surrounding environment of the rock art panel could be damaged by the construction of the embankment thus taking the opposite stance (Ulsan Metropolitan City 2019).

In December 2010, the KCHA registered the Bangudae Petroglyphs in the UNESCO World Heritage Tentative List under the name "Daegok stream Petroglyphs". This process adheres to the principle that the surrounding environment must be maintained without major interference, so that the rock art site can be later nominated for inclusion on UNESCO's World Heritage List. Nevertheless, the petroglyphs have been repeatedly flooded for several months each year in the last 50 years and KCHA is facing criticism regarding neglect of the situation. The Korean government is now seeking advice from professionals of international heritage conservation institutions, as to whether establishing a dike has any negative effects regarding listing as World Heritage. If a consensus regarding the effects of the dike's construction is reached, the petroglyphs are to be rescued as quickly as possible by installing the embankment in front of the cliff. In the long-term, having in mind the first proposal as noted above, alternative water resources and lowering the water level along Sayeon Dam will continue to be considered and actively researched to assure a more permanent strategy for the long-term preservation of the Bangudae Petroglyphs.

Conclusion

Conservation matters relating to the Bangudae Petroglyphs that are repeatedly flooded by water in the dam has been found to be beyond the scope of the scientific community, and as such has emerged as a major issue in South Korea. This issue was brought up in an academic seminar commemorating the 30th anniversary of the discovery of Bangudae Petroglyphs in 2000 and since Ulsan City began seeking ways actively to rescue the rock art from the dam (Lee 2011). The exemplar story of the preservation of petroglyphs at the Côa Valley in Portugal, also threatened by the construction of a dam (Baptista and Fernandes 2007), was first introduced to Koreans in 2005 by television and newspapers. This has gradually contributed to building a consensus regarding the need to follow a similar approach in the case of the Bangudae. However, ten years were lost due to disagreements between the local government and KCHA. The hope is that what happened in Côa Valley could also happen in Korea quickly turned into disappointment and frustration because the swift decision-making regarding the preservation of rock art cultural heritage in Portugal was not replicated in Korea. To that regard, the prospect of losing the source that supplied drinking water to around a million inhabitants of Ulsan was a major caveat.

In 2010, the Korean government proposed as a goal to register Bangudae Petroglyphs as a UNESCO World Heritage Site in order to elicit the consent and support of the people to preserve the petroglyphs (Lee 2011). From September to December 2015, with the help of the Coa Park Foundation in Portugal, Ulsan Petroglyph Museum at Bangudae hosted the special exhibition "Côa Valley Petroglyphs" (Lee, Baptista and Fernandes 2015). Some 27,000 people, including officers with relevant roles in Korea's cultural heritage department, visited the exhibition. Moreover, there was a special exhibition to introduce Bangudae Petroglyphs for the first time abroad from June to October in 2016 at the Coa Museum in Portugal. The conservation of the Bangudae Petroglyphs is at this point recognized as an important indicator of overall Korea Cultural Heritage Policy and it is obvious that the petroglyphs cannot be allowed to become periodically flooded any longer. The problem remains which method or methods to choose and when they will become effective. Even if a perfect conservation method is finally applied, it will be meaningless if the rock art has disappeared from the cliff. The recently elected new Mayor of Ulsan, Song Chul Ho laid out a new policy direction for preserving the Bangudae Petroglyphs recently. As a result, in September 2019, the KCHA and Ulsan City joined hands to sign a Memorandum of Understanding to preserve the Bangudae by lowering the dam level (Lee 2021). Behind this achievement was the conservation campaign effort by a civic group led by the voluntary participation of Ulsan citizens in 2018, as well as favourable reporting in the local media. It is now expected that the Bangudae Petroglyphs will finally be preserved once and for all in favourable conservation conditions (that is, not facing the negative impact of repeated flooding episodes) for the benefit of Korea, its citizens, and, above all, future generations.

References

Baptista, A. M. and Fernandes, A. P. B. (2007) Rock art and the Côa Valley Archaeological Park: A case study in the preservation of Portugal's Prehistoric parietal heritage. In Pettitt, P., Bahn, P. and Ripoll, S. (Eds.) *Palaeolithic Cave Art at Creswell Crags in European Context.* Oxford: Oxford University Press, pp.263–279.

Chegal, S. D., Cho, H. J., Kang, H. S., and Lee, S. O. (2014) An experimental study on hydraulic characteristics at Bangudae petroglyphs by changing management water level of Sa-Yeon Dam. *Korean Society of Hazard Mitigation,* 14(2), pp.277–287.

Choi Eun-ah (2020) *Results of Excavation of the Ulsan Hwangseong-dong remain, Whale on the Rock IV,* Ulsan Petroglyphs Museum, Ulsan. (South Korea).

Joowon Shin (2020) *A study of Changnyeong Bibong-ri site*, Whale On the Rock IV, Ulsan Petroglyphs Museum, Ulsan. (South Korea).

Laming-Emperaire, A and Baudez, C. (1968) *La Préhistoire.* PUF: France.

Lee, S. (2003) *Les gravures rupestres du site de Bangu-dae dans la partie méridionale de la péninsule coréenne.* PhD Thesis. Paris: École doctorale Sciences de la nature et de l'Homme - Évolution et écologie.

Lee, S. (2007) Coree, l'autre Neolithique. In *Les Grandes Dossiers Sciences Humaines,* 9. Éditeur Association de formation, d'études et de recherche en sciences humaines, pp. 52–54.

Lee, S. (2011) *Chasseurs de Baleines: La frise de Bangudae (Corée du Sud).* París: Editions Errance.

Lee, S. (2021) *The Preservation of Prehistoric Rock Art Sites in Korea.* París: IPH.

Lee, S., Baptista, A. M. and Fernandes, A. B. (Eds.) (2015) *Arte Rupestre do Vale do Côa. Exhibition Catalogue.* Ulsan, South Korea: Ulsan Petroglyph Museum, pp.164–186.

Mou-Chang Choi (1987) Le Paléolithique de Corée. *L'Anthropologie,* 91(3), pp.755–786.

Mung-Dae Moon (1984) *Petroglyphs of Bangudae,* Seoul (South Korea): Dongkuk University Press.

Pow-Key Son (1974) Les cultures paléolithiques. *Revue de Corée,* VI, pp. 15–16.

Sang-Il Hwang and Soon-Ok Yoon (2014) *Geographical Environment of Daekokcheon Stream, Bangudae Petroglyph in Daekok-ri Ulsan 67-54-71,* Ulsan Petroglyph Museum (South Korea).

Testart, A. (1982) *Les Chasseurs-cueilleurs ou l'origine des inégalités.* París: Ed. Société d'Ethnographie.

Ulsan Metropolitan City (2003) *Damage Diagnosis on the Bangudae Petroglyphs and Its Conservation Scheme* (South Korea).

Ulsan Metropolitan City (2019) *Reports on Preservation of Bangudae Petroglyphs* (South Korea).

Ulsan Petroglyphs Museum (2013) *Bangudae Petroglyphs in Daeko-ri, Korean Rock Art III, Ulsan* (South Korea).

17 Rock Art Conservation in the Serra Branca Valley, Serra da Capivara National Park, Piauí, Brazil

Thalison dos Santos and Cristiane de Andrade Buco

Introduction

To characterise rock art damage in the Serra Branca Valley, west side of Serra da Capivara National Park (Piauí, Brazil), field surveys took place, aiming to identify, describe and map the main agents of qualitative modification. However, in order to introduce the time equation in the approach, rock art conservation was related to both the whole span of human occupation in the area and environmental change.

It is assumed that the comprehension of rock art damage as a system provides precise parameters for the development of predictive models and curatorial actions to treat and reverse damage. This could help as well with the definition of long-term management activities, budgets more adapted to the local reality, and of protocols for monitoring rock art sites. As such, rock art conservation research is seen as a noteworthy source for setting up guidelines to achieve an ideal culture for preservation and conservation of the art of past societies at the Serra Branca Valley.

Archaeology in the Serra Branca Valley

Rock art studies at the Serra Branca Valley begun within excavation projects in a set of archaeological sites belonging to the area of the Serra da Capivara National Park, a World Heritage site (see Nash 2009). At the time, rock art was considered as part of a preliminary regional cultural characterisation and a classification was established, including the Nordeste, Agreste, Geométrica and Itacoatiaras traditions (Guidon 1975, 1985, 1986). Later, other rock art styles were integrated in the Nordeste tradition, such as Serra da Capivara, Serra Branca, Serra Talhada complex (Guidon 1986, 1989; Pessis 1992, 2003) and Angelim (Morales Jr. 2002).

Rock art attributed to the Nordeste tradition is very common in this area and constitutes the best studied prehistoric imagery group. Generally,

DOI: 10.4324/9780429355349-22

figures of the Nordeste tradition comprise scenes, with a richness of details expressing movement and action. These compositions usually describe aspects of everyday life, such as hunting, sexual intercourse, dancing, warfare, and others. The Serra Branca sub-style, for example, these scenes generally incorporate geometric patterns besides human and animal representations, especially of deer.

This precise rock art style is assumed to be autochthonous to the Serra Branca Valley (Santos 2010). Its recognition was firstly based on studies undergone at Toca do Vento, where the main characteristic of anthropomorphic and zoomorphic figures is their geometric bodies, which can also appear filled in with other smaller geometric motifs (Guidon 1975). However, some figures were only outlined and void inside, or, to the contrary were fully filled in with red, white or yellow colours, in monochrome or polychrome arrangements. Serra Branca style motifs range in dimension from 15 up to 160 cm.

Between the 1990s and the 2000s, excavation work intensified at the Serra Branca Valley, especially at Toca do Vento, Toca da Extrema II and in nine other rock shelters. By that time, landscape surveys were also taking place throughout the escarpments, slopes and ravines following the edges of the valley as at the top of the plateau. Consequently, 200 rock art sites were identified and registered at the Serra Branca valley (Buco 2012, vol.3).

In the 2010s, one of the authors (CAB) undertook PhD research on the Serra Branca Valley rock art. This investigation intended to relate archaeological contexts revealed by the excavations with the rock art in the panels above and below ground. This was possible due to overlapping figures, panels buried associated with archaeological stratigraphy contexts, and the possibility of reassembling rock fragments with rock art incomplete motifs found in the said contexts (Buco 2012).

A database helped with data systematisation regarding superimpositions, such as the presence and absence of sequential painting moments, quantities and types of figures, relative chronology of overlapping motifs, scene compositions, and production aspects. Gathered information correlated with excavated contexts, especially the equivalence between the quantity of occupational levels and the number of rock art categories and superpositions. This allowed the definition of a chronological model for human occupation at the Serra Branca Valley. The analysis of more than 10,000 figures and archaeological data from 12 excavated and dated rock shelters made possible to recognise the spatial distribution of the new rock art categories identified, which have been tentatively associated with different migration moments. Therefore, a new model for human movement in the valley was proposed in the form of at least four great migratory movements (Table 17.1).

Table 17.1 Chronology of human occupation at the Serra Branca Valley

Human Occupation	Chronology	Material Culture	Rock Art	Main Archaeological Sites
1st Movement Grandes Animais	Older than 10,800 BP	Not found	Large animal paintings	Toca do Vento, Toca do João Arsena, Toca do Veado, Toca do Pinga do Boi
2nd Movement Povos de Transição	Between 10,800 to 6,060 BP	Lithic tools such as scrapers and projectile points	Rock art panels with figures displaying movement, painted rock fragments, yellow and red ochres	Toca do Pau d'oia, Toca do Pica-Pau, Toca Nova do Inharé, Toca do Pinga do Boi, Toca da Extrema II, Toca do João Leite, Toca do Vento
3rd Movement Povos de Passagem	4,970 BP to 940 BP	Lithic tools such as polished hand axes, pestles and mortars, smooth and corrugated ceramics	Rock paintings, godets, lithic tools with pigment and engravings	Toca do Pinga da Escada, Toca do Morcego, Toca da Extrema II, Toca da Gamela, Toca do João Leite, Toca do Mulungu
4th Movement Histórico	400 BP to 1980s	Ceramics, working instruments, porcelains and glasses	Engravings, board games, mobile pestles, black, beige and white paintings	Toca do Caixa-Prego I to XII, Toca do Boqueirão do Cícero, Toca da Igrejinha, Toca da Mangueira do João Paulo, Toca dos Nomes

Source: Adapted Buco, 2012.

The first migration moment in the area is that of the "Grandes Animais" ("Great Animals"), and it took place at the end of the Upper Pleistocene, around 12,270 years BP. It is characterised by large animal figures, especially deer and rheas and possibly refers to nomadic hunter-gatherer cultures. These figures normally appear depicted in low areas of panels and are believed to be contemporary with the first human occupation levels at Serra Branca (Buco 2012).

The second occupation movement corresponds to the "Povos de Transição" ("Transition Peoples"), which refers to groups that reached the valley during the Early Holocene. These groups were also hunter-gatherers, but they introduced a more descriptive type of rock art, intensifying the composition of scenes, especially those reporting everyday life, namely activities like hunting, dancing and warfare. Figures very difficult to interpret were also produced, probably linked to the mythical universe (Buco 2012).

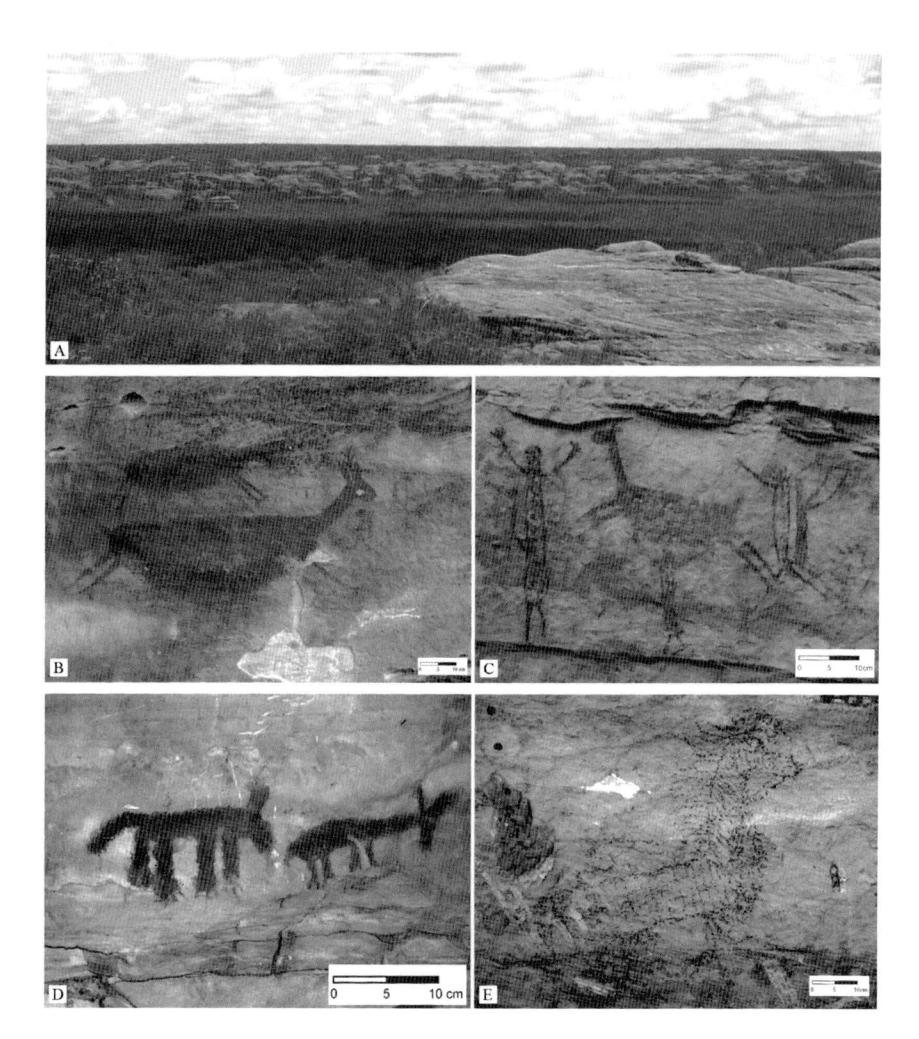

Figure 17.1 Landscape and rock-art of the four occupational movements at the Serra Branca Valley, Serra da Capivara National Park, Piauí, Brazil. (a) Partial view of the Valley. (b) Movement 1" Grandes Animais" (Toca do Veado archaeological site); (c) Movement 2 "Povos de transição" (Toca do Pinga do Boi archaeological site); (d) Movement 3 "Povos de Passagem" (Toca do Pinga da Escada archaeological site); (e) Movement 4 "Histórico" (Toca do Boqueirão do Cícero IV archaeological site). Credits: Buco 2012.

The third occupation movement is constituted by the "Povos de Passagem" ("Passage Peoples"), which introduced engravings in rock art production and increased the variability of painted themes, forms and techniques. It is important to mention that the introduction of engravings is also contemporary to technical alterations in lithic industry assemblages and to environmental change, as greener vegetation got scarce and became gradually substituted by semiarid deciduous thorn woodlands (Buco 2012). This phenomenon is dated to the Middle Holocene.

The fourth and last occupational movement refers to the "Histórico" ("Historic"), and it congregates the rock art produced in more recent periods, especially between the 1700s and the 1980s. This type of rock art comprises black, beige and white painted motifs like lines, circles, squares, rifles, cars, aeroplanes and people as well as written messages that involve names, ages and entire sentences. Engravings are also present, especially those produced with metal tools, which are easily distinguishable from those ones produced by stone tools due to the patinas and thicknesses. They consist mostly of grooves, smooth or polished surfaces, and board games (Buco 2012).

The images produced in colonial and historical periods have much to add to the study of rock art in Brazil, as they can function as time markers in chronological ordering, and as model to rock art differentiation, helping the comprehension of the standards that make them a diagnostic artefact. In the Serra Branca valley, a particular type of historical rock art is attributed to a group locally known as the "Maniçobeiros" (Buco et al. 2020). They were workers of the latex industry, which explored plant rubber of the genus *Manihot glaziovii* in the first half of the 20th century (Oliveira 2014).

Dynamic approach on rock art conservation

A dynamic approach to rock art conservation was conceived and applied at the Serra Branca Valley. In this framework, it was possible to analyse the conservation problems associated with rock art arising from human occupations in the area, dating back to the Pleistocene/Holocene transition until the recent periods. Therefore, it is argued that a holistic and historical view on rock art conservation could be achieved.

Threats to existing rock art in this area are as old as the first human occupations, dated to the Pleistocene/Holocene transition. Therefore, rock art conservation has a historical dimension, and is integrated into human sociocultural systems and the environment. Thereby, natural factors such as the climate, temperature, precipitation, humidity, vegetation, fauna, etc. need to be in the same explanation framework as human occupation.

In order to be able to state that there are agents of qualitative modification damaging the rock art, as well as to provide their characterisation and spatial distribution, it was necessary to define damage. The idea of damage systems regarding rock art conservation suggests that there is a gradual movement between two extremes of qualitative states. One extreme is an excellent condition of rock art motifs, while the other a poor condition. However, what one observes at the rock art sites is that it is difficult to affirm or demonstrate what would be an optimal quality condition. Thus, it is assumed that an optimal quality would be the instant right after rock art production. That is, the moment when weathering processes and agents of qualitative modification started to interact with fresh rock art motifs.

The agents of qualitative modification are those elements of intensity, strength, and frequency that can bring rock art from one quality situation to another. They have been operating since the introduction of the artwork in the sociocultural system and in the environment. Anthropogenic forces usually trigger damage to the rock art through the different uses and functions the society gives to the sites. For examples, use of the rock shelters for residence (Oliveira et al. 2020) or when performing sacred and ritual activities, such as the use of space for ex-votos (Cavalcante et al. 2007; Lage et al. 2009).

On the other hand, indirect human factors contributing to rock art damage are mostly those triggered due to the presence of a given sociocultural system near to the artistic territory of previous cultures. This may start a dynamic and instrumental web of agents of modification, which the intensities can remain unknown without detailed investigation. For instance, the use of wood as fuel to produce pottery, deforestation and horticulture, even if they occur kilometres away from a rock art area can trigger distinct patterns of mobility in the fauna and in other agents, leading to the emergence of rock art damage processes and features.

Sociocultural systems are entangled with natural systems forming a complex dynamic that involve agents of qualitative modification intensities that act as a single entity operating in synergy. Natural geological and geomorphological characteristics associated with climate dynamics eliminate or create conditions for agents of qualitative modification to set up and perform damage symmetrically or asymmetrically. At the same time, the cultural decision of establishing settlements in such an area triggers new damage processes interacting like a network. If this sociocultural system ages and develops itself culturally and demographically, more intense the rock art damage will be.

Issues in rock art conservation emerge from unfavourable situations regarding condition, integrity, and maintenance. These normally derive from the dynamics of agents of qualitative modification systematically related, and constantly moving the rock art from a higher quality status or ideal conservation scenario to a lower quality or worse conservation status.

Hence, we should endeavour to recognise conservation problems and relate them to their most likely triggering agents, in order to mitigate, neutralise or reverse unfavourable situations to the rock art. What is expected though is that the dynamics in the damage systems and the performance of the agents of qualitative modification become minimally controlled or predictable. This will be a step forward in avoiding threats and to prevent the development of irreversible rock art damage.

Materials and methods

This dynamic study of rock art conservation at Serra Branca took place in a context comprising a consistent background connecting the chronology of human occupation with specific artistic assemblages. This allowed for a more precise definition of human impact in rock art damage. To this end, a four-step protocol was developed.

The first step comprised the organisation of information gathered from surveys in the rock shelters. At this point, the evidence of artistic practice related to one or more occupational periods was identified, divided and compared with rock art styles. This helped establishing rapports between human activities in buried contexts with artistic practices in open air panels.

The second step was the acquisition of conservation data through the development and application of conservation formularies. Attributes considered the presence or absence of agents of qualitative modification, categorisation, measurement, sampling of deposits and visual record reproduction. Other guidelines concerned mostly with the rock art integrity were related to the identification of complete and incomplete figures. Aspects of visual quality such as the causes of pigment fading were also considered. Information was extracted from the surrounding context such as the presence of vegetation and its potential for protection of the rock art, geographical insertion and topographic position, sun and seasonal rain exposition, and the presence or absence of sedimentary packages. This protocol was applied in 200 rock shelters at the Serra Branca Valley distributed throughout a length of 22 km (Buco 2012, vol.3).

The data collected in the conservation formularies, the third step, were processed and turned into visual information. Especially, maps, in order to help in the spatial perception of rock art damage systems, and the characterisation of qualitative modification agents, as well as their symmetrical and asymmetrical performance and intensities, as to compose a more holistic interpretation.

The last step of the protocol involved the development of curatorial activities for the treatment and mitigation of damage to the rock art, as well as neutralisation/mitigation of qualitative modification agents. These interventions, however, only took place after acquiring a more complete comprehension about the behaviour and negative impact of these agents. A methodological evaluation was considered, in order to avoid technical mistakes, such as the imposition of alien and decontextualised techniques and materials not suited to effectively adapt to the specificities of the studied area. Each rock art site was understood as a subsystem, and therefore, the curatorial techniques were developed inductively for each one.

Physical damage

Identified physical agents of qualitative modification operating at Serra Branca Valley correspond to fracture systems, peeling processes, rock disaggregation, and detachments of stonewalls and stone-ceilings. These processes are influenced mostly by temperature oscillation, especially between day and night, characteristic of semiarid climate. During the day, while exposed to the sunlight and to higher temperatures, the rock concentrates thermal energy, which dissipates in the night, when temperature decreases. As an effect of this, the rocks contract and expand, fostering the emergence of internal and superficial fracture lines.

Other phenomena, such as rain, wind and gravity also play an important role in the fragmentation of rock art panels. Rainwater usually triggers chemical weathering, but it also penetrates in fractures, widening them through particle removal and dissolution. In drought periods, especially in the second semester of each year, wind erosion intensifies in sites where rock art is more exposed. This leads to rock disaggregation due to the clash of sediment particles, in saltation or in suspension, against decorated panels. This scenario is more evident in shelters placed on the higher slopes of the Serra Branca Valley. On the other hand, rock art sites in the low-lying topographies near to the base of the valley are more susceptible to mechanical damage processes related to wetter periods.

In the rainy season, water action intensifies leaving damp areas, sometimes inside archaeological sites. Water passage through the rock shelters erodes sedimentary packages and rocky surfaces also penetrating fractures in the sandstone and accelerating their fragmentation. As fracture lines increase, gravity contributes to the collapse of large panels holding rock art. The detached pieces of rock fall down with the decorated panels facing the ground, making them susceptible to weathering processes in the deposit.

Systems of fracture may vary in size and in number of interconnections. They spread superficially and internally in the sandstones, siltstones and conglomerates, and can be longstanding, related to geological processes like geological faults and seismicity. A more intense system of fracture is more effective in individualising sections from the walls and ceilings of the sites. Fractures may be set in association with rock-peeling or rock slab detachments. The first one refers to the fall of small and fine crusts from the surfaces of rocks, while the second one corresponds to the detachment of quadrangular, heavier and profound slabs which are thicker than 2 cm. Both compromise rock art panels by the breakage of painted and engraved surfaces.

The neutralisation of fracture systems, peeling and slab detachments is possible, as well as the refit of fallen fragments into their original position in the decorated panels. As most of the painted and engraved pieces of rocks are found buried in the deposit, this refitting must be preceded by systematic excavation. Analysis of these fragments and the whole decorated support is also required, in order to identify their correct place in the incomplete panels. Larger portions of panels are easier to refit unlike the fine superficial crusts resulting from rock peeling. Fragments of rock art panels were found within the stratigraphic deposit at Toca do Vento, Toca do Veado, Toca do Pinga do Boi, Toca da Extrema II and Toca do Pica-Pau archaeological sites in association with other cultural traces like lithic tools, bonfire structures and occupational soils.

Biological damage

Identified biological agents triggering mechanical and chemical processes (Casseti 2005) of qualitative modification at Serra Branca valley correspond to insects, especially, wasps, bees and termites, as well as vertebrate animals like small rodents, reptiles, and monkeys. In addition, other living organisms such as trees, fungi, lichens and algae also cause multiple damage to the rock art.

Insects often dwell in the rock shelters, where they construct nests and galleries. Wasps, for example, are persistent organisms in using rock shelters. They tend to recycle abandoned nests or even to reconstruct new ones in the same spots where older structures were established (Perioto and Lara 2018). This facilitates the creation of deposits of clay and mud upon the rock paintings and engravings.

Isopteran insects, which are very common in hot and dry tropical regions, have a huge seasonal impact on the environments they occupy. They modify landscapes, topographies and the physical-chemistry properties of the soil by building up huge nest structures (Holt and Lepage 2000; Ferreira et al. 2011). The construction of galleries on rock art panels induces to micro-chemical reactions, impairing the quality of ancient images. For instance, the architecture of termite galleries allows the stabilisation of the internal atmosphere and temperature, as moisture is very harmful to these organisms (Ratcliffe et al. 1952; Noirot and Darlington 2000; Ferreira et al. 2011). These internal environments allow exchanging optimal oxygen and carbon rates (Noirot and Darlington 2000; Ferreira et al. 2011), which tends to trigger the emergence of mineral deposits over the rock paintings, as well as pigment fading.

Other behaviour of these insects is polyphagia, which makes them to stock various types of materials, such as cellulose, wood, faeces and minerals. These materials mixed with the termites' saliva used in nesting, drive to cementation processes (Castro Junior 2002; Zanetti et al. 2010; Ferreira et al. 2011), creating patinas and thick deposits on rock art panels.

Rock shelters that are directly exposed to sunlight offer the best conditions for termites to establish colonies. This situation was found in Toca do Pica-Pau, where large termite galleries spread throughout the panels and in the stratigraphy. Galleries were constructed in the rock fractures binding their housing nucleus to the areas of food acquisition. Interactions between the termite constructions and thermal conditions turned some of these tracks into concreted deposits, accelerating the fragmentation of rock art panels. Pieces of rock art panels with cemented termite nest prints were found in stratigraphy and refitted into their original position.

Insects are the most frequent agents of qualitative modification in this area. But small mammal species adapted to rocky systems, such as the mocó (*Kerodon rupestris*) and monkeys (*Sapajus libidinosus* and *Callithrix*) may additionally contribute to the fragmentation of rock art panels due to climbing activity. They also leave organic deposits over the rock art panels like faeces, urine and food scraps. These materials interact with minerals modifying the properties of pigments and the natural colours of sandstones.

Other biological problems are related to penetration of plant roots in the fractures, which promotes rock detachments. Also, fungi, lichens and algae usually lead to the emergence of distinct features, like stains and patinas of multiple colours covering the paintings and provoking pigment sharpness loss. This is due to the symbiotic association with cyanobacteria, which spreads throughout the panels during the rainy season (Cavalcante et al. 2008). These organisms corrode pigments and rock, leaving spotted spongy-like surfaces.

Chemical damage

Agents of qualitative modification triggering chemical reactions that damage rock art at the Serra Branca valley are mostly rainwater and heat. These environmental phenomena associated with other conditions, such as rock permeability, relief, hydrostatic position, and chemical composition, also play an important role in the emergence of damage (Demattê 1974; Casseti 2005).

Rock art in this area was usually inscribed on sandstones cemented by quartz, iron oxides and hydroxides, as well as other heavy minerals of the Canindé group (Silva et al. 2003). These minerals react with rainwater and thermal conditions, causing the solubilisation of prehistoric pigments and rock material. Moreover, it may trigger the deposition of mineral layers over rock art panels.

Rainwater is by far the most intense force triggering chemical reactions that cause the loss of rock art in the area, especially during the rainy season.

It deposits numerous chemical compounds and removes others from the decorated rocks. In this process different deposits appear to lead to paint fading, corrosion, and pigment oxidation. Pluvial water also comprises acids that can interact with carbon dioxide in the atmosphere forming carbonic acid, which may modify qualitative property of rocks in a long-term interaction (Demattê 1974).

Saline efflorescence is the strongest chemical rock art modifier leading to quality loss. Soluble and insoluble inorganic salts brought by rainwater remain on the sandstones and usually form white and grey layers (Cavalcante and Rodrigues 2009) after the surfaces dry. These salts also migrate by capillarity from the interior of the rocks reaching the painted surfaces due to evapotranspiration (Cavalcante et al. 2008; Cavalcante and Rodrigues 2009).

Likewise, silica and calcium form crystalline micro layers leading to the formation of varnishes on top of rock art contributing to pigment fading and paintings loss of sharpness. Despite these irretrievable damage features, calcite deposits can assist in indirect dating of rock-art (Pessis et al. 2012). Furthermore, other chemical processes related to hydration, hydrolysis and dissolution (Casseti 2005; Macedo 2017) also bring damage to the rock art, especially dissolution, common at the Serra Branca Valley.

Anthropic damage

Human actions that resulted in damage to the Serra Branca rock art were carried out consciously or unconsciously, according to distinct circumstances, purposes and motivations. Most of the ancient forms of damage are the overlapping and the repainting of figures, which could have been practiced under territorial disputes and cultural substitution, or even under playful and naive aesthetic issues. These human actions are very common in the rock art produced in the Early Holocene attributed to the "Povos de Passagem", which overlaps the "Grandes Animais" art, dated to the Pleistocene/Holocene transition. This practice continues with the development of more recent types of rock art.

Other human activities, however, played an important role in the development rock art damage, such as living and housing in the rock shelters. These activities were common in pre-colonial times, but have been going on until the 1980s, especially, during the latex industry intensification between the 1900s and 1960s. Many of the latex workers (known as Catingueiros da Borracha and Maniçobeiros) in this area established family housing in the rock shelters, such as at the Toca do João Sabino, Toca da Mangueira do João Paulo and Toca do Juazeiro da Serra Branca (Oliveira 2014).

The recent use of rock art sites impacted the rock shelters and their surroundings. Human presence in these places attracted living organisms highly dependent on human habitats, like insects, rats and lizards. In addition, mud and wood constructions were normally used to create internal divisions in the sheltered areas, and sometimes, these walls were built directly on top rock art panels. In these contexts, engraved panels became subject of intentional coverings with clay pastes, in order to avoid insect proliferation, like wasps, scorpions and other venomous animals. However, the main problem linked to domestic use of the rock shelters is the spreading of kitchen soot on the decorated panels. In addition, cooking fires near to the rock art panels consumes the oxygen in the rocks, facilitating fractures and fragmentation.

Hunters are another group that used the Serra Branca rock shelters as camp areas. Their actions left plenty of irreversible damage features to the rock art and to the stratigraphic records. While camping at these sites, hunters usually set fire for cooking and for warming themselves during the night and dug up holes in the ground or in the rock walls, in order to suspend their sleeping hammocks. Another type of damage is related to the use of the decorated panels as grinding surfaces for knives, axes and other iron tools. Profound grinding grooves resulting from this activity have been identified in several rock shelters in this area.

These recent occupations in the rock shelters left, likewise, figurative and abstract drawings, as well as written messages overlapping the earlier rock art. These records usually refer to personal names, dates, phrases and toponyms, and are linked to at least, two groups. The first group is composed of functional literate people that inscribed written messages, and the second one is probably composed of illiterate people, which produced isolated figurative images like airplanes, cars and board games. These types of records imply different social situations and meanings in the expression of messages and cognitive content.

Rock art damage in this area is likewise linked to human activities taking place outside the rock shelters. The establishment of large economic activities and agricultural settlements affected natural systems, such as fauna and flora. Deforestation and the introduction of domestic animals in these areas influenced the mobility of native fauna, and several savage species started to be hunted and had to change their habitats. In this context, some species increased in numbers at the Capivara National Park, and this had implications to the use of rock shelters, principally by monkeys that are preyed on by large cats. Agricultural areas near to the Serra Branca Valley are also prone to fire outbreaks, especially in the long drought periods. Two major fire events affected Serra Branca and the rock shelters back in the 1980s, and later in the 2000s.

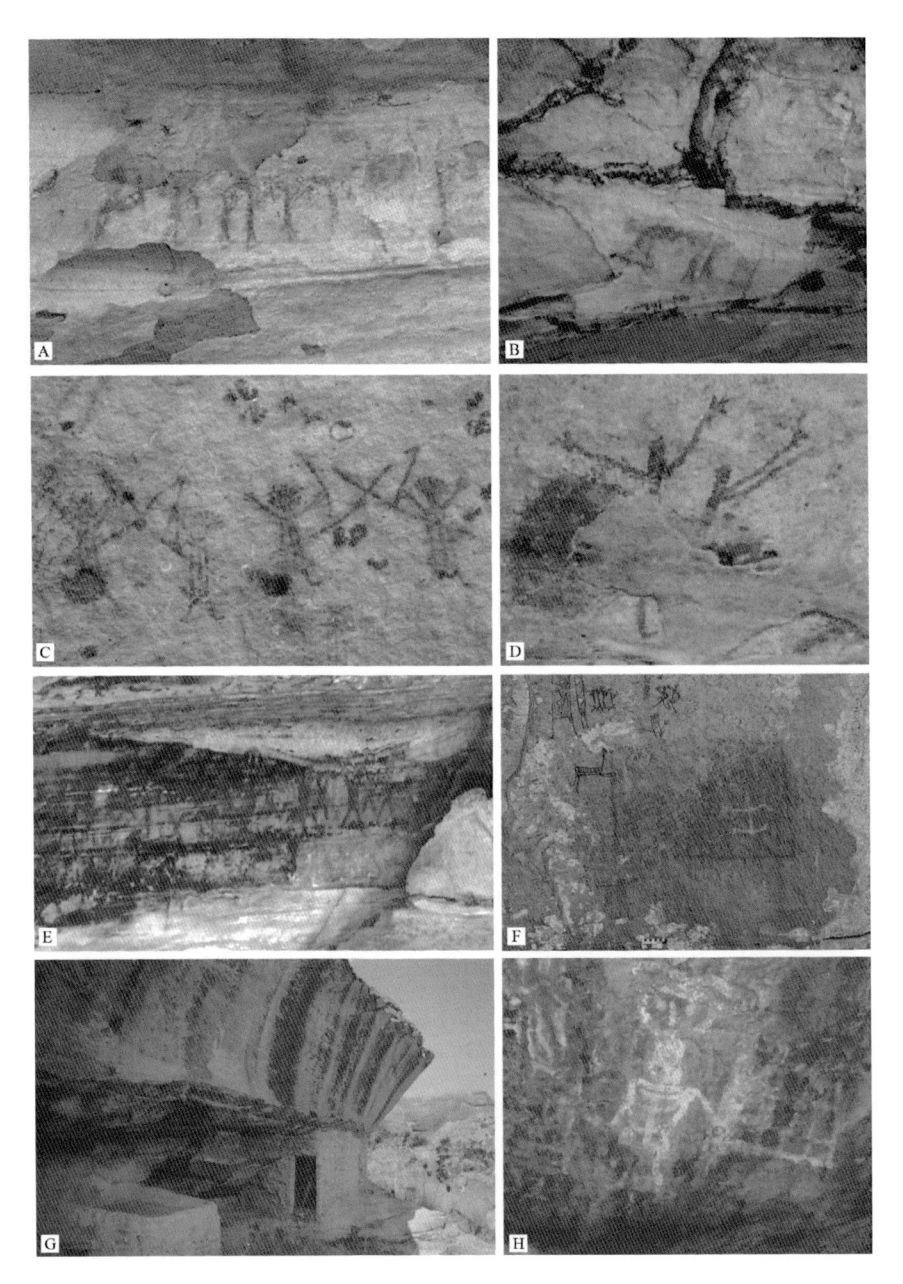

Figure 17.2 Physical, biological, chemical and anthropical damages in Rock-art of the Serra Branca Valley, Serra da Capivara National Park, Piauí, Brazil. (a) Cracking lines, plaquette detachments and Maria pobre galleries (Toca do Chaves I archaeological site); (b) Termite's galleries (Toca do Mondrongo archaeological site); (c). Fungi (Toca do Vento archaeological site); (d) Rock peeling (Toca do Gado archaeological site); (e) Rainwater and Lichens (Toca do Pinga da Escada archaeological site); (f) Saline (Toca do Morcego archaeological site); g) Rainwater and human habitat (Toca do João Sabino archaeological site); (h) Fire for cooking (Toca do Baixão do Caixa Prego II archaeological site). Credits: Buco 2012.

Entangled agents of qualitative modification

Actions driving qualitative modification and damage to the rock art are systematically entangled. Their interrelation is, however, mediated by their frequency and continuity through time, which results in more or less intense damage scenarios. Environmental aspects, such as semiarid climate conditions and seasonality play an important role in the rotation between pluvial water/landscape dryness. Droughts are not uncommon to last for years. In the lack of moisture, physical weathering and rock fragmentation occur mostly from the accumulation of thermal energy, wind, and sunlight exposition. On the other hand, in a context of extreme moisture and torrential rain, physical and chemical weathering are interrelated, accelerating the fragmentation of rocks, corrosion and deposition of mineral layers on the rock art panels. Whatever the case, there are interactions running between the agents of qualitative modification and several variables in the systems in which rock art is inserted in. The natural properties of rocks, such as their mineralogical and chemical composition, and depositional structures (Bigarella et al. 1994; Casseti 2005) also regulate the emergence and evolution of distinct damage features. This network of actions may result in reversible or irreversible scenarios.

Environmental and climate changes influence the emergence, evolution, and intensity of rock art damage. It is assumed that the intensification of biological agents at Serra Branca Valley, especially different types of plants and ectothermic insects, such as termites and wasps, is related to climate change. At the region, excavated sediment packages record one such incident in the Middle Holocene, around 6,000 years BP, resulting in the substitution of humid and fresh climate by a warmer and drier one (Buco 2012; Campos 2015). This event is contemporary to the 2nd occupational movement, when the Povos de Transição tradition gradually disappears in the archaeological record. At the same time, deciduous thorn woodlands expanded. This new situation would have favoured the establishment of termite and wasp habitats at the shelters, bringing biological damage to the rock art panels. Evidence acquired when excavating Toca do Pica-Pau point to that hypothesis, as large termite nests and galleries compromising the rock art above the ground and in stratigraphic deposit were dated indirectly to the mentioned period (Buco 2012). Most of the biological damage they produced in that rock art site corresponded to patinas and rock disaggregation (Buco 2012).

After the complete establishment of the semiarid climate, temperature fluctuations and chronic drought periods became a common trace in the area. The water supply decreased, and rock art damage was distributed in distinct patterns throughout the Serra Branca valley. The topographical position of the rock shelters is an apparent factor that determines the intensity, frequency and the evolution of agents and damage. The sites located on the high slopes tend to suffer more from physical weathering, mostly arising from the action of wind and heat, leading to rock disaggregation and thermal breakings. On the other hand, the sites in the low heights, or in moisture islands typical of the deep ravines, tend to receive more damage caused by biological agents, such as fungi and algae, as well as chemical reactions and mineral deposits.

Fungi and algae are very common during the rainy seasons in the deep and narrow ravines of the Serra Branca valley. These agents usually lead to the formation of black patinas on the painted and engraved figures, as well as the loss of sharpness, and liberation of acids that corrode grooves and produce perforations in distinct decorated areas. At Pinga da Escada rock shelter, where these living organisms have been covering up seasonally large portions of the rock art panels, some of them remained undetected for at least 20 years (Guidon et al. 2007). Only in the 2000s, due to curatorial actions aiming to deactivate several horizontal and vertical pluvial drainages was it possible to find several rock art panels up to then covered by algae and fungi black patinas.

Big fire events in the Serra Branca Valley led to the reduction of vegetal cover, increasing heat in the rock shelters and producing several thermal fractures in the rock art panels. To further complicate matters, hunting, a strong cultural activity in this area, created an imbalance in the food chain, as the anteaters and armadillo population, natural predators of several insects especially the termites, was reduced considerably. As a result, insect presence greatly increased in the area.

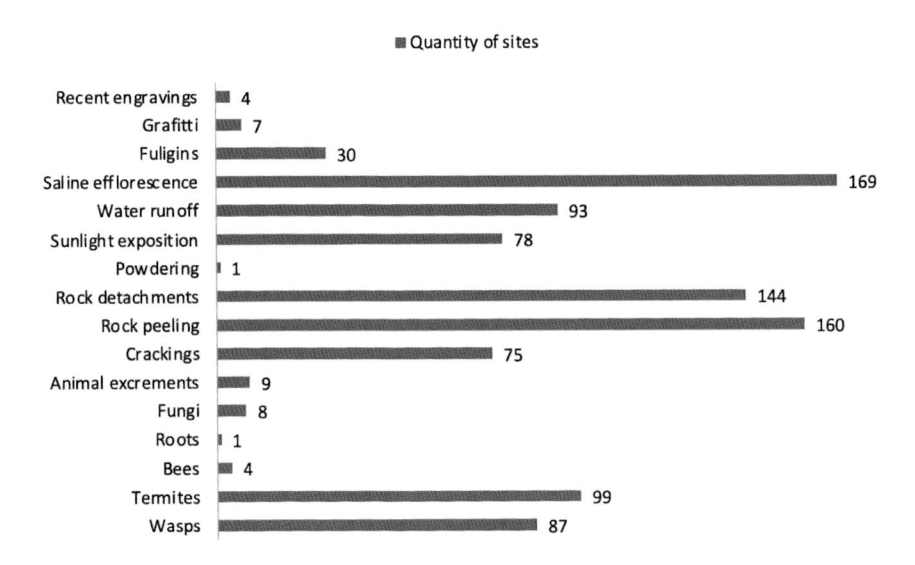

■ Quantity of sites

Agent	Quantity
Recent engravings	4
Grafitti	7
Fuligins	30
Saline efflorescence	169
Water runoff	93
Sunlight exposition	78
Powdering	1
Rock detachments	144
Rock peeling	160
Crackings	75
Animal excrements	9
Fungi	8
Roots	1
Bees	4
Termites	99
Wasps	87

Figure 17.3 Most common damage agents in the rock art of the Serra Branca Valley.

Rock art curatorial intervention

A dynamic approach to rock art conservation characterised damage to the Serra Branca valley rock art. This was the first step for the definition and application of techniques for damage mitigation, neutralisation, and reversal. These treatments were adapted to the specificities of sandstone located in a semiarid climate, combined with international recommendations for the intervention on cultural heritage sites, such as to those emanating from ICOMOS (2010). However, these recommendations were only considered when they correlating to the Serra Branca conservation issues, as rock art sites in the area are integrated into a demonstrated characteristic system in which different agents operate symmetrically and asymmetrically.

The fiercer agents leading to rock art damage in this area are mechanical fracturing, followed by runoffs, saline deposits and biological organism proliferation. Considering these principal damage features, curatorial strategies were developed separately. In the case of the runoffs, pluvial water passes through the rock art panels leaving deposits and patinas with different shades. To fix that situation, handmade plates were installed aloft the rock art panels in order to divert water run-off. These boards consisted of a mixture of Maxi Rubber© with local materials, such as clay, sand and iron oxides, and were painted with opaque hues similar to those of the local sandstones. This technique has shown itself extremely successful in saving rock art from damage and has been used in this area in since the late 20th century (Guidon 2001, 2003, 2005, 2006, 2009, 2012).

Damage resulting from biological agents, such as insect galleries, nests and their related processes, was treated without using fire or pesticides. Cemented wasp nests and termite galleries have been removed with spatulas and cleaned with toothbrushes and local water. Cleaning also focused on the removal of patinas, graffiti and soot. Multiple care was considered while handling spatulas and brushes to avoid hard rubbing in painted sectors.

Termites are one of the major biological agents compromising the rock art at the Serra Branca Valley and their removal is very difficult, as they tend to recolonise the same areas previously occupied leaving permanent marks on the support. Unfortunately, the hunt for the anteater, still existing in the region, contributes to the gradual disappearance of the main natural predator of termites.

In the case of the mechanical rock art breakage, fractures, peeling and slab detachments, a strategy for mitigation and stabilisation involved the production of a type of paste that counterweights those problems also avoiding their progression. That paste was also produced with Maxi Rubber©, local clays and pigments and was inserted in the fractures and in the peeling negatives in order to prevent their breakage spreading. Finally, the same paste was used to reassemble detached painted fragments found in the archaeological deposit to their original places in the rock art panels.

Figure 17.4 Rock-art curatorial intervention in Serra Branca Valley, Serra da Capivara National Park, Piauí, Brazil. (A, B) Before and after cleaning of biological and chemical damage (Toca do Tomás I archaeological site); (C, D, E) Process of collages of pictorial panel fragments (Toca do Pinga do Boi archaeological site); F) Panel design (Ignácio 2009); (G, H) Tourist infrastructure (Toca da Extrema II and Toca do Veado archaeological sites). Credits: Buco 2012.

In the last 20 years, at least four categories of damage treatment were conducted in the Serra Branca rock shelters by a local team of rock art conservators[1]: (1) cleaning, which took place in 78% of the rock art sites; (2) consolidation of fractures, which was applied in 38.50% of the sites; (3) installation of pluvial water diverting plates in 19.50% of the rock shelters; (4) and relocation of fallen painted fragments of rock into their original position in the rock art panel in 6% of the sites. It is important to mention that 18.50% of the rock art sites in this area have infrastructure, such as walkway, bodyguard, signs and information boards, trails, roads and parking areas for the tourist visit (Buco 2013).

Final considerations

Research on rock art conservation presented here was based on a dynamic approach, made possible by the identification, classification, and localisation of different agents of qualitative modification and damage features in the rock art of the Serra Branca Valley. It has been argued that the environmental and cultural dynamics influenced the emergence, intensity, frequency, and evolution of these agents, and that their actions are entangled as a great 'system'. A regional depiction of this system was provided according to the most common types of damage compromising the rock art on this gorge in the west side of the Capivara National Park.

The set of the damage features impacting the integrity of rock art and sites was classified as the result of biological, physical, chemical and anthropogenic agents. Examples include lichens, fungi, termites, wasps, plant roots, natural salt deposits, patinas, runoffs, painting sharpness loss, fractures, corrosion, rock-peeling and powdering and rock detachments. Besides, human actions in the rock shelters since the Pleistocene/Holocene transition until the contemporary era, mostly comprising graffiti, soot, digging holes, rock surface grinding, wood-mud constructions, or cooking fire structures have also been identified.

Finally, theoretical, practical, quantitative, and qualitative research, from micro to macro context, and curatorial actions are fundamental for the conservation and preservation of cultural heritage, in this case, the rock art of Serra da Capivara National Park.

Acknowledgements

We would like to thank CAPES for the "Full Doctorate Scholarship" abroad (UTAD-PT) that allowed this research to be conducted; Fundação Museu do Homem Americano (FUMDHAM) for its support in data collection and in particular the rock art conservation team, represented by Jorlan da Silva Oliveira; Chico Mendes Institute for Biodiversity Conservation (ICMBio) and Instituto do Patrimônio Histórico e Artístico Nacional (IPHAN - Brazilian government Cultural Heritage agency) for co-participation in the preservation project for the Serra da Capivara National Park rock art; Bete Buco for the illustrations; and to all who directly and indirectly contributed to this research.

Note

1 Between the 1990s and the 2010s, a conservation team composed of local technicians trained at the FUMDHAM labs and in the Serra da Capivara National Park applied the main curatorial techniques described in this manuscript. They worked under the supervision of the chemical-archaeologist Dr. Maria Conceição Soares Menezes Lage from the Federal University of Piauí-UFPI.

References

Bigarella, J. J., Becker, R. D. and Santos, G. F. (1994) *Estrutura e origem das paisagens tropicais e subtropicais.* Florianópolis: Editora da Universidade Federal de Santa Catarina, vol.1 and 2.

Buco, C. A. (2012) Arqueologia do Movimento: Relações entre Arte Rupestre, Arqueologia e Meio Ambiente, da Pré-história aos dias atuais, no Vale da Serra Branca. Parque Nacional Serra da Capivara, Piauí, Brasil. Vila Real: PhD Thesis, Universidade de Trás- os-Montes e Alto Douro. vol.1, 2 and 3.

Buco, E. F. (2013) *Turismo Arqueológico/Archaeological Tourism, Região do Parque Nacional Serra da Capivara/Serra da Capivara National Park region.* São Raimundo Nonato: FUMDHAM/Petrobras.

Buco, C. A., Galvão Neto, A. A., Oliveira, A. S. N. O. and Landim, J. P. P. (2020) Marcadores identitários rupestres: encontro de culturas no Vale da Serra Branca, Piauí, Brasil. In *V Congresso Internacional: santuários, cultura, arte, romarias, peregrinações, paisagens e pessoas — a morada como santuário (13–20/12/2020).* Caderno de Comunicações. Lisboa, PT, pp.275–283.

Campos, L. C. S. (2015) Paleoclima e comportamento humano no Holoceno: um estudo comparativo entre Brasil e a Península Ibérica. Vila Real. PhD Thesis, Universidade de Trás-os-Montes e Alto Douro-UTAD.

Casseti, V. (2005) *Geomorfologia.* https://geomorfologia.wordpress.com/2011/03/17/livro-do-valter-casseti-pdf.

Castro Junior, P. R. (2002) Dinâmica da água em campos de Murundus do planalto dos Parecis. PhD Thesis. São Paulo: Universidade de São Paulo.

Cavalcante, L. C. D., Abreuz, R. R de S., Lage, M. C. S. M. and Fabris, J. D. et al. (2008) Conservação de Sítios de Arte Rupestre: resultados preliminares do estudo químico de pigmentos e depósitos de alteração no sítio Toca do Pinga da Escada. *Revista de Arqueologia,* 21(2), pp.41–50.

Cavalcante, L. C. D., Lage, M. C. S. M., Santos, L. M., Farias Filho, B. and Fontes, L. M. (2007) Pedra do Castelo: arqueologia, fé, mistério e encantamento. *Clio Arqueológica,* 22(1), pp.215–229.

Cavalcante, L. C. D. and Rodrigues, P. R. A. (2009) Análise dos registros rupestres e levantamento dos problemas de conservação do sítio Pedra do Atlas, Piripiri, Piauí. *Clio Série Arqueológica,* 24(2), pp.154–173.

Demattê, J. L. I. (1974) Processos exógenos de elaboração do relevo: intemperismo químico. In Penteado, M. M. (Ed.) *Fundamentos de Geomorfologia.* Rio de Janeiro: Fundação IBGE, pp.63–71.

Ferreira, E. V. O., Martins, V., Vascocellos Inda Jr., A., Giasson, E. and do Nascimento, P. C. (2011) Ação das térmitas no solo. *Ciência Rural*, 41(5), pp.804–811.
Guidon, N. (1975) *Peintures Rupestres de Várzea Grande, Piauí, Brésil*. Paris: École des Hautes Études en Sciences Sociales, Cahiers d'Archéologie d'Amérique du Sud 3, pp.5–174.
Guidon, N. (1985) A arte pré-histórica da área arqueológica de São Raimundo Nonato: síntese de dez anos de pesquisa. *Clio Série Arqueológica*, 2, pp.2–80.
Guidon N. (1986) Unidades culturais da Tradição Nordeste na área arqueológica de São Raimundo Nonato. *Revista do Museu Paulista*, 30, pp.115–145.
Guidon, N. (1989) Tradições rupestres da área arqueológica de São Raimundo Nonato, Piauí, Brasil. *Clio Série Arqueológica*, 5, pp.5–10.
Guidon, N. (Org.) (2001) *Relatório MINC (Ministério da Cultura) sobre Conservação dos sítios arqueológicos no Parque Nacional Serra da Capivara, Piauí, Brasil*. 5p. São Raimundo Nonato: FUMDHAM, Fundação Museu do Homem americano [não publicado].
Guidon, N. (Org.) (2003) *Relatório Final "Projeto de Salvamento emergencial de 24 sítios arqueológicos no Parque Nacional Serra da Capivara, Piauí, Brasil"*, Convênio MINC/FUMDHAM, n.54/2003. 26p. São Raimundo Nonato: FUMDHAM, Fundação Museu do Homem americano [não publicado].
Guidon. N. (Org.) (2005) Relatório Pinturas rupestres, Patrimônio Cultural a serviço do desenvolvimento, Convênio FUMDHAM/CFDD, n.004/2004. "Projeto de Salvamento emergencial de 24 sítios arqueológicos no Parque Nacional Serra da Capivara, Piauí, Brasil", Convênio MINC/FUMDHAM, n.54/2003. 37p. São Raimundo Nonato: FUMDHAM, Fundação Museu do Homem americano [não publicado].
Guidon, N. (Org.) (2006) Relatório Parcial "Proteção, manutenção do Parque Nacional Serra da Capivara – Patrimônio Mundial da Humanidade" PETROBRÁS/PRONAC: 01 21 81 2006, 8p. São Raimundo Nonato: FUMDHAM, Fundação Museu do Homem americano [não publicado].
Guidon, N. (Org.) (2009) Relatório Parcial "Proteção, manutenção do Parque Nacional Serra da Capivara – Patrimônio Mundial da Humanidade" PRONAC: 07 25 22 2009, 41p. São Raimundo Nonato: FUMDHAM, Fundação Museu do Homem americano [não publicado].
Guidon, N. (Org.) (2012) Relatório Final referente aos "Serviços técnicos especializados na área de arqueologia, conservação de pinturas rupestres e restauração de obras de arte, para execução de conservação de registros rupestres em 20 (vinte) sítios arqueológicos, localizados no Parque Nacional Serra da Capivara e entorno" IPHAN contrato n. 02/2012, processo 01.402.000256/2010–37, 78p. São Raimundo Nonato: FUMDHAM, Fundação Museu do Homem americano [não publicado].
Guidon, N., Buco, C. A. and Ignácio, E. (2007) Toca do Pinga da Escada. Nota Prévia. *Fumdhamentos*, 6, pp.41–51.
Holt, J. A. and Lepage, M. (2000) Termites and soil properties. In ABE, T. et al. (Eds.) *Termites, Evolution, Sociality, Symbiosis, Ecology*. Dordrecht: Kluwer Academic, pp.389–407.
Ignácio, E. (2009) *A representação de cervídeos no complexo rupestre do Parque Nacional Serra da Capivara: morfologias, sintaxe e contextos arqueológicos: uma análise visual*. Vila Real: Master thesis, Instituto Politécnico de Tomar-IPT and Universidade de Trás-os-Montes e Alto Douro-UTAD.

Lage, M. C. S. M., Silva, J. C., Campelo, S. M., Cavalcante, L. C. D., Martins, K. and Ferraro, L. (2009) A restauração do sítio arqueológico Pedra do Castelo. *Clio Arqueológica*, 24(2), pp.67–82.

Macedo, I. S. (2017) Integração de dados geoquímicos na região de Sanga da Brandina, Caçapava do Sul, RS. Caçapava do Sul: Undergraduate thesis, Universidade Federal do Pampa-UFP.

Morales Jr., R. (2002) The Nordeste Tradition: Innovation and Continuity in Brazilian Rock Art. PhD thesis, Virginia: Virginia Commonwealth University.

Nash, G. (2009) Serra da Capivara: America's oldest art? *Current World Archaeology*, 37, pp.41–46.

Noirot, C. and Darlington, J. P. E. C. (2000) Termite nests: Architecture, regulation and defense. In Abe, T. et al. (Eds.) *Termites: Evolution, Sociality, Symbioses, Ecology*. Dordrecht: Kluwer Academic, pp.121–139.

Oliveira, A. S. de N. (2014) *Catingueiros da Borracha: Vida de Maniçobeiro no Sudeste do Piauí 1900–1960*. São Raimundo Nonato: FUMDHAM.

Oliveira, A. S. N. O., Landim, J. P. P., Galvão Neto, A. A. and Buco, C. A. (2020) O sagrado na Serra Branca: uma história de pertencimento dos Maniçobeiros e descendentes. In V *Congresso Internacional: santuários, cultura, arte, romarias, peregrinações, paisagens e pessoas — a morada como santuário (13–20/12/2020)*. Caderno de Comunicações. Lisboa, PT, pp.284–291.

Perioto, N. W. and Lara, R. R. (2018) Nest description, new parasitoid associations and geographical range of Trypoxylon (Trypoxylon) florale Richards (Hymenoptera: Crabronidae). *Revista Chilena de Entomología*, 44(3), pp.297–302.

Pessis, A. M. (1992) Identidade e classificação dos registos gráficos pré-históricos do Nordeste do Brasil. *Clio Série Arqueológica, Recife*, 1(8), pp.35–68.

Pessis, A-M. (2003) *Imagens da pré-história. Parque Nacional Serra da Capivara*. São Paulo: FUMDHAM/Petrobras, 304pp.

Pessis, A. M., Martin, G. and Guidon, N. (2012) Datations des peintures rupestres du Parc National Serra da Capivara: une construction issue de la confrontation des techniques archéométriques. In Clottes, J. (Ed.) *L'art pléistocène dans le monde*. Tarascon-sur-Ariège: Société préhistorique Ariège-Pyrénées, pp.711–717.

Ratcliffe, F. N. et al. (1952) *Australian Termites: The Biology, Recognition and Economic Importance of the Common Species*. Melbourne: CSIRO.

Santos, T. (2010) Pinturas rupestres do sítio arqueológico Toca da Gamela, Parque Nacional Serra da Capivara-PI. Undergraduate thesis, São Raimundo Nonato: Universidade Federal do Vale do São Francisco-UNIVASF.

Silva, A. J. P. et al. (2003) Bacias Sedimentares Paleozóicas e Meso-Cenozóicas Interiores - Paleozoic and Meso-Cenozoic Sedimentary Basins. In Bizzi, L. A., Schobbenhaus, C., Vidotti, R. M. and Gonçalves, J. H. (Eds.) *Geologia, Tectônica e Recursos Minerais do Brasil*. Brasília: CPRM - Serviço Geológico do Brasil, pp.55–85.

Zanetti, R. et al. (2010) *Manejo integrado de cupins: notas de aula da disciplina Entomologia aplicada*. Lavras: Departamento de Entomologia da Universidade Federal de Lavras-UFL.

18 Trials and Tribulations of Artificial Silicone Driplines
A Case Study from Kakadu National Park, Australia

Melissa Marshall, Kadeem May, Gabrielle O'Loughlin and Jeffrey Lee

Introduction

Undeniably, one of the most challenging impacts to affect the preservation of open-air rock art sites globally is that of water. Whether through indirect rain, water wash, condensation, frost or human interference (whereby throwing water over pigments was once considered the best means to illuminate them for photography), the management or mitigation of water on pictographs or pigment art is extremely difficult. In the extreme north of Australia and approximately 200km east of Darwin, Kakadu National Park includes the western edges of the Arnhem Land Plateau. This inspirational landscape has been recognised internationally for its significance, both cultural and natural. Subjected to a tropical monsoonal climate that brings torrential rains and extreme heat annually during the six months of the Wet Season (October–March), this is matched by the cooler and drier months of the Dry Season (April–September). These extreme weather conditions have a substantial influence on the long-term management of the rock art present here and efforts to mitigate this formed some of the earliest conservation trials in Australia.

With the establishment of Kakadu in the late 1970s and its subsequent inclusion on the World Heritage List (UNESCO 2014), early conservation efforts targeted water damage incurred during these seasonal influxes and sought to likewise address the multitude of associated impacts. Building on evidence-based work (Gillespie 1982, 1983a), artificial silicone driplines as techniques to support longer-term preservation efforts were introduced to Bininj and Mungguy (Aboriginal Traditional Owners from the Arnhem Land Plateau region) simultaneous to the rock art sites across the Park. This work intensified in the 1980s (Haskovec and Sullivan 1985, 1986, 1987) and 1990s which included training of rangers in techniques of application (Lambert 1997). While seeking at the time to primarily preserve sites, the intervention was not introduced in parallel with long-term monitoring and evaluation frameworks to ensure the conservation strategies were working. This unfortunate oversight has been a focus of the current annual Bim

DOI: 10.4324/9780429355349-23

(Rock Art) Monitoring and Maintenance Program. The learnings and strategic approach developed in response through collaborative efforts is the focus of this paper, which was originally presented at the European Archaeological Association (EAA) Conference in Barcelona in 2018. Interspersed throughout this chapter are reflections of the authors' and their efforts to address not only the challenges faced relating to the management of water as considered within the case studies, but also those related to monitoring, evaluating and managing intervention strategies in the longer term. In doing so, ultimately this is always in the context of looking after rock art across this extensive cultural landscape:

> *My name is Jeffery Lee. I'm from the Djok Land. Senior Traditional Owner of the Burrungkuy area, and I am a ranger and also sit on the Kakadu Board of Management. Why it's important to me looking after rock art in the Country... It's important because you see all the paintings on the rocks and the meaning they have is very strong and some of the rock art tells a story that goes along with it, the old people was walking around on the Country and what they got; or another country when they hunting, fishing. They draw the paintings on the rock to tell the story from there. So today like for us mob, me, myself and the young generation this is where we'll learn. From rock art is the story - the rock art on the painting itself from the old people. So songlines, the story about the Country and you know the places that's very important where old people been used that area. Like ceremony ground, that's very important. We need to know that because that's where it all happened in the ceremony ground and that's where old people were deciding how we look after rock art in our own way and how we can make it that strong and we can be looking after the paintings and continue to tell them that story to the young generation but it's very, very, very important that we need to get that because it comes from the land and the country.*
>
> Jeffrey Lee, Djok Traditional Owner and Kakadu National Park Ranger

Understanding from Jeffrey that culture must be the boss of the conservation techniques applied to protect and preserve sites, the lessons learned since the Park's establishment in the management of water through the extensive application of artificial silicone driplines, are only now being fully understood by all involved. Within the context of the theoretical knowledge underpinning the western scientific technique (Gillespie 1983a; Pearson and Pretty 1976), a review of the evidence-base from the 1970s will now be discussed followed by four case studies demonstrating success and failure of the technique. From this we will advocate that the conservation discipline can learn from these contemporary examples to assist in advancing the technique into the future based on the experience from this Australian perspective.

Background

Identified as one of the primary contributors in the deterioration of open-air rock art sites in Australia (Chaloupka 1974a; Pearson and Pretty 1976), mitigation strategies and intervention techniques to reduce or remove impacts associated with water was first considered widely in Australia from the late 1960s to mid-1970s. The early research efforts in rock art conservation and management methods ultimately led to the development of multiple techniques to address this issue. Of particular interest was the potential protection and improvements that could be gained through the use of artificial silicone driplines to manage water flow at rock art sites in order to reduce the associated damage such as fading pigments (Agnew et al. 2015; COR-LAB 1986, 1987, 1988, Gillespie 1983a, Hughes 1979, Hughes et al. 1984; Hughes and Watchman 1983; Lambert 1989, 2007; Marshall and Taçon 2014; May, Taçon et al. 2017; Rosenfeld 1985; Taçon and Marshall 2014; Watchman 2004). Most recently Marshall (2020, pp. 170–174) considered the development and implementation of various water management techniques as part of her doctoral studies, noting that while the threat water presents to the preservation of rock art may seem self-explanatory, this is not always the case. Two authors have summarised the forms that this impact can specifically take. Lambert (2007, pp. 17–22) described these as:

- direct water erosion (rapid water flow, especially from surface runoff, generally results in erosive action on pictograph surfaces);
- mineral accretion (a build-up or coating of a mineral that 'obliterates' painted surfaces); and
- frost damage (involving a spontaneous expansion of water from the liquid phase to the ice phase, thus increasing pressure under rock art created with applied techniques such as pigment, dislodging pieces from the rock surface).

With Thorn (1993) expanding this further defined the processes as:

- runoff down the rock surface (where water has washed away the painted surface, in some cases causing severe exfoliation at the edges of the main wash);
- pigment moisture (high readings conform to those anticipated for the various pigments);
- seepage from natural fissures or wash zones (when water passes through the rock geology materialising on the shelter wall flowing over imagery);
- condensation (surface measurements show the dew point is exceeded); and
- driven rain (that involves rain falling directly on the rock art rather than washing down from above).

Knowing the cause of the impact, Marshall (2020, p. 172) surmised that strategies and intervention techniques to mitigate, reduce or remove water damage have, for the past 40 years in Australia focused principally on the installation of artificial driplines with silicone products (involving strips of silicone attached to the natural curvature of the rock placed to improve the efficiency of the natural dripline of a shelter (Lambert 2007, p. 22)). Notably in Kakadu, there have also been irreversible trials introduced to assess the usefulness and applicability of artificial silica sprays (CORLAB 1986, 1987, 1988) to replicate the natural silica skins that often develop, particularly on siliceous sandstone and quartzite from wind and water (Rosenfeld 1985, pp. 21–25). These have been applied to both artificial sites such as the Koongarra trial (CORLAB 1986, 1987, 1988; Marshall et al. In Press), in addition to ancient open-air rock art sites. Many of these attempts were modelled on the research conducted by Gillespie in the late 1970s at the rock art complex of Ubirr in the East Alligator District of Kakadu National Park:

In October 1978 I joined the Australian National Parks and Wildlife Service as a project officer. My duties were to begin a programme of conservation for the rock art and archaeological sites of the proposed national park. In December 1978 I saw the art of Ubirr for the first time and I also met Big Bill Neiiji [sic] one of the senior traditional owners of Ubirr for the first time. I had a discussion with Bill about looking after the rock art - it was to be the forerunner or many such discussions. I was impressed with Neiiji's enthusiasm for the idea of a national park and for the idea of protecting the art. I decided that initially I would concentrate my efforts on the extraordinary rock art complex of Ubirr.

(Gillespie 1983b, p. 18)

Amidst a sea of problems that bedevilled sites the most significant cause of natural deterioration for the sites of Kakadu appeared to be water. It seemed a productive line of practical experimentation to look at the behaviour of water in the sites of Ubirr in the rapidly approaching Wet Season and to test the application of silicone driplines and diversion barriers and other methods of diverting water from painted surfaces.

(Gillespie 1983b, p. 28)

Working alongside senior Traditional Owners was a trademark of the formative joint management arrangement that was entered into as part of the establishment of Kakadu. This provided Gillespie with an enviable opportunity to sit on Country and watch the torrential rains of the monsoonal climate that covers much of northern Australia. This involved 'sitting still and being in the moment, observing and experiencing the tangible and intangible'; which is everyday living for Bininj/Mungguy and would involve watching water dribble, seep or rush over a rock surface and noticing its subtle and subline effects and actions on the art. This method applied by

Gillespie allowed him to consider the benefits and limitations of the recently developed artificial silicone driplines as one of the paramount intervention techniques that would be used in Kakadu:

> *In the Wet Season of 1979, I set up a temporary home in one of the shelters (SS91) and began to install driplines, observe their performance and examine the problem of mudnest building wasps in art sites. It was my practice to be dropped into the site by helicopter and have the machine return to collect me in five to seven days time. The shelter in which I lived, (which became known as the Hard Rock Motel) had been occupied recently by Aboriginal people who lived around the Cannon Hill ranger station. The shelter contained fire wood, metal cans and drums modified to serve as cooking containers.*
> (Gillespie 1983b, p. 28)

During this experimental research, Gillespie developed a solid, evidence-based methodology to replicate the installation of the intervention strategy to manage primarily water wash within rockshelters in the Park. Commencing with a site survey, mapping and photogrammetry, Gillespie identified two primary objectives (1983c p. 195):

1 To create artificial driplines and diversion barriers in rock shelters.
2 To caulk furrows and cracks in the roofs of shelters, and bedding planes at the rear of shelters.

As part of a seven-step process, Gillespie (1983c, p. 195) noted that the first task requires the selection of dripline materials – both the silicone product itself and a fastener or primer. At that time, Ramset Silicone Rubber (RB833 clear) was chosen supported by the use of a primer (in this case Ramset PR001) which was advised in preference to Ramset Fasteners (as these had left oil and mineral residue when used for conservation purposes elsewhere). Hughes (1979, p. 26) issued dire warnings against the use of surface consolidants in rock art – stating that there are substantial negative objections on the grounds of appearance, cost, limited life, ineffectiveness and increased damage to the stone. Gillespie (1983c, p. 195) echoed these limitations and noted that the use of these additional substances was ill-advised.

Following deliberation of the type of material to use, Gillespie (1983c, pp. 196–198) identified the following components were required for appropriate dripline management:

- Installation (surface preparation, silicone application);
- Assessment of failures (inadequate bonding, poor siting and installation, poor cross-sectional shape);
- Silicone caulking;
- Dripline maintenance;
- Removal of wasp nests;
- Removal of vegetation.

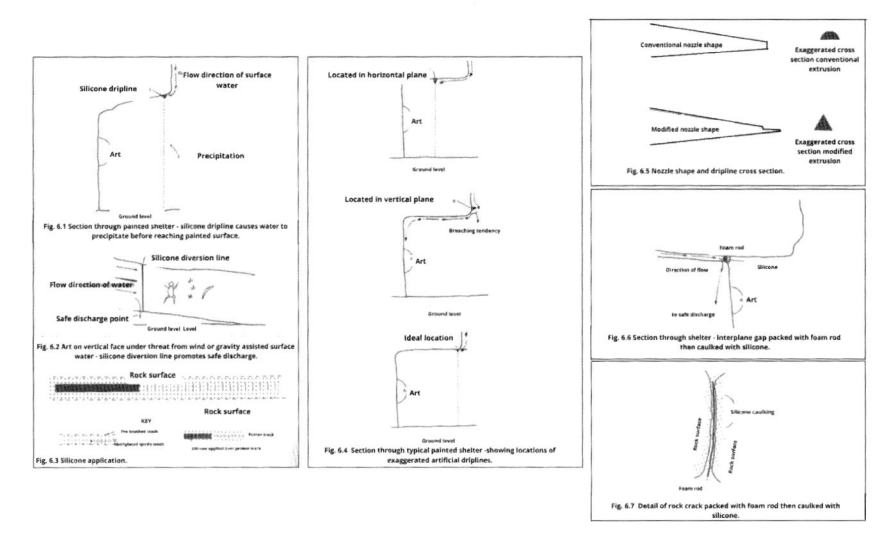

Figure 18.1 Application of artificial silicone driplines as illustrated by Gillespie (1983c, pp. 202–205) (Graphics by Jo Wilkins).

Utilising examples from both Ubirr and Nourlangie (now referred to by the Aboriginal name for this area, Burrungkuy), Gillespie illustrated best practice techniques for artificial dripline installation as reproduced in Figure 18.1.

What Gillespie evidenced, CORLAB advocated, and Thorn employed was that artificial silicone driplines need to be applied with an understanding of the movement of water through the site particularly during the monsoonal Wet Season. As CORLAB (1988, p. 8) noted, it is not how these trials succeed but how they fail that is of most value. Thus, whilst these innovative techniques received widespread application within Kakadu, we are now starting to understand 40 years on, how this technique can fail and the associated impacts that can be caused. Many of the early conservation activities considered potential long-term impacts and recommended that the driplines themselves be monitored and evaluated over the coming decades. For a myriad of reasons this had not happened and therefore, as part of an annual dedicated monitoring program we are now looking at ways to document these failings, to learn from them and ultimately improve current techniques for water management. Co-author Gabrielle O'Loughlin reflected on the history of conservation programs in Kakadu and where this now leads us to:

> *My name is Gabrielle O'Loughlin. I'm a senior project officer of cultural programs in Kakadu National Park. The national park was set up in the late 1970's as an amazing place of natural and cultural landscapes with thousands of rock art sites. The first workers that came here were very*

concerned about any deterioration, so they trialed a lot of different conservation methods and one of the main issues was to protect the art sites from water damage using silicone. Silicone was put up as a line that would create a bead that would then allow the water to hit the dripline so that the water would not run over the painting, and it would fall to the ground. There was a lot of trial and error in the initial application of this technique and at many places they found it to be quite successful. So, it became pretty much a standard practice for archaeologists or park staff that were working in Kakadu to use silicone as a tool to reduce water interacting with the rock art. Now, over time we've found that some of the expertise of applying this silicone has been left to Park staff who have perhaps not so much experience as previous staff members. So, there are some driplines now that we're finding that are applied inappropriately and it could actually be damaging the art. We are currently trialing and monitoring a number of sites to see whether or not the previous application is working today.

Assessing suitability of artificial silicone driplines

Through this ongoing monitoring and maintenance work, we have had the opportunity over the past decade to observe and understand some of the problems encountered through the over or inadequate use of artificial silicone driplines. Many of these were initially observed and evidenced or predicted by Gillespie (1983c), whilst other associated issues were previously unquantified. Thorn (1993, p. 23) subsequently observed dryness under the artificial silicone driplines at sites he reviewed in Kakadu. May, Taçon et al. (2017) more recently identified increased heat spalling under the artificial driplines from recent fire events, likely to have been exacerbated from the drier surface which had resulted from the removal of the natural moisture over the rock surface. Other previously unquantified examples we will describe in the case studies below. As reported in Marshall (2016), the list to date of identified impacts from the use of artificial silicone driplines are:

- Gaps (both large and small) in the artificial silicone dripline that is causing water to flow down over paintings that these were meant to protect; the perishing is both age-related and at times due to poor application;
- Incorrect installation that has included the placement of silicone on top of other paintings, which does not follow the natural curvature of the rock and/or is not necessarily capturing water it is meant to divert. Additional challenges are that there are instances where the artificial dripline was not required in the first place, such as when water damage was not near paintings at all (or there was already a natural silica over the rock surface). However, the installation of these interventions now requires ongoing attention and management.

Additional problems posing a threat to the long-term conservation, protection and/or preservation of rock art in Kakadu that has in cases been directly attributed to artificial silicone driplines:

- Creating an algae problem following the corking or blocking of a spring in a rock, whereby a strip of silicone captured this and fed the algae further.
- Dust is being captured above the silicone dripline and turning to mud, building up to a level equal to the silicone which means the water runs directly over the top of both the mud-like substance and the paintings it is meant to protect below.
- Salt crystals visibly increasing and being recorded through both photographic and measured monitoring at some sites in the north of the Park – there appears to be a correlation with an increase of salt accretions under artificial silicone driplines and a study is underway to ascertain whether the two are directly connected.
- A salt 'wash' directly under artificial silicone driplines has also been observed in a number of cases and photos prior to installation of the dripline are now being sought to ascertain whether this is coincidence or that there is a connection with the artificial silicone driplines or other issues such as climate change – this problem adds weight to the argument that there should be a detailed record of all paintings and panels within a site prior to any site works.
- Termites have taken a liking to the silicone substance and there are examples where termites have tunnelled over, under and next to the silicone, as well as other areas where it appears to have been nibbled or eaten away – a longer term study on this relationship is also under development at present.
- What appears to be a chemical reaction between the silicone used for the artificial dripline and minerals within the sandstone matrix has been observed at a number of locations across the Park and examining this impact further is now part of an additional research project.
- The moisture content within the sandstone itself appears to have reduced to the point that there is a greater fragility of the rock superstructure itself and increasing exfoliation, as well as increasing flaking of brittle pigment.
- Lack of long-term monitoring and maintenance plan for the management of the artificial silicone driplines within the Park, as these substances last only 10–15 years, possibly 20 years at the most, needing to be regularly checked and reinstalled as required.

Acknowledging that some of these may challenges be mitigated through strategic and directed maintenance regimes, others cannot and emerging research in this area will seek to advance techniques of this nature (Marshall 2020).

Case Studies

By way of example, we present four specific case studies to illustrate further several of the impacts identified above connected directly with the use of artificial silicone driplines for water management, as well as examples of where application of the technique has been successful or is still under assessment:

- Ubirr (mixed outcomes);
- Binjarrang (unnecessary failure);
- Nanguluwurr (mitigated);
- Nawalabila (under assessment).

Ubirr

As the Ubirr (formerly referred to as Obiri) rock art complex was the focus of Gillespie's (1983a) formative experimental research, we are currently assessing the suitability and applicability of artificial silicone driplines at two specific shelters. The first of these has a depiction of Naliyod or Kalarrabirri (Rainbow Serpent) and was one of the shelters observed by Gillespie:

> *At survey site 114 a painting of Kalarrabirri – the Rainbow Serpent dominates a vertical rock face. In the creation era the serpent is said to have placed her likeness on the rock during her creative travels. She is also said to have crossed the East Alligator River at a site near the present road crossing [Cahills Crossing] – the site is known as Kalarrabirri djorkeng which describes the act of crossing.*
>
> Gillespie (1983c, p. 200)

> *Traditional Owners were insistent that the painting was available for public viewing and in fact suggest its inclusion on the interpretative trail at Ubirr. Bill Neiiji requested that a silicone dripline be installed over the painting to diminish water wash damage. Both suggestions have been carried out.*
>
> Gillespie (1983c, p. 200)

The record keeping of maintenance activities relating to silicone dripline management has been interrupted over the course of the four decades since this initial work was applied. These driplines were checked as reported annually (Mahney 2009; Sullivan and Haskovec 1985, 1986, 1987) and in file notes (as discussed in Marshall 2020). However, it has been through the advancement of the current annual Bim program that an understanding of specific issues within a number of shelters at Ubirr has been correlated (as exemplified in Marshall 2014, 2016; Marshall et al. 2018).

As reported in Marshall (2019), monitoring of artificial silicone driplines was undertaken during rain at the site. It was observed and recorded that two driplines were located on the vertical rock face to protect the image of

Kalarrabirri. The dripline on the upper face was failing where there were gaps in the dripline and had been patched in places. However, where intact it continued to work as intended. The second lower dripline immediately above Kalarrabirri which did not have water wash flowing down the rock face towards it, had also perished in sections and was proving both ineffective and unneeded. As per the maintenance strategy reported below, the driplines were removed and the upper one reinstalled by Kakadu rangers. This is now being monitored periodically – before and after rain – to ensure continued effectiveness. At a second site on the Ubirr interpretative trail, an unusual stain has been observed on the periphery of the installed artificial silicone dripline running down the rock face (as illustrated in Figure 18.2). Perceived as a chemical reaction between the silicone product and the sandstone itself, there is also an observable decrease in moisture content of the shelter walls underneath the diverted water flow (Marshall et al. 2018) as evidenced by the level of exfoliation of the rock substrate and pigment where present. In terms of the chemical reaction specifically, the issue commences under one end of the silicone dripline and washes down the shelter wall. A preliminary investigation is underway to determine whether the relationship can be established through non-invasive Portable X-Ray Fluorescence (pXrf) analysis or whether samples would be required for Spectro-electron microscopy (SEM) analysis. Examination of these initial investigations continues with the pXrf data collected in 2017 and 2019. Analysis of the comparative results will be completed in 2022 for publication soon after.

Figure 18.2 Perceived chemical reaction between silicone product and sandstone (Photograph M. Marshall).

Binjarrang

The nearby site of Binjarrang has been the focus of recent doctoral research (Marshall 2020; Shine 2014; Shine et al. 2015) which sought to investigate the archaeological footprint and current conservation and management issues for the rock art. During this work, 11 individual artificial silicone driplines were recorded, installed previously to address water management concerns (Marshall 2020, pp. 139–242). As with Ubirr, Binjarrang was also a trial site for the use of this technique, however it was also a site that was utilised to train rangers in the intervention method (Lambert 1997). Interestingly, it now is one of the best examples of what not to do in terms of the utilisation of artificial silicone driplines where the range of associated impacts identified include:

- Incorrect application of the artificial silicone dripline causing failure;
- Salt accretions attaching to the artificial silicone dripline causing failure;
- Dust aggregation on top of the artificial silicone dripline causing failure;
- Termites using the artificial silicone dripline as a food source and/or incorporating it into trails and nests causing failure;
- Increased fragility of pigments as drying of the rock surface has been observed evidenced by recent exfoliation of the rock substrate and lifting paint.

One section illustrates these failures well and is shown in Figure 18.3 (reproduced from Marshall (2020, p. 287)). Whilst at first glance it may appear that the application of the silicone has been random, oral histories documented relate to this specific image with Shine et al. (2015, p. 105) noting that 'this male human figure with approximately six multi-barbed spears penetrating his body, neck and legs... represents a payback event that occurred in the late 1800s. It is likely that that intent was to provide extra protection for this image whereas the result is one that is unnecessary and subsequently contributing to deterioration of associated imagery.

A key issue that has subsequently been addressed is that when installed, whether through dedicated training sessions or other programs, these were often not part of strategic monitoring regimes resulting in periodic isolated reviews that focused on the durability of the silicone itself rather than the site in its broader cultural landscape. Given the increasing understanding of the impact that unmanaged artificial silicone driplines can have on the preservation and protection of rock art, this has since been addressed through the annual Bim program. This has included assessment during rain which is aiding in identifying those measures that can be removed completely.

Inappropriate or unnecessary installations of artificial driplines at this site are the primary issues; the further one identified initially here and

Figure 18.3 Artificial dripline going around paintings individually with an unusual termination below (Marshall 2020, p. 208).

subsequently elsewhere is that of the dust deposition. Here the deposited dust above the silicone driplines has now accrued to create hard mud which in some cases, has built up to the same level as the top of the silicone. This in turn has altered the intended water deviation from one that is meant to carry the water away to one that now encourages water to flow over it instead. What is now being investigated is whether the dust deposition obscuring paintings was there prior to the dripline installation and potentially self-managed by nature (such as the dust washing off each year with seasonal water) or if this is a new impact that has resulted due to the installation of the artificial dripline. Additionally, were these impacts also monitored prior to the installation of the silicone? Unfortunately, we do not currently have access to this data and after a thorough examination of available records, it is unlikely we will know. What this does tell us though is that monitoring water action throughout the year for a minimum of two and, where possible, five years prior to installation of an artificial silicone dripline assists to understand water action. This is essential at any given site if we are to mitigate future problems created by conservation interventions such as this.

Nanguluwurr

Travelling south in the Park to the Burrungkuy (formally Nourlangie) rock art complex, Marshall (2020) investigated the conservation and management of Nanguluwurr, a rock shelter that is open to visitors and accessible via the Barrk Walk. During initial field work, a failing dripline was observed. Failing to the extreme that a hand could be placed underneath it, the artificial silicone dripline was completely ineffectual. In consultation with the Traditional Owners for the site, the dripline was easily removed by Kakadu rangers along with a nearby silicone caulk that was plugging up a crevice (Marshall 2020, pp. 267–268). Neither the dripline nor the caulk was adhering to the rock surface and both lifted off easily. Returning six months later an unexpected result was observed – the cryptogamic deposit that had been growing on the periphery of the proximal painting had reduced substantially and effectively was gone within 12 months after removal of the silicone plug and perishing dripline (as illustrated in Figure 18.4). Ultimately what was observed was that the failing silicone had been retaining water in the affected area and in a sense fed the algal accretion. Once this was removed the associated impact was mitigated and no further impact to the exiting image has been reported as part of monitoring conducted at six-monthly intervals since this initial mitigation work in 2013.

This improvement was not anticipated when the plug and perishing dripline were removed, merely that the pieces were no longer providing the protection they were designed for. Rather than reinstall immediately, the decision was made with Traditional Owners to leave this image and monitor it. Nine years on, this remains the case with reviews continuing every six months. To date no observed changes to the preservation of the painting

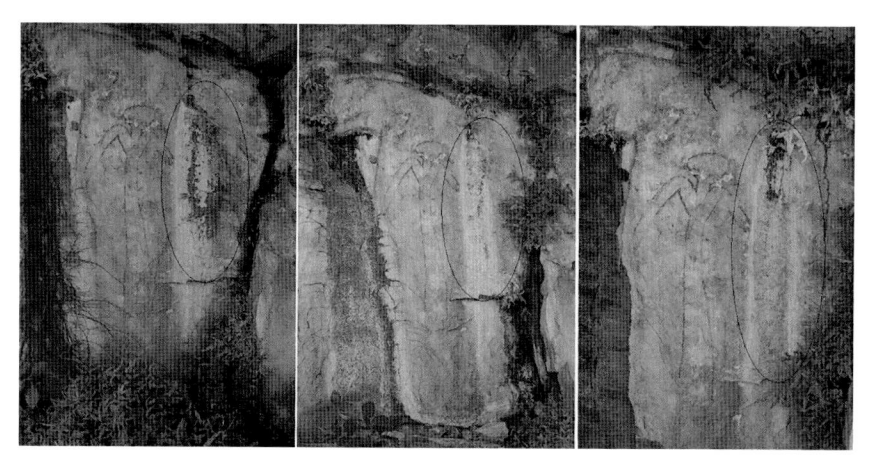

Figure 18.4 Silicone dripline feeding algae prior to removal in July 2013 and re-photographed in August 2014 and August 2021 (Photographs M. Marshall).

itself have been recorded. Additionally, the native vegetation growing in the crack above appears to regulate water flow over the area and is providing protection to the painting in question. This vegetation is now trimmed annually as part of the maintenance program and the monitoring point established will be used in the long-term to observe further impacts.

Nawalabila

Travelling south along the edges of the Arnhem Land escarpment, the area of Nawalabila and the broader region that it is located within the Jim Jim District has been of the subject of archaeological and rock art investigations (Chaloupka 1974a, 1974b, 1975; Jones 1985; Jones and Johnson 1985; Sullivan and Haskovec 1985, 1986, 1987). Visited periodically from 2014 onwards as part of the annual Bim program (Marshall 2014, 2016, 2019), systematic monitoring and maintenance activities have been implemented in the area. One of the key rock art assemblages here sits underneath the overhang of a large, isolated outcrop and the continued requirement of the installed artificial silicone dripline is currently under assessment.

The rock art present is extremely fragile and friable, with preservation efforts challenged by superimposition of thick pigments and potential drying of the rock surface from the redirection of the annual rains. The dripline as currently installed is starting to perish and is showing signs of failure. However, there is an accompanying photographic record of some decades illustrating the slow rate of deterioration of the imagery. What remains unclear is whether the artificial silicone dripline is contributing positively or negatively to this observed deterioration rate. Early trials conducted at Anbangbang (also in the Burrungkuy rock art complex) as part of a restoration project (CORLAB 1989) utilised poultices to reattach fragile pigments. This knowledge then questions whether this shelter at Nauwalabila would benefit from this type of intervention, with pigments re-adhered then rendering the need for the artificial silicone dripline unnecessary? Or would the torrential rains still negatively impact on the fabric of the site given the density of the pigments and their superimposition?

Correlating with this is the aforementioned reduction of moisture content in the rock superstructure. This problem has the potential to impact the rock art both directly and indirectly. Pigments themselves are flaking and brittle, however the direct impact of reduced moisture content indicates that this will increase substantially. Observations of the rock these are painted on also point to the compromise of the rock matrix itself, further increasing exfoliation. Indirectly, this fragility then poses supplementary threats to the preservation of the rock art from both fire and rain. The potential increase in the destruction of the site from seasonal bushfires due to the compromised sandstone is an issue, as well as the need to continue to maintain any artificial silicone driplines in the site as the reintroduction of water (particularly water wash from wet season rains) could also prove overwhelmingly destructive for the impacted paintings. Investigations continue to determine where reinstallation of the artificial silicone dripline is required (as opposed to potential removal) and results should be determined in the coming year.

Integrating monitoring and evaluation into annual programs

Kakadu National Park ranger and co-author Kadeem May has been involved in the annual monitoring and maintenance program since it commenced in 2014. Reflecting on this journey, he shared the following:

> *Hello, good afternoon. My name is Kadeem May. I am the assistant cultural heritage officer here in Kakadu. I been working with Mel now for the last nine years on a monitor and maintenance program that we've been running with rock art and our main focus now, we're looking at the deterioration of silicone driplines...*
>
> *Knowing that we've got 5500 recorded sites on our Kakadu database, we are trying to go around in ground truth all the sites now where a lot of the experimental silicone went in. So most of all our sites that we've got now have got silicone in them and we are seeing more problems with them. So we are trying to go back and audit all these sites where they have the silicone in them, because a lot of people did move away and they took a lot of information with them. So, we're just trying to go back and find where the silicone is, see what the problems and issues are with them and then if we got to deal with them, take them away because some of the sites are lacking in water because of this problem, some sites need them and some sites don't. So we just going back to have a good look at them now. So we're gonna try a good wet season program, so we can get out there and check these driplines during the full wet because a lot of the work happen with the pale of water and they poured it over the site, over the dripline and that's probably not the best sense of work but this was the work that was going on in at the time in Kakadu. So, everyone went with it. Flowed with it. So we're just going back, checking up on them. If we need to reinstall then we'll reinstall them, but the main thing is just going back to recheck and keep an eye on them at the same time.*

Through the systematic annual Bim monitoring and maintenance program underway since 2014, we are now beginning to understand the processes at work in relation to the installation, maintenance, and ongoing review of water management through artificial silicone driplines at rock art sites in Kakadu. Ultimately, what is understood is that there is a plethora of artificial silicone driplines installed within the Park and that a review of every piece of silicone installed over the past 40 years is overdue.

With more than 3,000 sites out of 5,500 identified on the Park's database as having at least one piece installed, often with more than half a dozen in many sites (in some instances these are more than 50m in length and above

20m high on the shelter ceiling), this task is overwhelming. As we consider that, of the sites we are visiting through the monitoring and maintenance program, 35% have been identified as containing silicone. Not all these sites have a previous record in the Park database, resulting in the task at hand increasing exponentially. With a perceived 15,000–20,000 sites in the Park, we are working towards locating, reviewing and either removing or reinstalling every piece of silicone in the Park within the coming decade or so, with a long-term view to continue this in perpetuity.

Watching rain fall through perishing dripline at Ubirr and the other case studies assisted greatly. This provided District staff with first-hand experience in the management of artificial silicone driplines and undertaking the required review, watching where the water fell, providing an opportunity to assess whether the artificial silicone dripline was required and if so, whether it is positioned correctly or needed at all. There is likewise the consideration that some of the rock art images were meant to be washed away as Aboriginal people have previously reported that there was an expectation it would not last forever (Brady et al. 2020). All these elements have combined to assist with the development of a new management strategy relating to the use of artificial silicone driplines within the Park. The following provides a summary of the steps as developed as part of the annual Bim program (Marshall 2016):

Initial site visit:
Locate any artificial silicone driplines within the rock art site;

- If the silicone is not perishing, revisit to review it again in 12 months;
- If the silicone is perishing, review it again in six months' time during the wet season:
  - For those sites where rain is running down the rock and entering via an overhang, watch during rain;
  - Where water is entering the site through cracks or fissures in the rock wall (between the wall and the ceiling), look the next day or so to allow time for water to penetrate through the rock.
- Assess during rain whether artificial dripline is working, correctly positioned or not required;
- As part of the next Bim program, remove or reinstall the silicone.

Removal of artificial silicone dripline:

- Remove all silicone in the site and review locations again the next two to three wet seasons (6 months after, 18 months after, 2.5 years after). If there is no visible change to the paintings, then review water management at the site every two to five years and consider additional strategies should the monitoring regime indicate that water damage is considerable or increasing.

Reinstallation of artificial silicone dripline:

- Make sure all the old silicone is removed including those pieces that are still sticking to the rock surface. If we do not do this and install new silicone over the top of the old one, when the old one eventually lets go of the rock surface, we are seeing that the newer silicone on top is also coming off. The silicone needs to be replaced in its entirety;
- Additionally, staff need to ensure that existing driplines are not patched up. Should only missing sections of the dripline be replaced, the new silicone will have a 10–15 year life span, but the remaining sections of dripline could have only one month, two years, five years – the timeframe is impossible to know as no records have been kept detailing when are where silicone has been installed. This would then require additional monitoring of the remaining silicone and increase the workload further. Rather, ensuring all the silicone in a site is replaced at the same time will reset the clock to 10–15 years for that location;
- Once a new dripline has been installed, review during the next two to three wet seasons (6 months after, 18 months after, 2.5 years after). If the monitoring shows that the artificial dripline is working, the next visit can be five to eight years' time. If not, go through the above procedure again.

Due to the large number of artificial driplines in the Park, introducing others is not ideal at present. However, that is not to say there will not be other sites that may require this action in the future. Therefore, any sites without artificial driplines should be monitored in relation to water for two to five years until damage from seasonal rains can be quantified and the need for this type of intervention evidenced. If photographic monitoring shows a deterioration, water management options could then be considered with Traditional Owners and site custodians. This could include alternatives such as a water diversion strategy from above, in addition to or as an alternative to the installation of artificial silicone driplines. Whatever the decision, any works then need to be time stamped and relevant monitoring regimes followed, such as the one outlined above for reinstalled silicone.

Practice analysis

The case studies presented here demonstrate the complexities associated with this type of scientific intervention. It is not as simple as identifying that water is damaging the integrity of rock art and the fabric of a site. An evidence-base model needs to be established to quantify the use of artificial silicone driplines, their subsequent placement, preparation of the surface and continued review as part of a systematic maintenance and management strategy. There is a place for the use of this type of technique taking care not to overuse it or over-rely on it. Innovation of alternative methods for water management at rock art sites (deviation or otherwise) remains and over the coming decades, further investment in this type of advancement should be prioritised. Nevertheless, its application should be only carried out under the cultural guidance of Bininj/Mungguy in Kakadu or Aboriginal and Torres Strait Islander First Nations people of the respective sites in question. There may be times where the deviation of water has cultural impacts that outweigh preservation concerns (Marshall 2020, p. 439) and the cultural authority of Traditional Owners and site custodians in relation to conservation actions is paramount.

A further complication is the knowledge-base from which this type of intervention can be applied. Lambert (1997, 2007) advocates that all rangers should be able to do this type of work. The challenge there is that there are so few opportunities for this type of training to occur. Additionally, were the steps advocated by Gillespie (1983c) not followed nor systematic processes such as that afforded by the Bim program in place, to usefulness of artificial silicone driplines could once again be called in to question if the negative impacts from this technique outweighed the positive ones. Kakadu exemplifies the challenges all management will face if this advice is not heeded.

This type of training and expertise in the installation of water management interventions such as artificial silicone driplines should be demanded, by Traditional Owners and practitioners alike. After all, no one can arrive at the Sistine Chapel, at the Louvre to conserve the Mona Lisa or other accepted artistic masterpieces of global significance and insist that they should be allowed to conserve those paintings with little or no training, so why should it be accepted at rock art sites in Australia or elsewhere?

The complexities associated with conservation techniques such as this can be understood through the following three statements that were made relating to the use of artificial silicone driplines at rock art sites in Kakadu. Each one illustrates the different perspectives on the use of this technique and will assist in contextualising this discussion (Marshall 2016):

> "Don't do it… tell them just don't do it"
> Senior Traditional Owner for northern areas of Kakadu National Park

> "all x-ray art should be protected at all costs – I don't know why they aren't used everywhere"
> Anonymous informant

> "we need to think of this like new Toyotas – when one comes off the factory line there is already another designed and ready for manufacture… – conservation techniques need to be thought of in this way and we should keep monitoring everything we do to keep improving the techniques that are available"
> Conservation specialist

Conclusion

It is a timely reminder that whatever we do in relation to conservation and management interventions at sites, these activities will have an impact – it is exactly what they are designed to do after all. However, the intention is obviously to reduce observed problems rather than increase or create additional ones. In Kakadu, a World Heritage Listed place, best practice standards should be the minimum to which work is undertaken. Thus, appropriate planning mechanisms need to be in place prior to works, as well as an ongoing monitoring and maintenance plan to look after the interventions and management activities in the longer term in addition to the rock art and associated cultural heritage in the sites themselves.

The proliferation of artificial silicone driplines installed across the Park since its inception now presents an overwhelming challenge for staff regarding the ongoing monitoring and maintenance of the technique, and thus no additional silicone has been installed post-2013. Since that time, this program has focused on relocating where the silicone is (as not all site locations were recorded at the time it was installed) and also, what state the silicone is in. To date, many of the installed driplines reviewed are perishing and contributing to additional impacts within rock art sites across the Park. Systematic monitoring regimes have since been embedded and are advancing improvements across the Park.

In conclusion, the overall goal for the long-term management of artificial silicone driplines within Kakadu National Park is to locate and monitor all silicone in the Park within ten years, as well as reducing the number in use as part of a strategic and directed program that sees them utilised only where they need to be. First and foremost, consultations with relevant Traditional Owners groups are paramount to any decision making regarding the management of any silicone driplines found on their country. Secondly, through the monitoring of water at sites during rain periods, those that are necessary will be identified and the Park then has a manageable task at hand through a long-term monitoring and maintenance program to look after the interventions. Embedded evaluations such as this will prove critical. Currently in Kakadu, the evidence for failure of this technique is outweighing its successes. The time for reverting the practice is now simultaneously innovating improvements for the future.

Acknowledgements

We would like to acknowledge the Bininj and Mungguy on whose Country we live and work. Without their support and enthusiasm, this research would not be possible. We would also like to acknowledge the pioneers of the Australian conservation profession, for without their innovation, these techniques applied with the authority of the Traditional Owners, would not have been possible. We also thank Parks Australia for their support of this research and the colleagues who have assisted us, particularly Dr. Sally K. May, Prof Paul S. C. Taçon and Dr Jillian Huntley.

The research for this paper was undertaken in the early stages as part of Marshall's doctoral candidature through the Australian National University (ANU) and funded through an Australian Postgraduate Award. The 2016 pXRF investigation was funded through the University of Notre Dame Australia's (UNDA) Research Incentive Scheme (R117013); with the 2019 pXRF investigation as part of the *Pathways: people, landscape and rock art* project based at the Place, Evolution and Rock Art Heritage Unit, Griffith Centre for Social and Cultural Research at Griffith University, funded by the Australian Research Council grant *Australian rock art: history, conservation and Indigenous well-being*, as part of Paul S. C. Taçon's ARC Laureate Project (FL160100123).

References

Agnew, N., J. Deacon, N. Hall, T. Little, S. Sullivan and P. S. C. Taçon (2015). *Rock Art: A cultural treasure at risk.* Los Angeles, CA, The Getty Conservation Institute.

Brady, L. M., S. K. May, J. Goldhahn, P. S. C. Tacon and P. Lamilami (2020). What Painting? Encountering and Interpreting the Archaeological Record in Western Arnhem Land, Northern Australia. *Archaeology in Oceania* 55(2):106–117.

Chaloupka, G. (1974a). *Report on the Causes of Damage and Suggested Conservation Measures at the Main Gallery of the Deaf Adder Creek Valley.* Northern Corridor Report. Unpublished report to Museums and Art Galleries of the Northern Territory, Darwin.

Chaloupka, G. (1974b). *Report on Site Survey Activities 1973–1974.* Unpublished report to Museums and Art Galleries of the Northern Territory, Darwin.

Chaloupka, G. (1975). *Report on Site Survey Activities 1974–1975.* Unpublished report to Museums and Art Galleries of the Northern Territory, Darwin.

CORLAB (1986). *Conservation of Post-Estuarine period Rock Art in Kakadu National Park: Report on Phase 1 Study: Pigment Identification.* Australian Nature Conservation Agency, Wilson.

CORLAB (1987). *Conservation of Post-Estuarine Period Rock Art in Kakadu National Park: Final Report on Phase 2 Study: Conservation Treatment Trials.* Australian Nature Conservation Agency, Wilson.

CORLAB (1988). *Conservation of Post-Estuarine Period Rock Art in Kakadu National Park: Final Report on Phase 3 Study: Conservation Treatment Trials.* Australian Nature Conservation Agency, Wilson.

CORLAB (1989). *Conservation of Post-Estuarine Rock Art in Kakadu National Park: Nourlangie Gallery Rock Art Restoration Project.* The International Centre for the Preservation and Restoration of Cultural Property and CORLAB Pty Ltd, Canberra.

Gillespie, D. (1982). *The Rock Art and Archaeological Sites of Ubirr, Kakadu National Park NT: The Beginning of a Management Strategy.* Unpublished report to Australian National Parks and Wildlife Service, Kakadu.

Gillespie, D. (Ed.) (1983a). *The Rock Art Sites of Kakadu National Park - Some Preliminary Research Findings for their Conservation and Management.* Canberra Australian National Parks and Wildlife Service.

Gillespie, D. (1983b). The Beginnings of a Conservation Strategy. In D. Gillespie *The Rock Art Sites of Kakadu National Park - Some Preliminary Research Findings for their Conservation and Management*. Canberra: Australian National Parks and Wildlife Service.

Gillespie, D. (1983c). The Practice of Rock Art Conservation and Site Management in Kakadu National Park. In D. Gillespie *The Rock Art Sites of Kakadu National Park - Some Preliminary Research Findings for their Conservation and Management*. Canberra: Australian National Parks and Wildlife Service.

Hughes, P. J. (1979). *The Deterioration, Conservation and Management of Rock Art Sites in the Kakadu National Park, NT*. ANU. Canberra, ANU.

Hughes, P. J., J. Flood, S. Sullivan, D. Lambert, M. J. Morwood, P. J. F. Coutts, R. G. Gunn, D. A. Gillespie, J. Clarke, W. R. Ambrose and J. L. Gordon (1984). The state of Australian rock art research and conservation in 1980. *Rock Art Research* 1(20):119–140.

Jones, R. (Ed.) (1985). *Archaeological Research in Kakadu National Park*. Canberra Australian National Parks and Wildlife Service.

Jones, R. and I. Johnson (1985). Deaf Adder Gorge: Lindner Site, Nauwalabila I. In R. Jones (Ed.) *Archaeological Research in Kakadu National Park*. Canberra: Australian National Parks and Wildlife Service. Special Publication 13: 165–228.

Lambert, D. (1989). *Conserving Australian Rock Art: A Manual for Site Managers*. Canberra, Aboriginal Studies Press.

Lambert, D. (1997). *Rock Art Conservation. Kakadu National Park: Final Report on First Field Visit April/May 1997*. Unpublished report to Kakadu National Park from the Cultural Heritage Services Division, NSW National Parks and Wildlife Service.

Lambert, D. (2007). *Rock Art Conservation Guidelines: A Manual for the Preservation of Aboriginal Rock Art*. Department of Environment and Climate Change (NSW), Sydney.

Mahney, T. (2009). *East Alligator District Rock Art Report*. Kakadu National Park. Jabiru, Kakadu National Park.

Marshall, M. (2014). *Kakadu National Park's Rock Art Monitoring and Maintenance Program: Pilot Evaluation Report*. Unpublished report for the Department of Environment.

Marshall, M. (2016). *Kakadu National Park's Rock Art Monitoring and Maintenance Year 3 Program: Evaluation Report*. Unpublished report for the Department of Environment.

Marshall, M. (2019). *Kakadu National Park Rock Art Monitoring and Maintenance Program: Year 6 Evaluation Report*. Unpublished report for Kakadu National Park.

Marshall, M. 2020. *Rock Art Conservation and Management: 21st Century Perspectives in Northern Australia*. Doctoral thesis, School of Archaeology and Anthropology, Australian National University, Canberra. DOI:10.25911/5f969812a2f22.

Marshall, M., J. Lee, G. O'Loughlin, K. May and J. Huntley (In Press). Preserving the Rock Art of Kakadu: Formative Conservation Trials during the 1980s. In P. S. C. Taçon, S. K. May, U. K. Frederick and J. McDonald (Eds.) *Histories of Australian Rock Art Research*. Terra Australis XX. Canberra: Australian National University.

Marshall, M., G. O'Loughlin, K. May and J. Wellings (2018). *Kakadu National Park Rock Art Monitoring and Maintenance Program: Year 5 Evaluation Report.* Unpublished report for Kakadu National Park.

May, S., P. S. C. Taçon, D. Wright, M. Marshall, J. Goldhahn and I. Domingo Sanz (2017). The rock art of Madjedbebe (Malakunanja II). In B. David, P. S. C. Taçon, J.-M. Geneste and J.-J. Delannoy (Eds.) *The Archaeology of Rock Art in Western Arnhem Land.* Canberra, Australian National University. Terra Australis 47.

Pearson, C. and G. L. Pretty, Eds. (1976). *Proceedings of the National Seminar on the Conservation of Cultural Material, Perth 1973.* The Institute for the Conservation of Cultural Material, Perth.

Rosenfeld, A. (1985). *Rock Art Conservation in Australia.* Canberra, Australian Government Publishing Service.

Shine, D. (2014). *Changing Places an Archaeological Study of Manilikarr Country in Western Arnhem Land.* Doctor of Philosophy, School of Geography and Environmental Science, Monash University, Melbourne.

Shine, D., M. Marshall, D. Wright, T. Denham, P. Hiscock, G. Jacobsen and S.-P. Stephens (2015). The Archaeology of Bindjarran Rockshelter in Manilikarr Country, Kakadu National Park. *Australian Archaeology* 80: 104–111.

Sullivan, H. and I. P. Haskovec (1985). *Annual Report for the Archaeological Section of the Kakadu National Park Scientific Services.* Australian National Parks and Wildlife Service, Canberra.

Sullivan, H. and I. P. Haskovec (1986). *Annual Report for the Cultural Resource Management Section of the Kakadu National Park Scientific Services.* Australian National Parks and Wildlife Service, Canberra.

Sullivan, H. and I. P. Haskovec (1987). *Annual Report for the Archaeological Section of the Kakadu National Park Scientific Services.* Australian National Parks and Wildlife Service, Canberra.

Thorn, A. (1993). *Condition Survey of Four Rock Art Sites in Kakadu National Park.* Unpublished report for Kakadu National Park, Jabiru.

UNESCO (2014). *Kakadu National Park.* http://whc.unesco.org/en/list/147.

Watchman, A. (2004). *Impacts of Water and Frost on Fire- Affected Rendezvous Creek Aboriginal Art Site in Namadgi National Park.* Unpublished report for Environment ACT, Canberra.

Index

Note: **Bold** page numbers refer to tables; *italic* page numbers refer to figures and page numbers followed by "n" denote endnotes.

Aboriginal Traditional Owners 42, 88, 352
Accelerator Mass Spectrometry Carbon-14 (AMS^{14}C) 67
AEMET weather station: environmental data 219, **219**; meteorological parameters 215
Ain Shallalah 307–309, *308*
Alameleh 311–313, *312*
Alqueva dam 6, 194, 201
Altamira 3, 5
aging test 237, 241
anthropomorphic figures 323
archaeological context 172, 320–322
archaeometry methods: gas chromatography 268; infrared spectroscopy by Fourier transforms 261; optical microscopy 258; pigment archaeometry analysis techniques 256; pigment samples *259, 260*; Raman spectroscopy 258, 261; red pigment archaeometric analysis and results **262–267**; scanning electron microscopy (SEM) 258; X-ray fluorescence spectroscopy 261
Area of Outstanding Natural Beauty (AONB) 135
artificial silicone driplines: application of *357*; assessing suitability of 358–359; background 354–358components for appropriate dripline management 356–357; CORLAB 357–358; reinstallation of 368; removal of 367; water management techniques 354–355
Australian rock art sites 28

Bangudae Petroglyphs (BP), Korea: anthropomorphic figures 323; archaeological context 320–322; artiodactyls 324; carnivores 324; Cheonjeon-ri Petroglyphs 318; chronology 326; discovery of petroglyphs 317–319; documentation work 318, *323*; environment 319–322; fishing and hunting 324, 326; general situation 322; geography 319–320; other animals 324; paleoenvironment 320; Petroglyph Museum 5; preservation of 327–329; Seokjang-ri 318; themes 322–323; Ulsan Petroglyph Museum 318–319; zoomorphic figures 323–324, *325*
Beckensall Archive of Northumberland Rock Art Project 147
binder 12, 253, 254, 255, 261, 268, 273
Binjarrang (case study) 362–363, *363*
biocides, use of 177
biofilm 10, 182, 187, 189, 305
biopatina *65*, 238
bioreceptivity 10, 177, 178, 181, 182, 187, 188, 189, 190
Burra Charter 32
Burrup Peninsula 38–40, *39,* 42–44, 47–49, 51–52
Burrup Rock Art Monitoring Management Committee (BRAMC) 47, 50

Cadw 121, 123–124, 127, 129, 131–132, 138, 155
calcium crust 6, 66
CaLoSiL® 11, 61, 231, 237, 242–245, *244*

376 Index

Campo Lameiro Rock Art Park 9
Canada do Inferno, Coa Valley 26, *27*
"Carib Stones"(at Waltham & Victoria) 103–104
Cathole Cave (case study), SWOT analysis: archaeological investigations 126–127; archaeological value 130; contextual value 130–131; digital 3D mapping survey 126; engraved torso of cervid *127*; entrance to *126*; insertion of a grille in 2014 *128*; location of 125, *125*; public appreciation and realm value 131–132; universal value 129; uranium-series disequilibrium dating 128; vandalism 129
Catingueiros da Borracha 341
Cerrado, rock art in: assessment of micro-fauna present at rock art shelters 294; cleaning of extensive termite trails 290; cleaning of termite trails at GO-Ja.26 *292*; Cluster A (Complexo do Diogo) 286–287; Cluster D (Pousada das Araras) 287–288; Cluster E (Veu do Muquem) 288–289; compounds regarding posterior elimination of graffiti 292–293; compounds to clean remnants left on rock surfaces 291; conservation 296–298; context and condition of sites 285–289; future work 295–296; GO-Ja.3 site at Pousada das Araras 283, *284*; graffiti removal at GO-Ja.13 *293*; methodology and undertaken actions 289–294; MRS Estudos Ambientais Ltda. 284; removal of vegetation, beehives, and debris 293–294
chromatic alteration 241
Church Hill Romano-British enclosure 131
Circinaria hoffmanniana 180, 180–181, *183*
cleaning: biocide cleaning 10, 189; chemical cleaning 177–190; laser cleaning 177–190, 291; mechanical cleaning 67; surface cleaning 66, 67, 183, 187
Coa dam 13, 194, 205–206
Coa Valley (Portugal) and Siega Verde (Spain) Archaeological Sites: bioreceptivity study 182; BI values 189, *189*; characteristics of laser systems 180–181; choice of removal method 177; CIELAB units 187; *Circinaria hoffmanniana 180,* 180–181, *183*; cleaning methods 179–181; Coa Museum 5; colorimetric differences 184, **186**; creation of integrated urgency intervention scale 25; evaluation of cleaning performance 181–182; laser-based treatments 177–178; laser cleaning *vs.* chemical cleaning for removal of lichen 10, 178; location of 179, *180*; materials and methods 179–182; mineralogical composition 179, **179**; Nd:YAG/Er:YAG 178, 180–183; results and discussion 183–190; samples 179; stereoscopic micrographs of samples 184, *185,* 186; uncolonized schists 179, *180*; variations in colour and *in vivo* fluorescence 187, *188*
Coa Valley Archaeological Park 29
collaborative approaches 1, 5–7, 15, 70
Collector™ 305
Complexo do Diogo 286–287
community approaches 1, 5–7
Condition Assessment and Risk Evaluation (CARE) project: erosion 97; promotion of 152, *153,* 154; toolkit 8, 149–152
conservation assessment 7, 59, 66
Conservation Management Plans (CMPs) 117
consolidation 6, 11, 26, 27, 57, 61, 66, 234–246, 348
Cova Remígia (Castelló, Spain) 235–236; calcium hydroxide nanoparticles testing 11, 242–243, 246n4; CaLoSiL® 243–245, *244*; consolidation of rock art paintings 241; geographic location of *235*; methodology 237–238; Nanorestore® 243–244, *244*; paintings 234–235; Paraloid B72® 240–242; Primal AC33® polymer 242; proposed treatments 240–243; purpose 236–237; results 243–245; rock surface alterations *238, 240*; state of conservation of 238–239; Valltorta-Gasulla Museum 234
crust removal/reduction 66–67
CSIRM Project 148

Dampier Archipelago, Australia 30, 38, *39,* 40
decohesion 239, 240
decolonization 2
durability 10, 85, 199, 362

Index 377

Early Upper Palaeolithic (EUP) 127
Ekain and Ekainberri 5
Environmental Impact Assessments (EIAs) 118
Environmental Statement (ESs) 118
Environment Protection and Biodiversity Act(1999) 43
Esri's Survey 123™ 305
ethics 5–7, 31, 256
European Archaeological Association (EAA) Conference 353
European settlement 38
ex situ conservation 5, 11, 14, 32, 34
4D model 60, 70; of La Covatina *69*

Galicia, NW Spain: distribution of petroglyphs 161, *162*, 163; European Union's INSPIRE Directive 164; georeferenced information management tools 164; IASGDCH of the Regional Government of Galicia 163; Open Geospatial Consortium 164; Rock Art Archaeological Park in Campo Lameiro (PAAR) 163
gas chromatography 12, 268
gelifraction 11, 230
georeferenced information management tools 164
GIS tools 9, 25, 98, 101, 161, 165, 295, 305
graffiti removal 2, 57, 289, *293*
Grenada: Caribbean tri-island nation 99; "Carib Stones" at Waltham & Victoria 7–8, 102, 103–104; Duquesne Bay and Mt. Rich 102; location of RASI-assessed rock art sites *103*
Gum Tree Valley 41

Hard Rock Motel 356
Heritage of Western Australia Act (1990) 43
Hisma Desert 302, *303*, 309
human threats 6, 55, 66

infrared spectroscopy 261
in situ conservation 14, 28, 31, 32, 206
INSPIRE (Infrastructure for Spatial Information in Europe) 9, 164, 172n2
International Council on Monuments and Sites (ICOMOS) 117
invasive 83, 88, 111, 256, 290, 291, 295, 299n1, 309
irreversibility 26, 67, 172, 241, 242, 337, 342, 344, 355

Kakadu National Park (World Heritage Area) 82, 82–86, *83, 85*; An-garregen, cultural heritage strategy 84; Bim (Rock Art) Monitoring and Maintenance Program 352–353, 367; Binjarrang (case study) 362–363, *363*; conservation practices 82, 82–83, *83*; CORLAB trials 85; cultural programs 84; cultural landscape 353; early interventions and related rock art research 83; East Alligator District of Kakadu National Park 355, 366–367; environmental threats and human impacts 84; establishment of Kakadu 352, 355–356; integrating monitoring and evaluation into annual programs 366–368; monitoring rock art 85; Nanguluwurr (case study) *364*, 364–365; Nawalabila (case study) 365–366; Ubirr (case study) 360–361, *361*
"Khazali Canyon" *see* Siq al-Khazali
Kimberley region (Australia) 86–88
Kinetic Dam Project 327
King Arthur's Cave 134, 136

La Covatina del Tossalet del Mas de la Rambla site 57
La Covatina project: aims and methods 59–63; archaeological approach 59–60; and contiguous rock shelter 215, *216*; digital recording techniques 60; 4D model of 68, *69*; general view in winter and summer time 56, *56*; images and digital reproductions 63, *64*; management plan and knowledge transfer 61, 63; rock art conservation 60–61; *in situ* tests of various consolidants and pigments used in rock art conservation 61, *62*
LArcHer project *216*
Lascaux 3, 5, 121–122
Late Upper Palaeolithic (LUP) 120, 128–129, 131, 137
legal protection 15, 208
Levantine rock art (LRA): AEMET weather station 219, *219*; ambient data analysis in daily time bands 220–221, *221*; analysis of temperature and incidence of light on rock surface 221–222; archaeological approach 63, 65–66; comparison between reach of line of sun 217, *218*; conservation assessment 66, 214; correlation between surface

temperature and illuminance 228, **229**; discovery of sites 4; distribution of 55, *56*; environmental data analysis 218–220; evaluating thermal-hygrometric dynamics at 11, 217, 229–232; illuminance range and thermal amplitude *226,* 226–228; La Covatina del Tossalet del Mas de la Rambla site 215, *216*; location of rock surface temperature measurement points 215, *216*; management plan 68; measurements at point A 222, *223*; measurements at point B 222, 224; measurements at point C 224; measurements at point D 224; measurements at point E 224–225; measurements at point F 225; measurements at point G 225–226; microclimatic monitoring 214–215; monitoring 215, 217; in open-air rock shelters and rock walls 55; project results and discussion 63, 65–70; site 58; surface cleaning and crust removal 67; temperature measurements and light exposure 217–218; transferring knowledge to society 68

lichen 10, 24, 77, 99, 106, 109, 148, 177–190; lichen removal 10, 178, 186, 190, 291

Little Doward Camp 135

Llethrid Tooth Cave 130, 131

luxmeter 217, 229

Maestrat 234

Maniçobeiros 335, 341

Merlin's Cave (case study), SWOT analysis: archaeological value 136–137; contextual value 135–136; entrance to *134*; limestone extraction 133; location of *125,* 133; public appreciation and realm value 137–138; universal value 134–135

monitoring 7–9, 76–88, 141–156: monitoring tools 8, 15, 148

mortar 27, 203, 241, 246n9

multidisciplinary 6, 55–71

multi-proxy archaeometric analyses on rock art pigments: archaeometric research methodology on rock art 256; archaeometry methods 256–268; pigment analysis objectives 253–254; pigment archaeometry analysis and results **269–270**; pigments and raw materials 254–255; results of pigments analysis on prehistoric rock art 252–253, 268; sampling proceedings on different rock-art painted sites *257*; technology of painted prehistoric rock art 255

Murujuga: Aboriginal cultural significance 40; Burrup Peninsula 38, *39,* 40; construction of TANPF 49–50; CSIRO studies 49; Dampier Archipelago, Australia 30; heritage engagement 40–43; HIPL and DSL 43; KGP facilities 44; "Murujuga Rock Art Strategy" 47; Net Benefit activities 42–43; question of impacts 46–50; rock art precinct 43–46

NADRAP 148–149

Naminidjbuk Estate (Wellington Range): and Arnhem Land 81; Malarrak and Maliwawa complexes 80–81; Naminidjbuk Development Plan 81; Picturing Change project 79–80; Traditional Owners 80

Nanguluwurr (case study) *364,* 364–365

Nanorestore 11, 61, 237, 242–245, *244*

National Heritage Lottery Fund funding (NHLF) 123

Native Title Act (1993) 41

Natural Resources Wales (NRW) 131–132

natural threats 31

natural weathering phenomena 25

Nawalabila (case study) 365–366

non-invasive 7, 78, 86, 97–113, 143, 149, 256, 268, 304, 361

Northern Australia, community collaborations in 78–88; Indigenous Traditional Owners 79; Kakadu National Park (World Heritage Area) *82,* 82–86, *83, 85*; Naminidjbuk Estate (Wellington Range) 79–82; range of opportunities 78–79; significance of paintings in Malarrak rock shelter 79, *80*; Traditional Owners of the Naminidjbuk Estate 79; Wanjina Wunggurr Wilinggin and Nyikina Mangala peoples in the Kimberley region 86–88; World Heritage area of Kakadu National Park 79

Obiri *see* Ubirr (case study)

open-air rock art conservation practice: at Canada do Inferno, Coa Valley 26, *27*; climate-induced weathering

25; community involvement 1; conservation interventions 26; effective management systems 1; ethical and aesthetical issues 27–28; GIS data referencing 25; interconnected weathering patterns 24; natural weathering phenomena or location attributes 25; need for interdisciplinary approaches 23–25; physical and cultural conservation practice 1; public and political awareness 1; removal for conservation purposes 29–33; Rock 2 at Ribeira de Piscos 32, *33*; unengraved outcrop relocated at time of dam's construction 29, *30*; use of stabilizing agents on rock art panels 25

open-air rock art sites: background 77–78; Colombian rock art 3; community collaborations in Northern Australia 78–88; Kakadu National Park 77; Levantine rock art in Castellon 4; need for graffiti removal 2; post-colonialism approach 3; Traditional Owners and Working on Country Aboriginal 77; Traditional Owners of the Naminidjbuk Estate 76

optical microscopy 258

over-visitation 4, 5, 13

oxalates 56, 66, 67, 239, 246n4

paleoenvironment 320, 326

Parc Le Breos Cwm Neolithic burial chamber 131

Parc Le Breos Limekilns 131

Participation Agreements with the Pilbara Traditional Owner groups 42

patina 57, 67, 104, 107, 179, 186, 236, 237, 239, 243, 246n3, 335, 339, 340, 344, 245, 246, 248

permeability 242, 340

Personal Protection Equipment (PPE) 120

petroglyphs 6, 9, 38, *39*, 40, 41, 43, 44, 46, 47, 48, 49, 50, 51, 102, 104, 111, 112, 161–172, 302–314, 317–330

physical weathering/biodeterioration 24–25, 344–345

pigment archaeometry analysis techniques 256

Pousada das Araras 283, *284*, 287–288

prehistoric rock art 6, 12, 31, 56, 119, 121, 129, 149, 177–178, 252–256

preventive conservation interventions 6, 57

Raman spectroscopy 258, 261

"red ochre" 255

red pigment archaeometric analysis and results **262–267**

repainting 2, 8, 341

replica 5, 6, 14, 28, 31, 122, 206, 208

rock art and geographical information technologies: distribution of petroglyphs in region of Galicia, NW Spain *162*; multi-layered architecture for SIPAAR (*see* SIPAAR)

Rock Art Stability Index (RASI): accessibility for non-specialists 101; CARE project 97; "Citizen Scientists" 101; ESRI products 97; geologic stability and rock weathering 7–8; Grenada's "Carib Stones" at Waltham & Victoria 102, *103*, 103–104; impending/future loss 99; incremental erosional loss 99, 305; informing local communities 111–112; intrinsic sandstone weaknesses 110–111; large erosion events 99, 305; open-air rock art management challenges 112; power of 99; previous implementation of 102; rock coatings 99; score range classifications 100; severity-of-occurrence scale 100; SHRA members 100; site setting 99, 305; socioeconomic factors 111; using scanning electron microscopy (SEM) 97; vandalism and issues 99; Victoria site RASI assessment *105*, 105–107, *106*; Waltham site RASI assessment 107, *108*, 109–110

Rock 2 at Ribeira de Piscos 32, *33*

"rock decay" ("stone decay") 98–102, 111–112, 113n1, 304–306, 311

Sabor Valley (Northwest Iberia): assessment of expected conditions after submersion 201–202; chronology 196; Coa Valley Archaeological Park 205–206; condition of intervened outcrops 200–201; condition of outcrops/surfaces/motifs 196; depiction of scenes 196; geological characterization of outcrops 199–200; Heritage Safeguard Plan (HSP) 195, 208; *in-situ* rock art preservation work 10, 202–203; location and rapport

with other sites 196; location of EP621 197, *198*; originality of figures 196; placing of successive layers of gauze, raw cloth and high-density geotextile blanket *204*, 205; position relative to reservoir water level 197; project implementation 203, 205; result of implemented protection at EP 621 206, *207*; selection of rock art heritage sites 195–199; superimposed motifs 196
sacred landscape 6, 38–51
San people, in South Africa 2
scanning electron microscopy (SEM) 258
Scheduled Monument Consent (SMC) 121
Scheduled Monuments (SMs) 117
SCHEP recruitment 304
Scotland's Rock Art Project (ScRAP) 145, 149, 154
Serra Branca Valley, Serra da Capivara National Park, Piauí, Brazil: anthropic damage 341–342; archaeology in 331–335; biological damage 339–340; chemical damage 340–341; chronology of human occupation **333**; common damage agents in *345*; dynamic approach on rock art conservation 335–337; entangled agents of qualitative modification 344–345; final considerations 348; Grandes Animais 333; "Historico" ("Historic") 335; indirect human factors 336; landscape and rock-art of four occupational movements *334*; materials and methods 337–338; physical, biological, chemical and anthropical damages *343*; physical damage 338–339; "Povos de Passagem" ("Passage Peoples") 334–335; "Povos de Transicao" ("Transition Peoples") 333; qualitative modification damaging the rock art 335–336; rock art curatorial intervention 346, *347,* 348; sociocultural systems 336
SIPAAR: forms for producing and editing data 167–168; geographic information standards and Esri's Geodatabase format 164–165; integration of archaeological information 165–166; management application *168*; markers in social landscape 168–171; 'Motifs' table 166; multi-layered architecture for 164–165; from risk management to dissemination 171–172; structure of database 166–167; zoomorphs 167
Siq al-Khazali 309–311, *310*
Skew Valley 41
solar radiation 11, 25, 55, 229, 231, 272
Spanish Heritage Act (1985) 56
stability 7, 27, 28, 97–113, 151, 202, 241, 273, 295, 304, 305, 306, 308, 309, 310, 311, 313, 314
sustainable tourism 8, 13, 80, 104, 296
SWOT (Strengths, Weaknesses, Opportunities and Threats) analysis 117; argued applicability to cultural heritage contexts 118–120; background and definition of 118; Cathole Cave (case study) 8, 119, *125,* 125–132; elements of 118; environmental considerations 123; financial constraints 120; funding sources 120; heritage benefits 123–124; human resources 119; implementation of 120–121; internal and external factors 121–122; legislation 120; limitations to 124; Merlin's Cave (case study) 119, *125,* 132–138; monitoring 120; past and present histories 119; physical environment 120; resources 119; used to 122–123; visitor intentions 120

Tadrart Acacus World Heritage site, Libya 26
thermal shock 177
thermoclasty 11, 230
thermo-hygrograph 215, *216*, 217, 229
thermometer 217, 229
3D models 60
Tito Bustillo 5
Trinity Well and Remains of a chapel 131
Tynedale Rock Art Project 149

Ubirr (case study) 360–361, *361*
UK and Ireland, rock art monitoring in: A5 flyer to promote the CARE app *153*; AOC Archaeology Group 147–148; Beckensall Archive of Northumberland Rock Art Project 147; CARE project 143–144, 149–152, *153,* 154; challenges 154–156; chronology 145–148; EH's 'Rock Art Management, Access, Study and Education Strategy' 147; extent

of the rock art 142–143; historical quarrying at West Lordenshaw *142*; international perspective 144–145; NADRAP 147, 148–149; RAPP 145, 147; RASI 145; regular monitoring 144; SAM status 141–142; scorecard's overall assessment 151; ScRAP 149; tangible threats 141; timeline of major UK rock art projects 145, *146*; Whitsunbank 3 in north Northumberland *143*

UNESCO World Heritage Site (WHS) inscription 117

University of Bristol Speleological Society (UBSS) 132, 137

Upper Palaeolithic European rock art sites 28

Valltorta-Gasulla Cultural Park 68

Valltorta Museum 68

vandalism 2, 23, 30, 56, 81, 99, 118, 124, 125, 129, 132, 137, 138, 145, 284, 292, 293, 298, 309, 310, 311, 312, 313

Victoria site RASI assessment 105–109; panel one assessment *105, 106*, 106–107; panel two assessment *105*, 107

Wadi Rum Protected Area (WRPA), Jordan: Ain Shallalah 307–309, *308*; Alameleh 311–313, *312*; comparison between RASI scores and category sums **306**; epigraphic and rock art documentation projects 303; geologic assessments of thamudic inscriptions and petroglyphs 13; Hisma Desert with stark red sand and tall inselberg mountains *303*; methods 304–305; RASI methodology 13; results 306–307; Rum Village 303–304; SCHEP recruitment 304; Siq al-Khazali 309–311, *310*; UNESCO World Heritage program 302

Waltham site RASI assessment: panel four assessment *108*, 109–110; panel one assessment 107, *108*; panel three assessment *108*, 109; panel two assessment *108*, 109

weathering: climate-induced weathering 25; from environmental conditions 77; interconnected weathering patterns 24; natural weathering phenomena or location attributes 25; physical weathering/biodeterioration 24–25, 344–345; rock weathering 7–8

Welsh Rock Art Organisation (WRAO) 118

Western Australian Museum 40–41

World Heritage declaration 56–57

X-ray fluorescence (XRF) spectroscopy 135, 261

zero intervention policy 5, 11, 31, 32, 33–34

zoomorphic figures 323–324, *325*

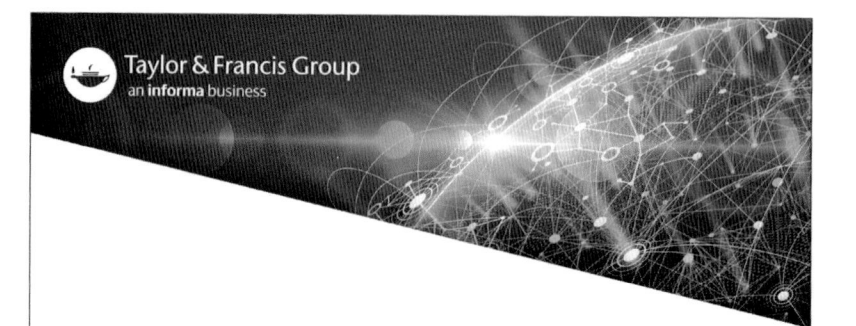

Taylor & Francis eBooks

www.taylorfrancis.com

A single destination for eBooks from Taylor & Francis with increased functionality and an improved user experience to meet the needs of our customers.

90,000+ eBooks of award-winning academic content in Humanities, Social Science, Science, Technology, Engineering, and Medical written by a global network of editors and authors.

TAYLOR & FRANCIS EBOOKS OFFERS:

- A streamlined experience for our library customers
- A single point of discovery for all of our eBook content
- Improved search and discovery of content at both book and chapter level

REQUEST A FREE TRIAL
support@taylorfrancis.com

Routledge — Taylor & Francis Group

CRC Press — Taylor & Francis Group